CW01022025

The Semantic Web Explained

The Semantic Web is a new area of research and development in the field of computer science, aimed at making it easier for computers to process the huge amount of information on the web, and indeed other large databases, by enabling them not only to read but also to understand the information.

Based on successful courses taught by the authors, and liberally sprinkled with examples and exercises, this comprehensive textbook describes not only the theoretical issues underlying the Semantic Web, but also algorithms, optimisation ideas and implementation details. The book will therefore be valuable to practitioners as well as students, indeed to anyone who is interested in Internet technology, knowledge engineering or description logics.

Supplementary materials available online include the source code of program examples and solutions to selected exercises.

Péter Szeredi is a Professor at the Budapest University of Technology and Economics (BUTE). In the mid 1970s he authored the first Hungarian Prolog interpreter and led the development of the MProlog system, a pioneering Hungarian software product sold worldwide in the 1980s. His main fields of interest include: declarative programming (logic programming, constraint programming, the Prolog language); semantic technologies (Semantic Web, semantic integration); exploiting parallelism and programming languages supporting parallelism; as well as the implementation of programming languages. He is the author and co-author of about 90 peer-reviewed publications, including 14 books or book chapters and eight journal publications. In recognition of his pioneering work in the field, he was honoured by the Association of Logic Programming as one of the 15 Founders of Logic Programming.

Gergely Lukácsy is a Software Architect at Cisco Systems, Ireland. He received his Ph.D. in Computer Science from the Budapest University of Technology, Hungary, in June 2008. The main contribution in his Ph.D. dissertation was a novel description logic reasoning approach that works effectively in cases when there are huge amounts of data. This result is particularly important for the Semantic Web area, where it is essential to have systems that can reason efficiently over large data sets. Dr Lukácsy has published more than 25 articles in journals, books, refereed conference proceedings and workshops. He has been working on various research projects involving semantic technologies and logic programming since 2000. His main results include the DLog reasoner, which uses logic programming techniques for efficient reasoning, including program analysis and transformation techniques and parallelisation. He has also been involved in the design and development of logic-based information integration systems that use knowledge representation, constraint logic programming and reasoning techniques.

Tamás Benkő is a Research Associate at the Digital Enterprise Research Institute, Ireland. He is involved in the development of the Semantic Web indexing project Sindice. His main fields of interest include declarative programming (logic programming, constraint programming, the Prolog language) and semantic technologies (Semantic Web, semantic integration). He is the author or co-author of several related conference papers and books.

The Semantic Web Explained

The Semantic Web Explained

The Technology and Mathematics behind Web 3.0

PÉTER SZEREDI

Budapest University of Technology and Economics (BUTE)

GERGELY LUKÁCSY

Cisco Systems, Ireland

TAMÁS BENKŐ

Digital Enterprise Research Institute, Ireland

With contributions by

ZSOLT NAGY

CAMBRIDGE
UNIVERSITY PRESS

CAMBRIDGE
UNIVERSITY PRESS

University Printing House, Cambridge CB2 8BS, United Kingdom

Cambridge University Press is part of the University of Cambridge.

It furthers the University's mission by disseminating knowledge in the pursuit of
education, learning and research at the highest international levels of excellence.

www.cambridge.org
Information on this title: www.cambridge.org/9780521700368

Originally published in Hungarian as *A Szemantikus Világháló Elmélete És
Gyakorlata* by Typotex, 2005
© Szeredi Péter, Lukácsy Gergely, Benkő Tamás, Nagy Zsolt, Typotex, 2005

First published in English by Cambridge University Press 2014
English translation © Cambridge University Press 2014

This publication is in copyright. Subject to statutory exception
and to the provisions of relevant collective licensing agreements,
no reproduction of any part may take place without the written
permission of Cambridge University Press.

Printed in the United Kingdom by Clays, St Ives plc

A catalogue record for this publication is available from the British Library

Library of Congress Cataloguing in Publication data
Szeredi, Péter, 1949– author.
[Szemantikus világháló elmélete és gyakorlata. English]
The Semantic Web explained : the technology and mathematics behind Web 3.0 / Péter Szeredi, Budapest
University of Technology and Economics (BUTE), Gergely Lukácsy, Cisco Systems, Ireland, Tamás Benkő,
Digital Enterprise Research Institute, Ireland ; with contributions by Zsolt Nagy.
    pages   cm
ISBN 978-0-521-70036-8 (paperback)
1. Semantic Web.   I. Lukácsy, Gergely, author.   II. Benkő, Tamás, author.   III. Title.
TK5105.88815.S9913   2014
006–dc23

                                                                              2014004717

ISBN 978-0-521-70036-8 Paperback

Additional resources for this publication are at http://www.swexpld.org

Cambridge University Press has no responsibility for the persistence or accuracy of
URLs for external or third-party internet websites referred to in this publication,
and does not guarantee that any content on such websites is, or will remain,
accurate or appropriate.

Contents

Introduction

The *Semantic Web* is a new area of computer science that is being developed with the main aim of making it easier for computers to process intelligently the huge amount of information on the web. In other words, as the common slogan of the Semantic Web says: computers should not only *read* but also *understand* the information on the web. To achieve this, it is necessary to associate metadata with web-based information. For example, in the case of a picture one should formally provide information regarding its author, title and contents. Furthermore, computers should be able to perform reasoning tasks. For example, if it is known that a river appears in a picture, the computer should be able to deduce that water can also be found in the picture.

Research into hierarchical terminology systems, i.e. ontologies, is strongly connected to the area of the Semantic Web. Ontologies are formal systems that allow the description of concrete knowledge about objects of interest as well as of general background knowledge. The *description logic* formalism is the most widespread approach providing the mathematical foundation of this field. It is not a coincidence that both OWL and its second edition, OWL 2, which are Semantic Web languages standardised by the World Wide Web Consortium (W3C), are based on Description Logic.

Ontologies and metadata, however, play an important role not only in the management of information on the web but also, for example, when one is dealing with business data bases and knowledge repositories. The amount of available information – be it on the web or anywhere else – is increasing very fast. Because of this, there is a growing need for the categorisation and integration of information sources. The tools and methods presented in this book can be used in this field as well.

Intended readership

The book is intended to be a textbook for courses on the Semantic Web and related topics. In writing the book the authors drew on their teaching experience in the courses "Foundations of the Semantic Web and ontology management" and "Introduction to semantic technologies", held at the Budapest University of Technology and Economics in the Faculty of Electrical Engineering and Informatics.

Moreover, the authors believe that the book is useful for everyone (whether she or he be an expert in informatics or not) who has ever been touched by the spirit of the Internet, ever wondered how search engines work, how the Web is built or what possibilities it offers. The book will prove useful to anybody who is fond of mathematics and interested in knowledge representation formalisms, Description Logic and the related reasoning methods.

Finally, the authors recommend the book to programmers because, complementing the theoretical coverage, the book also deals with algorithms, optimisation ideas and implementation details.

The structure of the book

The aim of this book is to present both the theoretical and practical side of the Semantic Web. In accordance with this, it consists of three parts. The first introduces the main idea of the Semantic Web, the second talks about the mathematical background, i.e. Description Logic (DL), while the last part deals with the combining of the first two: the usage of DL ontologies in the Semantic Web.

We now present a chapter-by-chapter summary.

Part I – The Semantic Web

Chapter 1 – The World Wide Web today

The aim of the first chapter is to introduce how Internet search engines work. To help the uninitiated reader, we first summarise some essential knowledge about the Internet, such as the concepts of static and dynamic pages. We discuss the main reasons why search engines do not behave intelligently. We examine the problem of non-processable information, the deep web, crawler traps and difficulties related to the lack of semantics. We also present solutions for these problems offered by the technologies widely used nowadays.

Chapter 2 – The Semantic Web and the RDF language

In the second chapter we introduce the concept of the Semantic Web and describe the languages that make it possible to associate meta-information with web resources and to perform reasoning on these. We outline how this approach can help in solving the problems discussed in the previous chapter. We describe in detail the basic languages of the Semantic Web, namely the RDF and the RDF schema languages, together with XML on which their syntax is based. We conclude the chapter by presenting several case studies.

Chapter 3 – Managing and querying RDF sources

In the third chapter we show several ways of storing and querying RDF-based meta-information. We introduce the XML and RDF query languages and argue that the standard XML query engines are not suitable for handling RDF sources. We examine what kind of reasoning tasks arise during RDF queries. At the end of the chapter we talk about possible optimisation approaches for making the execution of RDF queries more efficient.

Part II – Ontologies

Chapter 4 – Description Logic

Description Logic provides the mathematical foundation for knowledge representation systems. We introduce the TBox and the ABox: the former stores so-called terminological knowledge while the latter describes assertions about individuals. Subsequently, we describe several DL languages, from the simplest language, $\mathcal{AL}$, through $\mathcal{ALCN}$ and up to the fairly advanced language $\mathcal{SHIQ}$. We discuss the classification of reasoning tasks for both TBox and ABox inference. We also show the relationship between Description Logic and first-order logic. At the end, we briefly summarise advanced DL constructs that go beyond $\mathcal{SHIQ}$, including the language $\mathcal{SROIQ}$, which is the basis of the second edition of the Web Ontology Language, discussed in Chapter 8.

Chapter 5 – Reasoning on simple Description Logic

The chapter describes specific reasoning algorithms. First we introduce the structural subsumption algorithm, which is applicable for fairly simple DL languages only. Then we present the tableau algorithm for the $\mathcal{ALCN}$ language. The described techniques are illustrated with numerous examples, and the main properties of the algorithms are mathematically proved.

Chapter 6 – Implementing a simple DL reasoning engine

In this chapter we give an implementation of the $\mathcal{ALCN}$ tableau algorithm using the Haskell functional programming language. The aim is to show a compact and easily readable "reference implementation" for a fairly simple, but still useful, Description Logic. We do not presume any knowledge of Haskell: all the necessary language constructs are explained. The reader can execute the given program effectively. Moreover, because the implementation uses a notation very close to mathematics, we believe that it is easily understandable even for those who have never met a functional programming language before.

Chapter 7 – The $\mathcal{SHIQ}$ tableau algorithm

In this chapter we present a variant of the tableau algorithm that can accommodate the $\mathcal{SHIQ}$ language. The chapter concludes with a discussion of optimisation techniques for tableau algorithms.

Part III – Ontologies and the Semantic Web

Chapter 8 – The Web Ontology Language

In this chapter we introduce the Web Ontology Language OWL, which is based on Description Logic and is designed to be an extension of the RDF schema language. We describe the language constructs in detail and give their DL equivalent.

Supplementary materials

In addition to the book proper, we provide important web-based materials available at the website of the book `http://www.swexpld.org`. These include the source code of program examples and syntactic descriptions of various languages.

Authors of the book

Part I (Chapters 1, 2 and 3) and Chapter 8 were written by Gergely Lukácsy. Péter Szeredi wrote Chapters 4, 5 and all of 7 except for Section 7.9, which was written by Zsolt Nagy. Chapter 6 was written by Tamás Benkő and Zsolt Nagy. The book was edited by Péter Szeredi.

How to read the book

Naturally, the authors suggest that the book should be read in chapter order. However, some readers, for one reason or another, will wish to read only parts of the book and for those we illustrate the interdependence of the chapters in the figure.

The nodes represent the chapters (a node label refers to the contents of a chapter) and the dotted lines show the suggested entry points for reading the book.

Continuous arrows denote *strong*, and broken arrows *weak*, dependences. In the former case the authors feel that following the dependence graph is essential in order to understand the chapters, while in the latter case this is merely recommended.

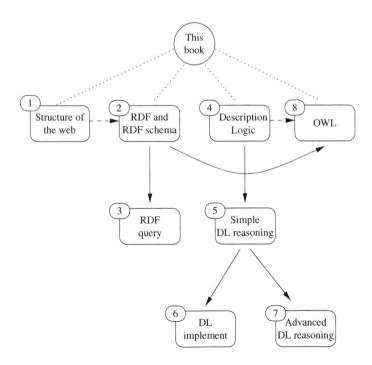

Examples of strong dependences are the chains of Chapters 4, 5 and 7 as well as those of Chapters 2 and 8. It would be very difficult to understand a DL reasoning algorithm without knowing what Description Logic is, or to understand the OWL language (which is based on RDF) without being familiar with the RDF formalism.

An example of a weak dependence is the relation between Chapters 4 and 8. In the latter we present the DL equivalent for each OWL construct. We believe, however, that the chapter can be read without a knowledge of Description Logic.

Acknowledgements

The authors would like to thank everybody who helped them in creating this book.

First, regarding the original Hungarian edition, thanks go to the reviewers, Dániel Varró and Szilvia Varró-Gyapai, for their diligent work and valuable remarks. The comments of Bálint Laczay and Péter Szabó helped a lot in making the book easier to understand and freer from errors. We are also very grateful to the students of the "Foundations of Semantic Web and ontology management" course who were the first "guinea pigs" to read the book and whose reactions helped us a lot in improving it. We also thank the Hungarian Ministry of Education for supporting the publication of the Hungarian edition of this book, and Typotex Electronic Publishing Ltd for their help in the process of publication.

Second, we would like to thank all the staff of Cambridge University Press, and especially David Tranah, for their help and patience in producing the English version. We are also most grateful to our former students who drafted the English translations of the book chapters, namely Lukács Tamás Berki, Tamás Ferenci, Viktor Fábián, Dávid Hanák, Levente Hunyadi, Rita Móga, Attila Németh, Péter Pallinger, Gergely Patai, Áron Sisak and Zoltán Windisch. The development of the English version of the book was supported by the grant TÁMOP–4.2.2.B-10/1–2010-0009.

The Semantic Web

Chapter 1

The World Wide Web today

The aim of this chapter is to introduce some major problems associated with the World Wide Web that have led to the development of its new generation, the Semantic Web.

The chapter has two main parts. In the first we describe the structure of the Internet, the different kinds of web pages (static and dynamic) and their role in the process of information storage. Here we also introduce the concept of web forms and Common Gateway Interface (CGI) technology and its more advanced alternatives.

In the second part of the chapter we examine how traditional search engines work, what their limits are and how they fare with heterogeneous information sources. We illustrate the problems associated with searching the Web and briefly describe possible solutions. One of these is the Semantic Web approach, which is described in more detail in later chapters.

For readers familiar with the Internet we suggest skipping the first section and starting at Section 1.2.

1.1. The architecture of the web

The World Wide Web is made up of *servers* and *clients*. Servers store different kinds of information in various ways. Most often these pieces of information are stored in the form of *web pages* (also called *homepages*), which are essentially standard text files with a special structure. Further to homepages, the web stores a variety of *documents*, including pictures, videos, Word and PDF documents and so on. A web page is also often referred to as an HTML page or document, where the abbreviation HTML stands for HyperText Markup Language [14].

It is important to know, however, that there are other ways to store information, such as databases and application programs. These are introduced later in this chapter.

The information stored by the servers is accessed by the clients. This can be done in many ways, depending on how the information is stored. Furthermore, for each such storage type usually there are several different access methods available. In the simplest case the client downloads a web page from the server (which normally corresponds to a file stored there) and displays it in a *browser*. Browsers are applications capable of displaying text files with a specific standardised syntax structure. For example, there is a special syntax for describing tables according to the HTML specification [14]. When such a syntactic construct is encountered in a file, it is displayed by the browser as a table with appropriate rows and columns. Similarly, if an HTML page contains picture references, the browser downloads the picture files one by one from the server and displays them in the proper place.

Browsers are capable of much more than that, of course. For example they understand pieces of program code embedded into HTML pages written in different scripting languages (such as JavaScript). This way, a page can be made interactive and more user friendly. Using scripts one can achieve special effects, e.g. changing the look of a piece of a text when the mouse moves over it, or displaying a sheep which constantly follows the mouse cursor, doing silly things all the time. Actually, scripts do serious things in most cases. The Google mail service, for example, is fast and comfortable because of JavaScript.

In many cases servers operate as clients, and vice versa. The reason is that the same computer can play the role of a server or a client, depending on the given scenario. For example, it often occurs that a server must contact another server in order to fulfil a client's request. During this new request our server behaves as a client, because it uses a service provided by another server.[1]

1.1.1. Web pages and HTML

We now introduce the two basic types of web pages, *static* and *dynamic*. We note, however, that in reality web pages cannot be categorised purely as static or dynamic as usually some parts of them are static, while others are dynamic.

Before describing these basic types, we briefly outline the HTML language as it is the language in which most web pages are written. We do not aim to describe the HTML in full detail, but only to remind the reader of its most important features. The basic knowledge of HTML we provide here also helps readers to understand the various examples in the book written in languages similar to HTML.

1.1.1.1. The basics of HTML

Files written in HTML are *plain text* files, so they can be created and modified using even the simplest text editors. One of the most important features of the HTML language is that it adds structure to text written in natural language. For this purpose, the language introduces special syntactic constructs, so-called *HTML elements*, which mark the title of the text, the titles of the chapters, the tables, the pictures and references to other pages, among other things. The introduction of references or *links* (also called *hyperlinks*[2]) is a major strength of HTML. A complex network of web pages, spread across the Internet, can be created using links. A page created by a person can include, of course, references to pages written by others.

In contrast with the above, there are several HTML elements that serve only for visualisation purposes. For example there is an element which draws a horizontal line separating parts of a web page.

---

[1] It is also possible that this request chain will eventually reach the very computer which initiated the original request.

[2] Sometimes the term *hyperlink* is used only for links referring to HTML pages.

The simplest HTML page contains at least a title element:

```
<title>Homepage of Stephen Taylor</title>
```

When displaying this example page, the browser will show an empty page with the given text appearing in the title bar.

HTML pages are ordinary files, so we can copy them to a data medium and transfer them to another computer. The browser on that computer will be able to display the page. We say that a web page "is on the web" if it is copied to a properly configured web server. Assuming that the above "web page" is saved under the name `first.html` (the extension `.html` is not mandatory, but recommended), on the web server named `www.swexpld.org` it can be accessed through the following link or URL (Uniform Resource Locator):

```
http://www.swexpld.org/first.html
```

Actually, in reality, the following happens: the *domain name* `www.swexpld.org` is translated to a unique identifier (so-called *IP address*) and the server is addressed and accessed through this identifier. The `http` prefix informs the browser that the file is to be processed using the protocol defined in the HTTP (HyperText Transfer Protocol) [16] standard and that the name of the file is `first.html`.

From URLs such as `http://www.swexpld.org/first.html` we often omit the trailing part of the URL, so that only `http://www.swexpld.org` remains. The reason why this works is that it is possible to specify in the web server a default file name. This default can be changed at will, but most often it is set to the file name `index.html`.

Within an HTML document, a link can be defined using the `<a>` element, for example:

```
A link to the <a href="http://www.w3.org/">W3C</a> page.
```

In this case the browser displays the text "A link to the W3C page" where the word "W3C" is shown in a different colour and style. Clicking on this word takes us to the homepage of the World Wide Web Consortium.

HTML offers numerous other opportunities to make our homepage more informative (highlighting, tables, frames etc.) and attractive (pictures, background images, colours, separators etc.). Figure 1.1 shows the code of a simple HTML page, which is displayed by a browser as shown in Figure 1.2.

Having introduced the basics of HTML, we continue with a discussion of the different web page types.

Exercise 1.1: Personalise the HTML source in Figure 1.1 to contain your name, hobbies etc. Consider adding other personal data. Try viewing this HTML page in your favourite browser.

1.1.1.2. Static pages

The notion of a *static web page* can be defined in several ways. One could say that static web pages are pages we create, put on the web (making them available to the clients) and update relatively rarely. In other words, we think about static pages as pages on which information is more or less stable for a long time. The main page of one's personal web, for example, needs to change rarely. Some new *links* can appear on such a main page (for example to the pages containing pictures from our last vacation), but on the whole the page remains relatively unchanged.

```
<!DOCTYPE html>
<html>
  <head>
    <title>Homepage of Stephen Taylor</title>
    <meta http-equiv="content-type"
          content="text/html; charset=utf-8"/>
  </head>

  <body>
    <h1>About me</h1>
    <h4>Hobbies</h4>
    <ul>
      <li>Running</li>
      <li>Swimming</li>
      <li>Fishing</li>
    </ul>
    Send me an
      <a href="mailto:stephen.taylor@swexpld.org">email</a>.
  </body>
</html>
```

Figure 1.1. A very simple HTML page.

The definition of a rare change can be broadly interpreted. We can certainly say that a page which remains the same for a month changes rarely. However, there could be a page the content of which changes daily, and yet it would still be considered static.

As a first approximation, we could define the notion of a static page as a page whose content changes "rarely". Although it contains a lot of truth, this is not a correct definition. We will soon show an example of a page whose content never changes, yet it is *not* considered static.

We will return to the definition of static pages after discussing their complement, dynamic pages.

1.1.1.3. Dynamic pages

In some cases it is not sufficient for the server to return a simple ready-made document to the client. Servers can often be regarded as real *service providers*, which return an answer to each query posted to them. This requires some interaction between the client and the server: the client provides some input, and the server answers with an output. For example, let us consider a web page which requires a number to be entered, and – when the Go button is pressed – returns Yes if the number is a prime, or No otherwise.

Actually, there are three distinct web pages involved in this example. The first web page contains the input field and the button (both can be found amongst the standard HTML elements). The second page contains the text Yes while the third page displays No. In this

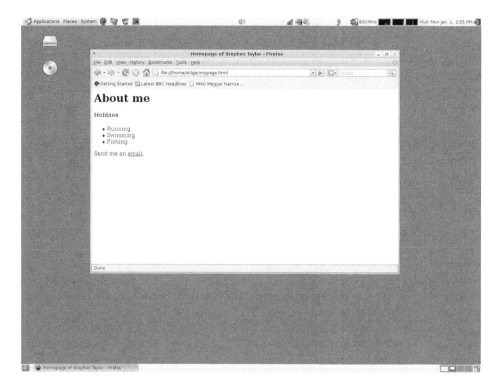

Figure 1.2.   The web page of Figure 1.1 in a browser.

example we also need some means for transferring the number entered to the server. In Subsection 1.1.3 we will show that this is actually nothing more than a new page request. The page returned in answer to this request is treated like a normal HTML page and is displayed by our browser.

It is clear, however, that some kind of processing has to be done on the server side, to decide whether the submitted number is prime. This is called the *(business) logic* of the page. In this simple example the business logic decides which of the two ready-made pages should be returned to the client.

In practice, the situation is often much more complicated. Let us imagine a web page that asks for two numbers to be entered and returns their sum as the result. In this case, the server-side logic is even simpler than before: the two numbers should be added and the page with the correct sum needs to be returned. But how do we produce such a page? Do we create numerous pages in advance which contain the answers to all the possible inputs? This sounds like a tremendous waste of resources and, of course, it is also physically impossible because we would need an infinite number of pages. The solution is to *generate dynamically* the web page containing the correct answer and return this page to the client.

This generated page is a normal HTML document. The client actually does not even know that the page is dynamically generated and displays it in just the same way as for pages retrieved from files.

Question–answer dialogues, like the one above, are not the only cases where dynamic web pages are required. Probably everyone has encountered web pages containing the current date. Let us think about that. The browser running on our client received an HTML page containing the current date. Do the creators of the homepage modify this part of the page daily? Are they waiting each night just to change the file immediately after midnight, so that a new request will see the updated page? Hardly. The returned web page is most likely a *dynamic* web page generated by the server at the moment it receives the request.[3] Notice that in this case we did not directly ask the server to do some service for us (such as adding up numbers). We only requested a normal file, yet the contents of this file have been dynamically generated.

1.1.1.4. Static pages, revisited

The concept of a static page can be better understood now that we have discussed dynamic web pages. The most important feature of a static web page *is not* the fact that its content changes rarely. The main point is that *there is no server-side logic behind static web pages.* The server only returns the requested, already existing, file to the client through the Internet. It does not need to do anything more. In contrast, if the server *generates* the resulting pages following the client's request, using some built-in mechanism, we speak about dynamic web pages. It must be noted that in extreme cases it is possible that a web page is dynamic but its content never changes. The server may generate the same page regardless of the request or other circumstances and, because the result page does not exist as a file on the server, the page will have to be classified as dynamic rather than static.

1.1.2. The Common Gateway Interface

While discussing dynamic web pages we saw that an HTTP server – in order to provide a specific service – may have to invoke some application program which actually performs the given service (such as deciding whether a given number is a prime). For this to work one needs a specification of the interface through which web servers and external applications can communicate. This is the *CGI* (Common Gateway Interface) specification.

The CGI specification can also be viewed as a means for providing a web-based user interface to an existing application. However, there is a major difference between the traditional graphical user interface (GUI) and the CGI-based interface. Using the traditional GUI one can invoke a specific function of the (already running) application, and multiple interactions such as this can happen during a single run. In contrast, with CGI the application is re-run every time a client request is received.

This specification does not impose any restrictions on the programming language used for the external application. For example, one can write an ordinary program in the language C, which will then be called with appropriate parameters by the web server each time a specific request is received.

The HTTP server will finally return an HTTP response to the client. An HTTP response contains header fields as well as an entity body. The latter can be an HTML page, some plain text, a picture in a binary format or an arbitrary sequence of data. The actual content

---

[3] It is also possible to get the current date using client-side technologies such as JavaScript.

of the HTTP response depends on what the CGI application returns on its standard output. Basically, there are two main types of such outputs:

(1) *Non-parsed output.* This means that the server forwards the output directly to the client without trying to interpret it. In this case the CGI application is responsible for providing a complete HTTP response message as described in the HTTP specification [16]. An example of a non-parsed CGI response with three header lines and a body containing a single line of text can be seen below:

```
HTTP/1.0 200 OK
Server: NCSA/1.0a6
Content-type: text/plain

This is plain text, not even HTML.
```

Using non-parsed outputs means a faster service time, as the overhead caused by the HTTP server is kept as low as possible. However, the CGI application has to take care of the creation of a proper HTTP-message.

(2) *Parsed output.* In this case the CGI application does not have to make a proper HTTP response message, because the server will take care of this. A parsed output starts with at least one line of text followed by an empty line (a so-called CGI header), which is interpreted by the HTTP server. Depending on this header the server performs different actions. In practice two kinds of header are used most often, the `Content-type` and the `Location` headers.

In case of the `Content-type` header, the server encapsulates the rest of the CGI output in an appropriate HTTP response message, taking into account the actual content type. A typical CGI response can be seen below, where the application returns a normal HTML page (see Figure 1.1).

```
Content-type: text/html

<html>
  <head>
    <title>Example output of a CGI program</title>
  </head>
  <body>
    <h1>About me</h1>
    <h4>Hobbies</h4>
    ...
  </body>
</html>
```

In the case of the `Location` CGI header, the server returns the document referred to by this header. An example is:

```
Location: /here/index.html
```

The empty line after the text line is also mandatory in this case. The given reference can be relative or absolute. In the case of an absolute path, the web server returns a redirect response to the client. The same happens in the case of a relative path but the server first resolves the relative path, making it absolute.

Either way, the client eventually receives the proper file. In the example above this is the file `http://server:port/here/index.html`, where the web server received the original request on the given `server` and `port`.

Having discussed the possible output formats, let us now turn to the issue of passing parameters to the application. The parameters can be supplied in two different ways: in the form of command line arguments or as environment variables. The CGI specification supports either technique, depending on the request method (see below and in Subsection 1.1.3).

Environment variables are also used for passing information about the server to the application, independently of the actual request. Such variables are for example the following.

SERVER_SOFTWARE The name and version of the server, in the form of name/version.

SERVER_NAME The IP address or the domain name of the server.

GATEWAY_INTERFACE The version of the CGI specification supported by the server, in the form of CGI/version.

The CGI specification defines a large number of environment variables whose value depends on the actual request. The most important are the following:

SERVER_PORT The port where the request actually arrived. Using this information the application can react in different ways depending on at which port the given request arrived.

REQUEST_METHOD The method used in the given HTTP request, which can be GET, POST or HEAD, for example. By knowing this, the CGI application can decide where to look for the parameters belonging to the request.

PATH_INFO The additional path information found in the request (see the examples below).

QUERY_STRING The part after the ? sign in the request (see the examples below) without any transformation. In the case of the GET method this literal contains the query parameters.

A CGI program can be accessed with an ordinary browser by the use of a specific web address. For example, when the link `http://swexpld.org/exacttime.cgi` is passed to a server, it will recognise it as a CGI request, provided the server was set up to treat paths matching the pattern `*.cgi` as CGI invocations (which is the default behaviour). Other such patterns can be specified, so it may not be obvious that a link involves a CGI request.

Some typical CGI call examples are listed below:

- `http://swexpld.org/whichday.cgi`

- `http://swexpld.org/whichday.cgi/2007/04`

- `http://swexpld.org/whichday.cgi?year=2004&month=2&day=9`

- `http://.../whichday.cgi/23?year=2004`

In the first example no parameters are forwarded to the CGI application by the server. In the second, the URL contains an additional path `/2007/04`, which can be accessed by the program through the environment variable `PATH_INFO`. In the third example three parameters are passed to the application, namely `year`, `month` and `day`. The CGI application finds these parameters in the environment variable `QUERY_STRING`. The last example involves both a parameter and an additional path.

As well as directly calling a CGI application, there is another option, using the so-called SSI (Server Side Include) feature. Web servers supporting SSI offer the opportunity to place specified directives into HTML documents that are to be replaced by dynamic content. These directives take the form of specific comments. When the server receives a request for a page, it examines the page source to see whether it contains any special comments and, if so, executes the specified operation. Such an operation can be, for example, the insertion of the current date or time or calling a CGI application and inserting its result into the page. The following example contains an SSI directive, involving a counter which records the number of visits to the page (it must be noted that this is not typical; such counters are normally implemented by other means):

```
<!--#include virtual="/cgi-bin/counter.pl" -->
```

Last, but not least, another possible way of calling CGI applications is by means of forms. This is what we come to now.

Exercise 1.2: Using your browser, try out all four invocation formats shown above for the `whichday` CGI application. Check what happens if you omit or misspell some input parameters, e.g. the year.

1.1.3. Forms

The most common way to invoke a CGI application is by using *forms*. A form is a group of special control fields which can be filled in or modified by the user in a browser. Such fields can be text input fields, where free text can be written, check boxes, which can be turned on or off, drop-down menus from which predefined item can be selected etc.

Every form has to contain a special button, the so-called *submit* button. Pressing this button instructs the browser to send a request to a server in a way specified at the head of the form. This request contains the values of the fields in the form. In this case a CGI application (or one of its improved variants) awaits the input data on the server-side and generates the result page.

Let us return to the example, introduced in Subsection 1.1.1.3, about calculating the sum of two numbers and generating a dynamic page for displaying the sum. In this example we need to provide some way for the user to specify which numbers she[4] would like to add. For this purpose we can use the form shown in Figure 1.3. The code of the form is placed between the `form` HTML elements. It contains three control fields, two of which are input fields for entering the numbers while the third is the button submitting the form itself.

---

[4] Our use of a female pronoun here and hereafter does not mean that the person in question has to be female; it is just done to simplify the formulation of text.

```
<html>
  <head>
    <title>Example web page containing a form</title>
  </head>
  <body>
  <h1>Sum of two numbers</h1>
  <form action="http://swexpld.org/cgi-bin/add_act.pl"
        method="get">
    First number: <input type="text" name="num1" size="5">
    Second number: <input type="text" name="num2" size="5">
    <input type="submit" value="Add them up">
  </form>

  </body>
</html>
```

Figure 1.3.   A form with two input fields and a button.

The head of the form shows the two most important attributes of the form element. The action specifies the CGI program whose task it is to process the data of the form. More precisely, we actually give a web address and expect that if we make a request to this address the proper answer will be returned. The method attribute specifies the actual HTTP method, which, in the case of forms, can be GET or POST.

In the case of the GET method, the fields of the form are sent by the client encoded into the URL after the ? sign; the CGI program can access these by querying the appropriate environment variable. For example if we entered the numbers 3 and 4, the following request would be issued after pressing the submit button:

`http://swexpld.org/cgi-bin/add_act.pl?num1=3&num2=4`

It is important to understand that such a URL can be manually entered into a browser and the resulting page (which displays the sum of the two numbers, if our CGI program operates correctly) will be identical to that received when submitting the form. In this sense, forms can be considered simply as a user-friendly way of invoking CGI applications.

By using the GET method the values of the fields of the form are sent without any encryption, so anyone glancing at our display sees not only that the result is 7 but also the above request. This is not an issue in this case, but let us imagine if someone sees the link / cgi-bin/login.pl?name=Tas&password=k28h in our browser. . .

As an alternative to the GET method we can use the POST method, where the fields of the form are encoded into the body of the corresponding HTTP request. These can be read by the CGI program at its standard input. In this way, the query parameters are no longer visible in the browser. From amongst numerous differences between the POST and the GET methods we mention just one more: the browsers can *cache* the answer to a GET request (i.e. remember the answer and reuse it for further identical requests), while in the case of POST this is disallowed by the specification. Also, it is worth noting that proper data security is not guaranteed using the POST method: additional techniques (for example the HTTPS protocol) should be used to achieve this.

Exercise 1.3: Try out the form shown in Figure 1.3 in your browser. Modify the text of the form to use the POST method instead of GET. Check how this change affects the URL generated by the submit button.

1.1.4. Advanced server-side solutions

We now discuss problems encountered using the CGI approach and outline some advanced server-side solutions addressing them.

1.1.4.1. Disadvantages of the CGI technology

The basic CGI approach introduced above has many disadvantages. These can be categorised into four different groups.

Efficiency problems. In order to understand why the efficiency of a CGI program is a crucial point, let us look at the life cycle of a CGI application. By default the server starts a new process for each HTTP request, which exits when the request is served.

This creation and termination of processes in itself carries a huge overhead, in terms of both space and time. Furthermore, if a large number of more complex CGI scripts are run then task switching will occur, with further time penalties.

If the CGI program needs to be interpreted (because it has been written in an interpreted scripting language), the problems mentioned above become even more serious.

Unfortunately, the life cycle of CGI applications causes other problems as well. For example, if a CGI program needs to connect to a database to do its job, it cannot do much better than to set up a new connection with the database at start-up and close it after finishing its work. This is an additional cost factor, decreasing efficiency.

Security problems. In the case of CGI applications security is a crucial point. This technology relies on executing remote programs with parameters specified by the (possibly malevolent) user. In principle, when writing a CGI program one should be as careful as if one were developing a web server itself. Unfortunately, such precautions are often neglected. Furthermore, system administrators rarely enforce proper checks on the CGI programs written by users before they permit their execution.

As CGI technology spread, hundreds of security leaks, large and small, were found in CGI programs. Today the general opinion is that CGI applications are serious threats to the security of web-based systems.

A well-known class of security leaks is based on *buffer overflow* errors. Here, the CGI application is called with parameters that cause an overflow in it, for example because the writer of the program assumed that the length of a parameter cannot be more than a certain number of bytes. The first really famous attack using this method was as early as in 1988, when an Internet worm called *Morris* initiated a 536 byte-long request to a *finger* server. The *finger* server is a very simple program, which forwards the request received to the local *finger* program and returns the output to the client (normally the program returns useful information about users such as their full name, last login time etc.). Unfortunately the server used the `gets()` library function to read the input, which simply copied the input data to a memory area referenced by the given pointer (512 bytes were allocated). The 24 byte excess resulted in the overwriting of certain code parts, and so the attacker could eventually run an arbitrary program on the server.

Other forms of attack are also possible, e.g. those relying on the peculiarities of pattern-based languages such as *awk*, which are often used for writing CGI programs.

Inconvenience. One inconvenience is that the request parameters must be parsed by the CGI application itself, which is a tiresome and sometimes dangerous task. Another problem is that the header information for the response, or at least part of it, must be manually created by the CGI programmer.

Finally, what may be the most important problem is that CGI does not offer any help for *session* management. By a session we mean a continuous, correlated, sequence of requests. A good example of using sessions is a web shop, where we can freely browse without "losing" the goods already put into our shopping cart. In the CGI setup, handling this is far from automatic, as visiting a new page means that a new request is sent to the web server. Because the HTTP protocol is stateless the server considers every request separately, without any consideration of what happened before.

To support sessions in the CGI setup, we have to encode the actual state information into each request. The new state must be placed on the answer page by the CGI program in such a way that it is automatically re-sent by the browser with the next request. The most common technique is to "roll" a single identifier along the requests, to which the server-side CGI program can associate the proper state information. Another way is to use *cookies*, which are stored on the client side by some browsers that support them.

As we can see, session management can be implemented in the CGI framework but in a cumbersome and error-prone way. The lack of "built-in" solutions for session management means that almost all CGI programs use their own tricks instead of a thoroughly tested and convenient solution.

Fundamental problems. The most serious and fundamental problem with the CGI technology is that it does not provide any support for separating visual appearance from business logic. Ideally, the business logic (which is what the CGI application really provides) should be reusable and independent of the output formatting. In contrast, a CGI program often contains an intertwined mixture of the logic and the code generating the HTML page.

In principle one can design a modular structure for the CGI program, with which the logic and output generation can be separated. However, this solution is difficult to enforce as the task of properly structuring the CGI program is entirely in the hands of the programmer.

1.1.4.2. Possible solutions

The *FastCGI* technology is capable of solving most efficiency problems mentioned. This is an extension of CGI with better support for life-cycle management. FastCGI applications are persistent, so they remain in the memory between requests. In this way the overheads of starting and terminating processes can be almost fully eliminated. Moreover, because of persistence, FastCGI programs are able to communicate with database systems efficiently.

FastCGI offers more efficient techniques for passing request parameters and the resulting pages. If the FastCGI application and the web server are located on the same computer, all communication between them occurs through a dedicated full-duplex *pipe*. FastCGI also supports communication over TCP/IP, which helps to run time-demanding FastCGI applications in a distributed manner.

The web server can start several single-threaded FastCGI programs (creating a *process pool*), so the service time can be decreased even at heavy load. Multi-threaded FastCGI programs can also be used, in which case the web server sends multiple concurrent requests to the application.

Besides FastCGI there exist other ad hoc solutions as well. An example is `mod_perl`, which is a Perl language interpreter embedded into the Apache web server. With this, Apache does not need any external Perl interpreter to run CGI applications written in Perl, since the web server "understands" programs written in that language. Likewise, solutions exist for encapsulating a PHP implementation into the Apache web server, as servers can be connected in a native way to applications written in the Python, Ruby etc. languages.

It must be noted, however, that these techniques do not solve most problems listed above concerning the CGI-based approach. Security problems and inconvenience still remain and there is no uniform way to separate the business and visualisation logic. More than that, most solutions have limitations, for example they can only be used with certain web servers. Despite that, PHP is one of the most popular server-side technologies today: the web hosting companies (where we store our web pages) generally support it.

A possible solution to all the problems outlined is provided by Java-based servlets and the JSP technology. Servlets, together with their respective frameworks such as Struts and JavaServer Faces, are popular technologies in certain server-side areas, particularly in the enterprise domain.[5]

1.2. Conventional web search engines

In this and subsequent sections we discuss the issues of information retrieval on the web.

This section introduces the subject. First, we give a brief overview of the web as an information source, then we outline how traditional search engines work. In subsequent sections we discuss problems of intelligent search and present some solutions to them.

1.2.1. Knowledge representation on the web

In the following, we consider the World Wide Web as a set of interlinked documents with *heterogeneous syntax and semantics* and *uncontrolled content*.

On the web, we can find documents of different types and formats. Some are plain text files, but most are written using the HyperText Markup Language (HTML). Other frequently used formats include PDF, as well as Microsoft Word and Excel. Images and video and audio streams available on the web may also be considered as documents. In addition, files that have been created by computer agents can also be found. Typical examples are the statistics of various applications, e.g. the monthly usage statistics of a web server.

Documents may differ greatly in the terminology they use. Different words or phrases can be used for the same concept; the numerical value of some datum can be supplied using

---

[5] From the technology point of view the greatest rivals of the servlet-based approach are the ASP and the ASP.NET technologies from Microsoft.

different units on different pages (e.g. in meters on one page and in feet on the other). The language of the documents may vary as well. Here we refer to both the natural and formal computer languages used in various source codes available on the web.

Because of the uncontrolled nature of the Internet, searching the web differs significantly from searching a corporate information base. The latter is a slowly changing well-controlled document repository, normally much more reliable than the information on the web. When searching the web, it is thus not sufficient to find and present a document that accurately matches the query: experience shows that expected results have other important characteristics as well (e.g. recent update time, quality, high reference count, popularity). Moreover, as most queries produce thousands of hits, the ordering of results is really essential. Of course, ranking is important in a well-controlled corporate environment as well! Here, however, a higher level of authenticity and reliability can be assumed, implying ranking strategies different from those in the case of web search.

Today a large number of search engines exist. Some are more popular, some are more user friendly, some are specialised in some way, but all work according to the same general principles. First, a set of web pages is collected by so-called crawlers. Second, the collected pages are analysed by an indexer, which produces a list somewhat similar to conventional book indices. Often search engines also store web pages themselves for faster future retrieval. Third, whenever a search engine is queried for documents, it interprets the query and the actual search is carried out using the index. Before presenting the results, the final step is ranking, which probably plays the most crucial part in judging how good a search engine is.

In the following, we give an overview of search engine components and also discuss some implementation-specific details, such as the Page Rank algorithm of the Google search engine.

1.2.2. Collecting and indexing pages

In the work cycle of search engines, visiting and downloading pages are the first tasks to be performed. For this purpose specialised software components, so-called *crawlers* (also known as *web robots* or *web spiders*) are used, which are continuously visiting and periodically re-visiting pages on the web. As a starting point, a web crawler may be initialised with a list of *seed* URLs to popular sites. Often, these links point to sites that contain a large number of reliable hyperlinks. The `Open Directory Project` [89] (which is discussed in greater detail in Subsection 2.7.2) and the `Yahoo!` directory [113] are good examples of popular sites with reliable URLs. Alternatively, the crawler may start working by using an existing database of its own.

Once the crawler has downloaded a specific page, it extracts the URLs from it and then passes the page to the indexer. Next, the crawler continues recursively: it processes referenced pages in the same way as that used for the URLs in the initial seed. Once again, the word "page" should be more broadly interpreted to include documents such as PDF files, images, plain text files or Excel worksheets. Crawling is definitely not restricted to HTML documents.

Pages are often not indexed immediately after having been visited. In other words, they do not immediately appear as results for search queries once they have been collected by the crawler. Intuitively, downloading and indexing web pages should be thought of as two independent tasks running in parallel. The crawler (a producer) is continuously collecting pages, while the indexer (a consumer) is processing these as its capacities allow.

One may think that web crawlers of different search engines operate very much alike, as their task is clear and simple. Crawlers themselves usually do not perform any analysis of the pages they visit, apart from following the hyperlinks they extract and downloading the referenced content (see Subsection 1.4.1). Clearly indexing, and especially ranking, contributes much more to the success of a search engine. However, this is not the whole story, as several differences can be found when one compares the behaviour of different web crawlers.

One of the most crucial questions a crawler has to answer is which URLs it should follow. In Subsection 1.3.3 we show that some crawlers tend to avoid certain types of hyperlinks while others are more willing to venture onto dangerous ground. Another difference is how crawlers traverse the search space; some crawlers visit only those pages that are referenced by pages already indexed. In addition, the handling of non-textual content (that is, images, audio streams etc.) is also a matter for consideration.

Another vital question is, how frequently should a robot revisit already indexed pages? The better search engines will visit a page more frequently if it has a high relevance rating. Also, pages whose content changes rapidly (such as news portals, electronic versions of newspapers etc.) may be revisited by a crawler very often. Furthermore, the content of these particular pages is indexed (made available for search) with much higher priority.

Search engines practically never use a single web crawler. Instead many such robots are executed in parallel, each looking for new unindexed pages or re-crawling indexed pages. This simultaneous execution produces high network traffic, of course. For this reason crawlers are designed to download pages thoughtfully: for instance, they do not continuously bombard a single web server with a myriad of requests but schedule these so that they are evenly distributed in time. In addition, web server administrators have the opportunity to prohibit crawlers from (1) indexing documents, (2) following hyperlinks extracted from documents and (3) archiving pages (the process during which a copy of the web page is saved in the internal database of the search engine). Prohibition may be accomplished in two different manners: globally or locally.

The globally scoped `robots.txt` file applies to the entire server as a whole. Its content is defined by the *Robot Exclusion Standard* [70]. An excerpt from such a file may be seen below; it forbids any crawler (the `User-agent` field) to index any file in the directory `secret` relative to the server root (the `Disallow` field).

```
User-agent: *
Disallow: /secret/
```

When we change the file `robots.txt`, the effect is not immediate. The contents of the changed file will be considered by a search engine only when the site is re-crawled and the file is read and interpreted again.

Another option to limit the crawlers' actions regarding a given web page is to use a special HTML `meta` element in the `head` section of the page in question. Using this, one may locally prohibit the three actions mentioned before (indexing, following links, archiving) from being performed by crawlers. As in the globally scoped case, any combination of these three actions could be used. In the example below, crawlers are forbidden to archive the given page and to follow the hyperlinks extracted from there:

```
<head>
  <title>Highly confidential material</title>
  <meta name="robots" content="noarchive, nofollow" />
</head>
...
```

One can prevent a robot from following a specific link on a page as well. To achieve this, a special attribute has to be inserted into the hyperlink HTML element in question.

When the globally scoped technique is used to exclude certain pages from being indexed, crawlers cannot even access the restricted directories and the files they contain. In the case of the second, local, technique, pages are visited but as soon as it becomes apparent that a restriction is in effect, crawlers immediately discontinue their action. All in all, the given page is prevented from being indexed, archived and/or hyperlink extracted, whichever is the case.

Nevertheless, taking restrictions into account is done at the discretion of the crawler. In fact, using solely the methods discussed above the creator of a page cannot be one hundred per cent sure that the restrictions imposed are actually complied with (see also Subsection 1.3.3). The good news is, however, that it is the search engines themselves that urge the web server administrators to use some of the features mentioned above. As an example, the attribute value `nofollow` was suggested by Google to prevent certain links from affecting its ranking algorithm (see Subsection 1.2.4 for details).

From the way crawlers work it follows that if no hyperlinks reference a web page, no crawler will find it. For newly created web pages it is therefore advisable to manually register the page for indexing on the appropriate search engine site. Search engines also make it possible to check whether a web page is indexed. The actual query for the retrieval of this information varies from engine to engine [105].

1.2.2.1. Indexing

The primary job of the *indexer* is to parse a downloaded document and collect the expressions relevant for search.

There are two immediate problems with this task. On the one hand, parsing documents on the web is by no means an easy thing to do. The reason behind this is not only the large variety of heterogeneous storage formats but also certain errors specific to each format. For example, a great proportion of HTML pages on the web contain typing errors in HTML element names, start or end tags are missing, special characters occur and sometimes non-standard HTML elements are used that are specifically intended for a given type of browser. An indexer should be prepared to handle these errors gracefully when parsing the document.

On the other hand, relevant and irrelevant expressions in a document should be clearly separated. It is obvious that not every expression that occurs in a document is relevant. In particular, a great many words are conjunction words, definite or indefinite articles or simple expletives. A possible approach is to exclude words with disproportionately low or high frequency. The former should be excluded because they are presumably not of real importance, the latter because they are most probably insignificant words as far as indexing is concerned and used only to structure the natural language text. As a refinement of the model, we may assume that the distribution of expletives and that of other words in a document differs, e.g. expletives form a Poisson distribution. By examining the distribution, a classification of words can hence be accomplished. Other techniques also exist that apply different clustering methods.

Nevertheless, a totally different approach has become widespread. A so-called *stop word list* is usually maintained, which simply contains words thought to be insignificant. These stop word lists are, of course, language dependent. The advantages of this method are easy implementation and fast execution during runtime. Despite its simplicity, it is surprisingly effective.

After discarding irrelevant words, the remaining ones are collected, together with their properties. For example, a property may describe the place of occurrence, e.g. whether the word is found in the title of the page or within an HTML `meta` element. In a more sophisticated model, one can store the relative position of the word within the document body as a property. The collected keywords and their properties are stored in a database and used by the actual search and ranking processes. This will be discussed in the sections that follow.

Exercise 1.4: Collect the set of relevant words from the paragraph above this exercise by omitting the words you consider irrelevant.

1.2.3. Query processing, the vector space model

Information retrieval techniques are not new, in the sense that they existed prior to the appearance and proliferation of the web. A common characteristic of these earlier techniques is that they search on a very limited set of documents compared with the number of pages available on the web today. We will discuss below one of the most widespread of these techniques. We also present the new challenges that web search poses for this method and describe the solutions available to tackle these difficulties.

One of the most popular and most frequently applied information retrieval techniques is the *vector space model* [73] (VSM). In this model, both the query and the documents are treated as vectors of dimension V and the aim is to find the vectors nearest to the vector representing the query, according to some metrics. Documents corresponding to these "nearest" vectors will be the results. The input of the VSM is a document set of N elements and a list of relevant expressions (either words or compound words) collected from it. If we have a total of V such relevant expressions, every single document and the query itself is assigned a vector of dimension V. Let us denote the vector that belongs to document i by w_i. The jth element of this vector (denoted by w_{ij}) is the relevance of the expression j in the document i, which may be calculated in different ways depending on which variant of the VSM is used.

In the most common approach, w_{ij} depends on two factors, (1) how many times the expression occurs in the given document (denoted by f_{ij}) and (2) in how many different documents the expression occurs in (denoted by d_j; obviously $d_j \leq N$). In other words, to determine the relevance of a given expression both the relative importance of the expression with respect to its container document and the global importance of the expression with respect to the entire document set is taken into account. The value of w_{ij} is computed as follows:

$$w_{ij} = f_{ij} * \log\left(\frac{N}{d_j}\right). \tag{1.1}$$

The role of the logarithmic factor is important. It gives high value to those expressions that occur frequently but only in a small proportion of the document set. In the extreme case, when an expression is found in every single document (d_j equals N), the value of the product and hence that of w_{ij} will be zero. This clearly shows that from the perspective of a text search this expression is completely irrelevant, as it occurs in all documents.

Let us denote by q the V-dimensional vector that belongs to the query. The elements of q are computed similarly to (1.1). However, unlike the frequency of expressions in documents, the frequency in the query is treated as a binary value. In other words, each expression in the query is counted only once, which reflects an assumption that no query contains an expression multiple times. Thus the query vector consists of the following components:

$$q_j = \begin{cases} \log \left(\frac{N}{d_j} \right) & \text{if expression } i \text{ occurs in the query,} \\ 0 & \text{otherwise.} \end{cases} \tag{1.2}$$

All we need now is a function that determines the measure of similarity between the query and a given document vector. Applying the function to every document vector and then arranging the function values in a decreasing order, we obtain a relevance ranking. The first few elements of the ranking are presented as results. The most commonly applied measure of similarity is the cosine of the angle between the two V-dimensional vectors. To do this, we simply use the two well-known definitions of a vector scalar product. The equation below shows the measure of similarity between the query q and the document w_i:

$$\text{similarity}(q, w_i) = \frac{\sum_{j=1}^{V} q_j * w_{ij}}{\sqrt{\sum_{j=1}^{V} q_j^2 * \sum_{j=1}^{V} w_{ij}^2}}. \tag{1.3}$$

In this equation the denominator is often referred to as the normalisation factor. Thanks to its presence, documents that use similar expressions will be a similar distance from the query independently of the length of these documents.

Exercise 1.5: Let the content of document A be "apple, banana, cherry" and the content of document B be "apple, banana, banana, cherry, apple, cherry". We do not have any more documents. Determine the measure of similarity between document A and the query "cherry". What can you say about the similarity between the same query and document B?

The VSM has been employed for many decades and has proved its usefulness in multiple fields of application. The model is a favourite of non-computer experts as they can formulate queries in natural language. The indexer analyses the query in the same manner as it analyses documents, and relevant expressions are gathered from queries just as they are from documents. In addition the model supports so-called *relevance feedback*. Relevance feedback means that the query is run several times: it is automatically extended with the most significant expressions appearing in the topmost hits of the previous run. Consequently, better-quality results and ranking may be obtained through the refinement of the original result set.

A further advantage of the VSM is that it eliminates the primary drawbacks of lexical search, which is based on the exact presence of words in documents. By default, lexical (also known as *full-text*) search engines provide poor performance when dealing with synonyms, homonyms etc. In particular, if the query uses a terminology different from that in a relevant document, the document will not be returned by the search. If the word "cat" occurs in the query, a strict lexical search engine does not fetch pages on which the word "cat" does not appear for some reason, even if the word "kitten" does. (This is also the reason for the common phenomenon that we get no results at all when our query consists of too many words.) In fact, from the perspective of a search engine, "cat" and "kitten" are two unrelated expressions. In the VSM the measure of similarity is a more flexible metric than binary matching and, using relevance feedback, the engine is able to achieve good results within even a few iterations. Nevertheless, the VSM does not associate any meaning with individual words and therefore, in this aspect, it is no different from lexical search. What happens is that, owing to its construction, the VSM does not require that every single word of the query should appear in a document returned as a result.

As far as Internet search is concerned, however, the VSM does not directly satisfy our needs. The available web search engines either use an extended variant of the basic VSM presented here or they use a totally different approach. A minor difficulty is that the values N and d_j in (1.1) are unknown: more precisely, they constantly change as more and more pages are indexed. Taking this into account can cause serious computational difficulties.

The major problem is that most search engine users under-specify their query. For instance, what most commonly comes out of the idea "I would like to learn more about koalas" is the query for the single word "koala". Using the standard VSM search technique, the best results would in general be those pages that contain the expressions in the query but relatively few other expressions besides. In this particular case, a web page that contains solely the word "koala", possibly illustrated by a few images, would be presented among the top results. It is obvious that much more informative results exist, which, in fact, are usually found by any of the most commonly used search engines today.

Exercise 1.6: Try to use your favourite search engine on the example above and check how many top hits contain a description of koalas.

One may argue that those who do not properly define their query should not expect good results. This is, however, not an appropriate approach from a business perspective: it must not be forgotten that web users often have minimal computer qualifications and search experience and will use the search engine that returns good results for their seemingly under-specified queries as well. Indeed, it is possible to return useful results for an under-specified query. The creators of the Google search engine mention the example of the query "Bill Clinton" (President of the USA between 1993 and 2001), for which their engine returns the White House, the Office of the President and major Clinton-related sites as topmost results [23]. These are exactly the results that the user who entered the query would most probably have required.

In fact, Google builds on the so-called *Boole model*, rather than VSM, and uses a lexical search engine (at least according to publicly available information). At the same time, it puts the real emphasis on the ranking of results [92]. Despite the fact that Google is undoubtedly the most popular search engine today, the VSM and the idea of doing "more" than full-text search is still a hot topic. Several attempts have been made to improve the VSM, to make it usable in web search [73], and there exist engines that make use of such improved VSM variants.

To measure the efficiency of a search engine on a given query, we can use two important properties of the document set returned for the query. The *precision* is a numerical value between 0 and 1 computed by dividing the number of relevant returned documents by the total number of returned documents for a query. The concept of relevance is undoubtedly a subjective one: we may, for instance, treat a document as relevant with respect to a given query if an expert committee considers it so. *Recall* is a concept similar to precision but the divisor is different: the number of relevant documents returned for a query is divided by the total number of relevant documents. Ideally both properties would have the value 1, which means that the engine returns all relevant documents without any superfluous results. In practice, however, this is unfeasible. We can say that in general an increase in the value of one property results in a decrease in the value of the other, and vice versa. Nowadays, lower precision and higher recall is more typical.

Finally, we mention that there is a hot debate between the creators of web search engines and the supporters of traditional information retrieval techniques. Notably, traditional information retrieval techniques (like the VSM) have been extended with methods that make them more applicable to web search. For example, it is worth distinguishing searches for an already seen page from the case when an unknown page is searched. In the latter case it is generally not problematic to display a set of results in which some of the specified expressions are left out: this fits the standard VSM approach. In the former case, however, it is vital that all expressions are present in the document.

For an in-depth comparison of web search engines and engines based on traditional information retrieval techniques, see Hawking and Craswell [50].

Exercise 1.7: Use your favourite search engine to search for the word "lion". Calculate the precision and recall for the first 20 elements of the returned document set (assume that the total number of relevant documents is r).

1.2.4. Ranking of the hits

As we have previously seen, the result of a query is a set of web pages all of which are related to the query entered. Probably the most crucial task of a search engine is to rank these pages, i.e. present them in the order which puts "good" hits at the top. A search engine that ignores any ranking considerations and shows web pages without any particular ordering would be completely useless, since a single query often returns several hundred thousand pages.

Actually, the precise ranking of results has become really important with the sharp increase in the number of indexed pages. The reason behind this is that the capabilities of users have not improved in parallel with the rise in data quantities; we are still able to go through only a very limited number of hits. Therefore, the first 10–20 results that the search engine displays are critical (a good test of a search engine is whether it finds itself, that is, what the results are for its own name).

In general the exact ranking criteria of particular search engines are not public, but the major ideas are well known. One of the most basic ranking criteria is to consider the *place* and *frequency* of occurrence of the particular expression we are seeking.

When our task is to search among books and all we are told is the phrase "computer science", it is almost certain that we would first check the titles of the books. Search engines follow similar ideas. Often, they assign higher ranks to pages in which the search expression occurs in the title than to pages where this is not the case. As an extension of this idea, one may take into consideration the place in the document where the expression first appears. The assumption here is that relevant expressions appear in the introductory part or at least in the first few sections of the document. For certain kinds of document (e.g. scientific publications) this is so true that often it is a requirement that the introduction or abstract highlights every relevant piece of information in the document.

A search engine may consider the properties of the character fonts used for a given piece of text to determine its relevance. It may also take into account the distance between the occurrences of query words in the document, as well as the presence of the query expression in the HTML meta-elements. Words with bigger fonts and/or colours different from the rest of the document can be considered more important. Observing the distance between words is the reason why querying a search engine for a person's name yields high-ranking pages when the given and family names occur one after the other (that is, the web page is indeed about the person we were looking for). The meta-elements of a page normally contain the summary of the web page and relevant keywords. These pieces of information might be used during ranking or search.

The *frequency of occurrence* is the other crucial thing to examine. The assumption is that if a given word occurs frequently in a document (provided that it is not on the stop word list) then it is important with regard to the content of the document (see Subsection 1.2.3). In addition to finding out the frequency of individual words, it is also important to do this for complex expressions.

Search engines can also record and analyse user behaviour. If a large proportion of users click on the second or third result displayed for a given query, it is probable that the ranking is not good and actually the page ranked first is not the most relevant. An example of this is the open-source Wiki-inspired search engine commonly known as Wikiasari.

In Subsection 1.2.1 we mentioned that the uncontrolled and unreliable nature of web documents creates completely new problems in searching and ranking. Pages often have to be given lower priority during ranking because of certain properties even if they seem to be a good hit. The reason is that, unfortunately, the criteria previously discussed allow the user to manipulate the results of the ranking processes relatively easily. Additional expressions can be inserted into the page title even if they do not match the content. Popular keywords may be placed in cunning ways in the page body (one keyword possibly hundreds of times) that remain unseen by the human reader. However, these keywords are parsed by the search engine, which thus considers the page a very relevant one. Certain low-ranked hits in a result set may be repeatedly clicked on (by humans, or even by computer programs) to give the impression that a particular hit is more relevant than others. And so on.

The battle between search engines and ranking manipulators is still raging. Consequently, ranking criteria that are easy to manipulate are continuously moved to the background and play a less significant role in determining the final ranking. They are being replaced by criteria that are more difficult to consciously influence; these include methods that take the link structure of the web documents into consideration.

Some search engines consider hyperlinked text or the text surrounding hyperlinks when they determine page ranking. More precisely, the hyperlinked text does not influence the ranking of the page on which it appears but, rather, that of the page referenced by the link. In fact a hyperlink has two ends, called *anchors*. The text around the source anchor of a hyperlink influences the relevance of the destination anchor. In fact, both the highlighted text of the anchor and the surrounding words can be taken into account here. This context is usually referred to as the *anchor text*.

For example, when our page is referred to by someone else as an excellent page on bear hunting, this might be a more significant piece of information for a search engine than it would be if we were to put the same description at the top of our page.

It is interesting that when the first search engine, the World Wide Web Worm [78], appeared in 1994 it already applied this technique. Later it became less popular while today it is flourishing again: nearly every search engine makes use of it.

A further advantage of anchors is that by using them we can collect information about documents that otherwise the search engine would not be able to index. For instance, a hyperlink that references an image may indeed tell us much about the image itself. However, one should be careful in returning unindexed, and hence unexamined, content as a result.

As many say, the popularity of Google is undoubtedly due to its ability to rank results significantly better than do other search engines. Google uses the general techniques discussed earlier but also implements a specialised algorithm that assigns importance to individual pages purely on the basis of the hyperlink structure. Together with other factors, this importance value is adequately weighed to determine the final ranking. Surprisingly, the technique is so powerful that, at the dawn of Google, the engine would have produced better results than its competitors with the application of this technique even if it had merely done a simple matching in the page title (completely discarding page content). We will now discuss this algorithm in more detail.

The PageRank algorithm of Google.   *PageRank* is a real number that indicates the *importance* of a page with respect to a given set of pages. It has both a theoretical lower and upper limit (to be discussed later). Google uses the PageRank algorithm during the ranking phase to determine the importance of indexed web pages. While many aspects are considered when determining the final ranking of a page, and the PageRank value is only one of these many aspects, it is unarguably very important.

The basic idea is to assume that if one web page contains a hyperlink to another then the source page in fact gives a vote of confidence to the referenced page. In other words, the creator of the web page, the voter, placed the hyperlink on her page because for some reason she considered the destination page relevant. It also matters, however, how important the voter is: a vote cast by an important page weighs more. This produces a recursive algorithm that basically says that a page is important if important pages reference it.

The validity of this model is debatable, as is that of most other models constructed. It might happen that certain pages are referenced via hyperlinks as bad examples and the creator by no means wishes to imply that those would be valuable pages. It seems, however, that it is far from true that these types of link dominate the web and anyway it is generally difficult to define the concept of "important" or "interesting" web pages. The reason why a hyperlink points to a page is essentially immaterial; if it does, it means that the referenced page has raised some interest.

The basic algorithm, first published in Page *et al.* [92], builds on an apparently trivial recursive equation which corresponds to the informal description given earlier (it is certain, however, that Google today uses a modified, non-public version of the algorithm discussed here). Actually, the authors erroneously published the first term of the equation in one of their papers and this has been the version that has become well known in the web community. Let us first look at this "erroneous" version:

$$PR(A) = (1-d) + d*(PR(t_1)/C(t_1) + \cdots + PR(t_n)/C(t_n)). \qquad (1.4)$$

The equation defines the PageRank value, i.e. the importance of page A. In the equation, $t_1, \ldots, t_n$ denote those pages that reference page A and $PR(t_i)$ denotes the PageRank value of the ith such page. The factor d that occurs in the equation is a scaling (damping) factor, the value of which was suggested to be 0.85 in [92]. Finally, $C(X)$ denotes the total number of outbound hyperlinks (or source anchors) on page X. For instance, if the value of $C(t_i)$ is 24, this means that page t_i contains a total number of 24 outbound hyperlinks, one of which has a destination anchor on page A.[6]

For the moment let us disregard the factor d; then the interpretation of the equation is as follows. Page A receives a number $PR(t_1)/C(t_1)$ of votes from the first page that contains links directed at A: that is, page t_1 evenly distributes its own importance among its outbound hyperlinks. If only a single outbound link is found on page t_1 then A receives all the $PR(t_1)$ votes; if three are found then a third of the votes; etc. This formula is applied to every page on which outbound links point to A. Summing up all resulting terms, we get the relevance of page A. Hence, it may be more desirable for our page to be referenced by a page with low PR value and few outbound links than by a more important page which has dozens of source anchors. Nevertheless, the more our page is referenced, the more its importance increases.

Thanks to the presence of the factor d, however, a page does not distribute its total relevance among the pages it references, but only 85% of it (assuming that $d = 0.85$). In order to fully understand the idea behind this, we need both the corrected version of the PageRank equation and a discussion of a newer, intuitive, meaning of the PageRank algorithm. The corrected PageRank equation has the following form, where N is the total number of indexed web pages:

$$PR(A) = (1-d)/N + d*(PR(t_1)/C(t_1) + \cdots + PR(t_n)/C(t_n)). \qquad (1.5)$$

Its authors, Sergey Brin and Lawrence Page, thought of the PageRank algorithm as a way of describing the behaviour of a "stochastic surfer". Such a person chooses a starting web page at random and proceeds by randomly following one of the outbound links. He does not even look at which link he clicks, just blindly chooses one among the outbound links following a uniform distribution. This explains why the relevance of a given page is divided by the number of outbound hyperlinks in the PageRank equation.

In this model the equation defines a distribution. The PageRank value of a page is a probability (a real number between 0 and 1) and hence the sum of the PageRank values of all existing pages is 1. Note, however, that this holds only if it is true that every page contains at least one outbound link to be followed (i.e. our surfer can always click on a link).

The probability that the surfer reaches page F from the starting page can be computed. If there are multiple paths reaching to F, the sum of the probabilities belonging to these paths is

---

[6] The original algorithm does not specify what happens if a page references another page multiple times. In what follows we assume that these links are treated as a single link.

taken. This is exactly what the PageRank equation says, with the extension that it reduces this probability by the factor d, because we assume that our imaginary surfer does not perpetually follow one of the outbound links on the page he currently visits but sometimes thinks it is time to choose a completely new starting page. Let us denote by $1-d$ the probability that the surfer chooses a new starting page; that is, d corresponds to the probability that the surfer continuously selects one among the available outbound links. The value $(1-d)/N$ is the theoretical minimum of a PageRank value: with this probability any page could be visited independently of the number of inbound links, i.e. hyperlinks that point to the given page.

For those readers with an interest in mathematics, we mention that if we consider web pages as states then the random walk realised by the PageRank algorithm can be considered as a Markov chain. The single-step transition probability p_{ij} is shown below. As before, $C(t_i)$ is the number of outbound links on page i. For simplicity we now assume that $d=1$:

$$p_{ij} = \begin{cases} \dfrac{1}{C(t_i)} & \text{if a hyperlink connects page } i \text{ to page } j; \\ 0 & \text{otherwise.} \end{cases} \tag{1.6}$$

The importance of a page is indicated by the probability that the Markov chain is in the state corresponding to the page. Hence the boundary distribution of the chain needs to be computed. Unfortunately the chain defined above is not guaranteed to be either irreducible or aperiodic, hence it is not necessarily stable. In addition it may contain closed sets ("webs") from which there are no outbound links. Therefore the boundary distribution will have states of probability 0 for pages outside these sets.

The problem of stability can be solved in many ways. For example, if we start the chain from a uniform distribution, that is, $P^{(0)} = (\frac{1}{N}, \ldots, \frac{1}{N})$, it can be proved that the distribution $P^{(n)}$ has a limit. This can be obtained as a solution to the usual $P = P\Pi$ equation. Actually, as we do not aim to get an exact solution, it is sufficient to perform the $P^{(n)} = P^{(n-1)}\Pi$ iteration until the ranking based on the distribution does not change.

Assuming that during his random walk the imagined surfer may jump with a small probability to any given page, the problem of closed sets can also be solved. This is the justification for the factor d in (1.4) and (1.5) from the mathematical perspective.

We now give a few examples showing how to compute PageRank values in practice. In these examples the "erroneous" equation will be used, since does not essentially differ from the corrected version: if we multiply the PR value that satisfies (1.5) by the number of web pages, we obtain the value we get from (1.4). Actually, it is the "erroneous" equation that is favoured by the scientific web community because if we use it then we do not need to take into account the total number of web pages.

Basics of calculating PageRank. In the simplest case we have two web pages denoted by A and B, which mutually reference each other. Here, according to (1.4) with $d = 0.85$, the PageRank values of A and B are given by the following formulae:

$$PR(A) = 0.15 + 0.85 * (PR(B)/1),$$
$$PR(B) = 0.15 + 0.85 * (PR(A)/1).$$

Evidently, the computation of $PR(A)$ relies on the PR value of B and vice versa. One possible way to obtain the PageRank values is simply to solve this linear equation system by using methods such as Gaussian elimination. For practical considerations, however, iterative methods are more widespread. For example, let us make an initial guess at the *PR* value of *B*, e.g. let us assume $PR(B) = 0.8$. The importance of page *A* is then $0.15 + 0.85 * 0.8 = 0.83$.

Note, however, that this value cannot be correct. If this were the PageRank value of *A* then importance of *B* could not be 0.8, as is obvious from the following formula:

$$PR(B) = 0.15 + 0.85 * (0.83/1),$$

which yields $PR(B) = 0.8555$.

We have now arrived at a new guess for $PR(B)$, and we can continue by repeating the above calculations. Fortunately, the iterated values of $PR(A)$ and $PR(B)$ converge and eventually produce the solutions of the above linear equation system. Thus the actual PageRank values may be computed with arbitrary precision if an adequate number of iterations is performed.

Exercise 1.8: Calculate the PageRank values of pages *A* and *B* above for a few more iterations. After this, guess the values to which these numbers converge and verify your assumption by substituting them into the equations. If you guess correctly then you reach a fixpoint, i.e. the values for $PR(A)$ and $PR(B)$ will not change after you evaluate the equations.

Web sites. By a *web site* we mean a set of connected pages that are related in some way. For instance, corporations often have web sites where pages present the products of the corporation, list its employees, advertise job vacancies, provide contact information etc.

It is in the interest of the administrators of a given web site that search engines, for example Google, assign the greatest possible importance to the site. For the sake of simplicity, we will consider a site to be a small independent structure whose pages may refer to external pages as well as be referred to from the outside world.

Actually, from the point of a search engine, the concept of a web site is purely theoretical. In fact search engines only consider a single global "site", that is, an enormous set of indexed web pages interconnected with links. Google, for example, applies the PageRank algorithm to this huge global network.

The PageRank value of a site is calculated by taking the sum of the PageRank values of all pages that belong to the site. If we consider web sites as individual units for the sake of example calculations, we will notice the following: the maximum PageRank value of a self-standing site equals the number of pages constituting the site. If every page is referenced by another and every page contains an outbound link then the web site gains its maximum PageRank value.

Two cases exist when an ineffective hyperlink structure results in a lower than maximum PageRank value. One is the trivial case when the site contains a page at which no links are directed. For instance, let us imagine a site comprising three distinct pages not connected by hyperlinks. The PageRank value of each page, according to (1.4), will be equal to 0.15: the sum of them is therefore considerably less than 3. In practice this case is irrelevant, as search engines by default do not even know of the existence of such isolated pages.

The other case is more interesting. If our web site contains a page which is referenced by hyperlinks but contains no outbound links then the site as a whole does not reach the

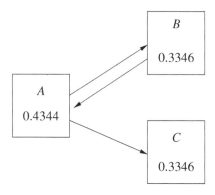

Figure 1.4. A web site with an ineffective link structure.

maximum PageRank value. Such "dead-end" pages are called *dangling pages* or *sinks*. Figure 1.4 depicts a site with the dangling page *C*. The numbers in the boxes are the computed PageRank values.

Actually, in the presence of dangling pages, Google uses a modified algorithm. Prior to performing the PageRank algorithm, it first removes those pages that contain no outbound links, as the presence of these does not fit the "stochastic surfer" model. If, because of this change, some other pages become dangling pages then these are repeatedly removed until no dangling pages remain. At this point the correct PageRank values are computed for the remaining well-formed structure. Finally, discarded pages are put back into the network, one by one, and the importance of these pages is computed from the available PageRank values. In our example the PageRank value of pages *A* and *B* is 1 while that of *C* is 0.575, as calculated by the modified algorithm. In this manner, pages with a "healthy" link structure do not lose importance owing to their dangling companions. In spite of this, the total PageRank value of the site still does not reach the maximum value 3.

From the discussion above it follows that it is worth paying attention to establishing an adequate link structure (notably, every single page should contain an outbound hyperlink) because otherwise Google, for example, will not rank our web site according to our expectations. However, dangling pages do not necessarily indicate a design flaw. When a hyperlink pointing to a PDF document is placed on a web page, the PDF file will be seen as a dangling page by search engines that index PDF content (provided that hyperlinks do not occur in or are not extracted from the PDF document).

Henceforth we will consider only sites that are regular in the sense that they contain pages with at least one inbound and at least one outbound link.

Exercise 1.9: Show that if the total number of web pages is N, the theoretical maximum for the PageRank value of a given page is $dN + (1 - d)$. Hint: a page may receive the theoretical maximum if every other page points only at it and if the page in question also contains a hyperlink to itself.

Distribution of PageRank values within a site. When a site of n pages is interconnected to form a complete graph (i.e. every page is connected to every other), the PageRank value for

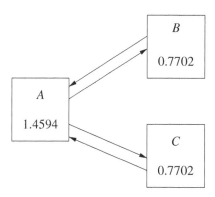

Figure 1.5. The importance of the site is concentrated on the main page.

every page will be 1: that is, the maximum importance achievable by a stand-alone site has been reached. In most cases, however, this is not adequate for our needs. Usually our aim is to increase the importance of certain pages, naturally at the expense of others. The main page of the site is generally a good example, as are all pages that contain relevant expressions as regards a search.

Thanks to the features of the PageRank algorithm, the cumulative importance of a site can in practice be almost freely distributed among the pages of the site. Let us consider the site in Figure 1.5. The cumulative PageRank value is the maximum obtainable value, 3, just as in the complete graph case, though page A is much more relevant than the two other pages. One may intuitively argue that there are two links to the main page, while the other two pages are referenced only by a single link each.

It should be realised that even though it may seem from the PageRank equation that if a page casts a vote for another then it loses no importance, this is not necessarily so. What we see, for sure, is that the importance of our page matters when computing the importance of other pages we are referencing. However, when computing the PageRank value of our page, the hyperlinks on our page are not taken into account. All that matters is which external pages cast a vote for our page. This process can be thought of as a shareholders' committee meeting in which the votes of some are worth more than those of others, because they possess more shares.

The twist is that while the number of shares possessed by all shareholders is constant, the importance of our page may depend on the importance of pages for which we either directly or indirectly voted. If a new link is added to our page then the weight of the vote transferred with each outbound link will decrease, which may finally result in a drop in importance for the set of pages to which we are referring. If our importance somehow depends on the importance of these referenced pages, the additional outbound link may actually decrease our PageRank value.

Let us consider a minimally modified version of Figure 1.5. This can be seen in Figure 1.6. A single new hyperlink has been added that connects page C to B. Performing the computations, we see that C has lost importance. Intuitively explained, C now shares its importance between A and B and hence transfers a smaller weight to A. As a result, the importance of A drops (even though this is offset to a small degree by the fact that A receives greater relevance

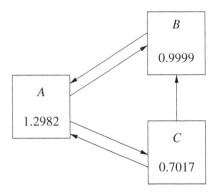

Figure 1.6. Outbound links may decrease importance.

from the now more important page *B*) and may thus transfer less importance back to *C* via the hyperlink from *A* to *C*.

All in all, we see that outbound links may cause a drop in page importance. This is not always the case, however, as it also may happen, though not very frequently, that an outbound link has a beneficial effect. It all depends on the way in which we are dependent on the importance of the pages to which we are referring.

To summarise, from the viewpoint of a site the outbound links on a page can be classified into two categories. One category includes links that connect two pages both of which belong to the same site. This may rearrange importance among the pages of the site but does not alter the cumulative importance. The other category includes links that point to a page external to the site, and this in most cases contributes to a loss in cumulative importance (which, as already mentioned, may in turn be offset by hyperlinks coming from external sites). Nonetheless, we have some control over the amount of loss as it depends to a great degree on the link structure of the site. With a clever link structure, the loss of importance due to externally directed hyperlinks can be minimised.

If the creators of web sites are cunning enough, they can completely hide hyperlinks directed at external sites so that Google, for example, does not take these hyperlinks into account when computing PageRank values. Hyperlinks may be placed on pages by means of JavaScript code, which, if cleverly written, is invisible to the Google engine. For example, we can store the script in a directory undisclosed to the search engine with `robots.txt`.

Finally, we mention that Google takes other factors besides link structure into account when determining the importance of a page. For instance, it often penalises pages for containing links to certain infamous, "black listed" sites. In addition, inbound links from the same domain or geographical unit transfer less importance than hyperlinks from more distant regions. It is worth more if someone "independent" votes for our site than if a "friend" does.

Exercise 1.10: Let us consider a modified version of the web site presented in Figure 1.5 in which there is a new hyperlink from page *B* to page *C*. Calculate the PageRank values for pages *A*, *B* and *C* in this modified site and compare these with the results shown in Figure 1.6.

1.3. Problems with searching the web

In this section we summarise the problems that the majority of today's search engines are striving to solve. These arise from the general characteristics of the Internet and web content. We have classified the problems into four main categories. General problems include difficulties due to the size of the web and its rapidly changing content. In the section on the deep web, we discuss questions related to dynamically generated pages and hard-to-access background databases. A separate section introduces the so-called crawler traps. Finally, probably the greatest problem of today's web, the lack of semantics, is discussed in detail.

1.3.1. General problems

The enormous size of the web is one of the basic factors that affects the applicability of information retrieval techniques. Handling billions of pages and terabytes of data poses an unprecedented challenge. One of the most famous series of conferences on traditional information retrieval techniques on large data sets is the Text Retrieval Conference (TREC) [87]. The first such conference was held in 1992 in Gaithersburg, Maryland. In the mid-90s, the size of the data set used for testing contained 20 gigabytes of data (articles, governmental data, news); by the end of the millennium the data set had grown to 100 gigabytes and was an abridged version of the Internet Archive [67].

These numbers at first might seem huge. Actually, the Google search engine even in its experimental phase was already handling 24 million web pages, which corresponded to 147 gigabytes of data. By the year 2004, the number of pages had increased by two orders of magnitude to billions. Now we can only guess how many pages are indexed, since at the end of the year 2005 Google stopped announcing the index size.

Size affects not only search but also the collection of web pages. Visiting web pages on the Internet is a time-consuming task: a complete crawl of the web would take too much time. In the time span of a full crawl, the content and structure of the Internet would change substantially [50].

Even if we managed to achieve a significant increase in crawling speed by some method unknown today, the Internet contains pages whose content rapidly changes, week by week, day by day or even minute by minute. Such pages include news portals, forums and blogs (web logs). It is a reasonable expectation that we can search among fresh news and current topics and not be confined to the state of the Internet weeks before.

1.3.2. The deep web

The *deep web* has become a frequently used phrase these days. The interpretation of "deep web" has been the target of arguments, with some giving a different meaning to the term than others, but nowadays a mainstream interpretation seems to be emerging. In this sense, the term deep web is used in two contexts, to denote

(1) either database content only available via web form submissions

(2) or documents available in non-textual formats.

Databases store data in various formats, generally in tables in some binary form. Data is accessed by queries through the database manager (DBM). This significantly differs from the direct access we are used to in the case of web pages. Queries addressed to against the database can be made by CGI programs, such as servlets or scripts, that generate dynamic content. Query results are presented to the user in a form completely different from their original storage format.

Parameters relating to a database query (which specify what is actually being queried) are frequently given by means of web forms (see Subsection 1.1.3). For instance, by asking us to fill in a form with our username and password, a CGI program may verify – by issuing an appropriate database query – whether we are authorised to enter a home page. If so, the page is presented to us; otherwise an error message is displayed. Similarly, in an online bookstore the user gets further information on the desired product after having filled in certain form fields (author, title, ISBN code etc.). In the background, queries are generated and executed against the database using the data entered into the form.

Pages with web forms seem friendly and secure to users. However, it is obvious that search engines are incapable of randomly completing and submitting a web form solely to stand a chance of obtaining a result worth processing. Moreover, such behaviour is beyond their aims.

Hence, such content is unavailable to search engines. This is more significant than it might at first seem. According to estimates, the data available on the web through background databases is *by orders of magnitude* greater than via conventional web pages. At the dawn of the web this was not so; on the contrary, databases available through the web were regarded as peculiarities and were often called *virtual directories*. With the advent of dynamic web pages, however, the need to access databases has greatly increased.

Actually, in certain situations, the data stored in databases is easily accessible by search engines. For instance, the majority of news portals store news in databases and the individual pages are generated and presented to the user upon request. Here, users do not need to complete web forms; simply by visiting the main page they trigger CGI programs to generate and return pages with fresh news. From the viewpoint of search engines, such a site is indistinguishable from a conventional static web page despite the fact that parts of it were generated on the fly. This kind of database content is hence *not* classified as part of the deep web.

The other kinds of content in the deep web are files available in non-textual formats. These include images, multimedia streams and, to some extent, Word, Excel or PDF files.

As opposed to the deep web, by the *surface web* we denote the statically available part of the Internet. Occasionally, the terminology *invisible web* is used instead of deep web, which is, however, in many senses unsuitable and illogical. On the one hand information is not invisible, only difficult to access by search engines; that is, the expression is search engine-oriented. On the other hand, it is somewhat paradoxical that search engines themselves represent deep web content since they store their indices in databases, which are available to users only through queries (i.e. by filling in web forms).

The border between the deep and surface web is not sharp. Between the two, there is the so-called *grey zone*, where the classification of content is not straightforward. Let us imagine that by filling in a web form the user gets a good result for her query. The address of the result page may be saved and reused to revisit the generated page without completing the web form again (in some cases, however, these dynamic links do not persist and do not allow later revisiting of the resultant page). Provided that we include this dynamic address on our homepage for some reason, a search engine may follow this link and index the related content. In other words, true deep web content can be reached by a search engine under such special circumstances.

Exercise 1.11: Look at the page `http://www.nasa.gov/multimedia/`, giving access to the NASA multimedia database, and search for any phrase related to space technology (try "alpha", for example). Try to use the same phrase in an ordinary search engine as well.

1.3.3. Non-indexable pages; cloaking

In this subsection we present two issues related to the process of crawling. First we discuss the fact that there is a large number of dynamically generated pages on the Internet which are not available to search engines. The reason for this is that crawlers are not willing to follow certain types of link. After this, we talk about the technique called "cloaking", i.e. how web servers can show different contents for the same URL, depending on whether the request comes from a crawler or a human visitor.

1.3.3.1. Dynamic links versus crawlers

The majority of search engine crawlers recognise dynamic links and do not follow them. In Subsection 1.1.2 we saw how request parameters are encoded in the query string, in the case of the HTTP GET method. This is easily recognised by crawlers, which immediately know that visiting the link involves the invocation of a CGI program. The link below is an example of such an invocation (crawlers may recognise other, much more sophisticated, dynamic links as well):

`http://swexpld.org/calendar.cgi?year=2004`   (1.7)

Each time a robot is entrapped in an infinite cycle or wastes valuable resources on downloading irrelevant pages, we say that the robot is in a *crawler trap* (also known as *spider trap*). Dynamic links can be dangerous to crawlers, as following dynamic links can snare them in crawler traps.

The reason behind the existence of crawler traps is that dynamic links often create huge or even infinite search spaces. The above link, for example, could occur on a page of a site that implements an online calendar; the dynamic link would take the user to the next year. From the perspective of the user, that she may advance as many years as she wishes is a useful service. If she so desires, she can check which days will be holidays in April 2029 etc. A crawler, however, would endlessly follow newer and newer links, misspending its resources as well as that of the web server.

It does not help very much either if the crawler is stopped after a given depth (which is a usual technique in the case of non-dynamic links as well) or if the links themselves disappear after a limit, e.g. the calendar functions only till the year 2049. Even in this case the crawler has visited dozens of nearly identical pages, which has absolutely no beneficial effect as regards a search. A similar thing happens when a session identifier parameter, which changes from visit to visit, is embedded in the query string. Because of this, the crawler may classify an already visited page as a completely new one.

It is of course possible that a dynamic link points, for instance, to the next element of an online catalogue, which contains relevant information. So it *would* be worth following it.

In spite of this, the majority of crawlers do not take the risk inherent in following dynamic links.

Beyond the issues discussed above, it is possible that the CGI program requires certain client data for its proper execution. Request parameters, frequently embedded in the link itself (e.g. `year=2004`) are ideally used for this purpose. Often, however, further information is also required, such as the content of cookies, which the crawler is not prepared to provide.

1.3.3.2. Cloaking

Actually, the phrase "crawler trap" can also be used for an arbitrary technique or program that can decide whether a given page is being visited by a crawler. If a robot is successfully identified, various actions may be performed such as blocking the generation of the page or returning a page different from that for a conventional user request. With this trick, called *cloaking*, some site administrators try to get crawlers to regard the page as an interesting and relevant one. The deceived visitors, lured to the site by the appealing ranking given to the page, are of course presented with the real content, which in most cases has nothing to do with the criteria that the users entered in the search engine. In a more positive scenario, the creator of the web page may present slightly dissimilar content to different search engines because she is aware that search engines have differing behaviours regarding which expressions to index and which to consider relevant. In other words all that involved is cosmetics, which is thought to be important owing to the heterogeneity of search engines.

It should also be noted that cloaking can actually be beneficial for both parties. For instance, additional information meaningful only to search engines (meta-information, textual description attached to links etc.) may be presented to them only. In such a way, regular user visits can result in the downloading of smaller files, which means faster access.

The identification of crawlers may be done in real time; that is, at the time of the request, or later by analysing web logs. In both cases, we need at least the visitor's IP address and the so-called user agent identifier. This includes the identifier of the software and its environment that initiated the request. When the site is accessed through conventional browsing (that is, the browser makes a request to the web server providing the dynamic content), this identifier contains textual information on the browser and desktop environment used. For instance, the identifier contains the following string if the browser is Microsoft's Explorer 9 running under Windows 7:

```
Mozilla/5.0 (compatible; MSIE 9.0; Windows NT 6.1)
```

The interesting thing in this example is that Explorer claims to be a different browser from what it actually is in order to get content specifically designed for Netscape's browser (the name Mozilla is the original development name of Netscape Navigator and is not intended to be a reference to the widespread, open-source, Mozilla browser). The idea is that Netscape used to be so widely available that the majority of web pages were targeted at this browser, even at the expense of deviating from web standards. CGI scripts, based on the user agent identifier in the HTTP header, detected that they were dealing with the most up-to-date browser at that time and provided the richest content exclusively in this case. Other browsers, such as Explorer, had become over time capable of displaying content of the same complexity; the first step, however, was to make CGI applications believe that it was worth providing the same content for them.

In the case of crawlers, the textual description generally contains the name of the crawler and contact information (e-mail address, homepage) to allow those interested to get information and ask questions related to what this robot actually does. The crawler of the most popular search engine today, Google, identifies itself in the user agent field as

```
Googlebot/2.1 (+http://www.googlebot.com/bot.html)
```

Two conclusions can be drawn from the discussion above. One is that the easiest method of recognising crawlers is by parsing the user agent field. The other is that user agent identifiers do not necessarily convey the truth. Therefore, a multitude of techniques have been developed to ascertain with high probability whether a visitor is actually a crawler. Such techniques include the analysis of IP-related information, Domain Name Service (DNS) verification, the placement of hidden hyperlinks that are followed only by robots, and so on.

1.3.4. Lack of semantics

One of the most crucial problems of web search today is that the *semantics* of documents and of the query are completely beyond the scope of search engines: they actually consider textual format only. However, this deficiency has far-reaching consequences. In this subsection we present the most significant problems arising from the absence of semantics. The examples aim to shed light on the same set of problems from different perspectives.

1.3.4.1. Language problems

In this context, by language problems we refer to the fact that information retrieval with today's tools relies heavily on the actual representation of textual information. From the perspective of a search engine, the expression, "the ears of a cat" has no meaning, these are just a few words one after the other. Accordingly, even if this phrase occurs in a web document, one will attempt in vain to get the document as a result for a query that concerns "the senses of pets" (assuming that the document does not actually contain these exact words).

The problem may be formulated at a much higher level of abstraction if we ignore the language of documents and of the query. It is common experience that if a query is formulated in English, hits will similarly be in English. Obviously, English words and expressions most probably occur in English pages. This is, on the one hand, a useful characteristic; the language of the results matches that of the query. On the other hand, one must realise that it is not necessarily the original question that is the one answered by the results.

For instance, if we seek information on human organs (such as "What kind of internal organs does a human being have?"), it is possible that not an English but a Dutch, a Greek or a Japanese page contains the most useful result. In fact, the most relevant results are pages about human organs with no regard to the language or the format. For example, an image that depicts the human body and its organs is an excellent result. Actually, this might be the result that answers best the original question; it is easy to comprehend as the size, shape and arrangement of organs are clearly seen.

1.3.4.2. Pictures and multimedia contents

The problem of semantics in the case of images and multimedia content bears a close relationship to the deep web. There, images and multimedia resources are classified as non-textual documents. Their exceptional status is due to the fact that the information they store usually cannot be automatically extracted, not even in particular cases. No design guidelines exist on how to construct an adapter that would allow us to parse the contents of images, as opposed to, say, PDFs, for which such adapters do exist. In fact, the difficulty is relatively easy to overcome in the case of PDFs because such a document mainly contains textual information, albeit not in a conventional format. The same applies to Microsoft Word or Powerpoint documents. It is possible that certain parts of a Powerpoint slide show are not comprehensible to or are misinterpreted by search engines, yet they are able to index the textual content within.

As far as images are concerned, a similar procedure is possible only if the image contains labels or inscriptions. If an image-processing algorithm that can extract texts from images is at our disposal, it might solve our problem mentioned before about the query "What kind of internal organs does a human being have?". The image depicting the organs presumably contains a heading and explanatory captions, which describe what is actually seen in the image. The language and the phrase must still match that of the query, of course.

Exercise 1.12: Use a search engine and search for pictures related to the phrase "sea mammals". How many relevant hits do you have? Try several different search engines to see if they provide different results.

Unfortunately, in many cases images contain no easily extractable text for processing. An image may show Big Ben in London and nothing else. Yet this image would be a relevant result for the query of "the most famous clock tower in London". The question is how search engines could become capable of recognising this.

1.3.4.3. Lack of reasoning capabilities

In some cases we need to reason using our own background knowledge. Let us recall the example about human organs and let us imagine that the image has no heading (such as "Major human organs") but contains captions connected to each individual organ. How is it then found out whether the image is a good result for the query? As human beings, we are clearly aware that the liver, the pancreas, the stomach and the heart are organs and any text, image or object that includes these could be a good result. The difficulty is that search engines lack this background knowledge and the necessary reasoning ability (which is fairly simple in this case).

A myriad of other examples can be brought up in the case of ordinary texts as well. If we formulate a query about mothers, we are undoubtedly interested in pages about women who have had children even if the word "mother" is absent from these pages. The meanings of the two expressions "mother" and "women who have had children" are identical: a search engine today, however, is unable to exploit this.

Summarising, if search engines are to answer users' questions as a wise old thinker would, what is needed is much more than textual search in a huge mass of data. We have to make the search engine aware of the meanings of the concepts (such as mother, woman), and of relationships between concepts (such as being a child of someone). We also very much need some means to derive knowledge about the content of non-textual documents.

1.4. Possible solutions

We now discuss what solutions are available for the problems outlined in Section 1.3. We will show that satisfactory solutions exist in many cases, yet the way to really grasp the semantics of web data remains an open problem. This is the area in which the Semantic Web approach, which is described in Chapter 2, has the potential for significant progress.

1.4.1. Special search engines managing size and variability

Owing to the enormous size and rapidly changing nature of the Internet, a search engine stands no chance of covering the entire web content. However, separate engines crawl the web independently, applying different algorithms and heuristics; hence the pages they index may significantly differ. Most people, after an unsuccessful attempt to find a page with their favourite engine, usually make a try with another engine.

The so-called *meta search engines*, such as `Mamma` or `WebCrawler`, follow the same logic; these are engines that search using other engines. A meta search engine forwards the query to multiple search engines and filters the results, which are then displayed to the user. Meta search engines have the advantage that they will reject web pages designed to deceive a particular engine in order to attain higher and higher ranking; these pages are usually focused on a particular engine and cannot simultaneously trick others.

One way to handle rapidly changing content is to use *focused crawling*. Here, our aim is not to follow every hyperlink but to narrow the search to a specific field of interest according to a set of criteria. For instance, general-purpose search engines can launch dedicated crawlers with the task of visiting well-known news portals. Indexing a limited set of pages of almost negligible size compared with the size of the Internet may naturally be performed in a much more efficient manner, meaning that search engines can return up-to-date information when handling queries regarding fresh news.

In fact, a search engine does not need to know which pages belong to news portals and which do not: it is sufficient if it discovers which pages change often. Supposing that such a page is also relevant (see Subsection 1.2.4), the search engine may assign the periodic downloading of the page to a *dedicated* crawler with adequate speed. As such, a dedicated crawler gets a small workload (few pages to process) and is able to revisit its pages frequently. *Normal* crawlers handle larger proportions of the web and are consequently slower. The range ends with *general-purpose* crawlers, which follow every possible link they can.

Focused crawlers are not only useful in the case of frequently modified pages but also enable the construction of search engines devoted to a specific field of interest. Some search engines index pages of medical content and return results for medical queries. The primary advantage of such specialised engines, as opposed to general-purpose ones, is higher precision and recall, as a narrower range of questions has to be answered on a smaller data set. These search engines may perform content filtering even at the crawler level as crawlers do not need to follow links that are totally unrelated to their field of interest. For this they use *text mining techniques* to decide whether a given page is relevant. Google Scholar [44], which appeared in late 2004 and which focuses on scientific journals and articles, is a good example of focused search within a specific field of interest.

Exercise 1.13: Using a meta search engine such as WebCrawler, compare the results it provides with the results of your favourite search engine.

1.4.2. Extracting information from the deep web

Generally, it is very difficult to automatically extract data from databases accessible through web forms or from non-textual documents. The existing techniques are classified into two categories depending on which requirement, generality or automation, they relax.

Some techniques relax automation requirements (yet they strive to retain generality) and use human intelligence to extract deep web content. The catalogues to be discussed in Subsection 1.4.4 could contain hyperlinks to web pages related to a given topic that rely on various databases. Here, people decide what the page actually contains, that is, what kind of result may be obtained by filling in web forms on the page. Accordingly, they may classify a page into, for example, the medical category. Another use of human intelligence is to add meta-information (either manually or semi-automatically) to databases accessible only via web forms. This may help to make a page a hit for certain queries. The benefits of meta-information will be discussed in more detail in Subsection 1.4.4.

The other major group of techniques for extracting deep web content preserves automation yet to some extent sacrifices generality. Some crawlers are capable of indexing PDF content despite the latter's being, strictly speaking, of non-textual content. A crawler may similarly be prepared to handle Word, Excel or Powerpoint documents or any other document format for which a wrapper is available. These are, however, ad hoc solutions, which do not address the original, more general, problem.

A popular hybrid technique, embedded into ordinary search engines, is to provide devoted services to search for news, job opportunities, things for sale etc. `AltaVista`, for instance, provides a dedicated search engine for news. Queries entered in such an engine can be forwarded to the individual search engines of the most popular newspapers, assuming that we know how to complete those particular web forms. This knowledge can be hardwired into the engine and, should another popular newspaper appear on the web, a small modification of the existing codes can extend the engine to access the search services of this new site as well.

Moreover, one may find search engines on the web that are dedicated to returning deep web content. The `CompletePlanet` directory is just such a specialised engine. For the query "environmental law", one of the first few results it displays is the page `http://www.wcel.org/search/`, which is basically a web form that allows users to enter the most important data (title, author) of a legal article in which they are interested. At the time of writing, CompletePlanet claimed to be displaying results covering over 70 000 databases, the largest 60 of which store around 750 terabytes of data. This is an order of magnitude greater than what the largest web search engines are able to index today.

Note that efforts to access deep web content are also driven by the recognition that deep web information is inherently much more specific and reliable than surface web content.

1.4.3. Making non-indexable pages available for searching

In Subsection 1.3.3 we showed that the majority of search engines deliberately avoid certain types of hyperlink, because of so-called crawler traps. Even though some search engine crawlers are willing to follow all such hyperlinks, it is often the case that dynamic links are followed only to a limited depth. As a special case, it is also common practice to follow only dynamic links that appear on static pages. Sometimes one has to explicitly submit a dynamic link to a search engine for indexing, otherwise it would not visit it.

Actually, crawlers can be made to believe that a hyperlink points to a static web page even if it does not. Even though a crawler has lots of ways for detecting or suspecting that a link is dynamic, if we really wish we can make our link indistinguishable from a static one. However, in a case when web form fields have to be supplied, we cannot really do much about making non-indexable pages available for searching (see also Subsection 1.4.2).

The most straightforward technique is to remove the request parameters from the hyperlink (that is, to use hyperlinks with no query string, in other words, without the section that begins with ?). To do this we can provide supplementary path information, as shown in Subsection 1.1.2, or use specialised tools such as the `mod_rewrite` module for the web server `Apache`. The latter is a general-purpose server-side program that enables the transformation of Internet addresses through rules using regular expressions. The dynamic link (1.7), for example, can be replaced by the following one:

```
http://swexpld.org/calendar2004.html
```

This link looks like a static one, so robots will follow it. All we need do now is instruct the server that such a link should be transformed into a dynamic one. This is done on the server side, behind the backs of the search engines. Informally, we ask the server to do the following. If a request address is of the form `calendarXXX.html`, where XXX is an arbitrary substring, then it should be rewritten to the address `calendar.cgi?year=XXX`. In the case of `mod_rewrite`, such a rule can be formally specified in the following form:

```
RewriteRule ^calendar([^.]+)\.html$ calendar.cgi?year=$1
```

When this rule is applied, the above request address is rewritten to the URL (1.7).

As far as other web servers are concerned, the way of specifying rewrite rules may differ, but the principles are the same. For example, Microsoft's Internet Information Service (IIS) provides the ISAPI_Rewrite tool for this functionality. The rewrite technique is widespread; for example, Amazon uses it, and so search engines are able to index the (dynamic) pages of the `Amazon` web store.

1.4.4. Capturing the semantics

We now present the major techniques available for overcoming the difficulties arising from the lack of semantics on the web. First, catalogues are discussed, which are search engines utilising human intelligence. Next, so-called query expansion engines will be introduced; these attempt to perform a better, more precise, search by transforming the original query. Finally, we talk about how meta-information can help bring semantics to the web. This topic will be covered in more detail in Chapter 2.

1.4.4.1. Catalogues

In Section 1.2 we presented the general architecture of conventional search engines. We showed that crawlers are responsible for the collection of web pages, which are in turn parsed by the indexers. There exists a completely different breed of search engines on the Internet. These provide services using a set of documents collected by humans, who manually perform the steps of page collection and indexing. These engines are called *catalogues* or *directories*; well-known examples are `Yahoo!` [113] or the Open Directory Project [89].

The main advantage of catalogues is that the set of pages they search through is manually selected by people, which, in principle, guarantees their quality. This immediately solves all the problems of web search that are related to the uncontrolled nature of the available documents. Namely, even if an automatic search engine recognises a page as a relevant hit, this is not necessarily so. The motto of one of the most popular catalogues is "Humans do it better".

From the perspective of a catalogue, it is irrelevant if the content of certain documents is difficult or even impossible to extract by automatic means. Capturing semantics is the task of those people who perform the collection and indexing of these pages. Of course, they see what images show, they are able to summarise the basic points of a longer essay and they are not disturbed by the heterogeneity of documents at all; the only requirement is that the documents should be readable, or visible or audible to them.

Nevertheless, catalogues typically still employ full-text search to return results for user queries. This means that if we were seeking "cats" or "animals" then we would not get a page of which the handmade summary uses the word "kitten" when describing the small creature dealt with by the site. Again, the engine has no knowledge that "kittens" are in fact young "cats" and thus also "animals". However, catalogues not only provide text search capabilities but also allow the user to browse the category tree. As the categorisation is performed by humans, it is probable that sites dedicated to the owners of cats are a subcategory of the main category on animals.

The most crucial drawback of catalogues, as compared with conventional automated search engines, is their inability to react quickly to the ever-changing content of the web. While a crawler immediately detects a new link that points to a brand new page on its regular revisiting tour, this new page can only become part of the catalogue if noticed by or brought to the attention of an editor, which is a significantly slower process.

Although catalogues provide a good coverage of popular topics, more exotic themes or less familiar pages of special fields of interest are often absent. For example, search engines are often queried for particular error messages. The idea is that somebody has probably encountered the message before and has found a solution to the problem. Topics such as this are usually discussed in web forums. It is almost certain that catalogues do not contain such pages: even if they did, it would be impossible for editors to keep pace with the daily appearance of new topics, all of which correspond to dozens of new pages and hyperlinks.

Exercise 1.14: Try the Directory Project at `http://www.dmoz.org`. Use the catalogue to navigate to your topic of interest and examine the quality of the pages you can find there.

Despite the manual collection of pages, catalogues still use full-text search to handle queries. In fact, queries are a much less popular means of accessing catalogues than browsing the category tree, which is the main service. Now we turn our attention to a generic technique that uses semantics during query processing.

1.4.4.2. Query expansion

The aim of *query expansion* is to gain a better understanding of a question asked by a user and to perform a search on the available indexed documents with an efficiency beyond that of full-text search. In this approach the query is first analysed linguistically. The result of this analysis is then used to construct a new query, which, according to our expectations, yields more precise and useful results than the original.

In order to do such a linguistic analysis and query transformation, some kind of *background knowledge* is needed, which should be given in some computer processable format. For instance, such knowledge could include the facts that a "cat" is an "animal" or that if an "animal" has "fleas" then it is not "healthy". Using this kind of knowledge, whenever we are looking for "animals" that are "not healthy" the engine is capable of transforming the query so that a page that describes how to remove fleas from the fur of a cat is yielded as a result.

Query expansion is usually built on top of a conventional search engine. Its task is to perform a query transformation that produces better results than a conventional engine on its own.

A search engine exploiting query expansion is generally highly complex. Linguistic analysis is itself a subtle task (and also extremely language-specific) and reasoning utilising a knowledge base requires powerful logic based methods and efficient optimisation techniques.

Polymeta [95] is a meta search engine, specialised for the Hungarian language, which uses query expansion. Hungarian is an agglutinative language, which basically means that affixes are added to the base of a word to express things like possession, plural, diminutives and so on. Consequently, words very rarely occur in documents in their base form, which makes text-based search difficult: a single character difference between two words may result in a significantly different set of documents.

PolyMeta uses linguistic technology to analyse a query and build a new one which contains the most important affixed variants of the words in the original query. For example, if we search for the expression "kocsi" (which means "car" in Hungarian, pronounced *coachee*[7]) then PolyMeta delegates the following question to Google:

```
(kocsi OR kocsit OR kocsik OR kocsija OR
  kocsival OR kocsinak OR kocsiban OR kocsira)
```

Here "kocsik" stands for "cars", "kocsija" for "his/her car", "kocsiban" for "in a car" etc.

Exercise 1.15: Try the PolyMeta search engine with the words "macska" (cat) and "kutya" (dog). Check the queries that PolyMeta forwards to the numerous underlying traditional search engines.

1.4.4.3. Meta-information on the web

Meta-information (in other words, information about information) is universally used for bringing meaning (i.e. semantics) to web content. There is already a fairly large amount of meta-information available on the web. Microsoft Office documents, for example, contain meta-information such as the name of the author, the date of last modification etc. The same applies to other file formats. Some image formats include information regarding the camera with which an image was recorded, when it was taken and in what circumstances. Meta-information can normally be extracted from databases themselves: what they store and in what format etc.

Sometimes we use available information as meta-information for a different purpose. A good example of this is the use of anchor text when indexing content (see Subsection 1.2.4).

---

[7] This is one of the very few English words of Hungarian origin, see [34].

Here, the text in or around the hyperlink provides information on the content anchored at the other end. Notably, the image of Big Ben (see Subsection 1.3.4.2) could be returned as a result for the query "a famous clock tower in London" using anchor text, assuming that someone has placed a link to this image on a page together with an appropriate textual description.

Another interesting real-world example of the use of meta-information concerns the query "Jehovah's Witnesses" posted to a database of scientific articles. The author of this chapter was surprised when this query returned a page on which there was no mention of Jehovah's Witnesses. However, the procedure described in that article required blood transfusions, which some patients may refuse for religious reasons. Actually the engine did not, as we might have expected, return the page as a result of being aware that Jehovah's Witnesses object to blood transfusion but because supplementary meta-information, indicating that the article was related to Jehovah's Witnesses was manually added to the page.

Returning results for the query about mothers mentioned in Subsection 1.3.4.3 also requires background knowledge. Namely, the engine should be aware that mothers are women who have had children. With this meta-information at hand it may be inferred that certain pages are in fact good results for the query entered.

The concept of meta-information has in fact been used in different situations throughout the current chapter (we have already mentioned anchor text above). Meta-information also includes additional attributes that search engines associate with web pages, such as the PageRank value. Similarly, the place and frequency of occurrence of index expressions is also meta-information. All these constitute background information that helps to generate more precise results for user queries.

Undoubtedly, meta-information is essential for returning adequate results for queries. However, meta-information today is stored in no less heterogeneous formats than the documents it is meant to describe. The aim of the Semantic Web approach is to provide a uniform way of attaching meta-information to documents and describing the necessary background knowledge, in order to make automated reasoning feasible. This approach is dealt with in the chapters that follow.

1.5. Summary

In this chapter we have described the structure of the World Wide Web, introduced the basics of how search engines work and presented problems that make the search more difficult to carry out. The following are the most important points in the chapter.

- The web is made up of *servers* and *clients*. Clients have access to information that the servers provide. In most cases the information is stored as web pages written in the HTML language. The most important feature of HTML documents is that they contain links that form the basis of the complex structure of references known as the Internet. We distinguish two kinds of web page. In the case of a *static* page the server simply sends back the stored document. In the case of a *dynamic* page, however, the server generates the response page in real time, according to the given request.

- The information on dynamic pages is usually supplied by external programs. A possible model of communication between the server and an external application is based on the

CGI specification. In this model the task of the application is to return a document on its standard output. This document is usually passed to the client without any change.

CGI applications are usually accessed by using web *forms*. A form consists of control fields which the users can fill in or modify as they wish. Every form has one or more specific buttons. Activating one of these instructs the browser to send a request containing the values of the fields of the form to a specific server in a specific way, as prescribed at the head of the form. On the server side, it is usually a CGI application that receives the incoming data and generates the response page.

The original CGI concept has several disadvantages. One of the main problems is the life cycle of the CGI application itself, since the server starts a new process for each request in order to fulfil it. In certain situations, e.g. when managing database connections, this may lead to an unacceptable loss of efficiency. Another drawback of the CGI model is that, from the point of view of servers, CGI applications are a major source of security holes. Furthermore the CGI specification lacks certain convenience services and does not provide any support for the separation of presentation and business logics.

The drawbacks of the CGI approach have led to the development of advanced server-side solutions such as *FastCGI*, *PHP*, *ASP*, Java *servlets* and *JSP pages*.

■ Having described the structure of the Internet, we started to introduce how *search engines* work. They consider the Web to be a huge pile of documents containing unchecked information of heterogeneous syntax and semantics. Search engines consist of several components. *Web robots (or crawlers)* collect the data, while *indexers* analyse these and extract relevant phrases. The actual query is interpreted and processed by the *query interpreter*, which carries out the search itself on the indexed pages. Finally, the engine ranks and displays the hits.

■ *Crawlers* collect the pages basically by following the links available on the web pages. Here, the two most important questions are which links should the crawler follow and how frequently should it visit these pages. Web servers can forbid crawlers from visiting certain pages, from following the links on some other ones and from archiving yet other pages. Such bans are regulated by the Robot Exclusion Standard.

■ The basic task of the *indexer* is to collect the relevant expressions from a page already visited. The techniques for finding these include taking into account the frequency of occurrences, examining the distribution of the expressions and using stop word lists. These lists contain those words and expressions that are irrelevant to indexing in a given language, such as conjunction words. Together with the relevant expressions, the indexer also extracts characteristics such as their context, the place of their appearance etc.

■ The task of the *query interpreter* is to find all those already indexed documents that are relevant to the given query. Information retrieval methods using more or less the same motivation were already known in pre-Internet times. In this chapter we have introduced one of the most widely used such techniques, the *vector space model*. The basic idea of this method is to create vectors from both the query and each element of the given set of documents, and to examine which document vector is the nearest to that corresponding to the query. There are many ways to define the distance between two vectors. In the simplest case we say that the distance is the value of the angle between them. When constructing the vectors, the extent of the relevance of a given expression is taken into consideration not only within the given document but with respect to the whole document set. The set of hits retrieved has two important indicators. The first is the *precision*, which can be calculated by dividing the number of relevant retrieved documents by the total number of retrieved documents. The other indicator is the *recall value*, which is equal to the quotient of the number of relevant documents retrieved and the total number of relevant documents. In the optimal case, both indicator values equal 1. Today's preference is for good recall values while accepting a lower precision.

The vector space model already has a considerable history; its two greatest advantages are ease of use, i.e. queries are allowed in free text format, and elimination of the worst drawbacks of full text search. Since the vector space model does not associate meaning with expressions, hits do not necessarily contain all the words of the given query text. This very successful model, however, cannot directly be used in Internet-based search. One reason for this is the size and the dynamically changing content of the World Wide Web. The other is that most Internet users under-specify their queries; this, with vector-space-model-based search, often leads to wrong results. To solve these problems the original model has been developed further in several ways.

- The uncontrolled nature of the documents on the web makes Internet search fundamentally different from a search of centralised, well-controlled data sources. Because of this, an important feature of search engines is that they present the retrieved documents to the user in the *order of relevance*. The exact details of the ranking algorithm of a search engine are usually unknown, but the basic concepts are known. During ranking, the place and frequency of occurrence of the search phrases in a given document are the most significant considerations. Some search engines consider the text of a link (the so-called anchor text) to belong to the page to which the link points rather than to the page that contains the link itself, and they do the ranking according to this principle.

- A special approach, based on the *PageRank equation*, is used by the Google search engine: the ranking is based on the structure of the web, i.e. on the links between pages. The basic idea of this recursive equation is to consider a page relevant if relevant pages point to it. The PageRank equation describes the behaviour of a "stochastic surfer", who starts randomly from a web page and proceeds randomly, choosing each link with equal probability. Actually, in this model the equation defines a probability distribution over the web pages, so the PageRank values of all web pages add up to the value 1. The value assigned to a given page is the probability that our surfer stays on it. We have shown how PageRank values can be calculated in practice and how a web site has to be built to achieve an appropriate PageRank distribution.

- After introducing the main components of search engines, we described problems that arise while searching the web. We divided these problems into four main categories. We discussed the difficulties resulting from the vast size and fast-changing contents of the Internet as general problems. A solution to the problem of managing this huge amount of data can be the use of meta searchers, which employ several search engines simultaneously, thus covering a considerable proportion of the web. A way of managing the rapidly changing content is to collect pages using the method known as focused crawling, i.e.

instead of following every link the search space is restricted to pages of a given domain, specified by a given set of principles.

- We introduced the concept of the *deep web* for Internet contents which are, in most cases, unavailable to search engines. These include the content of databases accessible on the web using some form of query and documents in non-textual format. In contrast with the deep web, the static and easily available part of the Internet is called the *surface web*. The amount of the data on the deep web is estimated to be larger by orders of magnitude than that on the surface web. There is no sharp division between the deep and surface web; there is a so-called grey zone, the contents of which cannot be unambiguously classified. A solution for the management of data on the deep web is to make meta-information about the contents of the databases available for search engines as well and to make various wrappers for non-text files (PDF, Excel etc.).

- A difficulty that arises is that crawlers do not follow the links that point to dynamic web pages, i.e. they have no access to a considerable part of the web. The explanation for this is that dynamic links often create huge or infinite search spaces, called *spider traps*, which crawlers try to avoid. It also often happens that certain servers try to camouflage themselves, and the content that they provide to crawlers is different from what they supply, for example, to browsers. There are widespread techniques to "force" the indexing of dynamic web pages. These are based on the idea of making the crawlers believe they are following static links.

- At the end of the chapter, we showed that the biggest problem in Internet search is that search engines do not work with the *meaning* of the available documents and the query, but only with their *textual representation*. This, on the one hand, results in the exclusion of non-textual materials, e.g. pictures, from the sphere of retrievable contents. An even bigger problem is, however, that search engines, having no access to the meaning, cannot reason; if "mothers" are looked for, "women who are known to have had children" will not be listed.

- A way to access the meaning, i.e. the *semantics*, of documents may be the use of *web catalogues*, in which a subset of pages, manually selected by human beings, is made available for search, thus saving the automatic phases of crawling and indexing. In spite of the fact that searching in catalogues is still a text search, it can be a great help that during categorisation the pages were read through by actual people. Another approach may be to understand, using automated methods, a user's query and then to transform it to a new, better, query which results in more suitable hits. Such query conversions require some formalised background knowledge.

- It is the *Semantic Web* concept which seems to be the most promising way forward for solving the problems outlined in this chapter. The basic idea behind it is to put semantics onto the web by associating the web contents with meta-information in standardised form, making it possible to reason about such metadata. The concepts involved in Semantic Web will be discussed in detail in the next chapter.

Chapter 2

The Semantic Web and the RDF language

The present chapter introduces the Semantic Web and its philosophy. This involves two main ideas. The first is to associate meta-information with Internet-based resources. The second is to reason about this type of information. We show how these two ideas can help in solving the problems mentioned in the previous chapter.

Having introduced the main concepts we continue the chapter by describing technologies that can be used for representing meta-information in a uniform way. First we introduce the XML language, which forms the basis of the Semantic Web as a standard information exchange format. Then we describe the RDF language; this has an XML notation as well as other representations and can be used to associate meta-information to an arbitrary resource. By doing this we can extend web contents with computer-processable semantics.

Subsequently, we introduce the RDF schema language, which provides the background knowledge that is essential to do reasoning on meta-information. We discuss the similarities and differences between RDF schemas and traditional object-oriented modelling paradigms.

We conclude the chapter by presenting several applications that directly or indirectly use RDF descriptions during their operation.

2.1. Introduction

The Semantic Web approach was originated by Tim Berners-Lee, the father of the World Wide Web and related technologies (URI, HTTP, HTML etc.). The approach is based on two fundamental ideas.

The first idea is to associate *meta-information* with Internet-based resources. Metadata are pieces of information about other data.[1] Examples of metadata are the title of a book, the creator and creation date of a homepage, the type and size of a file and the fact that a lion, a chimpanzee and a banana can be seen on a particular picture. For these examples, the "real data" are the specific bit-streams representing the book, the HTML code of the homepage, the file and the picture. The distinction between data and metadata is often not very sharp; something which acts like data in one situation becomes metadata in another, and vice versa.

---

[1] The concept of metadata comes from library science.

The Semantic Web approach interprets the concept of Internet-based resources rather broadly and asserts that it is possible to associate meta-information with practically anything which is uniquely identifiable. Such objects are, for example, a homepage or an arbitrary part of it, a picture, a video clip, a file or a hardware device. But, in a broader sense, a coffee mug or a pair of gloves are also such resources, granted that unique identifiers are assigned to them.

Besides the ability to associate meta-information with resources, the other fundamental idea of the Semantic Web is the ability to reason about the meta-information. For example, one must be able to figure out in some way that the picture with the chimpanzee on it shows *animals*, even though the meta-information mentions only a *chimpanzee* and a *lion*. No-one said that the picture displays an *animal*, let alone several *animals*.

2.1.1. New ideas

As a matter of fact, the idea of the Semantic Web is not entirely new. We can already find meta-information on the web, given both explicitly and implicitly, which helps us to exploit the semantic contents of the Internet. We mentioned in Section 1.4 that the information associated with individual web pages by search engines, such as their relevance and the text around the anchors, as well as the location, size and frequency of expressions gathered from the pages, can all be considered as indirectly given metadata.

We can also find examples of explicit metadata, supplied intentionally by the page creator. For example, we may provide certain meta-information about a web page using the META HTML-element in the head of the page. The two most important and most frequently used attributes of this element are `description` and `keywords`. The former is used to give a short summary of the page contents, which is displayed by the search engines in the search results page. This is definitely meta-information and, even though it is free text, its contents are meaningful for human beings and it can be fairly useful in text searches. Furthermore, with the `keywords` attribute we can specify (as the name suggests) keywords that are representative of the content. Below we reproduce some META elements from the homepage of W3C:

```
<meta name="keywords" content="W3C, World Wide Web, Web.../>
<meta name="description"
      content="The World Wide Web Consortium (W3C) is an
      international consortium where Member .../>
```

For more on the META elements in HTML documents and their support in various search engines, see the HTML specification [14].

Unfortunately, the use of the META element is very limited. First, the specification defines only a handful of attributes and does not allow the introduction of new attributes. Second, the metadata given in a META element is often not expressive enough. For example, we can specify – using the `keywords` attribute – that our homepage has something to do with Hungary, but there is no way to tell exactly what the relation is between the two. Does it contain pictures of the Hungarian landscape or analytical essays about the economical state of the country? Furthermore, we can assign meta-information only to an entire page not to arbitrary parts of it, e.g. we can specify the creator of the page but we cannot specify the photographer of a particular picture or the programmer who wrote the source code snippet embedded into the page.

It is important to note that meta-information is often used in cases which have little to do with the Internet. Examples include the `id3v1` and `id3v2` tags stored in MP3 files, information attached to various image formats, such as the EXIF tags in JPEG files or the author, last modification date, notes etc. information in Word documents. As a further example, think of any file system, which uses (implicitly or explicitly) attached meta-information to store access rights and times of individual files. The important idea in the Semantic Web approach is that these metadata are associated with arbitrary resources in a *uniform* and *structured* manner. The goal is that we should be able to attach meta-information to a Word document just as we would do it in the case of an MP3 file or a web page. At the present time this is clearly not possible, since the exact way in which the meta-information is stored is dependent on the format of the data itself, i.e. there is some binary format in the case of Word documents, free text inside a `META` element for web pages etc.

Exercise 2.1: Add `META` elements to your homepage (or if you do not have a homepage, use the HTML page in Figure 1.1) describing the content and keywords of it. Try this page in a browser to see what happens.

2.1.2. The usefulness of metadata

Using meta-information provides a generic means for associating meaning with various resources. If we are able to describe the properties of a resource in a format processable by and comprehensible to machines then we are making a huge step towards intelligent search. By using metadata, the deep web suddenly becomes searchable: we gain access to information stored in databases and flash-based web pages, images are returned as search results whose content it would be impossible to determine with automated tools if there were no metadata, and so on.

For any of these, all we need is that the databases provide metadata about themselves ("this database contains information on the works of Hermann Hesse", "this database stores specifications of Sony digital cameras"). Similarly, we should be able to figure out that a web page with a flash animation in fact presents information about the movie *Terminator 3*. The detail level of the metadata can vary, but even such generic, high-level descriptions as the above can help the search engines in, for example, forwarding the user to the login page of the appropriate web database, when they entered "Hermann Hesse" as the search query.

In fact, metadata can help in all situations where the real contents of a resource – such as a homepage – are not obvious to the web crawler from the source of the page itself. Imagine that our page contains pictures of the Amazon river and its various bridges but that the names of the files do not imply their contents and there is practically no textual information on the page. In such a case, if the `keywords` element contains the words "Amazon", "river" and "bridge", a search engine will probably return the page for a search on the Amazon river. However, without this piece of meta-information it would be almost impossible to automatically index the page as one that has something to do with the Amazon river. It would probably present difficulties even for a human being, to figure out, just by looking at the pictures, exactly which river they depict.

One of the biggest problems when providing meta-information is how to achieve a uniform way to do this. In the following section we present the Extensible Markup Language

(XML) language, a standard data exchange format which amply answers the requirements for a uniform data storage mechanism. This is followed by the introduction of the Resource Description Framework (RDF) language, the core language of the Semantic Web idea, which can be used to associate metadata with arbitrary resources.

2.2. The XML language

In order to become familiar with the XML syntax of the RDF standard, it is necessary to know XML itself at a basic level. It is especially important to know about the concept of XML namespaces. Extensible Markup Language, like RDF, is a recommendation of the World Wide Web Consortium (W3C) [21]. The primary purpose of XML is to describe data and their structure in a computer-processable format and to provide a standard means for inter-computer data exchange. The goal is to make the Internet suitable for machine-to-machine communication.

To better grasp the role of XML, think of it as a multi-layer model. In the lowest layer we ensure that textual data of an arbitrary natural language can be *represented* on the web; this is usually achieved by using Unicode encoding. Above this there is XML, which gives a syntactic structure to data, thus making them machine *processable*. Higher layers, such as RDF, provide various semantics to the data, making information on the web *comprehensible* to computers.

2.2.1. XML as a metalanguage

Extensible Markup Language is – as its name suggests – a general purpose, markup language for creating other, special purpose, markup languages.

The definition of a new language using XML is called an *application* of XML. A particular XML document is an *instance* of such a language or, using the terminology of formal languages, a *sentence* of a language.

In fact, XML is merely a simple subset of a very complex and generic description language which had existed long before the Internet became widely used. This language is *Standard Generalized Markup Language* (SGML), ISO Standard 8879:1986. There are numerous applications of SGML; it is good to know that one of these is none other than HTML. This is why there are so many syntactic similarities between XML and HTML documents.

In the following, first we will see how XML documents are constructed and what syntactic elements can be used in them. Then we show how one can define a new XML language using the so-called XML schemas. Finally we will talk about how XML documents can be presented and displayed.

2.2.2. Basic syntax; XML elements

An XML document is a text file that is designed to store data in a *structured manner*. It is very important to understand that an XML document does not *do* anything. Like any other text document, all it does is store information, nothing more. It is the task of the processing application to decide what to do with the data stored in the XML document. We can store in XML format our existing Word documents, emails, notes etc. Knowing this, we may consider XML merely as a means of storage that is aimed at being a data exchange format

```
<?xml version="1.0" encoding="iso-8859-1"?>
<message>
   <from>Little Red Riding Hood</from>
   <to>Granny</to>
   <body>I'll visit you this afternoon!</body>
   <ps>I'll bring some cookies</ps>
   <ps>they say there's a wolf in the forest</ps>
</message>
```

Figure 2.1.   A message from Little Red Riding Hood to Granny in XML format.

for systems wishing to cooperate, thereby providing the foundations of machine-to-machine communication.

The most important parts of an XML document are *elements* and *attributes*. An XML element consists of three parts: an opening tag, the data itself and a closing tag. For the sake of simplicity, if it will not lead to confusion we often refer to an element by its opening tag. HTML uses similar concepts to XML but, as we said, this is not a coincidence. An HTML source file also uses elements and attributes to structure our data, but the set of available elements is closed, their meaning having been defined in advance. XML, however, does not define elements like those in HTML, such as <HEAD>, <BODY> and <IMG>; this is the responsibility of the creator of the XML document, the choice of the appropriate set of elements being a design issue. It means that there are no "reserved words" in XML: that is to say, the name of an element can be an arbitrary character sequence (observing some simple rules, such as that a name cannot begin with a digit). Look at Figure 2.1. The first line specifies that this is an XML document and that it uses Latin-1 character coding.

Our example depicts a simple message in XML format. The *root element* of the document is <message>. An XML document must contain exactly one root element. The <from>, <to>, <body> and <ps> elements are all *children* of the root element and *siblings* of each other. On the basis of its contents, an XML element can be *complex, mixed, simple* or *empty*. Complex elements have children: such an element is <message> in the example. A simple element contains only literal or numerical data; such an element is <from>Little Red Riding Hood</from>. A mixed element contains both literals and child elements, while an empty element consists only of the opening and the closing tags.

The most striking property of an XML document is that it stores data in a hierarchy: the document defines a tree, with the root element at its root. In Figure 2.1 we define a two-level tree with one root and five child elements (see Figure 2.2). Thus an XML document defines not only the *name* and *contents* of individual elements but also their *hierarchical relations*. This makes XML also suitable for describing the structure of the data.

Figure 2.3 shows a second example of an XML document. Here we represent the employee database of a company in XML format. Employees have names, salaries and Social Security Numbers. Some also have phone numbers (perhaps more than one). It is clear that the database is easy to maintain: upon the arrival of a new employee a new <employee> element must be added and when someone leaves the appropriate entry must be deleted.

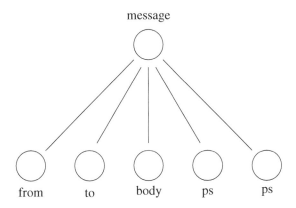

Figure 2.2. The XML tree of Little Red Riding Hood's message.

```
<?xml version="1.0" encoding="ISO-8859-1"?>
<employees>
    <employee>
        <name>Jane Doe</name>
        <salary>4500</salary>
        <SSN>965342876</SSN>
    </employee>
    <employee>
        <name>John Stiles</name>
        <salary>6100</salary>
        <SSN>823457201</SSN>
        <phone>555-136-8531/2465</phone>
        <phone>917-555-7642</phone>
    </employee>
</employees>
```

Figure 2.3. Employee database of a company in XML format.

Since an XML document is text based and uses elements to delimit data (with mandatory closing tags), it is necessarily larger than a corresponding binary file would be. This is a deliberate design decision, as the dense storage of data was not a priority of the XML recommendation. One advantage of the text-based format is that the resulting file is readable by human beings as well, so there is no need to run an application to transform or display it. Another important aspect is error handling. Imagine just how many problems we could run into when trying to open a corrupted binary file. What are the user's options when the application returns a "sorry, but the file cannot be opened" kind of error message? If the given document is in XML, it is much easier to find and fix the error in question. The verbosity can still lead to difficulties since no-one likes to store files of several hundred megabytes when the same in binary format would take up less than a tenth of that. The biggest problem, however, is not this (the present rate of increase in storage capacities can easily take care of it), but the much greater limitations of network *bandwidth*. XML files are often used for standard communication. As an example, consider the *SOAP protocol*, developed for web service interfaces, which uses XML to encode messages to be exchanged between applications. Fortunately most modern communication protocols, such as HTTP/1.1, are able to compress data on the fly, thereby significantly saving on bandwidth.

Exercise 2.2: Extend the XML source shown in Figure 2.3 to include the age of both employees. Examine the structure of the document by closing and opening parts of the XML tree (this can be done by clicking on the − or + sign in front of a composite element).

2.2.3. XML attributes

XML elements can have an arbitrary number of attributes (properties), but every attribute may occur at most once in each element. An attribute has a name and a value, separated by the equality sign. The well-known <IMG> element in HTML also uses attributes to identify a picture and its alternative text. We can see an example of this here:

```
<img src="dolphin.gif" alt="A cute dolphin">
```

An alternative XML representation of the message in Figure 2.1 is shown in Figure 2.4. There the sender and the recipient of the message are specified as attributes of the <message> element, rather than as its children elements. Note that an element with an attribute is always considered *complex*, but the values of attributes can only be *simple* (a literal, a numerical value etc.).

Using attributes instead of elements does not have any substantial benefits. This is more of a design and modelling decision. Attributes can be useful in cases when they carry only auxiliary information, not the core of the data. Their use can help to make the XML source more readable and structurally cleaner. An example of this is the following complex element:

```
<movie type="mpeg4">matrix.avi</movie>
```

In this example, the information that the format of the video is mpeg4 is less important than the file name from which it is available.

```
<?xml version="1.0" encoding="ISO-8859-1"?>
<message from="Little Red Riding Hood" to="Granny">
    <body>I'll visit you this afternoon!</body>
    <ps>I'll bring some cookies</ps>
    <ps>they say there's a wolf in the forest</ps>
</message>
```

Figure 2.4.   Message from Little Red Riding Hood to Granny with XML attributes.

2.2.4. XML namespaces

The XML element and attribute names that we have used so far are called *local names*. Local names are perfectly valid as names, although as soon as we try to merge multiple XML documents we must face the problem of conflicting names. It can happen, for example, that an XML document embedded into an HTML page also uses the `<body>` element name (like our message example). XML defines *XML namespaces* to avoid such conflicts.

The idea behind XML namespaces is very simple. It is advantageous to specify element and attribute names by adding a *prefix* such as this:

```
<n:body>...</n:body>
```

A local name extended with a prefix is called a *universal* or *qualified name*. We assume that the qualified name is unique, thereby avoiding any further conflicts. If the prefix is too simple, we are not much better off since the same prefix (n in this example) could accidentally be used in another XML document as well. The specification therefore requires that all prefixes must be associated with uniform resource identifiers (URIs), identifying XML namespaces. So, a prefix indirectly tells us to which namespace the given element actually belongs.

A URI is a literal with a well-defined structure. You can read more on URIs in Section 2.3. It is worth knowing in advance that a URI is generally assigned to an organisation or a person. An XML namespace can be considered unique because who is allowed to use it, namely its owner, can be determined unambiguously. When merging two such documents there will be conflicts, which must be resolved manually. Fortunately these conflicts happen very rarely.

To declare a new namespace prefix we must use special XML attributes, which can be added to arbitrary elements. There are two such attributes, and they are the following:

```
xmlns:prefix     xmlns.
```

The former is used to associate a namespace to the namespace prefix called `prefix`. The latter specifies the *default namespace*. All XML element names without a prefix automatically belong to this namespace. In the absence of default namespace, an unprefixed XML element is considered to be a simple local name. Note that default namespace declarations do not apply to attribute names.

All namespace prefixes have a scope. The specification prescribes that an XML namespace prefix is visible only within the element which declares it (including the opening and closing tags of the element). Therefore it matters where a namespace prefix is declared. If we want the namespace prefix to be visible throughout the entire document, it should be defined as an attribute of the root element.

Figure 2.5 shows an XML document declaring and using two namespaces. The element called `<priority>` is in the default namespace; all other elements are in the namespace with the prefix n. Note that attribute names are also prefixed.

It is important to note that the URIs have no other role than to act as globally unique identifiers avoiding name conflicts. This means that the URIs used do not have to be valid (e.g. they do not need to work in a browser), so we are allowed to write anything we like. Specific URIs, however, play an important role since the implementations of concrete web technologies may rely on them. In particular, by looking for elements belonging to a given namespace, applications can identify those parts of an XML document in which they are interested.

```
<?xml version="1.0" encoding="iso-8859-1"?>
<n:message
     xmlns:n="http://swexpld.org/"
     xmlns="uuid:BDC6E3F0-6DA3-11d1-A2A3-00AA00C14882"
     n:from="Little Red Riding Hood" n:to="Granny">

   <n:body>I'll visit you this afternoon!</n:body>
   <n:ps>I'll bring some cookies</n:ps>
   <n:ps>they say there's a wolf in the forest</n:ps>
   <priority>important</priority>
</n:message>
```

Figure 2.5.   A message from Little Red Riding Hood to Granny with XML namespaces.

For example, RDF applications process only those elements within an XML document that belong to the RDF namespace. More about this can be found in Section 2.3.

Finally, we mention that so-called *entities* can serve a role very similar to those of namespaces. An entity declaration can be used to instruct the XML parser to replace each reference to that entity with the value of the entity. The value can be an arbitrary character sequence, with the exception of a few special characters. For example, we declare entity s in the following snippet:

```
<!ENTITY s "http://swexpld.org/">
```

Following this declaration, anywhere within the XML document the reference `&s;wolf` becomes exactly equivalent to writing `http://swexpld.org/wolf` in that place.

Exercise 2.3: View the XML source in Figure 2.5 in a browser. Notice how the XML attributes and namespaces are displayed.

2.2.5. XML schemas; validity of documents

A piece of XML text is well formed if it adheres to the format requirements of XML documents; that is, all opening tags have a closing pair, the attributes are key-value pairs, and so on. However, well-formedness does not imply that the document satisfies any further, application-specific, requirements. In the example shown in Figure 2.3 we implicitly assumed that the names of people are string literals and not, say, numerical values. We also assumed that their salaries are non-negative and that they are guaranteed to have an SSN but not necessarily a phone number.

The real strength of XML stems from the fact that it is possible to check not only whether an XML document is well formed but also whether it is *an instance of a given language*. Without further information, it is impossible to figure out whether the language containing the example in Figure 2.3 allows further elements in the description of an employee (such as hobbies, marital status etc.). Likewise, there is no way to know whether the salary must be a numerical value or whether it could be something different; and so on. The reason is that an

XML document, as it is, can be an instance of multiple languages. When we are preparing an XML document, we are in fact creating a file according to an undetermined grammar. If we want to allow an application that can parse XML documents to be able also to verify whether these documents are instances of the language understood by the application, the language itself must be specified in a standard manner. This is what so-called *XML schemas* are for.

XML schemas describe which elements and attributes are allowed in the XML documents of the given language, what is allowed in the contents and the attributes of these elements and how they are related. For the document in Figure 2.1, for example, we can prescribe that there must be exactly one sender, one recipient and one body and there can be zero or more postscripts. We can also declare that the recipient must come first, followed by the sender, then the body and finally the optional postscripts. The schema corresponding to this verbal description can be seen in Figure 2.6. Provided that both the XML schema and an XML document are given, it is possible to tell whether the document is an instance of the language described by the schema.

In the schema we declared that all documents in our XML application begin with the `<message>` complex element. The `xs:sequence` element in the schema specifies that the given elements must follow each other in the given order. The `type` attribute, as expected, defines the type of the elements. In the case of the `<ps>` element, the `minOccurs` and `maxOccurs` attributes are used to prescribe that there can be an arbitrary number of these in a valid XML document. All the other elements (`from`, `to` and `body`) must occur exactly once, as in the absence of the occurrence indicators the default value, 1, is used.

By providing this schema, it becomes possible to reject messages that do not adhere to it (e.g. the sender is undetermined). One benefit of using XML as a data format is that the

```
<?xml version="1.0" encoding="ISO-8859-1"?>
<xs:schema xmlns:xs="http://www.w3.org/2001/XMLSchema"
           elementFormDefault="qualified">
<xs:element name="message">
   <xs:complexType>
      <xs:sequence>
         <xs:element name="from" type="xs:string"/>
         <xs:element name="to" type="xs:string"/>
         <xs:element name="body" type="xs:string"/>
         <xs:element name="ps" type="xs:string"
                     minOccurs="0" maxOccurs="unbounded"/>
      </xs:sequence>
   </xs:complexType>
</xs:element>
</xs:schema>
```

Figure 2.6. XML schema for messages.

processing applications can be simpler than otherwise. Imagine that we are applying for a job, and we provide our personal data in an XML document adhering to a schema given by the company. The submitted XML document will not surprise the processing application at the company because, once it passes the schema verification, it is guaranteed not to contain "invalid" entries, e.g. a numerical value where a boolean is expected, it is guaranteed to have a SSN field (the schema can also specify the required number of digits[2]), and so on.

XML schemas offer much more than we have described here. For example, one can specify the domain of certain elements (the value must fall into an interval or must be one of a number of predefined values, and so on). This is just one instance of a constraint – there can be many others. For further details, see the specification of the XML schema [107].

Exercise 2.4: Try a web-based XML schema validator, such as [31], to validate the XML document in Figure 2.1 against the XML schema presented in Figure 2.6. Modify the XML document, e.g. change the order of the elements from and to, and run the validator again.

2.2.6. Transformation and visualisation of XML documents

The *eXtensive Stylesheet Language Transformation* (XSLT) [28] is a language that can be used to transform one XML document into another. The transformation itself works by building a new XML tree from nodes matching certain patterns in the source document. The patterns are given using the so-called XPath [26] language, described in Section 3.3, where the XML query languages are also elaborated. The new XML document resulting from the transformation can differ arbitrarily from the source: elements can be omitted, new elements can be inserted and so on. For example, given an XML document storing employees, using an appropriate XSLT transformation we can easily create an HTML page which lists the workers and their data in a tabular form, setting the names in boldface.

The transformation defined by XSLT is called a *stylesheet* (hence the expansion of the XSLT acronym). This name was chosen because an original purpose of XSLT was to transform XML documents into XSL-FO [13] files. XSL-FO is a generic-purpose formatting language, which describes how to present various documents to people. In other words, an XSL-FO document represents a stylesheet. An XSL-FO document can in turn be translated into a PDF, PS or plain text using a *Formatting Object Processor* (FOP). Such an FOP can be seen in [2].

The XSLT, XPath and XSL-FO languages all belong to the same family, called *eXtensive Stylesheet Languages* (XSLs). They all share the basic idea of separating XML data storage and visual display. Consequently, the application processing the XML files does not have to be concerned with how, where or on what device the results will be presented. At the presentation stage, the "human readable" form can be generated using an XSLT transformation (or something similar).

The idea of separating the data and its appearance appeared in a precursor of XSL, the *Cascading Style Sheet* (CSS) language. The goal of CSS is to associate formatting rules

---

[2] Although it is still possible that we provided an invalid, non-existent, number.

```
<html>
  <head>
    <meta http-equiv="Content-Type"
          content="text/html; charset=iso-8859-1" >
    <title>Notice</title>
    <style type="text/css">
      h1     { color: red;
               font-weight: bold; }
      p      { color: black; }
      .thing { color: green;
               font-style: italic; }
    </style>
  </head>

  <body>
    <h1>Attention</h1>
    <p>Bring the following necessities to the excursion:
    </p>
    <ul>
        <li class="thing">Raincoat</li>
        <li class="thing">Electric torch</li>
        <li class="thing">Warm clothes</li>
        <li class="thing">Food</li>
    </ul>
  </body>
</html>
```

Figure 2.7. Using stylesheets: the separation of contents and appearance.

with HTML documents, for example, to specify that the contents of <H3> elements must be rendered in red font. Such a description is also called a stylesheet, although CSS is significantly different from XSL stylesheets. The CSS specifications have many fewer formatting options than those given in XSL-FO. However, the simplicity of CSS pages is often an advantage, because they are much easier and faster to write.

Figure 2.7 shows an HTML page using a CSS stylesheet. We have avoided using any formatting-oriented HTML elements. The example notifies the participants on an imaginary excursion what to bring with them. Here, the CSS specification itself is built into the page, for better readability, but in most cases it is stored in a separate file and there is only a link from the HTML code. The stylesheet specifies that the list items must be printed in green with italics. Figure 2.8 shows how a browser displays this page.

Exercise 2.5: Following the example shown in Figure 2.7, add a stylesheet to some simple HTML page of yours that uses no CSS at the moment. Check the resulting web page in a browser.

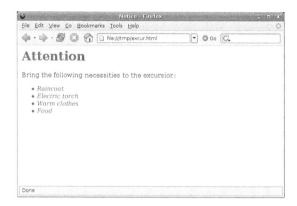

Figure 2.8.   Web page that uses a stylesheet.

2.2.7. An XML application: the XHTML language

We have already mentioned that HTML is a specific SGML *application*. That is, HTML is a language defined using the SGML metalanguage and, by using it, we can create an arbitrary number of documents (i.e. web pages). Naturally, we have to obey the rules of the language during the creation of web pages; in other words, we always have to construct a sentence of the HTML language. It is worth knowing that today's browsers are pretty lax when it comes to grammar strictness, and they often accept normally invalid HTML documents (missing closing tags etc.), eventually bringing more harm than comfort.

We have also seen that XML, similarly to SGML, is a metalanguage, which raises the question: can we write HTML in XML? The answer is yes, it has already been done by W3C. The resulting XML application is the XHTML language, which combines the benefits of HTML and XML. An XHTML document is also an XML document; therefore it is suitable for encapsulating snippets of XML-based languages (such as RDF, SVG, XSQL etc.), and XML-based technologies (XSLT, XPath etc.) can also be used on it. Furthermore it is important that the early XHTML standards (XHTML 1.0 and 1.1) differed only very little from regular HTML, so that browsers need only minor modifications in order to be able to parse XHTML documents.

The first draft of XHTML version 2 was published by W3C in August 2002; the latest at the time of writing this book is the eighth draft. Version 2 broke away from legacies and distanced itself from HTML. Many traditional HTML elements were removed, such as the `<b>`, `<i>`, `<br>` and `<hr>` elements. The last, for example, is a request for the browser to display a horizontal rule in the page where the markup appears. The elements that were removed determined how the page should look, but they did not say anything about the contents, and the importance and machine-processability of the contents is a key point of XML.[3] The idea is that an XHTML document merely specifies in a structured manner the data composing the bulk of the page. The presentation is taken care of by stylesheets given

---

[3] It is interesting also that HTML was originally been designed to define the structure of web pages, and new presentation-oriented elements as well as the formatting semantics of some existing elements were only added later.

in CSS or by XSLT transformations. These are responsible for deciding how certain parts of the document should be displayed.

This approach is very useful in practical applications, since it makes it possible to prepare a web page regardless of what kind of a device it will be displayed on (PDAs, mobile phones, customised browsers etc.), allowing the creator to concentrate on the content and the structure.

2.2.8. Evaluation of XML

Nowadays, XML is used practically everywhere: in deployment descriptors of web applications, in data files of word processors (Microsoft Office uses XML, for example), in database interfaces etc. The success of XML is all the more apparent knowing that it reached this level of popularity in only a couple of years.

However, XML is still basically a data-exchange format and in fact forms a very important milestone on the road to the creation of the Semantic Web. The first step was how the Internet changed the way in which applications communicate with each other. Before the dawn of the Internet various applications communicated on dedicated channels, using ad hoc protocols and techniques. This also included the case when someone wrote the data on a floppy disk and manually transferred it to another machine, to be read by the other application there. The Internet with its de facto standards and protocol families regularised the channels of communication.

Still, the problem of various applications using different data formats remained. Therefore a common syntax had to be assented to before each data interchange, since without this agreement no-one would have understood anyone else. No matter how badly a customer wants to buy a product, if the seller does not understand the request because the two sides represent the same data differently then a sale cannot be made. That XML is a standard data-exchange format is a huge step forward in this respect. Using XML there is no need to design and implement specific parsers for each communication channel. Using XML schemas, it can also be verified whether a received XML document adheres to our formal requirements.

2.3. The basics of the RDF language

With XML, a huge step forward was made towards the machine processability of web content by the standardisation of the syntax of data exchange.

However, the use of XML still requires that the meaning of the data to be transferred is agreed by the parties. XML is no help if one participant misinterprets a message and sends $100 instead of $100 000, just because the other counts everything in thousands! This is a general consideration: what if one party understands the same element differently from the other?

The Semantic Web, the next generation of the World Wide Web, is aimed at making not just the syntax but also the semantics of transmitted and stored data unambiguous to the parties involved. If this can be achieved then naturally a web crawler will also "understand" the contents of certain Internet resources. The general requirement is to be able to store data in such a way that it is processable and comprehensible for machines. The former is taken care of by XML and the latter is answered by RDF, which is to be presented shortly. Using RDF it is possible to associate meta-information – meaning, if you like – with arbitrary web contents in a standard way. However, providing such concrete information is not enough; one also has to provide some background knowledge to enable, for example, intelligent search based on automatic inference.[4] The computer-processable form of such background knowledge, for a specific field of interest, is called a *terminological system* or *ontology*.

The RDF language is only the first step towards the Semantic Web. However, it provides the foundations for further steps: the RDF schema extension uses RDF as its base notation to support the building of lightweight ontologies, suitable for describing simple terminological systems. Similarly, the web ontology language OWL, capable of describing heavyweight ontologies, uses both RDF and RDF schemas as its building blocks.

In the following we first define the concept of URIs and their role in RDF. We will then present a simple example of an RDF description. This is followed by an explanation of the RDF data model, which gives a syntax-independent means of making RDF statements. We then introduce the modelling paradigm of the language, where we show how best to describe real-world concepts in RDF. In the final part of this section we present the XML syntax of RDF and then explain the various language constructs which can be used during modelling.

2.3.1. URIs and their role

The *Resource Description Framework* is a language suitable for associating metadata with arbitrary *resources* [11, 69]. In the world of RDF, everything that has a *URI* (Uniform Resource Identifier) is a resource; URIs are string literals, which identify objects and resources usually found on the web. Examples of resources are web pages and parts thereof: an image, an arbitrary file, an audio sample, a group of resources etc. It is important that as far as URIs – and thus RDF – are concerned, resources do not have to be attached to the web: even a coffee mug standing on a desk can be a resource, granted that it has an associated URI (which can be achieved). Therefore, sometimes we say that everything which has a URI is *on the web*.

Uniform Resource Identifiers have a fundamental role in the Semantic Web. Their most important property is their uniqueness, which enables the construction of unambiguous statements. No matter where two metadata descriptions appear, if they use the same URI (e.g. that referring to a person) then they both state something about the very same resource. For example, that the given person has blue eyes on the one hand and that his or her height is $5'11''$ on the other. This implies that it is fairly easy to combine various pieces of meta-information originating from different sources, since they can be joined simply by using the same URIs. It can also be said that the usage of URIs embodies the "anyone can say anything" idea, since all one needs is the appropriate URI to make arbitrary statements about a particular resource.

It is important to distinguish URIs from the perhaps better known *Uniform Resource Locators* (URLs) and *Uniform Resource Names* (URNs); these are special URIs. The former identify resources by their location, while URNs are persistent, location-independent resource identifiers. For more information about URNs, we refer to the standard specification [82]. Here are a few examples of URIs:

---

[4] For example, it may be known that a specific picture on the web shows a fox terrier. To return this picture in a search for dogs, one has to know that fox terriers are dogs.

```
http://www.cs.uwyo.edu/index.html
```

```
mailto:lukacsy@math.bme.hu
```

```
file:///c:/examples/cat.rdf
```

```
urn:issn:1564-3417
```

```
uuid:BDC6E3F0-6DA3-11d1-A2A3-00AA00C14882
```

The first example URI identifies a web page, the second refers to a person via his email address and the third is a file in a local file system. All three are URLs. The fourth example, a URN, identifies a publication location independently via its ISSN number. Finally, the fifth URI is a unique 128-bit identifier (written in hexadecimal notation), called a *Universally Unique Identifier* (UUID); these are generated in such a way that it is reasonable to assume that they will be different from other, similarly generated, identifiers.

As far as RDF is concerned, it is important to make a distinction between two kinds of URI. *Absolute* URIs uniquely identify resources, no matter where and when they are used. *Relative* URIs are meaningful only in a given context, namely when a so-called *base* URI can be determined. The base URI is determined by several factors, as defined by the standard, along with their priorities. For example, if a particular document format is suitable for specifying a base URI explicitly, and a document in this format does so, then that will be the base URI. Otherwise, the base URI of the encapsulating resource (if there is such an object) is inherited. If the base is still unknown, the URI identifying the document itself will be used as a base.

Both absolute and relative URIs may have a *fragment identifier*, which is separated from the body of the URI by a # sign. According to the specification [17], "the fragment identifier component of a URI allows indirect identification of a secondary resource by reference to a primary resource and additional identifying information". The semantics of a fragment identifier depends on the media type [41] of the document actually retrieved. In a case where retrieval is not possible, the semantics is undefined.[5] As a typical usage, a fragment identifies part of a document, for example, in the case of an HTML page it refers to the element with the attribute name matching the fragment identifier.

It is also possible that a URI consists only of a fragment identifier, such as #Person. This refers to the specific part of the document identified by the actual base URI.

Exercise 2.6: Enter the Semantic Web Activity page of W3C [112] and within the navigation panel called "Further links", on the right, check the section entitled "On this page". Notice that navigation within the site is achieved using fragment identifiers.

In the following subsection we present a simple introductory example, which is intended to show the reader the basics of the RDF language.

---

[5] Recall that a URI in general is "only" an identifier, and is not necessarily associated with an accessible and downloadable document (even a desk lamp can have a URI).

2.3.2. An introductory RDF example

The fundamental idea of RDF is to associate – through given properties – resources identified by URIs with other resources or with plain literals. Such an association is called a
triple. Before going into further details about RDF, let us consider the RDF description of
the following informal *statement*: "The e-mail address of John Doe (who is a person) is
johndoe@freemail.org". This can be seen in Figure 2.9 in RDF graph representation using
three triples. The graph expresses the following facts: there is a resource identified by the
`http://freemail.org/~doe/#about` URI. The *type* of this resource is the URI
`http://www.w3.org/2000/10/swap/pim/contact#Person`, its *name* is John
Doe and its e-mail *address* is `mailto:johndoe@freemail.org` URI. In fact, the properties used in the graph (name, address, type) are also resources identified by URIs, but for
brevity we have used simple names here.

The RDF standard also defines an XML-based syntax. Figure 2.10 shows the XML equivalent of the graph seen in Figure 2.9. The process of transforming an RDF graph into an
equivalent XML description, or set of triples, is called *serialisation* or *linearisation*. Thus
Figure 2.10 is the serialisation of the graph in Figure 2.9.

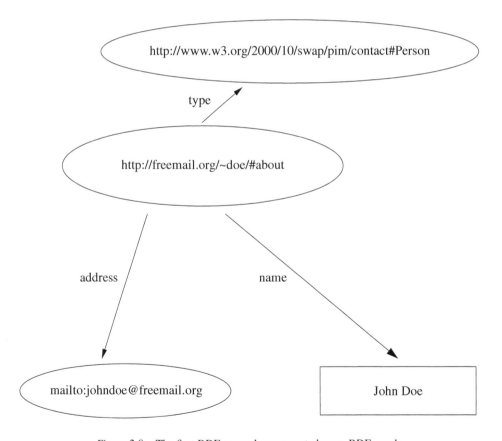

Figure 2.9. The first RDF example represented as an RDF graph.

```
<?xml version="1.0" encoding="ISO-8859-1"?>
<rdf:RDF
 xmlns:rdf="http://www.w3.org/1999/02/22-rdf-syntax-ns#"
 xmlns:s="http://swexpld.org/utils#">

 <rdf:Description rdf:about=
   "http://freemail.org/~doe/#about">
    <s:name>John Doe</s:name>
    <s:address rdf:resource="mailto:johndoe@freemail.org"/>
    <rdf:type rdf:resource=
     "http://www.w3.org/2000/10/swap/pim/contact#Person"/>
 </rdf:Description>

</rdf:RDF>
```

Figure 2.10. The first RDF example in XML form.

The XML elements used in this example will be described in detail in Section 2.4.

In the next section we introduce the data model of the RDF and describe the precise syntax and semantics of RDF statements.

2.3.3. The RDF data model

The principal use of RDF is to associate metadata with resources. In other words, RDF is a framework that, in order to attach semantics to the pieces of information found on the web, allows one to assign metadata to them. The strength of RDF lies in the fact that by using URIs and RDF descriptions it becomes possible to associate meta-information to almost anything.

The RDF specification defines the *RDF data model*, a data model based on set theory which is used to describe metadata. The model is composed of the following parts:

- *The set of resources.* This is the set of all things about which one can make RDF statements. The elements of this set are called *resources*. RDF resources are identified by URIs, with optional fragment identifiers. Examples of RDF resources are a web page, an image found on a page and in general everything that has a URI. Considering that practically everything (a book, a refrigerator etc.) can have a URI, this set includes all imaginable entities.

- *The set of properties.* The elements of this set are called *properties*. Properties are features with values that can be attached to resources. The properties themselves are also RDF resources (in other words, Properties is a subset of Resources), and as such they also are referred to by URIs. In the case of a property, one can determine what resources they can be attached to, what values they can take and their relation to other properties.

- *The set of literals.* The elements of this set are *literals*, i.e. character sequences.

■ *The set of statements.* The elements of this set are *triples* or *statements*[6] that consist of
   subject, *predicate* and *object*. The subject is an arbitrary RDF resource, the predicate
   is any RDF property and the object (that is, the value of the property) is either an RDF
   resource or a literal. As a consequence, an RDF statement is nothing other than a cohesive
   group of three resources or of two resources and a literal.

The RDF data model does not define the syntax of RDF statements. An *RDF description*
is a set of statements (that is, the set *Statements* represented in some syntax). Accordingly,
the order of the triples does not matter. The *meaning* (semantics) associated by the data
model to such a description is that the triples in the set are *true*.

Notice that in fact RDF describes *binary* (i.e. two-argument) relations between identifiable objects or, to put it another way, makes statements about them. It is a matter of taste
whether we look on an RDF triple as a statement or as an association binding values to a
resource.

In the next subsection we show how one can model the real world with this data model.

2.3.4. Basics of RDF-based modelling

We have just discussed how the RDF data model can be described in mathematical terms.
This does not require a strict computer-processable syntax. However, we do need the latter
since without it we would not be able to write down, store and transmit the statements, i.e.
the metadata. Therefore, the RDF specification defines three standard data-model representations, one of which also has a concrete syntax. RDF data can be represented as a *set of
triples*, as a *labelled directed graph* or as *XML data*. The graph model is of primary importance from the theoretical point of view but, as far as machine processability and data transfer
are concerned, the XML representation is the principal format.

As an example, take the following statement: a painting called "The Night Watch" was
created by Rembrandt van Rijn. For this we will need a URI which identifies the painting,
such as

`http://www.rembrandtpainting.net/rembrandt_night_watch.htm`

Then the decomposition of the statement into parts as required by the structure of RDF
triples can be seen in Figure 2.11. (Note that the RDF terminology is somewhat inconsistent
with the terms used in English grammar.)

subject (resource)	http://www.rembrandtpainting.net/rembrandt_night_watch.htm
predicate (property)	painted by
object (literal)	Rembrandt van Rijn

Figure 2.11.   Decomposition of an RDF statement.

---

[6] Sometimes the word "axiom" will also be used as a synonym of the word "statement".

{[http://...night_watch.htm], paintedBy, "Rembrandt" }

Figure 2.12. An RDF statement represented as a triple.

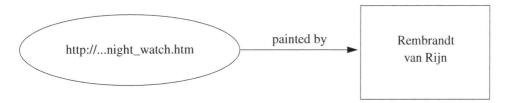

Figure 2.13. An RDF statement represented as a graph.

For the sake of simplicity we have listed the predicate ("painted by") in the example as a plain literal (in reality this must be a resource identified by a URI). The statement can also be depicted as a triple, as seen in Figure 2.12,[7] where the URI denoting the subject of the statement is delimited by square brackets [] and literals are surrounded by double quotes " ". We will use this notation for triples in the rest of the book.

The XML form of the statement will be given in Section 2.4, where the XML syntax of RDF is described.

Finally, the statement represented as a graph is shown in Figure 2.13. An RDF graph (not surprisingly) has nodes and arcs (directed edges). The nodes contain URIs optionally extended by fragment identifiers, or literals, thus the nodes represent RDF resources or literals, respectively. The arcs are labelled by (optionally extended) URIs: these identify RDF properties. It is important to note that an RDF graph *may only contain absolute URIs*. RDF is also suitable for making statements about properties: as properties are resources, they can appear as the subject or object of a statement.

From a modelling point of view it is rather unfortunate that the object of our example statement, the painter's name, is given as a literal, because a name does not identify the person unambiguously and, anyway, we might simply find it strange to have as a literal the painter of a painting. Let us not forget that RDF statements express *facts*, which are unconditionally true. Therefore it is better if we use as a URI an object which unambiguously identifies Rembrandt van Rijn (e.g. points to a web page describing his life and work). If we do not have such an unambiguous URI, we may still want to strengthen our statement by providing additional details about the painter. This can be achieved by introducing a so-called *intermediate* resource (also called a *blank* or *anonymous* resource), which is special in the sense that it cannot be identified at all: among other things, it does not even have a URI. Such a resource appears as a *blank* node in the graph, as can be seen in Figure 2.14. The graph expresses the fact that the painting was painted by someone whose name is Rembrandt van Rijn and who was born in 1606. The blank node in the graph provides a fairly exact identification of the artist without referring to the resource representing him.

---

[7] In the rest of this chapter we will shorten the URI of the painting and the name of the painter for typographical reasons.

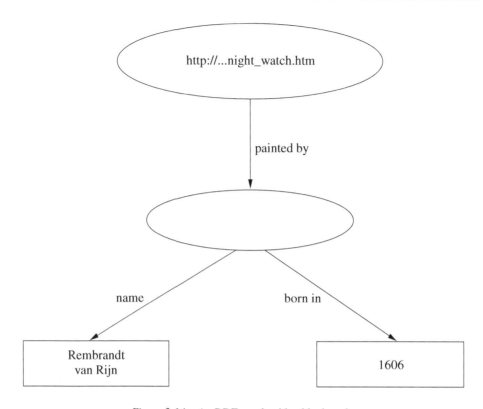

Figure 2.14.   An RDF graph with a blank node.

Blank nodes are often used to improve the structuring of the information. When, for example, we decide to represent an address as a structured entity rather than a single literal ("Shaftesbury Rd, Cambridge, CB2 8RU"), it helps to introduce an intermediate resource for the address itself. In this case, the street address, the city and the post code can be attached to this node as literals. Even though four new nodes have been created instead of one, it is well worth the added cost. The structured nature of the information can become a great asset in a later phase, when it is processed by machines. Note that a similar technique is used when higher-arity relations (i.e. relations with more than two arguments) are described in RDF (see Subsection 2.5.1).

When an RDF graph which contains blank nodes has to be serialised (written as triples or in XML form), naming these nodes is often unavoidable after all. These names should be easily distinguishable from URIs and literals appearing in the description, but they do not need to be globally unique as long as there is no name conflict within a single RDF description (it might be necessary to rename or renumber these when merging multiple descriptions) [69]. An example of such a serialisation can be seen in Figure 2.15, where the intermediate resource was simply named `im_resource1`.

Earlier we said that an RDF statement is nothing other than an ordered sequence of three resources, identified by URIs, or two resources and a literal. Now we have seen that an

```
{[http://......night_watch.htm], paintedBy, [im_resource1]}
{[im_resource1],name,"Rembrandt van Rijn"}
{[im_resource1],bornIn,"1606"}
```

Figure 2.15. An RDF statement with an intermediate resource.

intermediate resource can also appear in an RDF statement even though no URI is assigned to it. Extending thus our earlier definition, we state that the subject of a statement is either a resource identified by a URI or a blank resource. Similarly, the object of a statement is a resource identified by a URI; a literal or a blank resource. However, a predicate can still only be a resource identified by a URI; in other words, there can be no unlabelled arcs in an RDF graph.

Exercise 2.7: Consider the sentence "File `c:/project/house.jpg` is a picture made by Jim and it depicts a house painted white." Model this sentence in RDF. Describe your solution using both RDF graph and RDF triple representations.

Now we will proceed to the introduction of the XML-based syntax of RDF.

2.4. The XML syntax for RDF

This section introduces the use of the main XML constructs and namespaces in RDF descriptions. We show how intermediate resources can be described in XML and how relative URIs can be used.

2.4.1. Basic XML syntax

The XML syntax of RDF – the final version of which was published as late as 2004 – is a linear form of the RDF graph. Figure 2.16 displays the XML equivalent of the statement seen earlier (the given painting was painted by Rembrandt). Note that the XML description is rather verbose, given that the XML code seen in the figure represents exactly the same RDF expression as that depicted by the graph in Figure 2.13 and the triple in Figure 2.12.

The XML form of an RDF graph is a valid XML document: therefore such an XML description must start with the XML declaration introduced earlier:

```
<?xml version="1.0" encoding="ISO-8859-1"?>
```

This tells the processing application that there follows an XML data stream conforming to the specified version and using the given character encoding. The subsequent `<rdf:RDF>` XML element denotes that the enclosed content (which is delimited by the closing `</rdf:RDF>` tag) should be considered as RDF data. The significance of this is that the RDF contents can be inserted into other, larger, XML sources, and in that case one should be able to unambiguously isolate them.

```
<?xml version="1.0" encoding="ISO-8859-1"?>
<rdf:RDF
 xmlns:rdf="http://www.w3.org/1999/02/22-rdf-syntax-ns#"
 xmlns:s="http://swexpld.org/utils/">

 <rdf:Description rdf:about="http://...night_watch.htm">
   <s:paintedBy>Rembrandt van Rijn</s:paintedBy>
 </rdf:Description>

</rdf:RDF>
```

Figure 2.16. The XML form of an RDF statement.

Within the `<rdf:RDF>` element we find two attributes providing XML namespace declarations. The first assigns the prefix `rdf` to the namespace identified by the URI `http://`
`www.w3.org/1999/02/22-rdf-syntax-ns#`:

`xmlns:rdf="http://www.w3.org/1999/02/22-rdf-syntax-ns#"`

This namespace is part of the RDF specification. Using the `rdf:` prefix in qualified
names will make the corresponding local name part of the above namespace. We have already
seen an example of such a name in the element name `rdf:RDF` itself. Note that while the
namespace is required to be the above URI, the `rdf` prefix name is just a recommendation
and in theory we can use any other prefix for denoting the RDF namespace.

The second declaration is in the form

`xmlns:s="http://swexpld.org/utils/"`

which assigns the name `s` to the namespace identified by the given URI. Since these two
namespaces have been declared in the root element of the document, they are valid throughout the entire document according to the XML specification. Note that it is not compulsory
to place the namespace declarations in the root element, but with a few rare exceptions this
is the recommended procedure for RDF documents.

The next three lines describe the RDF statement represented by the graph in Figure 2.13:

```
<rdf:Description rdf:about="http://...night_watch.htm">
  <s:paintedBy>Rembrandt van Rijn</s:paintedBy>
</rdf:Description>
```

The subject of the statement can be described using the element `<rdf:Description>`
from the `rdf` namespace. The URI identifying the subject is given as the `rdf:about`
attribute of the `<rdf:Description>` element. Informally this first row means "here
follows the *description* of the resource identified by the given URI".

The second row contains the simple XML element `<s:paintedBy>`. Such an element
is called a *property element* and, together with its contents, it specifies the *predicate*
and the *object* of the statement, the subject of which was given by the enclosing
`<rdf:Description>` element. In our case the object of the statement is given by the
contents of the element `<s:paintedBy>`, which is a plain literal. The predicate of the

statement is provided by the name of the element itself, which is a qualified XML name. However,we know that the predicate of an RDF statement must be identified by a URI. In order to understand how the `s:paintedBy` qualified name becomes an appropriate URI, let us make a small diversion.

The XML syntax of RDF uses qualified XML names to represent URIs written on the *arcs* of RDF graphs. *Properties* identified by absolute URIs (and optional fragment identifiers) in an RDF graph must appear in the XML form as `prefix:local name`. In the case of RDF/XML syntax, a qualified name is actually a specific notation of *appending* names (this is an extension of the XML specification).

According to this, the name `s:paintedBy` can be considered the equivalent of the URI `http://swexpld.org/utils/paintedBy`: thus the triple represented by the XML code in Figure 2.16 is

```
{[...],[http://swexpld.org/utils/paintedBy],"Rembrandt..."}
```

This is almost the same as what we saw in Figure 2.12. The only difference is that in Figure 2.12 the predicate of the statement is written as a plain literal for brevity.

The XML code of our example is terminated with the closing tag of the `<rdf:RDF>` element.

Let us note that whenever the content of a property element is a literal (such as `Rembrandt van Rijn` in our example), it is possible to replace the property element by an attribute. The name of the attribute refers to the property while its value is the content of the property element. For example, the abbreviated alternative form of our example is the following:

```
<rdf:Description rdf:about="http://...night_watch.htm"
                 s:paintedBy="Rembrandt van Rijn" />
```

Finally, we mention that since qualified names in XML form are merely syntactic sugar, there are multiple ways of transforming a URI into a qualified XML name (depending on where the URI is split in two). We have to consider, however, that XML does not allow arbitrary characters in qualified names, which means that, theoretically, not every RDF graph can be serialised into XML format. The RDF specification [11] actually suggests that the URI should be split immediately after the last character that is not considered a letter by the XML standard.

In the next section we first demonstrate how to make more compact RDF descriptions if several statements share the same subject. We then show how to write down a statement whose object is not a literal but a resource.

2.4.1.1. Shared subjects

The RDF source in Figure 2.10 is the serialisation of the RDF graph in Figure 2.9. It is worth noting various properties of the XML form. First, the `<rdf:Description>` element in the example has multiple property elements: that is, this element has multiple children. This is a compact version of the full, more verbose, form shown in Figure 2.17. In the compact form, each property element defines the predicate and object of an RDF statement but the subject of all statements is common. Since it often happens that we would like to state several things about a resource, the compact form can come in very handy.

```
<?xml version="1.0" encoding="ISO-8859-1"?>
<rdf:RDF
  xmlns:rdf="http://www.w3.org/1999/02/22-rdf-syntax-ns#"
  xmlns:s="http://swexpld.org/utils#">

 <rdf:Description rdf:about=
  "http://freemail.org/~doe/#about">
    <s:name>John Doe</s:name>
 </rdf:Description>

 <rdf:Description rdf:about=
  "http://freemail.org/~doe/#about">
    <s:address rdf:resource="mailto:johndoe@freemail.org"/>
 </rdf:Description>

 <rdf:Description rdf:about=
  "http://freemail.org/~doe/#about">
    <rdf:type rdf:resource=
     "http://www.w3.org/2000/10/swap/pim/contact#Person"/>
 </rdf:Description>
</rdf:RDF>
```

Figure 2.17. Independent <rdf:Description> elements.

It is also worth noting that the declarations at the beginning of the XML document (XML version, character encoding, namespaces) only have to be written once, so larger RDF documents do not appear to be overly wordy. In fact, RDF triples can be translated into <rdf:Description> elements by computer in an automated manner. The XML syntax is based on such simple <rdf:Description> elements. Practically everything else is syntactic sugar, but for the sake of brevity we do not always stress this in the book.

2.4.2. Resources in object position

A further interesting point in the first example is the use of the rdf:resource attribute for referring to other resources. Let us recall that resource-to-resource relations are also present in the example in Figure 2.9. For example, the address of the resource identified by URI http://freemail.org/~doe/#about is also a resource, not a literal. Had we represented this part of the graph as

```
<rdf:Description rdf:about="http://freemail.org/~doe/#about">
    <s:address>mailto:johndoe@freemail.org</s:address>
</rdf:Description>
```

then we would have stated that the value of the s:address element is the mailto: johndoe@freemail.org *character sequence*, not the resource identified by the given URI.

As can be seen, the `rdf:resource` attribute is used for describing resource-to-resource relations. The value of this attribute is always interpreted as a URI. The attribute always belongs to an element which must be the child of an `<rdf:Description>` element. The subject of the resulting RDF statement is determined by the `<rdf:Description>` element, its predicate comes from the name of the element containing the attribute and its object is the resource identified by the URI in the value of the attribute. The latter can be given in full form (unfortunately we cannot use qualified names in attribute values) or we can use XML entities; see Subsection 2.2.4.

Another case where resources appear in the object position will be described in Subsection 2.5.4. For the time being, we continue our discussion by showing how RDF intermediate resources (blank nodes in the graph) can be represented in XML form.

2.4.3. XML format of blank nodes

Intermediate resources can be represented in the XML syntax of RDF in numerous ways. Here we introduce two of the most often used solutions. A third will be described in connection with RDF containers in Subsection 2.5.4. What is important is that, whichever approach we choose, the graph corresponding to the XML form will be the *same*.

The most obvious solution for describing intermediate resources is an adaptation for XML of the approach seen earlier. Namely, the blank resource is assigned an identifier which is locally unique within the document. This can be done using the `rdf:nodeID` attribute, which may appear instead of the `rdf:about` and `rdf:resource` attributes, as can be seen in the following example:

```
<rdf:Description rdf:about="http://...night_watch.htm">
   <s:paintedBy rdf:nodeID="local_identifier1"/>
</rdf:Description>

<rdf:Description rdf:nodeID="local_identifier1">
   <s:name>Rembrandt van Rijn</s:name>
   <s:bornIn>1606</s:bornIn>
</rdf:Description>
```

Another possibility for serialising blank nodes is to use the `rdf:parseType` attribute, with the value `Resource`. The `rdf:parseType` attribute is a generic means of changing the interpretation of the property element to which it belongs. If its value is, for example, `Literal` then the content of the given property element should be always interpreted as a literal value, no matter what it is. In the following example we use some HTML tags inside the text describing the object of a statement, which, without the `rdf:parseType` attribute, would cause trouble:

```
...
<rdf:Description rdf:about="http://128.30.52.45">
   <dc:Title rdf:parseType="Literal">
   This is <I>my</I> computer!
   </dc:Title>
   <dc:Creator>Compaq</dc:Creator>
</rdf:Description>
...
```

Let us return to the question of blank nodes. By setting the value of the
`rdf:parseType` attribute to `Resource`, we instruct the XML processor to encapsulate the property element into an additional `<rdf:Description>` element. This latter,
imaginary, element describes a blank resource providing the object of the RDF statement,
the predicate of which is determined by the name of the property element. The following
snippet is the XML equivalent of the graph shown in Figure 2.14:

```
<rdf:Description rdf:about="http://...night_watch.htm">
   <s:paintedBy rdf:parseType="Resource">
      <s:name>Rembrandt van Rijn</s:name>
      <s:bornIn>1606</s:bornIn>
   </s:paintedBy>
</rdf:Description>
```

Note that, unlike the solution based on `rdf:nodeID` shown above, here we have only
one `rdf:Description` element. The disadvantage is that the blank node described in
this way can no longer be referenced from a different place (if, for example, we would like
to add later a triple about the birthplace of the painter).

Exercise 2.8: Consider the RDF triples that you formulated as the solution of Exercise 2.7.
Write down these in RDF/XML form. Use the RDF validator of W3C [111] to check the
syntax of your document and to make sure that it really captures the set of triples with which
you started.

Next, we show that relative URIs are also allowed in the XML form of RDF. We
demonstrate how these relative URIs are resolved into absolute URIs.

2.4.4. Relative URIs in the XML syntax

The URIs in an RDF graph are present in the XML equivalent in various forms. We have
seen that the URIs on graph arcs appear as qualified (element) names in the XML source.
However, URIs in the nodes (those identifying the subjects and objects of statements) are
listed as the values of XML attributes. Such attributes, among others, are `rdf:about`, used
to describe subjects, and `rdf:resource`, used to specify objects of statements.

In our examples so far, the URIs defined as values of attributes were all absolute URIs,
and we also mentioned that qualified names are in fact syntactic sugar for absolute URIs. The
use of absolute URIs is hardly surprising, since we know that RDF graphs may only contain
absolute URIs for identifying resources and that the XML form is always the equivalent of a
graph.

However, the XML syntax of RDF allows the usage of *relative URIs* as well, in *all places*
where absolute URIs are allowed. This is acceptable because in the case of the XML form of
RDF the base URI is well defined, and the construction of an absolute URI from a relative
URI can be guaranteed to succeed. The base URI is the URI of the document by default, but
we may specify a different URI using the `xml:base` attribute.

Let us look at an example. In Figure 2.18 we see an XML document which uses a relative
URI as the object of the RDF statement (`people/John`). Let us assume that the document

```
<?xml version="1.0" encoding="ISO-8859-1"?>
<rdf:RDF
   xmlns:rdf="http://www.w3.org/1999/02/22-rdf-syntax-ns#"
   xmlns:dc="http://purl.org/dc/elements/1.1/">

   <rdf:Description rdf:about="http://128.30.52.45">
      <dc:contributor rdf:resource="people/John"/>
   </rdf:Description>
</rdf:RDF>
```

Figure 2.18.   The use of relative URIs in RDF.

is identified by the URI http://swexpld.org/tricky/ (for example, because it is
located there). Then the triple described by the document is the following:

```
{
  [http://128.30.52.45],
  [http://www.purl.org/dc/elements/1.1/contributor],
  [http://swexpld.org/tricky/people/John]
}
```

In some cases it might be necessary to specify the base URI of a document explicitly.
In this way we can ensure that the resolution of the relative URIs always happens using the
same base URI, independently of the location of the document. The base URI of an XML
element can be specified using the xml:base attribute, which it is best to place in the root
element. In that way we can determine the base URI for the whole document. Accordingly,
to set the base URI in our example to http://swexpld.org/base/, the root element
must be modified as follows:

```
<rdf:RDF
   xmlns:rdf="http://www.w3.org/1999/02/22-rdf-syntax-ns#"
   xmlns:dc="http://purl.org/dc/elements/1.1/"
   xml:base="http://swexpld.org/base/">
```

As a consequence of this modification of the base URI, the resolution of the relative URI
now results in a different absolute URI and the XML document represents a different triple:

```
{
  [http://128.30.52.45],
  [http://purl.org/dc/elements/1.1/contributor],
  [http://swexpld.org/base/people/John]
}
```

Below we introduce an alternative to the rdf:about attribute that relies heavily on
relative URIs.

2.4.5. The rdf:ID attribute

So far we have described resources in RDF that we assumed to have been identified by at
least one URI. This URI was used as the value of the rdf:about attribute to construct RDF

```
<?xml version="1.0" encoding="ISO-8859-1"?>
<rdf:RDF
    xmlns:rdf="http://www.w3.org/1999/02/22-rdf-syntax-ns#"
    xmlns:s="http://swexpld.org/general/"
    xmlns:p="http://swexpld.org/utils/">

    <rdf:Description rdf:ID="employee1">
        <s:name>Jane Doe</s:name>
        <s:salary>4500</s:salary>
        <s:SSN>965342876</s:SSN>
    </rdf:Description>

    <rdf:Description rdf:ID="employee2">
        <s:name>John Stiles</s:name>
        <s:salary>6100</s:salary>
        <s:SSN>823457201</s:SSN>
        <p:phone rdf:parseType="Resource">
            <p:base>555-136-8531</p:base>
            <p:extension>2465</p:extension>
        </p:phone>
        <p:phone>917-555-7642</p:phone>
    </rdf:Description>
</rdf:RDF>
```

Figure 2.19.   The use of the `rdf:ID` attribute (without any `xml:base`).

statements. In such a statement we claimed that the Night Watch was painted by Rembrandt van Rijn.

In many cases, however, we would like to make statements about things which do not yet have an associated URI or, if they do, we do not know what it is. For example, we might want to store the list of the employees or products of a company in RDF. Let us recall the employee database shown in Figure 2.3 in XML format. Figure 2.19 shows a representation of this data source in RDF.[8]

The main point of the example is that we used the `rdf:ID` attribute instead of the `rdf:about` to identify the subjects of the RDF statements. The meaning of the `rdf:ID` is similar to the `ID` attribute in the case of XML and HTML. Namely, `rdf:ID` defines a name which must be unique relative to the current base URI. In our example this allows us to "simulate" the process of assigning a unique identifier to a particular person (`rdf:ID` is also used for similar purposes in case of RDF reification, see Subsection 2.5.3 for the details).

---

[8] Unlike the original example, here the phone numbers with extensions are represented as structured entities; in this way the extension number and the base number are distinguished.

The rdf:ID attribute can be very useful when we would like to define many different, but in some way coherent things in a single RDF document (e.g. various employees of a company). The distinctness of these things is guaranteed by the a special property of the rdf:ID attribute mentioned above: it must be true for a well-formed RDF XML source so that, within the scope of a given base URI (which usually means the entire document), an identifier listed in an rdf:ID attribute must appear *exactly once*. RDF parsers should verify this property.

Coherence[9] is ensured by the fact that in the case of rdf:ID we actually specify a fragment identifier. In practice this means that all resources named with rdf:ID use the same base URI. More precisely, the URIs identifying the subjects are constructed using the following rule: take the current base URI, append the character # and finally append the value of rdf:ID.

According to this rule, the two absolute URIs in our example are the following (assuming that the location of the document is http://swexpld.org/stg.rdf):

```
http://swexpld.org/stg.rdf#employee1 (*1)
http://swexpld.org/stg.rdf#employee2 (*2)
```

If the example is depicted as an RDF graph, the above absolute URIs appear as the labels of the corresponding root elements. Such a graph is shown in Figure 2.20, which, for the sake of simplicity, shows only the root element of employee2, omitting the SSN and the second phone number too. As can be seen, nothing in the graph implies that rdf:ID was used instead of rdf:about.

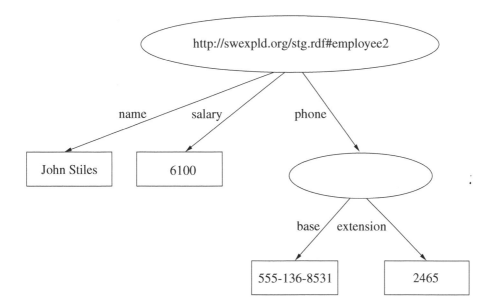

Figure 2.20. An RDF graph and the rdf:ID attribute.

---

[9] Note that by coherence we mean only syntactic similarity; RDF itself does not assume any relation between two resources simply because their URIs differ only slightly.

The base URI has a particularly important role when the `rdf:ID` attribute (or relative URIs in general) are being used, because, as we have seen, relative URIs are resolved using the base URI. Imagine what would happen if we published the document in Figure 2.19 on several sites on the web. Depending on the location we would get different subject identifiers (e.g. `http://swexpld.org#employee1` etc.), resulting in different RDF statements. To avoid that, it is vitally important to specify explicitly the base URI using the `xml:base` attribute, introduced in Subsection 2.4.4 (which is not the case for the RDF source shown in Figure 2.19).

Whenever an `rdf:ID` appears in the scope of an `xml:base` specification, the resulting absolute URI depends only on the value of these two attributes. For example, no matter where the enclosing document is located, the label of the root element of the RDF graph represented by the following XML example will always be the URI `http://swexpld.org/base/#something`.

```
<?xml version="1.0"?>
<rdf:RDF
  xmlns:rdf="http://www.w3.org/1999/02/22-rdf-syntax-ns#"
  xml:base="http://swexpld.org/base/">
  <rdf:Description rdf:ID="something">
     ...
  </rdf:Description>
</rdf:RDF>
```

A resource identified by an `rdf:ID` attribute can be referred to with the `rdf:about` attribute within the same document (strictly speaking, within the scope of the same base URI declaration). Note, however, that the `rdf:about` attribute has to be preceded by a # character. The last statement in the following RDF description adds to the employee database the information that Jane Doe has bought herself a mobile phone.

```
...
<rdf:Description rdf:ID="employee1">
   <s:name>Jane Doe</s:name>
   <s:salary>4500</s:salary>
   <s:SSN>965342876</s:SSN>
</rdf:Description>

<rdf:Description rdf:ID="employee2">
   <s:name>John Stiles</s:name>
   ...
</rdf:Description>

<rdf:Description rdf:about="#employee1">
   <p:phone>615-555-5588</p:phone>
</rdf:Description>
...
```

If we refer to a resource identified by an `rdf:ID` either from an external document or from outside the scope of the `xml:base` declaration then we have to use the full

```
<?xml version="1.0" encoding="ISO-8859-1"?>
<rdf:RDF
   xmlns:rdf="http://www.w3.org/1999/02/22-rdf-syntax-ns#"
   xmlns:n="http://swexpld.org/styles/"

   <rdf:Description
     rdf:about="http://swexpld.org/stg.rdf#employee2">
      <n:hasEyeColour
         rdf:resource="http://swexpld.org/colours#blue"/>
   </rdf:Description>

</rdf:RDF>
```

Figure 2.21.   External reference to an RDF resource.

URI, as expected. Figure 2.21 shows an example document which is different from that in Figure 2.19; it tells us that John Stiles has blue eyes.

The last example emphasises the point that information about a particular resource can be distributed on the Internet. Various places can store data about an employee of a given company. For example, it is possible that the author of the RDF document in Figure 2.21 could be the same as the author of that in Figure 2.19. If so, the author could have modified the original RDF source, instead of creating a new file, by adding a sixth child to the appropriate <rdf:Description> element. However, it is quite possible that two different people (or computers, for that matter) created these two files. This makes it clear that using RDF anyone can make arbitrary statements about any resource identifiable by a URI, without any practical limitations: a neat manifestation of the freedom of speech.

Exercise 2.9: What are the triples corresponding to the following RDF/XML document? Verify your solution using the W3C RDF validator [111].

```
<?xml version="1.0" encoding="ISO-8859-2"?>
<rdf:RDF
   xmlns:rdf="http://www.w3.org/1999/02/22-rdf-syntax-ns#"
   xmlns:s="http://swexpld.org/util/"
   xml:base="http://swexpld.org/base/">

<rdf:Description rdf:ID="id87">
   <s:address rdf:parseType="Resource">
      <s:street>Kossuth Lajos</s:street>
      <s:district>V</s:district>
      <s:city>Budapest</s:city>
   </s:address>
</rdf:Description></rdf:RDF>
```

2.4.6. Summary of and alternatives to the XML syntax

The XML syntax of RDF can be rather awkward to read for a human, but it has the huge benefit of being easily processable by machines because its base is XML. Furthermore, RDF sources written in XML are usually not generated by hand, or read directly by people, but in most cases we employ an RDF-based ontology editor, such as Protégé [104, 90], OilEd [6] or LORE [74]. Then the complexity of the format does not pose a problem. However, to make teaching RDF easier, and not to scare away novice users with an obscure and potentially unfamiliar XML syntax, Tim Berners-Lee created the *Notation 3* syntax [15], N3 for short. This notation is a practical alternative to the XML syntax given in the RDF specification; among other uses it is employed in the SPARQL query language, to be introduced in Subsection 3.3.6. The N3 syntax also serves as a basis for other RDF serialisations such as N-triples [9] or Turtle [8]. An example of a very simple N3 description can be seen below:

```
@prefix s:  <http://swexpld.org/utils/> .
<http://...night_watch.htm> s:paintedBy "Rembrandt" .
```

Thus, triples in N3 end with a period. A semicolon introduces another property of the same subject, while a comma introduces another object with the same predicate and subject. An example of such composite descriptions is shown below (we state that Bob, who is 34, has children Phil and Ryan):

```
...
p:Bob s:hasChild p:Phil, p:Ryan ;
      s:age 34 .
```

There are also other representations of RDF such as the JSON serialisation [39].

This concludes the introduction of the RDF XML syntax, and now we move on to the description of special RDF constructs.

2.5. Special RDF constructs

In this section first we observe how one can describe non-binary relations in RDF. Then we show how to state that a resource is an instance of a particular class. This is followed by the introduction of so-called reified statements, with which we can make RDF statements about RDF statements. Finally, we describe the containers and collections which can be used in RDF definitions and the concept of types as used by the RDF framework.

2.5.1. Non-binary relations in RDF

We have seen that one can describe binary relations between resources identified by URIs using RDF. In real life, however, we often encounter higher-arity, non-binary, relations as well.

For example, we call three integers a *Pythagorean triple* if a right-angled triangle can be constructed from segments of such lengths. For example, the numbers 3, 4 and 5 form a Pythagorean triple. The three numbers are connected by a single relation; only exactly three numbers *together* form a Pythagorean triple, so it is meaningless to ask what the relation is between 3 and 4 in the above triple.

As a further example, we could mention a `kick` relation, which relates a football player, a match and a number. Its meaning is that the given player scored the given amount of goals during the specified match. Similarly to the previous example, it is meaningless to try to explain the relation between the match and the number, or the player and the number, without the third value.

It appears that non-binary statements play a significant role in real life. However, it is important to note that everything can be described using only binary relations. For example, we can create an intermediate resource to represent a Pythagorean triple, and bind the three numbers to it with three separate statements (first number, second number, third number). This technique can be used to translate any non-binary relation into a group of binary relations. Note that this transformation often also makes the data representation more structured. With regard to higher-arity relations, the address relation might connect a person, a postal code, a street name and a house number. But perhaps it would be more informative to transform this into a set of binary relations and create an intermediate resource representing the address itself, associating postal code, street name, and house number with it and connecting it with a further binary relation to the resource representing the person.

Thus the limitation that RDF can only define binary relations does not pose a theoretical barrier. Nonetheless, in some special cases RDF provides a means of helping represent non-binary relations. We can use the rdf:value property for this. This property allows us to assign a "main value" to a relation. The interpretation of what this main value means is at the discretion of the processing application. A good example of the use of the rdf:value element occurs when there is something simple to express (e.g. the price of an object) but it is worth modelling this as a complex entity (for example, understandably we would want to provide the currency of the price as well).

The following example represents a graph which still uses binary relations only. A product is connected to an intermediate resource with an e:hasPrice property, and the intermediate resource has two further properties, rdf:value and e:hasCurrency specifying the price currency. The description might be considered as a non-binary relation between the product, the price as a number and its currency:

```
<rdf:Description rdf:about="http://.../products#item10245">
   <e:hasPrice rdf:parseType="Resource">
     <rdf:value>6</rdf:value>
     <e:hasCurrency rdf:resource="http://.../currency/euro"/>
   </e:hasPrice>
</rdf:Description>
```

In our example, instead of rdf:value we could have taken a user-defined property, such as e:amount. The only difference would be that in the case of the standardised rdf:value an application might be able to answer 6 when asked the price of a given product (even though the object of the e:hasPrice property is the intermediate resource, not the number itself).

Exercise 2.10: How would you decompose into binary relations the ternary relation "player–season–goal" (that is, how many goals a football player scored in a given season, e.g. Ryan Giggs scored seven goals in the season 2005–6)?

2.5.2. Instances in RDF

In this section we introduce the way in which an RDF resource can be declared to be an instance of a class. We also show the simplified (abbreviated) XML syntax for describing class instantiation.

The RDF language makes it possible to specify that a resource is an *instance* of a given *class*. This functionality is provided by the `rdf:type` property, the object of which identifies the particular class. Earlier we used the following statement to state that John Doe is a *person*:

```
<rdf:type rdf:resource=
    "http://www.w3.org/2000/10/swap/pim/contact#Person"/>
```

This is in fact a completely ordinary RDF statement, analogous to that in which we specified that the name of a resource was Rembrandt van Rijn.

It is fair to say that RDF instantiation closely resembles the "instance of" relation of the object-oriented world. That is, if an RDF resource is the instance of the class of animals then we actually say that this particular resource is *an* animal. In our example the class of people is identified by the following URI:

```
http://www.w3.org/2000/10/swap/pim/contact#Person
```

Here we are actually assuming that this URI means the same (i.e. the class of people) to everyone. This is very important, as without this the RDF statement above could have different meaning for different processing peers (humans, computers). Another example is that claiming that the `s:name` of a resource is John Doe makes sense only if the resource identified by the URI `s:name` is mapped to the same semantics by everyone.

To achieve this, we need some way to express that a resource is a class or property and to specify certain characteristics of it. The RDF language itself does not give us the means to define our own classes and properties, but RDF schemas, to be discussed in Section 2.6, are well suited for this. However, RDF does provide a handful of *built-in classes*, which can be used to declare instances and which facilitate the use of higher-order statements and containers. These are introduced in detail in the next couple of subsections.

Declaring instances is very common in RDF, therefore the XML syntax allows a simplified form. Here, the `rdf:type` property element is omitted and the enclosing `<rdf:Description>` element is replaced by a new element, the name of which is the value of the removed `rdf:type` property, but in a different format (the value of the `rdf:type` property is a long full URI. e.g. `http://www.w3.org/2000/10/swap/pim/contact#Person`, but what we use instead is `<n:Person>`). For example, the statement shown in Figure 2.10 can also be written as seen in Figure 2.22. The two forms are interchangeable, their RDF graph being the same in both cases.

An arbitrary number of `rdf:type` properties can be associated with a resource; in this case the resource is the instance of multiple classes at the same time. However, the simplified form can only be used for one of these; the rest must be declared in the more verbose form.

A great advantage of the simplified syntax is that it allows us to store relatively complex pieces of information in a very XML-like style (the resource is a piece of clothing, a person, a computer etc.). In some cases this may facilitate the transition from XML-based to RDF-based data storage.

```
<?xml version="1.0" encoding="ISO-8859-1"?>
<rdf:RDF
  xmlns:rdf="http://www.w3.org/1999/02/22-rdf-syntax-ns#"
  xmlns:s="http://swexpld.org/utils#"
 xmlns:n="http://www.w3.org/2000/10/swap/pim/contact#">

  <n:Person rdf:about="http://freemail.org/~doe/#about">
    <s:name>John Doe</s:name>
    <s:address rdf:resource="mailto:johndoe@freemail.org"/>
  </n:Person>

</rdf:RDF>
```

Figure 2.22. Simplified form of rdf:type.

Exercise 2.11: Let us assume that the employees in Figure 2.19 are actually instances of the class Employee. Modify the RDF source shown in the figure to represent this knowledge. Use the simplified syntax described above and compare your solution with the plain XML source presented in Figure 2.3.

In the following we show some examples of built-in RDF classes. First we introduce the Statement class, which includes so-called reified statements; this is followed by the definition of container classes.

2.5.3. Higher-order statements; reification

The RDF language lets us make statements about statements. Such statements are said to be *higher order*. Higher-order statements are necessary, since it is often important to know to whom a particular statement is attributed, when the statement was made and so on. A good example of a higher-order statement occurs when we state that *someone claims* that Rembrandt van Rijn was born in 1556.

The RDF equivalent of this natural language statement could be a statement the subject of which is the above mysterious someone (who is, by the way, not too well informed about dates), the predicate of which is that he or she claims and the object of which is the statement that Rembrandt was born in 1556. The problem is that the subject of an RDF statement must be a resource; therefore we need some way of modelling the statement as a special resource. This process is called *reification* and the resulting special resource is called a *reified statement*.

A reified statement is an instance of the rdf:Statement class. Therefore the meaning of the RDF statement

{[Uri1],[rdf:type],[rdf:Statement]}

is that the resource identified by [Uri1] is a reified statement, i.e. the model of another triple. The subject, predicate and object of the triple can be associated with the resource by using the `rdf:subject`, `rdf:predicate` and `rdf:object` properties, respectively. Assuming that the painter is identified by the URI `http://swexpld.org/painter #Rembrandt`, the triples are

```
{[Uri1],[rdf:subject],[http://swexpld.org/painter#Rembrandt]}
{[Uri1],[rdf:predicate],[s:bornIn]}
{[Uri1],[rdf:object],"1556"}
```

Finally, the reified statement can be used to construct the original statement (assume that the URI `http://swexpld.org/secret#he` identifies the mysterious stranger):

```
{[http://swexpld.org/secret#he],[n:claims],[Uri1]}
```

The reified statement is usually depicted as a blank resource. The final XML form of the original statement can be seen in Figure 2.23 and the corresponding graph is shown in Figure 2.24. According to the simplified syntax, the `rdf:type` property element could have been omitted had we replaced the line

```
<rdf:Description rdf:nodeID="identifier1">
```

by

```
<rdf:Statement rdf:nodeID="identifier1">
```

It is important to note that the fact that a reified statement is present in an RDF graph does not necessarily mean that the modelled statement is also part of it. In other words, the RDF

```
<?xml version="1.0" encoding="ISO-8859-1"?>
<rdf:RDF
 xmlns:rdf="http://www.w3.org/1999/02/22-rdf-syntax-ns#"
 xmlns:n="http://swexpld.org/utils/terms">

 <rdf:Description rdf:nodeID="identifier1">
  <rdf:type rdf:resource=
   "http://www.w3.org/1999/02/22-rdf-syntax-ns#Statement"/>
  <rdf:subject rdf:resource=
   "http://swexpld.org/painters#Rembrandt"/>
  <rdf:predicate rdf:resource=
   "http://swexpld.org/utils#bornIn"/>
  <rdf:object>1556</rdf:object>
 </rdf:Description>

 <rdf:Description rdf:about="http://swexpld.org/secret#he">
   <n:claims rdf:nodeID="identifier1"/>
 </rdf:Description>

</rdf:RDF>
```

Figure 2.23.   Reification in RDF/XML.

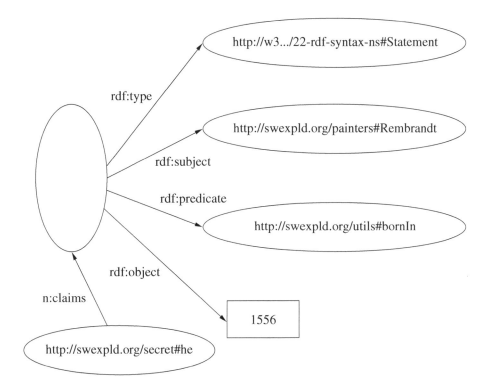

Figure 2.24. Reification in the RDF graph.

description in Figure 2.24 does *not* state that Rembrandt was born in 1556. All it says is that someone *claims* he was born in that year. This is a very important distinction because RDF statements express facts, which are considered true, and so which statements are represented by a graph is critical. Our example contains a single statement about an [n:claims] property, which has nothing to do directly with the birth date of the painter.

Note that a higher-order statement can also be created *without* reification if the triple in question already has a URI assigned to it (which means that someone else has already done the reification). For example, if U is a URI identifying a triple, the following statement is a higher-order statement (it is given in both XML and triple form):

```
<rdf:Description rdf:about="U">
   <n:author>John Doe</n:author>
</rdf:Description>
```

```
{[U],[n:author],"John Doe"}
```

We would also like to call the reader's attention to a peculiar feature and deficiency of RDF reification. A reified statement, according to the RDF specification, is about a *specific* triple in a *specific* RDF graph. This is obvious, since we use reification to declare who made a certain claim etc. However, statements containing the very same subject, property and object may appear in more than one graph. Therefore it can happen that several people made the mistake of giving the birth of Rembrandt van Rijn as 1556, and we would like to make a statement about a specific one of these claims.

The problem is that the reification syntax of RDF does not provide the means to directly attach the reified statement to the statement which reifies it. For example, in Figure 2.23 the reified statement identified by `identifier1` could include all triples where the subject, the predicate and the object assume the values specified. All we can do is try to refine which specific statement we are talking about (which statement was made at this time and in this place etc.)

Because of this (and because the syntax for reification introduced above is quite complex), the RDF recommendation actually provides a another way to "name" an RDF triple. More specifically, we can use the `rdf:ID` construct (already described in Subsection 2.4.5) for this purpose. In the following example we specify an RDF triple stating that Rembrandt was born in 1606.

```
<rdf:Description rdf:about="#Rembrandt">
  <s:bornIn rdf:ID="triple42">1606</s:bornIn>                    (2.1)
</rdf:Description>
```

Note that we have given an attribute `rdf:ID` for the property element `s:bornIn`. This notation tells the RDF parser to automatically create the appropriate reification triples. In other words, the RDF description above is equivalent to the following triples (`baseURI` stands for the base URI of our example above):

```
{[baseURI#Rembrandt], [s:bornIn], "1606"}
{[baseURI#triple42], [rdf:type], [rdf:Statement]}
{[baseURI#triple42], [rdf:subject], [baseURI#Rembrandt]}
{[baseURI#triple42], [rdf:predicate], [s:bornIn]}
{[baseURI#triple42], [rdf:object], "1606"}
```

Here, however, `baseURI#triple42` identifies exactly the triple in question. In some other RDF triple this URI can then stand as a subject or object providing information about the triple itself.

We should also note that, when using `rdf:ID` for reification purposes, the original RDF triple is actually placed in the resulting RDF graph (in this case, the triple stating that Rembrandt was born in 1606).

Exercise 2.12: Check the above statement by invoking the W3C RDF validator [111] on the RDF snippet (2.1) and ask the validator to draw the RDF graph for you. Note: do not forget to embed the piece of RDF code in question into proper `<rdf:RDF>` elements.

Finally, let us note that reification can be used in a natural way to create statements such as "he claims that she claims…", since nothing forbids us from reifying a statement which uses a reified statement as its object.

2.5.4. Containers and collections

In this subsection we introduce built-in RDF classes which can be used to gather resources into groups and to make statements about such groups.

We often consider a particular resource as a group of things. For example, the creators of a homepage or a program are such a group, one that has members which in this case are the creators themselves. Such groups are called *containers* in RDF. The RDF language allows the definition of containers and provides a set of built-in classes and properties for this.

The following three container classes are defined in RDF:

- *Bag* (rdf:Bag): This is a group of resources or literals where the same item can occur more than once and the order of the members is not significant. Examples of data that can be stored in an rdf:Bag are the list of employees working in a department, the publications of one person and the contents of a shopping cart. The latter may contain more than one of the same item.

- *Sequence* (rdf:Seq): This is an ordered rdf:Bag, i.e. a group where the same item can occur more than once but where the order of the items matters. Examples of data suitable for rdf:Seq are the list of employees working in a department (in alphabetical order), the contents of a shopping cart (in increasing order of the price of the items), and a person's publications (in order of appearance).

- *Alternative* (rdf:Alt): This is an unordered group of resources or literals where the same item can occur more than once and the items are in some sense interchangeable, being alternatives of each other. Examples of rdf:Alt are a group of synonyms and the list of mirror sites of a file accessible through the web. In distinction from the two other container classes an rdf:Alt cannot be empty, i.e. it must contain at least one item. The first item of the container is considered the default item: therefore in fact the order of items is not significant, with the exception of the first item.

Note that RDF does not define container classes corresponding to the concept of a set as used in mathematics.

A resource can be declared to be a container by using the rdf:type attribute. It is worth noting that, with RDF, containers are never "created" in the sense that we create a new array, as for example in a classical programming language. There we usually specify how many elements the array can have, what types of elements it may contain etc. Here we are merely declaring about an already existing resource that it is a container. The following snippet, using the rdf:type property, states that a resource is an rdf:Bag:

```
<rdf:Description rdf:ID="Rucksack">
  <rdf:type rdf:resource=
   "http://www.w3.org/1999/02/22-rdf-syntax-ns#Bag"/>
</rdf:Description>
```

A container resource identifies the container itself. This resource can be used in arbitrary RDF statements. For example, we may state about the above rucksack what it cost, what colour it is etc. We might also determine the number of people in the group of creators of a program or specify in some way the average employee morale; however, although the morale of the group as a whole might be high that would not necessarily mean that *everyone* in the group is so enthusiastic about his or her work.

The members of a container can be defined with special RDF properties. The form of these is rdf:_n, where n is a base 10 natural number. Such properties are rdf:_1, rdf:_2 etc. These properties are attached to the container; their values identify members of the container, as can be seen here (using the simplified syntax of instantiation):

```
<rdf:Bag rdf:ID="Rucksack2">
  <rdf:_1 rdf:resource="#Apple"/>
  <rdf:_2 rdf:resource="http://swexpld.org/things/laptop"/>
  <rdf:_3 rdf:resource="http://swexpld.org/stationery#pen"/>
</rdf:Bag>
```

As we have already mentioned, containers are not "created" in RDF; rathers, existing resources are thereby declared to be containers (this is true in general for RDF instantiation). Consequently, we have not declared that our rucksack contains *only* the listed items and nothing else. All we have said is that *these* objects are in the rucksack, even though there could be many more. Another RDF source might place further resources in the container; in fact, there could be many more such RDF sources doing this.

An `<rdf:Description>` element describing a container can have an arbitrary number of property elements, not just the `rdf:type` and `rdf:_n` properties. Accordingly, the following snippet specifies the model of the rucksack and places several resources in it:

```
<rdf:Bag rdf:ID="Rucksack3">
   <rdf:_1 rdf:resource="#Cookie"/>
   <rdf:_2 rdf:resource="#Candy"/>
   <rdf:_3 rdf:resource="#Gum"/>
   <s:model>Deuter 28</s:model>
</rdf:Bag>
```

Observe that even though RDF provides a means of specifying containers, `rdf:Bag` is just an ordinary class as far as RDF is concerned. In an RDF graph the above `Rucksack3` would appear as a resource connected to a URI via the `rdf:type` property and to a literal as the value of the `s:model` property. We could create an isomorphic graph structure which has nothing to do with containers; what makes containers special is that the processing applications should recognise the `rdf:Bag`, `rdf:Seq`, `rdf:_n` etc. URIs and associate the right meaning with them, *as defined by* the RDF specification.

A typical use of containers is as the objects of statements. For example, to model in RDF that a given homepage was created by John Stiles and company, we would have to represent the group of creators as a container and specify this container as the object of the appropriate RDF statement. This can be seen in a more complicated example in Figure 2.25. This example specifies the creators and the registered users of a web portal. Part of the example can be seen in Figure 2.26 in graphical form. The groups of creators and of users are both identified by anonymous containers. The example also demonstrates the use of two further, as yet unseen, features.

The `rdf:li` property can be used instead of `rdf:_n`; its first occurrence is replaced by `rdf:_1`, the second by `rdf:_2` etc. The members of the container are still attached to the container via `rdf:_n` properties (as can be seen in Figure 2.26): `rdf:li` is merely syntactic sugar, used so that we do not have to number the items manually.

Another interesting feature is a yet unseen construct for representing a resource as the object of a statement. The use of the `<rdf:Bag>` element is nothing other than the simplified form of instantiation already introduced, but since the container is represented as an anonymous resource, i.e. there is no URI assigned to it, the `rdf:about` attribute is missing. Writing this `<rdf:Bag>` element as a child element of the `<dc:creator>` element

```
<?xml version="1.0" encoding="ISO-8859-1"?>
<rdf:RDF
 xmlns:rdf="http://www.w3.org/1999/02/22-rdf-syntax-ns#"
 xmlns:s="http://swexpld.org/utils#"
 xmlns:dc="http://purl.org/dc/elements/1.1/">

 <rdf:Description rdf:about="http://swexpld.org/portal">
  <dc:creator>
   <rdf:Bag>
    <rdf:li>John Stiles</rdf:li>
    <rdf:li>Mary Major</rdf:li>
    <rdf:li>Richard Roe</rdf:li>
   </rdf:Bag>
  </dc:creator>

  <s:users>
   <rdf:Seq>
    <s:comment>Ordered by time of registration</s:comment>
    <rdf:li rdf:resource="http://swexpld.org/people/id15"/>
    <rdf:li>Lou</rdf:li>
   </rdf:Seq>
  </s:users>
 </rdf:Description>
</rdf:RDF>
```

Figure 2.25. An example of the use of containers.

is another way of specifying that the given resource is the value of the `dc:creator` property (see Subsection 2.4.3). The situation is analogous for the `<rdf:Seq>` container in the example.[10]

If the container appears as the object of a statement, in some cases it can be substituted by as many statements as the number of items in the container. The graph in Figure 2.26 implies that the given three people are all creators of the portal; therefore the following RDF description could be viewed as semantically equivalent to it:

```
{[http://swexpld.org/portal],[dc:creator],"John Stiles"}
{[http://swexpld.org/portal],[dc:creator],"Mary Major"}
{[http://swexpld.org/portal],[dc:creator],"Richard Roe"}
```

However, this is not true in general. It might happen that such a transformation changes the meaning of the graph. A classical counter-example is the following: consider a group

---

[10] Note that if a container is represented as an anonymous resource then it is practically closed, since other sources cannot refer to it owing to the lack of a URI.

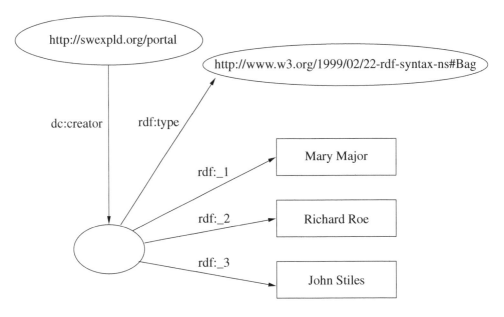

Figure 2.26. Containers presented as graphs.

of people who pass a resolution by plain majority voting. This can be written as follows in RDF:

```
<rdf:Description rdf:ID="Resolution">
   <n:acceptedBy>
      <rdf:Bag>
         <rdf:li>Gandalf</rdf:li>
         <rdf:li>Lord Elrond</rdf:li>
         <rdf:li>Frodo Baggins</rdf:li>
      </rdf:Bag>
   </n:acceptedBy>
</rdf:RDF>
```

If this is transformed in the above manner then we get three separate RDF statements declaring that the resolution has been accepted by all members of the group individually. However, this is not necessarily true in majority voting.

Finally we mention that RDF also allows the creation of groups of resources which are closed and contain only the listed items. Such a group is called an *RDF collection*, which is nothing other than a *list* of resources. RDF defines URIs for building such lists. A specific collection is an instance of the rdf:List class. The first item is given using the rdf:first property and the rest is *another* collection, attached to the main collection via the rdf:rest property. This second collection can also have a first item, and so on. The end of the collection is denoted by the rdf:nil resource. The container of the creators shown in Figure 2.25 can be closed, according to this, as follows:

```
<rdf:Description rdf:about="http://swexpld.org/portal">
   <dc:creator>
      <rdf:List>
         <rdf:first>John Stiles</rdf:first>
         <rdf:rest>
            <rdf:List>
               <rdf:first>Mary Major</rdf:first>
               <rdf:rest>
                  <rdf:List>
                     <rdf:first>Richard Roe</rdf:first>
                     <rdf:rest rdf:resource=
                      "http://.../22-rdf-syntax-ns#nil">
                  </rdf:List>
               <rdf:rest>
            </rdf:List>
         </rdf:rest>
      </rdf:List>
   </dc:creator>
</rdf:Description>
```

In some cases RDF permits the specification of collections in a simpler form very similar to that for declaring containers. In order to do this one must use the `rdf:parseType` attribute with the value `Collection`, described in more detail in the RDF specification [11]. It is worth knowing that for this kind of use of the `rdf:parseType` attribute, only collections containing RDF resources can be specified; so, those containing literals (such as the collection in our example) cannot.

Exercise 2.13: How many elements are there in the container called `Rucksack3` shown above?

In the following subsection we introduce the concept of data types in RDF, describe the two types of literal and show how these can be specified.

2.5.5. Data types in RDF

We distinguish two types of literals in RDF. Until now, we have seen only *plain literals*. These have the common trait of representing a character sequence. We have seen that it is often beneficial to store such data in a structured manner instead. As an example we suggested the splitting up of an address stored as a literal into logically separable segments and the use of an intermediate resource to connect them. Such segments were the postal code, the street name and the house number.

Even though adding structure to literals is a significant step forward, it is still true that literals are viewed as character sequences. This is unfortunate in the case of house numbers, for example, or in the case of numbers in general. The literal 12 in RDF is simply the characters 1 and 2 written side by side. It would be good if this could be interpreted as a number. However, then there would be the question of in which base it is interpreted.

All in all, it would be beneficial to introduce typed values for RDF literals. Literals with types are called *typed literals*. Sadly, RDF does not define built-in types, not even the simplest ones such as integers, floating point numbers etc. Nonetheless, it provides means to assign a URI to a literal which identifies its type. This can be done using the `rdf:datatype` attribute. This special attribute is added to the property element which contains the literal in question. For example, the literal value of the property element

`<n:age>23</n:age>`

"obtains" a type as follows:

`<n:age rdf:datatype="Int">23</n:age>`

(where `Int` is a URI which identifies a type – in this case the integer type).

The question remains: where can we find a URI which identifies the type that we need and which is recognised in a circle wide enough to contain the application which is going to process our RDF source? Fortunately the *XML schema* specification defines such types. We have seen that the type of the content of an XML element can be prescribed using XML schemas. The XML schema defines a number of primitive data types (integer, floating point etc.) and complex data types (date, time interval etc.). A data type defined in an XML schema can be referred to by appending a fragment identifier to the URI `http://www.w3.org/2001/XMLSchema`. For example, integers are identified by the following URI:

`http://www.w3.org/2001/XMLSchema#int`

It is important to note that as far as RDF is concerned the URI given as the value of the `rdf:datatype` attribute is irrelevant, even though usage of the XML schema is recommended. Actually, we could specify a URI which identifies something that is not a type or something that contradicts the representation of the literal (e.g. we could specify "integer" as the type of a literal containing characters). However, RDF ignores all this. All it does is to provide a way of attaching an external type to RDF literals in a standard manner. Everything else is the responsibility of the processing application. If the application in question "comprehends" the given URI then it will verify the correctness of the literal.

As a summary of the above consider Figure 2.27, which is the XML representation of the graph seen in Figure 2.14 in which we specify the date of birth of the painter "typed" as a date, this time correctly.

Exercise 2.14: Run the W3C RDF validator [111] on the RDF source using the typed literals shown in Figure 2.27 and also on the earlier version of the same knowledge base given in Figure 2.15. How does the use of typed literals change the resulting triples?

2.5.6. Summary and open issues

In the above we introduced the RDF framework, which allows us to make statements about resources identified by URIs. RDF descriptions can be represented in XML syntax, which thus presents meta-information in a form that can be easily processed – at least syntactically – by standard and automated methods. Metadata provided in RDF can be used by Internet search engines to facilitate a more intelligent and human-centric search.

The RDF approach is still very fresh and many questions naturally arise about its usability. A primary concern regarding RDF descriptions is that nothing guarantees or even requires

```
<?xml version="1.0" encoding="iso-8859-1"?>
<rdf:RDF
    xmlns:rdf="http://www.w3.org/1999/02/22-rdf-syntax-ns#"
    xmlns:s="http://swexpld.org/utils/">

    <rdf:Description rdf:about="http://...night_watch.htm">
        <s:paintedBy rdf:parseType="Resource">
            <s:name>Rembrandt van Rijn</s:name>
            <s:bornIn rdf:datatype=
             "http://www.w3.org/2001/XMLSchema#date">
            1606-07-15</s:bornIn>
        </s:paintedBy>
    </rdf:Description>

</rdf:RDF>
```

Figure 2.27. The date of birth of Rembrandt given as a typed literal.

that the creators of various web pages provide truthful and valid meta-information about their resources. It often happens even today that a page "lies" about what it contains in the hope that it will occur more often and in more distinguished positions in the result sets of search engines (there are even web pages dedicated to giving detailed tips and tricks to achieve such effects). We have also mentioned that web pages exist where the web server, detecting that a web crawler is trying to access a particular page, returns a page different from that which it would present for an ordinary page request.

Nonetheless, we saw in Subsection 1.2.4 that the question of the reliability of information found on the web is important from more than just the Semantic Web point of view. We believe that a future direction for the Internet is in developing its potential for distinguishing reliable and unreliable sources. Various techniques which are hard to manipulate, such as the PageRank algorithm, can help (and already do so today) to give a higher value to meta-information originating from more reliable pages than those from pages of low esteem. This idea also helps to answer the question what to do with contradictory meta-information. Namely, what should happen when someone claims that a particular file contains music while someone else states that it is the source code of a program? This question will have to be answered by future research.

Independently, solutions for extracting meta-information automatically have started to spread, which in part replaces the need to provide meta-information manually on an RDF basis and thus reduces any potential intentional imprecision. Such solutions are the so-called RDFizers [98], which try to extract semantically important information from different kinds of information source. There is RDFizer for converting pictures, email data, BibTEX, CSV files, GPS data, BitTorrent files etc. into RDF format. The extraction process itself may work with or without human intervention, depending on the source type. These tools may greatly increase the amount of RDF data available on the web, thus providing a sufficient amount of meta-information for the search engines to work with.

2.6. Representing background knowledge: RDF schema

RDF schema is a lightweight ontology language [22]. It provides constructs to build domain-specific classes and properties as well as to specify their characteristics and the hierarchical relations between them. An example could be the introduction of the class Human and the property hasChild. Such classes and properties could then be used in ordinary RDF descriptions, such as one stating {[Mary],[hasChild],[Bill]} and {[Mary], [rdf:type],[Human]}.

RDF schemas are actually written in RDF syntax, i.e. using triples. This means that RDF schema constructs are actually special RDF resources. This idea is outlined below.

2.6.1. RDF schema as a collection of RDF resources

We have seen before that the fundamental idea of the RDF framework is to construct triples from RDF resources identified by URIs. For this RDF provides some predefined resources, such as the rdf:type and the rdf:value properties or the rdf:Alt container class; RDF associates with these resources a meaning, which is understood by all RDF-aware applications and which thus can be designed to handle such resources. If, for example, a processing application sees a triple where the predicate is rdf:type, it will know that the URI in the subject position identifies a resource which is an *instance* of the object (and as a consequence, the resource in the object position must be a class). Similarly, if it encounters a triple where the predicate is rdf:type and the object is rdf:Alt, it will know that the subject of the triple in question is a resource that models a group of resources. Consequently it might treat this resource somewhat differently, e.g. it could answer a question which queries the default item in the group. As we will see, much depends on whether the processing applications have ample knowledge about the meaning associated with particular resources.

The Semantic Web is an Internet-based infrastructure facilitating *reasoning*. However, it is often difficult, if not impossible, to reason merely on RDF statements. Let us consider the following example. We are able to describe with RDF that a person is a friend of someone else. We can do this by constructing an RDF statement where the subject and the object are two people and the predicate is a resource about which we *know* that it somehow identifies the "friendship" relation. The RDF triple in question could be the following (assuming that the two people and the predicate are identified by the given URIs):

$$\{[U1],[http://swexpld.org/rel\#hasFriend],[U2]\}$$

Given this triple, can we determine whether one person *knows* the other?   (2.2)

For us human beings the answer is trivial, since we know for a fact that everyone knows their own friends, but notice that this is actually an implication for which we use some background knowledge. That is, two people cannot be friends if they do not know each other.

For a computer, stored knowledge is only available as RDF statements. In our example there is only one statement, which merely states that one resource is in an http://swexpld.org/rel#hasFriend relation with another. Since the "knows" relation is certainly identified by a *different URI*, the machine will return a negative answer to question (2.2). This is in fact the correct behaviour, since without additional knowledge the computer has no way of knowing what the resources identified by various URIs actually mean (that *different URIs* could easily identify a resource representing "hates").

In the field of artificial intelligence the meaning of various entities is usually determined by formally specifying their relation with other entities. In the present case we would need to be able somehow to determine the relation between the `n:hasFriend` and the `s:knows` properties. We need a statement such as "between any two resources, which are in `n:hasFriend` relation, the `s:knows` relation also holds". With this added knowledge, the computer would be able to figure out that the above two people know each other even though this information would still not have been given explicitly. It is very important that we should be able to specify this background knowledge in RDF, since we have stressed many times that RDF descriptions are fundamental in the Semantic Web. The most obvious solution is to make an RDF statement:

```
{[http://.../rel#hasFriend],
 [V1],
 [http://.../a#knows]}
```

where the intended meaning of the resource identified by the URI `V1` is exactly what we have just described. The only remaining questions are whether there is a resource which has this semantics and whether the resource itself is widely known.

In a different example we might want to formally describe a different relation between properties or classes as part of the background knowledge. It can also be important to enable the specification of various qualities of properties, such as that they are transitive, symmetric etc. Furthermore, we should be able to define our own classes and properties and to define their features. This leads us to the concept of the *RDF Schema*.

So, in a sense, the RDF Schema is nothing other than a handful of resources, with well-defined semantics, extending the base RDF library. These resources can be used in RDF statements, just like those we have already seen. For example, such a resource helps us to describe the relation between the "hasFriend" and "knows" RDF properties in the example above. But the reason why the special resources of RDF schema are not considered as base RDF resources is that their purpose is to describe information at a different *meta-level*. As an analogy, we could mention the difference between the object and model layers in the Unified Modeling Language (UML).

Before we introduce the constructs of the RDF Schema in detail, let us first present an example that demonstrates some possible uses of the schemas.

2.6.2. A simple example

Figure 2.28 shows an RDF description that uses some constructs of the RDF Schema. In this example we define two classes (the second definition uses the simplified syntax): the classes of buildings (1) and of bungalows (2). We also declare that the class "bungalows" is a *subclass* of the class "buildings", i.e. that all bungalows are buildings (3). Furthermore, we define an RDF property (4) which only applies to buildings (5), and its value is an integer (6). Following the conventions, class names have initial capitals while property names begin with lowercase letters. The base URI valid throughout the document is declared at the beginning of the RDF document: thus the URIs referring to parts of the schema are independent of where the schema is stored. For example, the class of buildings may be referred to by the URI `http://swexpld.org/houses#Building`. The `rdfs` namespace is also declared

```
<?xml version="1.0" encoding="ISO-8859-1"?>
<rdf:RDF
   xmlns:rdf="http://www.w3.org/1999/02/22-rdf-syntax-ns#"
   xmlns:rdfs="http://www.w3.org/2000/01/rdf-schema#"
   xmlns:base="http://swexpld.org/houses">

   <rdf:Description rdf:ID="Building">                     (1)
      <rdf:type rdf:resource=
       "http://www.w3.org/2000/01/rdf-schema#Class"/>
   </rdf:Description>

   <rdfs:Class rdf:ID="Bungalow">                          (2)
      <rdfs:subClassOf rdf:resource="#Building"/>          (3)
   </rdfs:Class>

   <rdf:Property rdf:ID="buildYear">                       (4)
      <rdfs:domain rdf:resource="#Building"/>              (5)
      <rdfs:range rdf:resource=
       "http://www.w3.org/2001/XMLSchema#integer"/>        (6)
   </rdf:Property>
</rdf:RDF>
```

Figure 2.28. A simple RDF schema description.

at the start of the document; this URI is used to access the RDF Schema constructs. The name of the namespace does not have to be `rdfs`, but this is the convention that we will follow throughout this book.

Observe that the example does not contain instances, only class and property definitions. This separation often increases the readability of RDF sources, and we will use this approach in the rest of this book. However, a source often contains both the schema and data-level RDF triples. In either case we get a regular RDF graph, since schema descriptions are also standard RDF triples.

Exercise 2.15: Use an ontology editor to visualise the RDF Schema shown in Figure 2.28. We suggest Protégé [104] for this purpose. Note how the editor displays the subclass relation and the fact that the RDF property `buildYear` is only applicable to the class `Building`.

2.6.3. Classes and their hierarchical relations

A resource can be declared to be a class using the `rdf:type` property. For this, the value (object) of the `rdf:type` property must be the `rdfs:Class` resource (in other words, a class is an instance of the `rdfs:Class` class, i.e. the `rdfs:Class` resource might be considered as a class of classes). The RDF language does not "create" new classes. It

```
<?xml version="1.0" encoding="ISO-8859-1"?>
<rdf:RDF
   xmlns:rdf="http://www.w3.org/1999/02/22-rdf-syntax-ns#"
   xmlns:rdfs="http://www.w3.org/2000/01/rdf-schema#"
   xmlns:base="http://www.w3.org/2000/03/example/classes">

   <rdf:Description rdf:ID="Animal">
      <rdf:type rdf:resource=
       "http://www.w3.org/2000/01/rdf-schema#Class"/>
   </rdf:Description>
</rdf:RDF>
```

Figure 2.29. The class of animals.

merely allows us to state with regard to a resource that it is a class, just as when we state that a resource is a container, a person or a computer. Figure 2.29 shows an example where a resource is declared to be a class. The class defined this way can be referred to as #Animal within the scope of the same base URI. For external access, the full URI must be specified, in this case by http://www.w3.org/2000/03/example/classes#Animal.

A class A can be declared to be a *subclass* of class B using the rdfs:subClassOf property. This means that all instances of A are also instances of B. For example, such a subclass–parent class relation exists between the classes of dogs and animals (all dogs are animals), mobile phones and telephones (all mobile phones are telephones) and squares and rectangles (all squares are rectangles). In RDF a class can have an arbitrary number of parent classes and an arbitrary number of subclasses (also known as child classes). The rdfs:subClassOf property is transitive, i.e. if A is a subclass of B and B is a subclass of C then A is also a subclass of C. For example, if we know that cats are mammals and that mammals are animals then we can figure out that cats are animals.

Figure 2.30 shows definitions of the classes of reptiles, mammals or humans. It also demonstrates the use of the rdfs:subClassOf and rdfs:comment properties. The latter allows the attachment of a short textual comment to any resource (including classes). The example uses the simplified syntax for class definitions.

Figure 2.30 calls attention to a further important detail. A schema, for example the definition of the class of reptiles, can refer to a class defined in another schema. This demonstrates how two schemas can be connected. As a generalisation, a schema might refer to a larger number of schemas, those schemas might refer to yet others, and so on, similarly to how HTML pages refer to each other using hyperlinks. Eventually, schemas can interweave the entire Internet.

The possibility of referring to another schema is very useful. The schema seen in Figure 2.30 reuses an existing class instead of defining another for the same purpose, thus avoiding redundancy and potential inconsistency. It can still happen that independent sources define similar, if not identical, classes without knowing about each other. A goal of the Semantic Web is to create the necessary connections between these classes (e.g. to be able to express the equivalence of two classes in two distinct schemas).

```
<?xml version="1.0" encoding="ISO-8859-1"?>
<rdf:RDF
  xmlns:rdf="http://www.w3.org/1999/02/22-rdf-syntax-ns#"
  xmlns:rdfs="http://www.w3.org/2000/01/rdf-schema#"
  xmlns:base="http://swexpld.org/thing/rdf/schemas/simple">

  <rdfs:Class rdf:ID="Reptile">
     <rdfs:subClassOf rdf:resource=
      "http://www.w3.org/2000/03/example/classes#Animal"/>
     <rdfs:comment>Latin: Reptilia</rdfs:comment>
  </rdfs:Class>

  <rdfs:Class rdf:ID="Mammal">
     <rdfs:subClassOf rdf:resource=
      "http://www.w3.org/2000/03/example/classes#Animal"/>
     <rdfs:comment>Latin: Mammalia</rdfs:comment>
  </rdfs:Class>

  <rdfs:Class rdf:ID="Human">
     <rdfs:comment>Latin: Homo Sapiens</rdfs:comment>
     <rdfs:subClassOf rdf:resource="#Mammal"/>
  </rdfs:Class>
</rdf:RDF>
```

Figure 2.30.   Connected RDF schemas.

We have seen earlier that a resource can be declared to belong to a class through instanti-ation. We also mentioned that RDF instantiation closely resembles the "instance of" relation of the object-oriented universe; therefore the following snippet can be read as follows: Willy is a mammal and his age is 23 years (the snippet refers to the class defined in the schema in Figure 2.30):

```
...
<rdf:Description rdf:ID="Willy">
   <rdf:type rdf:resource=
    "http://swexpld.org/thing/rdf/schemas/simple#Mammal"/>
   <s:age rdf:datatype=
    "http://www.w3.org/2001/XMLSchema#integer">
   23
   </s:age>
</rdf:Description>
...
```

This also specified that the literal value of the s:age property describing the age of Willy is an integer.

Notice that it is possible to do some reasoning about Willy. For example, we are able to determine that Willy is an animal, even though this is not stated explicitly,[11] thanks to the RDF schema. The reason is that we know that Willy is a mammal, and the schema in Figure 2.30 tells us that the class of mammals is a subclass of the class of animals.

In the rest of this book we use the term "class hierarchy" to refer to a directed graph consisting of RDF classes with the arcs of `rdfs:subClassOf` properties stretching between them.

2.6.4. Properties and their hierarchical relations

An RDF property is an instance of the `rdf:Property` class. Accordingly, we may declare a resource to be a property via instantiation. RDF allows us to define a hierarchy of properties just as in the case of classes. This is the purpose of the `rdfs:subPropertyOf` property. Thus, if A is a subproperty of B then, for all cases where A holds between two resources, B also holds. The `rdfs:subPropertyOf` property is obviously transitive, just like the `rdfs:subClassOf` property. Comments may also be attached to properties using the `rdfs:comment` property, giving us the ability to write RDF schemas which are easier for humans to understand. This is illustrated in Figure 2.31.

Defined in this way, RDF properties can be freely used in RDF sources as predicates of RDF statements. For example, using them we could express that two people are friends of each other (Figure 2.32). The example refers to two schemas specified earlier. One defined

```
<?xml version="1.0" encoding="ISO-8859-1"?>
<rdf:RDF
    xmlns:rdf="http://www.w3.org/1999/02/22-rdf-syntax-ns#"
    xmlns:rdfs="http://www.w3.org/2000/01/rdf-schema#"
    xmlns:base="http://swexpld.org/rel">

    <rdf:Description rdf:ID="knows">
        <rdf:type rdf:resource=
         "http://www.w3.org/2000/01/rdf-schema#Property"/>
        <rdfs:comment>Social relation</rdfs:comment>
    </rdf:Description>

    <rdf:Property rdf:ID="hasFriend">
        <rdfs:comment>Close acquaintances</rdfs:comment>
        <rdfs:subPropertyOf rdf:resource="#knows"/>
    </rdf:Property>
</rdf:RDF>
```

Figure 2.31. RDF properties and their hierarchical relations.

---

[11] More precisely, it is not stated that `Willy` is an instance of the `http://www.w3.org/2000/03/example/classes#Animal` class.

```
<?xml version="1.0" encoding="ISO-8859-1"?>
<rdf:RDF
  xmlns:rdf="http://www.w3.org/1999/02/22-rdf-syntax-ns#"
  xmlns:rdfs="http://www.w3.org/2000/01/rdf-schema#"
  xmlns:n="http://swexpld.org/thing/rdf/schemas/simple#"
  xmlns:s="http://swexpld.org/rel#">

  <n:Human rdf:ID="Eric_Clapton">
    <rdfs:comment>guitarist, AKA "Slowhand"</rdfs:comment>
  </n:Human>

  <n:Human rdf:ID="Mark_Knopfler">
    <rdfs:comment>Dire Straits lead</rdfs:comment>
    <s:hasFriend rdf:resource="#Eric_Clapton"/>
  </n:Human>
</rdf:RDF>
```

Figure 2.32.   Using defined RDF properties.

the class of humans (Figure 2.30), the other defined the hasFriend property (Figure 2.31). These schemas are identified by qualified names. For example, the s:hasFriend qualified name corresponds to the URI http://swexpld.org/rel#hasFriend, and this URI indeed identifies the desired property, according to the base URI seen in Figure 2.31. Also notice that this example – both in its syntax and semantics – is an RDF source just like those we encountered before we said anything about schemas. At that time we requested the reader simply to assume that this or that class was identified by the URI used. Such a resource was the class of humans, in the case of the example seen in Figure 2.9. Now we see that we ourselves are able to state with regard to certain resources that they are in fact properties or classes,[12] and we can also define the hierarchical relations between them. The latter is very important since this allows us to deduce that, for example, Eric Clapton is in the s:knows relation with Mark Knopfler, using the RDF information in Figures 2.31 and 2.32. Thus, we finally see that RDF schemas are truly suitable for representing the necessary background knowledge required to answer the question (2.2) posed in the introduction of this Section (see page 98).

2.6.5. Property restrictions

In addition to hierarchical relationships, RDF schemas allow us to express background knowledge by using *property restrictions*. Namely, the *domain* and/or the *range* of a property can be specified using schemas. If, for example, we specify the range of an RDF property to be the class n:Person then, for any specific RDF statement referring to this property, the object (value) will be known to be an instance of the n:Person class. Similarly, specifying

---

[12] Furthermore, we are able to do this in a standard RDF/XML syntax; therefore the processing application will also be able to figure out that some resources should be considered as classes.

the domain of a property implies that the subject of a statement is an instance of the class specified as the domain.

For example, let the domain of the `t:hasStudent` property (which means that the given person is a student of a specified university) be the `p:University` class, and let its range be the `n:Person` class. This definition signifies that the `t:hasStudent` property holds between universities and people: i.e. in the triple

`{[E1],t:hasStudent,[E2]}`

the `[E1]` resource is an instance of `p:University` and `[E2]` is an instance of `n:Person`.

RDF intentionally does not determine for what the domain and range information should be used. Certain applications may use this information to look for *inconsistencies* in RDF data. A good example of this is a statement where an instance of the `o:Television` class is connected to someone via a `t:hasStudent` property.[13] Other applications, e.g. interactive RDF editors, may use this information to provide default values during editing, facilitating efficiency. Reasoning engines may use domain and range specifications to figure out indirectly details which are not specified explicitly. For example, even if we do not know anything about the `[E2]` resource, we can reason that it must be a person. In these cases property restrictions are considered as background knowledge, which helps data-level reasoning.

The domain and range of an RDF property can be specified using the `rdfs:domain` and `rdfs:range` properties respectively. In the example in Figure 2.28 we specified that the `buildYear` property connects buildings with integers.

The domain and range of a property can be specified as classes. If the property does not have an `rdfs:domain` specification then its domain defaults to `rdfs:Resource`, which contains all existing resources. In other words, if a property has no domain restriction then it may be applied to resources belonging to arbitrary classes. Similarly, if we do not specify the range of a property then its value could be any resource or literal. A property may have multiple domain (and range) specifications; in such cases its domain (and range) will be the *intersection* of the specified classes. In the following example, a resource may have a `hasMaidenName` property if it is a person and a female at the same time:

```
<rdf:Property rdf:ID="hasMaidenName">
    <rdfs:domain rdf:resource="#Person"/>
    <rdfs:domain rdf:resource="#Female"/>
</rdf:Property>
```

It is worth noticing that multiple property restrictions are special in the sense that they indirectly allow us to speak about classes as intersections of other classes. There is no other way to do that in RDF. One might think that this can be achieved using an intermediate class, defined as a subclass of both the `Person` and `Female` classes. However, this would not represent the exact intersection class, but only a class which is a *subset* of the intersection.

---

[13] One must be very cautious in this case, since it may be that there is no contradiction even though the given resource is specified to be an instance of the class different from `p:University`. For example, if we have `q:Institute` instead of `o:Television` and we know that universities are institutes, then there is no contradiction.

A URI identifying a data type may also be specified as a range restriction, e.g. when we expect a property to connect people with numbers. However, when using such a property we still need to specify the type of the value using the `rdf:datatype` attribute.

The `rdfs:domain` and `rdfs:range` properties can also be used to specify formally the restrictions of other built-in RDF properties. For example, the domain and range of the `rdfs:subPropertyOf` property are both `rdf:Property` class resources. This is a formal way of saying that the subproperty relation holds between properties. Similarly, the domain and range of the `rdfs:subClassOf` property are both `rdfs:Class` resources. Consequently the subclass relation may exist between resources which are instances of the `rdfs:Class` class (in short, between classes). The `rdfs:domain` and `rdfs:range` properties also have a domain and a range. The domain of these properties is `rdf:Property`, and their range is `rdfs:Class`.

We can describe so-called *global* property restrictions using the `rdfs:domain` and `rdfs:range` properties. They are global because, once specified, the domain and/or range of a property are unchangeable and hold under all circumstances for that property.

Global property restrictions have some so far unmentioned drawbacks. For example, we might want to specify that the range of the `n:size` property must be the set of integers when the property is applied to instances of the class `c:Shoe`. However, we cannot declare that the value of the *same* property should be a literal when it is applied to T-shirts (e.g. one of the literals `S`, `M`, `L`, `XL`). Similarly, it would be beneficial to be able to say that if the value of a property is of a certain type or larger than a particular value then it can be applied only to instances of a given class. Generally speaking, there is no way to obtain domain-dependent range restrictions from global property restrictions; furthermore, there is no way to make domain restrictions depend on the value of the property.

The so-called *local* property restrictions, which are included in several schema languages that are richer than RDF schema, offer a solution to these problems. Such a language is OWL, which will be described in Chapter 8. The OWL language also provides various class construction operators missing in RDF including class intersection, discussed above.

Exercise 2.16: To what type of resources can we apply the property p2 using the following (stand alone) RDF description?

```
...
  <rdfs:Property rdf:ID="p1">
    <rdfs:domain rdf:resource="#Person"/>
  </rdfs:Property>

  <rdfs:Property rdf:ID="p2">
    <rdfs:subPropertyOf rdf:resource="#p1">
    <rdfs:domain rdf:resource="#Tall"/>
  </rdfs:Property>
...
```

2.6.6. Other RDF schema constructs

The RDF schema language provides a handful of generic resources in addition to the resources used for building class hierarchies and specifying property restrictions. The `rdfs:comment` property has already been used in an earlier example. This property allows us to attach a textual comment to an arbitrary resource. This can improve the readability for humans.

The `rdfs:label` property can be used to declare the verbose name of a resource in a way suited to human readers. The following example demonstrates how we can present for humans the resource identified by `http://swexpld.org/tantras/p12` as Richard Roe.

```
<rdf:Description rdf:about="http://swexpld.org/tantras/p12">
   <rdfs:label>Richard Roe</rdfs:label>
   <n:hasEyeColour
           rdf:resource="http://swexpld.org/colours#brown"/>
</rdf:Description>
```

The `rdfs:isDefinedBy` property helps us to specify an additional resource which more precisely defines the resource used as the subject of a statement (either formally or in plain text). An example occurs when we refer to a Wikipedia page to specify more elaborately the class `Human`. Additional information can also be linked to resources using the `rdfs:seeAlso` property. The full set of elements defined by RDF schema can be found in its specification [22].

Exercise 2.17: Design an RDF schema covering your own topic of interest. Try to use as many different RDF schema constructs as possible: class and property hierarchies, property restrictions, comments and labels. Make sure that your ontology also contains instances, i.e. data-level RDF statements such as `Bill loves Mary`. Load your RDF description into an ontology editor, Protégé [104] for example, to visualise it.

2.6.7. RDF schemas and the object-oriented world

This subsection compares the class, object, property and miscellaneous other concepts of the RDF schema language with their rough equivalents in the object-oriented world (such as UML).

2.6.7.1. Property as a primary modelling primitive

At first glance, UML shows many similarities with the RDF Schema language. Both have a concept of classes, and these classes can have instances. One of the most important differences is that there is no real UML equivalent of the property–predicate–relation concept in RDF schema,[14] even though it closely resembles UML associations and attributes.

RDF properties have an interesting character in that they are bound to resources only at "run time". That is, we define the properties with respect to classes which contain the instances to which the given property might be applied, and not vice versa. This is in contrast

---

[14] UML Standard 2.0 appears to make this gap smaller.

with the object-oriented world, where one has to decide at *modelling time* what attributes and associations a given class can have.

The following example is an attempt to demonstrate what we have said so far. Let us consider an RDF property `publishedBy`, without domain restriction and with `Publisher` as its range. This means that the `publishedBy` property connects two objects, the first of which can be practically anything and the second of which has to be a `Publisher`. For example, we can apply this property to an instance of the class `Book`. An object-oriented system, however (if we forget about associations for now), would first define the class of `Books`, which would have an attribute called `publishedBy`, of the type `Publisher`.

This difference stems from the distinct fundamental philosophies of modelling languages. On the one hand, in an object-oriented system, such as UML, in accordance with the object-oriented approach the primary modelling primitive is the class. On the other hand, property is the *primary modelling primitive* in RDF. The latter is not the only property-oriented language: there are also DAML+OIL and OWL, presented in Chapter 8, and numerous further knowledge-representation languages. These property-oriented languages model the world as if it consists of instances which have various characteristics. More precisely, an instance can be related to other instances, and these relations are the information providers about the instances themselves. Classes are "created" by specifying what common features characterise their respective instances. For example, the class of parents could be defined as follows: *a parent is someone who has at least one child*. After that, all instances that are known to have a child (i.e. they are on the appropriate side of a `hasParent/hasChild` relation in another instance) are also known to be *parent*s.

These property-oriented languages are very efficient when it comes to describing instances, since, contrary to the approach of object-oriented systems, there is no need to "allocate" all attributes of an instance at instantiation time. In the previous example, it is not necessary to store an array of children for each instance. We do not even know in the first place whether the given instance is a *human*, i.e. whether it can have children at all. It is possible that the particular instance is a flower, and that later someone will specify its colour.

This is closely connected to the other major benefit of the property-oriented languages (and thus RDF), namely that, rather like humans, they are able to efficiently store "knowledge crumbs" and perform reasoning on these. As we said, instances can be categorised into classes only through their attached properties: there is nothing to know about an instance in itself except its identifier. In the object-oriented world, however, an object can only exist as an instance of a specific class (or several classes), and this has two implications. First, the instance has only those and exactly those properties (attributes) which were declared with foresight during the definition of the class. This is fairly inflexible, since how are we able to place in memory a piece of *unexpected but potentially useful information*, such as that someone's favourite food is fried chicken, if there is no predetermined attribute in which to store it? Furthermore, when an object "appears", we must be able to categorise it, i.e. recognise to which class the instance belongs.

In many cases, however, there is not enough information available to do this categorisation. If, for example, we learn that an existing RDF resource (instance) `loves` another resource then the question arises whether we can recognise to which class this other resource belongs. The answer is no, since even if we know that the first resource represents a person, the second resource could still be a piece of music, a pet, a car, a book or another human being. Later, we might learn that the second resource has a child. This detail can be associated with the resource without any problem: furthermore, we could reason that this resource must be a *parent* and, if we also know that parents are people, then we know that the second resource is a *person*.

It should be clear that reasoning is often necessary to tell to which class a particular instance belongs. Accordingly, it is computationally more expensive to determine the class of an instance in a property-oriented language than in UML (this is a price to be paid for flexibility). In UML this class information is always explicitly present while in RDF, as we have seen, a resource can be a member of the class of humans without being explicitly declared as such.

Note that, in property-oriented languages which allow local property restrictions (such as DAML+OIL and OWL), one can be very "economical" with properties. The reason for this is that the same property can be used in multiple "roles"; for example, `size` could characterise a pair of shoes, a piece of clothing, a flat screen display etc. In UML an attribute or an association is always linked to a class and, even though two classes could have identically named attributes, these are always stored and treated separately by object-oriented systems.

2.6.7.2. Property-based approach and the web

The processing of the above-mentioned "unexpected but useful knowledge" is analogous to the fundamental notion of the Semantic Web, that is the association of meta-information with resources. According to what we have said so far, if we want to state that the server (resource, object) identified by the `http://128.30.52.45` URI[15] was made by IBM then this can be done even if the given object does not have an attribute named "brand". The corresponding RDF description can be seen in Figure 2.33.

In summary, property-oriented languages are much more suitable for Internet, a system famous for its flexibility and dynamics, than the more static object-oriented systems.

```
<rdf:RDF
    xmlns:rdf="http://www.w3.org/1999/02/22-rdf-syntax-ns#"
    xmlns:ns="http://swexpld.org/useful/thing#">

    <rdf:Description about="http://128.30.52.45">
        <rdf:type rdf:resource=
        "http://swexpld.org/computers#Server"/>
        <ns:brand>IBM</ns:brand>
    </rdf:Description>

</rdf:RDF>
```

Figure 2.33. The brand of the given computer is IBM.

---

[15] An IP address without the `http://` prefix is not a URI (not even a relative one) according to the specification; therefore it cannot be used as an RDF resource identifier.

2.7. Examples of RDF use

In the following, we present a few examples of the use of RDF sources in real, practical, applications. First we introduce the widely known and acknowledged web-based concept vocabulary called Dublin Core Metadata Initiative, which was created before the RDF era but is now accessible in RDF Schema form as well. This is followed by the description of a very promising, freely accessible, web catalogue, the Open Directory Project, which publishes its data in RDF form. Next we introduce the MusicBrainz meta-database, which was designed for the storage of additional information (CD track titles, album title etc.) about pieces of music and for serving this type of data to clients. The client–server communication is done via an RDF-based interface. Subsequently, we briefly describe the RDF Schema called RDF Site Summary, which can be used to describe information in web pages offered for other peers. Finally we introduce a web-based thesaurus which answers queries using RDF descriptions, automatically associating a URI to tens of thousands of expressions.

2.7.1. Dublin Core

For RDF to be used in a particular field one needs a commonly accepted RDF schema, describing resources which are used by all RDF sources in that field. RDF schemas give a means for everyone to prepare their own vocabularies, but this raises several problems. First, it is clear that it is inefficient if everyone reinvents the wheel and defines the properties of basic concepts such as author, address and name. Instead, a shared vocabulary accepted by all should be created. This can then be extended by specific local elements. For instance, one can declare a class called `Chief Executive Officer` (CEO) and state that it is a subclass of `Person`, which is acknowledged by everyone. As a consequence, those RDF-processing clients which know about this commonly accepted schema can reason about Peter, whom we declare to be a CEO, even though these clients do not know anything about chief executive officers.

Vocabularies accepted by many people have to be at a fairly high level. This means that they define generic things, thus providing building blocks for constructing lower-level schemas. The Dublin Core [32] is an initiative defining such high-level concepts. Using RDF terminology, Dublin Core is an RDF Schema which mainly defines properties.

The history of Dublin Core reaches back before the dawn of the RDF era. Dublin Core was constructed in 1995, on a workshop on metadata held in Dublin, Ohio. The goal was to create an element set which facilitates the automated discovery of electronic documents and resources in general [109]. The result was a collection of 13 entries, which describe certain characteristics of documents. This set was later slightly rearranged and extended by two further elements. This set is the foundation of the ISO Standard 15836 from 2003 as well. The 15 elements are the following:

Title: The title of the selected resource.

Creator: The name of the entity which is responsible for creating the contents of the resource. This can be a person, an organisation or a service.

Subject: The topic of the contents of the resource. Generally this is described by keywords, but the recommended procedure is to use a code defined by some sort of classification system.

Description: The summary of the contents of the resource. Typically this is free text, perhaps an abstract or the table of contents.

Publisher: The name of the entity which is responsible for the accessibility of the resource. This can be a person, an organisation or a service.

Contributor: The name of the entity which contributed to the preparation of the contents of the resource. It can be a person, an organisation or a service.

Date: The date of an event which is in some way connected to the resource, typically the date of preparation. It is recommended that the format of the date adheres to the ISO 8601 Standard.

Type: The type of resource or its contents (i.e. image, movie, service, software etc.). It is recommended that a word from a commonly accepted vocabulary is used here.

Format: The physical parameters of the resource. Examples are the size, length or MIME type of the resource.

Identifier: The unambiguous identifier of the resource. Typically URIs are used, but other unique identifiers such as the ISBN numbers of books may be given here as well.

Source: Reference to a resource during used as a source at the preparation of the contents.

Language: The language of the contents of the resource.

Relation: Reference to a resource which is in some way related to the selected resource.

Coverage: The coverage, i.e. scope, of the resource, often in the sense of geographical coverage.

Rights: Information about user and other rights of the resource and its contents.

The main benefit of an easily understandable element set like this is that through its simplicity it promotes its own spread and use. Nowadays many applications use the above fields to provide meta-information about several resources.

The goal of the Dublin Core vocabulary is not to cover all fields but, as mentioned earlier, to fulfil the role of a high-level vocabulary. Various communities might require new elements; furthermore, they would probably like to connect these to the existing Dublin Core elements in a standard manner.

This is greatly aided by the XML and RDF schema form of the Dublin Core vocabulary. The XML schema supports the use of Dublin Core elements in arbitrary XML documents. In Subsection 2.7.4 we will give an example of an XML file containing meta-information, published on a well-known web page, in which certain properties were defined using Dublin Core elements.

The RDF schema of the Dublin Core, however, offers even more ways of usage with respect to the RDF framework. Within an RDF description, Dublin Core elements can be used as building blocks in the definition of one's own RDF classes and properties, by simply referring to the RDF resources of the Dublin Core RDF schema. However, in the most widespread usage one simply refers to Dublin Core elements as RDF properties in RDF documents. An example of the latter can be seen in the RDF source shown in Figure 2.34, which gives meta-information about a file stored on a computer.

```
<rdf:RDF
   xmlns:rdf="http://www.w3.org/1999/02/22-rdf-syntax-ns#"
   xmlns:dc="http://purl.org/dc/elements/1.1/">

   <rdf:Description rdf:about=
                           "http://last.fm/...money.mp3">
      <dc:creator>Dire Straits</dc:creator>
      <dc:title>Money for Nothing</dc:title>
      <dc:description>
      The theme song of the album "Money for Nothing"
      </dc:description>
      <dc:date>1987-11-30</dc:date>
   </rdf:Description>
</rdf:RDF>
```

Figure 2.34. Using Dublin Core in an RDF source.

2.7.2. Open Directory Project

The *Open Directory Project* (ODP) [89] is a web catalogue. Web catalogues were described in detail in Subsection 1.4.4. The ODP differs significantly from other catalogues in that it is not affiliated to any profit-oriented company; the editorial and maintenance work is performed by unpaid volunteers and so the entire contents of the catalogue are freely accessible and usable.

The inclusion of one's own web site can be requested from the ODP editors by filling in a form, naming the appropriate category and providing a short summary of the site contents. If it is accepted, the site will be listed in the catalogue within a couple of weeks and in roughly the same time it will most probably also appear in the result pages of various search engines. This is due to the fact that many large non-catalogue-based engines use the data of the Open Directory Project as a starting point for their crawlers, and some offer it directly, in catalogue form, as a secondary service. Google, AOL Search and Excite are all examples of such engines.

The ODP editors are volunteers responsible for a specific field extensively known by them. Within this field, using their own experience they add new sites to the catalogue and edit and refine the descriptions of already listed sites. It is also the duty of the editors to review requests for the addition of new sites to the catalogue. Such an addition has very serious quality requirements: the editors of the ODP are very proud that their catalogue lists only particularly useful sites.

Anyone can become an editor. All one needs to do is to fill in an application form, where, apart from answering a couple of questions and specifying the field of expertise (a category), the applicant must list two or three web sites which they would add to that category. Applications are reviewed by more experienced editors, among other factors on the basis of how relevant the listed web sites are in that field. Editors have a great responsibility, so at first they work on a smaller category and only later receive the credentials to rename or move categories, create new ones etc. A number of guidelines have been created to support the editorial work, which are readable by everyone (thus one can see, for example, what considerations apply when one is reviewing a site addition request, what it is necessary to pay particular attention to etc.)

The ODP data can be downloaded in RDF form by anyone. However, one needs to be prepared for the huge size of the catalogue. The smaller of the two most important data files describes the structure of the ODP, the hierarchical layout and the characteristics of the individual categories; the size of this RDF source exceeds 300 megabytes. The larger of the two data files lists the web sites themselves, along with their descriptions, ordered into categories. This file is larger than 1 gigabyte. It first lists the various sites for each categories and then details the sites themselves. The following example shows part of the `Top/Arts/Movies/Titles/1984_-_1984` category, which lists links to pages about the film version of the famous novel by George Orwell.

```
...
<Topic r:id="Top/Arts/Movies/Titles/1/1984_-_1984">
  <catid>460423</catid>
  <link r:resource="http://.../aaronbcaldwell/1984.html"/>
  <link r:resource="http://orwell.ru/.../m84_01.htm"/>
  <link r:resource="http://.../.../filmography/014.html"/>
  <link r:resource="http://...batcave.net/1984.htm"/>
  <link r:resource=
            "http://www.filmtracks.com/titles/1984.html"/>
  <link r:resource="http://www.imdb.com/title/tt0087803/"/>
</Topic>

<ExternalPage
  about="http://.../aaronbcaldwell/1984.html">
  <d:Title>Top 100 Movie Lists: 1984</d:Title>
  <d:Description>Photos, sounds...</d:Description>
  <topic>Top/Arts/Movies/Titles/1/1984_-_1984</topic>
</ExternalPage>

<ExternalPage
  about="http://orwell.ru/a_life/movies/m84_01.htm">
  <d:Title>George Orwell's Movies - 1984</d:Title>
  <d:Description>Review.</d:Description>
  <topic>Top/Arts/Movies/Titles/1/1984_-_1984</topic>
</ExternalPage>
...
```

Both RDF files use the Dublin Core schema. In the above example, the `d:Title` URI refers to the `Title` property of the Dublin Core schema.[16]

The RDF sources of ODP (in most cases the RDF source describing the categories) are often converted into various other formats, e.g. into HTML or a relational database. Applications performing these conversions can be found readily on the web.

---

[16] The Open Directory Project uses version 1.0 of the Dublin Core, for some reason, in which property names begin with capital letters.

2.7.3. MusicBrainz

MusicBrainz (MB) is a musical meta-database edited by volunteers. It can be accessed either on the web (`http://musicbrainz.org/`) or by using some client application. Many CD and audio players are able to connect to the servers of MB, when the user inserts a CD into the drive or starts playing an MP3 file which does not contain any tags, and to request the necessary information. This information usually contains the title of the CD tracks and the album itself, the genre of the song etc. In the case of CDs, the identification is fairly simple because of the characteristics of the CD format. For MP3 and Ogg Vorbis files, identification is performed using a digital fingerprint of the file, which is extracted from a number of attributes (length, frequency distribution etc.).

Here we discuss briefly an earlier implementation of MusicBrainz (see `http://wiki.musicbrainz.org/RDF`) based on RDF. The present implementation uses relational databases and also makes the information available using a music ontology [97].

The RDF-based version of MusicBrainz defines three RDF schemas named `mm`, `mq` and `mem`.

The `mm` schema defines the basic classes and properties. It declares three classes, `Artist`, `Album` and `Track`. Furthermore, it defines exactly one dozen RDF properties such as `shortName`, `trackNum` (i.e. track number), `duration` etc. Some properties expect containers for values. For example, the value of `albumList` is an `rdf:Bag`, which contains all the albums of the given artist or band.

The `mq` schema defines those RDF classes and properties that are required for the questions proposed during a conversation between the MusicBrainz server and its clients. An instance of the `Result` class represents a specific answer, and the instances of the various query classes can be used to look for tracks, CDs, albums, artists etc. The following example issues a search for the band U2 and also specifies the search depth (which allows the client to specify the level of information that should be returned by the server):

```
<mq:FindArtist>
   <mq:depth>2</mq:depth>
   <mq:artistName>U2</mq:artistName>
</mq:FindArtist>
```

The above object is in fact an anonymous resource. The type of this resource is `mq:FindArtist`, and it has two properties. As an answer for this query, we receive an anonymous instance of `mq:Result` in RDF form, which informs us that the search was successful and that there are seven hits (the string U2 was found in the name of seven different formations, as in "Massive Attack and U2"):

```
<mq:Result>
 <mq:status>OK</mq:status>
 <mm:artistList>
  <rdf:Bag>
    <rdf:li rdf:resource=
     "http://musicbrainz.org/artist/a3cb23fc-acd3..."/>
    <rdf:li rdf:resource=
     "http://musicbrainz.org/artist/8ba42c7f-1ac8..."/>
    ...
```

```
   </rdf:Bag>
  </mm:artistList>
 </mq:Result>
```

The answer also contains the albums recorded by the various formations and the details of the songs on each such album.

The mem schema was set aside for future development; we will find properties here which can be used to attach lyrics to individual tracks and sound files.

According to the above, an RDF source using the schemas offered by MusicBrainz could look like this (this source does not use the mem schema but it does use the Dublin Core vocabulary):

```
<?xml version="1.0" encoding="UTF-8"?>
<rdf:RDF
    xmlns:rdf = "http://www.w3.org/1999/02/22-rdf-syntax-ns#"
    xmlns:dc  = "http://purl.org/dc/elements/1.1/"
    xmlns:mq  = "http://musicbrainz.org/.../mq-1.1#"
    xmlns:mm  = "http://musicbrainz.org/.../mm-2.1#">

 <mm:Artist rdf:about=
    "http://musicbrainz.org/artist/23d8426c-18c7...">
    <dc:title>Tangerine Dream</dc:title>
    <mm:sortName>Tangerine Dream</mm:sortName>
 </mm:Artist>
...
```

2.7.4. RSS: RDF site summary

Nowadays, so-called *web syndication* is the most widespread use of RDF. By syndication we mean that some kind of data is made available for external users. In television programming, it is often the case that various soap operas are not directly produced or ordered by the network; instead the broadcaster buys and airs some ready-made series. The creators of such television series expect that the television companies will buy their products, and so they offer them for buying. Similarly, the comic strips appearing in columns of daily newspapers are usually drawn not by the employees of the newspaper but by specialised studios and artist groups, from whom several newspapers buy their daily strips.

In web syndication parts of a web portal, normally including the most important news and events of the site, are made available for others, usually in XML format. These descriptions then are collected by RSS-reader client applications and presented to the user at the user's request. In this way, somebody can easily read the headlines of the web pages in which she is interested without the need to actually visit these sites one by one via her browser.

The most commonly used web syndication format is *RSS*, which has almost a dozen, partially incompatible, versions (the other popular format is *Atom*, supported by Google). In some versions RSS stands for *rich site summary*; elsewhere it is an acronym of *RDF site summary* or of *really simple syndication*.

Version 1.0 of RSS uses an RDF "dialect" similar to the first widely used version, 0.9, which was introduced by Netscape in 1999. Interestingly, the creator of RSS, Dan Libby, originally proposed a format very similar to version 1.0, but Netscape for some reason did

```
<rdf:RDF ...>
 <channel rdf:about="http://hardware.slashdot.org/">
  <title>Slashdot: Hardware</title>
  <link>http://hardware.slashdot.org/</link>
  <description>News for nerds, stuff that matters
  </description>
  <dc:language>en-us</dc:language>
  <dc:rights>Copyright 1997-2006, OSTG ...</dc:rights>
  <dc:date>2006-07-26T17:40:59+00:00</dc:date>
  <dc:publisher>OSTG</dc:publisher>
  <dc:creator>pater@slashdot.org</dc:creator>
  <dc:subject>Technology</dc:subject>
  <syn:updatePeriod>hourly</syn:updatePeriod>
  <syn:updateFrequency>1</syn:updateFrequency>
  ...
  <item rdf:about="http://hardware.slashdot.org/...">
   <title>Output Mouse</title>
   <link>http://rss.slashdot.org/...</link>
   <description>An anonymous reader writes "Combining
   unusual items together can sometimes produce interesting
   results. Over at MetkuMods one can find a computer mouse
   embedded with a cell phone display to show all sorts of
   information. For some people one TFT on the desktop just
   isn't enough."</description>
   <dc:creator>ScuttleMonkey</dc:creator>
   <dc:date>2006-07-25T22:57:00+00:00</dc:date>
   <dc:subject>inputdev</dc:subject>
   ...
  </item>
 ...
```

Figure 2.35. RSS in RDF form.

not support his proposal until later. ScriptingNews, the precursor of RSS, was designed by Dave Winer. It is he who has also been responsible for the more recent versions of RSS.

In spite of the differences, all versions agree in that they use XML syntax. Figure 2.35 shows a snippet of the RSS metadata published by the hardware section of the well-known nerd news syndication site Slashdot (http://slashdot.org) in RDF/XML form (using the default namespace). The example shows the most important details of the site, the title of a news entry, a link to the full entry and a short summary of its contents.

An RSS file can be linked from a page, and even referred to from the head of the HTML page, as follows (in this way RSS readers can easily reach it):

```
<link rel="alternate" type="application/rss+xml" title="RSS"
 href="http://www.w3.org/2000/08/w3c-synd/home.rss" />
```

The RDF version of RSS is an RDF Schema, which defines classes and properties that can be used in the definition of RDF data. The RDF variant, just like basic XML, can easily be extended later. For example, one schema defines the following three properties, where the syn namespace is associated with the URI `http://purl.org/rss/1.0/modules/syndication/` URI:

```
syn:updatePeriod
syn:updateFrequency
syn:updateBase
```

These properties are used to inform web crawlers collecting RSS data how often the published data are updated. Such RSS crawlers, for example, are RSSOwl [100] or AmphetaDesk [51]. Web syndication can be considered analogous to newsgroups, where subscribers regularly receive news updates in groups to which they have subscribed. In our case the users can select certain web sites which are regularly visited by their RSS crawlers, which then present the collected information in some, usually very stylish, format to them.

2.7.5. Wordnet

Wordnet [35] is a freely available online lexical reference system, which was developed in the Cognitive Science Laboratory at Princeton University. Wordnet contains more than a hundred thousand expressions, and it is unique in the sense that it also describes certain relations between words. If we search for the word *cat*, we first see that it has eight meanings as a noun plus two as a verb. Then we can ask, among other things, what parts a cat has (claws, fur...), to which taxonomy groups the cat belongs (feline, mammal...), and what kinds of cat there are (Persian, Egyptian...). Similarly, in the case of adjectives we can see that the antonym of high is low, the antonym of pretty is ugly etc. We can look up synonyms, words with similar meanings and many other things.

In the introduction to the Dublin Core schema in Subsection 2.7.1 we mentioned that one of the most difficult tasks when creating an RDF source is to use classes and properties accepted by the processing applications as well. What makes Wordnet particularly interesting for us is that it tries to provide a common terminology and, based on it, we may build RDF descriptions understood by others in the same way as by us.

As an experimental service, some Wordnet nouns have been associated with URIs. Different versions of Wordnet use different URIs. For example, version 1.6 uses the form of `http://xmlns.com/wordnet/1.6/XXX`, which identifies the entity described by XXX, where XXX must be an English noun listed in Wordnet. Wordnet 3 uses URIs of the form `http://purl.org/vocabularies/princeton/wn30/synset-XXX-noun-N`, where the number N distinguishes the different uses of the same word.

For example, a human being can be identified by the URI `http://purl.org/vocabularies/princeton/wn30/synset-person-noun-1.rdf`. This means that one can replace the probably undefined URI that we used in Figure 2.10 by the above link. The result can be seen in Figure 2.36. In this way, even if a particular processing application does not understand the s:name and s:address properties, it can easily notice that the given resource identifies a person.

Furthermore, even though we said that URIs do not necessarily denote actual downloadable documents in RDF, Wordnet URIs in fact do this! For example, the above

```
<?xml version="1.0" encoding="ISO-8859-1"?>
<rdf:RDF
 xmlns:rdf="http://www.w3.org/1999/02/22-rdf-syntax-ns#"
 xmlns:s="http://swexpld.org/utils#">

 <rdf:Description rdf:about=
   "http://freemail.org/~doe/#about">
     <s:name>John Doe</s:name>
     <s:address rdf:resource="mailto:johndoe@freemail.org"/>
     <rdf:type rdf:resource="http://purl.org/vocabularies/
                   synset/princeton/wn30/person-noun-1.rdf"/>
 </rdf:Description>

</rdf:RDF>
```

Figure 2.36.   Using a Wordnet concept in an RDF source.

link `http://purl.org/.../wn30/person-noun-1.rdf.` leads to an actual RDF document describing the notion of "person".

2.8. Summary

In this chapter we have presented the concept of the Semantic Web, the basic idea of which is to associate *meta-information* with Internet-based *resources* and to perform reasoning on them. We detailed the RDF and the RDF schema languages, the use of which is a standard-ised and recommended way of presenting meta-information. Below we summarise the most important points of the chapter.

- Describing the *meaning* of the information on the web is normally done through asso-ciating meta-information with it. Meta-information is present in the web languages; the HTML element called META is, for example, specifically used for providing meta-information although its usability is rather restricted. It is an important requirement in the Semantic Web approach that meta-information can be linked to an arbitrary resource in a uniform way that is easily processable by computers. Such a resource may be anything that can be identified uniquely.

- To support computer processing, meta-information is stored in *XML form*. An XML document is a text file designed to be capable of storing data in a structured form. The most important parts of an XML document are the *elements* and the *attributes* linked to them. An XML element may be complex, mixed or simple. Every XML document contains at least one element, the *root*. It is another feature of XML documents that they store the data in a hierarchical structure; a given document defines a *tree*, the root of which is the root element.

  The element and attribute names used in an XML description are only unique within the given document; these are called *local names*. If one merges several XML documents then the local names could clash, which might cause problems. Such problems can be eliminated by the use of XML *namespaces*. This means that the element and attribute names used in the document will be given a prefix. The prefixes are URIs; a local name supplemented by a prefix is called a *qualified name*. The only role of the URIs is to function as unique names.

One of XML's strong points is that it allows the user to check whether an XML document is an instance of the given language. This requires a standardised description of the *grammar* itself, which is made possible by the *XML schema* language. An XML schema describes the elements and attributes which can be used in XML documents belonging to it, as well as the contents of the elements and the relations between them.

Documents in XML in most cases focus on the contents; they do not contain formatting information. Presenting XML documents is done by converting them into a form suitable for human consumption. This conversion is carried out by the use of an appropriate *transformation language*, the XSLT, for example. In this way the data and their presentation can be separated. The CSS style sheets related to XHTML pages serve a similar purpose.

By itself, XML is not suitable for supporting communication between applications without prior agreement on the meaning of the language used during the transfer. The aim of the Semantic Web and the related RDF concept is, among other things, to eliminate the need for such a prior agreement. The *RDF language* is capable of linking metadata to any *URI-identified* resources. A fundamental role is played by URIs in the Semantic Web approach; they make it possible to *formulate assertions* unambiguously and to combine fragments of meta-information coming from different sources.

- The basic idea of the RDF language is to connect URI-identified resources with other resources or just with plain *literals* using *properties*. Essentially, RDF helps to describe binary relations between things identified in a given way. Accordingly, *RDF statements*, also known as *triples*, consist of a subject, a predicate and an object. An RDF description is a set of such triples. The meaning of *description* is that the statements it contains are true.

- Using RDF triples one can also build a *graph* where the nodes represent the subjects and objects appearing in descriptions, while the edges represent predicates. Identical resources, i.e. those referred to by the same URI, are denoted by the same node; this is the way in which the various component assertions make an organic whole. The RDF graph may also contain blank nodes representing resources to which no URIs are associated, for example because they were unknown at the time when the description was made. Blank nodes are also often used to make the given information better structured.

- The RDF language has multiple representations; among these the XML form is the most widely used. We therefore presented the XML format of RDF first. We introduced descriptions involving a *shared subject* as well as *intermediate* and *object-positioned* resources. We also showed the use of *relative URIs* in XML form and introduced the `rdf:ID` attribute.

- Subsequently, we dealt with the various special RDF constructs in turn. In the RDF language, non-binary relations can be represented by using the `rdf:value` property. With the help of the `rdf:type` property one can state that a resource is an instance of an RDF class. The *simplified XML form* of instantiation has the advantage that it strongly resembles the syntax of pure XML representation. This, too, may help to achieve in the near future the replacement of the XML-based storage of data in certain cases, by RDF-based representation.

- RDF has a few built-in facilities which can be used to create instances. One built-in class, for example, contains the instances of *higher-order statements*. We consider an RDF statement to be of higher order if it speaks about another statement. In order for it to do this the RDF statement should be modelled as a specific resource. This process is called *reification*, and the specific resource is a *reified statement*.

- Our second example of the use of built-in classes involved *containers*. RDF supports the use of three types of container classes, identified by the following URIs: `rdf:Bag`, `rdf:Seq` and `rdf:Alt`. RDF containers are *open*, i.e. the user can state only that certain resources are elements of a container. RDF also makes it possible to describe an aggregation of resources which is *closed*, i.e. it contains only the elements supplied. Such an aggregation is called an *RDF collection*, which, in fact, is a list.

- At the end of our presentation of the RDF language, we showed how to use *typed literals* in RDF descriptions.

- The RDF language alone is not sufficient to support reasoning during Internet queries, because it cannot express meta-knowledge. For example, using plain RDF it is not possible to find someone's friends when we are looking for whom that person knows, because the inference system does not have the knowledge that friends know each other. This problem is solved by introducing *RDF schema*, in which the meaning of a resource is made more specific by formally describing its relationship with other entities. For example one can declare that, between any two resources for which the `friendOf` relation holds the `knows` relation also holds.

  At first glance, RDF schema looks like nothing more than a few new resources, with well-defined meaning, added to the vocabulary of RDF. These resources can be used in RDF statements (e.g. for instantiation) in exactly the same way as before. So, it is important that no new language is introduced: the RDF notation is used. Looking more closely, however, one notices that the RDF schema extension allows users to define their "own" application-specific classes and properties as well as to describe the features of these resources and to specify the hierarchical relationships between them.

- A user-specific class can be defined by instantiating `rdfs:Class`. By using the property `rdfs:subClassOf`, one can state that class A is a subclass of class B. This means that any instance of A is an instance of B as well.

- A new property can be defined as an instance of the `rdf:Property` class. As in the case of classes, RDF schema allows hierarchical relations between properties. Such specifications can be made by using the `rdfs:subPropertyOf` property. RDF schema also supports the description of *data-level relations* between classes and properties. Namely, by using schemas one can describe the *domain* and *range* of a property. This information can be used for consistency checking as well as for reasoning or even to make the behaviour of an RDF editor more intelligent.

- The concepts used by RDF schema show similarities to those in object-oriented languages. RDF properties, however, have the interesting feature that they are only linked to resources at "run time". In object-oriented systems a class definition contains all the attributes of the objects which are created by the instantiation of the class. In contrast, in the world of RDF a property is defined in terms of the classes to which it is applicable, while a class is specified by the features of its elements. This shows that property-oriented languages such as RDF schema can nicely accommodate the anyone-can-say-anything philosophy of the Semantic Web.

- Finally, we presented a few real applications where the RDF language plays an important part. The first was the widely used Dublin Core dictionary, which is available as an RDF schema as well. We next presented one of the most popular web catalogues, the Open Directory Project, the data of which can be downloaded in RDF form. Then we examined a musical meta-database named MusicBrainz, which stores music-related data in RDF form and offers an RDF query interface. After that we described the RSS, one of the most widespread formats of web-based syndication, which has both XML and RDF versions. Finally, we briefly introduced the free Wordnet dictionary. As part of an experimental service the entities linked to the nouns in Wordnet are associated with URIs, which can be used in RDF descriptions.

Chapter 3

Managing and querying RDF sources

In this chapter we deal with the way in which RDF descriptions are stored, processed and queried as well as the applications and languages involved in the process.

In Section 3.1 we describe how to make RDF meta-information on the web available for search engines. Next, in Section 3.2, we give an overview of development tools which can be used to parse and manage RDF-based sources. In Section 3.3 we describe RDF query languages and show why XML query languages are not suitable for this purpose. Subsequently, in Section 3.4, we discuss the possible reasoning tasks involved in answering RDF queries. Finally, in Section 3.5, we describe problems which arise in the course of optimising RDF queries and outline possible solutions.

3.1. RDF descriptions on the web

The RDF language is a generic framework that helps to associate meta-information with resources in a uniform way. RDF is by no means limited to the web, because anything that is identified by a URI can be used in RDF statements. However, as we saw in the previous chapter, practically anything can have a URI: a person, a rucksack, a house etc. This allows us to use RDF in environments other than the web, for example, traditional databases, information integration and other knowledge-intensive systems.

In spite of this generality, a natural expectation is that the utilisation of RDF sources will help to create the basis of the Semantic Web. That is, one of the main goals is to make a step towards intelligent web search. For this, the search engines first need to obtain somehow metadata stored in the RDF format.

Because search engines use web crawlers that periodically and continuously surf the web, it pays to place RDF metadata in the context of a homepage. In this way, search engines can collect the background information that can be used for more intelligent search during their regular crawling process.

However, we should not forget that the meta-information associated with a homepage is not necessarily about the content of the page itself. The RDF description belonging to an Australian page can state that a file at a different location is actually some source code written in the programming language C. It can also state that the eyes of a certain person in Sweden are blue; URIs play a crucial role in making these bits of information finally converge to a consistent knowledge base. In other words, they allow us to merge various RDF graphs by unambiguously identifying the resources in them. In this way it is easy to recognise that some other homepage also gives meta-information about the same man, living in Sweden.

We now discuss the possible ways of associating RDF data with an HTML page.

3.1.1. RDF metadata embedded in HTML

In the previous chapter we saw that RDF descriptions can be represented either as graphs or as XML data. We mentioned that, from the semantics point of view, the graph representation is the primary one. The need for portability and machine processing, however, is reason enough for the existence of an XML form. In what follows, we use the term "RDF source" to refer to an appropriate XML document.

Because of their XML representation, XML parsers can handle RDF sources very easily, as syntactically they are simply normal well-formed XML documents. At the same time, mainly owing to the popularity of XHTML, XML data is already present on the web. Hence we can say that if RDF descriptions were embedded somehow in homepages, existing search engines would already be able to process them, at least syntactically. Actually, one can also say that the marriage of RDF and XHTML is obvious, because both are XML sources and so they can be easily integrated. We saw earlier that such integration is a central issue in XML: the notion of a namespace, for example, was introduced mainly for this purpose (see Subsection 2.2.4).

RDF data can be inserted into different parts of an HTML page. The head of an HTML document (i.e. between the `<HEAD>` and `</HEAD>` elements) would seem to be an ideal place for this purpose. Crawlers parse the heads of pages before indexing further, because this is where important pieces of meta-information are given, which are crucial for web robots (the character coding of the page, its author, the keywords, the title etc.). Figure 3.1 shows an example where an RDF description is inserted into the head of a homepage. The meta-information describes the authors of the homepage by means of an RDF container.

Unfortunately, this solution is far from perfect. If we open the page in a browser, most probably we will get something similar to the following:

```
Paul Smith  Bill Master  Steve Davidson
Hello World!
```

The reason for this is that most browsers display the content of the simple XML elements, no matter whether they recognise the element itself or not. In our case, this is obviously not acceptable, as metadata is not intended to be part of the visual display.

A solution to this problem is to use an abbreviated syntactic format of RDF (Section 2.4). This allows us to employ XML attributes to serialise predicate–object pairs where the object

```
<html>
   <head>
   <title>Simple Web Store</title>
   <meta http-equiv="content-type"
        content="text/html; charset=utf-8"/>

   <rdf:RDF
    xmlns:rdf="http://www.w3.org/1999/02/22-rdf-syntax-ns#"
    xmlns:s="http://swexpld.org/utils#">

   <rdf:Description rdf:about="">
      <s:creators>
         <rdf:Bag>
            <rdf:li>Paul Smith</rdf:li>
            <rdf:li>Bill Master</rdf:li>
            <rdf:li>Steve Davidson</rdf:li>
         </rdf:Bag>
      </s:creators>
   </rdf:Description>

   </rdf:RDF>

   </head>
   <body>
      <h1>Hello World!</h1>
   </body>
</html>
```

Figure 3.1. An RDF description embedded into the head of a web page.

is a literal.[1] As a reminder, the two descriptions shown below represent the same RDF graph:

```
<rdf:Description rdf:about="http://...night_watch.htm">
    <s:paintedBy>Rembrandt van Rijn</s:paintedBy>
</rdf:Description>

<rdf:Description rdf:about="http://...night_watch.htm"
                s:paintedBy="Rembrandt van Rijn" />
```

As we can see, this syntax actually helps to hide the content of simple XML elements by representing them as attribute values. As a result most browsers work as expected since they do not display the values of XML attributes.

There is only one more thing to consider. In our specific example, by using the abbreviated syntax we would get more than one `rdf:li` attribute in the case of the `<rdf:Bag>` element. Having multiple attributes with the same name, however, is not allowed in XML.

---

[1] If the object is a resource then this approach does not work.

```
<html>
   <head>
   <title>Simple Web Store</title>
   <meta http-equiv="content-type"
         content="text/html; charset=utf-8"/>
   <rdf:RDF
     xmlns:rdf="http://www.w3.org/1999/02/22-rdf-syntax-ns#"
     xmlns:s="http://swexpld.org/utils#">

     <rdf:Description rdf:about="">
        <s:creators>
           <rdf:Bag
               rdf:_1="Paul Smith"
               rdf:_2="Bill Master"
               rdf:_3="Steve Davidson"/>
        </s:creators>
     </rdf:Description>
   </rdf:RDF>
   </head>
   <body>
      <h1>Hello World!</h1>
   </body>
</html>
```

Figure 3.2.   RDF with abbreviated syntax in the head of a homepage.

To avoid this, we need to use the core RDF properties _1, _2, _3,... instead of rdf:li. The web page, with proper "non-displaying" RDF embedded into it, is shown in Figure 3.2.

Having presented this solution, we must also mention that the embedding of RDF data into a web page has its drawbacks. The biggest problem with this approach is that the resulting pages are not valid XHTML documents, since they are not validated against the XHTML schema (Subsection 2.2.5). The reason is simply that the embedded RDF data use XML elements and attributes that are not present in the XHTML schema. Having valid pages, however, is essential from the web point of view. Solutions include extending or changing the schema for XHTML using special XHTML elements (such as <object>) that may encapsulate arbitrary content or using the <link> element, to be discussed in the next subsection.[2]

3.1.2. RDF metadata linked to HTML

Instead of making metadata part of a web page, we can use a different approach, that of placing a link on the web page which points to the metadata. The assumption is that web robots follow these links, so they will finally get to the RDF descriptions.

---

[2] We note that the XHTML5 language supports RDF embedding.

```
<head>
  <title>The best homepage in the world</title>
  <link rel="meta" type="application/rdf+xml"
        href="metadata.rdf"/>
</head>
```

Figure 3.3. Linking RDF data to a web page.

Architecturally, this seems to be a clean solution. The problems due to embedding are eliminated. The metadata can be modified and managed independently from the web page. Browsers do not need to download the metadata; thereby bandwidth is saved. Finally, technically it is easier to simply retrieve a file and thus obtain its content rather than to extract it from an HTML page.

The appropriate link can be placed in the head of the page using the <link> element, whose task, in general, is to link our page to an external resource. The <link> element should point at the location of the RDF/XML data and the type attribute should be set to "application/rdf+xml", as shown in Figure 3.3.

Alternatively, we can utilise the usual <a> (anchor) element for this purpose in the body of the page:

```
...
<body>
  ...
    <a rel="meta" type="application/rdf+xml"
       href="metadata.rdf" />
  ...
</body>
...
```

Another advantage of using links is that they allow the use of RDF descriptions which are available in an alternative physical representation. For example, we can give our metadata both in RDF/XML serialisation and also in the so-called N3 notation (Section 2.3). This is shown below:

```
<link rel="meta" type="application/rdf+xml"
      href="metadata.rdf"/>
<link rel="alternate meta" type="text/rdf+n3"
      href="metadata.n3"/>
```

As in the case of metadata extraction from HTML pages, a solution based on links is supported by several tools. For example, the application called PiggyBank [66], which is an extension of the popular Firefox browser, extracts information from existing web pages and presents them to the user. This information typically comes from the RDF data linked to the page (although PiggyBank can extract data from pages with no RDF content by custom plug-ins called screen scrapers). It is also possible to let PiggyBank send the collected meta-information automatically to communal information repositories called semantic banks.

Exercise 3.1: Add a link to your homepage that refers to some RDF data encoded in RDF/XML format. Install PiggyBank and check whether it finds the metadata you have just added.

3.2. Parsing and processing metadata

Most programming languages have tools and libraries to parse and process RDF sources. We now briefly summarise the most important software solutions and their features. Because of the popularity of Java, we will focus on the RDF support in this language.

3.2.1. Available tools in a nutshell

Several comprehensive Semantic Web frameworks exist for the Java language. A very popular one is the Jena toolkit [3], which was originally developed in the Semantic Web Programme of the Hewlett Packard laboratories. Jena supports the RDF development life cycle, from parsing RDF sources through reasoning on RDF schemas[3] to supporting SPARQL-based RDF queries (more about SPARQL can be found in Subsection 3.3.6). Another Java tool is the Sesame [1] system, with support for RDF schema reasoning and querying, using its own query language. Sesame also supports several types of underlying storage mechanism for efficient RDF access (relational databases, file-based storage etc.), as well as several protocols for the remote access of RDF information, including the HTTP protocol.

Declarative programming language implementations also provide support for RDF. In the Prolog world, the developers of SWI Prolog [110] created libraries for supporting the use of RDF sources. Their Semantic Web library contains an RDF parser, a storage facility and a Prolog-based query engine. Furthermore, a Sesame-compliant HTTP server has been implemented in SWI Prolog; it provides access to the SWI library for Sesame clients.

The Wilbur [72] toolkit can be used for RDF processing in the context of the Lisp language. Wilbur was developed by Ora Lassila, who is one of the founders of the RDF paradigm. The LISP language is also interesting because it is the implementation language of leading reasoners for RDF and its ontology extensions (see Chapter 8).

Many implementations exist for the Python language as well, since Python is one of the favourite languages of RDF developers. The RDFLib Python library [71] consists of an RDF parser and storage module as well as support for SPARQL queries. The 4Suite [40] platform supports Python developers in generic XML processing, but it also contains RDF-specific components.

There are also RDF libraries for C. The Redland framework [10] provides full support for RDF processing, which includes parsing persistent and in-memory storage and SPARQL query execution. Redland was developed by Dave Beckett, who is a renowned RDF expert and active in the development of the RDF and SPARQL standards. RDFStore [99] is another well-maintained C/Perl library, with support for SPARQL queries.

---

[3] Jena also supports reasoning on OWL Light ontologies. For more details on OWL Light see Chapter 8.

3.2.2. Using the Jena toolkit

A typical reason for using an RDF toolkit is to support the creation and processing of information in RDF format within an application. In this subsection we first give a few examples of how to read RDF sources and navigate in them using the Jena 2.4 toolkit. These examples describe the basics of how to extract information from RDF descriptions that is relevant for our specific application. Next, we show examples of the other direction: how to create an RDF description from the internal representation built within our program. We do not aim to give a comprehensive guide to the Jena toolkit, just a brief introduction.

Below is the Java code of our first example, which refers to the RDF/XML document about Rembrandt shown in Figure 2.16. The numbers given on the left-hand side of the figure will be used to identify the lines of the source.

```
 1  import com.hp.hpl.jena.rdf.model.*;
 2
 3  public class ReadRDF {
 4    static String paintingURI  = "http://...night_watch.htm";
 5    static String fileURI = "file:/swbook/rembrandt.rdf";
 6
 7    public static void main (String[] args) {
 8      Model model =  ModelFactory.createDefaultModel();
 9
10      model.read(fileURI);
11
12      Resource painting = model.getResource(paintingURI);
13      StmtIterator iterator = painting.listProperties();
14
15      while (iterator.hasNext())
16        System.out.println(iterator.nextStatement()
17                           .getObject().toString());
18    }
19  }
```

In line 1 we import the appropriate Jena classes needed for our example. In lines 4–5 we specify the URI of the painting (we use an abbreviation for typographical reasons) and the name of the RDF file to read. In Jena, an RDF graph is represented by an object belonging to the class Model. We first create a new, empty, model (as shown in line 8), which is subsequently populated with RDF statements from the given file, as shown in line 10.

Having built the model we can navigate in it, collecting the relevant pieces of information. In this example we simply collect all the RDF properties attached to the resource specified by the URI paintingURI via any property and then display the values of these. In line 12 we obtain the resource itself. Next, in lines 13–17, we iterate through the properties of this resource and display their values. More precisely, the method invocation `painting.listProperties()` actually returns an iterator which loops over all the statements that have resource `painting` as a subject.

We can mention some shortcomings of Jena here. As a more sophisticated example, let us consider the RDF description shown in Figure 3.1 and determine how many known authors the given homepage has. This task is fairly complicated to implement in Jena, as we have to navigate explicitly to each element of the RDF bag in order to determine the cardinality of the bag (i.e. the number of elements that it possesses).

So far we have seen how to read RDF descriptions using Jena. In the reverse direction, we now show how to serialise our Jena model into an RDF/XML file. We will give some Java code in which we build a model on the fly and then save it. In the example below we build an RDF graph relating to the Rembrandt picture; see Figure 2.13.

```
import com.hp.hpl.jena.rdf.model.*;

public class RembrandtRDF {
  static String paintingURI = "http://...night_watch.htm";
  static String painterName = "Rembrandt van Rijn";
  static String propertyNS  = "http://swexpld.org/utils/";

  public static void main (String[] args) {
    Model model        = ModelFactory.createDefaultModel();
    Resource painting = model.createResource(paintingURI);
    Property property =
            model.createProperty(propertyNS,"paintedBy");

    painting.addProperty(property, painterName);

    model.write(System.out,"RDF/XML-ABBREV");
  }
}
```

After the necessary import declaration, in lines 4–6 we specify the URI of the painting, the name of the painter and the URI of the namespace for our `paintedBy` property.

At this point we have all the basic building blocks we need to create an RDF graph. In line 9 we create a new Jena model. Within this model we create a new resource identified by a URI. This can be seen in line 10. In lines 11–12 we create a new property using the namespace specified before and the name of the property. Finally, in line 14, we add this property to our newly created resource with the given value in the object position.

We have now built a model which can be used in different ways depending on the application itself. In our example here, we simply write this model out, in RDF/XML form, up to the standard output (line 16). The result can be seen below (cf. Figure 2.16).

```
<rdf:RDF
    xmlns:rdf="http://www.w3.org/1999/02/22-rdf-syntax-ns#"
    xmlns:j.0="http://swexpld.org/utils/" >
```

```
<rdf:Description rdf:about="http://...night_watch.htm">
  <j.0:paintedBy>Rembrandt van Rijn</j.0:paintedBy>
</rdf:Description>
```

```
</rdf:RDF>
```

Jena has several well-known built in RDF schemas, such as the Dublin Core (Subsection 2.7.1) or XML schema datatypes. When we use entities from these schemas the code can be much simpler. For example, if we used the Dublin Core property `creator` instead of `paintedBy`, we could get rid of lines 6 and 11–12. In this case, we would have to add one more import declaration (`import com.hp.hpl.jena.vocabulary.DC`) at the beginning of the Java program, and line 14 should be replaced by the following:

```
painting.addProperty(DC.creator, painterName);
```

Looking at the very simple examples above, we can get a feeling of how cumbersome it is to navigate through an RDF graph in a bigger model. Rather than to "dig out" the information by hand (or, more precisely, by program code) one would prefer to formulate expressive high-level *RDF queries* over a model. In fact the Jena framework has many other features not covered here, and one of these is exactly the support for RDF queries. The topic of querying RDF sources will be covered in subsequent sections.

Exercise 3.2: Write a Java program, using the Jena toolkit, that lists the names of the employees in the RDF source shown in Figure 2.19.

3.3. Querying RDF sources

Querying an RDF source means retrieving some pieces of information contained in it. This is normally done by formulating a query in some query language. For example, we could ask what pictures were produced by Rembrandt. To answer such a query we may use both RDF data (Night Watch is painted by Rembrandt) and schema information (if somebody painted a picture that means he produced it). Schemas are important when we would like to do some kind of reasoning in order to obtain data which is not given explicitly in the RDF source. In this section we focus on the base case, when no reasoning is performed. The scenario involving reasoning is discussed in Section 3.4.

A natural way of querying an RDF source is to use an XML query engine, as RDF documents are normally stored in XML format. In this section we first introduce the basic issues related to querying XML data and then argue why XML queries cannot be used effectively for RDF sources. Subsequently we describe some important languages created specifically for querying RDF sources, including the W3C standard, the SPARQL language.

3.3.1. XML queries

Early approaches addressed the problem of querying XML sources by suggesting storing these in relational databases and simply using SQL for formulating queries. It soon turned out, however, that to convert an XML document into a database table automatically we already need a language enabling us to navigate in the XML tree. Furthermore, such a conversion has other drawbacks. First, it is inconvenient and often very slow. Also, many XML queries can be formulated only in a very unintuitive way when the relational database representation is used.

In both the relational and the XML approach, separation of the schema and data information is advocated. However, XML documents can be queried on their own: navigating in an XML tree is possible with no knowledge of the schema. This is the reason why XML documents are sometimes referred to as self-describing information sources.

The World Wide Web Consortium launched a working group focusing on XML query languages in 1999. This group enjoys the support of industry, as several leading software companies participate in the work. The results (specifications of the XQuery, XPath, XQueryX and other languages) became W3C recommendations in January 2007.

We now introduce the XQuery and XPath languages and discuss to what extent are they suitable for querying RDF sources.

3.3.1.1. The XQuery and XPath languages

XQuery [38] is a strongly typed *functional language*. The most typical properties of functional languages are (1) single assignment variables, (2) execution based on function evaluation and (3) higher-order functions (functions which have other functions as arguments). As already mentioned, XQuery has recently become a W3C recommendation. However, it already has several implementations, such as the query engines in the Microsoft SQL Server [93] or in the GNU project called Qexo [20]. An interesting aspect of the latter is that it compiles an XQuery program either into Java bytecode or directly into a servlet. This is possible since queries written in XQuery are fully fledged programs. Moreover, as XQuery is designed to query XML data, these servlets are perfect tools for building web-based interfaces for XML information sources.

The XQuery language itself is not XML-based. However, there exists a W3C recommendation, called XQueryX [79], which specifies an XML syntax for XQuery. By avoiding XML syntax, programs in XQuery become more compact and readable for humans.

We can actually consider XQuery as a general purpose programming language extended with *XML-path expressions*, which serve for identifying nodes in the XML tree. As these path expressions form the bases of XML queries and of XQuery programs, we discuss them first.

The XPath language.   The path expressions used in XQuery 1.0 are almost the same as those allowed by XPath 2.0 [26], a language also developed by W3C. These two languages have a common basis: they share the notation, data model and semantics specifications.

We now briefly introduce the most common XPath constructs. For this we will use the sample XML source shown in Figure 3.4. We will evaluate our XPath-expression examples in the context of this XML document.

An XPath path expression selects XML elements (or attributes) from an XML document together with their descendants. In other words, an XPath expression actually selects a

```
 1  <AAA>
 2    <XXX>
 3      <DDD>
 4        <BBB/>
 5        <BBB id = "b1"/>
 6        <FFF id = "f1"/>
 7      </DDD>
 8    </XXX>
 9    <CCC>
10      <DDD name = "d1">
11        <BBB/>
12        <BBB/>
13        <FFF/>
14      </DDD>
15    </CCC>
16    <BBB>
17    Very important thing.
18    </BBB>
19  </AAA>
```

Figure 3.4. The XML used for evaluating XPath expressions.

complete subtree. For example, selecting the element starting in line 3 results in the following XML tree:

```
<DDD>
  <BBB/>
  <BBB id = "b1"/>
  <FFF id = "f1"/>
</DDD>
```

Selecting the element in line 16 gives the tree below:

```
<BBB>
Very important thing.
</BBB>
```

Path expressions starting with a slash / denote absolute paths in the XML tree. This means that the expression must be evaluated relative to the root. For example, the XPath expression /AAA selects the root element itself, so it returns the whole document. The expression /AAA/BBB selects the element <BBB> in line 16, the only <BBB> element located directly below an <AAA> element. An absolute path expression can select multiple elements: for example, the expression /AAA/CCC/DDD/BBB selects the elements in lines 11 and 12.

Expressions starting with // look in the whole document for the XML elements thus specified. The expression //BBB thus selects subtrees starting in lines 4, 5, 11, 12 and 16. The expression //DDD/BBB selects the same subtrees, except for that in line 16 as it is not located within a <DDD> element.

We can use * as a joker character in XPath expressions. This character matches an arbitrary element. For example, the expression /AAA/CCC/DDD/* selects lines 11, 12 and 13. The expression /*/*/*/BBB results in lines 4, 5, 11 and 12. Finally, the expression //* selects all elements in the document (12 altogether) unlike /AAA, which only selects the root element.

At the end of a path expression, a number or a function can be given within square brackets []. These constructs are called *predicates* and their purpose is to filter the resulting element sequence, by keeping some items and discarding others. An integer n placed here prescribes that only the nth element of the sequence should be kept. For example, the expression /AAA/XXX/DDD/BBB[1] selects only line 4 whereas the expression /AAA/XXX/DDD/BBB selects both lines 4 and 5. As an example involving a function, last() retains only the last element in the result sequence. Actually, this may still lead to multiple solutions since last() selects the last elements from amongst the siblings in a so-called *dynamic context* (for more details see [26]). For example, the expression //BBB[last()] selects elements in lines 5, 12 and 16. There are other built-in functions, which, among other things, let us filter the result sequence using element names, the number of occurrences of given elements and so on.

Attributes can be selected by using the @ construct. The expression //@id selects the attributes of elements in lines 5 and 6. When an attribute is used in square brackets, it filters the sequence by retaining only those elements that contain the specified attribute. For example, the expression //*[@name] selects line 10, while the expression //*[@*] selects all elements that have any attributes, in our case, lines 5, 6 and 10. The attribute value can also be included in the filtering condition, e.g. the expression //*[@id="b1"] selects the element in line 5.

The so-called *axes* are other important constructs of the XPath language. Axes let us traverse the XML tree by specifying where to go from the actual node. We can go, for example, to descendants, parents, ancestors, children or attributes. Axes are given as prefixes, separated by :: from a condition that holds for all elements selected by the given axis. For example, the expression //DDD/parent::* selects the parents of the <DDD> elements (with no condition), namely lines 2 and 9. Axes are fundamental constructs of the XPath language, whereas several language elements discussed so far can be viewed as syntactic sugar on an expression using axes. For example, [@id="b1"] is an abbreviation of [attribute::id="b1"].

The XPath language has many other useful constructs: more about these can be read in the specification of the language, [26].

Exercise 3.3: Write an XPath expression that selects the elements in lines 4 and 11. Verify your result by some XPath engine such as the GNU Qexo. Hint: a possible characterisation of these lines is that they are the first children of the <DDD> elements.

Running XQuery programs. The fundamental issue in querying XML is XML tree navigation, in other words, focusing on certain XML elements or attributes. Built on the XPath navigation features, XQuery lets us describe complex queries which can be executed by an XQuery engine. As an example, let us consider the XML document, shown in Figure 2.3, containing some records about the employees of an imaginary company. The XQuery query given below selects the names of the employees present in the document and lists the results in HTML form:

```
<html>{
let $employees := document("employee.xml")/employees
for $mt in $employees/employee
  return <h2>{$mt/name}</h2>
}</html>
```

When this query is executed on the document of Figure 2.3, the variable $employees will contain a single node, that corresponding to the <employees> element. By using the for construct, we iterate through the <employee> elements (there are two in the XML source) and return their <name> children elements. In the document in question there is a single name element below each employee, so the result will include a single <h2> element for both employees.

This program can be executed by an XQuery engine such as the GNU Qexo [20], using the following command (Kawa is the name of the underlying compiler of Qexo that is responsible for transforming the query into Java bytecode):

```
java -jar kawa-1.9.1.jar --xquery -f example_query.xq
```

The result of the execution is the following piece of HTML code:

```
<html>
  <h2>
    <name>Jane Doe</name>
  </h2>
  <h2>
    <name>John Stiles</name>
  </h2>
</html>
```

Summing up, we have shown how to use an XQuery program to select two elements from an XML document and how to embed the query results into HTML code.

Exercise 3.4: Modify the XQuery program shown above to include the phone numbers of the employees in the resulting HTML code. If an employee has more than one phone number then consider only the first. Run your XQuery program and check the output that it produces.

3.3.1.2. XML queries over RDF sources

As we have seen, the primary serialisation syntax for RDF is XML. Consequently, running XML queries on RDF descriptions would seem to be a quite natural method. The problem is that the same set of RDF statements can be represented by different XML documents. For example, we can choose the order of the XML elements at will, as the order of the triples does not matter in the RDF data model. We can also use the abbreviated syntax of RDF instead of the verbose one. It is important to notice that none of these variations deviates from the RDF standard, nor from the recommended RDF modelling practice.

We illustrate this issue with a simple example. Let us consider writing a query which returns the number of elements in a bag. Such a bag can appear in the following XML form, where the `Description` element has two children.

```
<rdf:Description rdf:ID="Team">
  <rdf:type rdf:resource=
   "http://www.w3.org/1999/02/22-rdf-syntax-ns#Bag"/>
  <rdf:li>John Smith</rdf:li>
</rdf:Description>
```

This XML document represents an RDF graph with three nodes and two edges (with labels `rdf:type` and `rdf:li`). The very same graph can also be given in a different way, as shown below:

```
<rdf:Bag rdf:ID="Team">
  <rdf:li>John Smith</rdf:li>
</rdf:Bag>
```

In this case there is no element named `Description` at all, and the element `Bag` has only one child.

Obviously, an XML query that works on one RDF source above may not behave well on the other. Hence using XML query engines for XML/RDF sources is cumbersome and inefficient – we need query languages specially designed for RDF.

Exercise 3.5: Write an XQuery program to count the elements of a bag, assuming the first XML representation, shown above. Next, write an XQuery program to perform the same task on the second representation. Finally, try to combine the two programs, so that your code will work on both representations.

Exercise 3.6: Try to find an XML representation form for the above "Team" for which your final program will not work properly.

3.3.2. Properties of RDF query languages

Several RDF query languages have been defined since the appearance of RDF. There has been a substantial improvement in this area in the past few years, in terms of the features of query languages, their implementation and their documentation.

Like the XML query languages and SQL, RDF query languages are *declarative*. In these languages the user has to specify *what* information she wants to get and not *how* to obtain the results. This means that the query should be formulated without any knowledge of the actual data storage, as this knowledge is only relevant within the query engine.[4]

Beyond declarativity, SQL sets a good example of how a query should be structured. An SQL query (1) specifies the sources that store the information to query, (2) sets the filtering criteria and finally (3) selects which part of the result shall be presented. These correspond

---

[4] It may happen, for example, that an RDF query engine finally executes SQL queries, if the RDF information is actually stored in a relational database. This, however, serves only for efficiency purposes and does not affect the way in which queries should be formulated.

to the SQL FROM, WHERE and SELECT constructs, respectively. The same idea can also be found in most RDF query languages.

RDF query languages should give as much direct support for specific RDF constructs (such as containers, reification etc.) as possible. They should also support RDF datatypes in some way. In Subsection 2.5.5 we mentioned that RDF has a generic type concept, supported by the rdf:datatype property. Despite this generality, XML data types play a significant role as they are used in most RDF applications. XML Schema seems to be a good choice as it offers several kinds of expansion mechanism for creating new data types.

In the following subsections we introduce several RDF query languages. The languages to be presented were selected either because they are widely used or because they have some special properties worth mentioning. For every language we will discuss its pros and cons.

We will use a common RDF source, shown in Figure 3.5, for demonstrating queries in these languages. In this RDF description we present metadata about three fictitious scientists. We give their names, their age, their position and their publications (including the titles and dates of publication). We also have some friendship relations between them. The information given is not exhaustive – some pieces of data are missing for some people – but this fits well with the RDF philosophy.

In the case of query languages we usually examine three important features, such as the *expressivity*, *closure* and *safety* [48] properties. The expressivity tells us how powerfully queries can be formulated in the given language; there is always a trade-off between expressivity and efficiency of query execution. A language has the closure property if the result of a query in this language can be represented in the same data model as that in which the language operates. Such languages support query encapsulation, as the result of a subquery can serve as the input to another query. The widely used SQL, for example, is just such a language: the result of an SQL query is actually a new database table, which can be a starting point for further queries. Finally, a language is called safe if, for an arbitrary query, its execution terminates in finite time. Recursion, negation and other built-in operations can all affect safety.

3.3.3. RQS: a database-oriented RDF query language

Certain types of RDF query language treat RDF as nothing other than an XML application. We call these languages *database-centric* query languages. The common property of such languages is that they assume that the structure of the RDF source to be queried is known to the user in advance, much as for SQL queries. There, we must know the names of the tables and columns before formulating any query. We could also say that database-centric RDF languages regard RDF information as data rather than metadata.

The *RDF Query Specification* (RQS) language [75], created back in 1998, is a database-centric RDF query language. It was created by Ashok Malhotra and Neel Sundaresan, who were working as IBM researchers at that time. Neel Sundaresan was a chief architect of IBM's RDF-based search engine, called Grand Central Station [114]. Since then, Ashok Malhotra has moved to Microsoft and, among other things, has participated in the development of the XQuery and XPath recommendations.

The RQS language was actually a short-lived proposal which disappeared soon after its initial publication. However, we still find it interesting, as it is one of the very few RDF query languages having an RDF syntax. This syntax is, however, somewhat different from the syntax introduced in Chapter 2, as in 1998 the RDF framework was far from being

```
<?xml version="1.0" encoding="UTF-8"?>
<rdf:RDF
  xmlns:rdf="http://www.w3.org/1999/02/22-rdf-syntax-ns#"
  xmlns:rdfs="http://www.w3.org/2000/01/rdf-schema#"
  xmlns:p="http://swexpld.org/util#"
  xml:base="http://swexpld.org/person">

<rdf:Description rdf:ID="JC">
  <p:name>John Carel</p:name>
  <p:born rdf:datatype="http://.../XMLSchema#int">1979</p:born>
</rdf:Description>

<rdf:Description rdf:about="http://swexpld.org/person#Peter">
  <p:name>Peter Bill</p:name>
  <p:position>associate professor</p:position>
  <p:publication>
    <p:Article>
      <p:publication_date>2001</p:publication_date>
      <p:title>Logic-based ontology management</p:title>
    </p:Article>
  </p:publication>
  <p:hasFriend rdf:resource="#JC" />
  <p:hasFriend rdf:resource="#George" />
</rdf:Description>

<rdf:Description rdf:ID="George">
  <p:name>George Cruise</p:name>
  <p:position>Ph.D. student</p:position>
  <p:born rdf:datatype="http://.../XMLSchema#int">1982</p:born>
  <p:publication>
    <p:Article>
      <p:publication_date>2004</p:publication_date>
      <p:title>Modeling the market</p:title>
    </p:Article>
  </p:publication>
  <p:hasFriend rdf:resource="#Peter" />
</rdf:Description>
</rdf:RDF>
```

Figure 3.5. The RDF source used by our RDF queries.

finalised and it has changed significantly since then. To avoid confusion, the RQS examples below have been adapted to the RDF framework presented in Chapter 2. We also note that, in the remaining part of this subsection, we will restrict our attention to rdf:Bag constructs (see Subsection 2.5.4) when speaking about containers.

The basic idea of RQS is that queries transform RDF containers into RDF containers. The result container is always a *subset* of the original container and also it might be empty. Accordingly, a result of a query can be used as the input of another query, so queries can be encapsulated into each other. Thus, the RQS language has the closure property.

As we have mentioned, RQS uses RDF syntax; in other words, an RQS query is an RDF description itself. A query always specifies the so-called *source container* by using the RDF property `rdfq:From`. If nothing else is given, the query returns all elements of the source container so the query result is the input container itself. An example of this is shown below (the URIs given in the container refer to the people in Figure 3.5):

```
<rdfq:rdfquery>
 <rdfq:From>
  <rdf:Bag>
   <rdf:li rdf:resource="http://swexpld.org/person#Peter"/>
   <rdf:li rdf:resource="http://swexpld.org/person#George"/>
  </rdf:Bag>
 </rdfq:From>
</rdfq:rdfquery>
```

The structure of this query can be understood better by looking at the corresponding RDF graph. This is shown in Figure 3.6. The query contains six nodes, two of them representing anonymous resources. The result of this query is the source container itself:

```
<rdf:Bag>
   <rdf:li rdf:resource="http://swexpld.org/person#Peter"/>
   <rdf:li rdf:resource="http://swexpld.org/person#George"/>
</rdf:Bag>
```

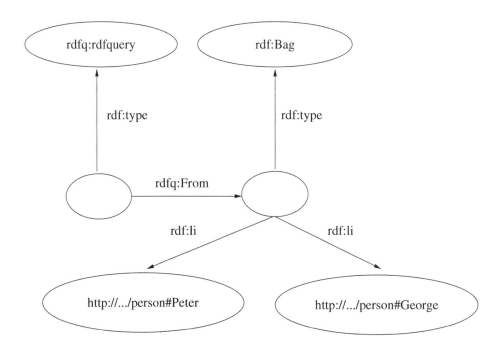

Figure 3.6.   RQS queries are also RDF graphs.

Usually we do not provide the source container in such an explicit form but simply refer to a URI where the appropriate container is deposited. The following RQL query represents the same query as before, provided that the resource `http://swexpld.org/pl#team` identifies a container with Peter and George as elements:

```
<rdfq:rdfquery>
  <rdfq:From rdfq:eachResource="http://swexpld.org/pl#team"/>
</rdfq:rdfquery>
```

Normally an RQS query contains a filtering condition. In its simplest form this specifies a single RDF property. The result of such a query is the set of resources that (1) can be found in the source container and (2) have at least one other resource or literal attached to them through the given property. This RDF property can be specified by the `<rdfq:Property>` construct within an `<rdfq:Select>` element:

```
<rdfq:rdfquery>
  <rdfq:From rdfq:eachResource="http://swexpld.org/pl#team"/>
    <rdfq:Select>
      <rdfq:Property rdfq:name="publication"/>
    </rdfq:Select>
  </rdfq:From>
</rdfq:rdfquery>
```

This query selects people from the given container having at least one publication.[5] This action is very similar to the `Select` and `Where` parts of SQL queries. Namely, it corresponds to an SQL query where (1) we would like to retrieve all columns and (2) we examine not the value of the property `publication`, but its existence. In other words, we select rows which contain a non-`NULL` value in the specified column:

```
SELECT * from team
WHERE publication is not NULL
```

We can also use the counterpart of conventional SQL *projection* in RQS queries. Projection is a relational algebra primitive which maps a table to a subset of its columns. We use projection when we specify column names in the `SELECT` part of an SQL query. In a database system this means that new temporary tables are created, at least virtually. Something similar happens in RQS: through projection we create new anonymous resources. The projection attributes can be given in the `rdfq:properties` attributes of the `<rdfq:Select>` element. An example is

```
<rdfq:rdfquery>
  <rdfq:From rdfq:eachResource="http://swexpld.org/pl#team"/>
    <rdfq:Select rdfq:properties="name position">
      <rdfq:Property rdfq:name="publication"/>
    </rdfq:Select>
  </rdfq:From>
</rdfq:rdfquery>
```

[5] In fact this does not do any filtering here, as both Peter and George have publications – we will refine the filtering condition later.

In this example people with a publication are selected, but only the `name` and `position` links are kept in the resulting graph.

Our concluding example is a query that returns the authors having relatively recent publications:

```
<rdfq:rdfquery>
  <rdfq:From eachResource="http://swexpld.org/pl#team" >
    <rdfq:Select rdfq:properties="name title">
      <rdfq:Condition>
        <rdfq:greatherThan>
          <rdfq:Property
           rdfq:path="publication/publication_date" />
          <rdf:Integer>2003</rdf:Integer>
        </rdfq:greatherThan>
      </rdfq:Condition>
    </rdfq:Select>
  </rdfq:From>
</rdfq:rdfquery>
```

Here we select those people who have at least one publication, the date of which is after the year 2003. If there is no `publication_date` attached to the given publication, the condition is evaluated to false.

Exercise 3.7: Write an RQS query which collects those people who are friends of scientists having at least one publication.

The RQS language has many other features, which we will not describe in detail here. Results can be sorted, we can use universal and existential quantifiers for complex queries etc. More can be read in the RQS specification [75].

As already implied, the RDF Query Specification language was not a big success. This could have been a consequence of its database-centric approach: RQS assumes that its user has full knowledge of the structure of the RDF source to be queried. In the case of SQL, it assumes that the user knows what tables are in the database and what columns these tables contain. This approach does not seem to be popular in the RDF world. The reason is – in the case of metadata retrieval – queries are very often related to unknown knowledge. For example, we may be looking for web pages that have *something to do* with the word `smith` but the exact relation is not known. The RQS language is not suitable for dealing with such queries since the RDF properties needed for navigation must be known when writing the query. As we saw earlier, we can look for someone having at least one recent publication; to formulate a query for this task, however, we need to know that the RDF source contains properties named `publication` and `publication_date`.

It is important to note that this problem is not related to the relational approach itself. Queries impossible to formulate in RQS can be easily written in SQL, if we use an appropriate data representation. For example, we can store RDF statements in a table called `statement` with three columns, which correspond to the three parts of an RDF triple. In this way the above query concerning `smith` can be easily formulated in SQL, as follows:

```
SELECT s1.subject
FROM statement s1, statement s2
WHERE s1.predicate='rdf:type' and s1.object='t:webpage' and
      s2.subject=s1.subject s2.object='smith'
```

3.3.4. Model-based RDF query languages - an overview

Most RDF query languages work directly on the RDF data model. These languages are called *model-based* query languages. We now give an overview of the generic features of this kind of query language. Concrete languages will be discussed later.

As discussed in Chapter 2, the RDF data model is a labelled directed graph. The edges of such graphs are always labelled with URIs; the nodes (1) can be blank, (2) can contain literals or (3) can be labelled with URIs. The meaning of the RDF data model is independent of the actual serialisation syntax, be it XML, N3 [15] or any other formalism. Accordingly, model-based query languages have to ignore the particular properties of serialisation formalisms, such as the order of the elements in an RDF/XML description.

Model-based query languages may utilise *RDF Schema* information (see Section 3.4 below). It is possible, for example, that when we search for the instances of a given class we will get results that are known only to be instances of a subclass. When the output of a query is presented, inferred results are often distinguished from those not requiring any reasoning. In the latter case the query engine uses only the information stored directly in the RDF graph. For example, the only resources considered to be the instances of a class are those which have an edge, labelled with `rdf:type`, pointing to the resource representing the class.

A further feature of model-based query languages is that they do not assume full knowledge about the structure of the so-called *RDF knowledge base* (the database storing RDF statements). Queries looking for "someone in some relation with someone else who has two cats" are very much acceptable in the case of model-based queries. It may turn out that the relation between the two participants is friendship, or one could be the boss of the other etc. The important thing is that the person writing the query does not need to know the possible relationships between the individuals in the given knowledge base.

3.3.4.1. The basic idea: graph patterns

Model-based RDF query engines use *subgraph matching* and *variable substitution* during execution. In this approach, as in the RDF data model, the queries themselves are labelled directed graphs. These graphs, however, may contain variables and therefore they are called *graph patterns*. The variables can be present in the graph in two places:

- as a label of a node – the variable denotes an RDF resource (or a literal) that is not known at the moment of query formulation;

- as a label of an edge – the variable denotes a property which was unknown when the query is written.

A query is executed in the context of an RDF knowledge base, i.e. a labelled directed graph corresponding to a set of RDF triples. The result of a query is a *subgraph of the knowledge base* which is isomorphic to the query graph, with possible variable substitutions.

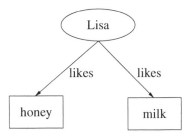

Figure 3.7. An example of a knowledge base: Lisa likes honey and milk.

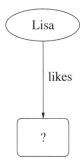

Figure 3.8. The query: "What does Lisa like?".

As an example, let us consider a very simple knowledge base, presented in Figure 3.7, stating that Lisa likes honey and she likes milk. In this world we may be interested in the query "What does Lisa like"? The graph pattern capturing this query is shown in Figure 3.8.

As results, we get two subgraphs. The first corresponds to the RDF statement "Lisa likes honey" with the variable substitution ?=honey. The second subgraph matches the statement "Lisa likes milk" with the substitution ?=milk. This "query language" needs a concrete syntax that nicely fits the RDF data model. Examples of such languages are introduced later, in Sections 3.3.5–3.3.7. It is worth noting that the result of a query is an RDF knowledge base (a graph without variables), so new queries can be formulated on it. This shows that the graph-pattern approach maintains the closure property and thus also ensures the ability to create embedded queries.

The simplest type of query in this approach consists of a single variable, which results in enumeration of all the nodes of the RDF graph. At the other extreme, very complex queries can be formulated using the graph-pattern approach. Unfortunately this kind of universality has its price, as subgraph matching is an NP-complete problem. In practice this means that, in the case of large knowledge bases and complex graph patterns, efficiency of execution can be an issue. Similar problems arise for almost all types of database system. Some systems are better than others exactly because they use optimisations and appropriate heuristics to overcome such problems.

3.3.4.2. Primitive and complex queries

The simplest graph pattern (excluding the extreme case of a single variable) is a labelled directed graph with two nodes and an edge between them, where the label of the edge and the labels of both nodes can be variables. We call these constructs *primitive queries* or *subqueries*, indicating that they can participate in the building of more complex queries. A primitive query corresponds to an RDF triple that may contain variables. In what follows, where it will not cause confusion, we will refer to the label of an edge simply as "the edge" and to the label of a node simply as "the node".

Practically speaking, we have eight different primitive queries, depending on which node (edge) positions are variables. The result of executing such a query is the set of possible variable substitutions or simply a yes/no result if the query contains no variables. An example of a primitive query has already been shown in Figure 3.8.

Primitive queries have several important properties. One is that this special case of the general subgraph-matching problem has linear time complexity in the number of edges in the knowledge base. In other words, primitive queries scale very well with the size of the knowledge base.

However, an RDF query language supporting only such simple graph patterns does not really satisfy our needs. Using patterns with two nodes we can ask only whether a partially specified RDF triple is present in the knowledge base. Although this already creates the possibility of retrieving the whole content of the RDF graph (if the edge and both nodes are variables) we usually would like to formulate queries involving *complex graph patterns*.

Complex patterns, also called complex queries or simply queries, are made by allowing the logical "and" operator between primitive queries. The meaning of a query with such an operator between two primitive queries is that both graphs must be present in the knowledge base. Primitive subqueries of a complex query are not necessarily independent, as they may be connected to each other via shared variables. In that case it is important that the matches of the subqueries assign the same value to the shared variables.

Note that a complex query represented by a conjunction of primitive queries is nothing other than a serialised format for a graph pattern. Each edge of the pattern corresponds to a triple in the conjunction, involving the labels of the endpoints and the label of the edge itself (each of which can be a variable).[6]

We now describe the way in which complex queries can be processed.

3.3.4.3. Execution of complex queries

We have just seen that a subquery can be answered by the use of subgraph matching and variable substitution. We now turn to a discussion of the execution mechanism for answering complex queries.

The basic idea of complex query execution is to take the primitive subqueries in turn (say, in the order in which these are enumerated in the complex query) and to try to find a match for each subquery in the knowledge base. When a variable is substituted, all its occurrences in further subqueries are replaced by the resource (or literal) assigned to this variable.

Assuming that we can perform this process for all subqueries, we reach a solution of the complex query. The problem is that we may end up with a subquery with no solutions (more exactly, with no solution for the given set of substitutions made until that point). In such a case we have to *backtrack* to an earlier subquery and continue from there with a solution

---

[6] Note that subqueries can share multiple variables. As an example, let us consider the first subquery as "Ryan is in some relation (?) with someone (??)" and the second subquery as "this someone (??) is in the same relationship (?) with Jack". A solution for this could be the substitution ? = loves, ?? = Kate. This informally corresponds to: "Ryan loves Kate, and Kate loves Jack".

different from earlier solutions. To make this search exhaustive, *lexicographic* backtracking is normally used, which means that we go back to the *most recent* subquery. An important requirement is that variable substitutions have to be undone during backtracking. Thus, when retrying a subquery (i.e. trying to find alternative solutions for it) we must use exactly the same variable assignments as when solving it for the first time.

We note that this approach corresponds to a depth-first traversal of the search space, in a way very similar to the execution mechanism of the logic programming language Prolog [68].

We now present an algorithm for the execution of complex queries in a more formal way. To this end, we introduce a counter n for keeping track of the current subquery. Furthermore, for each such n we maintain a list L_n which contains the solutions of the nth subquery found so far. This list is used at backtracking, to ensure that only new solutions of the given subquery are considered. Note, however, that there exist much more efficient approaches for ensuring the desired effect. Here we use the L_n data structure to make the algorithm easier to understand.

1 (*Initialisation*) Set the subquery counter n to 1.

2 (*Matching a subquery*) Set up a search for matching the (single-edge) subgraph that corresponds to the nth subquery against the knowledge base.

   2.1 Initialise the list L_n belonging to the subquery to an empty list, meaning no solutions have been found so far.

   2.2 Search the knowledge base for a match of the nth subquery (different from any matches stored in L_n). If this is unsuccessful, go to step 3.

   2.3 If a match is found:

      2.3.1 Record the match in the list L_n, so that a further search for alternative solutions can take this into account.

      2.3.2 Record any possible variable substitutions made during the matching process, so that they can be undone at backtracking.

      2.3.3 Increment the counter n. If the number of subqueries is greater or equal to n (i.e. the nth subquery does exist) then go to step 2. Otherwise we have reached the end of the complex query and so a solution has been found. If further solutions are needed, continue at step 3.

3 (*Backtrack*) This point is reached when the matching of the nth subquery has been unsuccessful.

   3.1 If $n = 1$ the execution of the complex query fails.

   3.2 Otherwise, look for an *alternative* match for the $(n-1)$th subquery:

      3.2.1 Undo all variable substitutions made during the previous match for this subquery.

      3.2.2 Decrement the counter n and continue at step 2.2.

Exercise 3.8: Does the execution of a query change if one or more edges of the RDF graph are duplicated?

The execution of a complex query *fails* if we get back to the first subquery in the process of backtracking and no new solution can be found for it. A special case of failure is when the graph corresponding to the first subquery cannot be matched against the knowledge base at all; in this case the query fails immediately.

The execution of a complex query succeeds if there exists a set of variable substitutions where (1) all variables present in the query are substituted and, (2) taking into account these substitutions, *all* the subqueries are present in the knowledge base.

In the case of success we can ask for alternative solutions (cf. the discussion of the example query in Figure 3.8). This can be viewed as explicitly asking the query engine to backtrack; see step 2.3.3 of the above algorithm.

To illustrate the process, let us consider the graph in Figure 3.9 and the corresponding RDF/XML serialisation in Figure 3.10. These describe a world where Ryan has a bag containing a watch and a cellphone. This is the knowledge base against which we will formulate our queries in the rest of this section.

We have a blank node in the example, which represents the bag itself. In Subsection 2.3.4 we have already discussed the fact that blank nodes actually need to be named during serialisation, to avoid ambiguity. We should do something similar here, as the result of our query

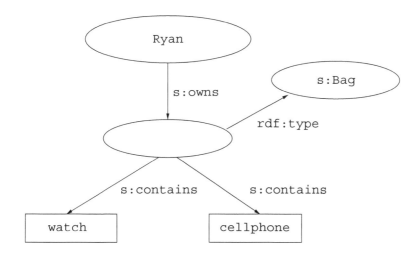

Figure 3.9.   An RDF knowledge base describing Ryan and his belongings.

```
<rdf:Description rdf:about="#Ryan">
  <s:owns>
    <s:Bag>
      <s:contains>watch</s:contains>
      <s:contains>cellphone</s:contains>
    </s:Bag>
  </s:owns>
</rdf:Description>
```

Figure 3.10.   The Ryan example in RDF/XML serialisation.

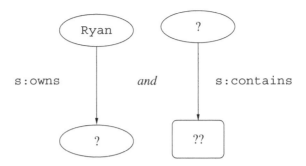

Figure 3.11. A complex query.

will contain this anonymous resource as well. We thus assign the name im_resource to the blank node.

Let us now consider the complex query in Figure 3.11. This query consists of two sub-queries. There is a single variable in the first subquery, while the second contains two variables. Note that the two occurrences of ? must refer to the same variable, while ?? denotes a (potentially) different variable. Informally, the query looks for "something whose owner is Ryan" and also for something else, which is contained in the thing owned by Ryan.

First, we try to find a triple in the knowledge base that can be matched with the first subquery. There is only one such subgraph, and matching requires the variable substitution shown below:

? = im_resource

Next, we try to match the second subquery against the knowledge base. We should notice, however, that the second subquery has to be changed as we have to take into account the above variable substitution. We thus have to look for something (denoted by the variable ?? contained in the im_resource. We can easily find a subgraph in the knowledge base that is isomorphic with this subquery, for example, by using the following variable substitution:

?? = watch

As we do not have any more subqueries, the query execution terminates successfully with the following two variable substitutions:

? = im_resource
?? = watch

If we ask for a different solution then we must continue to try to match the last subquery differently, after having undone the ??=watch variable substitution. This succeeds again, since there exists an appropriate subgraph using the variable substitution ??=cellphone:

? = im_resource
?? = cellphone

We can ask for a further solution again. Now we try to match the last subquery with the knowledge base in a yet another way. This, as it turns out, is not possible so we continue backtracking and try to find an alternative solution for the first subquery. This fails, too. Thus we conclude that there are no more solutions for this query.

As explained earlier, a complex query corresponds to a graph pattern with variables. The query shown in Figure 3.11, for example, actually represents a graph with three nodes created by unifying the ? nodes. Thus the execution algorithm presented here does indeed solve the subgraph matching problem.

Exercise 3.9: Let us consider a complex query composed of the following two primitive subqueries: ?? p:hasFriend ? and ?? p:publication ???. Describe how the steps of the execution algorithm above are applied to run this complex query against the knowledge base of Figure 3.5.

We now introduce some relevant model-based query languages. First, we present the RDQL language, which is the original query language of the Jena tool set (now it also supports SPARQL). Next, we introduce the new W3C query language SPARQL, which is already supported by nearly all RDF-based systems. Finally, we briefly introduce the prototype of the RDFLan language, built by the authors of this book.

3.3.5. The RDQL language

The *RDF Data Query Language* (RDQL) is model-based. It is part of the HP Jena system (see Section 3.2) and is the result of a long development process. The roots of the language go back to 1998, to the W3C query language conference held in Boston [77]. The paper [46], written by R. V. Guha and co-authors, can be considered as the foundation of model-based RDF queries. The RDQL language is itself an implementation of the language SquishQL [81], which in turn originates from the language of rdfDB [45], an RDF-based storage system also created by R. V. Guha. In fact several other RDF frameworks are based on SquishQL, such as the obsolete Inkling [80] and RDFStore [99]. A proposal for standardising RDQL was actually submitted to the W3C in January 2004.

The syntax of RDQL is similar to SQL but, of course, RDQL has no connection with the database approach of RQS (Subsection 3.3.3). The general structure of an RDQL query is the following:

SELECT Variables
FROM Documents
WHERE Pattern
AND Filters
USING Namespaces

The SELECT part lists the variables whose values form the result set. The FROM part specifies the RDF sources to be queried. The WHERE part contains the graph pattern for which we are looking. This pattern represents an RDF graph possibly containing variables, as introduced in Subsection 3.3.4. The AND part serves for specifying constraints over the variables, e.g. we can state that the value of a given variable must be larger than a specific number. Finally, the USING part defines the namespaces to be used in other parts of the query.

We now show some concrete examples of RDQL queries. We will still use the sample RDF knowledge base in Figure 3.5. In our first RDQL query example we list the names of the people in the knowledge base of Figure 3.5. Correspondingly, the graph pattern is a triple whose subject and object are variables (x and n) and whose predicate is the

URI `http://swexpld.org/util#name` (see Figure 3.5). The solutions of this query are substitutions of the variables *x* and *n*, corresponding to the triple {x, [name], n} present in the RDF graph. This graph (the RDF source) can be specified in the FROM part of the query. This is simply the name of the file (in this example `rdql_input.rdf`), containing the RDF description shown in Figure 3.5:

```
SELECT ?x ?n
FROM <rdql_input.rdf>
WHERE (?x, <http://swexpld.org/util#name>, ?n)
```

Note that variables are preceded by question marks; for example, the variable x is denoted by ?x in the RDQL query.

If we run the above query using the Jena system, we get the results in a tabular form. The system enumerates the values of all variables specified in the SELECT part of the query, as shown below.

```
x                                          | n
============================================================
<http://swexpld.org/person#JC>     | "John Carel"
<http://swexpld.org/person#Peter>  | "Peter Bill"
<http://swexpld.org/person#George> | "George Cruise"
```

As we can see, three people were found and, for example, the name of the person identified by `http://swexpld.org/person#JC` is John Carel.

In this example we used a primitive graph pattern: the result is all triples from the knowledge base that match this pattern. However, if we would like all the publication titles present in the knowledge base to be listed, we need to use a complex graph pattern. The first sub-query selects a publication, while the second retrieves its title (if there is any). These two patterns are joined through the shared variable p, denoting the publication, as shown below.

```
SELECT ?t
FROM <rdql_input.rdf>
WHERE (?x, <http://swexpld.org/util#publication>, ?p),
      (?p, <http://swexpld.org/util#title>, ?t)
```

Notice that the `http://swexpld.org/util#` prefix is used several times, which makes the query quite cumbersome. It therefore seems worthwhile to introduce an abbreviation for this URL and to use that in the pattern. This can be done by inserting a USING construct in our query, as seen below:

```
SELECT ?t
FROM <rdql_input.rdf>
WHERE (?x, <s:publication>, ?p),
      (?p, <s:title>, ?t)
USING s for <http://swexpld.org/util#>
```

Each solution of this query is a substitution of the variables x, p and t, for example, x=http://swexpld.org/person#George, p=1fddc31:1b90a59:-7fff and t="Modelling the market". Here the value of the variable p is an identifier assigned by the query engine to the blank node (cf. the use of im_resource in Subsection 3.3.4.3). This is needed, because we modelled the publications in our RDF description as anonymous resources (a publication is "something" that may have a title and does have a publication year).

However, as reflected by the SELECT part of the query, here we are interested only in the substitutions of the variable t. Accordingly, the reply of the Jena system is the following:

```
t
=================================
"Modeling the market"
"Logic-based ontology management"
```

In our next example query, we are looking for (the names of the) people who were born after 1980.

```
SELECT ?n
FROM <rdql_input.rdf>
WHERE (?x, <s:born>, ?b),
      (?x, <s:name>, ?n)
AND ?b > 1980
USING s for <http://swexpld.org/util#>
```

We have used the AND construct in this query for specifying an arithmetic constraint on the value of the variable b (it must be bigger than 1980). There is only one solution for this query, namely, the n = "George Cruise" substitution.

As a final example we present one more query, which nicely demonstrates navigation in the RDF tree; in this example we are looking for the friends of George Cruise together with their employment position:

```
SELECT ?fr ?frp
FROM <rdql_input.rdf>
WHERE (?x, <s:name>, ?n)
      (?x, <s:hasFriend>, ?fr)
      (?fr, <s:position>, ?frp)
AND ?n eq "George Cruise"
USING s for <http://swexpld.org/util#>
```

Some people argue that an RDF query language should have an RDF syntax and should return RDF descriptions as answers (see Subsection 3.3.3). There is some research aimed at providing such an RDF-based query interface over Jena. This involves designing an RDF-based query syntax, transforming that to RDQL and finally converting the tabular answers of Jena to RDF format.

Another double-edged feature of RDQL (and its implementation) is that it treats an RDF graph purely as data without using the underlying semantics (see Section 3.4 below). For example, RDQL does not know anything about containers or reification. Sometimes, when formulating queries on complex RDF constructs, RDQL proves to be rather difficult to use. Let us consider, for example, the following container, which is an extension of the RDF example in Figure 3.5:

```
<rdf:Description rdf:ID="team">
  <s:members>
   <rdf:Bag>
```

```
        <rdf:li rdf:resource="#Peter" />
        <rdf:li rdf:resource="#JC" />
        <rdf:li>Gregoris</rdf:li>
        </rdf:Bag>
    </s:members>
</rdf:Description>
```

If the task is to enumerate the members of this team, our first attempt could be (1) to find a node of the type `rdf:Bag` which is connected to the team via property `members` and then (2) simply to enumerate its contents. This would result in the following query:

```
SELECT ?member
FROM <rdql_input_ex.rdf>
WHERE (<k:team>, <s:members>, ?bag),
      (?bag, <rdf:type>, <rdf:Bag>),
      (?bag, <rdf:li>, ?member)
USING s for <http://swexpld.org/util#>,
      k for <http://swexpld.org/person#>,
      rdf for <http://www.w3.org/1999/02/22-rdf-syntax-ns#>
```

Unfortunately, this solution does not work since there is no such thing as `rdf:li` in the RDF graph. As discussed in Subsection 2.5.4, `rdf:li` is only syntactic sugar; the members are linked to the container through `rdf:_n` properties, i.e. the first element via `rdf:_1`, the second through `rdf:_2` and so on.

The following alternative solution uses the trick proposed by the Jena manual for dealing with containers.

```
SELECT ?y
FROM <rdql_input_ex.rdf>
WHERE (<k:team>, <s:members>, ?bag),
      (?bag, ?x, ?y)
AND ! ( ?x eq <rdf:type> && ?y eq <rdf:Bag>)
USING s for <http://swexpld.org/util#>,
      k for <http://swexpld.org/person#>,
      rdf for <http://www.w3.org/1999/02/22-rdf-syntax-ns#>
```

This solution enumerates all outgoing edges attached to the container, with the exception of the one whose label is `rdf:type` and which points to a resource with label `rdf:Bag`. Thus, we enumerate the members of the container but unfortunately also every other property belonging to the same container.[7]

Exercise 3.10: Formulate an RDQL query that enumerates the names of people having young friends (below the age of 30) with respect to the knowledge base of Figure 3.5.

---

[7] Recall that a container can be a subject of an arbitrary RDF statement, which allows us to formulate statements about the container itself, e.g. it can describe the brand name of a rucksack; see the example in Subsection 2.5.4.

3.3.6. The SPARQL family

In February 2004 the World Wide Web Consortium formed a working group dealing with RDF queries. The group was called the *RDF Data Access Working Group* (DAWG). The purpose of the DAWG was to create a standardised RDF query language, which would incorporate the most important properties of the existing RDF query languages. The plan was that the proposed language would enhance interoperability by being *the query language*, in the same way as SQL is the query language for relational databases. The other, equally important, task of the DAWG was to develop a HTTP/SOAP-based protocol which standardises the different methods of accessing remote RDF storage servers. The proposed new technologies were called the *SPARQL Protocol and the RDF Query Language*. As of January 2008, SPARQL became a W3C recommendation. We first describe the query language in detail and then give a brief overview of the SPARQL Protocol.

Forming the DAWG was an important step as this was the first official group dealing with RDF queries[8] since the previously mentioned W3C query conference in Boston, 1998 [77].

At the beginning of the work, the DAWG collected the requirements of the desired language and the protocol. Several case studies were made later on, for demonstrating the scenarios the new technologies should support.

3.3.6.1. The SPARQL query language

Regarding the SPARQL query language [96], the most important initial question was whether to use existing W3C technologies, such as the XQuery and XPath languages, as a basis for SPARQL. On the one hand, this would require the extension and modification of these languages because of the differences between the XML and RDF data models (see Subsection 3.3.1.2). On the other hand, it would be good to reuse W3C technologies. This issue was resolved by the definition of SPARQL as an independent, new, model-based RDF query language which borrows some elements (operators, regular expressions etc.) from XQuery and XPath.

Before proceeding to discuss SPARQL we should mention that this language has many features which will not be covered here. Our aim is to present a few introductory examples that illustrate the most important characteristics of the language.

The SPARQL language follows the idea of subgraph matching, introduced in Subsection 3.3.4. In our first example we look for those people in our usual knowledge base (see Figure 3.5), who have an employment position.

```
PREFIX s: <http://swexpld.org/util#>
SELECT *                                                                    (3.1)
WHERE { ?person s:position ?position . }
```

In its structure, this SPARQL query resembles closely an RDQL query (see the previous subsection): the `SELECT` and `WHERE` parts correspond to their RDQL counterparts, `PREFIX` serves the same purpose as `USING` in RDQL. The joker character `*` is an abbreviation that selects all the variables in the given graph pattern. The syntax of the graph pattern in the SPARQL language originates from the N3 notation [15] (see Section 2.3).

---

[8] W3C was also involved in the development of an RDF query language (different from SPARQL) where queries can be formulated in a pseudo-natural language. This language is called Metalog [76].

The answer of a SPARQL query engine, such as the ARQ engine in the Jena toolkit [3], may look like the following:

```
-------------------------------------------------------
| person                      | position              |
=======================================================
| <http://.../person#George>  | "Ph.D. student"       |
| <http://.../person#Peter>   | "associate professor" |
-------------------------------------------------------
```

There is a set of functions and operators in SPARQL that can be used for imposing restrictions on the values of the variables in the pattern (so-called *value constraints*). A subset of these functions and operators was taken from the XQuery language (this is an example where SPARQL uses existing technologies). Let us consider a query looking for publications whose title contains the word "logic":

```
PREFIX s: <http://swexpld.org/util#>
SELECT ?x ?title
WHERE
{
  ?x s:publication ?pub .
  ?pub s:title ?title .
  FILTER regex(?title, "logic", "i")
}
```

Here `regex` is a function which returns `TRUE` when the variable `?title` contains the substring `logic`. The third argument of the `regex` function tells the engine that we want a case-insensitive match. Accordingly, the result is the following:

```
-------------------------------------------------------
| x                        | title                    |
=======================================================
| <http://.../person#Peter> | "Logic-based ontology..." |
-------------------------------------------------------
```

SPARQL specifies four different *query result forms*. These forms tell the engine how to present the results of the query. We have already seen the `SELECT` result form, which displays a table containing the appropriate variable substitutions.

When the `CONSTRUCT` query result form is used, a new RDF graph, specified by a graph pattern (a template, in SPARQL terminology) is built. The result is a graph which consists of instantiations of the template for all solutions of the query formulated in the `WHERE` part.[9] In the following example we are looking for the friends of people with a known name and building a graph that states that the `knows` relation also holds between such people.

```
PREFIX s: <http://swexpld.org/util#>
CONSTRUCT { ?x s:knows ?friend }
WHERE {
```

---

[9] The `CONSTRUCT` result form closely resembles the way in which we build structures in the Prolog [68] language.

```
?x s:name ?name .
?x s:hasFriend ?friend . }
```

The result of this query is shown below:

```
@prefix s:      <http://swexpld.org/util#> .
@prefix rdfs    <http://www.w3.org/2000/01/rdf-schema#> .
@prefix rdf:    <http://www.w3.org/1999/02/22-rdf-syntax-ns#> .

<http://swexpld.org/person#Peter>
      s:knows           <http://swexpld.org/person#JC> ;
      s:knows           <http://swexpld.org/person#George> .

<http://swexpld.org/person#George>
      s:knows           <http://swexpld.org/person#Peter> .
```

We can see that the engine returned a complete RDF description in N3 notation containing three RDF statements. CONSTRUCT also allows us to create graphs with blank nodes. More details can be found in the original SPARQL specification [96] and its revisions [49].

There are two other query result forms in SPARQL, DESCRIBE and ASK. The former, similar to CONSTRUCT, returns an RDF graph. This graph contains some (or all) triples in which the selected resource appears in some position, as well as other details. The extent of the information provided depends on the SPARQL query engine. In the following example we look for people born before 1980 and ask for a description of each such person.

```
PREFIX s: <http://swexpld.org/util#>
DESCRIBE ?x
WHERE {
  ?x s:born ?birth .
  FILTER (?birth < 1980) .
}
```

Using the RDF knowledge base of Figure 3.5, the engine may return the following answer:

```
<http://swexpld.org/person#JC>
  s:born     "1979"^^<http://www.w3.org/2001/XMLSchema#int> ;
  s:name     "John Carel" .
```

Here all the information known by the engine about the resource JC is presented in the answer.

Finally, the ASK query-result form can be used simply to check whether a given pattern has a solution (i.e. has a matching subgraph in the RDF knowledge base). The SPARQL engine gives a yes/no answer to such questions. The example below checks whether the knowledge base contains at least one triple involving the property s:salary:

```
PREFIX s: <http://swexpld.org/util#>
ASK {?x p:salary ?salary}
```

This query, if run with respect to the knowledge base in Figure 3.5, will produce a "no" answer.

Exercise 3.11: Write a SPARQL query that enumerates the titles of those publications in Figure 3.5 that appeared after 2000.

3.3.6.2. The SPARQL Protocol

The SPARQL protocol [27] describes the communication between a SPARQL server and its clients. The RDF Net API [84] submission was used by the DAWG as the starting point for the specification. The RDF Net API is a network interface, first proposed in 2003, which provides query and modification capabilities on remote RDF knowledge bases. This network interface was not within the scope of the W3C DAWG working group, but the possibility of extending SPARQL in this direction later was left open. The SPARQL protocol specifies an abstract interface with a single operation. This takes a SPARQL query string as input and returns different kinds of results depending on which *SPARQL result form* was specified in the query. Thus the protocol actually defines the communication that should take place between a client and a remote server capable of answering SPARQL queries.

The SPARQL protocol specifies two bindings, for SOAP and HTTP. These provide the details of the concrete, invokable, version of the operation. For example, Joseki, the RDF server of the Jena toolkit [3], is a HTTP/SOAP-based implementation of the SPARQL protocol.

An example session can be seen below. First, the client sends a normal HTTP GET request to the server, including the URL-encoded representation of a SPARQL query. The client could be a web browser which helps a user to compose a query through a web form (see Subsection 1.1.3):

```
GET /people?query=PREFIX...SELECT...WHERE... HTTP/1.1
Host: sparqldemo.swexpld.org:3312
```

The string in the first line of the message is actually query (3.1) (see Subsection 3.3.6.1). The reply of the SPARQL server contains the following XML document, which is equivalent to the tabular result presented earlier:

```
<?xml version="1.0"?>
<sparql xmlns="http://www.w3.org/2005/sparql-results#">

 <head>
   <variable name="person"/>
   <variable name="position"/>
 </head>

 <results distinct="false" ordered="false">
  <result>
    <binding name="person"><uri>http://...#George</uri></binding>
    <binding name="position"><literal>... student</literal></binding>
    </binding>
  </result>

  <result>
    <binding name="person"><uri>http://...#Peter</uri></binding>
    <binding name="position"><literal>... professor</literal></binding>
```

```
   </binding>
  </result>
 </results>
</sparql>
```

3.3.7. The RDFLan language

The RDFLan language was originally developed by the authors of this book as a Prolog-based [68] RDF query language, to provide one component of the *SINTAGMA* information integration system [12]. The main points of RDFLan are (1) an intuitive syntax based on predicate logic, (2) Prolog execution for answering queries and (3) support for the rules to be used during query execution. RDFLan was first published in Benkő *et al.* [12].

The syntax of RDFLan supports special forms of primitive query, in addition to the generic triple format. When the predicate of a triple is known (i.e. it is non-variable), the triple can be written as predicate(subject, object), which is the usual first-order logic notation. The special case of an *instance query* of the form (x, rdf:type, class) can be written as a single-argument logic predicate: class(x). Some examples of such special primitive queries are:

s:Mammal(??)	– Who are mammals?
p:age(captain,?)	– How old is the captain?
r:publication(?,??)	– Who has which publication?
t:loves(?,jack)	– Who loves Jack?
r:position(?,"professor")	– Who is professor?
s:knows(?,??)	– Who know each other?
r:age(?,23)	– Who is 23 years old?

In composite queries conjunction is denoted by a comma, disjunction by a semicolon and negation by a backslash. RDFLan also automatically supports regular expression matching. The following example selects pages whose title contains the word computer but does not contain the word science.

```
ExternalPage(?),
(d:Title(?,'.*computer.*') , \ d:Title(?,'.*science.*'))
```

A variant of the above query, which looks for either of the same words, is:

```
ExternalPage(?),
(d:Title(?,'.*computer.*') ; d:Title(?,'.*science.*'))
```

As we saw earlier, querying special RDF constructs such as containers or reifications requires proper support from the query language (see Subsection 3.3.5). Supporting these constructs by providing a dedicated notation in the language increases readability and may help in formulating more robust queries. RDFLan provides language constructs for denoting a container, enumerating the elements of a container, obtaining the triple encapsulated by a reified resource etc. The full list of supported features can be found in the RDFLan specification.

In the following example we enumerate the authors of those web pages (in the variable ???) where the creators are given in a bag.

```
Homepage(?), dc:creator(?,bag(??)), rdflan:member(???, ??)
```

Here we have used the built-in `rdflan:member` subquery, whose task is to enumerate the members of a container specified in its second argument.

Like other languages, RDFLan supports the basic arithmetic operations. For example, we can search for people over 70 in an RDF knowledge base, using the query below:

```
Human(?), p:age(?, ??), ?? > 70
```

Last but not least, an interesting and useful feature of RDFLan is its ability to create *rules* and use them during queries. Rules are similar to SQL views, and they allow recursive definition as well.

As an example we may define the *virtual property* `ancestor`, which connects a person with her ancestors, using the following two rules.

```
ancestor(A, B) <--- p:parent(A, B)
ancestor(A, B) <--- p:parent(A, C), ancestor(C, B)
```

According to the definition above, B is the ancestor of A if it is true that either B is a parent of A or that B is an ancestor of a parent of A. This is very similar to how rules are formulated in Prolog.

The predicate defined by this rule can be used in an arbitrary RDFLan query as a subquery. The following example query lists those ancestors of `katie` who are older than 100 years:

```
ancestor(katie, ?), p:age(?, ??), ?? > 100
```

The RDFLan language has several other features. For example, it supports the detection of possible inconsistencies in an RDF knowledge base. More about this is presented in Subsection 3.4.3.

Exercise 3.12: Write an *RDFLan* rule that defines the relation "mother-in-law" using the properties "spouse" and "mother".

3.4. Reasoning during the execution of queries

When RDF queries are being answered, some reasoning may be done to deduce new facts from old ones and the background knowledge. In this section we discuss what kinds of reasoning tasks are needed, and what inference techniques are usable, when an RDF knowledge base is being queried.

There are two possibilities as to which component of query execution should perform these reasoning tasks. The first option is to do this in the query engine implementing the given language. The second option is to delegate the task of reasoning to the component responsible for managing the knowledge base. In this latter approach the knowledge base – in addition to concrete RDF data – also returns "virtual triples" to the query engine. Such triples are inferred from existing triples using background knowledge. The advantage of this second, more widespread, approach is that it is transparent to the query engine: no distinction is made between inferred triples and triples physically present in the RDF description. This is considered to be a nice architectural feature, as it separates reasoning capabilities and query execution.

This separation is useful as it makes possible the use of a query language, such as SPARQL, to query knowledge bases with semantics unknown to the SPARQL engine. This means that the engine is usable even for possibly new knowledge representation languages not available at the time when SPARQL was created. Another advantage is that SPARQL implementations may focus only on the query language itself, making them more compact and easier to write.

The importance of reasoning during the execution of RDF queries was discussed as early as 1988, in a famous paper by R. V. Guha [46]. A variant of the example presented in that paper can be seen in Figure 3.12. In this example we have a normal web page containing a link to a photo. The photo `depicts` a grey dolphin together with the author of the page. To support more sophisticated search engines, the author added RDF information to the photo in the head of the web page. The meta-information states that the file, designated by the URI `http://swexpld.org/dscp001.jpg`, is actually a `Photo` and was created with an

```
<html>
 <head>
 <rdf:RDF
  xmlns:rdf="http://www.w3.org/1999/02/22-rdf-syntax-ns#"
  xmlns:p="http://swexpld.org/util#"
  xmlns:t="http://swexpld.org/animals#>

  <rdf:Description about="http://swexpld.org/dscp001.jpg">
   <rdf:type rdf:resource="http://.../utils#Photo" />
   <p:date>2007-02-13</p:date>
   <p:resolution>1600*1200</p:resolution>
   <p:depicts>
    <t:Dolphin>
     <p:colour rdf:resource="http://swexpld.org/util#grey"/>
     <p:gender rdf:resource="http://swexpld.org/util#male"/>
    </t:Dolphin>
   </p:depicts>
   <p:depicts rdf:resource=
    "http://freemail.org/~doe/#about" />
  </rdf:Description>

 </rdf:RDF>
 </head>
 <body>
   <p>Hi all!</p>
   <img src="dscp001.jpg" width="400" height="240"/>...
 </body>
</html>
```

Figure 3.12. A photo with a grey dolphin on it.

acceptable resolution not long ago. It also states that someone can be seen on the photo who is identified by the URI `http://freemail.org/~doe/#about`. The photo also `depicts` "something" that is a `male Dolphin` with `grey colour`.

Using these pieces of RDF meta-information, a search engine could retrieve this photo as a hit for a question looking for pictures with dolphins. Moreover, the search phrase could even contain additional restrictions on the resolution and/or the date of creation as well.

Without reasoning, however, we would not be able to conclude that the photo is a good match for queries looking for photos containing a `SeaMammal`. For this, we need the straightforward piece of background knowledge that dolphins are sea mammals. More formally we need to know that dolphins form a subclass of sea mammals, so that every possible dolphin instance is also an instance of the class of sea mammals.

Considering a hierarchy of classes is actually the simplest case of inference. In Section 2.6 we discussed what other reasoning possibilities RDF schemas offer. These include utilising the property hierarchies and also the property restrictions. Using the latter we can, for example, conclude that something is an animal if we know that it has a `gender`.

We now describe the two basic types of RDF reasoning, schema- and data-level inferences. We also discuss several issues related to the consistency checking of RDF sources.

Before proceeding, however, let us note that in Chapter 8 we will introduce an extension of the RDF schemas, the OWL ontology language [7]. Fully exploiting the meaning of OWL descriptions requires much more sophisticated reasoning than that needed for RDF schemas. Reasoners working on OWL descriptions can be so complex that implementing them might easily turn out to be a larger task than building a query engine. This is another reason why the separation of query and reasoning is a good thing to achieve. The mathematical background of OWL reasoning tasks is discussed in Chapters 5 and 7.

3.4.1. Reasoning using schemas

Let us first consider what type of reasoning can be done on RDF schemas alone, in the absence of ordinary RDF (data) triples. Our goal here is to simplify certain schema constructs or infer new ones using the semantics of RDF schemas.

In Subsection 2.6.5 we mentioned that if more than one class is supplied as the `rdfs:domain` (or the `rdfs:range`) of a property then the effective domain (range) restriction of this property is defined as the intersection of the given classes. We presented there an example property called `maiden_name`, which is applicable to individuals who are instances of both the `Person` and `Female` classes. This scenario is represented by an RDF graph containing a node for the property `maiden_name` and two outgoing edges labelled `rdfs:domain`.

Usually, RDF knowledge bases are distributed, i.e. composed of several RDF fragments located in different places. One such fragment may state that the `rdfs:domain` of a given property is the class A. On processing another fragment, we might well find that the domain of this property is also restricted to class B. As an example, let us consider the following restrictions on the property `knows`:

```
<rdf:Property rdf:ID="knows">
  <rdfs:domain rdf:resource="#Human"/>                    (3.2)
  <rdfs:domain rdf:resource="#Animal"/>
</rdf:Property>
```

Here we state that the domain of knows is a subset of both the classes Human and Animal. However, if the knowledge base contains the statement "Human is a subclass of Animal" then we may simply remove the weaker of the two restrictions above, resulting in:

```
<rdf:Property rdf:ID="knows">
  <rdfs:domain rdf:resource="#Human"/>
</rdf:Property>
```

An obvious advantage of this simplification is that it helps to reduce the size of the RDF graph.

Of course, if the two classes are not above each other in the class hierarchy then we cannot apply this kind of simplification. For example, we should preserve the multiple restrictions for the maiden_name property, as neither of the classes Person and Female is the descendant of the other in the class hierarchy (an animal can also be female, for example). Another example may be a property with range restriction including classes Tall and Blonde.

A different kind of schema reasoning is based on the features of the subproperty hierarchy. Namely, if a subproperty holds between two resources then the parent property also holds between them. For example, if we know that two people are friends, we can be sure that they know each other (provided that the property hasFriend is a subproperty of knows). This means that the restrictions on the domain and range of a property are inherited by the descendant properties. This leads to the second case of schema-level reasoning: in the presence of a property restriction we should infer a new restriction for each of its subproperties. It should also be noted that a property can have multiple parent properties and so may inherit multiple restrictions. This may lead to RDF schema constructs similar to (3.2), for which the simplification technique can be applied.

The third type of schema-level reasoning utilises the fact that the RDF schema constructs rdfs:subClassOf and rdfs:subPropertyOf are transitive. Using this, for example, if we have a schema containing that the class Man is a subclass of Human and that Human, in turn, is a subclass of Animal, we can conclude that men are animals.

3.4.2. Instance-level reasoning

We now continue with a discussion of how RDF schema information can contribute to answering instance-level queries, such as "whose friend is Bob?". This process, called *instance-level reasoning*, can be classified according to the kind of RDF schema component used: (1) class hierarchies, (2) property hierarchies or (3) property restrictions.

Utilising class hierarchies is probably the most common way of reasoning. If we are looking for humans in an RDF source (namely, we want to enumerate the resources that are instances of the class Human), we would definitely want to include those who are known to be mothers. To do this, we need the knowledge that the class Mother is a subclass of the class Human, in other words, that every mother is also a human. It may even be that this is not given explicitly in the schema, as we only know that Mother is a subclass of Woman and that Woman is a subclass of Human.

Property hierarchies can be used for reasoning in a similar way to class hierarchies. Here, if the property hasFriend is a subproperty of the property knows then in every case where the former holds between two resources, the latter holds as well. Using this, if we are looking for those whom Bob knows then we should enumerate those people who are explicitly described only as friends of Bob.

We may also use the transitivity of the subclass and subproperty relations when there are multiple levels in the class or property hierarchy. For example, if we are to enumerate those people whom Bob knows then it is obvious that we should also list his best friends. To achieve this, the RDF schema should include the background knowledge that the property `hasBestFriend` is a subproperty of `hasFriend`.

Beyond class and property hierarchies, the domain and range restrictions can also be used to do reasoning. Here, we can infer that a resource that appears on the left- or right-hand side of a specific property instance has to belong to the class specified in the domain or range restriction. As an example, let us consider the property `hasAuthor`, which connects books with humans (these domain and range restrictions could actually be arrived at using some reasoning; see Subsection 3.4.1):

```
<rdf:Property rdf:ID="hasAuthor">
   <rdfs:domain rdf:resource="#Book"/>
   <rdfs:range rdf:resource="#Human"/>
</rdf:Property>
```

Now, given an RDF statement that the `hasAuthor` property of a certain *entity* is someone who is called Elaine Cunningham, two things can be inferred. On the one hand, it can be concluded that the *entity* in question is an instance of the class `Book`. This effectively results in creating a new (virtual) edge in the RDF graph, labelled `rdf:type`. On the other hand, we can deduce that Elaine Cunningham is a human: in other words, she is an instance of the class `Human`. This also results in a new virtual triple.

It may well be that specific pieces of information were already known about the resource in question. For example, if we already knew that Elaine Cunningham is a `Woman` then the range reasoning above does not yield any new information (assuming that we know that every woman is a human). Normally, the information that Elaine Cunningham is a human is not even worth storing (cf. the simplification described in Subsection 3.4.1). However, if nothing is known about the type of Elaine Cunningham or if we know something that is less specific or is of a "different" nature (e.g. Elaine Cunningham is `Blonde`) then we have to add a new edge to the RDF graph.

It can also happen that multiple domain or range restrictions belong to a property. For example, we can state that if someone is an author then she is human and studious as well:

```
<rdf:Property rdf:ID="hasAuthor">
   <rdfs:domain rdf:resource="#Book"/>
   <rdfs:range rdf:resource="#Human"/>
   <rdfs:range rdf:resource="#Studious"/>
</rdf:Property>
```

In this case, when using the `hasAuthor` property the resource on the right-hand side is inferred to be an instance of both classes.

It is often the case that the instance-level reasoning techniques can be combined. For example, let us consider a query that is looking for someone who knows a human. A resource can be inferred to be an answer to this query, for example, if it has a friend who is deduced to be a woman because she has a husband (i.e. she has an outgoing edge labelled with the `hasHusband` property). Here we have used all the techniques described above.

Exercise 3.13: Formalise the above example by writing down all the RDF and RDF schema triples involved (some of these can be found on the preceding pages). Next, try to perform schema- and instance-level reasoning on these triples, in as many ways as possible, and write down the resulting triples.

3.4.3. Detecting inconsistencies in RDF sources

The RDF framework does not have a construct for stating that two classes are disjoint, i.e. that there is no individual that is an instance of both classes. We may, of course, define our own RDF property, called `p:disjoint` for example. Then we can use this property as a predicate in triples whose subjects and objects are URIs identifying two classes. The RDF recommendation, however, simply does not define such a property, which means we cannot expect that the RDF applications, in general, will "understand" the meaning of triples using our `p:disjoint`.[10]

This feature of RDF schema is interesting, because without the notion of disjointness one is unable to prove that an RDF description contains contradictions. We note that the lack of disjointness actually goes against the intention of the RDF specification, as it explicitly mentions inconsistency detection as a possible advantage of RDF Schema.

Let us consider the following scenario. There are two classes, `Dog` and `Human`, and the property `hasSpouse`. The latter connects humans with humans, so both its `rdfs:domain` and `rdfs:range` are people. Furthermore, we know that `Kate` is human and `Sparky` is a dog. Having said that, the RDF triple stating that `Kate hasSpouse Sparky` seems to be a nonsense. How could a dog be the spouse of Kate?

Unfortunately, there is no chance of pinpointing this piece of nonsense if one has no notion of disjointness, i.e. if one cannot state that the classes `Human` and `Dog` do not share instances. After all, if Sparky had been known to be an instance of `Man` or `Tall` then there would be no problem at all. Without disjointness, however, we cannot distinguish a `Man` instance from a `Dog` instance.

This means that we cannot really warn the user that some RDF triples do not make much sense; actually, one might even say this is not a big problem and we should not care much about it. Unfortunately, this is not the end of the story. We have already seen that with the help of the `rdfs:range` restriction we can do instance-level reasoning. In our scenario this may result in concluding that `Sparky` is the instance of the class `Human`. In other words, when someone is looking for a person, she will receive a dog as an answer!

Anomalies can emerge during schema-level reasoning also. For example, when handling property inheritance, we could end up having more than one class as a domain or range (see Subsection 3.4.1). Most of the time this causes no problem, as we may either

---

[10] Using the OWL language, which is an extension of the RDF schema language, the disjointness of classes can be expressed. OWL is described in Chapter 8.

apply simplification (Human and Woman) or leave multiple classes as they are (Tall and Blonde). Sometimes, however, we arrive at disjoint classes, such as Human and Dog. A specific property having these classes as a domain restriction can be applied only to resources that are dogs and humans at the same time. In practice this signals a modelling error, i.e. it is meaningless to use this property in an RDF triple. Again, such an error cannot be pinpointed as RDF has no notion of disjointness.

An option for solving this problem, called *implicit disjointness*, was proposed by the authors of this book in connection with the RDFLan query engine [12]. This involves assuming that if certain conditions hold two classes should be considered disjoint. If this assumption leads to a contradiction, a warning message is issued.

In RDFLan we used the following single condition for implicit disjointness: two classes are disjoint if neither is the descendant of the other in the class hierarchy. In other words, neither can be reached from the other by navigating only through rdfs:subClassOf edges in the RDF graph.

The simplest example of implicit disjointness is to consider the children of a node in the RDF class hierarchy as pairwise disjoint. In the case of the usual hierarchy of living things, dogs and humans are the children of the class Animal, i.e. they are considered to be disjoint. The same holds for men and women as well as for men and dogs etc. However, some individual could easily be human and animal or man and animal at the same time, as these classes are not implicitly disjoint.

Thus it should be noted that assuming this kind of disjointness is not always right. For example, neither of the classes Tall and Human is the descendant of the other (it is not true that every human is tall or that every tall thing is a human), and it is quite feasible that we would like to state that someone is a human and tall at the same time. Our proposal would generate a false alarm in these cases.

We also note that our assumption about disjointness is actually applied to the class diagrams in the widespread modelling language UML [108]. As a matter of fact, the programming language Java also has the notion of *unrelated classes* with a definition similar to that above.

The checking of implicit disjointness is supported in the implementation of RDFLan. The user of RDFLan can ask the system to enumerate those instances in the RDF knowledge base whose type is inconsistent, i.e. which belong to disjoint classes. The RDFLan engine also marks those RDF triples where the usage of the RDF property does not match the schema. This is the case, for example, when a dog is given on the right-hand side of the hasSpouse property. We can also obtain those properties where the domain or range restriction contains an intersection of disjoint classes.

Moreover, the RDFLan implementation recognises RDF properties which break the principle that a subproperty can only narrow the constraints of its parents. This is important, since if a child property expands the inherited range then a problematic situation may occur. For example, imagine that the range of the property knows is the class Human, while the range of the property hasFriend is the class Animal (note that these two classes are not even implicitly disjoint). Then, we can state that Bob hasFriend Willy the dolphin (this is perfectly all right as we expected an animal here and got a dolphin). Even so, we are in trouble because Bob should also know Willy according to the property hierarchy, but Bob, by definition, may only know humans. However, dolphins and humans are implicitly disjoint.

3.5. Optimising RDF queries

In this section we discuss some query optimisation techniques. We will demonstrate these ideas using the RDFLan query language, but everything we say is applicable to any other model-based RDF query language. We first discuss various optimisation techniques and then present the pseudo-code of the algorithm used in the RDFLan implementation.

In the case of a generic database system the task of the query engine is to translate the queries (usually formulated in a high-level language) into a series of simple, consecutive, commands. Often the most difficult task of a query engine is query optimisation, i.e. the creation of a suitable *execution plan*. The execution plan is a sequence of queries to the underlying storage system that will answer the original query.

As in querying generic databases, an RDF query engine should also support some kind of query optimisation, i.e. it should minimise the number of times the engine accesses the knowledge base. To do this, we should first investigate how RDF queries are structured. Here we focus our attention on the model-based approach, where complex queries are built from primitive queries using the "and" logical connective (see Subsection 3.3.4). In this section we investigate how we should *reorder* the original query in order to ensure efficient execution.

We now introduce the basic idea of optimisation and then show what difficulties emerge when we try to implement it. We discuss these specific problems and present their partial or complete solution.

3.5.1. Initial strategy

First let us consider an example which shows how the order in which subqueries are made can affect the efficiency of execution. Let us consider the task of looking for photos together with the device with which they were made. If there are only a few photos in the knowledge base, while the number of devices is large, it is definitely worth enumerating the photos first and then determining the corresponding devices. Using this observation one may arrive at a strategy – used fairly widely – that subqueries should be ordered according to the number of answers they produce: the subquery with the least number of solutions comes first, then that with the second least number of solutions and so on.

Unfortunately, this is not a trivial task as often we can only guess how many solutions a subquery will produce, because reasoning can be used in answering the subquery, thus producing further solutions in addition to those explicitly stored in the knowledge base. Furthermore, the number of solutions produced by a subquery depends on which variables are known when it is executed. This is greatly influenced by where the given subquery is located relative to other subqueries. This phenomenon is called *dynamic dependence* and is discussed in more detail below.

3.5.2. Dynamic dependence

Let us imagine a scenario where we have photo and video materials, collectively referred to as multimedia information. Figure 3.13 depicts some background knowledge in this area, formalised using RDF schema. Thus, using RDF terminology, we say that, for example, an instance of the class Photo is also an instance of the class Multimedia. Furthermore, we

```
<rdf:RDF
    ...
  <rdfs:Class rdf:ID="Multimedia">
    <rdfs:comment>Generic multimedia</rdfs:comment>
  </rdfs:Class>

  <rdfs:Class rdf:ID="Photo">
    <rdfs:label>Photo</rdfs:comment>
    <rdfs:subClassOf rdf:resource="#Multimedia"/>
  </rdfs:Class>

  <rdfs:Class rdf:ID="Video">
    <rdfs:comment>Videos</rdfs:comment>
    <rdfs:subClassOf rdf:resource="#Multimedia"/>
  </rdfs:Class>

  <rdf:Property rdf:ID="isRecordedBy">
    <rdfs:domain rdf:resource="#Multimedia"/>
    <rdfs:range rdf:resource="#Device"/>
  </rdf:Property>
    ...
</rdf:RDF>
```

Figure 3.13. An RDF schema used for demonstrating dynamic dependences.

have a class called `Device`, and the properties `hasBrand` and `isRecordedBy` (a device may have a brand, a piece of multimedia information is recorded by a given device).

Consider the following query where, for readability, variables are denoted by capital letters, rather than the usual ?, ??, … notation. We are looking for a photo (A) which was made by a device B of brand C:

$$p:Photo(A), \quad p:isRecordedBy(A,B), \quad p:hasBrand(B,C) \qquad (3.3)$$

We expect this query to list all substitutions of the three variables A, B and C, so that A is a photo, B is the device using which the given photo was recorded while C is the brand of the device.

Correspondingly, the query can give the following answer:

```
A = dsc0001.jpg
B = im_resource34
C = Sony
```

In this world, a photo uniquely determines the device with which it was made. Similarly, a device belongs to a unique brand. These are quite natural assumptions. Accordingly, if the number of the photos in our knowledge database is n then the above query returns exactly n different solutions. The important question now is how many times do we need to turn to the RDF knowledge base to answer the above RDFLan query?

Subquery	No subst.	A subst.	B subst.
p:Photo(A)	5	1	—
p:hasBrand(A,B)	6	1	1
p:isRecordedBy(A,B)	10	1	1.67

Table 3.1.   The number of results of subqueries (estimated).

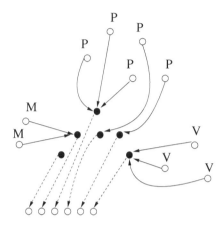

Figure 3.14.   Photos, videos and tools.

To calculate this, we need information about how many times specific subqueries may succeed. We present an example knowledge base in Figure 3.14 and the corresponding statistics in tabular form in Table 3.1.

In Figure 3.14, P denotes photos, V denotes videos and M denotes other types of multimedia resource. The broken lines correspond to the property p:hasBrand and the solid lines to the property p:isRecordedBy. We can see from the figure that, for example, all the video materials were recorded by the same device.

In the table, the column *No subst.* gives the number of solutions for each subquery, under the assumption that no variable is known at invocation time. The other two columns, *A subst.* and *B subst.*, list the number of solutions when variable A or variable B respectively is substituted. These columns contain estimations, as the exact number of solutions normally depends on the actual value of the variable. From the table we can see that the primitive query p:Photo(A) succeeds five times: in other words, the knowledge base contains five photographs. The subquery p:isRecordedBy(A,B) has 10 different solutions (which allows us to conclude that there are videos or other unknown multimedia resources in the knowledge base).

The column *A subst.* contains the number 1 for each subquery. This means that, for example, if the device is given then the corresponding brand can be determined unambiguously. In our world it is also true that each device belongs to a different brand (this can be seen from column *B subst.*, row 2).

We can also see in Table 3.1 that the property p:isRecordedBy(A, B) produces, on average, around two solutions if B is given. This figure is actually calculated as the average of the values 0, 2, 3, 1, 1, and 3. These values, in turn, come from Figure 3.14: that is, they correspond to the number of *incoming* continuous arrows, for each device (read from left to right).

It may seem feasible to order the subqueries according to the number of solutions, with no substitutions assumed (column 1 of Table 3.1). This results in the query:

```
p:Photo(A), p:hasBrand(B,C), p:isRecordedBy(A,B)
```

Let us calculate how many knowledge base requests this generates, i.e. how many times we need to access the knowledge base to answer primitive queries. We have to query the knowledge base five times in order to enumerate the solutions for p:Photo(A). For each photo, p:hasBrand(B,C) has six solutions (see the first column of Table 3.1). This means that we have accessed the knowledge base $5 + 5 * 6 = 35$ times. Finally, as variables A and B are already known, we have simply to check whether the triple p:isRecordedBy(A,B) is in the knowledge base. Actually, we have to do this 30 times, which gives us a final result of 65 knowledge base accesses.

We can lower the number of requests drastically if we notice that both isRecordedBy and hasBrand are functional properties, i.e. once their first argument is known, they return a single solution (see the second column of Table 3.1). If we order the subqueries according to this then we will get back to our query formulation (3.3).

Exercise 3.14: Calculate how many knowledge-base requests query (3.3) actually generates.

3.5.3. Estimating the number of solutions

In our example above we used the values in Table 3.1 for calculating the overall cost of a given query. On the basis of these calculations we can finally decide which query plan to choose in order to have optimal execution. The question is, how easily can we derive the values in such a table?

We have already mentioned that in certain cases we can only estimate values (see the third row in the column *B subst.*). The real difficulty, however, comes from the fact that it is not easy to determine the number of solutions even in simple cases, such as that of counting the multimedia resources in our example knowledge base.

Let us first deal with the even simpler case of photos. Here, our first try could be to count those nodes in the RDF graph which have an outgoing edge labelled with rdf:type and having a resource of the type p:Photo at its right-hand end. To do this we can execute the query p:Photo(A), which enumerates the photos, and then simply count the solutions.

This would seem to solve our problem, provided that sometimes we rerun the query to refresh the count, as the underlying RDF knowledge base may change over time. However, we should also take into account the fact that answering a query like this may require reasoning (see Subsection 3.4.2).

For example, if we would like to determine the number of multimedia resources in the knowledge base shown in Figure 3.14 then we cannot be satisfied with the two explicit solutions. From the corresponding RDF schema we know that photos and videos are also multimedia resources so we should also count these, and finally we would conclude that the p:Multimedia(A) subquery actually has 10 solutions.

Reasoning may be applied not only when enumerating class instances but also in queries involving properties. For instance, to obtain the number of solutions of the subquery `t:knows(A,B)` we should also consider the background knowledge that friends know each other.

All in all, to fill our table precisely we need reasoning. Luckily, as already mentioned in Section 3.4, this is usually performed by the software component managing the RDF knowledge base itself. Nevertheless, it needs to be considered that in the case of large knowledge bases it may not be feasible to execute every possible instance query and property query in order to collect statistics.

The `RDFLan` implementation works with a table, that similar to that in Table 3.1, which is filled in and refined dynamically during execution. This process is described now.

Below we distinguish between four types of estimate stored in the table for query optimisation. We will refer to these as estimates of type 1, type 2 etc.

(1) *The number of instances:* This value determines how many instances a class has in the given RDF knowledge base. Examples include the number of solutions for the classes `p:Photo`, `t:Human` or `z:Building`.

(2) *The number of property instances* (if both subject and object are unknown): This gives the number of times a specific property is used in instance-level RDF triples. For example, for the property `t:likes`, this value tells us the number of pairs in the knowledge base whose first member likes the second (such as `Bob likes Mary`).

(3) *The number of property instances* (if the subject is given): This value is an estimation telling us the average number of objects to which we may navigate via the given property, if the subject is given. For example, for the property `t:likes`, we first collect all the triples involving this property. Then we group the triples according to the subject. Next, we count how many individuals each distinct subjects `likes` and calculate the average of these counts for all subjects (cf. the column *A subst.* of Table 3.1).

(4) *The number of property instances* (if the object is given): This value is an estimation telling us the average number of subjects from which it is possible to navigate, via the given property, to somewhere else. Obviously this is different from an estimate of type 3 (cf. the last two columns of Table 3.1).

Note that by using average counts for types 3 and 4 we are basing our query ordering on estimates. At query optimisation time we are not able to determine the actual variable substitutions, so we use an estimate of the number of solutions. For example, imagine a world where only one of the photos was made by the first camera, three were made by the second and two were made by the third. Here, an estimation of type 4, for the property `p:isRecordedBy`, would be calculated as $(1+3+2)/3 = 2$. This gives a good approximation of the number of solutions no matter which camera actually appears in the given query.

3.5.4. The optimisation algorithm

We now present a simple optimisation algorithm, based on the estimation table described above, which is actually used in the implementation of `RDFLan` [12].

At the beginning we select the subquery which has the least number of solutions. This will be the first element of the optimised RDF query. Next, we enter a loop: we select the subquery with the least number of solutions at that point, and so on.

The key question is how the number of solutions is determined for a given subquery. To calculate this, we examine how many solutions a subquery would have if it were the next subquery in the final query plan. We keep track of which variables are substituted at the given point and, on this basis, we use the appropriate type of estimate. We distinguish three cases, depending on whether the subquery

(1) is fully instantiated (e.g. `p:loves(kate,jack)` or `p:Human(kate)`) or

(2) has two uninstantiated variables (e.g. `p:loves(A,B)`) or

(3) has a single uninstantiated variable (e.g. `p:loves(A,jack)`, `p:loves(kate,B)` or `p:Human(C)`)

If a subquery does not have any variables then it has at most one solution. If it has two uninstantiated variables then we use an estimate of type 2, from the table. Finally, if there is a single variable in the subquery then (depending on the type of query and the position of the variable) we use an estimate of the type 1, 3 or 4.

If our language supports arithmetic operators ($>, <, =<, >=$), invocations of these should appear at the first possible place in the query plan, that is, the first position where all their variables are instantiated and so can be evaluated.

Note that the estimation table used here is built during query execution. When estimates for a certain query are not yet available, an optimisation procedure will use some fixed default assumptions, which may result in suboptimal query execution. However, when the query is run, the appropriate counts are determined and the estimation table is filled in for the given primitive query. Thus subsequent query optimisations will be able to use the correct estimates.

3.6. Summary

At the beginning of this chapter we summarised the approaches for putting RDF-based meta-information on the web in such a way that search engines can find it. Following this, we introduced briefly a few development tools for the handling of RDF sources. The rest of the chapter dealt with RDF queries. We introduced the basic types of query engine, surveyed the reasoning tasks that arise during the queries and showed a possible way of query optimisation. In the following we summarise the most important points in the chapter.

■ Although RDF sources can be used independently of the web it is a natural requirement that search engines should also have access to them. The reason for this is that with the help of metadata provided by the RDF, search engines can give more intelligent replies to users' queries. The most obvious solution is to leave the gathering of meta-information to crawlers, which are continuously visiting the web pages anyway.

Since both RDF descriptions and XHTML documents are written in XML, the idea of *embedding RDF descriptions in web pages* naturally arises. This can be done in several ways. The head of the page would seem to be a good a choice, since search engines are almost certain to process the heads of the pages to be indexed. With a little transformation of the RDF descriptions, browsers can be prevented from displaying the contents of the

RDF elements. The disadvantage of this solution is that a web page created in this way will not be a valid XHTML document.

According to another scheme, we do not associate meta-information with a web page by making it part of the page but by putting a *link* on the page that points to the metadata. The crawlers will follow this link and, finally, reach a real RDF source. The suitable location of the link is the head of the page, where we can use the `<link>` element. This is a clear way to signal that, at the given address, meta-information can be found in RDF/XML format. Additionally to this, other physical representations of the metadata may be given as an alternative option.

- Our next topic was the *parsing and processing of RDF sources*. Tools exist for most programming languages which can perform this task. For the Java language we can use the Jena toolkit, for C the Raptor parser etc. Declarative languages also have suitable support: the Semantic Web library of SWI Prolog contains RDF support, while for the LISP language the Wilbur toolkit can be used.

- One possible way of making queries on RDF sources is to use *XML query languages*. Such a query language is *XQuery*, which is a strongly typed functional language augmented with *XPath path expressions*. An XPath path expression pinpoints an XML element, or an attribute, in a given XML document. By the use of such path expressions and the XQuery itself, complex queries can be formulated.

  In the case of RDF sources, the use of XML query languages is restricted, since XML is only one possible physical representation of an RDF graph. Moreover, an RDF model may be represented in the form of several different RDF/XML descriptions: thus, answering a given query may require various XML queries to be made. Therefore, it is preferable to use query languages which work on the basis of the logical model of the RDF.

- The early RDF query languages had a *database-oriented* approach to RDF sources. A common feature of these was that using them required exact awareness of the structure of the sources. This is similar to an SQL query, where it is necessary to know what tables and columns are in the database. A good example of such languages is *RDF Query Specification*. The basic idea of this language is that the allowed queries, which are RDF descriptions themselves, create RDF containers from RDF containers. The content of the resulting container will be a subset of the initial container; in the extreme case, the resulting container may be empty. The queries specify different filtering conditions, which select certain elements from the given container.

- Another large group of query engines works on the basis of the *RDF data model*. In this model-based approach the queries themselves are *directed labelled graphs* which *may contain variables*. A query of this type is often called a *graph pattern*. The query must always relate to an *RDF knowledge base*. The answer is a *subgraph* of the knowledge base which matches the query, possibly after variable substitution(s). Accordingly, the answer itself is an RDF knowledge base, which thus may be targeted by a further query. It is also conceivable that there is more than one answer that satisfies a given query. In this case the query engine is expected to list such answers.

- A simple graph pattern consists of two nodes and an edge between them, where the labels on the edge and on the nodes may be variables. Such primitive queries can be put together into complex graph patterns by connecting them with AND relations and using shared variables. Since more than one answer is possible for each subquery, querying complex patterns requires us to traverse a *search space* with, for example, depth-first search.

- A widely used model-based query language is *RDQL*. In spite of not being database-oriented, this language has an SQL-like syntax. In the SELECT part of the query, users can list the variables whose values they would like to know. The FROM clause serves for selecting the RDF sources to which the query relates. In the WHERE section we can specify the complex graph pattern that is the basis of the actual search. The AND clause can be used to impose restrictions on the variables. The RDQL language can be criticised for treating the RDF knowledge base purely as a graph; for example, it does not attribute any meaning to the specific edge labels. Accordingly, the handling of complex RDF constructions, for example, instances, reified statements or containers, is often rather clumsy.

- Another model-based query language is *SPARQL*, which became a W3C recommendation in January 2008.

- As our last example of query languages, we introduced the basics of the *RDFLan* language, which allows us to specify certain primitive queries more simply. With the help of an *instance query*, instances of a given class can be queried without the use of the <rdf:type> property. A *property query* can be used if the user wants to query an RDF statement where the predicate is given. In this case the subject and the object may be specified as well, but this is not obligatory. The RDFLan language natively (i.e. without the need for any extension) supports the built-in RDF constructions, for example, the containers and the reified statements. This language also supports the definition of so-called *rules*, which are constructs that resemble SQL views and also allow recursive definitions.

- During the execution of RDF queries there is often a need for certain kinds of *reasoning*. A reasoning ability can be built into the implementation of the query language, but it is more often provided within the RDF knowledge base. A knowledge base of this kind may show nodes and edges which are not present in the original graph.

  Certain types of reasoning can already be performed when processing the *schema information*. Multiple restrictions on the domain and the range of a property can often be simplified. For example, if we know that something is, at the same time, a musical instrument and a drum, then we can conclude that it is simply a drum. Inferences of this kind increase efficiency but have no other merit. There is another kind of reasoning, of more use, which is based on the following: if a subproperty holds between two resources then the parent properties also hold between the same two resources. Thus, all the restrictions on the domain and range of a property will be inherited by the descendants of the property. For example, if the domain is not specified for a given property then the application can infer it from knowledge relating to the parent properties.

  In the course of instance-level queries, so-called *data inference* can be made, exploiting schema information. There are different kinds of data inference, depending on which RDF construction plays a role in them. In the simplest case, the class or property hierarchy can be used in a query retrieval. A more complex kind of inference occurs when, for example, a resource is deduced to belong to a class because it occurs on the left- or right-hand side of a property whose domain or range is restricted by the schema.

- Discovery of *contradictions* is an issue closely connected to reasoning. In the case of RDF descriptions, contradictions can be examined at both the data and schema levels. The RDF framework does not allow us to state that two classes are disjoint, i.e. that there is no instance which belongs to both classes. Without this, however, there is no possibility of detecting contradictions in the RDF descriptions. Owing to this lack of disjointness inferences can lead to strange results, which differ greatly from those expected. A solution to these problems may be the introduction of the notion of *implicit disjointness*, where it is supposed that any two classes are disjoint if neither is a descendant of the other. This assumption can be found in other modelling languages as well. For example, the UML language imposes a similar restriction on class diagrams. Such implicit disjointness is used in the RDFLan implementation, which gives the possibility of discovering "suspicious" statements at both schema and data level.

- The last section of the chapter dealt with the *optimisation* of RDF queries. We showed a strategy in which the subqueries, i.e. the simple graph patterns, are sorted by number of solutions, in ascending order. The problem is that the number of solutions for a subquery may depend not only on the subquery itself but also on its relation to other subqueries. Even for a single query, because of the solutions involving inference it is not easy to determine this number. The recommended method is to store the estimated number of solutions for each subquery in a table which is continually updated during execution.

Part II

Ontologies and logics

Chapter 4

Description Logic

In this chapter we discuss the family of description logic (DL) languages. Following an introduction in Section 4.1, we present informally the most important language elements of Description Logic (Section 4.2). Next, we give the exact syntax and semantics of each language (Sections 4.3–4.5). Section 4.6 gives an overview of reasoning tasks for Description Logic while Section 4.7 deals with the simplification of reasoning tasks. Section 4.8 introduces the so-called assertion boxes (ABoxes). In Section 4.9 we explain the links between Description Logic and first-order logic, while Section 4.10 gives an overview of advanced features of DL languages.

In the present chapter and the rest of the book we follow a common notation: names in DL formulae are typeset using the grotesque font.

4.1. Introduction

Description Logic allows us to build a mathematical model describing the notions used in a specific area of interest, or in common knowledge [4]. Description Logic deals with *concepts* representing sets of individuals: for instance the concept "human" describes the set of all human beings. Furthermore, one can also describe *relationships* between individuals. In Description Logic, as in RDF, only binary (i.e. two-argument)[1] relationships can be used, which here are referred to as *roles*. For instance, the role "has child" holds between a parent and a child individual.

Description logic concepts are equivalent to RDF classes, whereas roles correspond to properties in RDF. Description Logic provides the mathematical formalism for building heavyweight ontologies and thus serve as the basis of the Web Ontology Language OWL (Chapter 8).

An important aspect of Description Logic is that it allows the construction of *composite concepts* from so-called atomic concepts and roles. For instance, the composite

---

[1] Of course, a DL concept can also be viewed as a "degenerate" unary relation.

concept "mother" can be described using the following *concept expression* (shown here in a non-formal notation):

"human and female and has a child".

In the example above "human" and "female" are atomic concepts referring to appropriate classes of individuals (objects). They are joined by the logical connective "and", which creates the intersection of these two classes. The third part of this concept expression describes the condition that a mother has a child, i.e. at least one individual connected to her through the "has child" role.

Why is it worth introducing a concept by defining it in terms of other concepts and relations? In this way we can describe our knowledge formally, so that it can be used by computers, e.g. in web search. For example, if the concept "mother" is defined as above, then a computer might be able to deduce that "Eve is a mother" if it knows that "Eve is a human", "Eve is female" and "Eve has a child Abel".

It is important to note that two different statement types are used in this deduction:

- the definition of the concept "mother", which assigns a meaning to the given word, and

- the specific knowledge about some named individuals (for instance "Eve has a child Abel").

A statement of the first type is called a *terminological axiom*, using which we can define new concepts and build a terminological system. A statement of the second type, which provides factual knowledge, is called an *assertion*.

Figure 4.1 shows a DL reasoning engine, together with its inputs and outputs. In the top part we see a *knowledge base*, which is a collection of statements to reason about. A knowledge base can be divided into two parts: the part that contains terminological axioms is called the *terminological box*, or *TBox*, while the part containing assertions is called the *assertion box*, or *ABox*. In the bottom left part of the figure we show example questions that can be submitted to the reasoning engine. For instance, we might ask it to enumerate the *instances* of a given concept, i.e. which individuals belong to the given concept ("Who are known to be mothers?"), or to enumerate the concepts to which a given individual belongs ("What is Eve?").

The reasoning process outlined in Figure 4.1 needs both the TBox and the ABox. However, important questions can be asked from a DL reasoning engine based on a TBox alone. Figure 4.2 shows some examples of these. Question (1) asks whether the concept "mother" is *satisfiable*. A concept is called *unsatisfiable* if it cannot have any instances. Obviously, defining an unsatisfiable concept is a modelling error.

Subsequent questions, (2)–(4), ask about the relationship of two concepts:

- concept subsumption (is a concept guaranteed to be a subset of another?): "Are all mothers parents?", "Are all parents men?";

- disjointness or overlap of concepts (is the intersection of two concepts empty?): "Can a mother be a man?".

Such questions can be useful for checking whether the created model satisfies our expectations (such as that every mother must also be a parent). If these are not met, this again indicates a modelling error.

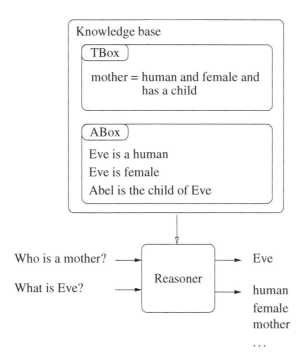

Figure 4.1. The process of reasoning in a description logic engine.

Question (5), the last in Figure 4.2, requires a complex task to be performed by the reasoning engine: the building of a hierarchy of the concepts present in the given TBox. This corresponds to a directed graph, the nodes of which are labelled with concepts while the edges denote concept inclusions. In the present example the hierarchy includes knowledge such as "all women are human" and "mothers are both parents and women". The task of building the concept hierarchy is sometimes called *TBox classification*.

The concept hierarchy normally includes all named concepts that occur in the TBox. For the sake of brevity we have omitted the concept "female" from the hierarchy shown in Figure 4.2.

Exercise 4.1: Add the following two statements to the TBox shown in Figure 4.2: "grandparent = human and has a child who is a parent" and "male = not female". Extend the concept hierarchy shown in the figure by the concepts female, male and grandparent.

One can ask why we need the DL formalism, as everything we have said so far could be described using classical mathematical logic: all we would need to do is to map concepts to unary relations and roles to binary relations. For instance, the three assertions given in the ABox of Figure 4.1 could be easily transformed to first-order logic (FOL), resulting in:

$$human(Eve), \qquad female(Eve), \qquad hasChild(Eve,Abel).$$

The main reason for not using FOL is that it is undecidable, i.e. no proof procedure for full FOL can be guaranteed to decide the truth of a statement within a time limit. However,

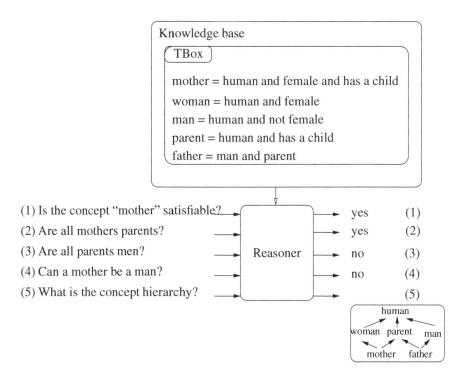

Figure 4.2. Pure terminological reasoning.

the DL languages used in practice (e.g. the members of the $\mathcal{AL}$ and $\mathcal{SHIQ}$ language families, described in detail in Sections 4.4 and 4.5) are all decidable, and efficient inference
algorithms have been developed for them.

Exercise 4.2: Consider the domain of higher education.

(a) List as many concepts as you can that occur in this domain of discourse, for example,
person, student, teacher.

(b) Collect the roles, i.e. the binary relations, of this domain, such as "is employed by", "is
enrolled in".

(c) Formulate statements in plain English sentences that link concepts and roles, such as "a
student is a person", "a student is enrolled in at least one course".

In subsequent sections we will focus on issues related to terminological reasoning. We
will re-examine ABoxes in detail in Section 4.8.

4.2. An informal introduction to the DL formalism

In this section we give an overview of the DL notation, i.e. the language in which one can
describe knowledge regarding the concepts and roles of a given domain.

---

(1) A Mother is a Human who is a Female and who has(a)Child.

$$\text{Mother} \equiv \text{Human} \sqcap \text{Female} \sqcap \exists \text{hasChild}.\top$$

(2) A Tiger is a Mammal.

$$\text{Tiger} \sqsubseteq \text{Mammal}$$

(3) Those who are in the relation hasChild are also in the relation hasDescendant.

$$\text{hasChild} \sqsubseteq \text{hasDescendant}$$

(4) The relation hasParent is the inverse of the relation hasChild.

$$\text{hasParent} \equiv \text{hasChild}^-$$

Figure 4.3. Statements that can be formalised using Description Logic.

Figure 4.3 shows four sentences written in plain English that can be formalised in DL. Each sentence is followed by its formal counterpart, i.e. a terminological axiom. Within the English sentences, the capitalised words typeset in Grotesque stand for concepts while non-capitalised grotesque words stand for roles.

The first two statements describe relationships between concepts, while the third and the fourth concern roles.

Sentence (1) says that the concept Mother (denoting the set of mothers) is the same as the set of Human beings who are Female and for whom there exists at least one individual who is in hasChild-relation with them. The formal counterpart of this sentence is a terminological axiom stating the *equivalence* ($\equiv$) of two *concept expressions*. The simplest concept expression is an atomic concept, such as Mother, Human or Female. Composite expressions can be built from these using concept constructors, i.e. operators creating complex concepts from simpler ones. In sentence (1) there are two constructors, the intersection ($\dots \sqcap \dots$) and the so-called limited existential restriction ($\exists$role.$\top$).

Note that intersection is denoted by $\sqcap$, a "square" version of the usual set-theoretic intersection sign $\cap$. This is an important distinction: $\sqcap$ is applied to concept expressions, which are DL language constructs, while the traditional $\cap$ is used to indicate the intersection of two sets. As we said before, concept expressions stand for sets, but they themselves are not sets. However, we will soon show that the semantics of $\sqcap$ is actually defined in terms of $\cap$ (see Subsection 4.3.2).

On the right-hand side of (1) we see two applications of $\sqcap$. In the first, the concept Human $\sqcap$ Female stands for the set of the individuals that belong to both the concepts Human and Female, i.e. they are female human beings. The concept expression Human $\sqcap$ Female can be read either as "human intersection female" or simply as "human and female".

The *limited existential restriction* $\exists$hasChild.$\top$ denotes the set of individuals who have a child. An individual belongs to this concept if there exists a second individual such that the first individual is in the hasChild relationship with the second. The sign $\top$ (pronounced "top") at the end of the expression denotes the universal concept, i.e. the set of all individuals in the domain of concern. Its presence here indicates that we pose no restriction on the child individual in the hasChild relationship.

The generalisation of this constructor, full existential restriction, allows for an arbitrary concept expression present in the place of $\top$. For instance, the expression $\exists$hasChild.Female describes a parent who has at least one daughter (and possibly some sons too). To be more precise, this expression denotes the set of those individuals who have a Female instance connected to them through the role hasChild.

Of course, the concept involved in the existential restriction can be composite. For example, the expression Human ⊓ ∃hasChild.∃hasChild.⊤ stands for those humans who have a child having a child, i.e. it denotes grandparents.

We now introduce some other important concept constructors before continuing with our explanation of Figure 4.3.

- Value restrictions are similar to existential but require *all* individuals in a given relationship to belong to a concept. For instance, the expression ∀hasChild.Female stands for the individuals every child of whom is female.[2] This kind of expression is usually called a *value restriction* because it poses a universal restriction on the second argument, often called the value of the role.

- The ¬ sign can be used to *negate* a concept, producing the complement of the set denoted by the concept after the sign. For instance, ¬Female stands for the individuals that are not female, while ¬∃hasChild.⊤ denotes childless individuals. Similarly ¬∀hasChild.Female describes those individuals for whom the statement "all their children are female" does not hold, i.e. those whose children are not all female. This is obviously equivalent to those who have a non-female child; therefore the above negated concept can be rewritten to ∃hasChild.¬Female.

- Besides intersection we can also use the *union* operation, which is denoted by the square version of the usual set-theoretic union sign. For example, Blonde ⊔ Tall denotes those individuals who either have fair hair or are tall. Because of this we often read the union operator as "or".

- Finally we introduce ⊥ (pronounced *bottom*), which is the complement (negation) of top. Thus ⊥ stands for the empty concept, to which no individual can belong. For instance, the concept "childless" can also be formalised as: ∀hasChild.⊥, i.e. those individuals whose children all belong to the empty set. As no individual can belong to the empty set, this statement only holds for childless people. As already mentioned above, an equivalent formulation of this concept is ¬∃hasChild.⊤.

Exercise 4.3: Transcribe the following concept expressions into plain English. Try to find the simplest characterisation of the set of individuals described by these concepts.

(a) Human ⊓ Female ⊓ ∀hasSpouse.⊥.

(b) Human ⊓ ¬Female ⊓ ∃hasSibling.∃hasChild.⊤.

(c) Book ⊓ ∃hasAuthor.Polish.

(d) Movie ⊓ ∀hasActor.¬German.

(e) Company ⊓ ∃hasLocation.UK ⊓ ¬∀hasLocation.UK.[3]

(f) Human ⊓ ∃worksFor.∀hasLocation.UK.

---

[2] Note that individuals who have no children at all will belong to this concept.

[3] The concept UK is special, in that it preferably has only a single instance. This type of concept, called a *nominal*, is discussed in Subsection 4.10.2.

Exercise 4.4: Formalise the following concepts, given in plain English, i.e. write down a corresponding DL concept expression. Whenever possible, use the concept and role names introduced in the previous exercise.

(a) Grandfathers.

(b) Single parents.

(c) Childless married men.

(d) Books all of whose authors are parents.

(e) Companies which have premises in the UK or in the USA.

(f) Parents working for a company that has premises outside the UK.

Let us now continue with discussing the statements in Figure 4.3. Sentence (2) states that a concept, viewed as a set, is a (not necessarily proper) subset of another; the set of tigers is a subset of the set of mammals. In general, the statement $C \sqsubseteq D$ expresses the fact that every instance of C is at the same time an instance of D: every tiger is a mammal. Statements similar to (2) are called *concept inclusion axioms*, and one can rephrase (2) as "the concept tiger is included in the concept mammal". Sometimes inclusion is referred to as subsumption: "the concept tiger is *subsumed* by the concept mammal".

Note that the $\sqsubseteq$ connective is a "square" version of the set-theoretic $\subseteq$ (subset-or-equal) operator.

Statement (2) provides less information about the concept on its left-hand side than statement (1). While (1) gives an exact definition of the concept "mother", (2) only reports that tigers are mammals; it does not define how they could be distinguished from other mammals. In a more sophisticated ontology one might consider dealing with this distinction as well. However, such "less informative" inclusion axioms are very common in, for example, lightweight ontologies, which correspond to RDF schema class hierarchies and consist of axioms of the form Concept1 $\sqsubseteq$ Concept2.

Axioms similar to (1) and (2) can be used not only for concept definition but also for describing background knowledge as well. For instance, we can formalise the fact that every child of a human being is also a human as Human $\sqsubseteq$ $\forall$hasChild.Human. Literally, this formula says that the concept consisting of those individuals all of whose children are humans includes the concept of humans. Thus, if someone is a human then he or she also belongs to the above composite concept, and hence all his or her children are humans.

Exercise 4.5: Using the notation introduced above, formalise the plain English sentences you listed as answers to part (c) of Exercise 4.2.

In Figure 4.3 two further sentences are given, (3) and (4). These are examples of inclusion and equivalence axioms applied to roles. We consider such role axioms as belonging to the TBox. Note, however, that in some publications, e.g. in Horrocks and Sattler [61], a TBox is defined as containing concept axioms only; the collection of role axioms is called the *RBox* (role-box) part of the knowledge base. We will sometimes use the term RBox to refer to the set of role inclusion and equivalence axioms in the TBox.

Sentence (3), hasChild ⊑ hasDescendant, says that the role hasChild is included in (or subsumed by) the role hasDescendant. In other words, hasDescendant is a more general relationship than hasChild. This means that whenever "A has child B" holds then "A has descendant B" has to hold as well. To clarify why this is called subsumption, let us view the binary relation represented by a role as a set of pairs of individuals which are in the given relation. Then, the role hasChild becomes a set of ⟨*parent, child*⟩ pairs, while the role hasDescendant contains ⟨*ancestor, descendant*⟩ pairs. Since each ⟨*parent, child*⟩ pair is – by definition – also a valid ⟨*ancestor, descendant*⟩ pair, the first set is subsumed by the second.

Sentence (4) is a role equivalence axiom, which states that the hasParent relation is the inverse of hasChild, i.e. hasParent ≡ hasChild⁻. Here, the upper index ⁻ is a role constructor that inverts a role, i.e. switches the two sides of the relation. When this constructor is applied to the role hasChild, then *parent–child* pairs become *child–parent* and so we obtain the has-Parent relationship. Syntactically hasChild⁻ is a role expression, which can be used in any place where a role name is allowed (e.g. in a value restriction). A role expression is built from role names, i.e. *atomic roles*, using role constructors.

In connection with inverse roles it is worth discussing some naming conventions. It is important to avoid confusing a role with its inverse. As suggested in the literature, we recommend that non-symmetric roles should be named in such a way that a proper English sentence is obtained when the role name is placed between the two individuals it connects. For example, the parent–child relationship should be named hasChild since, in the sentence "A hasChild B", it is clear which side is the child and which is the parent. For similar reasons the child–parent relationship should be named hasParent. Alternatively one could use the role name isParentOf instead of hasChild, since the sentences "A hasChild B" and "A isParentOf B" have the same meaning. Similarly hasParent could be replaced by isChildOf. What is important is to avoid using ambiguous role names, such as parent or boss, as it is unclear who is the boss and who is the subordinate in the sentence "Peter boss Adam".

Exercise 4.6: Transcribe the following DL statements into plain English sentences.

(a) ∃hasChild⁻.Blonde ⊑ Blonde.

(b) ∀hasChild⁻.Blonde ⊑ ∀hasChild.Blonde.

(c) Human ⊓ ∃hasFriend.Alcoholic ⊑ ¬Alcoholic.

(d) Human ⊓ ∃hasChild⁻.¬Alcoholic ⊑ ¬Alcoholic.

(e) Movie ⊓ ¬∃contains.Violence ⊑ SuitableForChildren.

Besides the inverse role constructor, one could consider other role constructors analogous to concept constructors. These include role intersection (for instance, hasFriend ⊓ hasRelative denotes a relationship where the individuals on the two sides are both friends and relatives), role union (for instance, hasHusband ⊔ hasWife is the same as the hasSpouse relationship), and role negation (for instance, ¬ hasFriend). Other, very useful, role operations can be defined, e.g. role composition (applying two roles, one after the other). For instance, composing the roles hasSpouse and hasFather means that we start with an individual, take his/her spouse (i.e. follow the hasSpouse role), and then follow the hasFather role. Thus the composition of these two roles defines the relation "the spouse's father", i.e. the hasFatherInLaw role.

The problem with these role constructors is that they make the DL language undecidable in most cases. Therefore the mainstream DL languages do not allow most such constructors. However, in the last few years a fairly weak, but at the same time very useful, special case of role composition has been identified which does not break the decidability barrier. In Section 4.10 we discuss this issue in more detail.

4.3. The $\mathcal{AL}$ DL language

We have informally introduced the most important elements of DL languages in the previous section. We have mentioned that concepts stand for sets of individuals and roles denote binary relations. In this section we refine this informal description and present the exact syntax and semantics of a very simple DL language.

4.3.1. Syntax of the $\mathcal{AL}$ language

We use a DL language to describe our knowledge in a given field. Such a knowledge base contains statements about concepts and roles, called *concept axioms* and *role axioms*. In the present section, as well as in the next one, we deal with simple DL languages in which no composite roles can be constructed and no role axioms are allowed. Thus, for now we focus on concept axioms.

If C and D are concept expressions, then

$$C \sqsubseteq D \quad \text{and} \quad C \equiv D$$

are concept axioms. The first kind of statement is called a *concept inclusion axiom*, stating that C is subsumed by D. Sometimes this axiom will be written as $D \sqsupseteq C$. The second kind is a *concept equivalence axiom*, claiming that C and D are the same. Note that the equivalence axiom $C \equiv D$ can be rewritten as two concept inclusion axioms: $C \sqsubseteq D$ and $D \sqsubseteq C$.

Let us now discuss how concept expressions are built. The simplest kind is the *atomic concept*, also called the *concept name*. We denote atomic concepts (such as Mother) by A. We can build composite expressions from atomic concepts and concept constants $(\top, \bot)$ using various concept *constructors*.[4] Different DL languages allow different sets of constructors.

The simplest DL language we discuss here is the $\mathcal{AL}$ *attributive language* [102].[5] In it, the following constructors are allowed: negation, intersection, value restriction and limited existential restriction. Figure 4.4 presents the formal grammar of the $\mathcal{AL}$ language. Here, A stands for an atomic concept, C and C_i for concept expressions and R for an (atomic) role.

In what follows we will often refer to concept expressions simply as concepts, and similarly for roles. In situations when composite concepts are to be excluded we will make this explicit by using the term "atomic concept".

Notice that the $\mathcal{AL}$ language involves serious limitations: composite concepts cannot be negated, the existential restriction is only allowed in its limited form and we cannot speak about the union of concepts. However, even in this simple language we can express some interesting concepts. For example, let us define the concept FatherOfGirls, by which we mean

---

[4] One could also view concept constants as concept constructors with no arguments.

[5] In the early stage of DL development, roles were called attributes; hence the name *attributive language*.

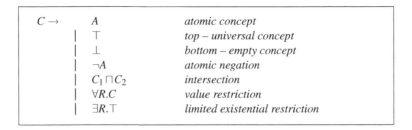

Figure 4.4. The concept expressions of the $\mathcal{AL}$ language.

a father all of whose children are female:

$$\text{FatherOfGirls} \equiv \text{Human} \sqcap \neg\text{Female}$$
$$\sqcap \forall\text{hasChild}.\text{Female} \sqcap \exists\text{hasChild}.\top. \qquad (4.1)$$

This concept is defined as an intersection of four simpler ones. The first two ensure that the individual in question is a man, the third one states that all his children are girls, while the last ensures that he is a parent (he has a child), since the previous value restriction (all his children are female) does not guarantee this.

We emphasise that defining a concept in a formal, computer-processable, way is important because natural language constructs are often ambiguous. For instance, one may interpret the expression "father of girls" as either a father who has at least two daughters, or as a father whose every child is a girl. A formal definition always resolves this kind of ambiguity.

Let us now return to the syntax of $\mathcal{AL}$ concepts. Figure 4.4 specifies how to build concept expressions using atomic concepts and roles, as well as some mathematical operators ($\top, \bot, \neg, \sqcap, \forall, \exists$). Furthermore, one should use parentheses to specify the proper nesting of constructs with multiple operators. As usual in mathematics, we adopt some conventions regarding the precedence of the operators: negation is the strongest, the quantifiers come next, while intersection has the weakest binding, i.e. it should be executed last. As the intersection operator is associative, we can use multiple $\sqcap$ operators without specifying the application order, as seen in the above definition of the concept FatherOfGirls.

Exercise 4.7: Decide whether the following concepts can be formalised in the $\mathcal{AL}$ language. If so, formulate a concept expression corresponding to the given concept.

(a) People not having a single blonde child.

(b) People having a blonde child.

(c) Grandparents.

(d) Childless married women.

4.3.2. Semantics of the $\mathcal{AL}$ language

In the previous section we informally stated that concept expressions actually denote sets of individuals. Now we present the exact semantics of concept expressions and assertions, using the techniques developed for first-order predicate calculus by A. Tarski (so-called Tarski semantics [106]).

In order to achieve this we introduce the notion of an *interpretation*, also called a *model*, a concrete world in which the atomic concepts and roles have a concrete meaning. To specify an interpretation, we have to supply a universe, i.e. the *domain* of the world, which can be an arbitrary *non-empty* set of individuals. Furthermore, for each atomic concept we have to specify a corresponding subset of the domain and, for each atomic role, the corresponding binary relation on the domain has to be supplied.

Given an interpretation, the semantics of a DL language describes how to determine the meaning of a composite concept (i.e. the subset of the domain to which it corresponds) and how to decide whether an axiom holds in the given interpretation.

Before proceeding further let us consider an example. We will introduce an interpretation in which the concept expression appearing on the right-hand side of (4.1) can be evaluated:

- the domain is {Nick,Mary,Ann,Steve,John};
- the meaning of the concept Human is the whole domain;
- the meaning of the concept Female is {Mary,Ann};
- the meaning of the role hasChild is
  {⟨Nick,Ann⟩,⟨Mary,Ann⟩,⟨Ann,John⟩,⟨Steve,John⟩}
  (i.e. Nick and Mary are the parents of Ann, while Ann and Steve are the parents of John).

Figure 4.5 depicts this interpretation: a broken line surrounds the set of Female individuals, while the role hasChild is shown as a set of arrows pointing respectively from the parents to their children.

Given our common sense, we can state that it is only Nick who can be considered a father of girls, in terms of (4.1), i.e. we expect the formal semantics to assign the singleton set {Nick} to the concept expression on the right-hand side of (4.1), for the above interpretation.

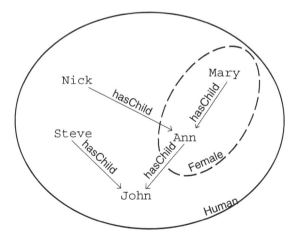

Figure 4.5. The example interpretation $\mathcal{I}_x$.

Continuing the example, let us consider statement (4.1) again; recall that so far we have only been considering its right-hand side. We provided this statement as the definition of the concept FatherOfGirls. For the sake of uniformity, when formalising DL semantics no distinction is made between axioms of this kind (often simply called *definitions*) and other equivalence axioms that describe background knowledge. This means that, in order to be able to assess the validity of (4.1), we have to extend our interpretation to include the meaning of the concept FatherOfGirls. Given this we can simply decide whether our interpretation satisfies (4.1): the axiom holds if, and only if, the concept expressions on the two sides have the same meaning (evaluate to the same subset of the domain). In our example this means that the condition for (4.1) to hold is that FatherOfGirls is defined as the singleton set {Nick}.

At the same time it is obvious that the meaning of FatherOfGirls is unambiguously determined by (4.1), given the meanings of the concepts and the role on the right-hand side of this equation. Therefore it makes sense to extend our formalism so that the meanings of concepts like FatherOfGirls need not be supplied. This will be dealt with in Section 4.6.

Let us now proceed to a formal description of DL interpretations. An interpretation is a pair $\mathcal{I} = \langle \Delta, I \rangle$, where Δ is the domain of the interpretation, i.e. an arbitrary non-empty set whose elements are called *individuals*; the second member of the pair is a function I which assigns a subset of Δ to every atomic concept and maps each atomic role to a binary relation on Δ, i.e. a set of pairs from Δ (a subset of $\Delta \times \Delta$). It is common to write the function I as an upper index; for instance, Human^I describes the set assigned to the atomic concept Human. The example introduced above can be formalised as the interpretation $\mathcal{I}_x = \langle \Delta, I \rangle$, where:

$$\Delta = \{\text{Nick}, \text{Mary}, \text{Ann}, \text{Steve}, \text{John}\};$$
$$\text{Human}^I = \Delta;$$
$$\text{Female}^I = \{\text{Mary}, \text{Ann}\}; \tag{4.2}$$
$$\text{hasChild}^I = \{\langle \text{Nick}, \text{Ann} \rangle, \langle \text{Mary}, \text{Ann} \rangle,$$
$$\langle \text{Ann}, \text{John} \rangle, \langle \text{Steve}, \text{John} \rangle\}.$$

A simplified notation is often used for the sake of brevity. Here, the domain of the interpretation $\mathcal{I}$ is denoted by $\Delta^{\mathcal{I}}$, and Human$^{\mathcal{I}}$ is used instead of Human^I (i.e. the upper index is the interpretation itself, rather than the interpretation function I). This is useful, because we do not have to explicitly "take apart" the interpretation (to a domain and an interpretation function) in order to speak about the meaning of concepts and roles. For the above interpretation example $\mathcal{I}_x$ we can thus refer to its domain as $\Delta^{\mathcal{I}_x}$, while Human$^{\mathcal{I}_x}$, Female$^{\mathcal{I}_x}$ and hasChild$^{\mathcal{I}_x}$ denote the concrete sets listed above.

Another way to understand the simplified notation is to view an interpretation as a function (written as an upper index) that maps the symbol Δ to the domain of the interpretation, while the atomic concepts and roles are mapped to their meaning in the given interpretation. This is why we often refer to $C^{\mathcal{I}}$ or $R^{\mathcal{I}}$ as the *interpretation* of the given concept or role, respectively.

Let us now turn to the semantics of concept expressions. Since an atomic concept is in itself a concept expression, its meaning (as an expression) obviously has to be the same as the set assigned to this atomic concept by the interpretation function. Therefore, we define the semantics of concept expressions by recursively *extending* the interpretation function, which so far has only dealt with atomic concepts, to apply to all concept expressions.

$$\top^{\mathcal{I}} = \Delta^{\mathcal{I}}$$
$$\bot^{\mathcal{I}} = \emptyset$$
$$(\neg A)^{\mathcal{I}} = \Delta^{\mathcal{I}} \setminus A^{\mathcal{I}}$$
$$(C_1 \sqcap C_2)^{\mathcal{I}} = C_1^{\mathcal{I}} \cap C_2^{\mathcal{I}}$$
$$(\forall R.C)^{\mathcal{I}} = \left\{ a \in \Delta^{\mathcal{I}} \mid \forall b. \left(\langle a,b \rangle \in R^{\mathcal{I}} \to b \in C^{\mathcal{I}} \right) \right\}$$
$$(\exists R.\top)^{\mathcal{I}} = \left\{ a \in \Delta^{\mathcal{I}} \mid \exists b. \left(\langle a,b \rangle \in R^{\mathcal{I}} \right). \right\}$$

Figure 4.6. The semantics of concept expressions in the $\mathcal{AL}$ language.

The semantics of the $\mathcal{AL}$ language is given in Figure 4.6. This defines the extension of the interpretation function to include the constructs allowed by the language $\mathcal{AL}$. Here we continue to use the simplified notation, i.e. the upper index is the interpretation $\mathcal{I}$ itself rather than its interpretation function.

The definition is given by considering all possible kinds of concept expression allowed by $\mathcal{AL}$. Let us go through these cases one by one.

The interpretation of the top symbol $\top$ is the complete domain while the interpretation of bottom ($\bot$) is the empty set, as we said earlier. The meaning of the negated atomic concept $\neg A$ is the complement, with respect to the interpretation domain, of the meaning of the concept A. The meaning of the intersection of two concepts is defined recursively as the intersection of their meanings. Because of this definition, the $\sqcap$ operator inherits the properties of set intersection, e.g. it is associative and commutative.

Next come the quantified expressions: the meaning of $\forall R.C$ is the set of all those individuals a for which it holds that any individual b connected to a via role R belongs to the set corresponding to C. The meaning of the limited existential restriction $\exists R.\top$ is defined as the set of individuals a that have at least one connection via role R.

As an example, let us follow how the meaning of the composite concept describing the notion "father of girls" is calculated in the interpretation $\mathcal{I}_x$ introduced in (4.2): see also Figure 4.5. The concept in question is formally defined as an intersection:

$$\mathsf{Human} \sqcap \neg\mathsf{Female} \sqcap \forall\mathsf{hasChild.Female} \sqcap \exists\mathsf{hasChild}.\top.$$

Let us go through the components of this intersection:

$$\mathsf{Human}^{\mathcal{I}_x} = \{\mathtt{Nick,Mary,Ann,Steve,John}\};$$
$$(\neg\mathsf{Female})^{\mathcal{I}_x} = \{\mathtt{Nick,Steve,John}\};$$
$$(\forall\mathsf{hasChild.Female})^{\mathcal{I}_x} = \{\mathtt{Nick,Mary,John}\};$$
$$(\exists\mathsf{hasChild}.\top)^{\mathcal{I}_x} = \{\mathtt{Nick,Mary,Ann,Steve}\}.$$

We can now derive the meaning of the "father of girls" concept expression as the intersection of these four sets, which is the singleton set $\{\mathtt{Nick}\}$ as expected.

Having discussed the meaning of concept expressions, it is very easy to define the semantics of concept axioms: $C \equiv D$ is true in an interpretation $\mathcal{I}$ if, and only if, $C^{\mathcal{I}} = D^{\mathcal{I}}$ and similarly $C \sqsubseteq D$ is true if, and only if, $C^{\mathcal{I}} \subseteq D^{\mathcal{I}}$.

Let us now introduce some further notation and terminology regarding the semantics of DL languages. Note that these apply to any DL language, not just to $\mathcal{AL}$.

The fact that axiom T is true in the interpretation $\mathcal{I}$ is denoted by $\mathcal{I} \models T$. This formula is often read as follows: the interpretation $\mathcal{I}$ *satisfies* axiom T, or $\mathcal{I}$ is a model of T. This notation can be extended to a TBox $\mathcal{T}$: an interpretation satisfies the set of axioms $\mathcal{T}$ ($\mathcal{I} \models \mathcal{T}$) if it satisfies all axioms of $\mathcal{T}$, and in this case the interpretation is also called a model of $\mathcal{T}$. Two axioms or two TBoxes are called *equivalent* if they have exactly the same models. Similarly, concept expressions C and D are said to be equivalent ($C \equiv D$), if they have the same meaning in all interpretations.

Exercise 4.8: Evaluate the meanings of the concept expressions appearing on the left- and right-hand sides of the following $\mathcal{AL}$ axioms, in the example interpretation $\mathcal{I}_x$; see (4.2). Next, decide whether the interpretation $\mathcal{I}_x$ is a model of the axiom.

(a) $\forall$hasChild.$\bot \sqsubseteq \neg$Female.

(b) $\forall$hasChild.Female $\sqsubseteq \exists$hasChild.$\top$.

(c) $\forall$hasChild.$\bot \sqsubseteq \forall$hasChild.Female.

(d) Female $\sqcap \forall$hasChild.Female $\sqsubseteq \exists$hasChild.$\top$.

(e) $\forall$hasChild.Female $\sqcap \forall$hasChild.$\neg$Female $\equiv \forall$hasChild.$\bot$.

Decide which of the above axioms will be satisfied by *all* their interpretations.

Exercise 4.9: Is there an interpretation which is a model of axiom (b) listed in Exercise 4.8? If so, give an example.

We now proceed to define the notion of semantic[6] consequence, analogously to that of semantic consequence in first-order logic. An axiom T is a consequence of TBox $\mathcal{T}$ if, and only if, T is satisfied by all models of $\mathcal{T}$. This fact is denoted by $\mathcal{T} \models T$. For example, if $\mathcal{T}$ is a TBox containing the axiom (4.1) then

$$\mathcal{T} \models (\text{Female} \sqcap \text{FatherOfGirls} \equiv \bot),$$

i.e. a father of girls cannot be female, assuming definition (4.1).

We now give a formal definition for semantic consequence:

$$\mathcal{T} \models T \leftrightarrow \text{for all interpretations } \mathcal{I} : (\mathcal{I} \models \mathcal{T} \to \mathcal{I} \models T).$$

Note that the $\models$ sign is overloaded. When there is an interpretation on its left-hand side then it states that this interpretation is a model of the axiom(s) on the right-hand side. However, when a TBox appears on the left of the $\models$ sign then it denotes semantic consequence.

---

[6] The "semantic" qualifier distinguishes this notion from that of syntactic consequence, used in proof theory. As this latter notion is not even mentioned in this chapter, we will often omit the "semantic" qualifier.

Exercise 4.10: Consider the DL axioms listed under (a)–(e) in Exercise 4.8, and let $T =$ Female $\sqsubseteq \exists$hasChild.$\top$.

(a) Decide which of the axioms (a)–(e) is a consequence of an empty TBox.

(b) Decide which of the axioms is a consequence of a TBox containing only the axiom T.

(c) Is there an axiom among these which is equivalent to T?

To overload the $\models$ sign even further, we can also use it with a TBox at each side: $\mathcal{T}_1 \models \mathcal{T}_2$ if, and only if, $\mathcal{T}_1 \models T$ for all $T \in \mathcal{T}_2$. That is, $\mathcal{T}_2$ is a consequence of $\mathcal{T}_1$ if every axiom of $\mathcal{T}_2$ is a consequence of $\mathcal{T}_1$. We can omit the TBox on the left-hand side of the $\models$ sign: $\models T$ denotes the fact that T is a consequence of an empty TBox. For example, it is obvious that the axiom Female $\sqcap$ Human $\sqsubseteq$ Human is true in any interpretation, so $\models$ Female $\sqcap$ Human $\sqsubseteq$ Human holds.

Using the notion of semantic consequence we can now reformulate the definition of TBox equivalence, introduced above: $\mathcal{T}_1$ and $\mathcal{T}_2$ are equivalent if, and only if, both $\mathcal{T}_1 \models \mathcal{T}_2$ and $\mathcal{T}_2 \models \mathcal{T}_1$ hold. Similarly, concept expressions C_1 and C_2 are equivalent if, and only if, $\models (C_1 \equiv C_2)$.

4.4. The $\mathcal{AL}$ language family

In the previous section the relatively simple $\mathcal{AL}$ language was introduced. We now define other DL language variants as extensions of $\mathcal{AL}$. First, in Subsection 4.4.1, we introduce three new concept constructors: union ($\mathcal{U}$), full existential restriction ($\mathcal{E}$) and full negation ($\mathcal{C}$, standing for *complement*). Following some examples in Subsection 4.4.2, we discuss language equivalence in Subsection 4.4.3 and show that, for example, the language $\mathcal{ALC}$ ($\mathcal{AL}$ extended with the full negation construct) is equivalent to the language $\mathcal{ALUE}$ ($\mathcal{AL}$ extended with the union and full existential restriction constructs). Finally, in Subsection 4.4.4 we introduce a fourth concept constructor, the number restriction ($\mathcal{N}$).

4.4.1. The language $\mathcal{ALC}$ and its sublanguages

In this subsection we introduce three further constructors: union, full existential restriction and full negation. These language constructs will be discussed one by one, as we introduce their syntax and semantics. Because full negation, denoted by $\mathcal{C}$, subsumes the other two constructs (see Subsection 4.4.3), all languages presented here are sublanguages of the $\mathcal{ALC}$ language.

First let us consider the *union* constructor. As was already informally discussed in Section 4.2, the union of concepts C and D is described by the expression $C \sqcup D$. For instance, the expression Blonde $\sqcup$ GreenEyed stands for the set of "blonde or green-eyed" people. As seen from this example the union operation is strongly related to the disjunction operation in first-order logic. Therefore, a concept of the form $C \sqcup D$ is sometimes referred to as a *disjunction*, while its subconcepts C and D as *disjuncts*.

The semantics of union expressions is fairly obvious:

$$(C_1 \sqcup C_2)^{\mathcal{I}} = C_1^{\mathcal{I}} \cup C_2^{\mathcal{I}}, \tag{$\mathcal{U}$}$$

i.e. the meaning of the union of two concepts is the union of the sets representing the meanings of these concepts.

We define the language $\mathcal{ALU}$ as $\mathcal{AL}$ extended with the union ($\sqcup$) constructor. The syntax of $\mathcal{ALU}$ is obtained from the grammar in Figure 4.4 by adding one more alternative to the right-hand side of the grammar rule: $C_1 \sqcup C_2$. The semantics of the language is defined by simply adding definition ($\mathcal{U}$) to Figure 4.6.

The next language construct, which has also been introduced informally, is *full existential restriction*. This has the form $\exists R.C$ and denotes the set of individuals that are R-related to some individual belonging to C. For instance, the expression $\exists$hasChild.Tall characterises the individuals (parents) who have tall children. More precisely, it denotes those parents who have at least one tall child. The formal semantics of the full existential restriction is the following:

$$(\exists R.C)^{\mathcal{I}} = \left\{ a \in \Delta^{\mathcal{I}} \mid \exists b. \left(\langle a,b \rangle \in R^{\mathcal{I}} \wedge b \in C^{\mathcal{I}} \right) \right\}. \qquad (\mathcal{E})$$

As indicated by the equation label ($\mathcal{E}$), full existential restriction is denoted by the letter $\mathcal{E}$. Thus, in addition to the languages $\mathcal{AL}$ and $\mathcal{ALU}$, we can now speak about a language $\mathcal{ALE}$ which adds full existential restriction to $\mathcal{AL}$, and about a language $\mathcal{ALUE}$ which further extends $\mathcal{ALE}$ with the union constructor. The exact syntax and semantics of these languages can be easily obtained by extending Figures 4.4 and 4.6, as was done for $\mathcal{ALU}$.

The third constructor to be introduced in this section is *full negation*. In the $\mathcal{AL}$ language one can apply the negation sign ($\neg$) only to atomic concepts. However, the language extension ($\mathcal{C}$) relaxes this constraint: the expression $\neg C$ contains an arbitrary concept expression C. For example, the expression $\neg$(Tall $\sqcap$ Blonde) describes individuals who do not belong to the set of tall blonde people. The formal semantics of the full negation constructor is:

$$(\neg C)^{\mathcal{I}} = \Delta^{\mathcal{I}} \setminus C^{\mathcal{I}}. \qquad (\mathcal{C})$$

An obvious consequence of the formula ($\mathcal{C}$) is that $\models \neg\neg C \equiv C$, because the meaning of $\neg\neg C$ is the same as that of C in any interpretation:

$$(\neg(\neg C))^{\mathcal{I}} = \Delta^{\mathcal{I}} \setminus (\neg C)^{\mathcal{I}} = \Delta^{\mathcal{I}} \setminus (\Delta^{\mathcal{I}} \setminus C^{\mathcal{I}}) = C^{\mathcal{I}}.$$

As the full negation constructor can be added to the four languages introduced so far, we can introduce languages $\mathcal{ALC}$, $\mathcal{ALCE}$, $\mathcal{ALCU}$, $\mathcal{ALCUE}$. In Subsection 4.4.3 we will show that these four languages have the same expressive power as the language $\mathcal{ALUE}$. This is why we use the shortest name (i.e. $\mathcal{ALC}$) to denote all these languages.

Exercise 4.11: Decide whether the following concepts can be formalised using the language $\mathcal{AL}$ and its extensions $\mathcal{C}$, $\mathcal{U}$ and $\mathcal{E}$. If so, formulate a concept expression corresponding to the given concept.

(a)   People with at least one tall child.

(b)   People with at most one tall child.

(c)   People with at least one child who is either blonde or tall.

(d)   People all of whose children are either blonde or tall.

(e)   People who do not have at least one tall child.

(f)   People none of whose children are either blonde or tall.

Try to give multiple equivalent formalisations of the concepts above. For each, list the single-letter abbreviations of the language extensions it uses.

4.4.2. Examples

Having presented the syntax and semantics of the $\mathcal{ALC}$ DL language, we give some simple examples. Let us examine, for instance, the TBox containing the following three axioms:

$$\mathsf{Father} \equiv \mathsf{Human} \sqcap \neg\mathsf{Female} \sqcap \exists \mathsf{hasChild}.\top; \qquad (4.3)$$

$$\mathsf{FatherOfGirls} \equiv \mathsf{Father} \sqcap \forall \mathsf{hasChild}.\mathsf{Female}; \qquad (4.4)$$

$$\mathsf{FatherOfGirls} \sqsubseteq \mathsf{Optimist} \sqcup \exists \mathsf{hasChild}.\mathsf{Optimist}. \qquad (4.5)$$

The first two axioms define the concepts Father and FatherOfGirls, the third states that every father of girls is either an optimist or has an optimistic child (i.e. if an individual is an instance of the concept FatherOfGirls then it is bound to be an instance of the concept Optimist $\sqcup$ $\exists$hasChild.Optimist).

Let us now construct an interpretation, so that we can discuss the semantics of the concepts introduced. This involves defining the domain and interpretation of all atomic concepts and roles. Subsequently, using the semantic rules in Figure 4.6 as well as those defined under ($\mathcal{U}$), ($\mathcal{E}$) and ($\mathcal{C}$), we can construct sets of individuals corresponding to arbitrary concept expressions and determine the truth values of axioms. Thus we can decide whether our interpretation is a model of the given set of axioms.

In our example interpretation we have to provide sets corresponding to all atomic concepts and roles present in the axioms above, i.e. the meanings of the concepts Human, Female, Optimist, Father and FatherOfGirls[7] and the meaning of the role hasChild. Let us build an extension of the example interpretation $\mathcal{I}_x$ introduced in (4.2). This extension, let us call it $\mathcal{I}_y$, includes the following concepts, in addition to the ones present in $\mathcal{I}_x$:

$$\mathsf{Optimist}^{\mathcal{I}_y} = \{\mathtt{Nick}, \mathtt{Steve}, \mathtt{Ann}\};$$
$$\mathsf{Father}^{\mathcal{I}_y} = \{\mathtt{Nick}, \mathtt{Steve}\}; \qquad (4.6)$$
$$\mathsf{FatherOfGirls}^{\mathcal{I}_y} = \{\mathtt{Nick}\}.$$

It is easy to see that this interpretation satisfies all the three axioms (4.3)–(4.5), so it is a model of this TBox.

Exercise 4.12: Evaluate the semantics of all the concept sub-expressions (i.e. *subconcepts*) occurring in (4.3)–(4.5), using the interpretation $\mathcal{I}_y$. Show that all three axioms are satisfied by this interpretation.

---

[7] Later, in Subsection 4.6.1 we will deal with the issue of *definitions*, such as (4.3) and (4.4) above, that extend our formalism so that no meaning has to be supplied for concepts like Father and FatherOfGirls.

Consider interpretations $\mathcal{I}_z$ and $\mathcal{I}_w$, which differ from $\mathcal{I}_y$ only in the meaning of the concept Optimist:

$$\text{Optimist}^{\mathcal{I}_z} = \{\texttt{Steve,Ann,Mary}\};$$
$$\text{Optimist}^{\mathcal{I}_w} = \{\texttt{Steve,John,Mary}\}.$$

Check whether the axiom (4.5) is true in interpretations $\mathcal{I}_z$ and $\mathcal{I}_w$.

Now let us discuss some examples illustrating the issue of whether two sets of axioms are equivalent. Let us assign the name $\mathcal{T}_1$ to the TBox (4.3)–(4.5). Let $\mathcal{T}_2$ stand for $\mathcal{T}_1$ with axiom (4.5) replaced by the following statement:

$$\text{Father} \sqsubseteq \text{Optimist} \sqcup \exists \text{hasChild}.(\text{Optimist} \sqcup \neg\text{Female}). \qquad (4.7)$$

Let us show that $\mathcal{T}_1$ and $\mathcal{T}_2$ are equivalent. We thus have to prove two semantic consequence statements: $\mathcal{T}_2 \models (4.5)$ and $\mathcal{T}_1 \models (4.7)$. Let us start with the first, and consider an arbitrary model $\mathcal{I}$ of $\mathcal{T}_2$ and an arbitrary individual a which belongs to the left-hand side of (4.5), i.e. to FatherOfGirls$^{\mathcal{I}}$. To prove that (4.5) holds, we have to show that a belongs to the concept expression on the right-hand side of (4.5), i.e. that a is in our *goal set* (Optimist $\sqcup$ $\exists$hasChild.Optimist)$^{\mathcal{I}}$. Because a is a father of girls, he also belongs to Father$^{\mathcal{I}}$. Consequently, due to (4.7), a either belongs to Optimist$^{\mathcal{I}}$ or to ($\exists$hasChild.(Optimist $\sqcup \neg$Female))$^{\mathcal{I}}$. In the former case i.e. when a is an optimist, he obviously belongs to the goal set. In the latter case, a has a child who is either optimistic or non-female. Because a is a father of girls all a's children are female, so the child in question has to be optimistic. This means that a has an optimistic child, and so a belongs to the goal set in this case too.

Proving the other direction of the equivalence is left to the reader, via the following exercise.

Exercise 4.13: Prove that $\mathcal{T}_1 \models (4.7)$, i.e. axiom (4.7) holds in an arbitrary model of $\mathcal{T}_1$.

Let us now replace the subset sign in (4.7) by an equivalence sign:

$$\text{Father} \equiv \text{Optimist} \sqcup \exists \text{hasChild}.(\text{Optimist} \sqcup \neg\text{Female}). \qquad (4.8)$$

Let TBox $\mathcal{T}_3$ consist of axioms (4.3), (4.4) and (4.8), i.e. the above axiom replaces (4.5) in $\mathcal{T}_1$. We claim that $\mathcal{T}_3$ is *not* equivalent to $\mathcal{T}_1$ and $\mathcal{T}_2$, because $\mathcal{T}_3$ implies that optimistic people have to be fathers and this does not follow from $\mathcal{T}_1$. All we need to prove this is to show an interpretation which is a model of both $\mathcal{T}_1$ and $\mathcal{T}_2$, but not of $\mathcal{T}_3$. Interpretation $\mathcal{I}_y$ is one such: it satisfies both $\mathcal{T}_1$ and $\mathcal{T}_2$ but it does not satisfy (4.8), the new axiom of $\mathcal{T}_3$: Ann is an optimist, but she is not a father.

Exercise 4.14: Using the semantics of the $\mathcal{ALC}$ language, as shown in Figure 4.6 and in formulae $(\mathcal{U})$, $(\mathcal{E})$ and $(\mathcal{C})$, prove that the following DL counterparts of De Morgan's laws hold:

(a) $\neg(C \sqcup D) \equiv \neg C \sqcap \neg D$;

(b) $\neg(C \sqcap D) \equiv \neg C \sqcup \neg D$;

(c) $\neg(\exists R.C) \equiv \forall R.\neg C$;

(d) $\neg(\forall R.C) \equiv \exists R.\neg C$.

Exercise 4.15: Using the semantics of $\mathcal{ALC}$ decide which of the following statements hold:

(a) $\{C \equiv \top\} \models \forall R.C \equiv \top$;　　(b) $\{\forall R.C \equiv \top\} \models C \equiv \top$;

(c) $\{C \equiv \bot\} \models \exists R.C \equiv \bot$;　　(d) $\{\exists R.C \equiv \bot\} \models C \equiv \bot$;

(e) $\models \forall R.C_1 \sqcap \forall R.C_2 \sqsubseteq \forall R.(C_1 \sqcap C_2)$;　　(f) $\models \forall R.C_1 \sqcap \forall R.C_2 \sqsupseteq \forall R.(C_1 \sqcap C_2)$;

(g) $\models \exists R.C_1 \sqcap \exists R.C_2 \sqsubseteq \exists R.(C_1 \sqcap C_2)$;　　(h) $\models \exists R.C_1 \sqcap \exists R.C_2 \sqsupseteq \exists R.(C_1 \sqcap C_2)$;

(i) $\models \forall R.C_1 \sqcup \forall R.C_2 \sqsubseteq \forall R.(C_1 \sqcup C_2)$;　　(j) $\models \forall R.C_1 \sqcup \forall R.C_2 \sqsupseteq \forall R.(C_1 \sqcup C_2)$;

(k) $\models \exists R.C_1 \sqcup \exists R.C_2 \sqsubseteq \exists R.(C_1 \sqcup C_2)$;　　(l) $\models \exists R.C_1 \sqcup \exists R.C_2 \sqsupseteq \exists R.(C_1 \sqcup C_2)$.

4.4.3. Equivalence of languages

We now turn to the issue of language equivalence: under what conditions can we say that two given languages have the same expressive power? A straightforward answer is to require that for any formula[8] of the first language one must be able to construct an equivalent formula in the second, and vice versa.

Using this definition we now proceed to show that $\mathcal{ALCUE}$ is equivalent to (1) $\mathcal{ALC}$ and (2) $\mathcal{ALUE}$. As the latter two are sublanguages of $\mathcal{ALCUE}$, it is enough to show that for any $\mathcal{ALCUE}$ concept expression there is an equivalent form containing no unions and no existential restrictions and another equivalent form in which only atomic negation is used.

To prove the first claim we can use the following transformation rules, which are slight variations of equations (a) and (c) of Exercise 4.14:

$$C \sqcup D \longrightarrow \neg(\neg C \sqcap \neg D);$$
$$\exists R.C \longrightarrow \neg(\forall R.\neg C).$$

These allow us to eliminate all $\sqcup$ and $\exists$ constructs from an arbitrary $\mathcal{ALCUE}$ expression. For example, we can transform $\mathsf{Blonde} \sqcup \exists \mathsf{hasChild.Blonde}$ to an equivalent formula $\neg(\neg \mathsf{Blonde} \sqcap \forall \mathsf{hasChild.}\neg \mathsf{Blonde})$.[9]

To show that claim (2) above is also true we have to eliminate the full negation from an arbitrary $\mathcal{ALCUE}$ expression. This can be done by bringing negation inside composite expressions, using the following transformation rules, similar to the De Morgan's laws of the propositional calculus (cf. Exercise 4.14):

$$\neg(C \sqcup D) \longrightarrow \neg C \sqcap \neg D;$$
$$\neg(C \sqcap D) \longrightarrow \neg C \sqcup \neg D;$$
$$\neg(\exists R.C) \longrightarrow \forall R.\neg C;$$
$$\neg(\forall R.C) \longrightarrow \exists R.\neg C.$$

---

[8] Here, in the context of DL, the term "formula" covers both concept expressions and axioms.

[9] Here the double negation has been omitted before the $\forall$ sign.

We apply these transformations repeatedly to any negated composite subconcept until there are no such subconcepts. For example, the concept

$$\neg(\forall \mathsf{hasChild.GreenEyed} \sqcap \exists \mathsf{hasChild}.\neg\mathsf{Blonde})$$

is transformed to an equivalent concept

$$\exists \mathsf{hasChild}.\neg\mathsf{GreenEyed} \sqcup \forall \mathsf{hasChild.Blonde},$$

in which negation only appears before atomic concepts.

Having shown that $\mathcal{ALCUE}$, $\mathcal{ALUE}$ and $\mathcal{ALC}$ are equivalent languages, it is obvious that $\mathcal{ALCE}$ and $\mathcal{ALCU}$ also belong to this equivalence group, as both are sublanguages of $\mathcal{ALCUE}$ and at the same time include $\mathcal{ALC}$. This group of equivalent languages is henceforth referred to as $\mathcal{ALC}$.

In addition to the $\mathcal{ALC}$ group, we have so far introduced three languages: $\mathcal{AL}$, $\mathcal{ALU}$ and $\mathcal{ALE}$. We claim that none of these four languages is equivalent to another. As an example, we give a proof that $\mathcal{AL} \neq \mathcal{ALU}$.

To demonstrate that two DL languages have different expressivity, it is enough to supply a concept expression C in the first language and to show an interpretation $\mathcal{I}$ such that the set $C^{\mathcal{I}}$ cannot be constructed as the meaning of some expression in the other language.

To prove that $\mathcal{AL} \neq \mathcal{ALU}$, let us consider the interpretation $\mathcal{I}_s$: $\Delta^{\mathcal{I}_s} = \{\mathsf{b}, \mathsf{g}, \mathsf{x}\}$, $\mathsf{Blonde}^{\mathcal{I}_s} = \{\mathsf{b}\}$, $\mathsf{GreenEyed}^{\mathcal{I}_s} = \{\mathsf{g}\}$. Let us now collect the subsets of $\Delta^{\mathcal{I}_s}$ that can arise in the process of interpreting $\mathcal{AL}$ expressions in $\mathcal{I}_s$. As there are no roles in $\mathcal{I}_s$, only intersections of negated or non-negated atomic concepts are allowed. Hence, in this interpretation, the semantics of an $\mathcal{AL}$ expression can only be the full domain, or the intersection of one or more sets assigned to the concepts, i.e. $\{\mathsf{b}\}$, $\{\mathsf{g}\}$, and their complements $\{\mathsf{x}, \mathsf{b}\}$, $\{\mathsf{x}, \mathsf{g}\}$.

In Figure 4.7 we collect the sets that can appear as the semantics of an $\mathcal{AL}$ expression in the interpretation $\mathcal{I}_s$. The sets corresponding to the atomic concepts are surrounded by thick lines, those for the negated atomic concepts by thin lines, and the only non-empty intersection of these is shown by a broken-line circle. The set $\{\mathsf{b}, \mathsf{g}\}$ which is the meaning of the $\mathcal{ALU}$ expression $\mathsf{Blonde} \sqcup \mathsf{GreenEyed}$ does not appear among these. Therefore there cannot exist an equivalent of this expression in the $\mathcal{AL}$ language in the given interpretation $\mathcal{I}_s$, so the languages $\mathcal{AL}$ and $\mathcal{ALU}$ cannot be equivalent.

Notice that the very same interpretation $\mathcal{I}_s$ provides us with a means of proving that $\mathcal{ALE}$ and $\mathcal{ALUE}$ cannot be equivalent. There are no atomic roles in $\mathcal{I}_s$, and therefore the extension

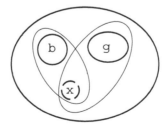

Figure 4.7. Interpretation $\mathcal{I}_s$ demonstrating that $\mathcal{AL} \neq \mathcal{ALU}$.

$\mathcal{E}$ does not add any new concept expressions to the language. Thus, in the interpretation $\mathcal{I}_s$, the set of meanings for $\mathcal{ALE}$ concept expressions is the same as that for $\mathcal{AL}$ expressions. Similarly, the sets of meanings of all possible $\mathcal{ALUE}$ and $\mathcal{ALU}$ expressions are the same. Since the $\mathcal{ALU}$ and $\mathcal{AL}$ meanings differ, the same holds for $\mathcal{ALE}$ and $\mathcal{ALUE}$ and thus the latter two languages have different expressive powers.

An alternative proof of $\mathcal{ALE} \neq \mathcal{ALUE}$, amongst others, is provided by the following exercise.

Exercise 4.16: Consider the interpretation $\mathcal{I}_t$:

$$\Delta^{\mathcal{I}_t} = \{\mathsf{a}, \mathsf{b}, \mathsf{c}\};$$
$$\mathsf{likes}^{\mathcal{I}_t} = \{\langle \mathsf{a}, \mathsf{b} \rangle, \langle \mathsf{a}, \mathsf{c} \rangle, \langle \mathsf{b}, \mathsf{c} \rangle\}.$$

Note that there are no atomic concepts in $\mathcal{I}_t$.

List those subsets of $\Delta^{\mathcal{I}_t}$ which can arise in the process of forming the meanings (interpretations) of arbitrary concept expressions allowed by the following DL languages: (a) $\mathcal{AL}$, (b) $\mathcal{ALU}$, (c) $\mathcal{ALE}$, (d) $\mathcal{ALUE}$.

Using these observations regarding interpretation $\mathcal{I}_t$, as well as those presented above for the interpretation $\mathcal{I}_s$, show that any two of the above four languages have different expressive powers.

4.4.4. Number restrictions

We now present the fourth language extension in the language family $\mathcal{AL}$. This involves two new constructs, the so-called *number restrictions*, denoted by $\mathcal{N}$. (Note that we did not include these in the informal introduction to DL languages in Section 4.2.) The two kinds of number restriction are the "at-least" and the "at-most" restrictions:

$$(\geqslant n R) \qquad \text{and} \qquad (\leqslant n R).$$

Here n is a positive integer,[10] while R is a role. The first formula stands for those individuals that have at least n R-connections, and the second for those with at most n R-connections. For instance, the expression $(\geqslant 3\,\mathsf{hasChild})$ stands for people having at least three children, while $(\leqslant 1\,\mathsf{hasFriend})$ selects those individuals who have at most one friend. The semantics of the number restrictions is the following, where $|S|$ stands for the cardinality of the set S, i.e. the number of elements it has:

$$(\geqslant n R)^{\mathcal{I}} = \left\{ a \in \Delta^{\mathcal{I}} \,\middle|\, \left| \{ b \mid \langle a, b \rangle \in R^{\mathcal{I}} \} \right| \geq n \right\};$$

$$(\leqslant n R)^{\mathcal{I}} = \left\{ a \in \Delta^{\mathcal{I}} \,\middle|\, \left| \{ b \mid \langle a, b \rangle \in R^{\mathcal{I}} \} \right| \leq n \right\}. \tag{$\mathcal{N}$}$$

We note that the number restriction $(\geqslant 1 R)$ is equivalent to the limited existential restriction $\exists R.\top$. However, the extension $(\mathcal{N})$ does not bring in the *full* existential restriction, because it allows us only to count *all* R-related individuals, not those belonging to a specific

---

[10] Sometimes the case $n = 0$ is also allowed in the number restrictions. However, this is not a proper extension as these special cases can be expressed using other constructors: $(\geqslant 0 R) \equiv \top$ and $(\leqslant 0 R) \equiv \forall R.\bot$.

concept. Thus while $\mathcal{ALN}$ permits the concept of a parent with at least three children, it does not allow the concept of a parent with at least three *tall* children.[11]

Exercise 4.17: Decide whether the following concepts and statements can be formalised in the $\mathcal{ALCN}$ language. If so, formulate the appropriate concept expression or terminological axiom.

(a) People with at least one blonde child.

(b) People with at most one child.

(c) People with exactly one child.

(d) People with exactly one blonde child, i.e. people who have one or more children among whom there is exactly one blonde.

(e) People with exactly one blonde child, i.e. people who have exactly one child, who is blonde.

(f) Mothers having at least three children are optimists.

(g) Anyone can have at most one spouse.

By appending the letter $\mathcal{N}$ to the four different languages introduced so far, we obtain four new members of the language family $\mathcal{AL}$: $\mathcal{ALN}$, $\mathcal{ALUN}$, $\mathcal{ALEN}$ and $\mathcal{ALCN}$. These languages can be shown to be different from each other and from the four languages introduced earlier [4].

The latter fact can be demonstrated using the following simple interpretation:

$$\Delta^{\mathcal{I}_u} = \{a,b\};$$
$$\mathsf{likes}^{\mathcal{I}_u} = \{\langle a,a\rangle, \langle a,b\rangle, \langle b,a\rangle\}.$$

It is easy to show (see Exercise 4.18 below) that in $\mathcal{I}_u$ any $\mathcal{ALC}$ concept expression evaluates either to an empty set or to the full domain $\Delta^{\mathcal{I}_u}$. It is obvious that the same has to hold for any sublanguage of $\mathcal{ALC}$. However, $(\geqslant 2\,\mathsf{likes})^{\mathcal{I}_u} = \{a\}$ and $(\leqslant 1\,\mathsf{likes})^{\mathcal{I}_u} = \{b\}$ hold. This means that any language allowing number restrictions, i.e. $\mathcal{ALN}$, $\mathcal{ALUN}$, $\mathcal{ALEN}$ or $\mathcal{ALCN}$, has a different expressive power from any of $\mathcal{ALC}$, $\mathcal{ALE}$, $\mathcal{ALU}$ or $\mathcal{AL}$.

Exercise 4.18: Show that any $\mathcal{ALC}$ concept expression evaluates either to an empty set or to the full domain $\Delta^{\mathcal{I}_u}$, in the above interpretation $\mathcal{I}_u$.

Now let us investigate the four languages involving number restrictions. Earlier we used the interpretation $\mathcal{I}_s$, introduced in Figure 4.7, to show that $\mathcal{AL} \neq \mathcal{ALU}$ and $\mathcal{ALE} \neq \mathcal{ALUE}$. When proving this last inequality we argued that the language extension $\mathcal{E}$ does not bring in new concept interpretations because there are no roles in $\mathcal{I}_s$. The same argument proves that the inequalities $\mathcal{ALN} \neq \mathcal{ALUN}$ and $\mathcal{ALEN} \neq \mathcal{ALUEN} \equiv \mathcal{ALCN}$ hold.

---

[11] A construct supporting this extension is called *qualified* number restriction and will be introduced shortly.

The remaining three inequalities are dealt with in the following exercise.

Exercise 4.19: Consider the following interpretation $\mathcal{I}_v$:

$$\Delta^{\mathcal{I}_v} = \{\mathsf{a},\mathsf{b},\mathsf{c},\mathsf{d}\};$$
$$\mathsf{likes}^{\mathcal{I}_v} = \{\langle \mathsf{a},\mathsf{c}\rangle,\langle \mathsf{a},\mathsf{d}\rangle,\langle \mathsf{b},\mathsf{a}\rangle,\langle \mathsf{b},\mathsf{c}\rangle\}.$$

Prove that $\mathcal{ALN} \neq \mathcal{ALEN}$, $\mathcal{ALEN} \neq \mathcal{ALUN}$ and $\mathcal{ALUN} \neq \mathcal{ALCN}$, by enumerating those subsets of $\Delta^{\mathcal{I}_v}$ which can arise in the process of forming the meanings (interpretations) of arbitrary concept expressions allowed by the above languages.

4.5. The $\mathcal{SHIQ}$ language family

This section introduces the $\mathcal{SHIQ}$ language,[12] a fairly expressive and widely used DL language. The $\mathcal{SHIQ}$ language extends the $\mathcal{ALCN}$ language in several ways: it allows the definition of role hierarchies and the use of transitive and inverse roles and introduces some new concept constructors as well.

We will present the $\mathcal{SHIQ}$ language step by step. First, we define the $\mathcal{S}$ language, which introduces transitive roles. Next, we add role hierarchies ($\mathcal{H}$), inverse roles ($\mathcal{I}$) and qualified number restrictions ($\mathcal{Q}$).

4.5.1. Transitive roles – the language $\mathcal{S}$

The evolution of DL language variants was influenced by application demands. Medical ontologies such as GALEN [91] as well as complex engineering and computer systems [33] are typical application domains. In all these the part–whole relationship plays an important role. For instance, in a medical taxonomy it is useful to include the part–whole relationship, by stating that e.g. a finger is a component of the hand, the hand of the arm, the arm of the upper body etc. At the same time it is important to introduce the transitive closure of the role "is component of", which is usually named "is part of". So, something is a part of something else if it is a component of it or a component of some of its components etc. The concept expression ∃isPartOf.Arm describes the parts of the Arm in whatsoever depth. Similar part–whole roles are needed in industrial terminologies: in the automotive industry we can speak about a valve being a component of a cylinder, a cylinder a component of an engine, an engine a component of a car etc.

In addition to part–whole relationships there are other situations where transitive roles are needed. In software engineering we can speak about some module providing information to another. Here, it can also be important to introduce the transitive closure of this role, which will connect a module with another if the former provides information to the latter, possibly in an indirect way through some other modules. Similarly, in the field of family relations, it may be interesting to introduce the transitive closure of the role "has child", i.e. the relationship "has descendant".

The first stop on our way towards $\mathcal{SHIQ}$ is the language named $\mathcal{S}$. This is derived from $\mathcal{ALC}$; i.e. we remove number restrictions from $\mathcal{ALCN}$, the most complex language

---

[12] The acronym $\mathcal{SHIQ}$ is pronounced "shicku".

introduced so far. (Number restrictions will be added later, in a more general form as qualified number restrictions.) We obtain the language $\mathcal{S}$ by adding transitive roles to $\mathcal{ALC}$.

Transitivity can be introduced in a DL language in several ways. The most natural way would be to allow the construction of the transitive closure of a role. This would require a new role constructor (denoted by, say, an upper index +), which, when applied to a role R, returns its transitive closure R^+. For example, one could then state a role equivalence axiom hasDescendant $\equiv$ hasChild$^+$. Note, however, that such an axiom cannot be expressed even in full first-order logic (see Subsection 4.10.3).

Therefore the language $\mathcal{S}$ provides a weaker form of transitivity: it allows us to state only that certain roles are transitive. For instance, we can state that the role hasDescendant is transitive but we cannot express the fact that it is the transitive closure of hasChild.

We write the axiom stating that a role R is transitive as Trans(R), e.g. Trans(hasDescendant).

The language $\mathcal{S}$ is also known as $\mathcal{ALC}_{\mathcal{R}^+}$, where the lower index $\mathcal{R}^+$ implies that roles can be declared transitive.

4.5.2. Role hierarchies – the language extension $\mathcal{H}$

We now introduce an extension $\mathcal{H}$ defining role *hierarchies*.

Above, we mentioned part–whole relationships, e.g. a car is in a "has component" relation with its subcomponents. Now, it may be useful to introduce the "has wheel" relation as a special case when the subcomponent in question is a wheel. Obviously, the wheel of the car is also a component of the car at the same time. This fact can be formally stated using a role inclusion axiom: hasWheel $\sqsubseteq$ hasComponent. Furthermore, it might be worth introducing further special cases, such as "has critical component". In this way a multi-level hierarchy of roles can evolve, for instance, hasWheel $\sqsubseteq$ hasCriticalComponent, hasBrake $\sqsubseteq$ hasCriticalComponent, hasCriticalComponent $\sqsubseteq$ hasComponent. Such a role hierarchy can be displayed as a directed graph, in a similar way to concept hierarchies. An example can be seen in Figure 4.8.

The language extension $\mathcal{H}$ introduces role inclusion axioms and thus makes it possible to describe role hierarchies. As already seen from the examples discussed above, a role inclusion axiom $R_1 \sqsubseteq R_2$ is similar to concept inclusion axioms but has roles (or role

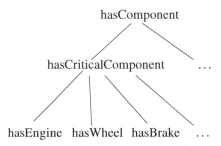

Figure 4.8. A simple role hierarchy.

expressions) on each side of the $\sqsubseteq$ sign, rather than concepts. To give yet another example of a role inclusion axiom: hasFriend $\sqsubseteq$ knows states that "knows" is a more general relationship than "has friend", i.e. one knows more than just one's friends. To be more precise: if the relation "has friend" holds between two individuals then the relation "knows" has to hold between them, too.

When we add role inclusion axioms to the language $\mathcal{S}$ we obtain $\mathcal{SH}$, in which a "weak" transitive closure operation can be expressed. Let us consider the following example:

$$\text{Trans(hasDescendant)};$$

$$\text{hasChild} \sqsubseteq \text{hasDescendant}.$$

These two axioms state that the role "has descendant" is transitive and is more general than the role "has child". Clearly, this implies hasChild$^+$ $\sqsubseteq$ hasDescendant, where $(\cdot)^+$ is the transitive closure operator (which is not allowed in the languages discussed in this section). We can thus express in $\mathcal{SH}$ the fact that hasDescendant is a *transitive* role subsuming the transitive closure of the relation hasChild. This is often rephrased in the following form: hasDescendant is a *weak transitive closure* of hasChild. Note that while the proper transitive closure is defined uniquely, a role normally has multiple weak transitive closures.

We have just said that the language extension $\mathcal{H}$ introduces role inclusion axioms. However, it is clear that role equivalence axioms can also be allowed here, because a role equivalence axiom $R_1 \equiv R_2$ can be replaced by two role inclusion axioms, $R_1 \sqsubseteq R_2$ and $R_2 \sqsubseteq R_1$. Note, however, that R_1 and R_2 can stand only for atomic roles (assuming that the language is $\mathcal{SH}$).[13] Thus, in the context of $\mathcal{SH}$, role equivalence axioms can be used only for aliasing one role to another. Such an axiom can be eliminated easily, by replacing e.g. the first role by the second throughout the knowledge base.

Exercise 4.20: Consider the following roles: hasParent, hasMother, hasFather, hasSpouse, hasAncestor, hasRelative. Build the role hierarchy of this set of roles, i.e. list all the role inclusion axioms involving these roles. Also declare the appropriate roles transitive.

4.5.3. Inverse roles – the language extension $\mathcal{I}$

The language extension to be discussed now is the inverse role constructor, which was introduced informally in Section 4.2. For example, we can state that hasParent is the inverse of hasChild and then use both roles in concept expressions. The abbreviation $\mathcal{I}$ refers to the *inverse*.

Like transitivity and role hierarchies, inverse roles are very important for applications. For example, they make it possible to name part–whole relationships in both directions, e.g. we can speak about the role "is part of" as the inverse of the role "has a part". Similarly, we can introduce "is a component of" as the inverse of the role "has a component". This brings in additional expressive power in describing the background knowledge of an application domain.

---

[13] This is not true for languages supporting inverse roles, introduced in the next subsection.

Let us illustrate this point with a simple example. Let the concept "good parent" denote a parent all of whose children are healthy, and let us call someone a "good child" if he or she has a good parent:

$$\text{GoodParent} \equiv \exists\text{hasChild}.\top \sqcap \forall\text{hasChild}.\text{Healthy};$$

$$\text{GoodChild} \equiv \exists\text{hasParent}.\text{GoodParent}.$$

Assuming that the notion of inverse role has been introduced and that hasChild is known to be the inverse of hasParent, then one can easily prove that the concept

$$\text{GoodChild} \sqcap \neg\text{Healthy}$$

is not satisfiable, since there cannot exist an individual who is not healthy while every child of one of its parents is healthy.

This result can also be formulated as the statement "good children are healthy", Formally we can state that

$$\text{GoodChild} \sqsubseteq \text{Healthy}$$

is a consequence of the above definitions. Thus inverse roles can help us in TBox classification (deducing the concept hierarchy), an important task in knowledge processing.

Now let us turn to the actual syntax of the language extension $\mathcal{I}$. We use the upper index $^-$ as the inverse role constructor: the inverse of role R is the role R^-. As expected, R^- denotes a relation obtained from the role denoted by R by switching the two arguments. For instance, the role expression hasChild$^-$ represents the same relation as hasParent.

In principle, a role constructor can be applied to an arbitrary role expression. For example, one can build the inverse of R^-, i.e. the expression $(R^-)^-$. This latter denotes the same relation as R: if we switch the two arguments of a relation twice, we get back the original relation. Hence $(R^-)^- \equiv R, ((R^-)^-)^- \equiv R^-$ etc. In order to avoid multiple inverse operations the following notation is introduced:

$$\text{Inv}(R) = \begin{cases} S & \text{if } R = S^-; \\ R^- & \text{otherwise.} \end{cases}$$

Inverse roles can be used wherever atomic roles can be used, i.e. in appropriate concept constructors, such as existential or value restrictions, and in role axioms.

At the end of the previous subsection we stated that, in the language $\mathcal{SH}$, role equivalence axioms can be eliminated by using a single name for all equivalent roles. Let us see whether this still holds in the presence of inverse roles. If we have a role equivalence axiom involving inverses, e.g. hasChild$^-$ $\equiv$ hasParent, we can still get rid of it by replacing all occurrences of hasParent by hasChild$^-$ throughout the knowledge base. However, there is one exception: the axiom

$$R^- \equiv R, \tag{4.9}$$

stating that the role R is symmetric, cannot be eliminated in this way. Nevertheless, this statement can still be replaced by two role inclusion axioms.

Exercise 4.21: Formalise the following concepts and statements using the $\mathcal{SHI}$ language. Use the hasParent, hasSibling and hasPart atomic roles only.

(a) People with at least one tall child.

(b) People who only have tall children.

(c) Children with at least one tall parent.

(d) The parts of a car.

(e) A car which has critical parts that are faulty is itself faulty.

(f) The children of a parent with at least one tall child are either tall themselves or have a tall sibling.

4.5.4. Qualified number restrictions – extension $\mathcal{Q}$

The *qualified number restriction* construct, denoted by $\mathcal{Q}$, is a generalisation of the (unqualified) number restriction $\mathcal{N}$ (see Subsection 4.4.4). While the latter can be used to describe, for example, the concept of a "parent having at least three children", the extension $\mathcal{Q}$ allows us to define a more refined concept of a "parent having at least three *tall* children":

$$(\geqslant 3\,\text{hasChild.Tall}).$$

Like the above at-least restriction, an at-most restriction can also be extended to include a qualification. For example, the notion of someone's owning at most two cars can be described in the following way:

$$(\leqslant 2\,\text{owns.Car}).$$

Qualified number restrictions are needed, for example, in applications for which the object-oriented or entity–relationship [25] modelling approach is appropriate. In such applications the *multiplicity* of a relation plays an important role. A typical example is that a person has exactly one surname and at least one forename. Such constraints can be transformed easily to DL formulae using qualified number restrictions [24].

The syntax of qualified number restrictions is the following:

$$(\geqslant n\,R.C) \qquad \text{and} \qquad (\leqslant n\,R.C), \tag{4.10}$$

where n is a positive integer, R is a role expression and C is a concept expression.

It is obvious that an unqualified number restriction ($\mathcal{N}$) is a special case of a qualified number restriction: $(\leqslant nR) \equiv (\leqslant nR.\top)$, $(\geqslant nR) \equiv (\geqslant nR.\top)$. Note that full existential restriction can also be expressed using a qualified number restriction: $\exists R.C \equiv (\geqslant 1\,R.C)$.

Let us also note that by using both kinds of number restriction one can describe a so-called *equality restriction*:

$$(\geqslant n R.C) \sqcap (\leqslant n R.C). \tag{4.11}$$

An individual belongs to this concept if it has *exactly* n R-relations which lead to individuals belonging to C. Formula (4.11) is often abbreviated as $(= n R.C)$.

When the extension $\mathcal{Q}$ is added to the language $\mathcal{SHI}$, introduced in the preceding sub-sections, we obtain the language $\mathcal{SHIQ}$. In this context it is usual to disallow certain combinations of extensions related to transitivity, role hierarchy and number restrictions: namely, the role R in formula (4.10) cannot be transitive nor can it subsume some transitive role.[14] For example, the concept expression $(\geqslant 4\,\mathsf{hasDescendant.Tall})$ ("has at least four tall descendants") is disallowed, assuming that the role $\mathsf{hasDescendant}$ is transitive.

To make this limitation more precise, the notion of a *simple role* is introduced. A role R is simple w.r.t. a TBox $\mathcal{T}$ if it does not follow from $\mathcal{T}$ that R is transitive or that R subsumes a transitive role. Here one should take into account that new role axioms can be deduced from a TBox in a variety of ways. First, we can use the fact that role inclusion itself is a transitive operation, i.e. if $R_1 \sqsubseteq R_2, \ldots, R_{n-1} \sqsubseteq R_n$ hold then the last role subsumes the first: $R_1 \sqsubseteq R_n$. Furthermore, if we have a role inclusion axiom of the form $R \sqsubseteq S$ then $\mathsf{Inv}(R) \sqsubseteq \mathsf{Inv}(S)$ also holds. Finally, if it is known that $\mathsf{Trans}(R)$ then $\mathsf{Trans}(\mathsf{Inv}(R))$ holds as well.

For example, if the TBox includes the statements

$$\mathsf{Trans}(R_0^-), \qquad R_0^- \sqsubseteq R_1, \qquad R_1^- \sqsubseteq R_2$$

then R_2 is not simple because the second axiom can be transformed to the form $R_0 \sqsubseteq R_1^-$, producing a chain of subsumption axioms between R_0 and R_2. Furthermore, R_0 is transitive because R_0^- is transitive.

Exercise 4.22: Consider the roles listed in Exercise 4.20, together with the role axioms provided by you as the solution to the exercise. Decide which roles are simple.

Having defined the notion of a simple role, we can formulate the limitation as follows: only simple roles can be used in number restrictions.

A special case of number restrictions, the *functional restriction*, deserves further attention. This construction (denoted by the letter $\mathcal{F}$) allows only concept expressions of the form $(\leqslant 1R)$ and $(\geqslant 2R)$, where R is still a simple role. Notice that this is a special case of an *unqualified* number restriction $\mathcal{N}$. For instance, $(\leqslant 1\,\mathsf{hasChild})$ denotes people having at most one child. The name "*functional* restriction" indicates that this construct can be used to express the fact that a role is a partial function (each individual has at most one individual associated with it through the given role). For example, the concept inclusion axiom

$$\top \sqsubseteq (\leqslant 1\,\mathsf{hasWife})$$

expresses the statement that everyone can have at most one wife.[15] To describe a total functional relationship (e.g. everyone has exactly one mother) we have to add an existential restriction as well:

$$\top \sqsubseteq (\leqslant 1\,\mathsf{hasMother}) \sqcap (\exists\mathsf{hasMother.}\top).$$

---

[14] This is for reasons of efficiency: if we allowed the use of such roles, the generated logic would become undecidable; see [64].

[15] The axiom states that the set of individuals who have at most one wife subsumes the whole domain. Therefore it is true for every individual in the domain that it has at most one wife.

The reason for inclusion of the formula $(\geqslant 2R)$ in the language extension $\mathcal{F}$ is that it is the negation of $(\leqslant 1R)$. As an example, consider a university regulation which requires that anyone obtaining a Ph.D. has to know at least two languages:

$$\textsf{PersonWithPhD} \sqsubseteq (\geqslant 2\,\textsf{knowsLanguage}).$$

In Chapter 7 we describe the so-called *tableau inference algorithms* for the $\mathcal{SHIQ}$ language family, starting with an algorithm for $\mathcal{S}$, and extending this in several steps until we reach $\mathcal{SHIQ}$. The last but one language on this path is $\mathcal{SHIF}$. It is included as a separate step there because it is the functional restriction which, in combination with inverse roles, leads to the loss of the so-called finite model property; see Subsection 7.5.1 for details. As a consequence, it also requires the introduction of so-called *pairwise blocking*, one of the most complex elements in $\mathcal{SHIQ}$ tableau reasoning.

Exercise 4.23: Formalise the following concepts and statement using the $\mathcal{SHIQ}$ language. Use the atomic roles hasParent and hasComponent.

(a) People with at least two tall children.

(b) Cars with at most two faulty components.

(c) A reliable system is not faulty if it has at most one faulty component.[16]

4.5.5. The syntax and semantics of the $\mathcal{SHIQ}$ language

In this subsection we give a complete syntactic description of the $\mathcal{SHIQ}$ language, summarising the preceding subsections. We also give a formal semantics for $\mathcal{SHIQ}$ expressions and axioms.

When constructing the $\mathcal{SHIQ}$ language, we started from $\mathcal{S} = \mathcal{ALC}_{\mathcal{R}^+}$ and then added extensions, indicated by the letters $\mathcal{H}$, $\mathcal{I}$ and $\mathcal{Q}$. Figure 4.9 gives a syntax summary of the $\mathcal{SHIQ}$ language: it shows how to build concept and role expressions (denoted by C and R, possibly with numeric indices) from atomic concepts A and atomic roles R_A. Here R_S denotes a simple role, as defined in the previous subsection. The bottom part of the figure describes how to build terminological axioms (denoted by T) using concept and role expressions. In the figure the rightmost column shows the language extension in which the given construct is introduced.

As concept and role expressions have already been discussed in detail, let us now focus on the terminological axioms T. The first two axiom types are *concept axioms*, stating the equivalence and inclusion of two concepts. The remaining three lines contain *role axioms*: using these, one can describe role equivalence, inclusion and transitivity.

The semantics of the $\mathcal{SHIQ}$ language is defined in the same way as for the $\mathcal{AL}$ language (see Subsection 4.3.2). We assume that an interpretation $\mathcal{I}$ is given which includes the non-empty domain of discourse, $\Delta^{\mathcal{I}}$, and which assigns a meaning to atomic concepts and roles. More precisely, an interpretation $\mathcal{I}$ maps every atomic concept A to a subset $A^{\mathcal{I}} \subseteq \Delta^{\mathcal{I}}$ and every atomic role R_A to a binary relation $(R_A)^{\mathcal{I}} \subseteq \Delta^{\mathcal{I}} \times \Delta^{\mathcal{I}}$.

---

[16] Reliable systems use certain techniques, such as the duplication of components, to achieve correct behaviour even if some of their components are faulty.

$C \to$	A	atomic concept	$(\mathcal{AL})$
	$\top$	top – universal concept	$(\mathcal{AL})$
	$\bot$	bottom – empty concept	$(\mathcal{AL})$
	$\neg C$	negation	$(\mathcal{C})$
	$C_1 \sqcap C_2$	intersection	$(\mathcal{AL})$
	$C_1 \sqcup C_2$	union	$(\mathcal{U})$
	$\forall R.C$	value restriction	$(\mathcal{AL})$
	$\exists R.C$	existential restriction	$(\mathcal{E})$
	$(\geqslant n R_S.C)$	qualified number restriction	$(\mathcal{Q})$
	$(\leqslant n R_S.C)$	qualified number restriction	$(\mathcal{Q})$
$R \to$	R_A	atomic role	$(\mathcal{AL})$
	R^-	inverse role	$(\mathcal{I})$
$T \to$	$C_1 \equiv C_2$	concept equivalence axiom	$(\mathcal{AL})$
	$C_1 \sqsubseteq C_2$	concept inclusion axiom	$(\mathcal{AL})$
	$R_1 \equiv R_2$	role equivalence axiom	$(\mathcal{H})$
	$R_1 \sqsubseteq R_2$	role inclusion axiom	$(\mathcal{H})$
	$\mathsf{Trans}(R)$	transitivity axiom	$(\mathcal{R}^+)$

Figure 4.9. The syntax of the $\mathcal{SHIQ}$ language.

Figure 4.10 gives a recursive extension of the $(\cdot)^{\mathcal{I}}$ interpretation function, mapping arbitrary concept and role expressions to their meaning in $\mathcal{I}$.

$$\top^{\mathcal{I}} = \Delta^{\mathcal{I}}$$
$$\bot^{\mathcal{I}} = \emptyset$$
$$(\neg C)^{\mathcal{I}} = \Delta^{\mathcal{I}} \setminus C^{\mathcal{I}}$$
$$(C_1 \sqcap C_2)^{\mathcal{I}} = C_1^{\mathcal{I}} \cap C_2^{\mathcal{I}}$$
$$(C_1 \sqcup C_2)^{\mathcal{I}} = C_1^{\mathcal{I}} \cup C_2^{\mathcal{I}}$$
$$(\forall R.C)^{\mathcal{I}} = \left\{ a \in \Delta^{\mathcal{I}} \,\middle|\, \forall b. \left(\langle a,b \rangle \in R^{\mathcal{I}} \to b \in C^{\mathcal{I}} \right) \right\}$$
$$(\exists R.C)^{\mathcal{I}} = \left\{ a \in \Delta^{\mathcal{I}} \,\middle|\, \exists b. \left(\langle a,b \rangle \in R^{\mathcal{I}} \land b \in C^{\mathcal{I}} \right) \right\}$$
$$(\geqslant n R.C)^{\mathcal{I}} = \left\{ a \in \Delta^{\mathcal{I}} \,\middle|\, | \{ b \mid \langle a,b \rangle \in R^{\mathcal{I}} \land b \in C^{\mathcal{I}} \} | \geq n \right\}$$
$$(\leqslant n R.C)^{\mathcal{I}} = \left\{ a \in \Delta^{\mathcal{I}} \,\middle|\, | \{ b \mid \langle a,b \rangle \in R^{\mathcal{I}} \land b \in C^{\mathcal{I}} \} | \leq n \right\}$$
$$(R^-)^{\mathcal{I}} = \left\{ \langle b,a \rangle \in \Delta^{\mathcal{I}} \times \Delta^{\mathcal{I}} \mid \langle a,b \rangle \in R^{\mathcal{I}} \right\}$$

Figure 4.10. The semantics of concept and role expressions in the $\mathcal{SHIQ}$ language.

Having defined the meaning of concept and role expressions, the semantics of the terminological axioms can be defined fairly easily. In Figure 4.9 we listed the five types

$$\mathcal{I} \models C_1 \equiv C_2 \Leftrightarrow C_1^{\mathcal{I}} = C_2^{\mathcal{I}}$$
$$\mathcal{I} \models C_1 \sqsubseteq C_2 \Leftrightarrow C_1^{\mathcal{I}} \subseteq C_2^{\mathcal{I}}$$
$$\mathcal{I} \models R_1 \equiv R_2 \Leftrightarrow R_1^{\mathcal{I}} = R_2^{\mathcal{I}}$$
$$\mathcal{I} \models R_1 \sqsubseteq R_2 \Leftrightarrow R_1^{\mathcal{I}} \subseteq R_2^{\mathcal{I}}$$
$$\mathcal{I} \models \mathsf{Trans}(R) \Leftrightarrow \forall a, b, c. \left(\langle a, b \rangle \in R^{\mathcal{I}} \wedge \langle b, c \rangle \in R^{\mathcal{I}} \rightarrow \langle a, c \rangle \in R^{\mathcal{I}} \right)$$

Figure 4.11. The semantics of the terminological axioms in $\mathcal{SHIQ}$.

of terminological axioms. Now, in Figure 4.11, we provide the precise conditions for an interpretation $\mathcal{I}$ to be a model of an axiom T, for each of the five axiom types T. The definitions are very simple: for concept equivalence and inclusion axioms we construct the meanings (domain subsets) corresponding to the concepts on the two sides of the given axiom and then simply check whether set equality or subsumption holds between these. Similar conditions are formulated for role equivalence and inclusion. Finally, for a transitivity axiom of we need to verify that the meaning of the role is in fact a transitive relation.

Exercise 4.24: Consider the following interpretation $\mathcal{I}_p$:

$$\Delta^{\mathcal{I}_p} = \{\mathsf{a}, \mathsf{b}, \mathsf{c}, \mathsf{d}, \mathsf{e}\};$$
$$\mathsf{Faulty}^{\mathcal{I}_p} = \{\mathsf{a}, \mathsf{d}, \mathsf{e}\};$$
$$\mathsf{ReliableSystem}^{\mathcal{I}_p} = \{\mathsf{a}\};$$
$$\mathsf{hasComponent}^{\mathcal{I}_p} = \{\langle \mathsf{a}, \mathsf{b} \rangle, \langle \mathsf{a}, \mathsf{c} \rangle, \langle \mathsf{b}, \mathsf{d} \rangle, \langle \mathsf{c}, \mathsf{e} \rangle\}.$$

Find out the meanings, in the interpretation $\mathcal{I}_p$, of the following concept expressions and terminological axioms:

(a) $\mathsf{Faulty} \sqcap \neg \mathsf{ReliableSystem}$;

(b) $\forall \mathsf{hasComponent}^-. \neg \mathsf{Faulty}$;

(c) $\exists \mathsf{hasComponent}^-. \neg \mathsf{Faulty}$;

(d) $\exists \mathsf{hasComponent}^-. \mathsf{Faulty}$;

(e) $(\leqslant 1 \mathsf{hasComponent}. \mathsf{Faulty})$;

(f) $(\geqslant 4 \mathsf{hasComponent}. \mathsf{Faulty})$;

(g) $(\leqslant 1 \mathsf{hasComponent}. \exists \mathsf{hasComponent}. \mathsf{Faulty})$;

(h) $(\geqslant 2 \mathsf{hasComponent}. \exists \mathsf{hasComponent}. (\neg \mathsf{Faulty} \sqcup (\geqslant 2 \mathsf{hasComponent}^-. \top)))$;

(i) $\mathsf{Trans}(\mathsf{hasComponent})$;

(j) $\exists \mathsf{hasComponent}. \mathsf{Faulty} \sqsubseteq \exists \mathsf{hasComponent}^-. \mathsf{Faulty}$;

(k) $\exists \mathsf{hasComponent}. \mathsf{Faulty} \sqsubseteq \mathsf{Faulty} \sqcup \exists \mathsf{hasComponent}^-. \neg \mathsf{Faulty}$;

(l) $\mathsf{Faulty} \sqcap \mathsf{ReliableSystem} \sqsubseteq (\geqslant 2 \mathsf{hasComponent}. \mathsf{Faulty})$;

(m) ReliableSystem ⊔ ∃hasComponent⁻.ReliableSystem ≡ ⊤;

(n) ¬Faulty ⊑ (⩽ 1hasComponent.Faulty).

Try to approximate the above concept expressions and axioms in plain English sentences.

4.6. Terminological reasoning tasks

In this section we discuss the building of terminological systems using Description Logics, and give an overview of reasoning tasks for these. Note that the design of inference algorithms for these tasks is the topic of the next chapters.

4.6.1. The structure of terminological systems

A terminological system (i.e. a TBox) is a collection of terminological axioms. In the case of the $\mathcal{AL}$ language family, the TBox consists of concept axioms only. Starting with the language $\mathcal{S}$, role axioms can also appear. Let us first discuss a classification of concept axioms:

Definitional axioms A *definitional axiom*, or simply a *definition*, serves as the definition of a new concept. As an example, consider the concept Mother, as introduced earlier in Figure 4.3 via the following axiom:

$$\text{Mother} \equiv \text{Human} \sqcap \text{Female} \sqcap \exists \text{hasChild}.\top.$$

A definition takes the form $A \equiv C$, where A is an atomic concept that does not appear on the left-hand side of any other definitions.

Background knowledge axioms Any terminological statement that is not a definition is considered background knowledge. For example:

$$\text{PersonWithPhD} \sqsubseteq (\geqslant 2 \text{knowsLanguage}).$$

As there is no restriction on axioms describing background knowledge, they can state the equivalence $(C \equiv D)$ or inclusion $(C \sqsubseteq D)$ of arbitrary concept expressions C and D. Because an equivalence axiom can be replaced by two inclusion axioms, quite often only inclusion axioms are considered. This type of statement is thus often referred to as a *general concept inclusion axiom* (GCI axiom).

In an analogous way we can categorise *role* axioms as definitions and background knowledge. However, in the $\mathcal{SHIQ}$ language there is only a single role constructor, namely the inverse. This means that $\mathcal{SHIQ}$ role definitions are very simple: they name the inverse of a role, e.g. hasParent ≡ hasChild⁻, or rename a role, e.g. wroteBook ≡ hasBook. As we have discussed most such axioms can be eliminated, the only exception being the statement that a role is symmetric, e.g. hasFriend ≡ hasFriend⁻. The background knowledge about roles is the role hierarchy, the statements describing the inclusion of roles or their inverses. Of course, in DL languages allowing more role constructors (see Section 4.10), the role axioms become more varied as well.

Because the role axioms in the $\mathcal{SHIQ}$ language are very simple, we will now focus on TBoxes containing concept axioms. Using the classification introduced above, such a TBox can be split into two parts: a *definitional part* and a *background knowledge part*. The former contains axioms of the form $A \equiv C$, where each atomic concept A appears only once on the left-hand side of an axiom within the definitional part. A *definitional TBox* is a TBox in which the background part is empty.

Given a TBox, one may distinguish between two types of atomic concepts, according to the role they play in the definitions. Concepts appearing on the left-hand side of definitions are called *name symbols*, while all other atomic concepts are called *base symbols*. Let us recall a former example about the concept "father of girls" (see Section 4.4.2): the statements (4.3) and (4.4), defining the concepts Father and FatherOfGirls, constitute the definition part here while the axiom (4.5) is the background part. The name symbols are Father and FatherOfGirls, while the base symbols are Human, Female and Optimist.

A TBox is called *definitorial* if the meaning of the name symbols can be determined *unambiguously* from the meaning of the base symbols. A definitorial TBox cannot have two models differing only in the meanings of the name symbols. This is the case, for instance, for the TBox (4.3), (4.4) cited above: if the meanings of the concepts Human and Female are supplied (together with the meaning of the role hasChild, of course) then the meanings of the concepts Father and FatherOfGirls are unambiguously defined by the TBox, as discussed earlier in Subsection 4.3.2.

When dealing with a definitorial TBox, the process of building interpretations can be simplified. A so-called *base interpretation* is an interpretation which assigns a meaning to base symbols only, the name symbols are left unassigned. Because the TBox is definitorial, a base interpretation determines unambiguously the (proper) interpretation. In the example above we do not need to assign a meaning to the name symbols Father and FatherOfGirls, because the axioms (4.3), (4.4), together with the meanings of the base symbols Human and Female present in the base interpretation, unambiguously determine the interpretation of the name symbols.

How can a TBox be *non*-definitorial? Essentially, this can only happen when a name symbol is used in its own definition, either directly or indirectly. For example, let us define the concept "Pessimist" as an individual all of whose friends are pessimists:

$$\text{Pessimist} \equiv \text{Human} \sqcap \forall \text{hasFriend.Pessimist}. \qquad (4.12)$$

It is easy to see that the TBox $\mathcal{T} = \{(4.12)\}$ is *not* definitorial. Recall that the condition for TBox (4.12) to be definitorial is that once we supply an *arbitrary* base interpretation (i.e. a domain, the meaning of the base symbol Human and the meaning of the role hasFriend), the meaning of the only name symbol, Pessimist, is determined unambiguously.

Figure 4.12 shows a base interpretation $\mathcal{I}$ for the TBox $\mathcal{T}$, which has a domain $\Delta^{\mathcal{I}}$ of four elements. In the interpretation $\mathcal{I}$ everyone is human and both the pairs $\langle a, b \rangle$ and $\langle c, d \rangle$ are mutually friends of each other. The statement (4.12) holds if, for instance, $\text{Pessimist}^{\mathcal{I}} = \{a, b\}$ (see the area delimited by the continuous line), but it also holds if $\text{Pessimist}^{\mathcal{I}} = \{c, d\}$ (see the broken-line area) and even if everybody is a Pessimist or nobody is. So the TBox consisting of the single axiom (4.12) is *not* definitorial.

The TBox above is called *cyclic*. To give the exact definition of this notion we first define a relation on the set of name symbols of a TBox: a name symbol A *relies directly on* a name symbol B if B occurs on the right-hand side of the axiom defining A. The relation *relies on* is defined as the transitive closure of *relies directly on*. A TBox is cyclic if it contains a concept that *relies on* itself. A TBox is *acyclic* if it is not cyclic.

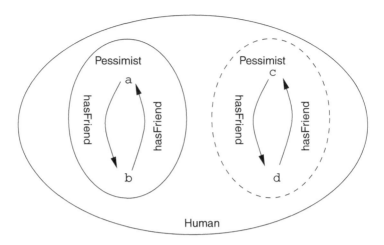

Figure 4.12. Interpretations of a cyclic TBox.

It is easy to prove that an acyclic TBox is definitorial. Let $\mathcal{T}$ be such a TBox. Let us choose one of its definition axioms, $A \equiv C$, and replace A with the concept expression C throughout the whole TBox, except for the left-hand side of A's definition. This results in a new TBox that is obviously equivalent to the original one, but in which the name symbol A appears only once, on the left-hand side of its definition (here we make use of the fact that the TBox is acyclic). When this operation is performed for every definition in the TBox, we get a TBox $\mathcal{T}'$, which is equivalent to the original one except that on the right-hand side of the definitions there are no name symbols, only base symbols. But $\mathcal{T}'$ is obviously definitorial, since for every name concept A introduced by an axiom $A \equiv D \in \mathcal{T}'$ the only correct interpretation is $A^{\mathcal{I}} = D^{\mathcal{I}}$. Because $\mathcal{T}$ and $\mathcal{T}'$ are equivalent, $\mathcal{T}$ is definitorial too.

Exercise 4.25: Transform the following English sentences into a TBox using the concepts Human, Man, Woman, MarriedMan, Female and the roles hasWife and hasSpouse.

(a) A man is a human who is not female.

(b) A married man is a man.

(c) A married man is a man who has a spouse.

(d) A wife of a man is a woman.

(e) A woman is a female human.

(f) No woman can be the wife of two men.

Split the above TBox into a definitional part and a background knowledge part. Show that this TBox is definitorial. Make a sample base interpretation and derive the meaning of the name symbols.

The TBox $\mathcal{T}'$ resulting from the above transformation is called the *expansion* of the original $\mathcal{T}$.[17] An important property of an expanded TBox is the following.

> Name symbols only appear on the left-hand side of definition axioms in the expansion of an acyclic TBox.   (4.13)

As an example, the expansion of the TBox (4.3)–(4.5) is the following:

$$\text{Father} \equiv \text{Human} \sqcap \neg\text{Female} \sqcap \exists\text{hasChild}.\top ;$$
$$\text{FatherOfGirls} \equiv \text{Human} \sqcap \neg\text{Female}$$
$$\sqcap \exists\text{hasChild}.\top \sqcap \forall\text{hasChild}.\text{Female};$$
$$\text{Human} \sqcap \neg\text{Female}; \sqcap\exists\text{hasChild}.\top$$
$$\sqcap \forall\text{hasChild}.\text{Female} \sqsubseteq \text{Optimist} \sqcup \exists\text{hasChild}.\text{Optimist}.$$

Exercise 4.26: Build the expansion of the TBox that you supplied as a solution to Exercise 4.25.

It can be proved that, given an arbitrary definitorial $\mathcal{ALCQ}$ TBox, there is an acyclic TBox which is equivalent to it [30]. Note that the statement "every definitorial TBox is acyclic" is obviously untrue as one can introduce "unnecessary" cycles, as in: $A \equiv C \sqcap (A \sqcup \neg A)$.

Note that a cyclic definition can be viewed as a constraint, requiring that the (meaning of the) given concept satisfies a fixed point equation. To illustrate this, let us consider our former example (4.12) and let us fix the interpretation domain, the meaning of the role hasFriend and the meaning of the base symbol Human. Let us now examine whether a given set X of individuals, as a candidate meaning for the concept Pessimist, satisfies the axiom (4.12). To check this, we have to evaluate the right-hand side of (4.12) using X as the meaning of Pessimist. If this results in the set X itself then the axiom is satisfied. Let us view the right-hand side of the axiom (4.12) as a function τ, the argument of which is the set representing the meaning of Pessimist and which returns the meaning of the right-hand side concept expression. With this view the axiom takes the form $X = \tau(X)$, i.e. the set X that satisfies the axiom is a fixed point of the function τ.

If certain conditions are satisfied, a partial order can be established among the models of a cyclic TBox. In such cases a specific fixed point can be chosen as the preferred solution, e.g. the least or the greatest. Further information on this topic can be found in, for example, Nebel [88].

4.6.2. Reasoning tasks

Let us assume that we have created a terminological system (i.e. a TBox). Let us examine what kinds of reasoning task can be performed on such a system.

The first question one should ask is whether the TBox is consistent, i.e. whether it has any models. It may happen that one makes modelling errors so serious that the TBox contains or implies a statement that obviously cannot have any models, such as $\top \sqsubseteq \bot$. (Recall that the

---

[17] The name refers to the fact that the expansion of a TBox can be substantially larger than the original TBox; the size of the former may be exponential in the number of name symbols of the original TBox.

notion of interpretation includes the condition that its domain cannot be empty.) Thus the first reasoning task that we identify is the verification of TBox consistency.

Even if a TBox $\mathcal{T}$ is consistent, there may still be trouble with it. We may have defined an atomic concept that is *unsatisfiable*, i.e. whose meaning is empty in every model of $\mathcal{T}$. Obviously, there are concept expressions that are unsatisfiable, e.g. $C =$ Female $\sqcap \neg$Female. However, if a TBox introduces an atomic concept which is not satisfiable then there is a very good chance that this is a modelling error.

A TBox is said to be *coherent* if every atomic concept that appears in the TBox is satisfiable [47]. Most DL reasoning engines provide a service to verify that a TBox is coherent.

Further modelling errors can be discovered by asking the reasoning engine whether a statement that we expect to be a consequence of the TBox can actually be deduced from it. For instance, a correct terminological system about family relations should imply that Father is included in Parent but that these two concepts are not equivalent. The concepts Father and Female should be disjoint also. Of course, composite concept expressions can appear in queries relating to such concept relationships, e.g. one may ask a DL inference engine to decide whether the concept $\exists$hasChild$^-$.$\forall$hasChild.Tall is subsumed by the concept Tall.

In the examples above there are three types of special concept relationship: *subsumption* (also called inclusion), where the meaning of one concept is contained in the meaning of the other; *equivalence*, where the two meanings are the same; and *disjointness*, when the two meanings are disjoint.

Let us summarise and define formally the four main kinds of terminological reasoning task, introduced above:

- *Satisfiability:* The concept C is satisfiable w.r.t. the TBox $\mathcal{T}$ if, and only if, $\mathcal{T}$ has a model $\mathcal{I}$ such that $C^{\mathcal{I}}$ is not empty, i.e. $\mathcal{T} \models C \equiv \bot$ does not hold.

- *Subsumption:* The concept D subsumes concept C w.r.t. the TBox $\mathcal{T}$ if, and only if, $\mathcal{T} \models C \sqsubseteq D$, i.e. if $C^{\mathcal{I}} \subseteq D^{\mathcal{I}}$ holds in every model $\mathcal{I}$ of $\mathcal{T}$. This subsumption relationship can also be denoted by $C \sqsubseteq_{\mathcal{T}} D$.

- *Equivalence:* The concepts C and D are equivalent w.r.t. the TBox $\mathcal{T}$ if, and only if, $\mathcal{T} \models C \equiv D$, i.e. if $C^{\mathcal{I}} = D^{\mathcal{I}}$ holds in every model $\mathcal{I}$ of $\mathcal{T}$. This equivalence is sometimes denoted by $C \equiv_{\mathcal{T}} D$.

- *Disjointness:* The concepts C and D are disjoint w.r.t. the TBox $\mathcal{T}$ if, and only if, $\mathcal{T} \models C \sqcap D \equiv \bot$, i.e. if $C^{\mathcal{I}} \cap D^{\mathcal{I}} = \emptyset$ holds in every model $\mathcal{I}$ of $\mathcal{T}$.

It is easy to see that these four reasoning tasks can be easily reduced to each other. This can be done, for example, by applying (possibly several of) the transformations below.

- *Unsatisfiability $\leftrightarrow$ Subsumption:* C is unsatisfiable if, and only if, C is subsumed by the empty concept $\bot$.

- *Subsumption $\leftrightarrow$ Disjointness:* C is subsumed by D if, and only if, $\neg D$ and C are disjoint.

- *Disjointness $\leftrightarrow$ Equivalence:* The concepts C and D are disjoint if, and only if, $C \sqcap D$ is equivalent to the concept $\bot$.

- *Equivalence $\leftrightarrow$ Unsatisfiability:* C and D are equivalent if, and only if, $(C \sqcap \neg D) \sqcup (D \sqcap \neg C)$ is not satisfiable.

For example, the reasoning task "Parent subsumes Father" can be reformulated in the following way.

- ¬Parent and Father are disjoint.

- ¬Parent ⊓ Father is equivalent to the concept ⊥.

- ¬Parent ⊓ Father is not satisfiable.

Notice that, in most of the above transformations, full negation was needed. This means that these transformations may not be valid in those simple DL languages, such as $\mathcal{AL}$, that only allow atomic negation. However, using only $\mathcal{AL}$ language constructs we can still reduce the other three reasoning tasks to a subsumption check, in the following way.

- *Unsatisfiability* ↔ *Subsumption:* C is unsatisfiable if, and only if, $C \sqsubseteq \bot$.

- *Disjointness* ↔ *Subsumption:* The concepts C and D are disjoint if, and only if, $C \sqcap D \sqsubseteq \bot$.

- *Equivalence* ↔ *Subsumption:* C and D are equivalent if, and only if, both subsumption relationships $C \sqsubseteq D$ and $D \sqsubseteq C$ hold.

Thus, all four types of reasoning task can be supported by an algorithm for subsumption checking, even for DL languages without full negation. In Subsection 5.1.3 we describe such an approach, called the structural subsumption algorithm. However, for languages that do allow full negation (i.e. which contain $\mathcal{ALC}$) it may be more efficient to base the reasoning tasks on a satisfiability algorithm. Notice that satisfiability only concerns a single concept, as opposed to the two concepts involved in subsumption, and so the reasoning algorithm can become simpler. In Chapters 5 and 7 we present various versions of the tableau algorithm which is one of the most widespread methods for checking satisfiability.

Finally, let us mention the reasoning task of *TBox classification*; see e.g. question (5) in Figure 4.2. The output of a classification task is the hierarchy of atomic concepts appearing in the TBox supplied as the input. In principle this task can be implemented by checking the subsumption relationship of all pairs of atomic concepts present in the TBox. In Subsection 7.9.10 we discuss various optimisations of this task.

In the rest of this chapter we assume a language that allows full negation, and hence we will focus on the question of concept satisfiability. Thus we can assert that the primary task of terminological reasoning is to answer questions of the following kind:

$$\text{Is the concept } C \text{ satisfiable w.r.t. } \mathcal{T}? \qquad (4.14)$$

Recall that solving this task requires finding an interpretation $\mathcal{I}$ which is a model of $\mathcal{T}$ and in which the meaning of C is non-empty: $C^{\mathcal{I}} \neq \emptyset$. Such an interpretation $\mathcal{I}$ will also be called a *model* of the concept C w.r.t. TBox $\mathcal{T}$.

Exercise 4.27: For each of the following reasoning tasks, construct a concept C such that the given reasoning task is equivalent to checking whether C is unsatisfiable.

(a) Is MarriedMan subsumed by Human?

(b) Does ∃hasWife.⊤ include Human?

(c) Is MarriedMan disjoint from Woman?

(d) Are the concepts $\exists$hasWife.$\top$ and $\exists$hasWife$^-$.$\top$ disjoint?

(e) Are the concepts Man $\sqcup$ Woman and Human equivalent?

In the context of the TBox of Exercise 4.25, decide which of the above reasoning tasks should return a positive answer.

As a concluding remark, we note that the first reasoning task mentioned in the present subsection, checking the consistency of a TBox $\mathcal{T}$, can also be reformulated as a satisfiability check of the form (4.14). This can be achieved by substituting $\top$ for the concept C: the task of checking whether "the concept $\top$ is satisfiable w.r.t. $\mathcal{T}$" is equivalent to checking that the TBox $\mathcal{T}$ is consistent.

4.7. Eliminating terminological axioms

So far all reasoning tasks have been considered in the *context* of some TBox $\mathcal{T}$. Of course, it may be interesting to consider some special cases, such when $\mathcal{T}$ is empty or contains role axioms only. Algorithms for handling such special cases may be much simpler than for the general case. Therefore it may be of interest to try to *simplify the TBox*, i.e. reduce the question of the satisfiability of some concept C w.r.t. $\mathcal{T}$ to the satisfiability of some (more complex) concept C' w.r.t. a TBox $\mathcal{T}'$ which is in some sense simpler than $\mathcal{T}$. For example, $\mathcal{T}'$ might not contain definitional axioms or, indeed, any concept axioms at all. The last condition, in the case of simpler languages such as $\mathcal{ALCN}$, means that the simplified TBox will be empty, as such languages do not allow role axioms at all.

To highlight the nature of the task of simplifying a TBox, let us briefly discuss an analogous issue in first-order logic. Given a finite set of axioms $\{\phi_1, \ldots, \phi_n\}$, the task of proving a statement ϕ_0 from this set of axioms can be trivially reduced to checking whether the single implication $\phi_1 \wedge \ldots \wedge \phi_n \to \phi_0$ is a tautology, i.e. true in all interpretations. This technique and TBox simplification are two analogous examples of the reduction of a more complex kind of reasoning task to a simpler one, at the expense of the formulae involved becoming more complicated.

We now proceed to discuss two important cases where the TBox can be simplified by getting rid of some concept axioms.

4.7.1. Acyclic TBoxes

Let $\mathcal{T}$ be a TBox with an acyclic definitional part, and let our aim be to examine the satisfiability of a concept C w.r.t. $\mathcal{T}$. To carry out this task, let us first build an expansion of $\mathcal{T}$, namely $\mathcal{T}'$. This is a TBox in which name symbols appear only on the left-hand side of definitions, as stated in (4.13). Let us also expand the concept C itself, in the following sense: take all definitions of the form $A_i \equiv C_i$ in $\mathcal{T}'$ and replace every occurrence of the atomic concept A_i in C with the right-hand side of its definition, i.e. with C_i. Let us call the resulting concept the expansion of C and denote it by C'. Finally let us omit all definitional axioms from the expanded TBox $\mathcal{T}'$ and call this TBox $\mathcal{T}''$.

We show now that C is satisfiable w.r.t. $\mathcal{T}$ if, and only if, C' is satisfiable w.r.t. $\mathcal{T}''$. First, let us assume that C is satisfiable w.r.t. $\mathcal{T}$, i.e. there exists an interpretation $\mathcal{I}$ which is a model of $\mathcal{T}$ and in which C is not empty. Because $\mathcal{T}$ and its expansion $\mathcal{T}'$ are equivalent, therefore the interpretation $\mathcal{I}$ is also a model of $\mathcal{T}'$, hence the axioms $A_i \equiv C_i \in \mathcal{T}'$ hold in $\mathcal{I}$. Therefore, when we replace the concept A_i in C with C_i, the meaning of C in the given interpretation $\mathcal{I}$ will not change. Consequently, the interpretations of the concepts C and C' are the same in $\mathcal{I}$. Furthermore, $\mathcal{I}$ obviously satisfies the axioms of $\mathcal{T}''$ since $\mathcal{T}''$ is a subset of $\mathcal{T}'$. Thus we have shown that $\mathcal{I}$ is a model of $\mathcal{T}''$ in which the meaning of C' is not empty, i.e. C' is satisfiable w.r.t. $\mathcal{T}''$.

In the other direction, let us take some arbitrary interpretation $\mathcal{I}$ which is a model of $\mathcal{T}''$ and in which C' is not empty. Let us expand the interpretation $\mathcal{I}$ to an interpretation $\mathcal{I}'$ which has the same domain but assigns meaning to the name symbols A_i occurring in $\mathcal{T}'$. In $\mathcal{I}'$ the name symbol A_i is mapped to the set obtained by evaluating the right-hand side C_i in the interpretation $\mathcal{I}$: $(A_i)^{\mathcal{I}'} = (C_i)^{\mathcal{I}}$, for each $(A_i \equiv C_i) \in \mathcal{T}'$. Otherwise, let $\mathcal{I}'$ be the same as $\mathcal{I}$. In the interpretation $\mathcal{I}'$ the definitional axioms $\mathcal{T}' \setminus \mathcal{T}''$ obviously hold. We also have the initial assumption that $\mathcal{T}''$ holds: thus all axioms of $\mathcal{T}'$ hold and so the TBox $\mathcal{T}$, which is equivalent to $\mathcal{T}'$, is satisfied as well. Therefore $\mathcal{I}'$ is a model of $\mathcal{T}$. Because the expansion C' does not contain any concepts introduced in $\mathcal{I}'$, the meaning of C' in $\mathcal{I}'$ is the same as in $\mathcal{I}$. We also claim that the meanings of C' and C are the same in $\mathcal{I}'$, by using the above argument. Thus we have obtained an interpretation $\mathcal{I}'$ which is a model of $\mathcal{T}$ and in which C is not empty, i.e. we have proved that C is satisfiable w.r.t. $\mathcal{T}$.

We have shown that, in case of an acyclic TBox $\mathcal{T}$, the task of checking concept satisfiability can be reduced to a simpler task: checking the satisfiability of the expansion of the given concept w.r.t. a TBox that is obtained by first expanding $\mathcal{T}$ and then removing all the definitional axioms from it. Specifically, if an acyclic TBox $\mathcal{T}$ consists of concept definitions only then the task of checking concept satisfiability w.r.t. $\mathcal{T}$ can be reduced to a satisfiability problem w.r.t. an empty TBox.

Exercise 4.28: Consider the TBox (4.3), (4.4) and the reasoning task of checking whether FatherOfGirls is subsumed by ¬Female. First, reduce this task into a satisfiability check. Next, apply the above transformation, so that the task is reduced to the satisfiability check of a concept C w.r.t. an empty TBox. What is this concept C?

4.7.2. Internalisation

Internalisation is a TBox simplification technique which can be used for removing all concept axioms from an arbitrary TBox. Without limiting the generality we can assume that all concept axioms in a TBox $\mathcal{T}$ are concept inclusion axioms, i.e. axioms of the form $C_i \sqsubseteq D_i$, $i = 1, \ldots, n$. The reason is that $C \equiv D$ can be replaced by two inclusion axioms. Stating that $C_i \sqsubseteq D_i$ holds is equivalent to stating that $\top \sqsubseteq \neg C_i \sqcup D_i$ is true, i.e. claiming that every element in the domain belongs either to the complement of C_i or to D_i. By making use of this fact one can easily formulate a single inclusion axiom $\top \sqsubseteq C_{\mathcal{T}}$ which is equivalent to the whole TBox. Here

$$C_{\mathcal{T}} = (\neg C_1 \sqcup D_1) \sqcap (\neg C_2 \sqcup D_2) \sqcap \cdots \sqcap (\neg C_n \sqcup D_n). \tag{4.15}$$

The concept $C_{\mathcal{T}}$ is called the *internalisation* of the TBox $\mathcal{T}$. It is obvious that an interpretation is a model of $\mathcal{T}$ if, and only if, every individual in it belongs to the concept $C_{\mathcal{T}}$.

Exercise 4.29: Consider the TBox $\mathcal{T}$ consisting of the following two axioms:

$$\text{Person} \equiv \exists \text{hasParent.Person};$$
$$\text{Person} \sqsubseteq \text{Man} \sqcup \text{Woman}.$$

Transform this TBox to a form which contains subsumption axioms only. Build the $C_{\mathcal{T}}$ internalisation concept of the TBox.

The internalisation of a TBox will be used in the next chapter to transform an $\mathcal{ALCN}$ tableau reasoning algorithm developed for an empty TBox into an algorithm that works for an arbitrary TBox. The tableau algorithm attempts to construct a model of the concept C in order to decide its satisfiability. Assume that we have an algorithm for checking concept satisfiability w.r.t. an empty TBox. Let us modify this algorithm in such a way that all individuals of the model being constructed belong to the concept $C_{\mathcal{T}}$ (the internalisation of the TBox $\mathcal{T}$). This means that, whenever a model satisfying C is constructed, this model also satisfies the TBox $\mathcal{T}$, thus showing that C is satisfiable w.r.t. $\mathcal{T}$. Using this approach, the details of which will be given in Subsection 5.4.3, we can derive a satisfiability algorithm applicable to non-empty TBoxes.

For a DL language that supports transitive roles and role hierarchy, such as $\mathcal{SH}$, internalisation can be used to simplify the TBox. This means that instead of modifying the tableau algorithm one can replace the reasoning task with another, simpler one. Specifically, instead of checking the satisfiability of some concept C w.r.t. $\mathcal{T}$, one can check the satisfiability of the concept

$$C_{C,\mathcal{T}} = C \sqcap C_{\mathcal{T}} \sqcap \forall U.C_{\mathcal{T}} \tag{4.16}$$

w.r.t. a TBox $\mathcal{T}_{C,\mathcal{T}}$ which contains no concept axioms, i.e. which consists of role axioms only. Here U is a newly introduced atomic role which is assumed to be different from all others appearing in C and $\mathcal{T}$. The TBox $\mathcal{T}_{C,\mathcal{T}}$ contains the role axioms of $\mathcal{T}$ and further role axioms stating that U is transitive and includes all roles (and their inverses) appearing in C and $\mathcal{T}$. Formally: $\mathcal{T}_{C,\mathcal{T}}$ contains all the role axioms in $\mathcal{T}$, the axiom $\text{Trans}(U)$ and the axiom $R \sqsubseteq U$ for every role R which appears in either C or $\mathcal{T}$. If inverse roles are also permitted by the DL language in question then the axiom $\text{Inv}(R) \sqsubseteq U$ is also to be included in $\mathcal{T}_{C,\mathcal{T}}$, for every role R appearing in either C or $\mathcal{T}$.

The newly introduced role is named U because it is related to the so-called *universal role*, which is a relation that holds between two arbitrary individuals. There is a DL language extension (see Subsection 4.10.3) that introduces the universal role symbol U as part of the language and interprets U in every interpretation $\mathcal{I}$ as $\Delta^{\mathcal{I}} \times \Delta^{\mathcal{I}}$. (This is analogous to interpreting the universal concept $\top$ as the full domain.) Note that the role U, as introduced in the definition of $\mathcal{T}_{C,\mathcal{T}}$, is a plain role whose "universal nature" is ensured by the role axioms included in the TBox. Such a role is sometimes called a *simulated* universal role.

The intuition behind the formula (4.16) is the following. Its first subterm, C, ensures that when $C_{C,\mathcal{T}}$ has a model, i.e. when there is an individual c belonging to it, then c belongs to C so C has a model as well. The remaining subterms ensure that all individuals of this model will belong to $C_{\mathcal{T}}$: the middle subterm ensures that c does, while the last states that anything related to c through the role U belongs to $C_{\mathcal{T}}$. Now, because U is transitive and subsumes all roles in our formulae, this means that any individual reachable from c through one or more role connections will belong to $C_\mathcal{T}$. Of course, there can be elements of the domain that cannot be reached from c but we will show that these can be removed without invalidating the model.

Let us proceed to prove the claim that checking the satisfiability of a concept C w.r.t. a TBox $\mathcal{T}$ is equivalent to checking the satisfiability of $C_{C,\mathcal{T}}$ w.r.t. $\mathcal{T}_{C,\mathcal{T}}$.

We first show that if the concept C is satisfiable w.r.t. $\mathcal{T}$ then $C_{C,\mathcal{T}}$ is also satisfiable w.r.t. $\mathcal{T}_{C,\mathcal{T}}$. The assumption means that $\mathcal{T}$ has a model $\mathcal{I}$ such that C is not empty, i.e. there exists an individual $c \in C^\mathcal{I}$. At the same time, because $\mathcal{I} \models \mathcal{T}$ holds, every element of the domain of $\mathcal{I}$ is an instance of the concept $C_\mathcal{T}$. As a consequence, c belongs to this concept as well: $c \in (C_\mathcal{T})^\mathcal{I}$. Because every individual of our model is in $C_\mathcal{T}$, every individual is also an instance of the concept $\forall U.C_\mathcal{T}$ that appears as the last term of formula (4.16), irrespective of how we interpret the role U (cf. formula (a) of Exercise 4.15).

Accordingly, we extend $\mathcal{I}$ with the role U and call the resulting interpretation $\mathcal{I}'$. Let us interpret U as the proper universal role, which connects any two elements of the domain: $U^{\mathcal{I}'} = \Delta^\mathcal{I} \times \Delta^\mathcal{I}$. As explained in the previous paragraph, $c \in (C_{C,\mathcal{T}})^{\mathcal{I}'}$ holds since c is an instance of all three terms on the right-hand side of formula (4.16), as interpreted in $\mathcal{I}'$. At the same time $\mathcal{I}'$ satisfies the newly introduced role axioms of $\mathcal{T}_{C,\mathcal{T}}$ because the universal role U is obviously transitive and subsumes every other role. Thus $\mathcal{I}'$ is a model of $\mathcal{T}_{C,\mathcal{T}}$ in which $C_{C,\mathcal{T}}$ is non-empty, and so we can conclude that $C_{C,\mathcal{T}}$ is satisfiable w.r.t. $\mathcal{T}_{C,\mathcal{T}}$.

Let us now consider the other direction. We thus assume that $C_{C,\mathcal{T}}$ is satisfiable w.r.t. $\mathcal{T}_{C,\mathcal{T}}$. Consequently there is an interpretation $\mathcal{I}$ which is a model of $\mathcal{T}_{C,\mathcal{T}}$, and an element c in the domain of $\mathcal{I}$, for which $c \in (C_{C,\mathcal{T}})^\mathcal{I}$. It is obvious that the meaning of C is not empty in $\mathcal{I}$, because the first subterm of formula (4.16) ensures that $c \in C^\mathcal{I}$ holds. The middle subterm claims that c belongs to $C_\mathcal{T}$, while the last guarantees that every element that is U-related to c is an instance of the internalisation concept $C_\mathcal{T}$. If U were a proper universal role, and thus connected c to all other individuals, then we could claim that $\mathcal{I}$ is a model of $\mathcal{T}$. Unfortunately the requirement that U is a proper universal role cannot be formulated within the $\mathcal{SH}$ language. However, because of the new axioms of $\mathcal{T}_{C,\mathcal{T}}$, we know that U is transitive and more general than any other role. This means that the relation U holds between any two individuals which are connected via one or more roles (including role inverses). Thus, points that cannot be reached from c through any number of role relationships are the *only* ones for which we cannot guarantee that $C_\mathcal{T}$ holds. Let us remove all such elements, i.e. those that are not U-related to c, from our interpretation $\mathcal{I}$. Thus we can build a new interpretation $\mathcal{I}'$ that has the domain $\Delta^{\mathcal{I}'} = \{c\} \cup \{x \mid \langle c, x \rangle \in U^\mathcal{I}\}$. The meaning of concepts and roles in $\mathcal{I}'$ is the same as in $\mathcal{I}$, but narrowed to the new domain: $C^{\mathcal{I}'} = C^\mathcal{I} \cap \Delta^{\mathcal{I}'}$ and $R^{\mathcal{I}'} = R^\mathcal{I} \cap (\Delta^{\mathcal{I}'} \times \Delta^{\mathcal{I}'})$. It is important to note that there cannot be a role relationship in $\mathcal{I}$ which connects a removed individual and an element of the new, narrowed, domain. If there were such a role relationship then the omitted individual would become reachable from c and thus would not be omitted.

Let us consider what happens when we remove an individual from an interpretation (which also requires the removal of all role connections in which it is involved). If we do this, the conceptual classification of certain individuals, namely those connected to the removed individual through a role, may change. This means that such an individual may cease to belong to a concept or become the member of a concept to which it did not belong previously. For example, if we remove the only child of a parent, this individual ceases to be a parent. This can propagate and influence the classification of other connected individuals, e.g. some other individual might cease to be a grandparent or uncle. However, let us notice that this kind of change can only propagate through role connections; it cannot have an effect on the part of the domain that is not reachable through role connections from the individuals being removed. Thus, in the narrowed interpretation $\mathcal{I}'$ the conceptual classification of the individuals does not change. The rigorous proof of this property is left to the reader, via the following exercise.

Exercise 4.30: Consider an arbitrary interpretation $\mathcal{I}$ in the $\mathcal{SHIQ}$ language, and let $c_0 \in \Delta^{\mathcal{I}}$ be an arbitrary individual. We say that an individual c_n, $n \geq 0$, is reachable from c_0 if there are individuals $c_1, \ldots, c_{n-1} \in \Delta^{\mathcal{I}}$ such that $\langle c_{i-1}, c_i \rangle \in (R_i)^{\mathcal{I}}$ holds for $i = 1, \ldots, n$, where R_i are arbitrary, not necessarily distinct, and possibly inverted atomic roles appearing in the signature of $\mathcal{I}$. (Note that this means that c_0 is considered reachable from itself.)

Let us define a sub-interpretation $\mathcal{I}'$ as follows:

$$\Delta^{\mathcal{I}'} = \{x \mid x \text{ is reachable from } c_0\};$$
$$A^{\mathcal{I}'} = A^{\mathcal{I}} \cap \Delta^{\mathcal{I}'}, \text{ for all atomic concepts A};$$
$$(R_A)^{\mathcal{I}'} = (R_A)^{\mathcal{I}} \cap (\Delta^{\mathcal{I}'} \times \Delta^{\mathcal{I}'}) \text{ for all atomic roles } R_A.$$

Show that for an arbitrary concept expresson C and an arbitrary role expression R the following equations hold:

$$C^{\mathcal{I}'} = C^{\mathcal{I}} \cap \Delta^{\mathcal{I}'};$$
$$R^{\mathcal{I}'} = R^{\mathcal{I}} \cap (\Delta^{\mathcal{I}'} \times \Delta^{\mathcal{I}'}).$$

Hint: use induction on the depth (maximal nesting) of the concepts. Thus, when proving the above equality for C, you can assume that it holds for all the subconcepts of C.

Exercise 4.31: Consider the DL language $\mathcal{AL}$ extended with role negation, to be defined later in Table 4.1, Subsection 4.10. This language allows, for example, the use of the role expression $\neg$loves, which holds between individuals x and y if, and only if, x does not love y. Thus the concept $\forall \neg$loves.Ugly contains those individuals all of whose not-loved ones are ugly.

Show that the statement of Exercise 4.30 does not hold for this DL language, by building a suitable interpretation which serves as a counterexample.

Let us now return to showing the correctness of internalisation. As c belongs to the concept $C_{C,\mathcal{T}}$ in the interpretation $\mathcal{I}$, it also belongs to this concept in the interpretation $\mathcal{I}'$. Because of the first subterm of (4.16), this means that C is not empty in $\mathcal{I}'$. At the same time, the interpretation $\mathcal{I}'$ has the property that every individual in its domain that is different from c is U-related to c. As a consequence, because of the middle and final subterms of (4.16), every individual in the domain of $\mathcal{I}'$ is an instance of the concept $C_{\mathcal{T}}$, i.e. $\mathcal{I}' \models \top \sqsubseteq C_{\mathcal{T}}$. This implies that $\mathcal{I}' \models \mathcal{T}$. To sum up: $\mathcal{I}'$ is a model of $\mathcal{T}$ and C is not empty in $\mathcal{I}'$, which means that the concept C is satisfiable w.r.t. TBox $\mathcal{T}$.

Thus we have shown that the concept C is satisfiable w.r.t. $\mathcal{T}$ if, and only if, the concept $C_{C,\mathcal{T}}$, which contains the internalisation of TBox $\mathcal{T}$, is satisfiable w.r.t. the TBox $\mathcal{T}_{C,\mathcal{T}}$, where the latter contains no concept axioms.

Exercise 4.32: Consider the task of checking the satisfiability of the concept C w.r.t. the TBox $\mathcal{T} = \{T\}$, where

$$T = \exists \mathsf{hasChild}^-.\mathsf{Optimist} \sqsubseteq \forall \mathsf{hasChild}.\mathsf{Optimist},$$
$$C = \mathsf{Optimist}.$$

(a) Construct the $C_\mathcal{T}$ internalisation concept of $\mathcal{T}$.

(b) Use the technique of internalisation to reduce the above satisfiability problem to a satisfiability problem w.r.t. a TBox containing no concept axioms, i.e. construct the concept $C_{C,\mathcal{T}}$ and the TBox $\mathcal{T}_{C,\mathcal{T}}$.

(c) Build an interpretation $\mathcal{I}_0$ consisting of a child, a parent and a grandparent. Select a non-empty interpretation of concept C such that $\mathcal{I}_0$ satisfies $\mathcal{T}$. Following the first part of the above proof, extend $\mathcal{I}_0$ to an interpretation $\mathcal{I}_1$ that demonstrates that $C_{C,\mathcal{T}}$ is satisfiable w.r.t. $\mathcal{T}_{C,\mathcal{T}}$.

(d) Construct an interpretation $\mathcal{I}_2$ which demonstrates that $C_{C,\mathcal{T}}$ is satisfiable w.r.t. $\mathcal{T}_{C,\mathcal{T}}$ (i.e. $\mathcal{I}_2 \models \mathcal{T}_{C,\mathcal{T}}$ and $(C_{C,\mathcal{T}})^{\mathcal{I}_2}$ is non-empty) but which, at the same time, is *not* a model of $\mathcal{T}$. Make the domain of $\mathcal{I}_2$ as small as possible.

(e) Consider the interpretation $\mathcal{I}_3$ defined by

$$\Delta^{\mathcal{I}_3} = \{a_1, a_2, a_3, b_1, b_2, b_3, c_1, c_2, c_3,\},$$
$$\mathsf{hasChild}^{\mathcal{I}_3} = \{\langle a_1, a_2 \rangle, \langle a_2, a_3 \rangle, \langle b_1, b_2 \rangle, \langle b_2, b_3 \rangle, \langle c_1, c_2 \rangle, \langle c_2, c_3 \rangle\},$$
$$\mathsf{Optimist}^{\mathcal{I}_3} = \{a_1, a_2, b_1, c_2\},$$
$$U^{\mathcal{I}_3} = \{\langle a_i, a_j \rangle | i, j \in S\} \cup \{\langle b_i, b_j \rangle | i, j \in S\} \cup \{\langle c_i, c_j \rangle | i, j \in S\},$$

where $S = \{1, 2, 3\}$. Show that $\mathcal{I}_3$ is a model of the TBox $\mathcal{T}_{C,\mathcal{T}}$. Using the interpretation $\mathcal{I}_3$ construct the meanings of the three subterms of $C_{C,\mathcal{T}}$, as shown in (4.16). Build the interpretation of $C_{C,\mathcal{T}}$ in $\mathcal{I}_3$.

Does $\mathcal{I}_3$ demonstrate that $C_{C,\mathcal{T}}$ is satisfiable w.r.t. $\mathcal{T}_{C,\mathcal{T}}$? Is $\mathcal{I}_3$ a model of $\mathcal{T}$?

Following the second part of the above proof construct the interpretation $\mathcal{I}_3'$ which is a model of $\mathcal{T}$ and in which C is non-empty.

4.8. ABoxes

Let us recall that a DL knowledge base has two main parts, as illustrated in Figure 4.1: the TBox, with which we have dealt so far, and the ABox, which constitutes the topic of this section.

4.8.1. The syntax and the semantics of ABoxes

In Figure 4.13 a simple ABox is presented. It is related to our example about fathers of girls; see (4.3) and (4.4). When introducing ABoxes one has to add a new type of name to the language, in addition to concept and role names (i.e. atomic concepts and roles). This

Father(NICK)
hasChild(NICK,ANN)
hasChild(MARY,ANN)
hasChild(ANN,JOHN)

Figure 4.13. A simple ABox.

new language element, analogous to constant names in first-order logic, serves for naming individuals and so is called an *individual name*. In the sample ABox of Figure 4.13 NICK, MARY, ANN and JOHN are the individual names. In general, in the examples we will use upper case identifiers as individual names while in formulae they will be denoted by the letters a, b, c etc.

An ABox can contain statements of the following two types:

$$C(a) \qquad \text{and} \qquad R(a,b),$$

where C is an arbitrary concept expression and R is an arbitrary role expression. The first statement is called a *concept assertion*, and it states that the individual name a is an instance of the concept C. The second statement is a *role assertion*, and it expresses the fact that a is R-related to b. In our example in Figure 4.13 the very first statement is a concept assertion which declares that NICK is an instance of the concept Father, whereas the final statement is a role assertion which tells that ANN and JOHN are related through the hasChild role. In the examples above we used only atomic concepts and roles, but an ABox can also include assertions that involve composite concepts and roles, for example $(\forall \text{hasChild.Tall})(\text{JOHN})$ and hasChild$^-$(JOE, JOHN).[18]

It is important to note that the individual *name* NICK is an entity different from the individual Nick, as shown in e.g. Figure 4.5. The former, NICK, is a symbol in the DL language *representing* an individual, such as Nick, which is an element of the interpretation domain. The relationship of the individual name NICK to the individual Nick is analogous to the relationship of the atomic concept Father to its meaning, i.e. the set of "father" individuals in a given interpretation. For the sake of readability, however, we will sometimes use the term "individual" instead of "individual name" provided that the context makes our intentions clear.

An ABox can include any finite number of statements of the above two kinds. In most cases the ABox is paired with a TBox that contains terminological information about the concepts and roles appearing in the ABox. We have introduced several kinds of terminological languages so far, from the simplest, $\mathcal{AL}$, to the most complex, $\mathcal{SHIQ}$. Each such language can be used in the construction of an ABox but, of course, more complex languages need more complex reasoning techniques.

To define the semantics of an ABox we have to extend the notion of an interpretation: we have to assign a meaning to individual names in addition to atomic concepts and roles. An interpretation $\mathcal{I}$ of a given ABox has to assign a meaning to every individual name a that

---

[18] The $\mathcal{SHIQ}$ language has composite role expressions, but in practice these can only have the form R_A^-, i.e. the inverse of an atomic role. These inverse roles can easily be eliminated from the ABox if their arguments are swapped. For example, one can replace the assertion hasChild$^-$(JOE, JOHN) by hasChild(JOHN, JOE).

appears in the ABox. This meaning, denoted by $a^{\mathcal{I}}$, is an individual, i.e. an element of the interpretation domain: $a^{\mathcal{I}} \in \Delta^{\mathcal{I}}$.

There is an important issue about whether to allow an interpretation to assign the same domain element to two different individual names. An interpretation $\mathcal{I}$ is said to satisfy the so-called *unique name assumption* (UNA) if, for every two distinct individual names a and b, we have $a^{\mathcal{I}} \neq b^{\mathcal{I}}$. For most ABoxes it makes sense to use UNA. For instance, in our sample ABox above we would be reluctant to accept an interpretation where two different individual names, e.g. JOHN and NICK, are assigned the same domain element. There may be some special cases, however, when UNA is not appropriate. For example, when we want to merge two knowledge bases that use different names for the same individual, it may be practical to keep both names and request that the same meaning is assigned to them. When UNA is not observed, it may thus become necessary to use special roles to declare instance equality and inequality. In our example of merging two knowledge bases, a special equality assertion can be used to declare that the two names have to be assigned the same meaning. At the same time, when this is important, an inequality assertion can state that two particular names are known to be different.

Let us consider an ABox and an interpretation $\mathcal{I}$ that assigns meanings to all concept, role and individual names occurring in the ABox. The fact that an ABox assertion α is satisfied by the interpretation $\mathcal{I}$ is denoted by $\mathcal{I} \models \alpha$. We now define the semantics of the ABox, i.e. the conditions under which $\mathcal{I} \models \alpha$ holds, for each kind of assertion α:

$$\mathcal{I} \models C(a) \Leftrightarrow a^{\mathcal{I}} \in C^{\mathcal{I}}; \tag{4.17}$$

$$\mathcal{I} \models R(a,b) \Leftrightarrow \langle a^{\mathcal{I}}, b^{\mathcal{I}} \rangle \in R^{\mathcal{I}}. \tag{4.18}$$

Furthermore, we say that $\mathcal{I}$ satisfies an ABox $\mathcal{A}$, denoted by $\mathcal{I} \models \mathcal{A}$, if, and only if, it satisfies all assertions in the ABox. If an interpretation $\mathcal{I}$ satisfies an ABox $\mathcal{A}$ or an assertion α then we also say that $\mathcal{I}$ *is a model of* $\mathcal{A}$ or α.

Let us now extend the example interpretation $\mathcal{I}_y$ introduced in (4.6) to an interpretation $\mathcal{I}_a$ such that it maps the individual name NICK to the individual Nick, i.e. NICK$^{\mathcal{I}_a} =$ Nick, and similarly for other individual names. It is easy to check that the interpretation $\mathcal{I}_a$ is a model of the ABox of Figure 4.13.

Exercise 4.33: Consider the interpretation $\mathcal{I}_a$ introduced above. Decide which of the following statements hold.

(a) $\mathcal{I}_a \models$ Optimist(NICK).

(b) $\mathcal{I}_a \models$ (Optimist $\sqcap \exists$hasChild.Optimist)(NICK).

(c) $\mathcal{I}_a \models$ ($\exists$hasChild.Optimist)(ANN).

(d) $\mathcal{I}_a \models$ ($\exists$hasChild.Optimist)(MARY).

It is often of interest to relate an interpretation to a complete knowledge base containing both an ABox $\mathcal{A}$ and a TBox $\mathcal{T}$. Let $\mathcal{I}$ be an interpretation that assigns meanings to all concept, role and individual names occurring in the knowledge base. We say that $\mathcal{I}$ satisfies $\mathcal{A}$ w.r.t. the TBox $\mathcal{T}$ if, and only if, $\mathcal{I}$ satisfies both $\mathcal{A}$ and $\mathcal{T}$. This fact is denoted by $\mathcal{I} \models_{\mathcal{T}} \mathcal{A}$, which is often read as "$\mathcal{I}$ is a model of $\mathcal{A}$ w.r.t. $\mathcal{T}$".

We can also extend the notion of (semantic) consequence to ABoxes. We say that an assertion α is a consequence of an ABox $\mathcal{A}$ w.r.t. a TBox $\mathcal{T}$ if α is satisfied in all interpretations that satisfy both $\mathcal{A}$ and $\mathcal{T}$. This is denoted by $\mathcal{A} \models_{\mathcal{T}} \alpha$ and is alternatively read as "α is a consequence of the knowledge base consisting of $\mathcal{A}$ and $\mathcal{T}$". Formally, semantic consequence is defined as follows:

$$\mathcal{A} \models_{\mathcal{T}} \alpha \leftrightarrow \text{for all interpretations } \mathcal{I} : (\mathcal{I} \models_{\mathcal{T}} \mathcal{A} \rightarrow \mathcal{I} \models \alpha).$$

For example, let TBox $\mathcal{T}$ contain (4.3), and let $\mathcal{A}$ consist of the single assertion Father(NICK). In this case the following statements obviously hold:

$$\mathcal{A} \models_{\mathcal{T}} \text{Human(NICK)};$$
$$\mathcal{A} \models_{\mathcal{T}} (\neg \text{Female})(\text{NICK});$$
$$\mathcal{A} \models_{\mathcal{T}} (\exists \text{hasChild}.\top)(\text{NICK}).$$

Exercise 4.34: Let our knowledge base contain the TBox $\mathcal{T}$ defined by

$$\exists \text{hasChild}^-.\neg \text{Alcoholic} \sqsubseteq \neg \text{Alcoholic},$$
$$\text{hasChild} \sqsubseteq \text{knows},$$
$$\text{hasChild}^- \sqsubseteq \text{knows},$$
$$\text{Mother} \equiv \text{Female} \sqcap \exists \text{hasChild}.\top$$

and the given by ABox $\mathcal{A}$

hasChild(NICK,ANN)	Female(KATE)
hasChild(MARY,ANN)	Female(ANN)
hasChild(ANN,JOHN)	Alcoholic(ANN)
knows(JOHN,KATE)	(¬Mother)(NICK).

Consider the α assertions listed below. For which of these does $\mathcal{A} \models_{\mathcal{T}} \alpha$ hold?

(a) knows(JOHN, ANN).

(b) (¬Female)(JOHN).

(c) (¬Female)(NICK).

(d) Mother(ANN).

(e) (¬Mother)(KATE).

4.8.2. Reasoning with ABoxes

The first question concerning ABoxes (as in the case of TBoxes) is whether an ABox is *consistent,* i.e. whether it has a model. A TBox is often needed to answer this question in a meaningful way. For instance, consider the ABox that states that Father(NICK) and Female(NICK) both hold. This ABox is consistent in itself, as there is absolutely no contradiction in NICK being an instance of the two unrelated atomic concepts Father and Female, about which no terminological knowledge is provided. However, the same ABox immediately becomes inconsistent as soon as a TBox containing the terminological axiom (4.3) is taken into consideration.

Formally, we say that an ABox $\mathcal{A}$ is consistent w.r.t. a TBox $\mathcal{T}$ if there is an interpretation $\mathcal{I}$ that is a model of both $\mathcal{A}$ and $\mathcal{T}$. This interpretation $\mathcal{I}$ obviously *satisfies* every statement in both $\mathcal{A}$ and $\mathcal{T}$ we will therefore also use the term *satisfiable* (w.r.t. $\mathcal{T}$) for such ABoxes. For example, the ABox in Figure 4.13 is consistent w.r.t. the TBox (4.3). If this ABox is extended with the statement Female(NICK), it becomes inconsistent w.r.t. the TBox (4.3).

In addition to consistency checking, the following three reasoning tasks, applicable to a knowledge base *KB* consisting of an ABox $\mathcal{A}$ and a TBox $\mathcal{T}$, are commonly identified:

- *Instance check:* Given an assertion α, decide whether the assertion is a consequence of the knowledge base, i.e. decide whether $\mathcal{A} \models_{\mathcal{T}} \alpha$ holds.

  An example instance check is the following: decide whether the assertion $(\neg \text{Female})(\text{NICK})$ is a consequence of the ABox in Figure 4.13, w.r.t. an empty TBox. This instance check fails. However, when a TBox containing the axiom (4.3) is used, the instance check succeeds. Further sample instance check problems were presented above in Exercise 4.34.

- *Instance retrieval:* Given a concept expression C, list those individual names a for which $C(a)$ is a consequence of the knowledge base. Thus, in instance retrieval we enumerate those individual names which *must* belong to the given concept C in all interpretations. Formally, an instance retrieval task for the concept C returns the following set:

$$\{a \mid a \text{ is an individual name in } KB, \mathcal{A} \models_{\mathcal{T}} C(a)\}.$$

  An example instance retrieval task is to determine all the instances of the concept Human $\sqcap \neg$Female, i.e. the individual names that can be deduced to be both human and male using the given knowledge base.

  An instance retrieval task can be defined similarly for roles. Given a role R, return a set of pairs of individual names such that the first component of the pair can be deduced to be R-*related* to the second:

$$\{< a, b > \mid a \text{ and } b \text{ are individual names in } KB, \mathcal{A} \models_{\mathcal{T}} R(a,b)\}.$$

  An instance retrieval task can be reduced to a series of instance checks. For a given concept C, we consider every individual name a which occurs in the ABox and check whether $\mathcal{A} \models_{\mathcal{T}} C(a)$ holds. Similarly, we could check every pair of individual names, for instance-retrieval tasks involving roles. However, this is far from optimal.

- *Realisation:* Given an individual name a, return the narrowest atomic concept C that is known to contain the given individual name ($\mathcal{A} \models_{\mathcal{T}} C(a)$). The term "narrowest" means the minimal atomic concept w.r.t. the concept inclusion relation $\sqsubseteq$. Thus a concept C is an answer to a realisation task for a if, and only if, $C(a)$ is a consequence of the knowledge base but, for all atomic concepts D in the knowledge base such that $\mathcal{T} \models D \sqsubset C$ holds,[19]

---

[19] Following usual mathematical practice, the statement $\mathcal{T} \models D \sqsubset C$ is said to hold if, and only if, $\mathcal{T} \models D \sqsubseteq C$ holds and $\mathcal{T} \models D \equiv C$ does not hold.

$D(a)$ is not a consequence of the knowledge base. Note that, in general, a realisation task can return multiple such minimal concepts.

As a further example, let us consider the instance retrieval task for the concept Human, in the context of the ABox of Figure 4.13 and the TBox (4.3). This returns NICK as the only answer. This may be surprising, but do not forget that our TBox lacks some background knowledge, such as "those who have a child are human": $\exists$hasChild.$\top \sqsubseteq$ Human and "those who have a parent are human": $\exists$hasChild$^-$.$\top \sqsubseteq$ Human. If we add these axioms to the TBox, the instance retrieval query will return all four individual names occurring in the ABox of Figure 4.13.

Exercise 4.35: In the context of the knowledge base of Exercise 4.34, what are the answers to the following instance retrieval tasks?

(a) Mother	(b) ¬Mother
(c) Female	(d) ¬Female
(e) Alcoholic	(f) ¬Alcoholic
(g) ∀hasChild.⊥	(h) knows

Exercise 4.36: Given the knowledge base of Exercise 4.34, what is the output of the realisation task for the individual name (a) ANN, (b) NICK or (c) KATE?

There are two kinds of instance-check problem, those for concepts and those for roles. Regarding concept assertions, an instance-check task can be easily reduced to a consistency check using the following observation:

$$\mathcal{A} \models C(a) \text{ if, and only if, } \mathcal{A} \cup \{(\neg C)(a)\} \text{ is not consistent.}$$

Note that such a reduction cannot be performed for role assertions if one is to remain within the $\mathcal{SHIQ}$ language, because role negation is not allowed in $\mathcal{SHIQ}$. However, checking a role assertion is a fairly easy task, because of the very limited role expression format allowed in the $\mathcal{SHIQ}$ language (only inverse roles) and the relatively simple format of role axioms (only role inclusion and transitivity).

It is interesting to note that an ABox inference engine can be used for terminological reasoning too. To decide whether a concept expression C is satisfiable w.r.t. a TBox $\mathcal{T}$, one can compose the single-assertion ABox $\{C(a)\}$ and check whether it is consistent w.r.t. $\mathcal{T}$, where a is an arbitrary individual name. As discussed in Subsection 4.6.2, any terminological reasoning task can be reduced to checking concept satisfiability (assuming a language which supports full negation). This means that practically all TBox and ABox reasoning tasks can be reduced to checking ABox consistency w.r.t. a TBox.

Exercise 4.37: Show that a concept C is satisfiable w.r.t. a TBox $\mathcal{T}$ if, and only if, the ABox $C(a)$ is consistent w.r.t. the TBox $\mathcal{T}$.

4.8.3. Internalisation of ABoxes

Let us consider the task of determining whether an ABox $\mathcal{A}$ is consistent w.r.t. a TBox $\mathcal{T}$. Given the concluding remark of the previous subsection, this covers the majority of TBox and ABox reasoning tasks.

If the TBox $\mathcal{T}$ is acyclic then the definitional concept axioms can be eliminated in a way similar to that for terminological reasoning. In other cases we can use the technique of internalisation: the reasoning task is transformed to a consistency check of a larger ABox $\mathcal{A}_{\mathcal{T}}$ w.r.t. a TBox $\mathcal{T}_{\mathcal{A},\mathcal{T}}$ that contains only role axioms. This is under the assumption that role hierarchy and transitivity axioms are allowed (i.e. $\mathcal{SH}$ or a stronger DL language is used).

The new TBox is built in similarly to how the internalisation of a concept satisfiability task was performed, as described in Subsection 4.7.2. First, we build the TBox $\mathcal{T}_{\mathcal{A},\mathcal{T}}$ in such a way as to contain all role axioms of $\mathcal{T}$, the axiom $\mathsf{Trans}(U)$ and the axioms $R \sqsubseteq U$ for every role R for which R or $\mathsf{Inv}(R)$ appears in either $\mathcal{A}$ or $\mathcal{T}$.

Next, the ABox $\mathcal{A}_{\mathcal{T}}$ is constructed. It contains all the assertions of the ABox $\mathcal{A}$ and further assertions, of the form $(C_{\mathcal{T}} \sqcap \forall U.C_{\mathcal{T}})(a)$, for each individual name a occurring in the ABox $\mathcal{A}$. Here $C_{\mathcal{T}}$ is the internalisation of the TBox $\mathcal{T}$ defined by (4.15). It can be proved that the ABox $\mathcal{A}$ is consistent w.r.t. $\mathcal{T}$ if, and only if, the ABox $\mathcal{A}_{\mathcal{T}}$ is consistent w.r.t. the TBox $\mathcal{T}_{\mathcal{A},\mathcal{T}}$. This is done by following a series of arguments similar to those given for the internalisation of TBoxes: see Subsection 4.7.2.

Exercise 4.38: Consider the instance-check task for $\mathsf{Optimist}(a)$ in the context of a knowledge base consisting of the TBox $\mathcal{T}$ and the ABox $\mathcal{A}_0$, where

$$\mathcal{T} = \{\exists\mathsf{hasChild}^-.\mathsf{Optimist} \sqsubseteq \mathsf{Optimist}\}$$
$$\mathcal{A}_0 = \{\mathsf{hasChild}(\mathsf{NICK},\mathsf{ANN}),\ \mathsf{Optimist}(\mathsf{NICK})\}.$$

(a) Reduce the above instance-check problem to the task of checking the consistency of an ABox $\mathcal{A}$ w.r.t. $\mathcal{T}$. Construct this ABox $\mathcal{A}$.

(b) Using internalisation, reduce the consistency-check task to another task where the TBox contains only role axioms. Construct this TBox $\mathcal{T}_{\mathcal{A},\mathcal{T}}$ and the corresponding ABox $\mathcal{A}_{\mathcal{T}}$.

4.8.4. Open and closed world assumption

A DL ABox is similar to a relational database. For example, the ABox in Figure 4.13 corresponds to a relational database with two tables: the table Father has a single column, while the table hasChild has two columns. Continuing the analogy, a concept expression may correspond to a query. For example, the concept parent: $\exists\mathsf{hasChild}.\top$ corresponds to a query involving the hasChild table, which returns the values that appear in the first column of the table. Furthermore, database schema information can be transformed to TBox axioms. For example, the fact that both columns of the table hasChild contain data of the type Human can be expressed with the axioms: $\top \sqsubseteq \forall\mathsf{hasChild}.\mathsf{Human}$ and $\top \sqsubseteq \forall\mathsf{hasChild}^-.\mathsf{Human}$.

There is, however, a fundamental difference between ABoxes and relational databases, namely the issue of semantics. A specific relational database describes a single universe in which given relations hold between given individuals; database queries concern this single interpretation. In this *closed world* only the relationships enumerated in the database are true; every other statement is considered false.

As opposed to the closed world of databases, the semantics of ABoxes uses the *open world assumption*. As explained in the previous section, we consider an assertion α to be the consequence of an ABox $\mathcal{A}$ if α holds in *every* model of $\mathcal{A}$ ($\mathcal{A} \models \alpha$). The fact that α is not a consequence of $\mathcal{A}$ by no means implies that its negation is a consequence of $\mathcal{A}$. Contrastingly, in the closed world of databases, missing information is interpreted as a negative statement.

For example, if an individual, such as JOHN, does not occur in the first column of the hasChild table then a database query engine will consider this individual childless. In contrast with this, a DL inference engine would not infer that JOHN is childless, i.e. it would not claim that the assertion $(\forall \text{hasChild}.\bot)(\text{JOHN})$ is a consequence of the ABox in Figure 4.13. The reason is that the given ABox has models in which JOHN does have children. At the same time, the DL inference system will give the same, negative, answer when asked whether JOHN has at least one child. Thus, when the open world assumption is used there can be three different outcomes regarding an instance check $C(a)$: (1) a belongs to C in all models, (2) a belongs to $\neg C$ in all models and (3) neither (1) nor (2) holds, i.e. the given knowledge base has models in which $C(a)$ holds and also models in which $C(a)$ does not hold. In this last case we can say that the relation of a and C is unknown or, more precisely, not decided by the knowledge base.

Exercise 4.39: Given the knowledge base of Exercise 4.34, list those assertions involving the concepts Mother, Female and Alcoholic that are not decided by the knowledge base.

As another example let us consider a database in which the table "has child" has only a single row, with NICK in the first column and ANN in the second. If ANN is also known to be female then the database query engine will answer "yes" to the question whether all children of NICK are female. A DL reasoning engine, however, should not give a positive answer to such a query since the given ABox has models where NICK has a son, too. Hence we cannot conclude that every child of NICK is Female. However, if we add to our ABox the assertion $(\leqslant 1 \text{ hasChild}.\top)(\text{NICK})$, i.e. we state that NICK has at most one child, then the DL reasoning engine will be able to prove that all children of NICK are female.

There is an interesting example illustrating the open world assumption which is often mentioned in DL textbooks and papers, e.g. in [4]. This example is based on the well-known story of Oedipus from ancient Greek mythology. Figure 4.14 shows four child–parent relations from the Oedipus family, both as a graph and as role assertions.[20] Two concept assertions are also given: Oedipus is known to be a patricide while Thersandros is known not to be a patricide. We attempt to visualise the fact that Oedipus is a patricide by surrounding this name with "+" signs, and for similar reasons Thersandros is surrounded by "−" signs.

---

[20] An ABox can be represented by a directed labelled graph similarly to an interpretation (as e.g. in Figure 4.5): individual names become the nodes of the graph; a role assertion of the form $R(a, b)$ is transformed to an edge from a to b bearing the label R; and, finally, a concept assertion $C(a)$ causes the concept expression C to be added to the label of a. Note that a node label is thus the set of concept expressions to which the given individual name is expected to belong. This representation is very similar to tableau graphs, to be discussed in Chapters 5–7.

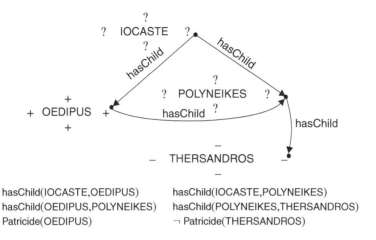

hasChild(IOCASTE,OEDIPUS)   hasChild(IOCASTE,POLYNEIKES)
hasChild(OEDIPUS,POLYNEIKES)   hasChild(POLYNEIKES,THERSANDROS)
Patricide(OEDIPUS)   ¬ Patricide(THERSANDROS)

Figure 4.14. The ABox $\mathcal{A}_{OE}$.

We do not know whether either of the other two individuals[21] is a patricide; hence we have put question marks around their names.

We would like to ask the following question regarding this ABox:

> Does Iocaste have a child who is a patricide and who, in turn, has a child who is not a patricide?

This can be reformulated as the following instance-check task, where $\mathcal{A}_{OE}$ denotes the ABox of Figure 4.14:

$$\mathcal{A}_{OE} \models (\exists \mathsf{hasChild}.(\mathsf{Patricide} \sqcap \exists \mathsf{hasChild}.\neg\mathsf{Patricide}))(\mathsf{IOCASTE})? \qquad (4.19)$$

First, let us consider how can this question be interpreted in the world of relational databases. The data table belonging to the binary relation "hasChild" has four rows, while the table "Patricide" has a single row claiming that "Oedipus is a patricide". We are in trouble with the negative statement about Thersandros because, according to the closed world of databases, any individual not mentioned in the "Patricide" table has to be treated as non-patricide. So we simply ignore the negative statement about Thersandros. Notice that the world of databases is "black and white": we can always decide whether a person is a patricide; there cannot exist anyone with "question marks" around his or her name.

Having clarified the interpretation of the input data we can easily answer the relational database counterpart of the question (4.19): yes, Iocaste has a child, namely Oedipus, who is a patricide and who has a non-patricide child, Polyneikes. Notice, however, that here we have considered Polyneikes to be non-patricide simply because no one has said that he is a patricide.

Let us now have a look at the DL interpretation. Here we have two individuals who are neither known to be patricide nor known to be non-patricide. One way of reasoning is the

---

[21] Formally, from the DL point of view, we should have used the term *individual name* here. However, to make our phrasing simpler, we refer to IOCASTE, OEDIPUS etc. simply as individuals.

following: Iocaste has two children, Oedipus and Polyneikes. We know that Oedipus is a patricide but his son, Polyneikes is not known to be a non-patricide. *Therefore Oedipus does not meet the requirements in question.* Let us now consider Polyneikes as the child of Iocaste: we know that he has a non-patricide child, but we have no information on whether Polyneikes himself is a patricide. *Thus Polyneikes does not meet our requirements either.* Therefore we come to the conclusion that the answer to question (4.19) is negative.

This reasoning is incorrect, because it tries to decide whether a certain named individual satisfies a *sub-condition* of the search. The argument of the previous paragraph is correct in claiming that neither Oedipus nor Polyneikes can be proved to satisfy the condition (Patricide ⊓ ∃hasChild.¬Patricide). However, the answer to (4.19) is still positive, because every interpretation of the ABox can be shown to contain a child of Iocaste satisfying the above condition but this individual will be Oedipus in some interpretations and Polyneikes in others. Thus the proof of (4.19) has to use case analysis.

The case analysis goes as follows. We have to examine whether the concept assertion on the right-hand side of (4.19) – let us call it α – is a consequence of the ABox $\mathcal{A}_{OE}$. To prove this we have to show that α holds in every model of $\mathcal{A}_{OE}$. Let us distinguish between two kinds of such models: those in which Polyneikes is a patricide[22] and those in which Polyneikes is not a patricide. Note that we are speaking now of interpretations where every element of the domain is either patricide or non-patricide. Let us look at a model of the first kind. Here α holds because Iocaste has a patricide child, Polyneikes, who has a non-patricide child, Thersandros. However, if we take a model of the second kind then Iocaste also has a patricide child, Oedipus, who has a non-patricide child, Polyneikes. Thus we have shown that α holds in every model of $\mathcal{A}_{OE}$, i.e. the answer to the question (4.19) is "yes".

This example highlights the fact that ABox reasoning is a much more complex task than executing database queries and that case analysis may be needed in its implementation.

Exercise 4.40: Consider the following TBox $\mathcal{T}$:

$$\exists \text{hasParent}.\neg\text{Alcoholic} \sqsubseteq \neg\text{Alcoholic},$$
$$\exists \text{hasFriend}.\text{Alcoholic} \sqsubseteq \neg\text{Alcoholic},$$

and the following ABox $\mathcal{A}$:

$$\text{hasParent}(\text{JOHN}, \text{ANN})$$
$$\text{hasParent}(\text{ANN}, \text{NICK})$$
$$\text{hasParent}(\text{ANN}, \text{MARY})$$
$$\text{hasFriend}(\text{MARY}, \text{NICK})$$

Notice that there is no concept assertion in the ABox. Nevertheless there are concept assertions that can be inferred from the knowledge base, using case analysis, as follows.

(a) Show that $\mathcal{A} \models_{\mathcal{T}} \neg\text{Alcoholic}(\text{ANN})$.

(b) Show that $\mathcal{A} \models_{\mathcal{T}} \neg\text{Alcoholic}(\text{JOHN})$.

---

[22] More precisely: the interpretation of the individual name POLYNEIKES belongs to the interpretation of the concept Patricide.

(c) Replace assertion "hasFriend(MARY,NICK)" by "hasFriend(JOHN,ANN)". Which individuals can you deduce to be non-alcoholic in the modified knowledge base?

(d) Try to find other ABoxes with no concept assertions from which, using the above TBox $\mathcal{T}$, concept assertions can be inferred.

(e) Can you find an ABox of this kind in which there are only role assertion(s), and furthermore the only role is hasFriend?

4.9. Mapping DL languages to first-order logic

In the preceding sections we have described different DL languages and presented their syntax and semantics. We now show that all these languages can be considered sublanguages of first-order logic and that their semantics (as described before) can also be expressed in first-order logic (FOL). Obviously, it is enough to show this for the most complex DL variant described so far, the $\mathcal{SHIQ}$ language.

As explained earlier, concepts correspond to unary relations while roles to binary relations. Keeping this in mind we map an atomic concept A to a first-order formula $A(x)$ and an atomic role R_A to $R_A(x,y)$. We will now define an extension of this mapping in such a way that each composite concept is mapped to a first-order formula with a single free variable. This formula will be true for an individual if, and only if, the individual belongs to the concept. Similarly, we will map a role expression to a formula with two variables, thereby expressing the fact that the two arguments are related through the given role.

Let us first look at some example mappings. The concept expression $\exists$hasChild.$\top$ is mapped, in a natural way, to a formula with a free variable x:

$$\exists y.\text{hasChild}(x,y). \tag{4.20}$$

The much more complex notion "father of girls", Human $\sqcap$ ¬Female $\sqcap$ $\forall$hasChild.Female $\sqcap$ $\exists$hasChild.$\top$, is transformed to the following first-order formula:

$$\begin{aligned}\Phi_{FoG}(x) = \ &\text{Human}(x) \wedge \neg\text{Female}(x)\\ &\wedge \forall y.\,(\text{hasChild}(x,y) \rightarrow \text{Female}(y))\\ &\wedge \exists y.\text{hasChild}(x,y).\end{aligned} \tag{4.21}$$

Number restrictions require a slightly more complicated translation. For instance, we can map the concept "has at least two rich children", $(\geqslant 2\,\text{hasChild.Rich})$, to a first-order formula $\Phi_1(x)$, defined below:

$$\Phi_1(x) = \exists y_1, y_2.\,(\text{hasChild}(x,y_1) \wedge \text{hasChild}(x,y_2) \wedge \text{Rich}(y_1) \wedge \text{Rich}(y_2) \wedge y_1 \neq y_2).$$

The translation of the concept expression $(\leqslant 1\,\text{hasChild.Female})$ is shown below as $\Phi_2(x)$. This formula states that if x has two female children then these have to be the same:

$$\begin{aligned}\Phi_2(x) = \forall y_1, y_2.\,&(\text{hasChild}(x,y_1) \wedge \text{hasChild}(x,y_2)\\ &\wedge \text{Female}(y_1) \wedge \text{Female}(y_2) \rightarrow y_1 = y_2).\end{aligned}$$

Note that the size of the translation of the $(\geqslant nR.C)$ and $(\leqslant nR.C)$ constructs is quadratic in n, because it involves equality or inequality relations applied to all pairs of n variables.

TBox axioms are mapped to closed formulae. For example, the axiom

$$(\geqslant 2\,\mathsf{hasChild}.\mathsf{Rich}) \sqsubseteq \mathsf{Happy},$$

stating that "those who have at least two rich children are happy" is transformed to the following FOL sentence:

$$\forall x.(\Phi_1(x) \to \mathsf{Happy}(x)),$$

i.e. for all x individuals in the domain, if $\Phi_1(x)$ holds then $\mathsf{Happy}(x)$ has to hold as well, where Φ_1 is the formula defined above.

To transform a knowledge base involving an ABox, we have to deal with individual names. We map an individual name a to a first-order constant name, also denoted by a. Using this convention, ABox assertions are transformed to first-order sentences in a trivial way, e.g. the concept assertion $(\exists \mathsf{hasChild}.\top)(\mathsf{JOHN})$ is transformed to the formula (4.20) with the substitution $x = \mathsf{JOHN}$:

$$\exists y.\mathsf{hasChild}(\mathsf{JOHN}, y).$$

Finally, the first-order equivalent of a DL knowledge base is the conjunction of the translation of all TBox axioms and ABox assertions. As an example, consider the following knowledge base:

$$\mathcal{T} = \{\mathsf{FatherOfGirls} \equiv \mathsf{Human} \sqcap \neg\mathsf{Female} \sqcap \forall\mathsf{hasChild}.\mathsf{Female} \sqcap \exists\mathsf{hasChild}.\top,$$
$$\mathsf{FatherOfGirls} \sqsubseteq \mathsf{Happy}\}.$$

This knowledge base (consisting of terminological axioms only) is mapped to the following first-order sentence:

$$\forall x.\big(\mathsf{FatherOfGirls}(x) \leftrightarrow \Phi_{FoG}(x)\big) \wedge \forall x.\big(\mathsf{FatherOfGirls}(x) \to \mathsf{Happy}(x)\big),$$

where $\Phi_{FoG}(x)$ is the first-order formula which is the translation of the "father of girls" concept expression in (4.21).

To sum up this informal overview, the non-logical symbols[23] occurring in the first-order translation of DL formulae are the following:

- every atomic concept A serves as a unary predicate name;

- every atomic role R_A serves as a binary predicate name;

- every individual name a serves as a constant name (i.e. a *nullary* function name).[24]

Let us now give a systematic formal overview of how to map DL constructs to FOL, following the handbook [4]. Let E denote an arbitrary DL construct: a concept expression, a role expression, an individual name, a TBox axiom, an ABox assertion or a complete knowledge base. The translation of E to first-order logic is denoted by Φ_E. Figure 4.15 defines the mapping Φ for concept and role expressions of the $\mathcal{SHIQ}$ language. As expected, the definition is recursive and mirrors the syntactic description of $\mathcal{SHIQ}$; cf. Figure 4.9.

---

[23] The non-logical symbols are the predicate and function names which, together with their arities, comprise the so-called *signature* of a first-order language.

[24] A function is nullary if it has no arguments.

$$\Phi_A(x) = A(x)$$
$$\Phi_\top(x) = \text{TRUE}$$
$$\Phi_\bot(x) = \text{FALSE}$$
$$\Phi_{\neg C}(x) = \neg\Phi_C(x)$$
$$\Phi_{C_1 \sqcap C_2}(x) = \Phi_{C_1}(x) \wedge \Phi_{C_2}(x)$$
$$\Phi_{C_1 \sqcup C_2}(x) = \Phi_{C_1}(x) \vee \Phi_{C_2}(x)$$
$$\Phi_{\forall R.C}(x) = \forall y.\,(\Phi_R(x,y) \rightarrow \Phi_C(y))$$
$$\Phi_{\exists R.C}(x) = \exists y.\,(\Phi_R(x,y) \wedge \Phi_C(y))$$
$$\Phi_{\geqslant nR.C}(x) = \exists y_1,\ldots,y_n.\,\big(\,\Phi_R(x,y_1) \wedge \cdots \wedge \Phi_R(x,y_n)$$
$$\wedge\, \Phi_C(y_1) \wedge \cdots \wedge \Phi_C(y_n) \wedge \bigwedge_{i<j} y_i \neq y_j\big)$$
$$\Phi_{\leqslant nR.C}(x) = \forall y_1,\ldots,y_{n+1}.\,\big(\,\Phi_R(x,y_1) \wedge \cdots \wedge \Phi_R(x,y_{n+1})$$
$$\wedge\, \Phi_C(y_1) \wedge \cdots \wedge \Phi_C(y_{n+1}) \rightarrow \bigvee_{i<j} y_i = y_j\big)$$
$$\Phi_{R_A}(x,y) = R_A(x,y)$$
$$\Phi_{R_A^-}(x,y) = R_A(y,x)$$

Figure 4.15. First-order equivalents of $\mathcal{SHIQ}$ concept and role expressions.

$$\Phi_{C_1 \equiv C_2} = \forall x.\,(\Phi_{C_1}(x) \leftrightarrow \Phi_{C_2}(x))$$
$$\Phi_{C_1 \sqsubseteq C_2} = \forall x.\,(\Phi_{C_1}(x) \rightarrow \Phi_{C_2}(x))$$
$$\Phi_{R_1 \equiv R_2} = \forall x,y.\,(\Phi_{R_1}(x,y) \leftrightarrow \Phi_{R_2}(x,y))$$
$$\Phi_{R_1 \sqsubseteq R_2} = \forall x,y.\,(\Phi_{R_1}(x,y) \rightarrow \Phi_{R_2}(x,y))$$
$$\Phi_{\mathsf{Trans}(R)} = \forall x,y,z.\,(\Phi_R(x,y) \wedge \Phi_R(y,z) \rightarrow \Phi_R(x,z))$$
$$\Phi_{C(a)} = \Phi_C(a)$$
$$\Phi_{R(a_1,a_2)} = \Phi_R(a_1,a_2)$$

Figure 4.16. First-order equivalents of the $\mathcal{SHIQ}$ language axioms.

In Figure 4.16 we present the first-order equivalents of the axioms and assertions of the $\mathcal{SHIQ}$ language.

To complete the definition of the mapping function Φ_E, we define how to transform a knowledge base to a first-order formula. Let us consider a knowledge base KB which consists of terminological axioms and/or assertions. The knowledge base KB is mapped to a conjunctive formula whose conjuncts are the first-order equivalents of the axioms and assertions of the knowledge base:

$$\Phi_{KB} = \bigwedge_{S \in KB} \Phi_S \wedge \Phi_{\text{UNA}}.$$

Here, Φ_{UNA} is the axiom describing the unique name assumption, if needed; otherwise $\Phi_{\text{UNA}} = \text{TRUE}$. The unique name assumption can be spelled out in first-order logic in the following straightforward way:

$$\Phi_{\text{UNA}} = \bigwedge_{i < j} a_i \neq a_j,$$

where $\{a_1, \ldots, a_n\}$ are the individual names appearing in the knowledge base KB.

Having defined the mapping function Φ, let us discuss the relationship between the notions of interpretation in Description Logic and in first-order logic. Recall that an FOL *signature* enumerates the predicate and function names together with their arities. An FOL interpretation consists of a domain and of an interpretation function which assigns a meaning to the predicate and function names present in the signature of the language. The signature of a first-order sentence generated from a DL knowledge base KB has to contain the following symbols: unary predicate names A, representing atomic concepts; binary predicate names R_A, standing for atomic roles; and nullary function names a, representing individual names. If we build a first-order interpretation $\mathcal{I}$ for such a signature, we will notice that $\mathcal{I}$ can also be viewed as a DL interpretation in which the knowledge base KB can be evaluated. We claim that $\mathcal{I}$ is a first-order model of Φ_{KB} if, and only if, $\mathcal{I}$ is a DL model of KB. To prove this, let us follow the stages of construction of the mapping function Φ.

In the first stage we mapped DL concept expressions to first-order formulae with a single free variable. This formula $\Phi_C(x)$ was designed to hold for the individual x if, and only if, the individual belonged to the concept C. Thus the equation linking a concept expression D with its first-order counterpart $\Phi_D(x)$, when both are evaluated in the same interpretation $\mathcal{I}$, is the following:

$$D^{\mathcal{I}} = \left\{ x \in \Delta^{\mathcal{I}} \mid \Phi_D(x) \right\}.$$

This equation can be proved fairly easily by induction. A similar equation can be written down for role expressions:

$$R^{\mathcal{I}} = \left\{ \langle x, y \rangle \in \Delta^{\mathcal{I}} \mid \Phi_R(x, y) \right\}.$$

Given these two equations and the form of the first-order counterparts of the DL axioms and assertions, it can be easily seen that, for an arbitrary terminological axiom or assertion T,

$$(\mathcal{I} \models T) \leftrightarrow (\mathcal{I} \models \Phi_T),$$

which can be trivially extended to a whole knowledge base KB:

$$(\mathcal{I} \models KB) \leftrightarrow (\mathcal{I} \models \Phi_{KB}).$$

This completes our overview of the relationship of Description Logic to first-order logic.

Exercise 4.41: Using the transformation Φ described above, translate the knowledge base of Exercise 4.40 to first-order logic.

4.10. Advanced DL languages

In the final section of this chapter we present some advanced DL constructs that go beyond the $\mathcal{SHIQ}$ language. The first two subsections discuss the most important extensions from the Semantic Web point of view, introducing concrete domains and nominals. We continue with an overview of advanced concept and role constructors and then present the language $\mathcal{SROIQ}$, the mathematical basis of the Web Ontology Language OWL2.

4.10.1. Concrete domains

When constructing a terminological system one often encounters roles that have some concrete domain as the range, e.g. the set of the integers. For instance, the role hasAge can be thought of as a relation between a person and integer number. Using this role in an existential restriction, we can define the concept "adult" as a person who is at least 18 years old. Note that, to do this, we have to be able to name a concrete subset, the set of integers greater than or equal to 18.

As a motivating example, let us first try to build the concept "adult" without using concrete domains:

$$\text{Adult} \equiv \text{Human} \sqcap \exists\text{hasAge}.\text{AdultAge};$$
$$\text{AdultAge} \sqsubseteq \text{Age};$$
$$\text{Age} \sqsubseteq \text{Integer}.$$

Here we have used an "abstract" concept Integer in the definition of the concept Adult. We call it abstract because there is absolutely no restriction on the individuals that may belong to the concept Integer. All we know about it is that it includes another concept, Age, which in turn includes the concept AdultAge. We probably think of the latter two as integer intervals, e.g. $[0, \infty)$ and $[18, \infty)$, but we cannot express this in the $\mathcal{SHIQ}$ DL language. We can define the concept Teenager in a similar way, using an auxiliary concept TeenagerAge that is intended to mean the interval $[13, 19]$, and in the same way we can define infants, pensioners etc.

One problem of the approach sketched above is that we cannot assign concrete intervals to the subconcepts of the concept Integer. From this follows a bigger problem, namely that an inference engine is not able to deduce various important relationships between the subconcepts of Age, for example that infancy and adult age are disjoint or that pensioner age is subsumed by adult age. Consequently, such an engine cannot deduce the relationships of the corresponding subconcepts of Human, namely that Infant and Adult are disjoint or that Adult subsumes Pensioner. One could add appropriate axioms to the TBox, but this is a laborious and error-prone task.

These problems can be avoided if concrete domains are introduced. This extension is normally denoted by a suffix (**D**) appended to the name of the language, e.g. $\mathcal{SHIQ}(\mathbf{D})$. The character **D** refers to the word *data type* or *domain*, since the programming language counterpart of a concrete domain is a simple data type such as integer, real, string etc. However, the word *data type* has a broader meaning in DL than in programming languages, as subsets of data types such as even numbers, positive integers less than 18 etc. are also considered to be data types (these are sometimes called subtypes); cf. the `rdf:datatype` attribute in RDF and OWL.

The theory of Description Logic does not prescribe which concrete domains can or should be introduced. Instead, it sets out a general framework for adding concrete domains to a given Description Logic. For this, first a domain has to be chosen (e.g. the integers or strings), together with the relevant subsets of this domain that are needed by the application in question. In our motivating example we needed the concrete domain of integers, together with interval subtypes.

To extend a DL language with concrete domains, we thus have to decide which simple data types to allow and which subsets of these should be considered subtypes. We also have to introduce symbols into our language that represent these subtypes, so that we can refer to the subtypes chosen from the DL formulae. Let us denote by **D** a given set of data type symbols, each representing a subset of a concrete domain. The union of the subsets corresponding to the data type symbols is called the *concrete domain* and is denoted by $\Delta_{\mathbf{D}}$. For a given **D**, $\Delta_{\mathbf{D}}$ will always be part of the universe of discourse. It is assumed to be disjoint from the domain $\Delta^{\mathcal{I}}$ (also called the *abstract domain* in this context), which varies from interpretation to interpretation. The meaning of a type symbol $d \in \mathbf{D}$, i.e. the set of concrete values belonging to d, is denoted by $d^{\mathbf{D}}$, where $d^{\mathbf{D}} \subseteq \Delta_{\mathbf{D}}$.

Let us consider an example extension **D** which can be used to solve our introductory problem. We choose the set of integers as the concrete domain and allow integer intervals as subtypes. We thus introduce the following set of data type symbols: $\mathbf{D} = \left\{ \mathsf{intv}_{i,j} \mid i \leq j \text{ integers} \right\} \cup \left\{ \mathsf{leq}_j \mid j \text{ integer} \right\} \cup \left\{ \mathsf{geq}_i \mid i \text{ integer} \right\}$. The interpretation of a symbol $\mathsf{intv}_{i,j}$ is the closed interval of integers between i and j: $\mathsf{intv}_{i,j}^{\mathbf{D}} = \{k \mid i \leq k \leq j, k \text{ is an integer}\}$. The other two kinds of symbol map to infinite intervals: geq_i represents the integers greater than or equal to i: $\mathsf{geq}_i^{\mathbf{D}} = \{k \mid i \leq k, k \text{ is an integer}\}$; leq_j stands for the integers less than or equal to j: $\mathsf{leq}_j^{\mathbf{D}} = \{k \mid k \leq j, k \text{ is an integer}\}$.

Having introduced concrete domains, we will distinguish between two kinds of roles in our DL language: abstract and concrete roles. An abstract role provides a link between two elements of the abstract domain while a concrete role specifies a relationship between an abstract and a concrete individual. In our example hasAge is a concrete role since it links (abstract) people to their age. Age is an integer, an element of the concrete domain. In contrast with this, the roles introduced earlier, such as hasChild, hasParent, are abstract roles.

A concrete role name R_D can only be used in an existential restriction $\exists R_D.de$ or in a value restriction $\forall R_D.de$. Here *de* is a so-called concrete concept expression built from data types $d \in \mathbf{D}$ using the union, intersection and negation DL constructors. For example, we can describe the concept "Person of non-working age" as $\exists \mathsf{hasAge}.(\mathsf{intv}_{0,18} \sqcup \mathsf{geq}_{65})$. Note that number restrictions are not allowed for concrete roles because most (including hasAge) represent a function.

To build an inference engine for a Description Logic with concrete domains, one has to be able to perform reasoning tasks, involving concrete concept expressions *de*, such as deciding their disjointness, subsumption etc. One can reduce these tasks to deciding whether a concrete concept expression evaluates to an empty interval. This can be done analogously to how TBox reasoning tasks were reduced to the checking of satisfiability (see Subsection 4.6.2). The task of checking whether an expression is empty can be further simplified to the problem of deciding whether the intersection of one or more, possibly negated, atomic data types is empty. This means that an algorithm is required for deciding whether an expression $dnd_1 \sqcap \cdots \sqcap dnd_n$ is empty, where dnd_i is of the form d or $\neg d$ and d is a data type, i.e. $d \in \mathbf{D}$.

Exercise 4.42: Using the concrete data type of integers and its interval subtypes introduced above, formalise the following advertisement for a house to buy:

> Looking for a house with a price tag of 200 000 to 250 000 euros, with three or four bedrooms, with at least two bathrooms, and with either a living room of size at least 50 square metres or a study and a living room, each at least 30 square metres.

Introduce appropriate concrete role names, such as hasBedrooms or hasStudyOfSize.

4.10.2. Nominals

A *nominal* is a concept whose interpretation contains only a single individual.

For instance, in a terminological system about geography, one introduces the concepts Continent, Country etc. and a role isIn, which can hold between two individuals (e.g. between a country and a continent). Using these we would like to define the concept European-Country as a country which is in Europe: EuropeanCountry $\equiv$ $\exists$isIn.Europe. Let us discuss now what kind of language construct can Europe be in this definition. At first, one is tempted to consider Europe as an individual name, but this would not be correct, because individual names may only appear in an ABox, for example isIn(HUNGARY,EUROPE) where HUNGARY and EUROPE are both individual names. However, the above axiom defines the concept of EuropeanCountry and as such clearly belongs to a terminological box.

The construct Europe in "$\exists$isIn.Europe" is in the syntactic position of a concept expression. Obviously, we would like to think of this concept as having a single individual as its meaning (namely the member of the concept Continent which represents Europe). This can be achieved by declaring Europe to be a nominal concept.

To justify the introduction of nominals, let us discuss what happens in our example when no nominals are used. In this case the continents are denoted by ordinary concepts. We then formulate axioms stating that the concept Continent is the union of the concepts denoting the individual continents and that the latter are pairwise disjoint:

$$\text{Continent} \equiv \text{Europe} \sqcup \text{Asia} \sqcup \text{America} \sqcup \cdots ;$$
$$\text{Europe} \sqcap \text{Asia} \sqsubseteq \bot;$$
$$\text{Europe} \sqcap \text{America} \sqsubseteq \bot;$$
$$\cdots$$

This is a good approximation, but not fully accurate.[25] For instance, let us define the concept LargeCountry to denote a country located in at least two continents. Let us also assert the fact that every EUCountry is located only in Europe:

$$\text{LargeCountry} \equiv (\geqslant 2\,\text{isIn}.\text{Continent});$$
$$\text{EUCountry} \sqsubseteq \forall\text{isIn}.\text{Europe}.$$

Obviously, we think that the concepts LargeCountry and EUCountry are disjoint, i.e. it is true that no EUCountry covers two continents. However, to be able to prove this the inference engine has to be made aware of the fact that the concept Europe has exactly one individual.

For reasons such as this the notion of nominals was introduced into Description Logics. This extension is denoted by the letter $\mathcal{O}$, the initial of the word "object" (a synonym of "individual"). By adding nominals to the various languages introduced so far we obtain new languages, $\mathcal{SHOIN}$, $\mathcal{SHOQ}$, $\mathcal{SHOQ}(\mathbf{D})$ etc.

The language extension itself is very simple: we only have to make it possible to declare that some concepts are nominals. Syntactically, an option is to introduce a new type of axiom, e.g. Nominal(C), to denote the fact that concept C is a nominal. However, there is a more popular syntactic notation for nominal concepts: an individual name enclosed in braces, e.g. {EUROPE}. This has the advantages that it introduces an individual name which can be used in the ABox and, together with the unique-name assumption, makes it clear that the nominals are to be considered disjoint. This notation also allows for a sort of "syntactic sugar": by placing multiple concepts in braces, e.g. {EUROPE, ASIA}, a union of the corresponding nominal concepts is built, e.g. {EUROPE} $\sqcup$ {ASIA}.

Exercise 4.43: Using nominals to denote the colour and sweetness of wines, build a simple wine ontology. Include axioms stating that a red wine has red or ruby colour, a white wine is white or yellow etc. Add appropriate axioms such that a DL reasoner is able to deduce that the concepts of red and white wine are disjoint.

4.10.3. Further language extensions

We mentioned in Section 4.2 that, in a way analogous to concept constructors, a rich set of *role constructors* can also be introduced into Description Logics. So far we have defined a single role constructor, the inverse operation. Table 4.1, taken from the appendix of [4], gives a summary of the most important role constructors other than the inverse operation.

The rightmost column of the table shows the semantics of role constructors. Here we have used several mathematical operators, of which the composition of binary relations (denoted by $\circ$) requires some explanation. The relation $Rel_1 \circ Rel_2$ holds between a and c if, and only if, there is a b for which both $Rel_1(a,b)$ and $Rel_2(b,c)$ hold:

$$Rel_1 \circ Rel_2 = \{\langle a,c \rangle \mid \exists b.\,(\langle a,b \rangle \in Rel_1 \wedge \langle b,c \rangle \in Rel_2)\}.$$

---

[25] A similar approximation was used in mapping the web language OIL (a predecessor of OWL, to be discussed in Chapter 8) to the DL language supported by the FACT reasoning engine [55], which lacks nominals.

Name	Syntax	Semantics
Universal role	U	$\Delta^{\mathcal{I}} \times \Delta^{\mathcal{I}}$
Intersection	$R_1 \sqcap R_2$	$R_1^{\mathcal{I}} \cap R_2^{\mathcal{I}}$
Union	$R_1 \sqcup R_2$	$R_1^{\mathcal{I}} \cup R_2^{\mathcal{I}}$
Complement	$\neg R$	$\Delta^{\mathcal{I}} \times \Delta^{\mathcal{I}} \setminus R^{\mathcal{I}}$
Composition	$R_1 \circ R_2$	$R_1^{\mathcal{I}} \circ R_2^{\mathcal{I}}$
Transitive closure	R^+	$\bigcup_{n \geq 1} \left(R^{\mathcal{I}}\right)^n$
Reflexive–transitive closure	R^*	$\bigcup_{n \geq 0} \left(R^{\mathcal{I}}\right)^n$
Role restriction	$R|_C$	$R^{\mathcal{I}} \cap \left(\Delta^{\mathcal{I}} \times C^{\mathcal{I}}\right)$
Identity	$id(C)$	$\left\{ \langle d, d \rangle \mid d \in C^{\mathcal{I}} \right\}$

Table 4.1. Advanced role constructors.

For example, hasMother∘hasFather is a relation linking grandchildren with their maternal grandfather.[26]

Having introduced composition, we give an inductive definition for the operation Rel^n (used in Table 4.1 in the semantics of transitive and reflexive–transitive closures):

$$Rel^0 = \left\{ \langle d, d \rangle \mid d \in \Delta^{\mathcal{I}} \right\};$$
$$Rel^{n+1} = Rel^n \circ Rel.$$

Thus Rel^0 is the identity relation, Rel^1 is Rel itself and Rel^n, for $n > 1$, is the relation obtained by composing n copies of Rel.

All the constructors in Table 4.1, except for the transitive and reflexive–transitive closures, can be expressed in first-order logic. The facts that R^+ is transitive and that it includes the role R can be easily expressed in FOL. The statement that cannot be expressed in FOL is that R^+ is the *smallest* relation which is transitive and subsumes R. It cannot be thus expressed because of the so-called *compactness theorem* of first-order logic [18].

In Subsection 4.6.1 concept axioms are classified as definitions and statements expressing background knowledge. If complex role constructors such as in Table 4.1 are permitted, a similar classification can be made, which distinguishes between role definition axioms and *general role inclusion axioms* (abbreviated as RIA or g-RIA), which describe background knowledge.

Let us consider some role definition examples using our newly introduced constructors. We define complex family relations building on the roles hasChild hasParent $\equiv$ hasChild$^-$ and

---

[26] This is similar to the well-known function composition $f \circ g$. However, note that in the function composition $f \circ g$ we apply g first and then pass the result to f. In contrast with this, in the relation composition $R \circ S$ we navigate first along R and afterwards along S. For instance, the statement "gc has maternal grandfather gf" can be described using function composition as $gf = (f_{\text{father}} \circ f_{\text{mother}})(gc)$, while the same statement takes the form $(R_{\text{mother}} \circ R_{\text{father}})(gc, gf)$ when one is using relations.

on the concept Female:

$$\text{hasGrandparent} \equiv \text{hasParent} \circ \text{hasParent};$$
$$\text{hasMother} \equiv \text{hasParent}|_{\text{Female}};$$
$$\text{hasMaternalGrandparent} \equiv \text{hasMother} \circ \text{hasParent};$$
$$\text{hasSibling} \equiv (\text{hasParent} \circ \text{hasChild}) \sqcap \neg id(\top); \tag{4.22}$$
$$\text{hasSon} \equiv \text{hasChild}|_{\neg\text{Female}};$$
$$\text{hasAncestor} \equiv \text{hasParent}^{+};$$
$$\text{hasAncestorOrSelf} \equiv \text{hasParent}^{*};$$
$$\text{hasBloodRelation} \equiv (\text{hasAncestorOrSelf} \circ \text{hasAncestorOrSelf}^{-}) \sqcap \neg id(\top).$$

Let us now give some help in interpreting these definitions. The role "has grandparent" denotes a parent of a parent. The role "has mother" is obtained from "has parent" if we restrict the right-hand side of the relation to female individuals, using the *role restriction* construct. A maternal grandparent is a parent of a mother. The relation "has sibling" is defined as a child of a parent, with the exclusion of self. In more detail: the role hasParent $\circ$ hasChild holds for x and y if x and y are siblings *or* if $x = y$. To obtain the relation "has sibling" we have to exclude the case of equality, and so we intersect this composition with $\neg id(\top)$, the relation holding between any two distinct individuals. The "has ancestor" role is the transitive closure of the role "has parent", while "has ancestor or self" is the reflexive–transitive closure of "has parent". The only difference between the two ancestor roles is that "has ancestor or self" allows identity; an equivalent definition for it could be hasAncestorOrSelf = hasAncestor $\sqcup$ $id(\top)$. The notion of a blood relative is defined as a person with whom one has a common ancestor, allowing the person itself as an ancestor. Thus if we follow the relation "ancestorOrSelf" and then continue with its inverse, we reach either a blood relative or ourselves. Because we want to exclude ourselves from the set of our blood relatives, we intersect the previous composition with the relation "not self", just as we did in the definition of "has sibling".

Exercise 4.44: Using the advanced role constructors introduced in this section define the following roles, using the roles hasChild, hasParent and hasSpouse and the concept Female.

(a) hasWife	(b) hasCousin
(c) hasMotherInLaw	(d) hasSisterInLaw
(e) hasSonInLaw	(f) hasUncle

Be careful to include e.g. an aunt's husband as an uncle. If in doubt about the meaning of these family relationships, consult Wikipedia.

Having discussed how to construct roles from roles, we now present a concept constructor using roles only: the *role–value map*. This has two forms:

$$(R \subseteq S) \quad \text{and} \quad (R = S),$$

where R and S are both role expressions. The above constructs look very similar to role axioms, but the latter use the $\sqsubseteq$ and $\equiv$ signs as opposed to $\subseteq$ and $=$, as above. The distinction is very important, as a role–value map denotes a concept while a role axiom has a truth value.

An individual a belongs to the concept $(R \subseteq S)$ if any object b connected to a through R is also connected to a through S. For example, the concept expression (hasParent $\subseteq$ hasFriend) denotes those children whose parents are also their friends. Similarly, a belongs to $(R = S)$ if the set of objects connected to it through R is the same as the set of objects connected to it through S. Formally, the semantics of role–value maps is the following:

$$(R \subseteq S)^{\mathcal{I}} = \left\{ a \in \Delta^{\mathcal{I}} \mid \forall b. \left(\langle a,b \rangle \in R^{\mathcal{I}} \rightarrow \langle a,b \rangle \in S^{\mathcal{I}} \right) \right\};$$
$$(R = S)^{\mathcal{I}} = \left\{ a \in \Delta^{\mathcal{I}} \mid \forall b. \left(\langle a,b \rangle \in R^{\mathcal{I}} \leftrightarrow \langle a,b \rangle \in S^{\mathcal{I}} \right) \right\}.$$

Exercise 4.45: Solve the following problems using role–value maps and possibly other advanced role constructors. Use the role names hasParent, hasFriend, hasSpouse, knows, killed.

(a) Define the concept SafeChild. A child belongs to this concept if all his or her friends are known by at least one of his or her parents.

(b) Define the concept GoodMother. A mother is good if she is a friend of at least one of her children.

(c) Define the concept OedipusLike, containing people who have married their mother.

(d) Define the concept NonPatricide, containing people who have not killed their father.

(e) Define the concept FriendlyPerson, containing people who are friendly with their friends' friends.

Unfortunately adding role–value maps to $\mathcal{SHIQ}$ makes the resulting language undecidable [101]. This is the case for role composition and also for most other constructors introduced in Table 4.1 [5]. However, an important exception, a special form of a role axiom using role composition, occurs frequently in applications.

Let us consider the statement that the owner of a car must also own the parts of this car. This is an important piece of background knowledge regarding the ownership relation. If the latter is denoted by the atomic role hasProperty, we can formalise this statement as:

$$\text{hasProperty} \circ \text{hasPart} \sqsubseteq \text{hasProperty.} \tag{4.23}$$

Similar axioms may be needed in a medical ontology. Here, the role hasLocation is often introduced; this connects an illness with its location in the human body. This location is normally non-unique since the illness of some body part is considered an illness of any larger body part encapsulating it. For example, the deficiency of a heart valve is classified as a heart disease, because a heart valve is part of the heart; a broken forearm is a broken arm, since the forearm is a part of the arm etc. Thus, in general, given an illness a that has a location b, and that b is part of c, then c should also be considered a location of a. This statement can be captured by the following DL axiom:

$$\text{hasLocation} \circ \text{isPartOf} \sqsubseteq \text{hasLocation.}$$

Because of these applications, allowing axioms of the above form becomes an important issue. Adding role composition to $\mathcal{SHIQ}$ is out of the question, because this makes the language undecidable; even if role composition were only allowed within axioms of the form $R \circ S \sqsubseteq T$, the extended language would still be undecidable.

However, we note that our examples are even more specific: both have the form $S \circ R \sqsubseteq S$. Let us consider the consequences of allowing such axioms.

A role inclusion axiom remains true if both its sides are inverted. Because $\mathsf{Inv}(S \circ R) = \mathsf{Inv}(R) \circ \mathsf{Inv}(S)$, the above schema can also be restated as $R^- \circ S^- \sqsubseteq S^-$. Thus, if axioms of the form $S \circ R \sqsubseteq S$ are allowed then the schema $R' \circ S' \sqsubseteq S'$ should also be supported.

Exercise 4.46: Apply the inverse operation to both sides of the axiom (4.23). Restate it using the role names isPartOf and isPropertyOf. Check to which of the above schemas this axiom belongs.

Because of the importance of axioms of the above form, the language incorporating these was given a name, $\mathcal{RIQ}$.[27] This language is the extension of $\mathcal{SHIQ}$ with general role inclusion axioms of the form

$$S \circ R \sqsubseteq S \quad \text{and} \quad R \circ S \sqsubseteq S.$$

However, to ensure decidability, $\mathcal{RIQ}$ imposes a further restriction on the set of role inclusion axioms: these role axioms have to form an acyclic RBox in the sense explained below.

To define whether a TBox $\mathcal{T}$ is considered "acyclic" w.r.t. role composition axioms, we first extract the relevant role axioms from it. We thus replace all role equality axioms in $\mathcal{T}$ by two role inclusions. We then form the set of all role inclusion axioms present in $\mathcal{T}$ (including "plain" axioms of the form $R \sqsubseteq S$ as well as those involving composition, $R \circ S \sqsubseteq S$ and $S \circ R \sqsubseteq S$). Finally we extend this set with the inverses of the axioms in it, i.e. statements obtained by inverting both sides of the inclusion. Let $\mathcal{R}_\mathcal{T}$ denote the RBox obtained in this way.

A role R is said to *directly affect* some other role S w.r.t. the TBox $\mathcal{T}$, if $R \neq S$ and $(R \sqsubseteq S) \in \mathcal{R}_\mathcal{T}$, or $(R \circ S \sqsubseteq S) \in \mathcal{R}_\mathcal{T}$, or $(S \circ R \sqsubseteq S) \in \mathcal{R}_\mathcal{T}$. The transitive closure of the relation "directly affects" is called "affects". The RBox $\mathcal{R}_\mathcal{T}$ is called acyclic if there is no role in it that affects itself w.r.t. the TBox $\mathcal{T}$.

For example, the role hasPart affects directly the role hasProperty because of the axiom (4.23). Let us construct an example of a cyclic RBox: let it include (4.23) together with the statement

$$\text{hasProperty} \circ \text{hasPart} \sqsubseteq \text{hasPart}.$$

The above axiom implies that the role hasProperty directly affects the role hasPart, and thus a cycle is formed. This axiom states that if a owns b, and b has a part c, then this c is a part of the owner a, which does not make much sense. It is unclear whether a meaningful cyclic RBox can be constructed.

The $\mathcal{RIQ}$ language was introduced in the paper [62], which also contains the proof that it is decidable.

---

[27] The name $\mathcal{RIQ}$ comes from combining the acronym $\mathcal{SHIQ}$ with the initial letter of the word *role*, referring to the introduction of role axioms.

4.10.4. The $\mathcal{SROIQ}$ language

The next extension step was made by the authors of the paper [57], introducing the language $\mathcal{SROIQ}$. Notice that the name is formed by replacing the letter $\mathcal{H}$ in $\mathcal{SHOIQ}$ by the letter $\mathcal{R}$. The reason is that $\mathcal{SROIQ}$ goes even further than $\mathcal{RIQ}$ in extending role hierarchy axioms to support role composition.

Before discussing the precise definition of the language, let us first give an overview of the new features with respect to the $\mathcal{SHOIQ}$ language.

Overview.   As in $\mathcal{RIQ}$, the $\mathcal{SROIQ}$ language allows role inclusion axioms involving role composition. However, certain limitations are lifted, making it possible to use the axiom

$$\text{hasParent} \circ \text{hasSibling} \circ \text{hasParent}^- \sqsubseteq \text{hasCousin}. \tag{4.24}$$

This expresses the knowledge that the children of one's parent's sibling are one's cousins. Notice that $\mathcal{SROIQ}$ allows more than one role composition on the left-hand side of the inclusion axiom and it does not insist that the right-hand side role occurs at the beginning or at the end of the composition chain, as in $\mathcal{RIQ}$. The left-hand side of a role inclusion axiom is now a *finite sequence* of role compositions, involving possibly inverted role names. Such a composition sequence can contain an arbitrary number of roles and this includes the degenerate case of a single role. In this degenerate case the axiom has the form $S \sqsubseteq R$, i.e. we get back the "classical" role hierarchy axiom of $\mathcal{SHIQ}$.

Role inclusion still has to be acyclic; for example, given the above axiom, any axiom of the form

$$\cdots \circ \text{hasCousin} \circ \cdots \sqsubseteq \text{hasSibling} \tag{4.25}$$

is disallowed. However, as in $\mathcal{RIQ}$, the right-hand side role can occur at the beginning or at the end of the composition sequence (but not at both ends), without making the role axioms cyclic. For example, this allows for expression of the knowledge that the parts of the engine of a car are owned by the owner of the car:

$$\text{hasEngine} \circ \text{hasPart} \circ \text{hasOwner} \sqsubseteq \text{hasOwner}.$$

The only exception, when the right-hand side role *can* appear at both ends of the left-hand side, occurs when nothing is between. For example, the axiom

$$\text{hasAncestor} \circ \text{hasAncestor} \sqsubseteq \text{hasAncestor}$$

states that one's ancestor's ancestors are themselves one's ancestors, which is exactly the same as stating that the hasAncestor relationship is transitive. Recall that a role inclusion axiom can also be used to express that a relationship is symmetric; see equation (4.9). For example,

$$\text{hasSpouse}^- \sqsubseteq \text{hasSpouse}$$

states the fact that the spouse relationship is symmetric, i.e. one is a spouse of one's spouse.

In addition to allowing role compositions in inclusion axiom, $\mathcal{SROIQ}$ provides several new kinds of role axiom. One can state that a role R is reflexive, i.e. that $R(x,x)$ holds for all individuals x in the domain. For example, the axiom Ref(knows) expresses the knowledge that everyone knows herself or himself.

Similarly, one can state that a role R is irreflexive, i.e. that $R(x,x)$ does not hold for any individual x. Thus Irr(hasSpouse) states that no one is a spouse of herself or himself.

Furthermore, $\mathcal{SROIQ}$ supports disjoint roles: the axiom Dis(R,S) states that roles R and S are disjoint, i.e. it cannot be the case that $R(x,y)$ and $S(x,y)$ both hold for some individuals x and y. For example the axiom Dis(likes, dislikes) expresses the knowledge that one cannot both like and dislike the same person.

Regarding concept expressions, $\mathcal{SROIQ}$ adds two new features. First, in concept expressions, wherever a role is needed one can use the universal role U, presented in Table 4.1. Next, a new kind of concept expression is introduced: $\exists R.\mathsf{Self}$. This *self restriction* describes the concept containing those individuals x for which $R(x,x)$ holds. For example, the concept definition Narcissist $\equiv \exists$likes.Self states that narcissists are those (people) who like themselves.

Finally, $\mathcal{SROIQ}$ extends ABoxes by allowing *negated role assertions*. For example, one can state that Thersandros is *not* a child of Oedipus: ¬hasChild(OEDIPUS, THERSANDROS).

Syntax.   We now proceed to present the formal syntax of the new features of the $\mathcal{SROIQ}$ language, following [57].

We first discuss the requirements regarding role inclusion axioms (RIAs). To ensure that a set of RIAs is acyclic, we require that a strict partial order[28] $\prec$ is given on the set of role names and their inverses. To forbid cyclic inclusion, we require each role S_i occurring on the left-hand side of an inclusion axiom to come before the role R on the right-hand side: $S_i \prec R$. If this condition is enforced, it is obvious that there can be no cyclic inclusions. If there is a cycle, e.g. if a TBox contains both axioms (4.24) and (4.25), and the above condition holds, it is easy to show that a contradiction arises.[29]

A strict partial order on the set of role names and their inverses is called regular if it satisfies the condition that role inverses compare in the same way as the original roles:

$$S \prec R \quad \leftrightarrow \quad S^- \prec R^-.$$

A $\mathcal{SROIQ}$ role inclusion axiom has the form $S_1 \circ \cdots \circ S_k \sqsubseteq R$, $k \geq 1$, where S_i are possibly inverted role names and R is a role name.[30] The axiom $w \sqsubseteq R$ is called $\prec$-regular, where '$\prec$' is a regular partial order, if, and only if:

- $w = R \circ R$ (R is transitive);   or
- $w = R^-$ (R is symmetric);   or
- $w = S_1 \circ \cdots \circ S_n$,   and $S_i \prec R$, for all $1 \leq i \leq n$; or

---

[28] A strict partial order is a binary relation which is transitive and irreflexive.

[29] Because of the ordering condition both hasCousin $\prec$ hasSibling and hasSibling $\prec$ hasCousin have to hold, from which it follows that hasCousin $\prec$ hasCousin holds because of transitivity. This is a contradiction, as $\prec$ is irreflexive.

[30] Disallowing inverse roles on the right-hand side of role inclusion axioms does not limit the expressive power of the language, as $S_1 \circ \cdots \circ S_n \sqsubseteq R^-$ can be replaced by the equivalent axiom $\mathsf{Inv}(S_n) \circ \cdots \circ \mathsf{Inv}(S_1) \sqsubseteq R$.

- $w = R \circ S_1 \circ \cdots \circ S_n,$ and $S_i \prec R$, for all $1 \leq i \leq n$; or
- $w = S_1 \circ \cdots \circ S_n \circ R,$ and $S_i \prec R$, for all $1 \leq i \leq n$.

Notice that the transitivity axiom of $\mathcal{SHIQ}$ is now replaced by a role inclusion axiom (see the first bullet point above). The second bullet point introduces the special case of symmetric roles, while the remaining ones treat the general cases when the right-hand side role R: (1) does not occur on the left hand side; (2) occurs at the beginning; or (3) occurs at the end of the left-hand side.

A *regular role hierarchy* is a set of role inclusion axioms such that there exists a regular partial order $\prec$ for which each RIA in the set is $\prec$-regular.

Having defined the notion of regular role hierarchy, we now turn to extensions relating to concept and role expressions and to TBoxes.

The $\mathcal{SROIQ}$ concept and role expressions are built using the concept and role constructors of the $\mathcal{ALCOIQ}$ language, with the following extensions.

- A concept expression can take the form of a self restriction $\exists R.\mathsf{Self}$, where R is a possibly inverted role name.

- A role expression can be the universal role U.

A $\mathcal{SROIQ}$ TBox consists of:

- a set of concept inclusion and equivalence axioms, involving $\mathcal{SROIQ}$ concept expressions, as defined above;
- a regular role hierarchy;
- the additional role axioms

  - $\mathsf{Ref}(R)$: Role R is reflexive,
  - $\mathsf{Irr}(R)$: Role R is irreflexive,
  - $\mathsf{Dis}(R,S)$: Roles R and S are disjoint;

  where R and S are possibly inverted role names.

A $\mathcal{SROIQ}$ ABox is a set containing:

- concept assertions of the form $C(a)$;
- role assertions of the form $R(a,b)$;
- negated role assertions of the form $\neg R(a,b)$.

Here, C is a $\mathcal{SROIQ}$ concept expression, as defined above; R is a possibly inverted role name; while a and b are individual names. Note that the first two kinds of assertion are already present in $\mathcal{SHOIQ}$ ABoxes, while negated role assertions are introduced in the $\mathcal{SROIQ}$ language.

Recall that the definition of the $\mathcal{SHIQ}$ language involves the notion of *simple roles*, i.e. roles that had no transitive subrole. We had to constrain number restrictions to contain simple roles only, in order to ensure decidability.

Obviously, there has to be a counterpart of this in the $\mathcal{SROIQ}$ language. Intuitively, a $\mathcal{SROIQ}$ role is said to be simple if it does not subsume a role obtained by composition. Notice that there is no need to mention transitive roles, as these are declared using composition.

Formally, consider a set $\mathcal{R}$ of RIAs. The set of simple roles with respect to $\mathcal{R}$ is defined by induction:

- an atomic role R is simple if neither R nor R^- occurs on the right-hand side of an RIA in $\mathcal{R}$;

- the role R^- is simple if R is simple;

- a role R occurring on the right-hand side of some RIAs in $\mathcal{R}$ is simple if, for all $w \sqsubseteq R \in \mathcal{R}$, it holds that $w = S$ (i.e. the left-hand side does not contain a composition), where S is a simple role.

In order for a $\mathcal{SROIQ}$ knowledge base to be valid, only simple roles should be used in the following contexts:

- the axioms $\mathsf{Irr}(S)$ and $\mathsf{Dis}(R,S)$;

- negated role assertions in the ABox;

- number restrictions (just as in $\mathcal{SHIQ}$);

- self restrictions $\exists R.\mathsf{Self}$.

Semantics. To complete the description of the $\mathcal{SROIQ}$ language we now discuss the semantics of the new features, as an extension to the description of $\mathcal{SHIQ}$ language semantics in Subsection 4.5.5.

The semantics of $\mathcal{SROIQ}$ concept and role expressions is obtained by extending Figure 4.10 with the following equations:

$$(\exists R.\mathsf{Self})^{\mathcal{I}} = \{x \in \Delta^{\mathcal{I}} | \langle x,x \rangle \in R^{\mathcal{I}}\};$$
$$(U)^{\mathcal{I}} = \Delta^{\mathcal{I}} \times \Delta^{\mathcal{I}}.$$

Having added these equations, the semantics of the concept inclusion and equivalence axioms, as seen in the first two rows of Figure 4.11, remains unchanged.

The semantics of role inclusions and of further role axioms is given below:

$$\mathcal{I} \models S_1 \circ \cdots \circ S_k \sqsubseteq R \Leftrightarrow \forall x_0, \ldots, x_k. \left(\langle x_0, x_1 \rangle \in S_1^{\mathcal{I}} \wedge \cdots \right.$$
$$\left. \wedge \langle x_{k-1}, x_k \rangle \in S_k^{\mathcal{I}} \to \langle x_0, x_k \rangle \in R^{\mathcal{I}} \right);$$
$$\mathcal{I} \models \mathsf{Ref}(R) \Leftrightarrow R^{\mathcal{I}} \supseteq \left\{ \langle x,x \rangle | x \in \Delta^{\mathcal{I}} \right\};$$
$$\mathcal{I} \models \mathsf{Irr}(R) \Leftrightarrow R^{\mathcal{I}} \cap \left\{ \langle x,x \rangle | x \in \Delta^{\mathcal{I}} \right\} = \emptyset;$$
$$\mathcal{I} \models \mathsf{Dis}(R,S) \Leftrightarrow R^{\mathcal{I}} \cap S^{\mathcal{I}} = \emptyset.$$

Finally, we extend the ABox semantics given by equations (4.17) and (4.18) to cover negated role assertions:

$$\mathcal{I} \models \neg R(a,b) \Leftrightarrow \langle a^{\mathcal{I}}, b^{\mathcal{I}} \rangle \notin R^{\mathcal{I}}.$$

The article [57] presents a decision algorithm for concept and ABox satisfiability within the language $\mathcal{SROIQ}(\mathbf{D})$, thus proving that this language is decidable. It serves as the mathematical basis of OWL 2, to be discussed in Chapter 8.

Exercise 4.47: Decide whether the following sentences (each to be taken by itself) can be formalised as $\mathcal{SROIQ}$ TBox axioms. If so, provide an appropriate formalisation.

Note that the first four sentences correspond to concept axioms, while the remaining ones correspond to role axioms. Be aware that these latter sentences refer to the *roles* hasBrother, hasParent, hasUncle etc. and not the concepts brother, parent, uncle etc.

(a) A palindrome is a string whose reverse is the same as itself.

(b) Self-employed people cannot employ others.

(c) Self-employed people cannot be employed by others.

(d) People who are friends of themselves are happy.

(e) A brother of one's parent is one's uncle.

(f) A husband of one's parent's sister is one's uncle.

(g) A wife of one's uncle is one's aunt.

(h) A husband of one's aunt is one's uncle.

(i) An enemy of one's enemy is one's friend.

(j) A friend of one's enemy is one's enemy.

(k) A friend of one's friend is one's friend.

(l) An enemy of one's friend's enemy is one's friend.

(m) An enemy of one's enemy's friend is one's friend.

(n) One is a friend of one's friends.

(o) A subordinate of an employee x is an employee of x's employer, for all individuals x.

(p) No one is both x's enemy and x's friend, for all individuals x.

(q) No one is an enemy of herself or himself.

Which of the above sentences can be formalised in $\mathcal{RIQ}$? Which ones can be formalised in $\mathcal{SHIQ}$?

Select sentence pairs such that both individual sentences can be formalised in $\mathcal{SROIQ}$ but the resulting two axioms, when put together, do not form a valid $\mathcal{SROIQ}$ TBox.

Try to find all such pairs of sentences.

4.11. Summary

In this chapter we have introduced logic languages for the formal description of terminological knowledge. The most important building blocks of this formalism are *concepts*, representing sets of objects, and *roles*, describing binary relationships between objects. As known from mathematics, the latter can be regarded as sets of pairs of objects.

To describe the terminological knowledge of a given field, some *atomic* concepts and roles need to be established. From these one can build *composite* concept or role expressions using *concept constructors* or *role constructors*. Finally, *terminological axioms* can be stated that express the equality or subsumption of concepts or roles. A set of terminological axioms describes the general knowledge in a given field. Such a set is called a *terminological box* or *TBox*.

Knowledge about individuals can be described using assertions: a *concept assertion* expresses the fact that an object denoted by a given *individual name* is an instance of a given concept, while a *role assertion* is used to state that a relationship defined by a given role expression holds between two given objects. A set of concept and role assertions is called an *assertion box* or *ABox*.

Well-known methods of classical mathematical logic were used to define the meaning (semantics) of terminological axioms and assertions. We introduced the concept of *interpretation,* which consists of a domain and an interpretation function. This function maps each atomic concept to a subset of the domain, each atomic role to a binary relation on the domain and each individual name to an element of the domain. The *semantics* of a description logic language defines how to map a composite concept expression to a subset of the interpretation domain, how to assign a binary relation to a composite role expression and how to decide whether a terminological axiom or an assertion is true in a given interpretation. We defined the semantics recursively, following the structure of the axioms and expressions.

We also showed another, indirect, method of characterising the semantics of description logic languages: by providing a translation of language elements to *first-order mathematical logic* formulae. When speaking of the semantics of assertion boxes, we pointed out the importance of the *open world* assumption used in ABox inference. This is in contrast with the *closed world* approach used in the mathematical modelling of relational databases.

We introduced, one by one, the concept and role constructors used in the various DL languages and discussed the axiom types allowed. The simplest language, $\mathcal{AL}$, allows *atomic negation, intersection, value restriction* and *limited existential restriction*. Only atomic roles can be used, and no role axioms are allowed. The language extension denoted by $\mathcal{U}$ introduces the *union* operation, $\mathcal{E}$ adds full *existential restriction* and $\mathcal{C}$ extends the language by *full negation.*

We showed that the $\mathcal{ALCUE}$ language has the same expressive power as $\mathcal{ALC}$. As the final language element of the $\mathcal{AL}$ family of languages we introduced *number restrictions*, denoted by $\mathcal{N}$.

Next, we discussed the languages of the $\mathcal{SHIQ}$ language group. The language $\mathcal{S}$ is an extension of $\mathcal{ALC}$ allowing transitivity axioms. This means that in the language $\mathcal{S}$ it is possible to declare roles as being *transitive*. The language extension $\mathcal{H}$ introduces role hierarchy, i.e. it allows role inclusion axioms and role equality axioms to be used. The letter $\mathcal{I}$ denotes the extension that enables the use of *inverse roles,* while the extension $\mathcal{Q}$ allows *qualified number restrictions* to be imposed.

Knowledge described and formalised by terminological axioms and assertions can be used to perform reasoning. In *inference tasks* that relate to TBoxes only, the *satisfiability check* has a special role. This reasoning task involves deciding whether a given concept is satisfiable with respect to a given TBox, which means that one needs to check whether there is an interpretation that makes every axiom of the TBox true and in which the meaning of the given concept is a non-empty set. Other terminological inference tasks, such as checking *subsumption, equivalence* and *disjointness,* are all reducible to the satisfiability check provided that the language in question allows full negation.

The most important case of inference tasks involving ABoxes is the *consistency check,* i.e. deciding whether, for a given ABox and TBox, there exists an interpretation in which all their axioms are true. Further ABox inference tasks, such as *instance check, instance retrieval* and *realisation*, can all be reduced to a consistency check. We also showed that a TBox satisfiability check is reducible to a consistency check of a special ABox.

Internalisation is an important technique for replacing one inference task with another, equivalent, task. Using this transformation one can reduce the satisfiability check of a concept with respect to a general TBox to the satisfiability check of a more complex concept with respect to a TBox that contains only role axioms. Thus, using internalisation, concept axioms can be eliminated from the TBox. It is important to remember that this method is only applicable to $\mathcal{SH}$, or stronger, languages. Internalisation can be employed analogously for ABoxes too.

In the final section of the chapter we examined advanced description logic constructs that go beyond the $\mathcal{SHIQ}$ language. The language extension (**D**) introduces *concrete domains*, for example, integers, strings etc. The extension denoted by $\mathcal{O}$ allows the use of *nominals*, i.e. concepts that have only a single instance. The inverse construct is the only role operation allowed by the $\mathcal{SHIQ}$ language; however, the language can be extended by a number of further *role constructors* such as intersection, union, complement, composition. Most of these extensions result in an undecidable logic. However, there are extensions related to role composition that allow for the convenient and concise specification of, for example, medical terminology systems. We discussed two languages based on such extensions, $\mathcal{RIQ}$ and $\mathcal{SROIQ}$. Both languages are decidable and $\mathcal{SROIQ}(\textbf{D})$ forms the mathematical basis of OWL 2, the second edition of the Web Ontology Language.

Chapter 5

Reasoning on simple DL languages

This chapter gives an overview of inference algorithms for simple description logic (DL) languages. First, in Section 5.1, we present the *structural subsumption algorithm* for reasoning in the $\mathcal{AL}$ language. In the remaining sections we discuss the *tableau algorithm* for the $\mathcal{ALCN}$ language.

5.1. Reasoning in the $\mathcal{AL}$ language

In this section we present inference algorithms for the $\mathcal{AL}$ language, for the case of an empty TBox. For such a very simple task the process of reasoning can be based on the analysis of the concept structures, under the assumption that the concept expressions in question are brought to an appropriate normalised form. In Subsection 5.1.1 we thus first discuss the issue of normalisation. Then we present algorithms for checking the satisfiability and subsumption of $\mathcal{AL}$ concepts in Subsections 5.1.2 and 5.1.3.

5.1.1. Normalising $\mathcal{AL}$ concepts

A complex concept expression can be written in many equivalent forms. Obviously, a reasoning algorithm becomes simpler if it has to deal only with a specific, *normalised*, concept format. Note that different reasoning approaches may require different normalisation techniques. Let us now introduce a normal form of $\mathcal{AL}$ concept expressions, suitable for structural reasoning algorithms.

As an example, consider the following $\mathcal{AL}$ concept expression:

$$\forall \mathsf{hasChild}.\mathsf{Tall} \sqcap \exists \mathsf{hasChild}.\top \sqcap \mathsf{Tall} \sqcap \forall \mathsf{hasChild}.\neg\mathsf{Tall}.$$

Let us simplify this expression. First, notice that the first and the last terms of the intersection are both value restrictions using the role hasChild. Here we can use the following equivalence (see Exercise 4.15):

$$\forall R.C_1 \sqcap \forall R.C_2 \equiv \forall R.(C_1 \sqcap C_2). \tag{5.1}$$

This allows us to join the two value restrictions, which results in the concept expression

$$\forall\mathsf{hasChild}.(\mathsf{Tall} \sqcap \neg\mathsf{Tall}).$$

Notice that here we have a subconcept of the form $C \sqcap \neg C$, which can obviously be replaced by $\bot$. Thus, the transformations so far result in the following simplified form:

$$\forall\mathsf{hasChild}.\bot \sqcap \exists\mathsf{hasChild}.\top \sqcap \mathsf{Tall}.$$

The first two terms are complements of each other since $\neg(\forall\mathsf{hasChild}.\bot) \equiv \exists\mathsf{hasChild}.\top$, and so we can replace the intersection of these two terms by the expression $\bot$. Finally, $\bot \sqcap \mathsf{Tall}$ can be simplified to $\bot$. Thus we have shown that the above expression is equivalent to $\bot$, and so it is not satisfiable.

Let us now try to generalise the above transformations. We can join those value restrictions which use the same role, i.e. use the equivalence (5.1) from left to right. We should repeatedly perform such transformation steps until no intersection contains two value restrictions with the same role name. Also, it is important to detect sub-expressions that are equivalent to bottom, i.e. intersections which contain either an atomic concept together with its negation or a value restriction $\forall R.\bot$ together with its negation, the existential restriction $\exists R.\top$.

Using these observations we can define a normalised form for $\mathcal{AL}$ concepts. A concept expression is said to be $\mathcal{AL}$-normalised if, and only if, it is either one of the $\bot$ or $\top$ symbols or a construct of the following form:

$$
\begin{aligned}
& A_1 \sqcap \cdots \sqcap A_k \sqcap \neg B_1 \sqcap \cdots \sqcap \neg B_l \\
& \sqcap \exists R_1.\top \sqcap \cdots \sqcap \exists R_m.\top \\
& \sqcap \forall S_1.C_1 \sqcap \cdots \sqcap \forall S_n.C_n.
\end{aligned}
\tag{5.2}
$$

Here, $A_1, \ldots, A_k, B_1, \ldots, B_l$ are different atomic concepts (i.e. even $A_i = B_j$ is disallowed); $R_1, \ldots, R_m$ are different atomic roles, and so are $S_1, \ldots, S_n$ (but $R_i = S_j$ is allowed); $C_1, \ldots, C_m$ are *normalised* concept expressions, where $C_i \neq \top$. Finally, if $R_i = S_j$, then $C_j \neq \bot$ must hold.

The following simple properties of the $\mathcal{AL}$ language can be used to bring an arbitrary concept expression to the above normal form:

- properties of intersection, i.e. associativity $(C_1 \sqcap (C_2 \sqcap C_3) \equiv (C_1 \sqcap C_2) \sqcap C_3)$, commutativity $(C_1 \sqcap C_2 \equiv C_2 \sqcap C_1)$ and idempotence $(C \sqcap C \equiv C)$;

- an atomic concept and its negation are disjoint, $A \sqcap \neg A \equiv \bot$;

- the concepts "has at least one related instance" and "has no related instance" are disjoint, $\exists R.\top \sqcap \forall R.\bot \equiv \bot$;

- the distributivity of the value restriction over the intersection, see (5.1);

- identities for the concepts $\top$ and $\bot$, i.e. $C \sqcap \top \equiv C$, $C \sqcap \bot \equiv \bot$ and $\forall R.\top \equiv \top$.

Exercise 5.1: Transform the following concept expressions to an equivalent $\mathcal{AL}$-normalised form:

(a) $\forall R(\forall S.\top \sqcap \forall S.\neg A) \sqcap \forall R.\forall S(A \sqcap B)$;

(b) $\forall R \exists S. \top \sqcap \forall S.(A \sqcap \forall R.B) \sqcap \forall S. \forall R(\neg A \sqcap \neg B)$;

(c) $\forall R \forall S. \bot \sqcap \forall S.(\forall R. \top \sqcap \forall S.A) \sqcap \forall R.(\forall S \top \sqcap \forall R. \forall S. \neg A)$.

According to the above definition, the basic building blocks of $\mathcal{AL}$ concept expressions, namely $\top$, $\bot$, the atomic concepts, their negations and limited existential restrictions, are all in normalised form. We have only two "proper" concept constructors in $\mathcal{AL}$: value restriction and intersection.[1] The following exercise is fairly easy to prove by induction (w.r.t. the number of proper constructors in the concept).

Exercise 5.2: Show that any $\mathcal{AL}$ expression has an equivalent $\mathcal{AL}$-normalised form.

It is also easy to show that a normalised concept different from $\top$, cannot be equivalent to the $\top$ concept. That is, for an arbitrary concept C in $\mathcal{AL}$-normalised form, it holds that

$$C \equiv \top \qquad \Leftrightarrow \qquad C = \top \qquad (5.3)$$

This can be proved indirectly: assume that (5.3) does not hold and choose a smallest concept $C \neq \top$ which is in normal form and is equivalent to $\top$. Obviously, C cannot be an atomic concept or its negation or a limited existential restriction, because it is easy to produce an interpretation in which the meaning of such a construct is different from that of $\top$. Moreover, C cannot be an intersection $C_1 \sqcap C_2$ either, because then the smaller concepts C_1 and C_2 would have to be equivalent to $\top$, too. Futhermore, there can be no intersection inside C because replacing the intersection by one of its sides would give a simpler concept, which would subsume C and thus be equivalent to $\top$. This leaves us with a concept C of the form

$$C = \forall R_1. \forall R_2. \cdots \forall R_n. D,$$

where $R_1, \ldots, R_n$ are not necessarily distinct role names and D is a concept expression which is neither a value restriction, nor $\top$. Now, as $C \equiv \top$ holds for an *arbitrary* interpretation of the atomic roles occurring in it, this equivalence should also hold if we replace the role names $R_1, \ldots, R_n$ with a single role name R. Similarly, if D is an atomic concept or its negation then $C \equiv \top$ should still hold if we replace D with $\bot$. Finally, if $D = \exists S. \top$, we can replace S by R. Our indirect assumption thus leads us to the fact that one of the following two concept expressions has to be equivalent to $\top$:

$$\forall R. \forall R. \cdots \forall R. \bot; \qquad (5.4)$$

$$\forall R. \forall R. \cdots \forall R. \exists R. \top \qquad (5.5)$$

Proving that this cannot be the case is left to the reader.

Exercise 5.3: Show that neither (5.4) nor (5.5) can be equivalent to $\top$, by constructing appropriate interpretations in which the meaning of these concept expressions is a proper subset of the interpretation domain.

---

[1] These are the only constructors which build a concept from one or two other general concepts.

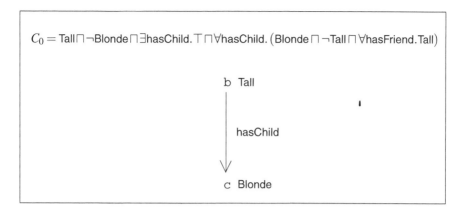

$C_0 = \mathsf{Tall} \sqcap \neg\mathsf{Blonde} \sqcap \exists \mathsf{hasChild}.\top \sqcap \forall \mathsf{hasChild}. (\mathsf{Blonde} \sqcap \neg\mathsf{Tall} \sqcap \forall \mathsf{hasFriend}.\mathsf{Tall})$

b Tall

hasChild

c Blonde

Figure 5.1. An $\mathcal{AL}$ concept and its model.

It is also true that a concept in normal form which is different from $\bot$ cannot be equivalent to $\bot$ and so is guaranteed to be satisfiable. We discuss this issue in detail in the next subsection.

5.1.2. Satisfiability of $\mathcal{AL}$ concepts

Given an $\mathcal{AL}$ concept expression in normal form (5.2), we will now show that an interpretation can be constructed in which the given concept has a non-empty meaning. Given that $\top$ is always satisfiable, this proves the proposition that a normalised $\mathcal{AL}$ concept expression is satisfiable if, and only if, it is not equal to the $\bot$ bottom sign.

Let us first consider an example. Figure 5.1 shows a normalised $\mathcal{AL}$ concept expression C_0 and a corresponding model $\mathcal{I}$ in which the meaning of C_0 is not empty. The domain of the interpretation is $\Delta^{\mathcal{I}} = \{\mathrm{b}, \mathrm{c}\}$, b is the only individual who is Tall and c is the only Blonde person. There is only a single hasChild link, namely between b and c, and no individuals are in the hasFriend relation. It can be easily verified that $\mathcal{I} \models C_0(\mathrm{b})$.

Notice that this interpretation is built simply by trying to ensure that the concept C_0 is satisfied. We thus start by including an individual, namely b, which is expected to belong to C_0. Consequently, b is classified as Tall but not Blonde. Because of the third subterm in C_0, a child of b, named c, is added. The final subterm of C_0, the value restriction, causes c to be classified as Blonde but not Tall. Individual c belongs to the interpretation of the concept $\forall \mathsf{hasFriend}.\mathsf{Tall}$, because c has no friends.

As a generalisation of this example, we now present an algorithm for building an interpretation satisfying an arbitrary concept expression C of the form (5.2). This interpretation will be a directed tree, the edges of which correspond to role links. The recursive algorithm consists of the following steps.

(1) Create a domain containing a single root node (b in our example), make the interpretation of all concepts and roles empty. The *current node* is the root.

(2) Add the current node to the interpretation of all those atomic concepts A_i that appear non-negated as members of the intersection C (in our example it is only the concept Tall which is affected).

(3) Create new individuals (nodes) for all existential restrictions $\exists R_i.\top$ that are members of the intersection C. Such a new node is called an R_i-*successor* of the current node. This means that the relation R_i holds between the current node and the successor node. (In our example we insert node c and extend the meaning of hasChild so that b hasChild c holds.)

(4) Consider each new node x inserted because of an $\exists R_i.\top$ existential restriction. If the intersection C has a value restriction $\forall S_j.C_j$ as its member, such that $R_i = S_j$, then recursively apply steps (2)–(4) for $C = C_j$, with x considered as the current node. (In the example, we proceed with the recursion because of the value restriction in C_0. We then apply step (2) for the node c, with the result that c becomes Blonde. Steps (3) and (4) are not applicable in the recursive phase of our example.)

When C contains no value restrictions then the current node will belong to C in the interpretation constructed because, in steps (2) and (3), we made the necessary provisions for this. In the presence of value restrictions we can use an inductive argument: assume that all recursive invocations of the algorithm ensure that x belongs to C_j, and from this it clearly follows that the current node also must belong to any value restriction in C. Thus the root node belongs to C in this interpretation, and so the interpretation demonstrates that C is satisfiable. Note that this model is *minimal* in the following sense: if D is a non-negated atomic concept, or a limited existential restriction that is not a member of the intersection C, then the root node will not belong to D. In general, the reasoning algorithms presented in this book follow the *minimality principle*, i.e. they construct a minimal model in the above sense.

Exercise 5.4: Using the above algorithm, construct an interpretation satisfying the following $\mathcal{AL}$ concept:

$$\exists\mathsf{hasChild}.\top \sqcap \forall\mathsf{hasChild}.(\exists\mathsf{hasChild}.\top \sqcap \forall\mathsf{hasChild}.(\exists\mathsf{hasChild}.\top \sqcap \exists\mathsf{hasFriend}.\top)).$$

In Subsection 4.6.2 we discussed the issue of reducing various reasoning tasks to the checking of satisfiability. Unfortunately, if we want to reduce a subsumption task to a satisfiability check, we have to use full negation (C is subsumed by D if, and only if, $\neg D \sqcap C$ is not satisfiable). Because the $\mathcal{AL}$ language lacks full negation, we cannot use the satisfiability check algorithm for subsumption tasks. Therefore a separate algorithm is needed to decide the subsumption relation of two concepts. We describe this algorithm now.

5.1.3. The structural subsumption algorithm

The *structural subsumption* algorithm takes as input two normalised $\mathcal{AL}$ concepts and decides whether the first is subsumed by the second.

Recall that a subsumption algorithm can be used to support other reasoning tasks (see Subsection 4.6.2). Checking whether C is satisfiable is equivalent to checking that C is *not* subsumed by $\bot$. To decide whether concepts C and D are disjoint one can check whether $C \sqcap D$ is subsumed by $\bot$. Finally, the task of checking the equivalence of concepts C and D can be reduced to checking whether C is subsumed by D and D by C.

The $\mathcal{AL}$ subsumption algorithm, presented below, is based on the following main idea. Given two $\mathcal{AL}$-normalized concepts C and D, $C \sqsubseteq D$ holds if, and only if, either $C = \bot$ or, for each D_i a member of the intersection D, there is a member C_j of the intersection C such that $C_j \sqsubseteq D_i$.

As an example, let us consider the question whether the following subsumption holds:

$$\text{Blonde} \sqcap \neg\text{Tall} \sqcap \forall\text{hasChild}.\bot \sqsubseteq \neg\text{Tall} \sqcap \forall\text{hasChild}.\,(\text{Tall} \sqcap \exists\text{hasFriend}.\top)\,.$$

Here, the first member of the right-hand side, $D_1 = \neg\text{Tall}$, can be found on the left-hand side also. The second member of the right-hand side, $D_2 = \forall\text{hasChild}.\,(\ldots)$, can be paired with the subconcept $C_3 = \forall\text{hasChild}.\bot$ of the left-hand side, so that D_2 subsumes C_3 (if someone has no children then it is true that all her children belong to an arbitrary concept). Thus the above subsumption relation does hold.

Let us now consider the general case. The normal form (5.2) contains four parts: atomic concepts, negated atomic concepts, limited existential restrictions and value restrictions. The first three types are used in the structural subsumption algorithm in the same way as each other. Accordingly, we introduce a simplified notation for non-bottom normalised concepts described by (5.2):

$$A_1 \sqcap \cdots \sqcap A_K \sqcap \forall R_1.C_1 \sqcap \cdots \sqcap \forall R_L.C_L, \tag{5.6}$$

where the A_i cover the first three types of subconcept and the value restriction part is the same as in (5.2). For completeness, let us reformulate the constraints introduced earlier in the above notation. Thus, each A_i can be either an atomic concept, a negation of an atomic concept or a limited existential restriction. Furthermore, R_i is an atomic role while C_i is either the $\bot$ concept or an expression of the form (5.6). The concepts A_i and roles R_j are all different, and it may not be the case that both a concept A and its negation $\neg A$ occur among the A_i. Let us note that the concept $\top$ is a degenerate case, in which the above intersection has no members, i.e. $K = 0$ and $L = 0$. It is also important to note that this degenerate case is not allowed as a C_i within the value restrictions, because the original normal form (5.2) prescribed that the C_i sub-expressions are different from the $\top$ concept.

Let C and D be two arbitrary expressions of the $\mathcal{AL}$ language. We claim that $C \sqsubseteq D$ holds if, and only if,

- either $C = \bot$
- or $C \neq \bot$ and the normal form (5.6) of C is

$$A_1 \sqcap \cdots \sqcap A_K \sqcap \forall R_1.C_1 \sqcap \cdots \sqcap \forall R_L.C_L, \tag{5.7}$$

and $D \neq \bot$ and the normal form (5.6) of D is

$$B_1 \sqcap \cdots \sqcap B_M \sqcap \forall S_1.D_1 \sqcap \cdots \sqcap \forall S_N.D_N, \tag{5.8}$$

and furthermore

(1) for every i, $1 \leq i \leq M$, there exists a j, $1 \leq j \leq K$, such that $B_i = A_j$;
(2) for every i, $1 \leq i \leq N$, there exists a j, $1 \leq j \leq L$, such that $S_i = R_j$ and $C_j \sqsubseteq D_i$.

It is evident that the above conditions are sufficient for $C \sqsubseteq D$ to hold: the conditions (1) and (2) ensure that, for every member D' of the normalised intersection on the right-hand side, there is a member C' on the left-hand side such that $C' \sqsubseteq D'$ holds. Condition (1) ensures this for the case of $D' = B_i$ (and here even $C' = D'$ holds), while condition (2) handles the case of $D' = \forall S_i.D_i$.

Let us think over how to tackle the issue of proving that the above conditions are necessary. For this, it is enough to show that if the conditions do not hold for a particular pair of concepts C and D then there is an interpretation in which $C \sqsubseteq D$ is not true. Thus for $C \sqsubseteq D$ to hold in all interpretations, the above conditions have to hold too.

Before proceeding to the general case, let us discuss some examples. Consider the following question:

$$\text{Blonde} \sqcap \forall \text{hasChild}.\bot \overset{?}{\sqsubseteq} \neg\text{Tall} \sqcap \forall \text{hasChild}. (\text{Tall} \sqcap \exists \text{hasFriend}.\top).$$

Here, the concept $\neg\text{Tall}$ appears on the right-hand side, but not on the left; thus condition (1) is not satisfied. It is easy to construct an interpretation demonstrating that the above subsumption does not hold: let the domain contain only a single node, which is both Tall and Blonde, and let both roles be empty. In this interpretation the only node is an instance of the left-hand side concept but not of the right-hand side concept.

Let us consider another, more sophisticated, example:

$$\text{Blonde} \sqcap \forall \text{hasChild}.\text{Tall} \overset{?}{\sqsubseteq} \forall \text{hasChild}. (\text{Tall} \sqcap \exists \text{hasFriend}.\top). \tag{5.9}$$

Here, condition (2) has to be checked, leading to the following recursive question:

$$\text{Tall} \overset{?}{\sqsubseteq} \text{Tall} \sqcap \exists \text{hasFriend}.\top. \tag{5.10}$$

For this question, condition (1) is not satisfied because the existential restriction is not present on the left-hand side. We now build an interpretation $\mathcal{I}_0$ which shows that subsumption (5.10) does not hold. Let $\mathcal{I}_0$ contain only a single individual c, where c is Tall but has no friends, i.e. the hasFriend relation is empty. In this interpretation c is an instance of the left-hand side of (5.10) but is not contained in the right-hand side.

We now show how to use the interpretation $\mathcal{I}_0$ to construct another interpretation which disproves the original subsumption claim (5.9). Such an interpretation will have to contain an individual belonging to the left-hand side concept: it has to be Blonde and all its children have to be Tall. At the same time this individual should not be included in the concept on the right-hand side of (5.9). To achieve this, let us extend the interpretation $\mathcal{I}_0$, so disproving the recursive subsumption query, with a new individual b which is Blonde and which has c as its child. In this new interpretation $\mathcal{I}$ the individual b demonstrates that the subsumption (5.9) does not hold.

Let us now consider the general case for two concepts C and D. Let us assume that the normal form of $C \neq \bot$ is (5.7) and the normal form of $D \neq \bot$ is (5.8). We will now show that if *at least one* of the following two conditions hold then C is *not* subsumed by D:

(1) there exists $1 \leq i \leq M$ such that B_i does not occur among the A_j, i.e. for all $1 \leq j \leq K$ $B_i \neq A_j$ holds; or

(2) there exists $1 \leq i \leq N$ such that either S_i does not occur among the R_j or, if it does, then, for the corresponding C_j, $C_j \sqsubseteq D_i$ does not hold. In other words, for all $1 \leq j \leq L$, $S_i = R_j$ implies that $C_j \not\sqsubseteq D_i$.

If the first condition holds then it is easy to build an interpretation where $C \sqsubseteq D$ is not true. First, consider the case where B_i is a positive atomic concept or a limited existential restriction. Let us build an interpretation in which C is satisfied, using the algorithm of Subsection 5.1.2 (recall that $C \neq \bot$). In this interpretation tree the root node belongs to C but not to B_i (because of the minimality principle and the fact that B_i does not occur in C). Because the intersection D contains B_i as one of its members, the root node does not belong to D either. This proves that $C \not\sqsubseteq D$ holds in this case.

Next, let us consider the case when the concept in question is a negated atomic concept, $B_i = \neg B$. Here, let us build an interpretation tree demonstrating that the concept $C' = C \sqcap B$ is satisfiable. In this tree the root node will belong to C but not to D, because this latter intersection has $\neg B$ among its members.

Now, let us switch to the slightly more difficult case where condition (2) is true. Here again we have two sub-cases. In the first the role S_i occurring on the right-hand side also occurs on the left-hand side, i.e. there is a j such that $R_j = S_i$. In this case, according to condition (2) above, $C_j \not\sqsubseteq D_i$ holds. We will continue from this point in the next paragraph, but let us first consider the case when S_i does not occur at all on the left-hand side. In this case, in order to unite the two sub-cases let us transform the concept C to the form $C \sqcap \forall R_j.C_j$, where $j = L+1$, $R_j = S_i$ and $C_j = \top$. This is equivalent to C because $\forall R.\top \equiv \top$. With this transformation we have shown that $C_j \not\sqsubseteq D_i$ holds in this case too, because D_i cannot be $\top$.[2]

Thus in both sub-cases it is true that $C_j \not\sqsubseteq D_i$. Using an inductive argument, there must be an interpretation $\mathcal{I}_0$ and an individual $b \in \Delta^{\mathcal{I}_0}$ that demonstrate this fact, i.e. for which $b \in C_j^{\mathcal{I}_0}$ and $b \notin D_i^{\mathcal{I}_0}$. Let us now remove from the intersection C the member $\forall R_j.C_j$, and also, if it contains a limited existential restriction, the member $\exists R_j.\top$, which uses the same role R_j. Let us call the resulting concept C'. Now let us construct a tree interpretation $\mathcal{I}_1$ that demonstrates that C' is satisfiable, as described in Subsection 5.1.2. Let a be the root of this tree, so that a belongs to C' in $\mathcal{I}_1$. We can assume that the domains of $\mathcal{I}_0$ and $\mathcal{I}_1$ are disjoint.

Next, let us build an interpretation $\mathcal{I}$ which combines the models $\mathcal{I}_0$ and $\mathcal{I}_1$. Thus let the domain of $\mathcal{I}$ be the union of the domains of $\mathcal{I}_0$ and $\mathcal{I}_1$, let the meaning of a concept (role) in $\mathcal{I}$ be the union of the meanings of the given concept (role) in $\mathcal{I}_0$ and $\mathcal{I}_1$. Let us also extend the meaning of role R_j with a single link between individuals a and b.[3] This completes the construction of an interpretation disproving $C \sqsubseteq D$.

Exercise 5.5: For each subsumption below build an interpretation which demonstrates that the given subsumption does not hold, following the above construction.

(a) $A \sqsubseteq \forall S.\forall R.B$

(b) $\forall R.\exists R.\top \sqsubseteq \forall R.\forall R.\neg A$

(c) $\forall R.\bot \sqsubseteq \forall S.\forall S.A \sqsubseteq \forall R.A \sqsubseteq \forall S.\forall S.B$

---

[2] The expression D_i cannot be the $\top$ symbol, according to the definition of the normal form. Also, D_i cannot be equivalent to $\top$ because of (5.3).

[3] To be more precise, $R_j^{\mathcal{I}} = \{\langle a, b \rangle\} \cup R_j^{\mathcal{I}_0} \cup R_j^{\mathcal{I}_1}$.

Proving that the interpretation $\mathcal{I}$ resulting from the above general construction demonstrates that $C \not\sqsubseteq D$ is left to the reader, via the following exercise.

Exercise 5.6: Show that for the root node a of the tree-shaped interpretation $\mathcal{I}$ constructed above, both $a \in C^{\mathcal{I}}$ and $a \notin D^{\mathcal{I}}$ hold.

Using the statement we have just proved, we can formulate the following recursive *structural subsumption algorithm* for answering the question whether C is subsumed by D. Here both C and D are $\mathcal{AL}$ concepts in the $\mathcal{AL}$-normal form introduced above.

(a) If $C = \bot$ then return the answer that $C \sqsubseteq D$ holds.

(b) Otherwise, if D contains a member of the form $\forall R.D'$ such that there is no value restriction for the same role in C, i.e. C contains no member of the form $\forall R.C'$, then return that $C \sqsubseteq D$ does not hold.

(c) Otherwise, if the intersection D has a member D' which is not a value restriction and which is not a member of the intersection C then return that $C \sqsubseteq D$ does not hold.

(d) Otherwise, consider all value restrictions $\forall R.D'$ that occur in the intersection D and for each find the corresponding $\forall R.C'$ value restriction in C (such a value restriction must be there in C because otherwise, in step 2, we would have already exited the algorithm). For each such value restriction pair apply this algorithm recursively to check whether $C' \sqsubseteq D'$ holds. If all recursive invocations of the algorithm are successful then return that $C \sqsubseteq D$ holds; otherwise, return that $C \sqsubseteq D$ does not hold.

Exercise 5.7: Using the structural subsumption algorithm, build the concept hierarchy, i.e. list all valid subsumption relationships that hold between the following normalised $\mathcal{AL}$ concepts $C_1, \ldots, C_7$:

$$C_1 = A \sqcap \forall S.\forall R.\bot \sqcap \forall R.B;$$
$$C_2 = A \sqcap \forall S.(B \sqcap \forall R.\neg A) \sqcap \forall R.(B \sqcap \neg A);$$
$$C_3 = A \sqcap \forall S.\forall R.\neg A;$$
$$C_4 = \forall S.B \sqcap \forall R.\neg A;$$
$$C_5 = A \sqcap \forall S.\bot \sqcap \forall R.\bot;$$
$$C_6 = \forall S.(B \sqcap \neg A) \sqcap \forall R.(\neg B \sqcap \neg A);$$
$$C_7 = \forall R.B.$$

The structural subsumption algorithm can be extended to support the $\mathcal{ALN}$ language [19]. However, this approach is not capable of handling the constructs union, full negation or full existential restriction. For more complex DL languages requiring such constructs, one can use instead the tableau algorithm, to be discussed in the next section.

5.2. The $\mathcal{ALCN}$ tableau algorithm – an introduction

We now proceed to discuss the *tableau algorithm* for the $\mathcal{ALCN}$ language, following Baader *et al.* [4] and Horrocks and Sattler [60]. This section presents some introductory examples while the next describes the tableau algorithm for empty TBoxes. The following two sections extend the algorithm to handle non-empty TBoxes and ABoxes.

The tableau algorithm decides the satisfiability of a concept by trying to build a model for it. If it is successful in building a model then of course the concept is satisfiable. The tableau algorithm uses systematic and exhaustive search, so that a failure implies that the concept has no model, i.e. it is not satisfiable.

Consider the following simple question, which will form the basis of our introductory examples. We know that somebody has a tall child and also that she has a blonde child. Does it necessarily hold that she has a child who is both tall and blonde?

Obviously, the answer is "no". Nevertheless, it is interesting to follow how this answer is derived by a formal inference algorithm.

Let us first formulate the above question as a DL inference task. We have to name the concepts "tall" and "blonde" as well as the role "has child". To save space we will abbreviate these names as T, B, hC, respectively. Using this naming convention the above question can be transformed into the following subsumption check:

$$(\exists hC.T) \sqcap (\exists hC.B) \overset{?}{\sqsubseteq} \exists hC.(T \sqcap B). \tag{5.11}$$

First, let us transform this inclusion problem into a satisfiability question. For this, we use the "$C \sqsubseteq D \Leftrightarrow C \sqcap \neg D$ is not satisfiable" transformation; see Subsection 4.6.2. So the question is whether the following concept is satisfiable:

$$(\exists hC.T) \sqcap (\exists hC.B) \sqcap \neg(\exists hC.(T \sqcap B)).$$

We have seen the advantages of concept normalisation in the structural subsumption algorithm. The tableau algorithm also relies on normalisation, but a different kind. It uses the so-called *negation normal form* (NNF), which allows only atomic negation, i.e. $\mathcal{ALUEN}$ concepts. Using *de Morgan*'s *laws* and their counterparts for quantified concept expressions, it is easy to transform an arbitrary concept expression to NNF, by "bringing negation inside" composite concepts, as discussed in Chapter 4; see e.g. Exercise 4.14. When this transformation is applied to our example, we obtain the following concept in NNF:

$$C_0 = (\exists hC.T) \sqcap (\exists hC.B) \sqcap \forall hC.(\neg T \sqcup \neg B). \tag{5.12}$$

5.2.1. Constructing an $\mathcal{ALC}$ tableau

We now give an informal overview of how the satisfiability of the $\mathcal{ALC}$ concept (5.12) can be proved using the tableau algorithm.

Our aim is to construct an interpretation $\mathcal{I}$ in which the meaning of the concept C_0 is not empty. We do this by building a structure called the *tableau graph*, which is a labelled directed graph.[4] The nodes of the graph represent the individuals of the interpretation and they are assigned a *label*, which is a set of arbitrary concept expressions. Intuitively, a concept expression appears in the label of a node if the given node *must* belong to the given concept in the interpretation being constructed. Where it will not cause confusion, we will

---

[4] Except for the ABox tableau algorithm, this graph will always be a tree.

sometimes refer to a concept which appears in the label of a node as a *label* of the given node.

Each directed edge of the tableau is labelled with a role name. This implies that the start and the end nodes of the edge have to be related through the given role in the interpretation. When speaking about edges of a tableau we will extensively use the notion of a *successor*, already introduced in Section 5.1: we call node y an R-successor of node x if, and only if, the tableau graph contains an edge with label R that goes from x to y.

The tableau graph is the main (and, for the moment, the only) component of the tableau state, i.e. the data structure manipulated by the tableau algorithm. For brevity, we often refer to this data structure simply as the *tableau*. The tableau algorithm starts with a very simple initial tableau and then applies *transformation rules* which extend the tableau structure either by adding new nodes or by introducing new concepts into node labels. Let us now follow how the tableau algorithm works for the above simple example.

Initially the tableau graph consists of a single node, say b, called the *root*. The label of the node contains a single concept, whose satisfiability is to be decided. We will refer to this concept as the *root concept*. So, in our example, the label of the root node will be the singleton set $\{C_0\}$, where C_0 is defined by (5.12). The corresponding tableau graph is as follows:

$$(1) \qquad\qquad\qquad b \;\bullet\; \{C_0\}$$

The concept C_0 is an intersection of three simpler concepts. If node b has to belong to C_0 then obviously it has to belong to each of these three simpler concepts too. Therefore we extend the label of the node b as follows:

$$(2) \qquad\qquad\qquad b \;\bullet\; \{C_0, \; \exists hC.T, \; \exists hC.B, \; \forall hC.(\neg T \sqcup \neg B)\}$$

The intersection rule: If the label of a node contains an intersection then this is *unfolded*, i.e. the members of the intersection are added to the label of the given node.[5]

Of course, this *unfolding transformation* (and other transformations, described below) should be applied only once. We postpone until the next subsection the issue of how to prevent multiple applications of a rule.

Let us now examine the second and third concept expressions in the tableau (2). For the node b to belong to the concept $\exists hC.T$, there has to be another node which belongs to concept T and which is an hC-successor of b. A similar statement holds for the concept $\exists hC.B$. Therefore we extend the tableau graph with two new nodes, c and d, and add two directed edges from b to the new nodes, each labelled with the role hC. The new nodes are thus hC-successors of b. Nodes c and d are labelled with a singleton set containing the concept in the corresponding existential restriction (T and B, respectively):

---

[5] The intersection itself could be removed from the label, in principle, but we will not deal with such optimisations until later.

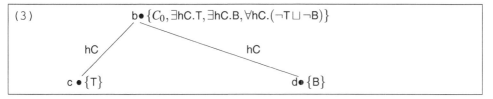

The existential restriction rule: If the label of a node a contains an existential restriction concerning role R then a new node is introduced and made an R-successor of a. The label of the new node contains a single concept, the one appearing in the existential restriction.

One may ask why two new nodes are introduced into the tableau graph (3) instead of just a single hC-successor having both concepts T and B in its label. This would not be consistent with our intentions, because tall and blonde hC-successors are not necessarily the same.[6] This reflects an important issue of the tableau algorithm, the *minimality principle*: only minimal necessary extensions should be added to the tableau graph. In other words, if a transformation rule adds some new elements to the tableau then the constraints represented by these elements should be logical consequences of the constraints represented by the original tableau. It is this principle which ensures the soundness of the tableau algorithm: if it cannot build an interpretation then there is no model satisfying the given concept.

Let us now continue with our example. We now examine the value restriction appearing in the label of node b. The fact that b is an instance of the concept $\forall$hC.D implies that all hC-successors of b should belong to the concept D. Let us extend the labels of these successors, c and d, accordingly:

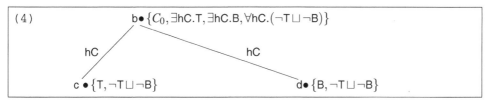

The value restriction rule: If the label of a node a contains a value restriction for role R then the concept appearing in this value restriction is added to the label of every R-successor of the node a.

As seen so far the tableau algorithm simply applies certain transformation rules, deriving more and more complex tableau trees. Notice that, as the tableau tree grows, the concepts appearing in new node labels become simpler. In the tableau above, in the second layer there are no quantified expressions. This means that no new nodes will be added to the tree, so eventually we could reach a state in which no transformation rule is applicable. Such a tableau is called *complete*. If it contains no conflicts then we will be able to build an interpretation which satisfies our root concept.

Exercise 5.8: Transform the following subsumption checks to concept-satisfiability checks. For each, build an initial tableau graph and apply the tableau transformation rules for as long

---

[6] Interestingly, the reasoning task being discussed now, (5.11), is about this very issue.

as you can. Next examine the resulting complete tableau and decide whether you can build an interpretation using this graph.

(a) $\forall R.A \sqsubseteq \forall R.\bot$;

(b) $\forall R.\bot \sqsubseteq \forall R.A$;

(c) $\forall R.A \sqcap \forall R.\neg A \sqsubseteq \forall R.\bot$;

(d) $\forall R.A \sqsubseteq \exists R.A$;

(e) $\forall R.A \sqcap \exists R.B \sqsubseteq \exists R.A$.

A conflict arises in the building of a tableau graph if, for example, the bottom concept $\bot$ or both C and $\neg C$ appear in the label of a node. In tableau terminology such a conflict is called a *clash*. Obviously, a node cannot belong to $\bot$ or to both C and $\neg C$ at the same time; in the absence of so-called *non-deterministic* rules this would indicate that the root concept is not satisfiable.

A non-deterministic rule transforms its input to several, alternative, new tableau graphs. When such a rule is applied, one of these alternatives is tried first. If further transformations of the resulting tableau graph lead to a clash-free complete tableau then the tableau algorithm terminates with a positive answer. However, a clash occurring in such a branch of execution does not indicate failure; instead, the next possible alternative of the non-deterministic rule is tried. The tableau algorithm terminates with failure only if all alternative branches of a non-deterministic rule lead to tableau graphs containing a clash.

This non-deterministic exploration is sometimes referred to as branching tableau execution.

A typical example of a non-deterministic rule is the rule handling the union concept constructor. If the label of a node contains the concept $C \sqcup D$ then C is added to the label as the first alternative, and D as the second. As for the $\sqcap$-rule, this rule is often said to *unfold* the union concept.

Let us now show what happens when the above rule is applied to the union occurring in the label of node c when the first member of the union, $\neg T$, is added to the label:

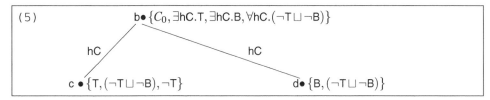

(5)   b• $\{C_0, \exists hC.T, \exists hC.B, \forall hC.(\neg T \sqcup \neg B)\}$

hC

hC

c • $\{T, (\neg T \sqcup \neg B), \neg T\}$ d• $\{B, (\neg T \sqcup \neg B)\}$

The union rule: If the label of a node a contains a union then two alternative branches are created. On the first branch the label is extended with the first member of the union while on the second branch it is extended with the second member. If the transformations on the first branch lead to a clash then the second branch is tried.

Notice that the tableau graph resulting from the first alternative of the union rule contains a clash: both T and $\neg T$ occur in the label of c. Because the first choice causes a conflict we continue with the second branch, adding the second member of the union expression, $\neg B$, to the label of c.

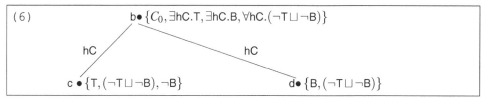

As this choice does not cause a conflict the algorithm continues, looking for further transformation possibilities. We now apply the union rule to the expression $(\neg T \sqcup \neg B)$ at node d. When we add the first member of this union, $\neg T$, to the label of d we obtain a complete and clash-free tableau graph:

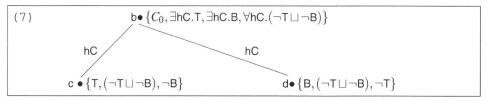

This tableau is *complete*, as no new transformation rules can be applied to it. Given a complete clash-free tableau, one can easily build an interpretation in which the root node satisfies the root concept. The domain of this interpretation is the set of the nodes in the tableau. A role R holds between two nodes if, and only if, there is an edge labelled R from the first node to the second. A node belongs to an atomic concept if, and only if, the given atomic concept appears in its label.

To put this into a simpler form: the tableau graph itself can be viewed as an interpretation if we remove the non-atomic concepts from the node labels:

```
        b• {}
   hC /    \ hC
    /        \
c • {T}     d• {B}
```

The above interpretation, let us call it $\mathcal{I}$, can be formally described in the following way:[7]

$$\Delta^{\mathcal{I}} = \{b, c, d\};$$
$$T^{\mathcal{I}} = \{c\};$$
$$B^{\mathcal{I}} = \{d\};$$
$$hC^{\mathcal{I}} = \{\langle b, c \rangle, \langle b, d \rangle\}.$$

And yes, b satisfies the concept C_0 in the interpretation $\mathcal{I}$: $b \in (\exists hC.T)^{\mathcal{I}}$, $b \in (\exists hC.B)^{\mathcal{I}}$ and $b \in (\forall hC.(\neg T \sqcup \neg B))^{\mathcal{I}}$, and thus $b \in C_0^{\mathcal{I}}$. This means that the individual b in the interpretation $\mathcal{I}$ demonstrates that (5.12) is satisfiable: b has both a tall child and a blonde child, but she does not have a child who is both tall and blonde.

---

[7] Here we have typeset the node labels a, b and c in a font different from that used earlier to indicate that these are now considered as individuals in a domain of an interpretation rather than as tableau node labels.

To conclude the example considered in this subsection, we can state that the answer to our original question (5.11) is negative:

$$(\exists hC.T) \sqcap (\exists hC.B) \not\sqsubseteq \exists hC.(T \sqcap B).$$

Exercise 5.9: Transform the following subsumption checks to concept-satisfiability checks. Use the tableau algorithm to decide whether the subsumption holds.

(a) $\exists R.(A \sqcup B) \sqsubseteq \exists R.A \sqcup \exists R.B$;

(b) $\forall R.(A \sqcup B) \sqcap \exists R.T \sqsubseteq \exists R.A$;

(c) $\forall R.(A \sqcup B) \sqcap \exists R.T \sqsubseteq \exists R.A \sqcup \exists R.B$;

(d) $\forall R.(A \sqcup B) \sqsubseteq \exists R.A \sqcup \exists R.B$;

(e) $\forall R.(A \sqcup B) \sqsupseteq \exists R.A \sqcup \exists R.B$.

5.2.2. Viewing the tableau as an ABox

We have given an informal description of the tableau algorithm for the $\mathcal{ALC}$ language. If we want to understand why the algorithm works, we have to introduce some logical interpretation for the tableau graphs. This can be done in several ways but perhaps the most useful is the following approach, which we discuss here following the handbook by Baader *et al.* [4]. The mapping of the above tableau graph to an ABox is described now.

- The nodes of a tableau graph are considered as individual names. In the example these are b, c, and d.[8]

- Each occurrence of a concept expression C in the label of a node a is mapped to the concept assertion $C(a)$. In tableau (7) of the above example, the node c gives rise to concept assertions $T(c)$, $(\neg T \sqcup \neg B)(c)$ and $(\neg B)(c)$.

- A directed edge of the tableau graph going from a to b and labelled with R is mapped to the role assertion $R(a,b)$. Tableau (7) has two edges, which are mapped to the role assertions $hC(b,c)$ and $hC(b,d)$.

Let us transform the tableau graphs (1)–(7) to the above ABox format. They are listed below as the ABoxes $\mathcal{A}_1$–$\mathcal{A}_7$. For completeness we also include an ABox $\mathcal{A}_8$ which corresponds to the second branch of the union expression processed in tableau (6) (we did not deal with this branch of the union because the first branch led to a satisfiable tableau):

$$
\begin{aligned}
\mathcal{A}_1 &= \{C_0(b)\}; \\
\mathcal{A}_2 &= \mathcal{A}_1 \cup \{(\exists hC.T)(b), (\exists hC.B)(b), (\forall hC.(\neg T \sqcup \neg B))(b)\}; \\
\mathcal{A}_3 &= \mathcal{A}_2 \cup \{hC(b,c), hC(b,d), T(c), B(d)\}; \\
\mathcal{A}_4 &= \mathcal{A}_3 \cup \{(\neg T \sqcup \neg B)(c), (\neg T \sqcup \neg B)(d)\}; \\
\mathcal{A}_5 &= \mathcal{A}_4 \cup \{(\neg T)(c)\}; \\
\mathcal{A}_6 &= \mathcal{A}_4 \cup \{(\neg B)(c)\}; \\
\mathcal{A}_7 &= \mathcal{A}_6 \cup \{(\neg T)(d)\}; \\
\mathcal{A}_8 &= \mathcal{A}_6 \cup \{(\neg B)(d)\}.
\end{aligned}
\tag{5.13}
$$

---

[8] Since we are converting a tableau graph to an ABox, we do not need to adhere to the convention of using all-upper-case identifiers for individual names.

The initial ABox, $\mathcal{A}_1$, contains only a single axiom, the concept assertion $C_0(\mathsf{b})$. The satisfiability of this assertion, as already discussed at the end of Subsection 4.8.2, is equivalent to the satisfiability of the root concept C_0.[9] We will argue that the tableau transformation rules preserve satisfiability in the sense discussed below.

The ABoxes $\mathcal{A}_2$, $\mathcal{A}_3$ and $\mathcal{A}_4$ were generated by extending the preceding ABox. It is easy to verify that the applied transformations preserve satisfiability, i.e. $\mathcal{A}_{i+1}$ is satisfiable if, and only if, $\mathcal{A}_i$ is satisfiable also (for $i = 1, 2, 3$). The "only if" direction is obvious, because the newer ABox extends the older one: if $\mathcal{A}_i$ is not satisfiable then the larger $\mathcal{A}_{i+1}$ cannot be satisfiable either. For the "if" direction, each transformation rule should be examined separately. Let us consider, for example, the use of the existential rule for the transformation $(2)\rightarrow(3)$.

If $\mathcal{A}_2$ is satisfiable then it must have a model $\mathcal{I}$ where its axioms hold. Thus, for example, $\mathcal{I} \models (\exists \mathsf{hC}.\mathsf{T})(\mathsf{b})$ holds. According to the semantics of the existential restriction this means that there is a $\mathsf{c} \in \Delta^{\mathcal{I}}$ such that $\langle \mathsf{b}^{\mathcal{I}}, \mathsf{c}\rangle \in \mathsf{hC}^{\mathcal{I}}$ and $\mathsf{c} \in \mathsf{T}^{\mathcal{I}}$. Let us extend the interpretation $\mathcal{I}$ with the individual name c, which is mapped to the individual c. This new interpretation obviously satisfies the assertions about c in the ABox $\mathcal{A}_3$, i.e. $\mathsf{hC}(\mathsf{b},\mathsf{c})$ and $\mathsf{T}(\mathsf{c})$. An interpretation for the individual name d can be provided in a similar way, to show that the whole ABox $\mathcal{A}_3$ is satisfied.

The transformation $(2)\rightarrow(3)$ introduced two new individual names, c and d. Let us discuss whether we should apply the unique name assumption (UNA) here. We argue that we should not use UNA because this would invalidate our proof above. In particular, if the interpretation $\mathcal{I}$, demonstrating that $\mathcal{A}_2$ is satisfiable, happens to be such that the blonde child and the tall child of b are the same then the new interpretation constructed above, intended to show that $\mathcal{A}_3$ is satisfiable, would obviously violate the UNA. Even worse, in the presence of UNA, if we extend both ABoxes with the assertion $(\leqslant 1\mathsf{hC})$ then these two ABoxes would no longer be equivalent w.r.t. satisfiability; the extension of $\mathcal{A}_2$ would be satisfiable, but that of $\mathcal{A}_3$ would be not.

Earlier we argued that the minimality principle does not allow us to "reuse" a successor when processing multiple existential restrictions for a role, say hC, because this would add the new constraint that the children in question are the same. In a similar way UNA would add the new constraint that the children are different. In both cases it would mean that the tableau transformation in question does not preserve the satisfiability of the corresponding ABoxes.

Let us now continue with further transformations. When non-deterministic rules are used, as in the transformations $(4)\rightarrow(5)$ and $(4)\rightarrow(6)$ we can still speak about preserving satisfiability, but in a somewhat different way. From the tableau (4) we created (5), which turned out to contain a clash, so we tried the other alternative of the union rule to obtain the tableau (6). Correspondingly, ABox $\mathcal{A}_5$ extends $\mathcal{A}_4$ with an assertion corresponding to the first member of the union while $\mathcal{A}_6$ does the same with the second member. We claim that $\mathcal{A}_4$ is satisfiable if, and only if, one of the two ABoxes $\mathcal{A}_5$ and $\mathcal{A}_6$ is satisfiable.

If either of the latter two ABoxes is satisfiable then so is $\mathcal{A}_4$, because both are extensions of $\mathcal{A}_4$. Conversely, let us assume that $\mathcal{A}_4$ is satisfiable and so has a model $\mathcal{I}$ in

---

[9] In Subsection 4.8.2 we introduced the term "*satisfiable* ABox" as a synonym of a "*consistent* ABox", because in the context of the tableau algorithm it often makes the wording of our explanations simpler if we can speak about *satisfiable* concepts being mapped to *satisfiable* ABoxes rather than to *consistent* ABoxes.

which $\mathcal{I} \models (\neg T \sqcup \neg B)(c)$ holds. Again, according to the semantics of the union operator, at least one of the assertions $\neg T(c)$ and $\neg B(c)$ should hold in the interpretation $\mathcal{I}$.
This means that either $\mathcal{A}_5$ or $\mathcal{A}_6$ is satisfiable. Thus we have shown that the above claim
is true.

We would like to view tableau transformations as operations preserving satisfiability, even
in the presence of non-deterministic rules such as the union rule. To achieve this, we will
view the process of tableau reasoning as a sequence of operations applicable to a set of
tableau graphs rather than to single tableau graph. For example, in the above case of the
union rule we can claim that the set $\{\mathcal{A}_5, \mathcal{A}_6\}$ *contains at least one satisfiable* ABox if, and
only if, this is also true for the set $\{\mathcal{A}_4\}$.

Let us call a set of ABoxes $\{\mathcal{A}_1, \ldots, \mathcal{A}_n\}$ *satisfiable* if the set has at least one element
which is satisfiable. Given this definition we can claim that the tableau transformations of
our introductory example can be viewed as satisfiability-preserving transformations on sets
of ABoxes:

$$\{\mathcal{A}_1\} \Leftrightarrow \{\mathcal{A}_2\} \Leftrightarrow \{\mathcal{A}_3\} \Leftrightarrow \{\mathcal{A}_4\} \Leftrightarrow \{\mathcal{A}_5, \mathcal{A}_6\} \Leftrightarrow \{\underline{\mathcal{A}_5}, \mathcal{A}_6\} \Leftrightarrow \{\underline{\mathcal{A}_5}, \mathcal{A}_7, \mathcal{A}_8\}. \quad (5.14)$$

Here, we have underlined those ABoxes that are known to contain a clash. Let us reiterate
that the sign $\Leftrightarrow$ means that if there is a satisfiable ABox within the set on either of its sides
then there must be a satisfiable ABox in the set on the other side, too. We have shown that
$\mathcal{A}_7$ is satisfiable by constructing an appropriate interpretation. If we accept that all tableau
transformation rules preserve satisfiability in the above sense then this proves that $\mathcal{A}_1$ is
satisfiable also.

Exercise 5.10: Transform the sequence of tableau graphs you produced as a solution for
Exercise 5.8(c) to a sequence of ABoxes, using the above mapping. Show how this process
can be viewed as a series of equivalence transformations on sets of ABoxes, such as those in
(5.14).

Perform the same tasks for your solutions of Exercise 5.9(a), (b), (c).

We have shown that both the existential and the union rules preserve satisfiability. Proving
this for the remaining two transformation rules is left to the reader.

Exercise 5.11: Consider a tableau graph in which the intersection (value restriction)
rule can be applied. Assume that the ABox corresponding to this tableau is satisfiable.
Using the semantics of the intersection (value restriction) constructor show that the ABox
corresponding to the tableau graph resulting from the transformation is satisfiable too.

5.2.3. An unsatisfiable tableau; at-most restrictions

Let us modify our initial question to the following: if somebody has both a blonde child and
a tall child and we also know that *she has at most one child* then is it true that she has a child
who is both tall and blonde? The formalised version is shown below:

$$(\exists hC.T) \sqcap (\exists hC.B) \sqcap (\leqslant 1\, hC) \stackrel{?}{\sqsubseteq} \exists hC.(T \sqcap B). \quad (5.15)$$

As in the previous example we reduce this question to a satisfiability check for the concept C_0 below, which has already been transformed into negation normal form:

$$C_0 = (\exists hC.T) \sqcap (\exists hC.B) \sqcap (\leqslant 1\,hC) \sqcap \forall hC.(\neg T \sqcup \neg B).$$

Let us start the process of tableau construction for the concept C_0. We first build the initial tableau graph (1) (see the start of Subsection 5.2.1). Next, we unfold the intersection:

$(2')$ b $\bullet$ $\{C_0,\ \exists hC.T,\ \exists hC.B,\ (\leqslant 1\,hC),\ \forall hC.(\neg T \sqcup \neg B)\}$

We continue, analogously to the previous example, by applying the existential restriction rule, which results in the addition of two hC-successors:

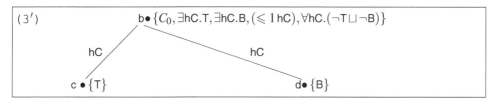

$(3')$ b$\bullet\{C_0, \exists hC.T, \exists hC.B, (\leqslant 1\,hC), \forall hC.(\neg T \sqcup \neg B)\}$

       hC   hC

    c $\bullet$ $\{T\}$ d$\bullet$ $\{B\}$

Here we could continue using the value restriction rule, as we did before. However, let us now introduce a new rule which handles number restrictions. There is an *at-most* restriction in the label of node b: $(\leqslant 1\,hC)$. This restriction implies that b can have at most one hC-successor. However, the tableau already contains two children of b: c and d. Given such a situation the at-most rule will *identify* the two successor nodes. Identifying two nodes means merging them into a single node. Note that this is possible because the unique name assumption is not enforced. In practice, this identification can be carried out by removing one node and moving both the concepts in its label and its outgoing edges to the other node. Let us thus remove d and add the concept B to the label of node c:

$(4')$ b$\bullet$ $\{C_0, \exists hC.T, \exists hC.B, (\leqslant 1\,hC), \forall hC.(\neg T \sqcup \neg B)\}$

           hC

    c $\bullet$ $\{T, B\}$

The at-most rule (draft version): If the label of a node a contains the at-most restriction $(\leqslant nR)$ and a has $n + 1$ R-successors then two of these are identified.

We should point out that for $n > 1$ this rule is non-deterministic. For example, let the at-most restriction $(\leqslant 2\,hC)$ appear in the label of a node a which has three hC-successors: b, c and d. In this case the tableau algorithm should try three alternative branches: identifying b with c, identifying b with d or identifying c with d. As with the union rule all these three branches should be tried, until one branch leads to a complete clash-free tableau.

Note that the at-most rule reduces the number of successors by one. If the tableau contains more than one "superfluous" successor then the rule should be applied repeatedly. For example, let us consider a node a, with a label containing $(\leqslant 2\,hC)$, which has four hC successors. In this case the rule prescribes that we select *arbitrary three-successors*,[10] identify two of these and then apply the rule again for the three remaining successors.

Now let us continue with the solution of the satisfiability problem (5.15). Having performed the identification required by the at-most rule, we now apply the value restriction rule, which extends the label of c as follows:

(5′)	b• $\{C_0, \exists hC.T, \exists hC.B, (\leqslant 1\,hC), \forall hC.(\neg T \sqcup \neg B)\}$
	$\mid$ hC
	c • $\{T, B, (\neg T \sqcup \neg B)\}$

Note that we could have switched the last two transformation steps: we could have executed the value restriction rule first, extending the labels of both c and d, and then used the at-most rule to identify c with d. At this point c inherits the labels of d and so we obtain the same tableau graph as above. It is true in general that we can choose an arbitrary rule, which is applicable at a certain tableau state, without endangering the correctness of the tableau algorithm. However, with a good rule-selection strategy the efficiency of the algorithm can be improved significantly.

Next, let us unfold the branches of the union at node c in the tableau (5′). In the first alternative, which we will call (6′), the concepts T and ¬T appear in the label of c. On the second branch, call it (7′), the concepts B and ¬B appear. Thus both branches contain a clash. Because we have explored all branches of all non-deterministic rule applications and all these led to tableau graphs containing a clash, the tableau algorithm reports that the concept C_0 is not satisfiable and so the subsumption (5.15) holds. We have thus proved that if somebody has both a blonde child and a tall child, and furthermore if she has at most one child, then she has a child who is both tall and blonde.

Let us now build the ABoxes $\mathcal{A}_1, \ldots \mathcal{A}_7$ which correspond to the tableau graphs (1), (2′), (3′), ..., (7′) constructed in the above reasoning process:

$$\mathcal{A}_1 = \{C_0(b)\};$$
$$\mathcal{A}_2 = \mathcal{A}_1 \cup \{(\exists hC.T)(b), (\exists hC.B)(b), (\forall hC.(\neg T \sqcup \neg B))(b), (\leqslant 1\,hC)(b)\};$$
$$\mathcal{A}_3 = \mathcal{A}_2 \cup \{hC(b,c), hC(b,d), T(c), B(d)\};$$
$$\mathcal{A}_4 = \mathcal{A}_2 \cup \{hC(b,c), T(c), B(c)\}; \qquad\qquad (5.16)$$
$$\mathcal{A}_5 = \mathcal{A}_4 \cup \{(\neg T \sqcup \neg B)(c)\};$$
$$\mathcal{A}_6 = \mathcal{A}_5 \cup \{(\neg T)(c)\};$$
$$\mathcal{A}_7 = \mathcal{A}_5 \cup \{(\neg B)(c)\}.$$

In the transition $\mathcal{A}_3 \to \mathcal{A}_4$ we have applied the at-most rule for $(\leqslant 1\,hC)$. We can reformulate this rule as an ABox transformation in two ways. First, we could simply add the new assertion c = d, where the = sign represents the equality role: the relation c = d is valid in an

---

[10] Note that it is not required here that all possible selections should be tried. In general, it is often the case that several rules are applicable in a specific tableau graph or that a rule can be applied for multiple (sets of) nodes – as in our present example with four successors. In such situations we can freely choose the rule or the nodes to use, without the need to explore all possibilities. This is in contrast with non-deterministic rules, which explicitly prescribe that a given tableau graph should be transformed to multiple alternative new graphs.

interpretation if, and only if, the meaning of the two individual names is the same. The other way of performing this ABox transformation is to replace all occurrences of one individual name, say d, with the other, c. This latter form is shown above as $\mathcal{A}_4$, the result of applying the at-most rule to the ABox $\mathcal{A}_3$. Given the semantics of ABoxes, it is obvious that the two variants are equivalent w.r.t. satisfiability, i.e. $\mathcal{A}_4$ is satisfiable if, and only if, $\mathcal{A}_3 \cup \{c = d\}$ is satisfiable.

Let us now examine whether the above application of the at-most rule preserves the satisfiability of the corresponding ABoxes. If $\mathcal{A}_4$ is satisfiable then $\mathcal{A}_3$ is also satisfiable, because the former is equivalent to $\mathcal{A}_3 \cup \{c = d\}$, which contains $\mathcal{A}_3$ as its proper subset. However, if the ABox $\mathcal{A}_3$ has an interpretation $\mathcal{I}$ then the statements $\mathcal{I} \models \mathsf{hC}(\mathsf{b},\mathsf{c})$, $\mathcal{I} \models \mathsf{hC}(\mathsf{b},\mathsf{d})$ and $\mathcal{I} \models (\leqslant 1\,\mathsf{hC})(\mathsf{b})$ clearly imply that $\mathsf{c}^{\mathcal{I}} = \mathsf{d}^{\mathcal{I}}$. Because of this, interpretation $\mathcal{I}$ is also a model of $\mathcal{A}_4$.

Let us now view the above tableau reasoning process as a series of equivalence transformations:

$$\{\mathcal{A}_1\} \Leftrightarrow \{\mathcal{A}_2\} \Leftrightarrow \{\mathcal{A}_3\} \Leftrightarrow \{\mathcal{A}_4\} \Leftrightarrow \{\mathcal{A}_5\} \Leftrightarrow \{\underline{\mathcal{A}_6},\ \mathcal{A}_7\} \Leftrightarrow \{\underline{\mathcal{A}_6},\ \underline{\mathcal{A}_7}\}.$$

Here, the unfolding of the two branches of the union expression is performed in the transitions $\mathcal{A}_5 \Rightarrow \mathcal{A}_6$ and $\mathcal{A}_5 \Rightarrow \mathcal{A}_7$. Both branches lead to clashes, as shown by the underlining. Thus $\{\underline{\mathcal{A}_6},\ \underline{\mathcal{A}_7}\}$ does not contain a satisfiable ABox and so the same holds for $\{\mathcal{A}_1\}$ because the two sets of ABoxes are equivalent w.r.t. satisfiability.

Exercise 5.12: Transform the following subsumption checks to concept-satisfiability checks. Use the tableau algorithm to decide whether the subsumption holds. Show how this process can be viewed as a series of equivalence transformations on sets of ABoxes such as those in (5.14).

(a) $\exists R.A \sqcap \exists R.B \sqsubseteq (\geqslant 2R)$;

(b) $\exists R.A \sqcap \exists R.\neg A \sqsubseteq (\geqslant 2R)$;

(c) $\exists R.A \sqcap (\leqslant 1R) \sqsubseteq \forall R.A$;

(d) $\exists R.(A \sqcap B) \sqcap \exists R.(A \sqcap \neg B) \sqcap (\leqslant 2R) \sqsubseteq \forall R.A$.

5.2.4. Number restrictions

We now turn to a final example, which demonstrates the use of both at-most and at-least restrictions. Let us see how the tableau algorithm behaves when given the following concept, which is obviously not satisfiable:

$$C_0 = (\leqslant 1\,\mathsf{hC}) \sqcap (\geqslant 2\,\mathsf{hC}). \tag{5.17}$$

We start with an initial tableau containing only the node b, with $\{C_0\}$ as its label. Next, we unfold the intersection in C_0. Now, the label of b contains two number restrictions in addition to C_0. The first of these, the at-most restriction $(\leqslant 1\,\mathsf{hC})$, can trigger the at-most rule only if b already has at least two hC-successors. This is not the case in the current tableau; therefore a rule for the number restriction $(\geqslant 2\,\mathsf{hC})$ will be applied. This *at-least* rule, quite naturally, adds two hC-successors. The new nodes have empty labels, as the (unqualified) number restrictions do not pose any constraints on the successors. The resulting tableau is as follows:

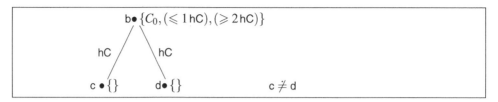

The constraint $c \neq d$ at bottom right of the tableau indicates that the two individuals have to be different. In the absence of this constraint the at-most rule for the concept $(\leqslant 1\,hC)$ would be applicable and would identify the two newly created nodes. If such an identification is performed, b ceases to have two hC-successors and this would trigger the at-least rule to create two hC-successors again, and so on. In order to prevent this infinite chain of events, we modify the main data structure used in tableau reasoning: in addition to the tableau graph we store a set of inequalities of the form $x \neq y$, where x and y are nodes of the tableau. This extended data structure, containing the tableau graph and a set of inequalities, is the *tableau state*.

The inequalities are added to the tableau state by the at-least rule. At the same time, the earlier version of the at-most rule is modified so that it will not identify nodes x and y, if $x \neq y$ or $y \neq x$ holds. We will call nodes x and y identifiable if the tableau state does not contain the inequalities $x \neq y$ and $y \neq x$. In this case we will also say that x and y can be *identified*. We will call two nodes *non-identifiable* or simply *distinct* if the nodes are not identifiable.

Let us formulate the transformation rules for both types of number restrictions.

The at-least rule: If the label of the node a contains an at-least restriction $(\geqslant nR)$ then n R-successors of a, each with an empty label, are created. For each pair x, y of newly created successors the inequality $x \neq y$ is added to the tableau state.

The at-most rule: If the label of the node a contains an at-most restriction $(\leqslant nR)$, a has $n+1$ R successors and there is an identifiable pair of nodes among these then one such pair is identified (and this is performed in a non-deterministic way for every identifiable pair).

Let us return to the tableau of the problem (5.17). The modified at-most rule, introduced above, will not be applicable at the node b for the concept $(\leqslant 1\,hC)$ because the two successors of b cannot be identified. At the same time, b has two successors and thus does not belong to $(\leqslant 1\,hC)$. Obviously, such a situation is a contradiction and therefore has to be classified as a clash.

To handle number restrictions we thus introduce a third type of clash in addition to the first two types, where the $\bot$ concept, or both C and $\neg C$, appear in the label of a node. A node a represents a clash of this new type if the label of a contains the at-most restriction $(\leqslant nR)$ and a has $n+1$ R-successors, no two of which can be identified.

Because of this newly introduced clash condition, the tableau algorithm will detect that the concept (5.17) is not satisfiable.

Exercise 5.13: Transform the following subsumption checks to concept-satisfiability checks. Use a tableau algorithm to decide whether the subsumption holds. Show how this process can be viewed as a series of equivalence transformations, on sets of ABoxes, such as (5.14).

(a) $(\geqslant 2R) \sqsubseteq \exists R.\top$;

(b) $\top \sqsubseteq (\leqslant 1R) \sqcup (\geqslant 3R)$;

(c) $\exists R.\forall R.\bot \sqcap \exists R.((\exists R.\top) \sqcap (\leqslant 1R)) \sqcap \exists R.(\geqslant 2R) \sqsubseteq (\geqslant 3R)$.

5.3. The $\mathcal{ALCN}$ tableau algorithm for empty TBoxes

In this section we provide an exact description of the $\mathcal{ALCN}$ tableau algorithm. This algorithm decides whether an $\mathcal{ALCN}$ concept is satisfiable w.r.t. an empty TBox.

5.3.1. Preliminary definitions

The tableau algorithm requires that the concepts it handles are in negation normal form (NNF), i.e. they contain negation only in front of atomic concepts. Figure 5.2 shows simple equivalence transformations using which negation can be moved inwards or eliminated from an arbitrary composite $\mathcal{ALCN}$ concept. We apply these transformations repeatedly, to arbitrary subconcepts (i.e. sub-expressions) of the concept in question, until no more transformations are applicable. Clearly, at this point the concept is in negation normal form.

In our forthcoming definition of a tableau graph, the main data structure used by the tableau algorithm, we will have to specify which concepts can appear in the labels of the nodes. We claim that node labels can contain only subconcepts of the root concept (i.e. the concept whose satisfiability is being checked). By reviewing the informal versions of the transformation rules presented in the previous subsection it is easy to ascertain that each concept added to a node label is a subconcept of another concept already present in the label of a tableau node, and thus it is a subconcept of the root node.

$$\neg\neg C \Rightarrow C$$
$$\neg(C \sqcap D) \Rightarrow \neg C \sqcup \neg D$$
$$\neg(C \sqcup D) \Rightarrow \neg C \sqcap \neg D$$
$$\neg(\exists R.C) \Rightarrow \forall R.\neg C$$
$$\neg(\forall R.C) \Rightarrow \exists R.\neg C$$
$$\neg(\leqslant nR) \Rightarrow (\geqslant mR) \ \text{where } m = n + 1$$
$$\neg(\geqslant 1R) \Rightarrow \forall R.\bot$$
$$\neg(\geqslant nR) \Rightarrow (\leqslant mR) \ \text{where } m = n - 1 \text{ and } n > 1$$

Figure 5.2.   The transformation rules for negation normal form.

$$sub(A) = \{A\} \text{ if } A \text{ is an atomic concept}$$
$$sub(\neg C) = \{\neg C\} \cup sub(C)$$
$$sub(C \sqcap D) = \{C \sqcap D\} \cup sub(C) \cup sub(D)$$
$$sub(C \sqcup D) = \{C \sqcup D\} \cup sub(C) \cup sub(D)$$
$$sub(\exists R.C) = \{\exists R.C\} \cup sub(C)$$
$$sub(\forall R.C) = \{\forall R.C\} \cup sub(C)$$
$$sub(\leqslant nR) = \{(\leqslant nR)\}$$
$$sub(\geqslant nR) = \{(\geqslant nR)\}$$

Figure 5.3. The notion of a subconcept.

We use $sub(C)$ to denote the set of all subconcepts of the concept expression C. The recursive definition of this set is presented in Figure 5.3.

Exercise 5.14: Transform the following concept C_0 into an equivalent concept C_1 in NNF:

$$C_0 = \neg((\geqslant 1R) \sqcap \forall R.(\neg B \sqcup \exists R.\neg B) \sqcap \exists R.(\leqslant 5R) \sqcap (\geqslant 2R)).$$

List the elements of the set $sub(C_1)$.

5.3.2. The tableau algorithm

Let C be an arbitrary $\mathcal{ALCN}$ concept expression in negation normal form. The tableau algorithm manages so-called tableau states, which consist of a labelled tableau graph and a set of inequalities.

The tableau graph for the concept C is a directed graph $\langle V, E, \mathcal{L} \rangle$, where V is the set of nodes, $E \subseteq V \times V$ is the set of edges and $\mathcal{L}$ is the function which assigns *labels* to the nodes and edges. The function $\mathcal{L}$ labels every node $x \in V$ with a set of concepts $\mathcal{L}(x) \subseteq sub(C)$ and every edge $\langle x, y \rangle \in E$ with a role $\mathcal{L}(\langle x, y \rangle) = R$, where R is a role name appearing in C. In addition to the tableau graph, the tableau state stores a set I of inequalities of the form $x \neq y$, where $x, y \in V$ are nodes of the graph.

Thus, a tableau state $\mathbf{T}$ can be described by the quadruple $\langle V, E, \mathcal{L}, I \rangle$. We will often refer to a tableau state simply as a tableau.

Given the above characterisation of the tableau state, let us now formalise the definitions of some related notions. Given a tableau state $\langle V, E, \mathcal{L}, I \rangle$, a node y is called the *R-successor* of a node x if, and only if, there is an edge, labelled R, which goes from x to y: $\langle x, y \rangle \in E$, $\mathcal{L}(\langle x, y \rangle) = R$. Nodes x and y are called *identifiable* if, and only if, $x \neq y \notin I$ and $y \neq x \notin I$ hold. A tableau state is said to contain a *clash* if, and only if, the tableau graph has a node $x \in V$, for which one of the following conditions holds:

- $\perp \in \mathcal{L}(x)$, or

- $\{C, \neg C\} \subseteq \mathcal{L}(x)$, or

- $(\leqslant nR) \subset \mathcal{L}(x)$ and x has $n+1$ R-successors, no two of which can be identified.

The input of the tableau algorithm is a concept expression C, called the *root concept*. It can return either a positive or a negative answer. The first case indicates that C is satisfiable and the second that it is not.

The tableau algorithm starts from an initial state $\mathbf{T}_0(C) = \langle \{x_0\}, \emptyset, \mathcal{L}_0, \emptyset \rangle$. Here the graph contains only a single node x_0, which is called the *root node*. There are no edges and no inequalities in the initial state. The labelling function maps the root node to a singleton set containing the concept expression whose satisfiability is being checked: $\mathcal{L}_0(x_0) = \{C\}$.

The $\mathcal{ALCN}$ tableau algorithm proceeds by repeatedly applying the rules shown in Figure 5.4. A given rule is applicable in a tableau state $\mathbf{T} = \langle V, E, \mathcal{L}, I \rangle$ if there exists a node

---

The $\sqcap$-rule

Condition:	$(C_1 \sqcap C_2) \in \mathcal{L}(x)$ and $\{C_1, C_2\} \not\subseteq \mathcal{L}(x)$.
New state $\mathbf{T}'$:	$\mathcal{L}'(x) = \mathcal{L}(x) \cup \{C_1, C_2\}$.

The $\sqcup$-rule

Condition:	$(C_1 \sqcup C_2) \in \mathcal{L}(x)$ and $\{C_1, C_2\} \cap \mathcal{L}(x) = \emptyset$.
New state $\mathbf{T}_1$:	$\mathcal{L}'(x) = \mathcal{L}(x) \cup \{C_1\}$.
New state $\mathbf{T}_2$:	$\mathcal{L}'(x) = \mathcal{L}(x) \cup \{C_2\}$.

The $\exists$-rule

Condition:	$(\exists R.C) \in \mathcal{L}(x)$ and there is no y such that $\mathcal{L}(\langle x, y \rangle) = R$ and $C \in \mathcal{L}(y)$.
New state $\mathbf{T}'$:	$V' = V \cup \{y\}$ ($y \notin V$ is a new node),
	$E' = E \cup \{\langle x, y \rangle\}$, $\mathcal{L}'(\langle x, y \rangle) = R$, $\mathcal{L}'(y) = \{C\}$.

The $\forall$-rule

Condition:	$\forall R.C \in \mathcal{L}(x)$ and x has an R-successor y such that $C \notin \mathcal{L}(y)$.
New state $\mathbf{T}'$:	$\mathcal{L}'(y) = \mathcal{L}(y) \cup \{C\}$.

The $\geqslant$-rule

Condition:	$(\geqslant n R) \in \mathcal{L}(x)$ and x does not have n R-successors of which no two can be identified.
New state $\mathbf{T}'$:	$V' = V \cup \{y_1, \ldots, y_n\}$ ($y_i \notin V$ are new nodes),
	$E' = E \cup \{\langle x, y_1 \rangle, \ldots, \langle x, y_n \rangle\}$,
	$\mathcal{L}'(\langle x, y_i \rangle) = R$, $\mathcal{L}'(y_i) = \emptyset$, for every $i = 1 \leq i \leq n$,
	$I' = I \cup \{y_i \neq y_j \mid 1 \leq i < j \leq n\}$.

The $\leqslant$-rule

Condition:	$(\leqslant n R) \in \mathcal{L}(x)$ and x has R-successors $y_0, \ldots, y_n$, among which there are at least two identifiable nodes.
New state $\mathbf{T}_{ij}$:	For every $\langle i, j \rangle$ ($0 \leq i < j \leq n$), where y_i and y_j are identifiable:
	$V' = V \setminus \{y_j\}$, $\mathcal{L}'(y_i) = \mathcal{L}(y_i) \cup \mathcal{L}(y_j)$,
	$E' = E \setminus \{\langle x, y_j \rangle\} \setminus \{\langle y_j, u \rangle \mid \langle y_j, u \rangle \in E\} \cup \{\langle y_i, u \rangle \mid \langle y_j, u \rangle \in E\}$,
	$\mathcal{L}'(\langle y_i, u \rangle) = \mathcal{L}(\langle y_j, u \rangle)$, for every u, such that $\langle y_j, u \rangle \in E$,
	$I' = I[y_j \to y_i]$ (every occurrence of y_j is replaced by y_i).

Figure 5.4. The transformation rules of the $\mathcal{ALCN}$ tableau algorithm.

$x \in V$ such that the condition of the rule, as shown in the table, is satisfied. This condition is sometimes called the *firing* condition and the act of applying a rule the *firing* of the rule.

Notice that in addition to node x each rule involves a concept present in the label of node x and possibly one or more successors of x (cf. node y in the $\forall$-rule and nodes $y_0, \ldots, y_n$ in the $\leqslant$-rule). The nodes x, y etc. as well as the concept involved are called the *parameters* of the rule.

The result of a rule application is a new tableau state, denoted by $\langle V', E', \mathcal{L}', I' \rangle$, or a set of such new tableau states. These are given in the figure under the heading "*New state*". These descriptions show only those components of the new state that are different from those of the old one. Thus if the value of V', E' or I' is not shown in a new state, this means that $V' = V$, $E' = E$ and $I' = I$, respectively. Similarly, unless a new value of the labelling function is explicitly specified for a node u or a pair $\langle u, v \rangle$, the old value is preserved in the new state: $\mathcal{L}'(u) = \mathcal{L}(u)$ and $\mathcal{L}'(\langle u, v \rangle) = \mathcal{L}(\langle u, v \rangle)$.

The $\exists$- and $\geqslant$-rules are called *expansion* rules, because they add new nodes to the tableau graph. It is important to note that these rules never "reuse" existing nodes, i.e. the nodes y and y_i added by these rules are always new ones, different from the existing nodes of the graph. Such a re-use would violate the minimality principle and thus constraints not implied by the preceding tableau state would be added to the new state.

Notice that for every rule there is a subcondition, which, once the rule has been applied, prevents the algorithm from reapplying the rule with the same node and concept parameters. For example, the intersection rule adds the two members of the intersection to the node label. At the same time the last condition specified in the rule forbids its application when both intersection members are already present in the node label.

To sum up, Figure 5.4 should be interpreted in the following way. Given a tableau state $\mathbf{T}$, a node x in $\mathbf{T}$ and a transformation rule whose condition-part holds for $\mathbf{T}$ and x, the figure specifies the output of the transformation rule as a *set* $S_\mathbf{T}$ of tableau states. If, for a given rule, this set can contain multiple elements then the rule is called *non-deterministic*. Otherwise, i.e. when the result is always a singleton set, the rule is said to be *deterministic*.

Let us first consider the non-deterministic rules. In the case of the $\sqcup$-rule, the set $S_\mathbf{T}$ will contain the two new tableau states $\mathbf{T}_1$ and $\mathbf{T}_2$, as defined in the description of the $\sqcup$-rule. In the case of the $\leqslant$-rule, for every identifiable pair from amongst the nodes $y_0, \ldots, y_n$ listed in the condition part of the rule a new state is created, and thus:

$$S_\mathbf{T} = \left\{ \mathbf{T}_{ij} \mid 0 \leq i < j \leq n, \ y_i \text{ and } y_j \text{ are identifiable} \right\}.$$

In this case $S_\mathbf{T}$ is a finite non-empty set, since the condition of the rule ensures the presence of at least one identifiable pair.

In the case of deterministic rules (all rules other than the $\sqcup$-rule and the $\leqslant$-rule), $S_\mathbf{T}$ is a singleton set $\{\mathbf{T}'\}$ where $\mathbf{T}'$ is the new state described in the appropriate part of Figure 5.4.

A tableau state is called *complete* if no transformation rule is applicable for it.

Exercise 5.15: Consider the following tableau state, obtained in the process of deciding the satisfiability of the concept $C_0 = \exists hC.\exists hC.\top \sqcap \exists hC.\exists hC.B \sqcap (\geqslant 2\,hC) \sqcap \forall hC.(\leqslant 1\,hC) \sqcap ((\exists hC.(\geqslant 2\,hC)) \sqcup (\leqslant 1\,hC))$:

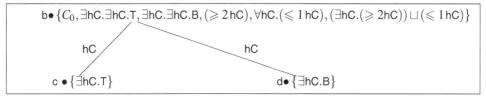

Consider the transformation rules of Figure 5.4. Which of these are applicable in the above tableau, and at which nodes? For each applicable rule construct its output, the set $S_{\mathbf{T}}$.

We can formulate two versions for the tableau algorithm. The *first version* defines a recursive Boolean procedure *sat_tableau*($\mathbf{T}$), where $\mathbf{T}$ is a tableau state. The procedure *sat_tableau*($\mathbf{T}$) can return "true" or "false" and is defined in Figure 5.5.

The tableau algorithm for the concept C corresponds to the execution of the recursive procedure *sat_tableau*($\mathbf{T}_0(C)$). If this returns true then C is satisfiable, otherwise it is not.

Notice that there are two points in the above algorithm where arbitrary choices can be made: in the selection of the applicable rule in step 3 and in the selection of the next tableau state to process in step 4. These are cases of so-called *don't care non-determinism*, i.e. there is no need to explore the choices systematically; any choice will do.

In contrast with this, the $\sqcup$- and $\leqslant$-rules represent proper non-determinism (sometimes also called *don't know non-determinism*). This is reflected in the loop in steps 4–8, which implements a depth-first exploration of the tableau search tree. The nodes of the search tree are labelled with tableau states (which are themselves trees) and the edges correspond to tableau transformations. The choice made in step 4 is non-deterministic if the set S contains more than one element. In this case we may speak about creating a *choice point*. This is a node of the search tree with multiple outgoing branches, each representing an alternative tableau transformation. Step 7 corresponds to the detection of a clash in the subtree rooted

The procedure *sat_tableau*($\mathbf{T}$):

1. If the state $\mathbf{T}$ contains a clash then return "false".

2. Otherwise, if $\mathbf{T}$ is complete (i.e. no transformation rule is applicable for it) then exit with the result "true".

3. Otherwise, select an arbitrary rule, and an arbitrary node in $\mathbf{T}$, such that the given rule is applicable for the given node in $\mathbf{T}$. Perform the corresponding tableau transformation step, according to Figure 5.4, and so produce a set of tableau states $S = S_{\mathbf{T}}$.

4. Select an arbitrary tableau state $\mathbf{T}' \in S$, and remove it from S, i.e. modify set S to $S \setminus \{\mathbf{T}'\}$.

5. Execute *sat_tableau*($\mathbf{T}'$) recursively.

6. If the recursive execution returns "true" then exit with the result "true".

7. Otherwise, if $S = \emptyset$ return "false".

8. Otherwise, continue at step 4.

Figure 5.5. The $\mathcal{ALCN}$ tableau algorithm – recursive version.

The procedure *decide_concept_satisfiability(C)*:

1. Let $S = \{T_0(C)\}$.

2. If all elements of S contain a clash then return "false".

3. Otherwise, if S contains a tableau state which is clash-free and complete then return "true".

4. Otherwise S must contain a clash-free tableau state which is not complete. Choose an arbitrary such tableau state $\mathbf{T} \in S$. Select an arbitrary rule, and an arbitrary node in $\mathbf{T}$, such that the given rule is applicable for the given node in $\mathbf{T}$. Perform the corresponding tableau transformation step, according to Figure 5.4, and so produce a set of tableau states $S_{\mathbf{T}}$.

5. Replace $\mathbf{T}$ with $S_{\mathbf{T}}$ in S, i.e. let the new value of S be $S \setminus \{\mathbf{T}\} \cup S_{\mathbf{T}}$.

6. Go to step 2.

Figure 5.6.   The $\mathcal{ALCN}$ tableau algorithm – iterative version.

at the node being examined. Step 8 and the repeated application of step 4 can be viewed as *backtracking* to the given choice point, in order to explore an alternative branch of the search space.

The *second version* of the tableau algorithm is iterative and is more general than the first, in that it allows other search regimes such as breadth-first. It uses a variable S to store the as yet unexplored tableau states. This second version of the tableau algorithm for checking the satisfiability of the concept C is shown in Figure 5.6. Again, if it returns "true" (resp. "false") then C is satisfiable (resp. not satisfiable). Note that the choices in step 4 are again of the "don't care" type.

Exercise 5.16: Consider the concept C_0 of Exercise 5.15. Use the first version of the tableau algorithm to check the satisfiability of C_0. Present a view of this transformation sequence which follows the second version of the algorithm.

5.3.3. An example execution

Let us present an example which highlights most features of the tableau algorithm. Consider the problem of checking the satisfiability of the following concept C_0, which uses the role hC (has a child) and the concept B (blonde):

$$C_0 = C_1 \sqcap C_2 \sqcap C_3 \sqcap C_4;$$
$$C_1 = (\geqslant 2\,\mathsf{hC});$$
$$C_2 = \exists\mathsf{hC}.\mathsf{B};$$
$$C_3 = (\leqslant 2\,\mathsf{hC});$$

$$C_4 = C_5 \sqcup C_6;$$
$$C_5 = \forall hC.\neg B;$$
$$C_6 = B.$$

Figure 5.7 presents an execution of the $\mathcal{ALCN}$ tableau algorithm for checking the satisfiability of the concept C_0. We follow the first, recursive, variant of the tableau algorithm; see Figure 5.5. In the case of "don't care" choices we always select the rule applicable to the leftmost subconcept of C_0.

Notice that Figure 5.7 shows a search tree, the nodes of which are framed tableau states (which are themselves trees). The edges of both kinds of tree are always directed downwards. Each edge of the outer tree corresponds to a tableau transformation and is labelled with the name of the transformation rule. A framed node with multiple outgoing edges corresponds to a tableau state where a non-deterministic rule has been applied.

Within a framed tableau state we show both a tableau graph and a set of inequalities, if any. To aid readability, we have omitted the edge labels in the tableau graphs. The edges are assumed to have a label hC, the only role in the concept being processed. Also, mostly we use abbreviations for the concepts appearing in the node labels. A subconcept is spelled out in detail only when it is participating in an operation where its structure is important.

Let us discuss the tableau states in turn. The tableau T_0 contains only the root node b. Here the $\sqcap$-rule is applied several times, until all members of the intersection are added to the label of b.[11] Next, we apply the $\geqslant$-rule for the concept $C_1 = (\geqslant 2\,hC)$ at node b. We thus introduce two hC-successors for b, namely c and d, and also add the inequality constraint for the new nodes (tableau state T_4). Then we apply the $\exists$-rule for the concept $C_2 = \exists hC.B$, thereby introducing a new hC-successor e, the label of which is $\{B\}$.

Now the $\leqslant$-rule is applied with respect to the concept expression $C_3 = (\leqslant 2\,hC)$: as b has three hC-successors, two of them must be identified. Because c and d are not identifiable, either c and e or d and e must be identified, resulting in the tableau states T_6 and T_7, respectively. The $\sqcup$-rule is applicable at T_6, leading to the tableaux T_8 and T_9. In the first of these, the $\forall$-rule can be applied to both successors of b. This results in the tableau T_{10}, where the label of c contains both B and $\neg$B, producing a clash. We thus return to the tableau T_6, where the last non-deterministic rule was applied, and take the other branch of the union rule there, that leading to T_9. This contains no clashes, and no rule is applicable, so we reach here a complete and clash-free state.

This means that the tableau algorithm terminates at state T_9 and reports that C_0 is satisfiable. For the sake of completeness, we also show what happens in the other subtree, rooted at T_7, although with some details omitted. The transformations in this subtree would have been followed if we had chosen to first identify d with e (rather than c with e) in the tableau T_5. Notice that the subtree rooted at T_7 has the same structure as the one rooted at T_6: the branch T_{11}–T_{13} leads to a clash, while T_{12} is a complete and clash-free tableau state.[12]

---

[11] Strictly speaking, the label of b also contains sub-intersections, e.g. $C_1 \sqcap C_2 \sqcap C_3$, which are intermediate results in this transformation. We do not show these concepts because they play no further role in the algorithm.

[12] This similarity is not accidental: nodes c and d were created in the same application of a $\geqslant$-rule and are thus in practice indistinguishable. In fact, there are optimisations of the tableau algorithm that make it possible to avoid creating such useless branches in the search tree; see Subsection 7.9.1. Such an optimisation, when applied in our example, would create just a single successor at state T_4 and so the $\leqslant$-rule would not be needed at all.

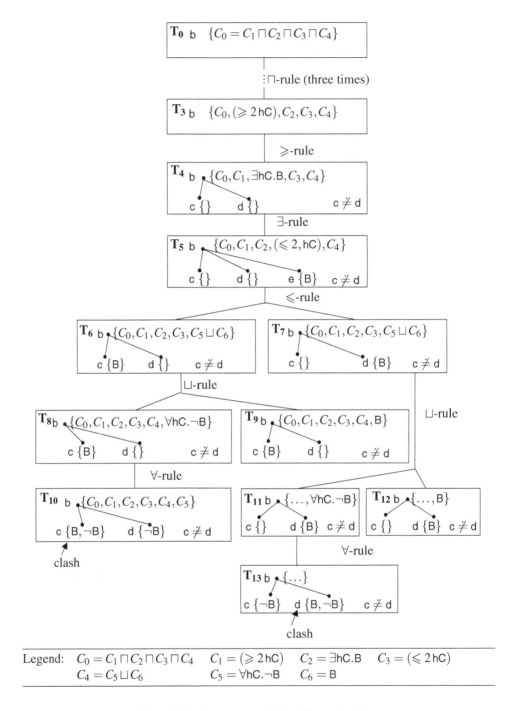

$$\text{Legend:} \quad C_0 = C_1 \sqcap C_2 \sqcap C_3 \sqcap C_4 \quad C_1 = (\geqslant 2\,\mathsf{hC}) \quad C_2 = \exists \mathsf{hC.B} \quad C_3 = (\leqslant 2\,\mathsf{hC})$$
$$C_4 = C_5 \sqcup C_6 \qquad\qquad\quad C_5 = \forall \mathsf{hC.\neg B} \qquad C_6 = \mathsf{B}$$

Figure 5.7. An execution of the tableau algorithm.

Exercise 5.17: Consider the following variant of the concept discussed above:

$$C_0' = C_2 \sqcap C_3 \sqcap C_4';$$
$$C_2 = \exists hC.B;$$
$$C_3 = (\leqslant 2\,hC);$$
$$C_4' = C_5 \sqcup C_6';$$
$$C_5 = \forall hC.\neg B';$$
$$C_6' = C_7 \sqcap C_8;$$
$$C_7 = \exists hC.(\neg B \sqcap T);$$
$$C_8 = \exists hC.(\neg B \sqcap \neg T).$$

Note that the subconcepts C_2, C_3 and C_5 have not changed.

Execute the tableau algorithm for deciding the satisfiability of the concept C_0'. Draw the search tree, following the same principles as in the above example.

In the second version of the tableau algorithm, discussed above, we manage a set S of tableau states. Let us follow how the steps of the above example can be viewed as transformations of the set S. While we apply deterministic rules, the set S contains only a single member, $S_i = \{T_i\}, i = 0, \ldots, 5$. The non-deterministic $\leqslant$-rule results in $S_6 = \{T_6, T_7\}$. In the above overview of Figure 5.7 we continued the algorithm with the transformation of the tableau T_6, i.e. we explored the left-hand branch of the search tree. Had we continued with T_7 we would have traversed the right-hand part. When we apply the non-deterministic $\sqcup$-rule in the state T_6 the new set $S_7 = \{T_8, T_9, T_7\}$ contains three members, as our search space has already been decomposed into these three states.

Although we applied depth-first search in our example, the search space can also be traversed using other strategies. In the second variant of the tableau algorithm we have the freedom to select any tableau state in the set S and expand the corresponding node of the search tree. In Figure 5.8 we have reproduced just the search tree of Figure 5.7 and indicated certain states of expansion by broken lines. Line 1 represents the singleton set of states $S_5 = \{T_5\}$ and line 2 corresponds to the state $S_7' = \{T_6, T_{11}, T_{12}\}$. We can reach this state from S_6 by applying the union transformation rule to T_7 instead of T_6. Line 3 is typical of a breadth-first search: in this case the $\sqcup$-rule is applied in both T_6 and T_7. Finally, line 4 represents a *final* state, when the whole search space has been explored: $S_f = \{T_{10}, T_9, T_{13}, T_{12}\}$. Here, all elements of S_f are leaves of the search tree, i.e. *complete* tableau states.[13]

5.3.4. Properties of the algorithm

We now discuss certain important properties of the $\mathcal{ALCN}$ tableau algorithm. Throughout this section C_0 stands for the root concept, i.e. the concept whose satisfiability is being checked by the algorithm.

---

[13] Note that S_f cannot be normally reached in the execution of the tableau algorithm, as it contains two complete clash-free tableau states; the algorithm terminates as soon as one of these is encountered.

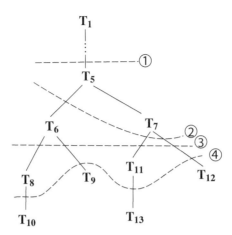

Figure 5.8. The search space of the example.

The tableau algorithm terminates. This is a simple consequence of the fact that the tableau graph is actually a labelled tree, where upper bounds can be provided for the depth and the branching factor of the tree as well as for the number of concepts in the node labels. These upper bounds are actually functions of certain characteristics of the root concept.

In the analysis below we consider the first version of the tableau algorithm, which uses non-deterministic search. We will show that the length of a path in the search tree, i.e. the number of consecutive transformation steps, has a limit which is a function of C_0. Next, we will show that the branching factor of the search tree is limited too.

Let sc denote $|sub(C_0)|$, i.e. the number of subconcepts of C_0, and let d be the so-called *role depth* of C_0, i.e. the maximal nesting depth of concept constructors involving roles (i.e. $\exists, \forall, \leqslant, \geqslant$). Let al denote the sum of the numbers appearing in at-least restrictions in C_0 and let e be the number of existential restrictions in C_0.

Given these characteristics of C_0, let us calculate some upper bounds on the number of possible tableau states. First we claim that the depth of the tableau tree can be at most d. If a is a node and b is its successor then the maximal role depth of the concepts in the label of b is always less than that in the label a, because a concept added to the label of b is always a proper subconcept of an existential or value restriction appearing in the label of a. Thus the role depth decreases by at least 1 when one goes from a node to its successor. This means that at depth d there can be no quantified concept expressions in the labels, and so no expansion rules can be applied.

Let us now calculate the branching factor of the tableau tree, i.e. the maximal number of outgoing edges. Such edges are created only by application of the $\exists$- and $\geqslant$-rules. The former creates one successor and the latter n successors, where n is the number appearing in the at-least restriction. A rule can fire at most once for any node and any concept expression. Therefore the branching factor cannot be more than $al + e$.

As the depth and the branching factor of the tableau are limited, there is an upper bound on the number of unlabelled tableau trees that can be built during the execution of the tableau algorithm. The nodes are labelled with the subsets of $sub(C_0)$; thus the number of possible node labels is less than or equal to 2^{sc}. Furthermore, the edge labels are roles appearing in

C_0. Hence the number of labelled tableau trees is also limited. The same holds for tableau states, as the inequality sets are just sets of node pairs, and the number of such sets is limited by a function of the number of nodes.

Summing up, there is a function (having certain characteristics) of the concept C_0 which gives an upper bound on the number of possible tableau states that can be reached during the tableau algorithm deciding the satisfiability of C_0. Recall that each tableau transformation step is associated with the occurrence of a concept in a node label, and only a single transformation step can be associated with each concept occurrence. Since the number of the latter is limited, so is the number of transformation steps. Thus we have shown that the paths in the search tree have a limited length.

To conclude the proof of termination we show that there is an upper bound on the branching factor of the search tree. A union rule gives rise to two alternative branches, while an at-most rule for the concept $(\leqslant nR)$ can generate at most $n(n-1)/2$ branches. Thus the branching factor of the search tree has an upper bound which is $\max(2, N(N-1)/2)$, where N is the largest number occurring in at-most restrictions. Given that the depth and the branching factor of the search tree is limited, the tableau algorithm terminates.

Exercise 5.18: Consider the concept C_0' of Exercise 5.17. Calculate the four main characteristics of C_0', i.e. sc, d, al and e, as defined above. Following the above discussion determine the theoretical limit for the depth and the branching factor of the search tree constructed by the tableau algorithm for C_0'. Compare this with the parameters of the actual search tree built as your solution to Exercise 5.17.

The tableau algorithm is complete. We now prove that the tableau algorithm is complete, i.e. whenever the given concept C_0 is satisfiable the algorithm will deliver the answer "satisfiable". We will proceed by contradiction: we assume that the algorithm returns the answer "not satisfiable" and show that in this case the concept C_0 cannot be satisfiable.

In this proof we use the mapping from tableau states to ABoxes introduced informally in Subsections 5.2.2 and 5.2.3. Consider a tableau state $\mathbf{T} = \langle V, E, \mathcal{L}, I \rangle$ constructed by the tableau algorithm checking the satisfiability of the concept C_0. Let us now formally define the result of the mapping of this tableau to an ABox $\mathcal{A}_\mathbf{T}$:

$$\mathcal{A}_\mathbf{T} = \{C(x) \mid x \in V, C \in \mathcal{L}(x)\} \tag{5.18}$$
$$\cup \{R(x,y) \mid \langle x,y \rangle \in E, R = \mathcal{L}(\langle x,y \rangle)\} \tag{5.19}$$
$$\cup \{x \neq y \mid x \neq y \in I\}. \tag{5.20}$$

Recall that the nodes of the tableau serve as individual names in the ABox constructed. Naturally, the concept and role names (the atomic concepts and roles) of the ABox are those appearing in the node and edge labels of the tableau (i.e. those occurring in the concept C_0). If a concept expression C is present in the label of a node x of the tableau then the assertion $C(x)$ appears in the ABox; see (5.18). Similarly, if an edge $x \to y$ in the tableau is labelled R then the role assertion $R(x,y)$ is added to the ABox; see (5.19). Finally, the system of inequalities I of the tableau state is represented in the ABox by assertions using the special role $\neq$; see (5.20). The inequality $x \neq y$ is considered to hold if, and only if, the meanings of the individual names x and y are different.

Using the mapping from tableau states to ABoxes, we call a tableau state $\mathbf{T}$ *satisfiable* if, and only if, the corresponding ABox $\mathcal{A}_\mathbf{T}$ is satisfiable.[14] Similarly, a set of tableau states S is called satisfiable if one of its members is satisfiable.

Recall that each $\mathcal{ALCN}$ transformation rule, when applied at tableau state $\mathbf{T}$, produces a set $S_\mathbf{T}$ of tableau states. We claim that each transformation rule preserves satisfiability, i.e. that $S_\mathbf{T}$ is satisfiable if, and only if, $\mathbf{T}$ is satisfiable showed this. In Section 5.2 we showed this informally for some of the rules (existential restriction, union and at-least restriction), while a similar task for intersection and value restriction rules was set as Exercise 5.11. These arguments can be easily reformulated using the definition (5.18)–(5.20). Working out the details is left to the reader, via the following exercise.

Exercise 5.19: Consider each of the six transformation rules of Figure 5.4. Using the above mapping of tableau states to ABoxes, show for each of these rules that the input state $\mathbf{T}$ is satisfiable if, and only if, the set of output states $S_\mathbf{T}$ is satisfiable.

Because each transformation rule preserves satisfiability, the same is true for a sequence of transformations. Let us now focus on the second, iterative, version of the tableau algorithm, as shown in Figure 5.6. Here, if the set of tableau states S' is obtained by a series of tableau transformations from the set S then S and S' are equivalent from the satisfiability point of view.

The tableau algorithm starts with an initial singleton set of tableau states $S_0 = \{\mathbf{T}_0(C_0)\}$. By definition, this set of tableau states is satisfiable if, and only if, the corresponding ABox $\mathcal{A}_{\mathbf{T}_0(C_0)}$ is satisfiable. This ABox contains a single concept assertion, $C_0(a)$, and thus its satisfiability is equivalent to the satisfiability of the concept C_0 (see the end of Subsection 4.8.2).

The last two paragraphs, put together, lead to the following proposition:

> A set S of tableau states obtained during the execution of the tableau algorithm for a concept C_0 is satisfiable if, and only if, C_0 is satisfiable $\qquad$ (5.21)

The proof of completeness can be concluded easily using the above statement. Assume that the tableau algorithm returns the answer "C_0 is not satisfiable". This can only happen when the tableau algorithm reaches a set of states S such that every member of S contains a clash (see step 2 of the algorithm in Figure 5.6). If a tableau state contains a clash then it cannot be satisfiable, because the corresponding ABox contains an evident conflict. Because all members of S contain a clash, S itself is not satisfiable. Consequently, owing to (5.21), C_0 is not satisfiable. This means that the above negative answer is appropriate, and thus the algorithm is complete.

The tableau algorithm is sound; model construction. We now proceed to prove the soundness of the tableau algorithm. This amounts to showing that whenever the algorithm returns "C_0 is satisfiable", C_0 is indeed satisfiable.

Let us assume that the tableau algorithm returns a positive answer. This means that a complete clash-free tableau state $\mathbf{T}$ has been obtained; see step 3 of the algorithm in Figure 5.6. If we can show that every clash-free complete tableau state is satisfiable then our soundness

---

[14] Recall that for ABoxes the terms "satisfiable" and "consistent" are used interchangeably.

proof can be concluded simply by referring to statement (5.21), i.e. as a satisfiable tableau state is reached by the tableau algorithm, C_0 itself has to be satisfiable.

To prove this "missing link" let us consider an arbitrary complete clash-free tableau state **T**. We will actually construct an interpretation which is a model of the corresponding ABox, $\mathcal{A}_{\mathbf{T}}$. This process, called *model construction*, will be repeated several times later in this book, to cater for more and more complex versions of the tableau algorithm.

Before proceeding to discuss model construction for the $\mathcal{ALCN}$ tableau algorithm, let us first introduce some definitions.

Let $\mathcal{A}$ be an arbitrary non-empty ABox. We build an interpretation, called the *natural interpretation* of $\mathcal{A}$, which is denoted by $\mathcal{I}^{nat}(\mathcal{A})$, using the following principles.

- The domain of the interpretation contains the individual names of the ABox.

- The meaning of an individual name is itself.

- The meaning of an atomic concept A consists of those individuals a for which a concept assertion $A(a)$ is present in $\mathcal{A}$.

- The meaning of an (atomic) role R consists of those pairs $\langle a,b \rangle$ of individuals for which the role assertion $R(a,b)$ is present in $\mathcal{A}$.

Formally, the interpretation $\mathcal{I} = \mathcal{I}^{nat}(\mathcal{A})$ is defined as follows:

$$\begin{aligned}
\Delta^{\mathcal{I}} &= \{a \mid C(a) \in \mathcal{A}, \text{ or } R(a,x) \in \mathcal{A}, \text{ or } R(y,a) \in \mathcal{A}\}; \\
a^{\mathcal{I}} &= a, \qquad \text{for every individual name } a \in \Delta^{\mathcal{I}}; \\
A^{\mathcal{I}} &= \{a \mid a \in \Delta^{\mathcal{I}}, A(a) \in \mathcal{A}\}, \qquad \text{for every atomic concept } A \text{ of } \mathcal{A}; \\
R^{\mathcal{I}} &= \{\langle a,b \rangle \mid a,b \in \Delta^{\mathcal{I}}, R(a,b) \in \mathcal{A}\}, \qquad \text{for every atomic role } R \text{ of } \mathcal{A}.
\end{aligned} \qquad (5.22)$$

For instance, consider the ABox $\mathcal{A}_7$, see (5.13), used in one of our earlier examples. The natural interpretation of this ABox, $\mathcal{I} = \mathcal{I}^{nat}(\mathcal{A}_7)$, is the following: $\Delta^{\mathcal{I}} = \{\mathsf{b},\mathsf{c},\mathsf{d}\}$, $\mathsf{T}^{\mathcal{I}} = \{\mathsf{c}\}$, $\mathsf{B}^{\mathcal{I}} = \{\mathsf{d}\}$, $\mathsf{hC}^{\mathcal{I}} = \{\langle \mathsf{b},\mathsf{c} \rangle, \langle \mathsf{b},\mathsf{d} \rangle\}$.

An ABox $\mathcal{A}$ is called *self-realising* when its natural interpretation $\mathcal{I}^{nat}(\mathcal{A})$ is the model of the ABox $\mathcal{A}$, i.e. $\mathcal{I}^{nat}(\mathcal{A}) \models \mathcal{A}$. For example, the ABox $\mathcal{A}_7$, referred to above, has this property. However, the very simple singleton ABox $\{(C \sqcup D)(a)\}$ is not self-realising, as concepts C and D are both empty in its natural interpretation.

Having introduced the above definitions we now embark on the task of model construction. We claim that if $\mathbf{T} = \langle V,E,\mathcal{L},I \rangle$ is a complete clash-free tableau state, then the corresponding ABox $\mathcal{A}_{\mathbf{T}}$ is *self-realising*.

To prove this we have to show that the given $\mathcal{I} = \mathcal{I}^{nat}(\mathcal{A}_{\mathbf{T}})$ satisfies all assertions appearing in $\mathcal{A}_{\mathbf{T}}$. These assertions can be of five kinds:

- Atomic concept assertions and role assertions. These are true in $\mathcal{I}$ by definition see (5.22).

- Top assertions. The statement $\top(x)$ is always satisfied by any ABox.

- Bottom assertions. The statement $\bot(x)$ cannot appear in $\mathcal{A}_{\mathbf{T}}$, because this would imply a clash at node x in the tableau **T**.

- Concept assertions of the form $(\neg A)(x)$. The tableau state from we started is clash-free, hence no tableau label can contain both $\neg A$ and A. Therefore $(\neg A)(x) \in \mathcal{A}_{\mathbf{T}}$ implies that

$A(x) \notin \mathcal{A}_{\mathbf{T}}$, from which, again through (5.22), it follows that $x \notin A^{\mathcal{I}}$ and so $(\neg A)(x)$ holds in $\mathcal{I}$.

- Other assertions, i.e. those not covered by the previous four bullet points. These are concept assertions of the form $C(x)$, where C is neither an atomic nor a negated atomic concept and is different from $\top$ and $\bot$.

Let us now elaborate on the last case. We will consider the outermost concept constructor of C and proceed with an inductive proof using case analysis. That is, for each concept constructor allowed by $\mathcal{ALCN}$ except negation,[15] we show that if C is a concept formed using the given constructor, and $C(x) \in \mathcal{A}_{\mathbf{T}}$, then $C(x)$ holds in $\mathcal{I}$, i.e. $\mathcal{I} \models C(x)$. In the course of this proof we make use of the inductive assumption that, for each proper subconcept D of C, if $D(y) \in \mathcal{A}_{\mathbf{T}}$ then $\mathcal{I} \models D(y)$ holds.

We now provide such a proof for the case of the existential restriction. Let us assume that $C = (\exists R.D)$ and $C(x) \in \mathcal{A}_{\mathbf{T}}$. Because of the way in which the ABox $\mathcal{A}_{\mathbf{T}}$ has been constructed, this implies that there is a node x in $\mathbf{T}$ whose label contains the concept assertion in question: $(\exists R.D) \in \mathcal{L}(x)$. The tableau state $\mathbf{T}$ is complete, so no rule can be applied to any node, and thus specifically the $\exists$-rule *cannot* be applied to node x. However, the condition of this rule can fail only if there exists a node y such that $\mathcal{L}(\langle x, y \rangle) = R$ and $D \in \mathcal{L}(y)$. Consequently, again referring to the ABox construction, $\mathcal{A}_{\mathbf{T}}$ contains the assertions $R(x,y)$ and $D(y)$. As D is a subconcept of C, we can use the inductive hypothesis, together with the presence of $D(y)$ in the ABox, to deduce that $\mathcal{I} \models D(y)$, i.e. $y \in D^{\mathcal{I}}$. At the same time the presence of $R(x,y)$ in the ABox implies that $\langle x, y \rangle \in R^{\mathcal{I}}$, simply because of the definition of $\mathcal{I}$. Using the semantics of the existential restriction (Subsection 4.4.1) we can now conclude that $x \in (\exists R.D)^{\mathcal{I}}$ is true, i.e. $\mathcal{I} \models C(x)$, which is the statement we wanted to prove.

Notice how the completeness of the tableau $\mathbf{T}$ is used in the above proof. Because no transformation rule is applicable to $\mathbf{T}$, we can intuitively state that the ABox $\mathcal{A}_{\mathbf{T}}$ already includes all relevant consequences of the assertions it contains. This is the property which ensures that this ABox is self-realising.

Providing similar proofs for other concept constructors is left to the reader.

Exercise 5.20: Consider each of the following $\mathcal{ALCN}$ concept constructors:

(a) intersection;

(b) union;

(c) value restriction;

(d) at-least restriction;

(e) at-most restriction.

Assume that $\mathbf{T}$ is a complete and clash-free tableau state. For each of the above constructors, show that for an arbitrary concept expression C formed using that constructor, $C(x) \in \mathcal{A}_{\mathbf{T}}$ implies that $\mathcal{I} \models C(x)$, where $\mathcal{I} = \mathcal{I}^{nat}(\mathcal{A}_{\mathbf{T}})$, the natural interpretation of the ABox corresponding to the tableau state $\mathbf{T}$. You can assume inductively that, for any concept D whose size is smaller than that of C, $D(y) \in \mathcal{A}_{\mathbf{T}}$ implies that $\mathcal{I} \models D(y)$.

---

[15] We can exclude negation, as all concepts in the tableau state are in negation normal form. Thus negation can appear only in front of atomic concepts, and this case is covered by the above discussion.

Using the results of the exercise we can conclude that the ABox $\mathcal{A}_{\mathbf{T}}$ is *self-realising*, provided that $\mathbf{T}$ is a complete clash-free tableau state. Taking into account (5.21) we have thus shown that the tableau algorithm is complete, i.e. if it returns the answer "C_0 is satisfiable" then C_0 really is satisfiable.

As an alternative to using (5.21) in the above argument, we can show that concept C_0 is satisfiable by simply examining the ABox $\mathcal{A}_{\mathbf{T}}$ itself.[16] The reason is that the label of the root node x_0 of all tableau states contains the initial concept C_0. Because the ABox $\mathcal{A}_{\mathbf{T}}$, shown to be satisfiable, contains the assertion $C_0(x_0)$, it follows that concept C_0 is satisfiable.

This concludes the proof of three important properties of the $\mathcal{ALCN}$ tableau algorithm: termination, soundness and completeness.

5.4. The $\mathcal{ALCN}$ tableau algorithm for non-empty TBoxes

In the previous section we described an algorithm which decides the satisfiability of a concept C in itself, i.e. without terminological axioms. When a TBox is present, but is acyclic and contains only definitional axioms, it can be eliminated by following the techniques described in Subsection 4.6.1. This permitted the use of the presented algorithm for checking the satisfiability of a concept with respect to an acyclic definitional TBox. In the present section we discuss the case when such elimination is not possible, either because the TBox is cyclic or because it contains general inclusion axioms.

We first describe some interesting examples and then discuss *blocking*, a new feature of the tableau algorithm introduced to guarantee termination in the presence of non-empty TBoxes. Finally, we provide a formal description of the new features of the tableau algorithm for non-empty TBoxes.

5.4.1. Examples of satisfiability checks involving a TBox

Consider the following example: assuming the background knowledge that the children of optimistic people are also optimistic, we would like to determine whether it is possible for someone to be optimistic and to have a grandchild who is not optimistic. Formally, the question is whether a concept C is satisfiable w.r.t. the TBox $\mathcal{T}$, where

$$C = \mathsf{O} \sqcap \exists \mathsf{hC}.\exists \mathsf{hC}.\neg \mathsf{O},$$
$$\mathcal{T} = \{\mathsf{O} \sqsubseteq \forall \mathsf{hC}.\mathsf{O}\}.$$

Here, as usual, hC denotes the role "has child" and O stands for the concept "optimist".

We use the technique of internalisation as described in Subsection 4.7.2. First the TBox $\mathcal{T}$ is internalised, using the formula (4.15). This produces the following concept:

$$C_{\mathcal{T}} = \neg \mathsf{O} \sqcup \forall \mathsf{hC}.\mathsf{O}. \tag{5.23}$$

---

[16] Here $\mathbf{T}$ is a complete clash-free tableau obtained in the course of execution of the tableau algorithm for deciding the satisfiability of C_0.

We know that $\mathcal{T}$ is equivalent to the statement $\top \sqsubseteq C_\mathcal{T}$. The latter expresses the fact that every individual must belong to $C_\mathcal{T}$.

In accordance with this, the tableau algorithm is modified as follows.

- The concept $C_\mathcal{T}$ is added to the label of the root node in addition to C (since the individual satisfying C must also satisfy $C_\mathcal{T}$).

- Every time a new node is created (in our example this can only happen within the $\exists$-rule), the concept $C_\mathcal{T}$ is added to its label, because this new individual must satisfy the concept $C_\mathcal{T}$ as well.

Let us follow the execution of the tableau algorithm with the above modifications. The label of the root node in our initial tableau $\mathbf{T}_0$ contains two concepts: C and $C_\mathcal{T}$. The former is an intersection, so it is unfolded using the $\sqcap$-rule, and we obtain a tableau $\mathbf{T}_1$ still containing only a single node (the root node) with label

$$\{\mathsf{O},\ \exists\mathsf{hC}.\exists\mathsf{hC}.\neg\mathsf{O},\ (\neg\mathsf{O} \sqcup \forall\mathsf{hC}.\mathsf{O})\}.$$

Next, the $\sqcup$-rule is applied. The first branch yields a tableau $\mathbf{T}_2$ with a clash, as it contains both O and $\neg$O in a single label. The other branch yields a tableau $\mathbf{T}_3$ where the label of the root node is

$$\{\mathsf{O},\ \exists\mathsf{hC}.\exists\mathsf{hC}.\neg\mathsf{O},\ (\neg\mathsf{O} \sqcup \forall\mathsf{hC}.\mathsf{O}),\ \forall\mathsf{hC}.\mathsf{O}\}.$$

Notice that the concept $\forall\mathsf{hC}.\mathsf{O}$ has just appeared in the label of the root node, because the root node is an "optimist" and the TBox states that "children of optimistic people are optimists". Note how the union rule, applied to the internalised TBox (5.23), performs this inference: the presence of the concept O causes a clash on the first branch of the union, and so the second branch adds the expression $\forall\mathsf{hC}.\mathsf{O}$ to the node label.

We now apply the $\exists$-rule at the root node for the concept $\exists\mathsf{hC}.(\exists\mathsf{hC}.\neg\mathsf{O})$; an hC-successor is created and the concept $C_\mathcal{T}$ is added to its label, in addition to the concept $\exists\mathsf{hC}.\neg\mathsf{O}$, as follows:

$$
\begin{array}{l}
\mathbf{T}_4 \qquad\qquad\qquad b\bullet\{\ldots,\exists\mathsf{hC}.(\exists\mathsf{hC}.\neg\mathsf{O}),\forall\mathsf{hC}.\mathsf{O},\ldots\} \\[2mm]
\qquad\qquad\qquad\qquad\quad \Big|\ \mathsf{hC} \\[2mm]
\qquad\qquad\qquad c\bullet\{(\exists\mathsf{hC}.\neg\mathsf{O}),(\neg\mathsf{O}\sqcup\forall\mathsf{hC}.\mathsf{O})\}
\end{array}
$$

Next, the $\forall$-rule is applied for the concept $\forall\mathsf{hC}.\mathsf{O}$ in the label of the root node, extending the label of the child c with the concept O (i.e. the child c inherits the optimism of its parent):

$$
\begin{array}{l}
\mathbf{T}_5 \qquad\qquad\qquad b\bullet\{\ldots,\forall\mathsf{hC}.\mathsf{O},\ldots\} \\[2mm]
\qquad\qquad\qquad\qquad\quad \Big|\ \mathsf{hC} \\[2mm]
\qquad\qquad\qquad c\bullet\{(\exists\mathsf{hC}.\neg\mathsf{O}),(\neg\mathsf{O}\sqcup\forall\mathsf{hC}.\mathsf{O}),\mathsf{O}\}
\end{array}
$$

Now the $\sqcup$-rule is applied at node c. The first branch of the union, let us call it $\mathbf{T}_6$, yields another clash. The other branch results in the tableau $\mathbf{T}_7$, where the label of c is extended with the concept $\forall\mathsf{hC}.\mathsf{O}$ (i.e. every child of c is optimistic too). Then we apply the $\exists$-rule again, creating grandchild d:

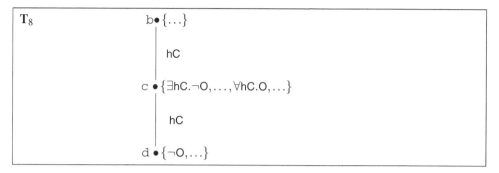

The label of node d contains the concept $\neg O$ coming from the existential restriction. It also contains the concept $C_\mathcal{T}$ but, as we shall soon see, this plays no further role in the algorithm and therefore it is not shown in the above tableau. Next, we apply the value restriction transformation for the concept $\forall hC.O$ in the label of c. The resulting tableau $\mathbf{T_9}$ has a clash: the label of d contains both $\neg O$ and O (the latter having been introduced by the last $\forall$-rule).

The search space explored by the tableau algorithm discussed is shown in Figure 5.9. Each branch resulted in a clash during the traversal of the search tree; therefore the tableau algorithm returns the answer "C is not satisfiable w.r.t. TBox $\mathcal{T}$". Thus the answer to our initial question is negative: if all children of optimistic people are optimistic then grandchildren of optimistic people are optimists, too.

Exercise 5.21: Consider the following TBox $\mathcal{T}_0$:

$$A \sqcup B \sqsubseteq \neg C;$$
$$\exists R.B \sqsubseteq A;$$
$$(\leqslant 1R) \sqsubseteq B.$$

Using the extended tableau algorithm introduced above, determine the satisfiability of the concept C with respect to:

(a) the TBox $\mathcal{T}_0$;

(b) the TBox $\mathcal{T}_0 \cup \{\top \sqsubseteq (\leqslant 1R)\}$.

Let us now consider another example, which demonstrates an important issue: the extended tableau algorithm, as used in the example, can fall into an infinite loop for certain kinds of terminological axiom. Let us examine the satisfiability of the concept $\top$ w.r.t. the TBox $\mathcal{T} = \{\top \sqsubseteq \exists hC.\top\}$. Informally, we are asking here whether there can be an interpretation where everyone has a child.

The only terminological axiom in TBox $\mathcal{T}$ is of the form $\top \sqsubseteq C$, so we obtain $C_\mathcal{T} = C$ after internalisation.[17] In principle, the label of the root node in the initial tableau should be

---

[17] This is true because the only property of $C_\mathcal{T}$ exploited in Subsection 4.7.2 was that $\top \sqsubseteq C_\mathcal{T}$ is true. However, we also get this result when we actually evaluate the formula (4.15): $C_\mathcal{T} \equiv \neg\top \sqcup C \equiv C$.

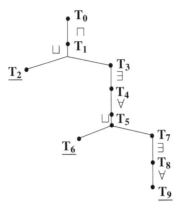

Figure 5.9. The search space of the example with a TBox.

the set $\{\top, C\}$. However, including $\top$ in a node label is unnecessary, because it represents a concept that puts no restriction on the node it labels (and accordingly, it plays absolutely no role in the tableau algorithm). So, from now on, the $\top$ concept will not be shown in node labels.

Thus we start the algorithm with a root node whose label only contains the concept $C = \exists hC.\top$. We use the $\exists$-rule: an hC-successor is created and C is added to its label. Because the label of the new node is the same as that of the root node, the same rule can be applied to the new node, and this can be repeated ad infinitum:

Obviously, this infinite chain of "has child" roles represents an interpretation $\mathcal{I}$ which satisfies the TBox $\mathcal{T} = \{\top \sqsubseteq \exists hC.\top\}$: $\Delta^{\mathcal{I}} = \{x_0, \ldots, x_n, \ldots\}$, $hC^{\mathcal{I}} = \{\langle x_i, x_{i+1} \rangle \mid i \geq 0\}$. However, this TBox has finite models too, namely those where the chain of hC-successors forms a cycle. The simplest model of $\mathcal{T}$ contains a single element which is hC-related to itself.

To ensure termination, the tableau algorithm must be stopped if it reaches situations similar to the one outlined above. As a more general example, consider a tableau where the label of a node is the same as that of a node somewhere above it. Obviously, such a situation may lead to an infinite loop: if the transformation steps leading from the upper node to the lower one are applied to the lower node then a third node is created with the same label,[18] and this

---

[18] Note that the $\mathcal{ALCN}$ transformation rules do not "look upwards", i.e. they do not depend on nodes above the one in question. This implies that if we have two nodes in the tree with identical labels then they will unfold to identical subtrees.

process can be repeated ad infinitum. However, there is no need to unfold the lower node. If we view the tableau algorithm as a search for clashes, we can argue informally as follows: any clashes that appear while one is unfolding the lower node have to appear also during the unfolding of the upper node. Thus the unfolding of the lower node cannot yield any new clash (compared with the upper node), so it is unnecessary. We will address this issue more precisely in the next subsection.

Exercise 5.22: Consider the following TBox:

$$\top \sqsubseteq \exists hC.\exists hC.\mathsf{Tall} \tag{5.24}$$

Using the extended tableau algorithm introduced above, determine the satisfiability of the concept Tall with respect to the above TBox. Whenever you reach a node whose label is the same as that of a node above it, stop exploring the given branch.

5.4.2. Blocking

As we have seen above, when the $\mathcal{ALCN}$ tableau algorithm is extended to support general terminological axioms it will not terminate for certain TBoxes. If this happens, one should stop applying certain transformation rules. To characterise situations in which the danger of looping arises we introduce the following notion: a node is said to *block* another one below it in the tableau tree if certain conditions are satisfied, for example if the labels of the two nodes are the same. We use the term "blocking" because at a blocked node the application of certain transformation rules is disallowed. Typically, rules that *extend* the tree can only be applied when the node to which they are applied is not blocked.

In order to handle DL languages of different expressive power, it is necessary to define different variants for the notion of blocking [60]. So-called *equality blocking* requires equality of the two node labels. In the $\mathcal{ALCN}$ tableau algorithm it is sufficient to use a weaker form of blocking, called *subset blocking*. The condition for subset blocking is that the label of the blocked node is a *subset* of the label of the upper, blocking, node. Our earlier argument, that the unfolding of the lower, blocked, node cannot result in a "new" clash, is true in this case as well.

Another important aspect of classification is to differentiate between *static* and *dynamic* blocking. We say that the blocking is dynamic if the blocked status of a node can change several times during the execution of the algorithm (the node gets blocked, gets unblocked, gets blocked again ...). If we pose no restriction on the rule application order, this can happen even with the $\mathcal{ALCN}$ tableau algorithm. For example, consider the following scenario.

- A successor y of a node x is created using the $\geqslant$-rule. According to this rule, the label of y is empty. This means that y is blocked by every node above it (recall that subset blocking is used).

- A $\forall$-rule which extends the label of y with a concept C is applied at node x. Assume that C does not occur in the label of the nodes above y. This means that y is unblocked.

- A $\forall$-rule which adds the concept C to the label of x is applied to the node above x. From now on, y is blocked by x and so on.

These chaotic changes concerning the blocked status of nodes in the $\mathcal{ALCN}$ tableau algorithm can be eliminated simply by a restriction on the rule application order. Let us prescribe that the expansion rules, i.e. rules that add new nodes to the tree, can be used only when no other rules are applicable.

With this restriction in place, if a node has at least one successor then its label cannot change any further. This is again due to the fact that the $\mathcal{ALCN}$ tableau rules do not depend on, and do not modify, any nodes above the node in question. This, together with the fact that we examine the blocking status of a node only when the expansion rules are to be applied, guarantees that once a block appears, it persists. This is called *static blocking*.

Exercise 5.23: Consider the following concept:

$$C = \forall hC.(\geqslant 1hC)$$
$$\sqcap \; \forall hC.\forall hC.\mathsf{Tall}$$
$$\sqcap \; \forall hC.\mathsf{Tall}$$
$$\sqcap \; \forall hC.\mathsf{Blonde}$$
$$\sqcap \; (\geqslant 1hC).$$

Show that concept C is satisfiable with respect to the empty TBox using the tableau algorithm. Experiment with applying the transformation rules in various orders:

(a) Reproduce the above generic scenario when a node gets blocked, unblocked and blocked again (using subset blocking).[19]

(b) Apply the principle that expansion rules are used last. Observe the blocking status of nodes when expansion rules are to be applied. Show that the principle used ensures static blocking.

5.4.3. The tableau algorithm with TBoxes

We now summarise the changes necessary to the $\mathcal{ALCN}$ tableau algorithm described in Section 5.3 to support TBoxes. First, we provide some important definitions.

When introducing the idea of blocking, we used the expressions "x is a node below/above y in the tableau tree". We will now make this notion more precise. The "*successor of*" relationship between two nodes has already been defined in Subsection 5.2.1. The inverse of this relation is called "*predecessor of*": x is a predecessor of y if there is an edge in the tableau from x to y. Node x is an "*ancestor of*" z if x can be reached from z by repeated application of the "predecessor of" relation. In other words, the "ancestor of" relation is the transitive closure of "predecessor of". Similarly, the transitive closure of the "successor of" relation is called "*descendant of*".

A node is called *stable* if no transformation rules can be applied to its ancestors and only expansion rules (the $\exists$- and $\geqslant$ -rules) can be applied to the node itself.

Let us now discuss the tableau algorithm with TBoxes. Here, the task is to decide the satisfiability of a concept expression C (which we assume to be in negation normal form) with respect to a TBox $\mathcal{T}$. The first step is to compute $C_{\mathcal{T}}$, the internalisation of the TBox $\mathcal{T}$,

---

[19] Note that blocking is not strictly necessary in this example, as the TBox is empty.

∃-rule	
Condition:	$(\exists R.C) \in \mathcal{L}(x)$, there is no y such that $\mathcal{L}(\langle x,y\rangle) = R$ and $C \in \mathcal{L}(y)$, furthermore x is stable and not blocked
New state **T′:**	$V' = V \cup \{y\}$, $E' = E \cup \{\langle x,y\rangle\}$, $\mathcal{L}'(\langle x,y\rangle) = R$, $\mathcal{L}'(y) = \{C, \underline{C_{\mathcal{T}}}\}$.
⩾-rule	
Condition:	$(\geqslant n R) \in \mathcal{L}(x)$, x does not have n R-successors of which no two can be identified, furthermore <u>x is stable and not blocked</u>
New state **T′:**	$V' = V \cup \{y_1, \ldots, y_n\}$, $E' = E \cup \{\langle x, y_1\rangle, \ldots, \langle x, y_n\rangle\}$, $\mathcal{L}'(\langle x, y_i\rangle) = R$, $\mathcal{L}'(y_i) = \{\underline{C_{\mathcal{T}}}\}$, for every $i = 1 \leq i \leq n$, $I' = I \cup \{y_i \not\doteq y_j \mid 1 \leq i < j \leq n\}$.

Figure 5.10. Transformation rules of the $\mathcal{ALCN}$ tableau algorithm modified to support TBoxes.

according to the formula (4.15). We will assume as well that $C_{\mathcal{T}}$ has already been brought to negation normal form.

The tableau algorithm is started from the state $\mathbf{T}_0 = \langle \{x_0\}, \emptyset, \mathcal{L}_0, \emptyset \rangle$, where $\mathcal{L}_0(x_0) = \{C, C_{\mathcal{T}}\}$. Here, the underlining indicates those parts of the formula which have been introduced to cater for TBoxes. Figure 5.10 shows the two transformation rules that need to be modified in order for them to handle terminological axioms (here, the changes are again indicated by underlining). The extended $\mathcal{ALCN}$ tableau algorithm uses the ⊓-, ⊔-, ∀- and ⩽- rules of the original algorithm (see Figure 5.4) and the modified ∃- and ⩾- rules shown in Figure 5.10.

The control flow of the tableau algorithm, shown in Figure 5.6, remains unaltered. However, the "true" answer should be interpreted as "C is satisfiable w.r.t. $\mathcal{T}$" and the "false" answer as "C is not satisfiable w.r.t. $\mathcal{T}$".

Exercise 5.24: Consider the TBox (5.24) of Exercise 5.22. Determine the satisfiability of the following concepts with respect to this TBox. Use the above tableau algorithm with subset blocking.

(a) ⊤

(b) ∃hC.Tall

(c) ∀hC.⊥

(d) ∃hC.∀hC.⊥

(e) ∀hC.∀hC.∀hC.⊥

5.4.4. Properties of the algorithm

Let us now examine whether the properties of the tableau algorithm described in Subsection 5.3.4 still hold.

The tableau algorithm terminates. In the modified algorithm it is no longer true that the maximum role depth of the concepts decreases as we get deeper into the tableau tree, because the concept expression C_T is added to every new node. However, it is still true that only a limited number of concepts can appear in the labels, namely the subconcepts of C and C_T. Let $m = |sub(C) \cup sub(C_T)|$ be the number of concepts that can appear in the labels. This means that at most 2^m distinct labels can be created, i.e. any path of length $2^m + 1$ necessarily contains a label repetition. This causes blocking, so the tree stops growing along the given path.

Furthermore, as in the case of the empty TBox, the branching factor of the tableau tree has an upper bound which depends only on the $\geqslant$- and $\exists$- expressions in C and C_T. Hence the modified tableau algorithm always terminates.

The tableau algorithm is complete. We used a mapping from tableau states to ABoxes in the proofs of the soundness and completeness of the tableau algorithm for empty TBoxes: a tableau state $\mathbf{T}$ was mapped to the ABox $\mathcal{A}_\mathbf{T}$, as defined by formulae (5.18)–(5.20). A tableau $\mathbf{T}$ was said to be satisfiable when the corresponding ABox $\mathcal{A}_\mathbf{T}$ was satisfiable.

We now use the same mapping, but the definition of a satisfiable tableau has to be changed slightly to take care of the TBox. A state $\mathbf{T}$, constructed while the tableau algorithm is checking the satisfiability of a concept C w.r.t. a TBox T, is said to be satisfiable when $\mathcal{A}_\mathbf{T}$ is satisfiable w.r.t. the TBox T. It can be shown (analogously to the case of an empty TBox) that the transformation rules preserve satisfiability: the input tableau state $\mathbf{T}$ of a transformation rule is satisfiable if, and only if, the output set of states $S_\mathbf{T}$ is satisfiable (recall that a set of tableau states is said to be satisfiable if it contains at least one satisfiable state).

Exercise 5.25: Consider a tableau graph in which the $\exists$-rule ($\geqslant$-rule) rule can be applied. Assume that the ABox corresponding to this tableau state is satisfiable w.r.t. T. Using the semantics of the $\exists$ ($\geqslant$) constructor show that the ABox corresponding to the tableau state resulting from the transformation is satisfiable w.r.t. T, too.

Continuing the analogy, we can easily convince ourselves that the following variant of statement (5.21) holds:

> A set S of tableau states obtained during the execution of the tableau algorithm (Figure 5.6) for a concept C w.r.t. a TBox T is satisfiable if, and   (5.25) only if, C is satisfiable w.r.t. T.

Using the above statement, completeness is easy to see. If the tableau algorithm returns a negative answer, it means that it has arrived at a set of states every member of which contains a clash. This set of states is not satisfiable and thus, because of (5.25), C is not satisfiable w.r.t. T either. Consequently, the negative answer of the tableau algorithm is appropriate, and thus the algorithm is complete.

The tableau algorithm is sound. The soundness of the algorithm means that its positive answer is correct. We thus have to show that the positive answer returned when a complete and clash-free $\mathbf{T}$ tableau state is reached implies that the root concept is indeed satisfiable w.r.t. the TBox in question.

For the case of an empty TBox we showed that the ABox $\mathcal{A_T}$ is self-realising, assuming that the tableau state **T** is complete and clash-free. In the presence of a non-empty TBox we should ensure that the ABox is self-realising *w.r.t. the given TBox*. By this we mean that the natural interpretation of the ABox is a model of both the ABox and the TBox.[20]

Thus we should examine whether the ABox $\mathcal{A_T}$ is self-realising w.r.t. the TBox in question. First let us discuss whether the ABox is self-realising w.r.t. an empty TBox, i.e. whether its natural interpretation satisfies the ABox. Unfortunately, this is no longer true, because some successors may be missing, owing to blocked nodes.

For example, assume that there is a concept $D = \exists hC.\mathsf{Tall}$ in the label of a node y which is blocked by the node x. For the assertion $D(y) \in \mathcal{A_T}$ to be true, we need a node which has a label containing Tall and which is hC-related to y. Notice, however, that there is already a node in the tableau tree with the required label. Because y is blocked by x, the label of y is a subset of that of x and hence the concept D appears in the label of x, too. As the tableau is complete no transformation rule can be applied, so x has to have an hC-successor z which has Tall in its label. We will utilise this node z by simply adding a new role assertion $hC(y,z)$ to the ABox. If we add such role assertions for all blocked nodes containing concepts of the form $\exists R.C$ and $(\geqslant nR)$, the extended ABox will become self-realising.

Before formally defining this ABox extension, let us introduce some notation. Let **T** be a complete tableau and let x be one of its non-blocked nodes. If there is a concept $\exists R.C$ in the label of x, let $succ^{\mathbf{T}}_{\exists R.C}(x)$ denote an R-successor of x which contains C in its label. There must be such a node, because otherwise the $\exists$-rule could be applied at node x and so the tableau would not be complete. In a similar fashion, if there is a concept $(\geqslant nR)$ in the label of x, let $succSet^{\mathbf{T}}_{\geqslant nR}(x)$ denote a set of nodes $\{z_1, \dots, z_n\}$ such that every z_i is an R-successor of x. Again, x must have n distinct R-successors because otherwise the $\geqslant$-rule could be applied to x, which is not possible as the tableau is complete.

Let us now proceed to the general case. Let **T** be a complete clash-free tableau state, and let y be a node in this tableau that is blocked by x. If the label of y contains the concept $\exists R.C$, the label of x must also contain this concept (because subset blocking is used). So x must have a successor bearing the concept C in its label, such as the node $z = succ^{\mathbf{T}}_{\exists R.C}(x)$. For every such y we extend the ABox with the role statement $R(y,z)$, thus ensuring that y has an R-successor as required. Similarly, if the label of y contains a $(\geqslant nR)$ concept, the role statements $R(y,z_i)$ $(i = 1, \dots, n)$ are added to the ABox, where $\{z_1, \dots, z_n\} = succSet^{\mathbf{T}}_{\geqslant nR}(x)$, thus creating n R-successors for every blocked node y the label of which contains the concept $(\geqslant nR)$. The formal definition of the extended ABox is

$$\mathcal{A'_T} = \mathcal{A_T} \cup \{R(y,z) \mid y \text{ is blocked by } x, (\exists R.C)(y) \in \mathcal{A_T} \text{ and } z = succ^{\mathbf{T}}_{\exists R.C}(x)\}$$
$$\cup \{R(y,z) \mid y \text{ is blocked by } x, (\geqslant nR)(y) \in \mathcal{A_T} \text{ and } z \in succSet^{\mathbf{T}}_{\geqslant nR}(x)\}. \quad (5.26)$$

It can be shown easily that the constructed ABox is self-realising, i.e. the interpretation $\mathcal{I}^{nat}(\mathcal{A'_T})$ satisfies the ABox $\mathcal{A'_T}$. As this ABox contains the assertion $C_{\mathcal{T}}(x)$ for each x individual appearing in it, it is clear that the natural interpretation also satisfies the TBox $\mathcal{T}$ (thus the ABox is self-realising w.r.t. $\mathcal{T}$). This means that $\mathcal{A'_T}$ is satisfiable w.r.t. TBox $\mathcal{T}$.

---

[20] We will keep referring to this notion simply as a "self-realising ABox", i.e. we will not include the phrase "w.r.t. the given TBox" if it is clear from the context that a TBox is involved.

Consequently, $\mathcal{A}_{\mathbf{T}}$, which is a subset of $\mathcal{A}'_{\mathbf{T}}$, is satisfiable as well. By referring to (5.25) we can now conclude that C, the root concept of the tableau, is satisfiable w.r.t. the TBox $\mathcal{T}$.

We will refer to the above approach as the *redirection* technique. The name comes from the fact that in the absence of number restrictions (i.e. for the language $\mathcal{ALC}$) the approach can be simplified: the blocked nodes are removed and the edges terminating at blocked nodes are *redirected* to the blocking node (see Subsection 7.2.4 below).

We thus have shown that if the extended tableau algorithm reaches a complete clash-free tableau state, and thus gives a positive answer, then the root concept is indeed satisfiable w.r.t. to the given TBox. This means that the extended tableau algorithm is sound.

Let us illustrate this with an example. We will use the extended tableau algorithm for checking the satisfiability of the concept $\top$ with respect to the following TBox:

$$\mathcal{T} = \{\top \sqsubseteq (\geqslant 2\,\mathsf{hC}), \top \sqsubseteq \exists \mathsf{hC}.\exists \mathsf{hC}.\mathsf{B}\}. \tag{5.27}$$

(as usual, B and hC denote the concept "blonde" and the role "has child"). Viewed informally, the reasoning task is to decide whether a universe is possible where everyone has at least two children and everyone has a blonde grandchild. Figure 5.11 shows the complete and clash-free tableau graph $\mathbf{T}$ which is the result of the extended tableau algorithm. In the figure, the solid lines mark the successor-of relationship and the broken arrows point back from blocked nodes to their respective blocking node. For sake of clarity, we omit from the figure the concepts resulting from internalisation. This means that the label of each node is understood to contain implicitly the concept $C_{\mathcal{T}} = (\geqslant 2\,\mathsf{hC}) \sqcap \exists \mathsf{hC}.\exists \mathsf{hC}.\mathsf{B}$ as well as the concepts $(\geqslant 2\,\mathsf{hC})$ and $\exists \mathsf{hC}.\exists \mathsf{hC}.\mathsf{B}$ that result from applying the $\sqcap$-rule to $C_{\mathcal{T}}$.[21]

Figure 5.12 shows the natural interpretation $\mathcal{I}^{nat}(\mathcal{A}'_{\mathbf{T}})$, built from the tableau $\mathbf{T}$ of Figure 5.11. Here arrows denote the hC (has child) relation and the only instance of the concept B is the individual x. To aid readability, the upward arrows are replaced by short stubs displaying the name of their target nodes.

At first sight the model that we have obtained seems to be too complex for the task. Notice that the satisfiability of the TBox $\mathcal{T}$ in (5.27) could be demonstrated by a very simple interpretation, containing just two blonde individuals who are connected both to themselves

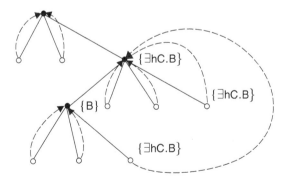

Figure 5.11.   A complete and clash-free tableau with blocking.

[21] Notice that the concepts shown in Figure 5.11 are all subconcepts of $\exists \mathsf{hC}.\exists \mathsf{hC}.\mathsf{B}$: every non-blocked node has a successor with the label $\exists \mathsf{hC}.\mathsf{B}$ and of these successors the only non-blocked node has a successor with the label B.

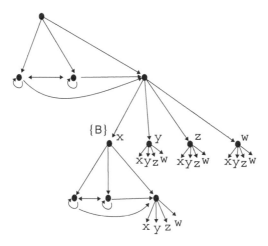

Figure 5.12. The interpretation corresponding to the tableau in Figure 5.11.

and to the other through the "has child" relation. The complexity of the tableau built for the above example is due to the minimality principle: the algorithm identifies individuals introduced by different subconcepts only when it is forced to by a $\leqslant$-condition.

Exercise 5.26: Consider the complete and clash-free tableau **T** built as your solution to task (b) of Exercise 5.24. Construct the ABox $\mathcal{A}_{\mathbf{T}}$, and extend it with the necessary role assertions to an ABox $\mathcal{A}'_{\mathbf{T}}$. Check that this ABox is self-realising.

5.5. Handling ABoxes in the $\mathcal{ALCN}$ tableau algorithm

The tableau algorithm described above can be extended to support ABoxes as well. Here, the main task is to decide the consistency of an ABox w.r.t to a TBox. As shown in Subsection 4.8.2, every inference problem concerning ABoxes can be reduced to such consistency checks (though the efficiency of this approach is far from optimal).

5.5.1. The tableau algorithm with ABoxes

The following algorithm for checking the consistency of an ABox $\mathcal{A}$ w.r.t. to TBox $\mathcal{T}$ was suggested in Hollunder [53]. The main idea here is to reduce the ABox consistency problem to a finite number of concept satisfiability checks. The algorithm consists of the following three main phases.

- **Construction of the initial tableau**: An initial tableau state $\mathbf{T}_0$ is constructed from an ABox $\mathcal{A}$ by essentially inverting the transformation described by formulae (5.18)–(5.20), as follows.

  - The set of individual names $\{a_1, \ldots, a_n\}$ that appear in the ABox $\mathcal{A}$ forms the set of nodes of the initial tableau.

- An edge with the label R runs from a_i to a_j if, and only if, a role assertion $R(a_i, a_j)$ is present in $\mathcal{A}$.
- The label of a node a_i contains the internalised concept $C_{\mathcal{T}}$ and all concepts D for which a concept assertion $D(a_i)$ is present in $\mathcal{A}$.
- All pairs of individual names are added to the inequality system of the tableau state in order to ensure the unique name assumption (if necessary).

Note that if we apply the transformation (5.18)–(5.20) to the above tableau state $\mathbf{T}_0$, we get an ABox $\mathcal{A}_{\mathbf{T}_0}$ which differs from $\mathcal{A}$ only in that the assertions of the form $C_{\mathcal{T}}(x)$ are present in it for every individual x. Also note that $\mathbf{T}_0$ is a general graph, rather than a tree as has been the case so far for the tableau states.

- **Preprocessing**: The tableau algorithm described in Subsection 5.4.3 is applied to the initial tableau state $\mathbf{T}_0$ and the TBox $\mathcal{T}$, with the following restrictions.

  - The expansion rules can be applied only to the nodes of the original ABox; they cannot be applied to their newly created successors. Furthermore, blocking is not used.[22]
  - If a node a_i is identified with a node x that is not present in the original ABox, a_i is kept; that is, the concepts in the label of x are added to the label of a_i and not the other way round.
  - If two nodes are identified and both are present in the original ABox, the node that is kept inherits the edges going to the deleted node as well as the edges leaving from it.

Note that, in the presence of non-deterministic rules, the preprocessing phase returns a set of tableau states. From these we remove those tableau states which contain a clash. The set of remaining, clash-free, states is called $S_{\mathcal{A}}$.

- **Satisfiability test**: The tableau states $\mathbf{T} = \langle V, E, \mathcal{L}, I \rangle \in S_{\mathcal{A}}$ produced by the preprocessing stage are checked one by one, until one of them is found to be satisfiable in the following sense.

  - For each individual name a_i of the ABox $\mathcal{A}$ a concept expression C_i is constructed which is the intersection of the concepts in the label of the node a_i in $\mathbf{T}$: $C_i = \bigcap_{D \in \mathcal{L}(a_i)} D$.
  - We determine whether each concept C_i is satisfiable w.r.t. the TBox $\mathcal{T}$ by applying the tableau algorithm described in Subsection 5.4.3. If all such concepts are satisfiable then the tableau state is said to be satisfiable, and the algorithm terminates with the answer "$\mathcal{A}$ is consistent w.r.t. $\mathcal{T}$".
  - Otherwise the algorithm proceeds with the next tableau in $S_{\mathcal{A}}$.

If no tableau state in $S_{\mathcal{A}}$ is found satisfiable, the algorithm terminates with the answer "$\mathcal{A}$ is not consistent w.r.t. $\mathcal{T}$".

Let us summarise the reasoning process described above. We first transform the ABox to a tableau and then apply the tableau algorithm, as described in Subsection 5.4.3, with the restriction that expansion rules can be applied only to the nodes originally present in the

---

[22] An alternative formulation of this restriction could be the following: the original ABox nodes are never blocked; the newly created successors are always blocked.

ABox. We thus obtain one or more such preprocessed tableau states. Next, we throw away the states containing a clash and, for each remaining state we try to show that it is satisfiable. If one such is found, the algorithm gives a positive answer; otherwise it gives a negative answer.

To check the satisfiability of a preprocessed tableau, we consider those of its nodes that were originally present in the input ABox. The tableau is said to be satisfiable if all these nodes are found to be satisfiable.

5.5.2. Examples of ABox reasoning

We now discuss a few example executions of the tableau algorithm with ABoxes. The first example demonstrates how concepts using the $\leqslant$ constructor are handled. Then we examine the tableau algorithm with two examples from Chapter 4.

Handling $\leqslant$-concepts.   Let us examine the consistency of the following ABox w.r.t. an empty TBox:

$$\mathcal{A} = \{hC(a_1,a_2),C(a_1)\} \quad \text{where} \quad C = \exists hC.B \sqcap \exists hC.\neg B \sqcap (\leqslant 2\,hC). \tag{5.28}$$

Following the algorithm, first we have to create a tableau $\mathbf{T}_0$ the nodes of which are a_1 and a_2. There is an edge with label hC from a_1 to a_2, the label of a_1 is $\{C\}$ and the label of a_2 is empty. We start the preprocessing stage with this tableau, apply the $\sqcap$-rule to the node a_1 (twice) and then apply the $\exists$-rule to both unfolded existential restrictions. We thus reach the following tableau state:

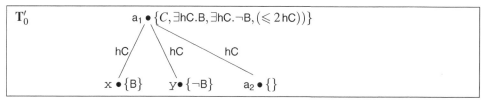

Here a_1 has three hC-successors. Because of the concept $(\leqslant 2\,hC)$ in the label of a_1, we have to identify two of these. The identification of x and y would cause a clash, so a_2 has to be identified with either x or y. Let us call the tableaux resulting from these two cases $\mathbf{T}^x$ and $\mathbf{T}^y$, respectively. Thus the outcome of the preprocessing is $S_{\mathcal{A}} = \{\mathbf{T}^x, \mathbf{T}^y\}$.

We now subject each element of $S_{\mathcal{A}}$ individually to a satisfiability test. Consider first $\mathbf{T}^x$, which looks like this:

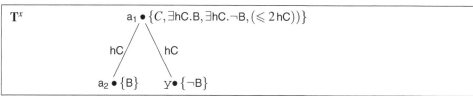

We notice that this, in fact, is already a complete and clash-free tableau.[23] However, let us proceed with the algorithm as prescribed, i.e. let us consider the labels of nodes a_1

---

[23] Of course, this is not always the case. The tableau produced by the preprocessing phase will not be complete if, for example, existential concepts appear in the label of a non-ABox node such as y above.

and a_2 and examine the satisfiability of the concepts $\sqcap\{C, \exists hC.B, \exists hC.\neg B, (\leqslant 2\,hC)\} \equiv C$ and B separately. The following complete and clash-free $\mathbf{T}_1^x$ tableau is constructed for the concept C:

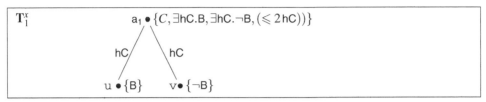

A complete and clash-free tableau $\mathbf{T}_2^x$ in which the label of the single node a_2 is $\{B\}$ is trivially derived for the concept B. Once we have found these two concepts to be satisfiable separately, the algorithm terminates and gives the answer that the ABox $\mathcal{A}$ is consistent.

Exercise 5.27: Consider the following reasoning task.

(1) We know that all children of optimistic people are optimistic as well.

(2) We are aware of two concrete individuals, a and b, where b is a child of a and we know that all grandchildren of a are optimistic.

(3) The task is to show that this last property holds for b, i.e. that also all grandchildren of b are optimistic.

Formalise the above reasoning task by transforming sentence (1) to a TBox statement, sentence (2) to two ABox assertions and sentence (3) to an instance check problem. Next, reformulate this task as an ABox consistency problem. Finally, use the algorithm of Subsection 5.5.1 to solve the reasoning task.

The Mother example. The very first example considered at the beginning of Chapter 4 dealt with the following knowledge base:

$$Mother \equiv Human \sqcap Female \sqcap \exists hasChild.\top$$
$$Female(EVE)$$
$$Human(EVE) \hspace{4cm} (5.29)$$
$$hasChild(EVE, NICK)$$

We claimed that a DL-based reasoning system can infer the statement Mother(EVE) from this knowledge base. Let us see how this can be done using our ABox tableau algorithm.

We would like to decide whether EVE is an instance of the concept Mother, i.e. we face an instance check problem. In Subsection 4.8.2 we explained that this can be reduced to a consistency test by adding the negation of the given concept assertion to the ABox. Hence we extend the knowledge base with the negated $(\neg Mother)(EVE)$ assertion and try to prove that this results in an inconsistent ABox.

There is only one terminological axiom and it is acyclic, so the concept name Mother can be eliminated: the axiom $(\neg Mother)(EVE)$ is replaced with the assertion $C(EVE)$, where $C = (\neg Human \sqcup \neg Female \sqcup \forall hasChild.\bot)$. The concept C is obtained by first negating the definition of Mother and then transforming the result to negation normal form. Thus we have to examine the consistency of the following ABox $\mathcal{A}$:

$$\text{Female}(\text{EVE})$$
$$\text{Human}(\text{EVE})$$
$$\text{hasChild}(\text{EVE}, \text{NICK})$$
$$C(\text{EVE})$$

We now construct a tableau from this ABox, apply the $\sqcap$-rules and omit the intersection expressions from the label of node EVE:

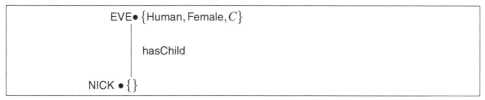

The preprocessing stage for this tableau proceeds as follows. We apply the $\sqcup$-rule for the concept $C = (\neg\text{Human} \sqcup \neg\text{Female} \sqcup \forall\text{hasChild}.\bot)$. The first two branches of this lead to an immediate clash at the node EVE. In the third branch the concept $(\forall\text{hasChild}.\bot)$ is added to the label of EVE. When we apply the $\forall$-rule to node EVE and her child NICK, a clash is obtained at the latter node. All three branches of preprocessing lead to a clash; thus $S_\mathcal{A} = \emptyset$. Consequently, the algorithm reports that ABox $\mathcal{A}$ is not satisfiable. This proves that the assertion Mother(EVE) does in fact follow from the knowledge base (5.29).

Exercise 5.28: We had an empty TBox in the above proof, as the acyclic definition of the concept Mother could be eliminated. Rework the proof for the case where our knowledge about motherhood is given as the following general concept inclusion axiom:

$$\text{Mother} \sqsupseteq \text{Human} \sqcap \text{Female} \sqcap \exists\text{hasChild}.\top$$

The Oedipus problem. Let us now examine the Oedipus example presented in Subsection 4.8.4. In this instance-check problem we consider the following ABox:

hasChild(IOCASTE,OEDIPUS)	hasChild(IOCASTE,POLYNEIKES)
hasChild(OEDIPUS,POLYNEIKES)	hasChild(POLYNEIKES,THERSANDROS)
Patricide(OEDIPUS)	$\neg$ Patricide(THERSANDROS) .

We would like to decide whether IOCASTE is an instance of the concept C_0, with respect to an empty TBox, where C_0 is defined as follows:

$$C_0 = (\exists\text{hasChild}.(\text{Patricide} \sqcap \exists\text{hasChild}.\neg\text{Patricide})) \tag{5.30}$$

We reduce this instance check to a consistency check by taking the negation of C_0 and transforming it to negation normal form: $C_1 = \neg C_0 = (\forall\text{hasChild}.C_2)$, where $C_2 = (\neg\text{Patricide} \sqcup \forall\text{hasChild}.\text{Patricide})$. Let $\mathcal{A}$ denote the above ABox extended with the statement

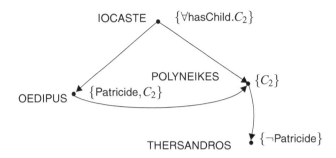

Figure 5.13. The tableau for the Oedipus problem.

C_1(IOCASTE). Let us construct the initial tableau and start the preprocessing. Figure 5.13 shows the tableau in a state where the $\forall$-rule has already been applied twice for the node IOCASTE, and so its children are known to belong to the concept C_2.

The $\sqcup$-rule can be applied to the node OEDIPUS and to the concept $C_2 = (\neg \text{Patricide} \sqcup \forall \text{hasChild.Patricide})$. The first branch of the union immediately leads to a clash. In the second branch, the concept ($\forall \text{hasChild.Patricide}$) is added to the label of the node OEDIPUS. Applying the $\forall$-rule at this node, we get a tableau where the label of POLYNEIKES becomes $\{C_2, \text{Patricide}\}$, i.e. it is the same as the label of the node OEDIPUS in Figure 5.13. Now the steps are the same as earlier with OEDIPUS: the first branch of the union leads to a clash while in the second branch the label of the node POLYNEIKES is extended with the concept ($\forall \text{hasChild.Patricide}$). When the $\forall$-rule is applied to this concept, Patricide appears in the label of THERSANDROS and causes a clash. Thus, we have applied two $\sqcup$-rules and explored three alternative branches. All branches led to a tableau state with a clash. Consequently, the ABox $\mathcal{A}$ is found to be unsatisfiable and IOCASTE has been shown to be an instance of the concept C_0.

Exercise 5.29: Consider the following ABox:

hasChild(IO,OE)	hasChild(IO,P$_1$)	hasChild(IO,P$_2$)
hasChild(OE,P$_1$)	hasChild(P$_1$,P$_2$)	hasChild(P$_2$,TH)
Patricide(OE)		$\neg$ Patricide(TH).

Using the tableau algorithm for ABoxes show that IO is an instance of the concept C_0, as defined by formula (5.30), with respect to an empty TBox.

5.5.3. Properties of the algorithm

Consider an execution of the ABox tableau algorithm that checks the satisfiability (consistency) of an ABox $\mathcal{A}$ w.r.t. an TBox $\mathcal{T}$. Assume that the set of individual names occurring in $\mathcal{A}$ is $\{a_1, \ldots, a_n\}$.

Recall that the algorithm first converts $\mathcal{A}$ and $\mathcal{T}$ to a tableau $\mathbf{T}_0$. Next, it performs the preprocessing phase, which transforms $\mathbf{T}_0$ to a set of tableaux $S_{\mathcal{A}}$. Finally, the satisfiability-check phase follows. The algorithm gives a positive answer if, and only if, there is a tableau state $\mathbf{T} \in S_{\mathcal{A}}$ such that the label of each node a_i in $\mathbf{T}$ is found to be satisfiable w.r.t. $\mathcal{T}$.

The tableau algorithm terminates. The number of tableau states created in the preprocessing phase, as well as their size, is limited by the characteristics of $\mathcal{A}$ and $\mathcal{T}$; thus the preprocessing phase is guaranteed to terminate.

The satisfiability test phase involves n executions of the tableau algorithm for checking concept satisfiability, where n is the number of individual names in the ABox in question. As the satisfiability-check algorithm is known to terminate (see Subsection 5.4.4), so also does the ABox tableau algorithm.

Note that the satisfiability-check phase of the ABox algorithm involves at most kn independent concept-satisfiability tests, where $k = |S_{\mathcal{A}}|$, i.e. the number of alternative tableaux produced in the preprocessing phase.

The tableau algorithm is complete. Assume that the ABox tableau algorithm returns a negative answer. This means that every tableau state in the set $S_{\mathcal{A}}$ contains a node whose label is unsatisfiable. Thus all tableau states in $S_{\mathcal{A}}$ are unsatisfiable, which, by definition, means that $S_{\mathcal{A}}$ itself is not satisfiable.

Note that the ABox tableau algorithm uses the transformation rules of the TBox tableau algorithm discussed in Section 5.4. We showed there that the tableau transformation rules preserve satisfiability. Thus the fact that the output of the (restricted) tableau algorithm, $S_{\mathcal{A}}$, is not satisfiable implies that this holds for the input tableau $\mathbf{T}_0$ as well. This, in turn, means that the initial ABox $\mathcal{A}$ is not satisfiable either.

We have thus shown that the negative answer of the algorithm is justified, i.e. the algorithm is complete.

The tableau algorithm is sound. Now assume that the ABox algorithm gives a positive answer for the ABox $\mathcal{A}$ and the TBox $\mathcal{T}$. We will show that this implies that the ABox $\mathcal{A}$ is satisfiable w.r.t. $\mathcal{T}$, which means that the positive answer is correct.

As the answer is positive, there is a tableau $\mathbf{T}$ in which all ABox individuals were found to be satisfiable. This means that, for each ABox individual name a_i, we constructed a concept C_i as the intersection of the concepts in the label of a_i in the tableau $\mathbf{T}$ and successfully executed a satisfiability check for C_i. It is obvious that, instead of building the concept C_i, we can start the satisfiability check using the node a_i and its label as the initial tableau state. Let $\mathbf{T}_i = \langle V_i, E_i, \mathcal{L}_i, I_i \rangle$ denote the complete and clash-free tableau state obtained from this initial state a_i. Without loss of generality we can assume that the node sets V_i of these tableaux are disjoint.

In order to prove that the original ABox $\mathcal{A}$ is satisfiable we will now put together the $\mathbf{T}_i$ tableaux, add edges corresponding to the role assertions of $\mathcal{A}$ and show that the resulting tableau $\overline{\mathbf{T}}$ contains $\mathbf{T}_0$ and is satisfiable.

The unified tableau $\overline{\mathbf{T}} = \langle \overline{V}, \overline{E}, \overline{\mathcal{L}}, \overline{I} \rangle$ is formally defined as follows:

$$\overline{V} = \bigcup_{i \le n} V_i;$$

$$\overline{E} = \bigcup_{i \le n} E_i \cup \left\{ \langle a_i, a_j \rangle \mid \text{ there is some role } R \text{ such that } R(a_i, a_j) \in \mathcal{A} \right\};$$

$$\overline{\mathcal{L}} = \bigcup_{i \le n} \mathcal{L}_i \cup \left\{ \langle a_i, a_j \rangle \mapsto R \mid R(a_i, a_j) \in \mathcal{A} \right\};$$

$$\overline{I} = \bigcup_{i \le n} I_i.$$

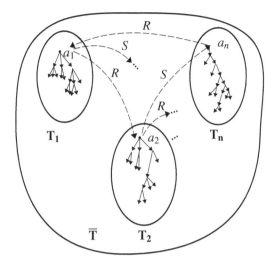

Figure 5.14. Construction of a unified tableau.

The construction of $\overline{\mathbf{T}}$ is illustrated graphically in Figure 5.14. The edges of the tableaux $\mathbf{T}_i$ are shown as solid lines and the edges added during the construction of $\overline{\mathbf{T}}$ are shown as broken lines.

Recall that the tableau $\mathbf{T}$ is the result of the preprocessing stage. At this stage all transformation rules were applied for as long as possible, except for the expansion rules for certain nodes. This means that all nodes in $\mathbf{T}$ are stable. Also note that if a node is stable then its label cannot change any further, because no rule changes the label of nodes above the current node.[24] Since every node of $\mathbf{T}$ is stable, the same holds for the initial states that belong to the root nodes a_i. This means that for every node a_i its labels in $\mathbf{T}$ and in $\overline{\mathbf{T}}$ are the same.

The unified tableau $\overline{\mathbf{T}}$ is clash-free because every tableau $\mathbf{T}_i$ is clash-free. Thus there can be no clashes of the first two types, i.e. those involving the concept $\bot$ and complementary concepts appearing in a single label. Also, there cannot be a clash involving a node with a $(\leqslant kR)$ concept, because this would imply a clash in the preprocessing phase, in which case $\mathbf{T}$ would have been removed from $S_{\mathcal{A}}$.

The tableau $\overline{\mathbf{T}}$ is "almost complete" in the sense that the only rule which can possibly be applied to it is the $\leqslant$-rule. Furthermore, this rule can only fire at the nodes a_i of the original ABox, because neither the label nor the set of the successors of the nodes different from a_i has changed; the $\sqcup$-, $\sqcap$-, $\exists$- and $\geqslant$- rules are not sensitive to the addition of new edges (their firing condition cannot become true when a new successor is added) and the condition for the $\forall$-rule cannot become true because the labels of the respective successors a_j have already been extended in the preprocessing stage.

However, the unified tableau is not necessarily complete as the $\leqslant$-rule can fire because of the newly added edges. Assume that the label of a_i contains the concept $(\leqslant mR)$. Then, in the tableau $\mathbf{T}_i$, a_i has at most m R-successors. This may no longer be true in the unified

---

[24] This is true for the tableau algorithm for the $\mathcal{ALCN}$ language but not for languages supporting inverse roles. In the algorithms for such languages there will be rules that change the label of a predecessor node.

tableau $\overline{\mathbf{T}}$, owing to the additional edges. However, if this is the case then such a situation must have occurred during the preprocessing stage as well. The reason is that no restriction in the preprocessing phase applies to the nodes of the original ABox, and so all successors of a_i were created then. This means that we had to perform one or more node identifications in the preprocessing phase, when going from $\mathbf{T}_0$ to $\mathbf{T}$. If two new successors of a_i were identified and this did not cause a clash then the two successors that have the same label in $\overline{\mathbf{T}}$ can also be identified. If we identified a new successor with a node a_j, the node a_j has "inherited" the label of the new successor. Thus, when a_j is identified with the respective a_i-successor in $\overline{\mathbf{T}}$ the label of a_j does not change, that is, no rule can fire.

This means that the identifications required by the $\leqslant$-rules can be performed in $\overline{\mathbf{T}}$, and thus a complete and clash-free tableau state $\overline{\mathbf{T}}'$ can be obtained. The tableau $\overline{\mathbf{T}}'$ is satisfiable (see Subsection 5.4.3) and it contains, as a subset, the tableau $\mathbf{T}_0$ whose satisfiability is, in turn, equivalent to that of $\mathcal{A}$. Furthermore, each node label in $\overline{\mathbf{T}}'$ contains the internalisation $C_{\mathcal{T}}$, and so the model of $\overline{\mathbf{T}}'$ also satisfies the TBox $\mathcal{T}$. Thus $\mathcal{A}$ has a model w.r.t. $\mathcal{T}$. Hence the positive answer of the algorithm is justified.

Let us now show an example of the tableau-unification process discussed above. Recall the example (5.28), which involved the construction of two complete and clash-free tableau states $\mathbf{T}_1^x$ and $\mathbf{T}_2^x$. Let us see how the unified tableau $\overline{\mathbf{T}}$ can be constructed in this example. We take the union of $\mathbf{T}_1^x$ and $\mathbf{T}_2^x$ and add an edge $\mathsf{a}_1 \to \mathsf{a}_2$ bearing the label hC:

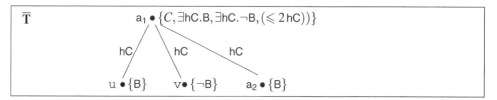

This tableau is not complete because the $\leqslant$-rule can be applied. However, we can perform the same identification that we applied in the transition $\mathbf{T}_0' \mapsto \mathbf{T}^x$, namely of a_2 with the node u (also bearing the label $\{\mathsf{B}\}$). This step does not result in a clash because a_2 has already inherited the label of the node x, corresponding to u, during the identification in the preprocessing phase. Thus we reach a complete and clash-free tableau state, which proves the consistency of the original ABox (5.28).

5.6. Summary

In this chapter we discussed *reasoning methods* for relatively simple description logic languages. We first introduced the structural subsumption algorithm for the very simple $\mathcal{AL}$ language. Next, we discussed the tableau algorithm for the $\mathcal{ALCN}$ language. We presented three versions of this algorithm. The simplest version is applicable to empty TBoxes only. Next, we discussed the version supporting TBoxes and finally the version handling both TBoxes and ABoxes.

A concept expression can be written in a many equivalent forms, so reasoning methods need to use some *normalisation*. This may vary from one algorithm to another. A specific normalisation was used for the structural subsumption algorithm, while the so-called *negation normal form* was applied in the tableau algorithm.

The basic idea of the *structural subsumption algorithm* is the following: if the concept expressions have been converted into a suitable normal form then, by examining the structure of the expressions, the subsumption relations of the two concepts can be determined. This approach, however, cannot treat full negation so it cannot be applied to the $\mathcal{ALC}$ language.

The *tableau algorithm* is suitable for more complex description logic languages. Its task is to decide the satisfiability of a concept C with respect to a (possibly empty) TBox $\mathcal{T}$. The main idea is to try to build a model of the concept. If the construction is successful then the concept is obviously satisfiable. Because the search for the model is exhaustive, an unsuccessful traversal of the search space means that the given concept is unsatisfiable.

The interpretation is constructed using a so-called *tableau graph*, the nodes of which, in the simplest cases, form the domain of the interpretation while the edges correspond to the role relations. The label of a node x is a set of concept expressions to which x has to belong. The edges are labelled with role expressions, so that the given role relation must hold between the endpoints of the edges. For tableau algorithms supporting number restrictions, a set of inequalities needs to be included in addition to the tableau graph. Thus, in the general case, these two data structures together form the so-called *tableau state* handled by the algorithm. In most cases the tableau graph has a tree structure; general graphs are only needed for ABox consistency algorithms.

We have given the tableau state an *ABox interpretation*, where elements of the node labels are mapped to concept assertions and edge labels to role assertions. The ABox corresponding to the initial tableau state is satisfiable w.r.t. TBox $\mathcal{T}$ if, and only if, this is true for the concept C.

The *transformation rules* specified in the tableau algorithm map a tableau state into one or more new, expanded, states. According to the *minimality principle* the tableau may be expanded only by such information as can be inferred from it, if it is viewed as an ABox. If this inference involves non-deterministic operations (such as union), the transformation results in a set of alternative tableau states. In such cases the tableau algorithm must keep traversing the search space spanned by the alternative branches as long as it does not find a satisfiable state. It is important that the transformation rules *preserve satisfiability* in the following sense: the ABox corresponding to the input tableau state is satisfiable if, and only if, the set of states resulting from the transformation has an element for which the corresponding ABox is satisfiable.

When reasoning over a non-empty TBox, the tableau algorithm may get into an infinite loop. This problem can be eliminated by introducing the technique called *blocking*. A node is said to be *blocked* by another node above it in the tree if the label of the former is a subset of the latter (*subset blocking*). The expansion rules, i.e. the rules adding new nodes to the tableau graph, must not be applied to the blocked nodes.

A tableau state is contradictory if, for example, the label of a node contains a concept together with its negation. In such a case, as well as in a few other cases corresponding to obvious contradictions, the tableau state is said to contain a *clash*. A tableau algorithm terminates if it reaches a state which does not contain a clash and where no transformation rules are applicable (the latter is called a *complete* state). In this case the algorithm returns the answer "C is *satisfiable* w.r.t. $\mathcal{T}$". We showed that this response is justified: given a complete and clash-free tableau, we built up an interpretation which is a model of $\mathcal{T}$ and in which C is not empty.

Naturally, for different versions of the algorithm this *model construction* process is different too. In the simplest case the tableau itself serves as a model. Having introduced blocking, however, this simple model-construction approach is no longer suitable, because certain edges may be missing for the blocked nodes. This problem is resolved by *redirection*: blocked nodes receive additional outgoing edges which go to appropriate successors of the blocking node.

The tableau algorithm also terminates if it has found clashes in all branches of the search space; in this case it returns the answer that C is *unsatisfiable* w.r.t. $\mathcal{T}$. This response is justified because all branches lead to contradictions and because the transformation rules preserve satisfiability.

In the different versions of the tableau algorithm we used different techniques to show that *the tableau algorithm terminates*, i.e. it cannot get into an infinite loop. In the simplest case, the depth of the tableau tree can be shown to be less than the *role depth* of the root concept. In the case of blocking, the fact that there can be only a finite number of possible node and edge labels ensures that, in a long enough branch of the tableau tree, blocking is certain to occur.

Chapter 6

Implementing a simple DL reasoning engine

This chapter presents an implementation of a description logic reasoning engine. Building on the theoretical foundations discussed in the previous chapters we present a program, written in the Haskell functional programming language, which is able to answer concept satisfiability queries over an arbitrary TBox using the $\mathcal{ALCN}$ language.

Following the introduction we give some examples illustrating the use of the program to be described. We then present the data structures of the program. Next, we describe the transformation of $\mathcal{ALCN}$ concepts into negation normal form and present the entry point of the tableau algorithm. The bulk of the chapter deals with the implementation of the main components of the tableau algorithm: the transformation rules and blocking. Finally, we describe the auxiliary functions used in the preceding sections and discuss possible improvements to the reasoning engine.

6.1. Introduction

The $\mathcal{ALCN}$ tableau algorithm considered in this chapter is implemented in Haskell, a functional programming language with lazy evaluation [65]. Haskell has been chosen for this task because it allows us to present the inference engine in a concise, simple and easily understandable way which is quite close to the mathematical notation employed in the previous chapters. No prior knowledge of Haskell is required to understand this chapter, since the various features of the Haskell programming language are explained at their first use. Further information on how to write Haskell programs and on the Haskell language itself can be found in Hudak, Peterson and Fasel [65] among other publications.

The program presented in this chapter is a fully fledged executable $\mathcal{ALCN}$ inference system. The complete source code can be downloaded from the URL [103]. We suggest that the reader experiments with this program as that will help him or her to understand the principles of this chapter.

Note that we do not deal with the external textual representation of concepts and axioms and with the issues of parsing, as our primary goal is to present the principles of DL reasoning.

6.2. Executing the reasoning engine

As a warm-up, in this section we solve a few simple reasoning tasks using the down-loaded reasoning engine. The details of execution are not important here; the goal is just to give a feeling of how the engine can be used to solve various tasks related to $\mathcal{ALCN}$ reasoning.

First let us make the reasoning engine decide whether the subsumption relation

$$\exists\mathsf{hasChild.Tall} \sqcap \exists\mathsf{hasChild.Blonde} \sqsubseteq \exists\mathsf{hasChild.}(\mathsf{Tall} \sqcap \mathsf{Blonde})$$

holds w.r.t. an empty TBox. This reasoning task has already been presented as (5.11) in Section 5.2. We showed there that the tableau algorithm gives a negative answer to this question. Let us see whether our reasoning engine gives the same result. To try the examples in this section, start the GHCi interpreter [43] like this: `ghci ALCN.hs`, where `ALCN.hs` is the file containing the program code downloaded from [103].[1]

Next, enter the following expressions (without the `*Main>` or `*Main|` prompt). Note that the lines with the braces are necessary for GHCi when the input is spread over several lines. The last line, with no prompt, displays the answer of the Haskell interpreter.

```
 1  *Main> :{
 2  *Main| subsumes
 3  *Main|     (Exists "hasChild" (Atomic "Tall" `And`
 4  *Main|                             (Atomic "Blonde")))
 5  *Main|     ((Exists "hasChild" (Atomic "Tall")) `And`
 6  *Main|      (Exists "hasChild" (Atomic "Blonde"))
 7  *Main|     )
 8  *Main|     []
 9  *Main| :}
10  False
```

The function `subsumes`, to be discussed in Section 6.5, has three input arguments: the first (lines 3 and 4) is the subsumer concept, i.e. the concept on the right-hand side of $\sqsubseteq$; the second (lines 5–7) is the subsumed concept; while the third (line 8) is the list of TBox axioms, which is empty in this case. Note that the input concepts are built by so-called constructor functions of the corresponding Haskell datatype. For example, the function **Atomic** builds an atomic concept from its name, given as a string. The functions **Exists** and `And` (the latter is used as an infix operator) build composite concepts which correspond to the DL constructors $\exists$ and $\sqcap$.

Exercise 6.1: Download and install the the GHCi interpreter [43] (or any other Haskell environment). Load the $\mathcal{ALCN}$ reasoning program [103] into your Haskell environment.

(a) Execute the above subsumption query and experiment with other queries, including the variants (b) and (c) below.

---

[1] This file is actually a concatenation of the code snippets presented in this chapter, with some minor editing: the **import** declarations have been brought to the beginning of the file.

(b) Replace the `And` operator in line 3 of the query by `Or` and run the same query. Check whether the answer is correct.

(c) Switch the first two arguments of subsumes, i.e. move lines 3 and 4 to a position before line 8. Again, check whether the answer of the program is correct.

The function subsumes is an entry point of the program. The interactive nature of Haskell implementations makes it easy to call other, internal, functions as well. This is vital during the testing phase, and it also facilitates the learning process. As an example, let us convert the concept expression $\neg(C \sqcap D)$ into its negation normal form using the function nnf:

```
*Main> nnf (Not (Atomic "C" `And` Atomic "D"))
Not (Atomic "C") `Or` Not (Atomic "D")
```

This function call produces the expected result, using *de Morgan*'s laws.

Let us now consider a more complex example with a non-empty TBox.

```
*Main> :{
*Main| let {
*Main|   concept = (Exists "hasChild" (Atomic "Mother")) `And`
*Main|                   (All "hasChild" (Atomic "Man"))
*Main| ; tbox = [Atomic "Woman" `Implies`
*Main|               (Atomic "Human") `And` (Atomic "Female"),
*Main|             Atomic "Man" `Implies`
*Main|               (Atomic "Human") `And` (Not (Atomic "Woman")),
*Main|             Atomic "Mother" `Implies`
*Main|               (Atomic "Woman") `And` (Exists "hasChild"
*Main|                                       (Atomic "Human"))
*Main|           ]
*Main|       }
*Main| in satisfiable concept tbox
*Main| :}
False
```

Here, we first construct the arguments and name them as concept and tbox. Next, in line 14, we call the function satisfiable with these two arguments.

Even though the TBox contains just a few axioms, these are enough to detect that the argument concept is not satisfiable: if someone has a child who is a mother, it is not possible for all his or her children to be male.

6.3. Data structures

The first step in writing a DL inference system is to define a datatype which describes the notion of $\mathcal{ALCN}$ concept expressions. This definition mirrors the syntax of the $\mathcal{ALCN}$ language.

```
 1  data Concept = Top
 2                | Atomic ConceptName
 3                | Not Concept
 4                | Concept `And` Concept
 5                | Concept `Or` Concept
 6                | Exists RoleName Concept
 7                | All RoleName Concept
 8                | AtLeast Int RoleName
 9                | AtMost Int RoleName
10                  deriving (Eq, Ord, Show)
11
12  type ConceptName = String
13  type RoleName = String
```

Haskell datatypes can be defined using the keyword **data**. This keyword is followed by the name of the type, an equals sign and the set of alternative constructors of this type together with their arguments. The alternatives are separated by the | character.

We have chosen **Top** to denote the top symbol $\top$, standing for the universal concept (line 1), while **Atomic ConceptName** denotes atomic concepts (line 2). The remaining *type constructors* of the datatype (lines 3–9) denote composite $\mathcal{ALCN}$ expressions. The constructor functions **Not**, **And**, **Or**, **Exists**, **All**, **AtLeast** and **AtMost** correspond to the $\mathcal{ALCN}$ constructs $\neg, \sqcap, \sqcup, \exists, \forall, \geqslant$ and $\leqslant$, respectively.

Line 10, the last line of the type definition for **Concept**, needs further explanation. The declaration **deriving (Eq, Ord, Show)** tells the Haskell compiler to automatically generate trivial implementations of the operations provided by the type classes **Eq**, **Ord** and **Show**. The class **Eq** includes the operations **==** and **/=**, whose task is to decide whether two concepts are identical or different. For instance, the trivial implementation of the operation **==** compares two **Concept** values and returns the boolean value **True** if they have identical constructors and if, furthermore, the **==** relation also holds for all their respective arguments (here we take advantage of the fact that the types **Int** and **String** are also instances of the **Eq** class). The operations of the class **Ord** consist of the trivial implementations of ordering relations (compare, <, <=, >, >=, min, max) [65]. The **Show** class is responsible for converting the concepts to strings; this is used for displaying the instances of the data structure.

Exercise 6.2: Consider the concept-equality function **==** outlined above.

(a) Provide a trivial implementation for it in pseudo-code or in Haskell.

(b) Consider the impact of using strings for identifying atomic concepts and roles. Devise an approach that makes it possible to decide the equality of atomic concepts and the equality of atomic roles in constant time, i.e. in a way that does not depend on the length of the string used as the name.

We use character sequences, i.e. the **String** type of Haskell, to name atomic concepts and roles. The corresponding data structures (in lines 12 and 13 of the code extract above) are defined using *type synonyms*. The first states that the type **ConceptName** is equivalent to **String**, and the second states the same for the type **RoleName**. Such type synonyms make data structure definitions more readable and also make the program easier to modify.

Note that the definition of the datatype **Concept** does not include a symbol for $\perp$. There is no need for the bottom symbol, because **Not Top**, i.e. $\neg\top$ can be used instead. If the label of a node contains this concept, or any other equivalent to $\perp$ such as $C \sqcap \neg C$, then the program reports an inconsistency.

Exercise 6.3: Modify the program to include $\perp$ as a **Concept**. As a first step, modify the definition of the **Concept** datatype. Later, when you have become familiar with the whole program, add further modifications to handle the $\perp$ symbol.

In order to make the notation easier to read, the **And** and **Or** constructor functions are declared to be *left associative infix operators*. An operator (such as addition) is left associative if it is applied from left to right. That is, the expression $3+4+5+6$ is evaluated as if it were explicitly parenthesised as $(((3+4)+5)+6)$. We declare the constructors **And** and **Or** to be infix, so that one can write them between their two operands (i.e. instead of $\sqcap\, A\, B$ one can write $A \sqcap B$). Furthermore, we give **And** a higher precedence than **Or** so that **And** binds more tightly than **Or**. This is accomplished by the following piece of code, where the keyword **infixl** declares the operator to be infix and left associative, while the integer which follows is the specified precedence value:

```
infixl 5 `Or`
infixl 6 `And`
```

Exercise 6.4: Consider the concepts listed in Exercise 4.2.

(a) Write down the Haskell expressions that are equivalent to these concepts.

(b) Check the subsumption relationships between these concepts, i.e. find their full classification using the program. Hint: the function subsumes can be used to check whether one concept subsumes another. For example, to check whether concept c1 subsumes concept c2, evaluate the Haskell function-call subsumes c1 c2 [].

Let us now proceed to define the tableau data structure. The notion of a tableau state was introduced in Section 5.3 as a finite directed graph, extended with a set of inequalities. Formally, a tableau state is a quadruple $(V, E, \mathcal{L}, I)$, where V is a set of nodes, E is a set of edges, $\mathcal{L}$ is a function mapping nodes and edges to their labels and I stores the $\neq$ relation between pairs of nodes from V. The corresponding Haskell data structure is somewhat different, as nodes and edges store their labels themselves. Furthermore, we need to maintain some global data, i.e. the internalisation of the TBox, to be added to each node, and a node counter. The latter is a non-negative integer used to provide a unique identifier for the nodes. The Haskell datatype definition of the data structure for representing tableau states is thus the following:

```
1  data Tableau = Tableau { nodes :: [Node],
2                           edges :: [Edge],
3                           tboxConcept :: Concept,
4                           nextId :: Id,
5                           ineqs :: [(Id,Id)]
6                         } deriving (Eq, Show)
```

The above piece of Haskell code defines a composite data structure whose fields can be referred to with the names supplied (nodes, edges, tboxConcept, nextId, ineqs). These names automatically become functions which, given an argument of the type **Tableau**, return the value of the corresponding field in the tableau data structure.

Let us give a brief description of the fields of the **Tableau** record type:

nodes denotes the list of tableau nodes (of the type **Node**);[2]

edges is the list of the tableau edges (of the type **Edge**);

tboxConcept is a value of the type **Concept** which stores the *internalisation* of the TBox, as described in Subsection 4.7.2;

nextId is the lowest non-negative integer value not yet used to identify a tableau node;

ineqs is the list of distinct node pairs, i.e. those belonging to the $\neq$ relation.[3] We ensure that the following invariant holds: the node with the smaller identifier takes the first place in every pair.

We now introduce a type synonym **Id**, declaring it to be an integer. The datatype **Id** stands for node identifiers. It is used in the **Node** and **Edge** types identifying the nodes of the tableau.

```
1   type Id = Int
2
3   data Node = Node { nid :: Id,
4                      concepts :: [Concept]
5                    } deriving (Eq, Ord, Show)
6
7   data Edge = Edge { parentId :: Id,
8                      role :: RoleName,
9                      childId :: Id
10                   } deriving (Eq, Ord, Show)
```

Let us explain the meaning of the fields of the above two data structures:

nid is the identifier of the node;

concepts is the list of concept expressions in the label of the node, containing the concepts to which the individual denoted by the node has to belong;

---

[2] Notice that a type name such as **Node**, when enclosed in square brackets, denotes a list whose elements are of the given type: [**Node**] means a list of nodes.

[3] Recall that identification is needed in a tableau algorithm in the $\leqslant$-rule. However, the $\geqslant$ transformation rule requires that no two nodes added by it are ever identified. The ineqs field stores this information.

parentId is the identifier of the parent node (i.e. the upper end) of the edge;

role is the name of the role with which the edge is labelled;

childId is the identifier of the child node, i.e. the lower end of the edge.

Exercise 6.5: Write down the `Tableau` data structure corresponding to the complete tableau built as your answer for item (a) of Exercise 5.8. Concentrate on the `nodes` and `edges` fields of the data structure.

6.4. Transforming concepts to negation normal form

The tableau algorithm assumes that the concepts stored in node labels are in negation normal form. The node labels contain subconcepts of the internalised TBox and of the concept whose satisfiability is being checked. Thus the latter two concepts have to undergo a conversion to negation normal form.

Before implementing the conversion, we introduce the syntax of Haskell functions. As an example, let us write a Haskell function computing the square of an integer:

```
1  -- sqr n = the square of n.
2  sqr :: Int -> Int
3  sqr n = n * n
```

The first line of the above code extract is a comment. Comments start with the characters `--` and are terminated by a newline character.

Line 2 contains a type declaration which tells us that `sqr` is a function mapping an integer to an integer. Type declarations are optional. Line 3 contains the definition of the function. The argument of the function `sqr` is n, and its value is n `*` n. The part before the equals sign, `sqr n`, is called the head of the function.

Using the function `sqr` as a template, let us implement a function that calculates the value b^e (b raised to the eth power), where b and e are positive integers.

```
1  -- pow (b,e) = b raised to the eth power.
2  pow :: (Int,Int) -> Int
3  pow (b,1) = b
4  pow (b,e) = b * pow (b,e - 1)
```

The two arguments of the function `pow` (b and e) are passed to the function as a single value, the pair `(b,e)`. This is necessary because, strictly speaking, Haskell functions have at most one argument. The type of the function is `(Int,Int) -> Int`, showing that it transforms a pair of integers into an integer.

Lines 3 and 4 have to be written in the given order. Depending on the value of e, Haskell executes exactly one of the *cases* represented by these lines, namely the first one, read from top to bottom, whose argument *matches* the value of e. For instance, the argument of the function-call `pow (3,2)` matches the second case. Haskell then proceeds to calculate the value of the right-hand side of this case, calling the function `pow` recursively `pow (3,1)`. This, in turn, matches the first case and thus the following sequence of calculations is performed:

$$\text{pow } (3,2) \;\rightarrow\; 3 \; * \; \text{pow } (3,1) \;\rightarrow\; 3 \; * \; 3 \;\rightarrow\; 9.$$

Let us now show another way of implementing the function pow. This second version is invoked as pow b e. This looks like a function-call with two arguments, contradicting our earlier statement that such functions are not allowed by Haskell. However, it is parenthesised as (pow b) e and, in fact, involves two function-calls, each with a single argument. Here we make use of the fact that the value of a function can itself be a function. In our example, the function pow applied to the argument b results in the *function* (pow b), which is then called with e as its argument. The latter is an integer and so is the expected output value, b^e. Therefore, (pow b) has to be a function of the type **Int -> Int**, i.e. a function which takes an integer and returns an integer.

Consequently, pow is a function that takes an integer b and returns an integer-to-integer function (pow b). Formally, the type of pow is pow **:: Int -> (Int -> Int)**. This can also be written without parentheses: pow **:: Int -> Int -> Int**, since the type operator **->** is right associative. Therefore, strictly speaking, it is still true that the function pow accepts a single argument. However, to make our explanations simpler we will speak about the first, second etc. arguments of functions similar to the second formulation of pow.

The complete code for the second version of pow is the following:

```
-- pow b e = b raised to the eth power.
pow :: Int -> (Int -> Int)
pow b 1 = b
pow b e = b * (pow b (e - 1))
```

To illustrate the use of functions as return values of other functions, let us consider an example which uses the second version of pow to define a new function:

```
-- powOf2 n = The nth power of 2.
powOf2 :: Int -> Int
powOf2 = pow 2
```

The function powOf2 takes an integer and raises the integer 2 to a power equal to that integer. The type of powOf2 is **Int -> Int**, since it is the special case of (pow b) where b equals 2. For example,

$$\text{powOf2 } 3 \;\rightarrow\; (\text{pow } 2) \; 3 \;\rightarrow\; \text{pow } 2 \; 3 \;\rightarrow\; 8.$$

Note that the expression pow 2 in line 3 above is called a *partial application* of pow, as not all the arguments of pow are supplied.

Exercise 6.6: Functions can also occur as parts of complex data structures. Define a function distance **:: Int -> (Int -> Int, Int -> Int)** which takes an integer i and returns a pair of functions: the first member of the pair returned maps its argument x to $x - i$ and the second to $x + i$. Feel free to define auxiliary functions if needed.

Before proceeding, let us introduce some conventions to be used throughout the present chapter. Each Haskell function starts with a *head comment*, which explains what the function is expected to do. The more complicated local definitions also have such a comment, although as we progress through the chapter they become less frequent. The code of the function is followed by a detailed explanation of how it works. Especially at the beginning, the head comment might be too terse to be understood at first sight. In such a case the comment can be skipped and used only later for quick reference.

The variables denoting concept expressions and roles are named c and r, respectively, possibly with a numeric suffix. Collections (lists) are named by making the variable plural, i.e. by adding a suffix s. Integers are usually denoted by k.

Let us now continue by considering the function nnf, the task of which is to convert an arbitrary $\mathcal{ALCN}$ concept expression into an equivalent concept in negation normal form:

```
 1  -- nnf c = the negation normal form of the concept c.
 2  nnf :: Concept -> Concept
 3  nnf (Not (Not c)) = nnf c
 4  nnf (Not (c1 `And` c2)) = nnf (Not c1) `Or`  nnf (Not c2)
 5  nnf (Not (c1 `Or`  c2)) = nnf (Not c1) `And` nnf (Not c2)
 6  nnf (Not (Exists r c))   = All r (nnf (Not c))
 7  nnf (Not (All r c))      = Exists r (nnf (Not c))
 8  nnf (Not (AtMost k r))   = AtLeast (k + 1) r
 9  nnf (Not (AtLeast k r))  = if k > 0 then AtMost (k - 1) r
10                                      else Not Top
11  nnf (c1 `And` c2) = nnf c1 `And` nnf c2
12  nnf (c1 `Or`  c2) = nnf c1 `Or`  nnf c2
13  nnf (Exists r c)  = Exists r (nnf c)
14  nnf (All r c)     = All r (nnf c)
15  nnf c = c
```

Line 2 declares that both the argument and the return value of the function are of the type **Concept**, as defined earlier. The type definition is followed by the function definition containing 12 cases, which cover all possible concepts.

The first seven cases (lines 3–9) are simply transcriptions of the transformation rules shown in Figure 5.2. For instance, when the function is applied to the Haskell representation of the concept $\neg \forall R.C$ the following happens. The first case that matches the given concept is in line 7. The right-hand side prescribes that a concept of the form $\exists R.C'$ is to be returned, where C' is obtained by recursively applying the function nnf to $\neg C$.

The last five cases deal with the situations where the concept at hand is not a negation of a composite concept. They prescribe that the nnf conversion should be applied to each subconcept. In all cases but the last, this is achieved by decomposing the concept, applying the function nnf recursively and then rebuilding the converted form. The last case covers concept expressions which are already in negation normal form, namely $\top$, $\neg\top$, A, $\neg A$, $(\geqslant nR)$ and $(\leqslant nR)$, where A denotes an atomic concept. Obviously, in such a case the concept itself should be returned, with no change.

Exercise 6.7: Verify your solution to Exercise 5.14 by invoking the function nnf with appropriate arguments.

6.5. The entry point of the tableau algorithm

The tableau algorithm decides whether a concept is satisfiable with respect to a TBox $\mathcal{T}$. First, we introduce a new type that represents the axioms of $\mathcal{T}$:

```
infixl 4 `Implies`
data Axiom = Concept `Implies` Concept
```

The priority of the operator `Implies` is lower than that of `Or`; therefore it has a weaker binding. Consequently, no parentheses are needed when transcribing the subsumption axiom $C \sqsubseteq D$ to its Haskell representation C `Implies` D, even if the concepts C and D are composite. Note that we do not introduce a Haskell syntax for the axiom $C \equiv D$, as it can be expressed using two subsumption axioms, $C \sqsubseteq D$ and $D \sqsubseteq C$.

Exercise 6.8: Check your answers to item (b) of Exercise 4.10 using the appropriate functions of the program.

Exercise 6.9: Extend the definition of **Axiom** to include a constructor **Equivalent** which takes a single argument, the list of equivalent expressions.

The set of axioms in the TBox is converted to a single concept using the technique of internalisation; see Subsection 4.7.2. This internalisation concept is added to every node of the tableau. The internalisation is based on the idea that an axiom of the form $C \sqsubseteq D$ is equivalent to $\top \sqsubseteq \neg C \sqcup D$. This latter form makes it explicit that every individual in the interpretation has to be an instance of the concept $\neg C \sqcup D$. Therefore the concept $\neg C \sqcup D$ has to appear in the label of each node of the tableau for each axiom $C \sqsubseteq D$.

The single internalised concept is derived from the TBox axioms by first transforming each axiom $C \sqsubseteq D$ to the concept expression $\neg C \sqcup D$, then taking the intersection ($\sqcap$) of these concepts. Finally, the resulting concept is converted to negation normal form:

```
-- axiomConcept a = the concept derived from the axiom a.
axiomConcept :: Axiom -> Concept
axiomConcept (Top `Implies` c) = c
axiomConcept (c1 `Implies` c2) = Not c1 `Or` c2

-- tboxInternalise tbox = the concept derived from the list of
-- axioms tbox representing a TBox.
tboxInternalise :: [Axiom] -> Concept
tboxInternalise [] = Top
tboxInternalise tbox = nnf (foldl1 And cs)
     where cs = map axiomConcept tbox
```

The function `axiomConcept` is responsible for converting an axiom to a concept. In order to make the resulting concept simpler, the first case (line 3) handles the conversion of the axiom $\top \sqsubseteq C$ separately, since the concept $\neg\top \sqcup C$ is equivalent to C.

Exercise 6.10: Extend the function `axiomConcept` so that it supports the axiom constructor **Equivalent**, as introduced in Exercise 6.9.

To understand how the function `tboxInternalise` works, some new elements of Haskell have to be introduced.

- A *list* in Haskell is written as a sequence of comma-separated elements enclosed in square brackets. For instance, the list containing the elements 2, 4 and 6 is written as `[2,4,6]`. The empty list is denoted by `[]`.

- The function `map` applies a function to each element of a list separately and returns the list of the resulting values. For example, using the function `sqr`, introduced in Section 6.4, the value of `map sqr [2,4,6]` is `[4,16,36]`.

- `foldl1` processes a list by applying a binary function to its elements, from left to right. For instance, `foldl1 (+) [2,4,6]` yields $(2+4)+6 = 12$. The name of the function is a combination of *fold* and *left*,[4] and it refers to the fact that the function "folds" the elements of the list supplied in the argument into a single value using the binary function provided.

- The **where** keyword allows us to provide definitions which are local to the function `tboxInternalise`. The identifiers introduced after a **where** keyword can be used only within the function; they are not visible from outside. However, identifiers defined in the function are available in the **where** clause. Thus, for instance, the function argument `tbox` can be used in the definition of the local name `cs`.

The list `cs` in line 11 of the procedure is obtained by applying the function `axiomConcept` to each element of the list `tbox`. As explained above, the function `axiomConcept` transforms a TBox axiom into a concept. The intersection of these concepts is built in line 10, via the function `foldl1` using the constructor function **And** for folding. In line 9, `tboxInternalise` handles the case when the TBox is empty by returning the concept ⊤.

Having dealt with the internalisation of the TBox, we can turn to the issue of checking the satisfiability of a concept w.r.t. a TBox. In Section 6.6 we will define a function `tableau`, which, given a list of tableau data structures as input, computes all complete and clash-free tableaux that can be obtained from the input using the tableau algorithm, and returns them in a list.

In order to supply an initial input argument to the function `tableau` we now implement the function `initTableau`, which assembles a tableau data structure of the type **Tableau**, as defined in Section 6.3. This function takes two concept arguments: c, the concept whose satisfiability is to be checked, and `tbox`, the internalisation of the TBox in question:

```
1  -- initTableau c tbox = the initial tableau state
2  -- for checking the satisfiability of the concept c
3  -- w.r.t. the TBox, whose internalisation is the concept tbox.
```

---

[4] The suffix `1` in `foldl1` is needed to distinguish it from a variant which takes an initial value and "adds" all list elements to it, e.g. $((0+2)+4)+6 = 12$.

```
4  initTableau :: Concept -> Concept -> [Tableau]
5  initTableau c tbox = [Tableau [n] [] ntbox 1 []]
6      where n = Node 0 [nnf c,ntbox]
7            ntbox = nnf tbox
```

In line 5, a list containing a single tableau structure is constructed. The values of the fields of the **Tableau** record are specified as arguments following the **Tableau** data constructor. The order of the arguments corresponds to the order of the fields in the definition of the **Tableau** datatype. The tableau created has a single node n, whose label contains the concept to be satisfied and the expression created from the TBox, both converted to negation normal form (line 6).

Let us introduce some further naming conventions. The variable names n and e, possibly with a numeric suffix, denote tableau nodes and edges. Similarly, tableau structures are denoted by t. Lists of these are formed by adding the suffix s.

Using the function initTableau, let us now implement the function that executes the tableau algorithm for given input data:

```
1  -- models c tbox = the list of complete and clash-free tableau
2  -- states representing models of the concept c w.r.t. the
3  -- TBox tbox.
4  models :: Concept -> [Axiom] -> [Tableau]
5  models c tbox = tableau (initTableau c (tboxInternalise tbox))
```

The function models has two arguments: a concept c and a TBox tbox. The latter takes the form of a list of **Axiom** expressions. The function returns a list of tableau states, which represent models of the concept c w.r.t. the TBox tbox. For the sake of brevity, in this chapter we will often use the term *model* to mean a complete and clash-free tableau, constructed in the process of checking the satisfiability of a concept w.r.t. a TBox. This explains the naming of the function models: it returns the list of *models* of the given concept and TBox.

The body of the function models is very simple. The axioms of the TBox are converted to an internalised concept by the function tboxInternalise, presented earlier. This concept, together with the concept whose satisfiability is being checked, is passed to the function initTableau. This, in turn, builds an initial tableau to be passed to the function tableau, which implements the reasoning process (for details of the latter see Section 6.6).

Exercise 6.11: Verify your solutions to Exercise 5.8 using the program considered in this chapter. Compare the results with your answer to Exercise 6.5.

Using the function models, we can easily implement the satisfiability check:

```
1  -- satisfiable c tbox = True iff the concept c
2  -- is satisfiable w.r.t. the TBox tbox.
3  satisfiable :: Concept -> [Axiom] -> Bool
4  satisfiable c tbox = not (null (models c tbox))
```

The function invocation satisfiable c tbox returns the Boolean value true if, and only if, the concept c is satisfiable w.r.t. the TBox tbox. Here, null is a function that takes a list as an input argument and returns a value of the type **Bool**: **True** if the list is empty and **False** otherwise. The function not implements the Boolean negation.

The function call satisfiable c tbox returns a positive answer as soon as the first model of the input concept has been found. This is due to the fact that Haskell uses *lazy evaluation*: an expression whose value is not needed for solving the task is not evaluated. If there is no doubt that the concept to be satisfied has a model, i.e. models c tbox returns a list containing at least one element, then null (models c tbox) immediately evaluates to **False** without calculating the remaining elements of the return value of the function models.

We showed in Subsection 4.6.2 that several TBox-reasoning tasks can be reduced to deciding the satisfiability of a concept. This reduction can be easily implemented in Haskell. For example, the subsumption check can be performed as follows:

```
1  -- subsumes c1 c2 tbox = True iff concept c1 subsumes
2  -- concept c2 w.r.t. the TBox tbox.
3  subsumes :: Concept -> Concept -> [Axiom] -> Bool
4  subsumes c1 c2 tbox = not (satisfiable (Not c1 `And` c2) tbox)
```

Exercise 6.12: Using subsumes as an example, implement the functions equivalent, disjoint and consistent, for checking concept equivalence, concept disjointness and TBox consistency, respectively. Verify your solutions to Exercises 5.12 and 5.13 using the program.

6.6. Tableau transformation rules

The tableau algorithm consists of the repeated execution of the transformation rules shown in Figures 5.4 and 5.10. There is a transformation for each $\mathcal{ALCN}$ constructor except negation, i.e. for $\sqcap, \sqcup, \forall, \exists, \geq, \leq$. We examine the node labels, looking for a concept for which the firing conditions of a transformation rule hold. If such a node is found, the corresponding transformation rule is executed. This results in one or more new tableau states.

The type of the functions implementing the transformation rules is given by the following:

```
1  type TableauTransformation = Tableau -> [Tableau]
```

The type-synonym TableauTransformation denotes the type of tableau transformation functions. These functions map a tableau state to a list of tableau states. First they determine which nodes and concepts satisfy the firing conditions of the corresponding transformation rule and then they perform the transformation. We can distinguish the following possible outcomes of the function.

- If the input tableau state contains a clash then the function returns an empty list.

- If the transformation is deterministic, i.e. it does not create choice points, then the value of the function is a list with a single element. Note that all tableau transformations change their input in some way. This means that the single list element returned in this case is *different* from the input tableau.

- If the transformation is not applicable, i.e. its firing conditions are not satisfied, then the function returns a singleton list, with the unchanged input tableau state as its element.

- If the transformation is non-deterministic, i.e. a choice point is to be created, then the result is a list with multiple elements representing all possible new tableau states.

Exercise 6.13: Note that the four possible outcomes of a tableau transformation are all represented as lists. Define a variant of the type `TableauTransformation` which makes the four outcomes explicit. Use a new auxiliary type for representing the output of the transformation functions.

The implementation of the function `tableau`, introduced in the previous section, is shown in Figure 6.1. Before discussing the function itself, we present the new Haskell language features used here.

The *head* of a list is the first element, while its *tail* is the list of all the other elements. For instance, the head of the list `[1,2,3]` is the element `1` and its tail is the list `[2,3]`. Lists can be constructed using the `:` ("cons") operator. The `:` operator allows us to insert an element in front of a list, thereby producing a list whose head is the inserted element. For example, the value of `1:[2,3]` is `[1,2,3]`.

```
1   -- tableau ts = the list of complete and clash-free tableaux
2   -- which can be derived from the elements of the input
3   -- tableau list ts by repeatedly applying transformation rules.
4   tableau :: [Tableau] -> [Tableau]
5   tableau ts = applyTransformations transformations ts
6     where -- applyTransformations fs ts = the result of executing the
7           -- tableau algorithm on the tableau list ts, assuming
8           -- that only the transformations in fs can be used to
9           -- process the first element of ts.
10          applyTransformations _ [] = []
11          applyTransformations [] (t : ts) = t : tableau ts
12          applyTransformations (f : fs) (t : ts) =
13                      if c then tableau ts'
14                      else applyTransformations fs (t : ts)
15             where -- c is true if the firing condition of the
16                   -- transformation rule f holds, i.e. new
17                   -- tableau state(s) are formed.
18                   -- ts' denotes the list of states obtained
19                   -- from the successful application of
20                   -- the rule f for the tableau t, prepended
21                   -- to the list ts.
22                   (c,ts') = apply f t ts
23          transformations = [clash,applyAnd,applyAll,applyAtMost,
24                             applyOr,applyExists,applyAtLeast]
```

Figure 6.1. The main loop of the tableau algorithm.

Note that the : operator is a constructor function, and as such it can also be used to decompose lists by means of pattern matching. For instance, if the head of a function definition contains an argument of the form t : ts, we can use the name t to refer to the head of the list and ts to denote its tail within the body of the function. The expression t : ts also implies that the list to be matched is not empty, because an empty list has no head and therefore does not match the pattern t : ts.

The underscore character _ matches any pattern, and it differs from a variable name in two aspects. First, it can be used more than once in patterns for matching arguments, successfully matching all of them regardless of the values supplied. Second, it cannot be used in expressions; therefore it is impossible to refer to values matched by the character _. Because of these properties, it is used in patterns to denote explicitly those values which are not relevant in the given context. For example, the use of _ in line 10 of Figure 6.1 makes it explicit that the list of applicable tableau transformations is irrelevant if the list of tableau states is empty.

Exercise 6.14: Implement the function null using the features introduced above.

In the Haskell conditional expression **if** c **then** expr1 **else** expr2, the type of expression c must be **Bool**, and the types of expr1 and expr2 must be identical. The **else** branch is mandatory. If c evaluates to true, the value of the whole conditional expression is the value of expr1; otherwise it is the value of expr2.

Let us now turn to the function tableau. Its task is to apply tableau transformation rules for as long as possible. The auxiliary function applyTransformations takes a list of transformation functions as its first argument and a list of tableau states, as its second argument. Its task is to try to apply all the transformation functions to all the given tableau states. The list transformations (defined in lines 23–24) is the initial value of the first argument of applyTransformations (line 5). If a transformation does not fire, applyTransformations tries to apply the remaining transformations (line 14). If a transformation does fire (line 13) then the resulting tableau list is passed to a recursive invocation of the function tableau, which means that we again attempt to apply all transformations on the new tableaux. If no transformation fires for the tableau at hand, we have a complete and clash-free tableau and thus it is included in the list returned by the function tableau (line 11).

Note that the tableau algorithm has the property that, from any input state, only a bounded number of transformation steps can be performed (see Subsection 5.4.4). This ensures that the algorithm reaches a state where no transformation rules can be applied, and so the algorithm terminates.

The application order of the transformation rules is specified by the transformation list. The elements of this list are Haskell functions: the first performs clash detection, while the remaining ones attempt to apply the transformation rule corresponding to intersection, value restriction, at-most restriction, union, existential restriction and at-least restriction, in that order. Note that clash detection is not a proper transformation rule, but it is treated as such in our implementation.

Inspecting the order of transformations in the transformations list we notice that non-deterministic rules are in the middle of the list: the last two places are taken by the ∃- and ⩾- rules. The reason is that the latter are the *expansion* rules, which add new nodes to the tableau. The labels of the new nodes contain the internalised TBox, which is normally an intersection of unions. Unfolding the intersection, we would obtain a possibly large number of union concepts, leading to very costly non-deterministic union rule applications. This is the reason why the expansion rules are placed after the non-deterministic rules.

Exercise 6.15: By changing the `transformations` list, experiment with various transformation orders. Try various reasoning tasks. How does the optimal order depend on the input? Why? Can you find an order which always performs better than the one given in Figure 6.1?

Let us now discuss the three cases in the definition of `applyTransformations`. In the first case (line 10) the list of tableaux is empty, i.e. there are no more tableaux to transform. In the second case (line 11), there are no more applicable transformation rules, and `t` is thus a complete and clash-free tableau. The last case (line 12) is responsible for the actual work: we apply rule `f` to the tableau `t` by calling the function `apply` (see line 22 in the **where** clause).

The definition of the function `apply` is the following:

```
1  -- apply r t ts = a pair (b,ts'), where the Boolean value b is
2  -- True iff the transformation rule r fires for the tableau t;
3  -- the list ts' contains the transformed tableaux produced
4  -- by the rule r, prepended to the list ts.
5  apply :: (TableauTransformation -> Tableau ->
6            [Tableau] -> (Bool,[Tableau]))
7  apply r t ts =
8      (changed transformed_tableaux, transformed_tableaux ++ ts)
9      where transformed_tableaux = r t
10           changed [t'] = t /= t'
11           changed _ = True
```

The value of the expression `apply r t ts` is a pair whose first element is true if, and only if, the transformation rule has fired.[5] The second element is of interest only if the rule in question has fired. It is the concatenation (denoted by the operator `++`) of two lists. The first list is the output of the transformation rule `r` as applied to the tableau `t`. The second is the list of the remaining tableau states `ts`. The `++` operator concatenates two lists, e.g. the value of `[1,2,3] ++ [5,6]` is `[1,2,3,5,6]`. The `/=` operator is a function that returns true if, and only if, its arguments are different. In other words, `/=` is the negation of the `==` operation. It is used when the transformation returns a singleton list (line 10). Here, the rule is deemed to have fired if the output tableau is different from the input tableau.

The function `apply` is always invoked so that its `r` argument is a member of the `transformations` list, as defined in line 22 in the function `tableau`. These transformation rule functions are applied to the tableau specified by the argument `t`. In the following subsections we discuss the implementation of the tableau transformation functions.

---

[5] Note that detecting a clash counts as a rule firing in this context.

6.6.1. Detection of clashes

We have to look for clashes in every tableau created during reasoning. As discussed in Subsection 5.3.2, the following three conditions have to be satisfied for an $\mathcal{ALCN}$ tableau to be clash-free:

(a) the $\bot$ ($\neg\top$) concept must not appear in the label of any node;

(b) for an arbitrary concept C, the label of any node must not simultaneously contain C and $\neg C$;

(c) if a node label contains a concept of the form $(\leqslant kR)$, $k > 0$, then that node cannot have $k + 1$ distinct R-successors.

In the program we will use the following reformulation of condition (c): if the label of a node contains both $(\geqslant k_1 R)$ and $(\leqslant k_2 R)$ then $k_1 \leq k_2$. If the latter condition is violated, i.e. a node label contains two such concepts, with $k_1 > k_2$, then the $\geqslant$-rule is bound to create k_1 distinct R-successors, and this violates the original condition (c). The converse is also true, because only the $\geqslant$-rule can create non-identifiable nodes. Thus if (c) is violated, and so a node with the concept $(\leqslant k_2 R)$ has $k_2 + 1$ distinct R-successors ($k_2 > 0$), then the label of the node has to contain a concept expression $(\geqslant k_1 R)$, where $k_1 \geq k_2 + 1$, which, in turn, means that the new condition is violated.

Note that the new formulation of clash condition (c) has the advantage that it requires the inspection of nodes only, while for checking the original condition the edges have to be examined as well.

The function `clash`, shown in Figure 6.2, checks whether any of the three conditions is violated. If a tableau `t` contains a clash, `clash t` returns an empty list. This means that

```
-- clash t = [] if tableau state t contains a clash,
--             [t] if t is clash-free.
clash :: TableauTransformation
clash t = if any check (nodes t) then [] else [t]

-- check n = True, if any of the clash conditions is met
-- in the label of node n, False otherwise.
check :: Node -> Bool
check n = (Not Top) `elem` cs ||
          any checkPair [(c1,c2) |
                         (c1 : c2s) <- tails cs, c2 <- c2s
                        ]
    where cs = concepts n
          checkPair (a,Not b) = a == b
          checkPair (Not b,a) = a == b
          checkPair (AtLeast k1 r1,AtMost k2 r2) =
              r1 == r2 && k1 > k2
          checkPair (AtMost k1 r1,AtLeast k2 r2) =
              r1 == r2 && k2 > k1
          checkPair _ = False
```

Figure 6.2. Checking clashes in the tableau.

a tableau with a clash will be ignored by the rest of the algorithm. If there is no clash, the function returns a list containing the input tableau t as its only element. Recall that this is interpreted by the calling function apply as a signal that the clash "rule" did not fire, and so other rules are checked.

Consider now the definition of the function clash in line 4. The value of the expression any check lst is **True** if, and only if, the function check returns true for at least one element of the list lst. The expression nodes t refers to the list of nodes in the tableau t, as defined by the **Tableau** data structure in Section 6.3. Thus the function clash works by calling check for each node of the tableau.

The function check detects contradictions in the label of the node it receives as its argument. Let us first look at the local definitions in the **where** clause. First, we define the value cs (line 13) to be the list of concept expressions in the label of the node. Next the auxiliary function checkPair is introduced, which returns true in the following two cases, corresponding to the clash patterns (b) and (c) above.

- The argument of the function is a pair of concepts where one concept is the negation of the other (lines 14 and 15).

- The argument is a pair of concepts of the form $(\geqslant k_1 R)$ and $(\leqslant k_2 R)$, in either order, where $k_1 > k_2$ (lines 16–19).

Note that the function checkPair returns true for a pair of concepts C and $\neg C$ only if C is an atomic concept. The reason is that our concepts are in negation normal form, and so negation can only occur directly in front of atomic concepts.[6]

In order to see how the function check operates, we need to get familiar with more Haskell language features. The operator || denotes to the Boolean *or* relation of two expressions that yield a value of type **Bool**. That is, the expression x || y is **True**, if either x or y evaluates to **True**. Similarly, the operator && denotes the Boolean *and* relation of its two operands.

The expression e `elem` lst evaluates to **True** if e is an element of the list lst, and to **False** otherwise. The function elem is an ordinary Haskell function which we made into an infix operator using the ` (open quote) signs. This can be done for any function: the expression f x y is equivalent to x `f` y. In fact, the same infix notation has already been used for the constructor functions `And`, `Or` and `Implies`.

The expression below, copied from lines 10–12, needs to be explained in more detail:

$$ [(c1,c2) \mid (c1 : c2s) \; \text{<-} \; tails \; cs, \; c2 \; \text{<-} \; c2s]. \qquad (6.1) $$

The function tails has not been encountered so far. This function returns a list consisting of all possible tails of a list, starting with the complete input list, and ending with the empty list. For instance, tails [1,2] evaluates to the list of lists [[1,2],[2],[]]. We use this function to obtain the tails of the concepts list found in a node. Each element of this list is matched *one by one* with the pattern (c1 : c2s); then each element of the list c2s is matched one by one with c2. The pairs (c1,c2) are collected for all possible matches.

---

[6] Our reasoning system would be more efficient if we could determine easily whether two composite concepts are negations of each other. To do so, at present, we need to negate one concept and convert the result to negation normal form. However, this is an expensive operation, and it does not pay off. If efficiency is of major concern then an alternative concept representation, the lexical normal form, see Subsection 7.9.2, may be used (see Exercise 6.28).

The notation $[\cdots \mid \cdots]$, used in (6.1), is called *list comprehension* and resembles mathematical set notation. The square brackets surrounding the list comprehension correspond to braces, the operator `<-` to the set membership operation $\in$ and lists to sets.

We will illustrate this with a simple example. Let us collect the set of pairs (x,y) such that $x,y \in \{1,2,3\}$ and $x > y$. This can be specified in the following way, using the conventional mathematical notation:

$$\{(x,y) \quad \mid \quad x \in \{1,2,3\}, y \in \{1,2,3\}, x > y\}.$$

This formula can be rewritten as a Haskell list comprehension with just a few syntactic modifications, as outlined above:

```
[(x,y) | x <- [1,2,3], y <- [1,2,3], x > y].
```

Now let us return to the list comprehension expression (6.1). This can be read in the following way: collect a list of (c1,c2) pairs, where c1 **:** c2s is an arbitrary element of the list of lists `tails cs` and c2 is an arbitrary element of the list c2s. Thus the expression (6.1) evaluates to a list of pairs composed of two elements of the list cs such that the first element in the pair appears before the second. Informally, if the list cs is viewed as a set S then (6.1) describes the set of all unordered pairs from S.

Let us now return to the definition of `check` in Figure 6.2, lines 9–12. First the function checks whether the label of the given node, cs, contains the bottom concept (line 9). Next, it applies the function `checkPair` (line 10) to all pairs of concepts occurring in cs. If either of these checks returns true, we have found a clash and the function `check` returns **True**.

An **import** declaration has to be included in the program, so that we can use the function `tails`. The declaration tells the compiler that the Haskell function `tails` is defined in the module **Data.List**:

```
import Data.List (tails)
```

Note that each import declaration has to be placed at the *beginning* of the source code.

Exercise 6.16: Consider our strategy for detecting inconsistencies.

(a) The implementation shown here is very eager in detecting clashes: a check is made after each transformation. Experiment with alternative implementations, e.g. where a check for clashes is made only after all deterministic transformations have been executed.

(b) Are there transformations which cannot bring inconsistencies to the surface? If yes, modify the program so that such transformations are not followed by clash detection.

6.6.2. The intersection rule

The $\sqcap$-rule performs a deterministic transformation. It looks for concept expressions of the form C `And` D in the labels of the tableau nodes and "unfolds" them. Formally, if $C \sqcap D \in \mathcal{L}(x)$ holds for a node x then the $\sqcap$-rule adds the concepts C and D to the $\mathcal{L}(x)$ label of node x, assuming that these concepts are not already present in the label.

We will implement a slight extension of this rule: we will look for concepts of the form

$$C_1 \sqcap \cdots \sqcap C_n, \qquad n \geq 2, \tag{6.2}$$

and extend the label of the node in question with the concepts $C_1, \ldots, C_n$. Note that the expression (6.2) can be parenthesised in various ways and thus has several representations in our implementation using the binary operator `And`. We assume that (6.2) is maximal in the following sense: none of the concepts $C_1, \ldots, C_n$ is an intersection. If C_i is a member of the above intersection (6.2), we will say that C_i is an *and-visible* component of this intersection concept.

The function `applyAnd` is responsible for performing the above transformation on the whole tableau:

```
-- applyAnd t = [t'], where tableau t' is derived from t by
-- applying the intersection rule to each node of t, i.e.
-- unfolding each and-visible concept in the node.
applyAnd :: TableauTransformation
applyAnd t = [t {nodes = map andRule (nodes t)}]
```

Functions of the type `TableauTransformation` require a tableau as their input argument and return a list of tableaux. In the case of `applyAnd` the return value is a singleton list which differs from the input only in the `nodes` field. We use the *record update syntax* to describe the changes necessary to obtain the new tableau record from the old record. This is done by writing down a *record expression* (the second occurrence of `t` in line 5) followed by the field names and values that we want to change, enclosed in braces. In this specific case, the `nodes` field of the tableau record is modified: its new value is produced by the function invocation `map andRule (nodes t)`. Recall that the function `map` applies the transformation prescribed in its first argument to all elements of its second, list, argument (see Section 6.5). Thus the new value of the `nodes` field is obtained by applying the function `andRule` to every node of the tableau. The other four fields of the tableau are copied from the input tableau `t`. This is true in general: in the value of a record update, all fields not present within braces get their values from the respective fields of the original record.

The bulk of the work is done by the function `andRule`, which executes the ⊓-rule for a single node. Note that if no node is changed by this function then `applyAnd` returns an unmodified tableau, thereby indicating that the intersection rule did not fire:

```
-- andRule n = a node obtained from n by extending the
-- label of n with the and-visible components of its
-- intersection concepts.
andRule :: Node -> Node
andRule n = n {concepts = usort (andRule' (concepts n))}
  where -- andRule' cs = the list of non-intersection concepts
        -- and and-visible concepts found in cs.
        andRule' [] = []
        andRule' (c:cs) = c : unfold c (andRule' cs)
          where -- unfold c as = the list of and-visible
                -- components of c prepended to as
                unfold (c1 `And` c2) as = unfold c1 (unfold c2 as)
                unfold c as = c : as
```

The only new function here is `usort` in line 5, which sorts the list in its argument and filters out duplicate elements. This means that all elements will be unique (i.e. occur exactly once) in the output list produced by `usort`. For example, the value of `usort [3,1,3,2]` is `[1,2,3]`. Haskell provides only the function `sort`, which does not remove duplicates: therefore we have to add `usort` ourselves. The implementation of the function `usort` will be discussed in Section 6.8, after the tableau algorithm has been presented.

The function call `andRule n` returns the node record n with all and-visible concepts (see above) occurring in the node label added to the label.

This function works as follows. In line 5 the auxiliary function `andRule'` is invoked with the list of concepts in the node n. Its task is to extend the list with all and-visible expressions occurring in it. This is done by returning a list containing the first concept c, the and-visible components of c and the recursively expanded list of the remaining concepts cs (line 9). The recursion in `andRule'` terminates when the unprocessed list becomes empty (line 8).

The function `unfold` is used to find the and-visible components. It is called by `andRule'` with a concept to unfold and the list of already expanded concepts (line 9). If the first argument of `unfold` is an intersection then it decomposes it and afterwards recursively processes both its components, adding them to the list as (line 12). Otherwise, the recursion stops and the first argument is prepended to the second, which contains the already expanded concept list (line 13).

In the last step of the processing, the function `usort` is used to remove the duplicate elements from the concept list collected by `andRule'` (line 5).

Note that we have ignored the firing condition, which prevents the application of the rule if the concepts being intersected are already present in the label. The main purpose of this condition is to disallow repeated application of the rule. We can omit this check because the second and later firings of the rule for the same expression do not change the tableau, as it never produces duplication in the node labels.

Exercise 6.17: Consider how **And** expressions are processed.

(a) Derive the type of the function `andRule'`.

(b) How would the execution of the program change if a single transformation unfolded only the topmost **And** expression instead of all visible ones? For what kind of input would this behaviour be favourable and when would it make the reasoning slower?

(c) Modify the implementation so that the ⊓-rule does not fire if all the and-visible concepts are already included in the label. Compare the performance of the two implementations.

6.6.3. The value restriction rule

If a concept of the form $\forall R.C$ appears in the label $\mathcal{L}(x)$ of node x, and x has an R-successor y such that the concept C is not present in the label $\mathcal{L}(y)$, then the $\forall$-rule inserts C into $\mathcal{L}(y)$.

Like the intersection rule, the $\forall$-rule is deterministic and affects only the nodes of the tableau. The implementation of this rule follows the usual pattern: first we define a function which applies the transformation to all nodes of the tableau passed to it:

```
1  -- applyAll t = [t'] where t' is a tableau state not more
2  -- constrained than t that contains all possible changes
3  -- resulting from the application of the "forall" rule.
4  applyAll :: TableauTransformation
5  applyAll t = [t {nodes = allRule (nodes t) (edges t)}]
```

Since the ∀-rule modifies only some node labels, it is only the `nodes` field of the tableau record which has to be changed. To produce the new node list we need to know both the node list and the edge list of the input tableau. Accordingly, these two pieces of information are extracted from the tableau data structure and passed to the function `allRule` which does the main work.

Before looking at `allRule`, let us define a couple of auxiliary functions. Sometimes we need to look up nodes using their identifiers. This is done by the function `findNode`; the other function is `removeNode`, which is used when a given node has to be deleted from the tableau:

```
1   -- findNode ns id = the list of nodes that contains those
2   -- elements of the node list ns whose identifier is id.
3   findNode :: [Node] -> Id -> [Node]
4   findNode ns id = filter f ns
5     where f n = nid n == id
6
7   -- removeNode ns id = the list of nodes obtained from ns by
8   -- omitting the nodes with identifier id.
9   removeNode :: [Node] -> Id -> [Node]
10  removeNode ns id = filter f ns
11    where f n = nid n /= id
```

The expression `filter f lst` applies the function f, which returns a **Bool** value, to each element of the list `lst` and returns the list of elements where f evaluates to true. For instance,

$$\text{filter (> 2) [2,3,4]} \rightarrow \text{[3,4]}.$$

Thus the function `findNode` returns the list of nodes whose identifier is equal to `id`.[7] The function `removeNode` has a complementary task: `removeNode ns id` returns the list of those nodes in `ns` whose identifier is different from `id`.

Since node identifiers are unique in this program, the value of `findNode ns id` is a list of at most one element: if there is no node with the identifier `id`, it returns an empty list; otherwise it returns the node with the identifier `id` made into a singleton list. Thus we can use the function `findNode` to check whether a node with a given identifier is present in the tableau and to get hold of the node in question if the answer is positive.

Let us now implement the function `allRule` (see Figure 6.3). When the expression `allRule ns es` is evaluated, it considers each node in the list `ns` and extends the label

---

[7] In several places the program refers to the identifiers of the nodes using the name `id`, which is a built-in function in Haskell. The original definition is hidden by our declaration. Since we do not use the function `id`, this does not pose any problems for us.

```
 1  -- allRule ns es = the list of nodes obtained by applying
 2  -- the value restriction rule to all "forall" concepts in
 3  -- all nodes of the tableau whose list of nodes is ns
 4  -- and whose list of edges is es.
 5  allRule :: [Node] -> [Edge] -> [Node]
 6  allRule ns es = if null toDo then ns else allRule ns' es
 7   where -- toDo = the list of firings of the rule.
 8          toDo = [x | e <- es, n <- ns,
 9                      parentNode n e, x <- needAll e n]
10          -- parentNode n e = true, iff the node n is the starting
11          -- point of the directed edge e.
12          parentNode n e = nid n == parentId e
13          -- needAll e n = list of (id,c) pairs specifying that the
14          -- concept c has to be added to the label of the node with
15          -- identifier id. The identifier points to the end point
16          -- of edge e.
17          needAll e n = [(cid,d) | c <- concepts n, d <- match e c,
18                                   d `notElem` ccs]
19              where cid = childId e
20                    ccs = concepts (head (findNode ns cid))
21          -- match e c = [d], if c is a concept of the form
22          -- (All r d), where role r is the label of edge e,
23          -- [] otherwise.
24          match e (All r d) = if r == role e then [d] else []
25          match _ _ = []
26          -- ns' = the list of nodes ns with the concepts
27          -- specified in toDo added to the corresponding labels.
28          ns' = foldl op ns toDo
29          op ns idC = map (insert idC) ns
30          -- insert (id,c) n = if the identifier of node n is id,
31          -- then insert the concept c into n's label, otherwise
32          -- leave n unchanged. Return the possibly modified node.
33          insert (id,c) n0 = if nid n0 == id
34                             then n0 {concepts = c : concepts n0}
35                             else n0
```

Figure 6.3. Applying the value restriction rule to the nodes of a tableau.

of the node by concepts, as required by the ∀-rule. To apply the ∀-rule, we have to consider successor nodes. Therefore, the edges of the tableau are supplied in the `es` argument.

When the ∀-rule extends the label of a node, it can make this rule applicable to another node. For instance, if the node x contains $\forall R.\forall R.C$ in its label and there exists an R-successor, say y, for which the rule fires then `allRule` first adds the concept $\forall R.C$ to the label of y. This opens the possibility of applying the value restriction rule to y: the concept C has to be added to the label of the R-successors of y wherever necessary. If C itself is a value restriction, the recursion continues even further. All these changes are performed by the implementation of `allRule`.

Accordingly, `allRule` is a recursive function. The recursion goes on as long as there exists a concept of the form $\forall R.C$ in the label of a node that has an R-successor without the concept C in its label. Such concepts are collected in the list `toDo`. The decision about terminating or continuing the recursion is made in line 6. If `toDo` is empty then the function terminates and returns the list of nodes in the tableau, which might have been transformed by previous calls of `allRule` in the **else** branch.

Before discussing further details of `allRule`, we introduce the function `foldl` used in line 28. This is a generalisation of the function `foldl1` described in Section 6.5. Let us see how `foldl` works by looking at a simple example. We define the function `op`, which calculates the sum of its integer and Boolean arguments, interpreting **True** as 1 and **False** as 0:

```
op :: Int -> Bool -> Int
op x y = if y then x + 1 else x
```

The function `foldl` differs from `foldl1` in that it takes an initial value whose type may be different from that of the list elements. This is the case when we want to calculate the sum of a list of Boolean values:

foldl op 0 [**True,False**] $\rightarrow$ op (op 0 **True**) **False** $\rightarrow$ op 1 **False** $\rightarrow$ 1.

Generally, if the initial value `start` in the call `foldl op start lst` has the same type as the elements of `lst`, then the expression `foldl1 op (start:lst)` can be used instead. Since a list cannot hold elements of different types, the above example, in which the sum of Booleans is calculated, cannot be implemented using the function `foldl1`.

Let us now return to the function `allRule`. The simpler local functions can be understood from the program code and the head comments. The more complex functions are explained below in detail.

- The function `needAll` is called with an edge `e` and a node `n` as its arguments. Here `n` is the starting point of `e`; see `parentNode n e` in line 9. The function `needAll` collects those concepts that have to be added to the label of the endpoint of `e` by an application of the $\forall$-rule. The function returns a list of pairs of the form (ID, C), where ID is the identifier of the endpoint of `e` and C is the concept to be added to the label of this endpoint. The function is defined using a list comprehension (lines 17 and 18), which works as follows. All concepts in the label of node `n` are processed one by one. We look for a concept `c` for which the expression `match e c` produces a non-empty list (line 17), i.e. where `c` is of the form **All** `r d` and `r` is the label of the edge `e`. Then, in line 18, we check that concept `d` does not occur in the list `ccs`, which contains the concepts found in the label of the child node of edge `e`. Note that the built-in Haskell function `notElem` is the negation of the function `elem` presented earlier: e `notElem` lst returns **True** if, and only if, `e` is not an element of the list `lst`.

  The function `needAll` uses two local definitions: `cid` denotes the identifier of the child node of edge `e`, while `ccs` (*child concepts*) is the list of concepts found in the label of the child node of edge `e`. Since Haskell is a lazy language, these local definitions are only calculated if necessary, i.e. if the generator expressions in line 17 produce results.

- The function `match` (lines 24 and 25) either returns a singleton list or an empty list. This enables it to serve a double purpose in the list comprehension in lines 17 and 18: first, it refuses to deal with a concept unless it is an **All** expression with the required role; second, it delivers the concept d to be added to the child node.

- In order to obtain the toDo list (lines 8 and 9), we consider each node n and each edge e such that n is the starting point of e. For each such node and edge we invoke the function needAll and collect the pairs x returned by all invocations of needAll in the list toDo. Consequently, this list contains all pairs (ID, C) such that concept C is to be added to the label of the node with the identifier ID.

- Our final task is to obtain the list of transformed nodes: we have to add each concept appearing in the toDo list to the label of the appropriate node. In line 29 we define an auxiliary function op, which takes two arguments: the list of tableau nodes and an element of the toDo list. This auxiliary function performs the task "to be done": it adds the specified concept to the appropriate node label. In line 28 we use the function foldl to process all elements of the toDo list. The output of this process is the node list ns', which is then used in the recursive invocation of allRule in line 6.

6.6.4. The at-most restriction rule

The $\leqslant$-rule is one of the two non-deterministic $\mathcal{ALCN}$ transformation rules. If the label of the node x contains the concept $(\leqslant kR)$ and x has R-successors $y_1, y_2, \ldots, y_{k+1}$ then the $\leqslant$-rule prescribes that two of these R-successors should be identified. This is to be done in a non-deterministic way, considering all possible identifications as alternative choices.

We will use a generalisation of this rule: if a node label contains a concept of the form $(\leqslant kR)$ and, at the same time, the node has n R-successors $(n > k)$ then several pairs of R-successors are identified (in all possible ways), so that only k R-successors remain.

It is obvious that the original rule is a special case, for $n = k + 1$, of the general case. However, the effect of the general rule can be achieved by repeated application of the original rule. This shows that the generalisation is similar to that used for the $\forall$-rule, in Section 6.6.3: each generalisation covers several consecutive applications of the same rule.

We can reduce the task of finding appropriate node identifications to a graph-colouring problem. Let x be a node whose label contains a concept $(\leqslant kR)$ and to which the $\leqslant$-rule is to be applied. We build an undirected graph, the nodes of which are the R-successors of x. There is an edge between two successors y and z if $y \dot{\neq} z$ or $z \dot{\neq} y$ holds, i.e. if the two successors are non-identifiable. We will set ourselves the task of colouring this graph with exactly k colours. This means that each node is assigned one of the k colours in such a way that neighbouring nodes (i.e. those connected by an edge) have different colours and each colour is assigned to at least one node.

Having obtained such a colouring, solving the identification task is easy: we identify two nodes if they have the same colour. Because of the way in which the graph is constructed, nodes with the same colour are identifiable. Because exactly k colours are used, exactly k successors remain after identification. We will use the term *colour partition* or simply *partition* to denote a set of nodes with a given colour.

We use the function colourings for graph colouring. It is invoked by an expression of the form colourings k ns es, where ns is the list of node identifiers, es is the list of edges of the undirected graph to be coloured and k is the number of colours. The edge list es contains pairs of node identifiers, where the smaller identifier is always the first member of the pair. The function `colourings` colours the given graph with *exactly* k colours in all possible ways. The value returned by the function is the list of all possible *colourings*. We will call this list a *colouring choice*. Each colouring is itself a list whose elements correspond to *colour partitions*. A colour partition is represented by the list of node identifiers that make up the partition.

Let us demonstrate an example invocation of the function `colourings`, in which a graph containing three nodes and a single edge is coloured using two colours:

$$\text{colourings 2 [1,2,3] [(1,2)].}$$

The nodes with identifiers 1 and 2 obviously end up in different colour partitions, since they are neighbours. The node with identifier 3 is isolated: therefore it can go into the partition of either 1 or 2. At the end the function `colourings` returns a colouring choice which is a list with two elements, `[[[3,1],[2]],[[3,2],[1]]]`. Here each element describes a colouring. A colouring such as `[[3,1],[2]]`, is a list of colour partitions, each listing nodes of the same colour; so this particular colouring assigns the first colour to nodes 3 and 1 and the second colour to node 2.

It is not always possible to colour a graph using k colours. The example above would have no solutions if we tried to use only a single colour. In such a case the function `colourings` returns an empty list, as the set of possible colourings is empty.

We will not discuss further the details of the function `colourings` at this point; its implementation can be found in Section 6.8, where auxiliary functions are discussed.

Let us assume that the concept expression $(\leqslant kR)$ appears in the label of node x. In order to perform the identifications possible using the graph-colouring algorithm or to ascertain that there is no need for identifications, we need to generate the R-successors of x. This is implemented in the following function, using a simple list comprehension:

```
1  -- successors pid r t = the list of node identifiers in
2  -- the tableau t that are the r-successors of the node with
3  -- identifier pid ("parent identifier").
4  successors :: Int -> RoleName -> Tableau -> [Id]
5  successors pid r t =
6                 [childId e | e <- edges t, match e]
7     where match (Edge pid' r' _) = pid == pid' && r == r'
```

Let us briefly recollect the tasks to be performed when two nodes are identified (see Figure 5.4): one node is removed from the tableau and the other, which we call the *new* node, inherits the concepts and edges of the removed node. Furthermore, the set of inequalities has to be updated: each occurrence of the removed node is replaced by the new node.

The task of identifying two nodes is performed by the function `identifyNodes` (see Figure 6.4), which receives two node identifiers and a tableau data structure. The function carries out the identification of the specified nodes and returns a pair containing the identifier of the new node together with the modified tableau.

Because the task of identification involves the merging of sets of concepts and edges, the function `identifyNodes` relies on the function `usort` presented in Subsection 6.8.1, which sorts a list and removes duplicate elements.

In line 6 of Figure 6.4 we specify that `id1` is the identifier of the new node. In lines 6–8 we build the modified tableau. Its node list contains the new node n, followed by the list

```
1   -- identifyNodes id1 id2 t = a pair (id,t'), where t' is the
2   -- tableau obtained from t by identifying nodes specified by
3   -- id1 and id2, and id is the identifier of the new node.
4   identifyNodes :: Id -> Id -> Tableau -> (Id,Tableau)
5   identifyNodes id1 id2 t =
6           (id1,t {nodes = n : ns',
7                   edges = usort (map modifyEdge (edges t)),
8                   ineqs = usort (map modifyIneq (ineqs t))})
9       where -- n = The node obtained by identifying n1 and n2.
10          n = n1 {concepts = usort (concepts n1 ++ concepts n2)}
11          -- n1, n2: the nodes with identifiers id1 and id2.
12          ([n1],[n2]) = (findNode ns id1,findNode ns id2)
13          ns = nodes t
14          ns' = removeNode (removeNode ns id2) id1
15          -- modifyEdge e = if either end of the edge is the node
16          -- with identifier id2, then it is replaced by id1 in
17          -- the return value. Otherwise the return value
18          -- equals e.
19          modifyEdge :: Edge -> Edge
20          modifyEdge e =
21              if      parentId e == id2 then e {parentId = id1}
22              else if childId  e == id2 then e {childId = id1}
23                  else e
24          -- modifyIneq (x,y): if one of the elements of (x,y)
25          -- is id2, then it is changed to id1, and the elements
26          -- are swapped if necessary to have the smaller value
27          -- in the first place.
28          modifyIneq :: (Id,Id) -> (Id,Id)
29          modifyIneq (x,y) =
30              if x == id2 then pair id1 y
31              else if y == id2 then pair id1 x else (x,y)
```

Figure 6.4. Identifying two nodes of a tableau.

ns', which is obtained from the node list of the original tableau by removing the nodes to be identified (see lines 13 and 14). The new node n is built in line 10, inheriting all its fields from the node n1, with the exception of the concepts field (the node label): this is the union of the concepts in nodes n1 and n2. The latter two nodes are to be identified: these are retrieved from the node list ns in line 12. Note that the union of concept sets is obtained by concatenation, followed by an invocation of usort to remove duplicates (line 10).

In lines 7 and 8 we build the edges and the inequalities of the modified tableau. To obtain these we first apply an appropriate function to each edge and inequality of the old tableau (modifyEdge and modifyIneq, respectively). These functions replace the occurrences of id2 by id1 in the data structures concerned. Because such changes can result in duplicates, the function usort is applied again.

The functions for modifying edges and inequalities are defined in lines 19–23 and 28–31, respectively. Both functions are fairly straightforward. The function `modifyIneq` is the more involved of the two. It relies on an auxiliary function `pair`, shown below, which builds a pair of node identifiers so that our invariant for inequality pairs is observed, i.e. the smaller of the two identifiers is the first element of the pair:

```
1 -- pair x y = the pair containing x and y such that the first
2 -- element of the pair is not greater than the second element.
3 pair :: Id -> Id -> (Id,Id)
4 pair x y = if x < y then (x,y) else (y,x)
```

Recall that our graph-colouring algorithm collects the nodes to be identified in lists called colour partitions. Because of this, it is useful to define an operation that performs the identification for a set of nodes. The function `identifyNodeList` takes a tableau and a list of node identifiers and returns a new tableau in which the given nodes are identified:

```
1 -- identifyNodeList t ids = a tableau derived from t by
2 -- identifying the nodes specified by a list of identifiers ids.
3 identifyNodeList :: Tableau -> [Id] -> Tableau
4 identifyNodeList t [] = t
5 identifyNodeList t (id : ids) = t'
6     where (_,t') = foldl op (id,t) ids
7           op (id1,t) id2 = identifyNodes id1 id2 t
```

If the list of identifiers is empty then the tableau is left unchanged, since there are no nodes to be identified (line 4). If the list of identifiers is not empty then the identifications are performed one by one using the function `foldl` (lines 6 and 7). Note that the function `op`, used for folding, takes a pair of the form `(id1,t)` as its argument, where `id1` represents the last new node produced in the process of identification. This node identifier is thrown away when the final output of `foldl` is processed; see the use of `_` in line 6.

In Figure 6.5 we present the function `applyAtMost`, which implements the $\leqslant$-rule. It uses the auxiliary functions presented above as well as the built-in Haskell function `minimum`, which returns the smallest element of a list.

The implementation of the function `applyAtMost` relies on the `toDo` list constructed in lines 8–11. The list comprehension, appearing within the value of `toDo`, collects triples of the form `(id,k,r)`. Each such triple represents an occurrence of an at-most restriction **AtMost** k r in the label of a node whose identifier is `id`. The invocation of `foldl` in line 8 passes each such triple to the function `needAtMost`. The task of this function is to generate a colouring choice if the triple at hand refers to a node–concept pair for which the $\leqslant$-rule should fire. The return value of `foldl` is thus the list of all applicable colouring choices, which is deposited in the variable `toDo`.

Before looking at the definition of `needAtMost`, let us discuss how the `toDo` list is used in lines 5–7. If this list is empty, no $\leqslant$-rule can fire and so the transformation rule returns the original tableau in a singleton list (line 5). If `toDo` contains an element that is an empty list then we return an empty list, indicating a clash (line 6), because an empty colouring choice means that it is impossible to identify enough nodes for the given at-most restriction to be satisfied. Finally, if we have a non-empty list of non-empty colouring

```
1  -- applyAtMost t = the list of tableau states derived from t
2  -- by applying an at-most transformation, which results in
3  -- the least number of non-deterministic branches.
4  applyAtMost :: TableauTransformation
5  applyAtMost t = if null toDo then [t]
6                   else if any null toDo then []
7                        else atMostRule (minimum (map lpair toDo))
8      where toDo = foldl needAtMost [] [(nid n,k,r) |
9                                        n <- nodes t,
10                                       AtMost k r <- concepts n
11                                      ]
12         -- needAtMost ccs (id,k,r) = a list of colouring choices
13         -- which includes the list ccs, as well as the
14         -- colouring choice obtained for the k-colouring of the
15         -- r-successors of node id in the tableau t, if the
16         -- number of r-successors of node id is more than k.
17         needAtMost ccs (id,k,r) =
18             if length rss <= k then ccs
19             else (colourings k rss (ineqs t)) : ccs
20               where rss = successors id r t
21         -- lpair lst = a pair whose first element is the length
22         -- of the list lst and whose second element is lst itself.
23         lpair lst = (length lst,lst)
24         -- atMostRule (l,cc) = list of tableau states derived
25         -- from tableau t by applying the node identification
26         -- transformations specified by each colouring
27         -- in the colouring choice cc
28         atMostRule (_,cc) = map (foldl identifyNodeList t) cc
```

Figure 6.5.   Applying the at-most restriction rule to a tableau.

choices then we choose the one which has the smallest number of elements (line 7). This is accomplished by first pairing each colouring choice with its length (see the function `lpair` defined in line 23) and then using the function `minimum` to obtain the shortest colouring choice.

Exercise 6.18: Note that the function `applyAtMost` is capable of detecting any violations of the clash condition (c) in Subsection 6.6.1. Remove the code dealing with condition (c) from the function `clash` and check whether this improves the efficiency of the reasoner.

The shortest colouring choice `cc` is passed to the function `atMostRule`, defined in line 28. This function builds a new tableau state for each colouring contained in `cc` by applying the function `identifyNodeList` to each partition in the colouring.

Finally let us discuss the function `needAtMost`, as shown in lines 17–20. It receives a list `ccs`, the colouring choices collected so far, and a triple `(id,k,r)`. First it collects the r-successors of the node with identifier `id` in the variable `rss` (line 20). If there are no more than `k` such successors then no new colouring choice has to be added, so `ccs` is returned unmodified (line 18). Otherwise, a colouring choice is obtained from the function colourings[8] and the function needAtMost returns the list ccs extended with this new colouring choice.

Exercise 6.19: In the current implementation the function applyAtMost chooses a node which gives rise to the minimal number of non-deterministic choices. Experiment with other heuristics.

Exercise 6.20: Implement the ⩽-rule according to the original definition. Compare the behaviour of the two versions.

6.6.5. The union rule

If a node label contains an expression of the form $C \sqcup D$ but neither C nor D occurs in the label on its own then we have to unfold this concept. This involves generating two tableaux using the non-deterministic union rule: the label containing the concept $C \sqcup D$ is extended with C in the first tableaux and with D in the second. This rule is implemented by the function applyOr (Figure 6.6).

First the function searches for nodes where the firing conditions of the ⊔-rule hold. Appropriate node–concept pairs are collected in the toDo list (lines 5–7). If this list is empty then the original tableau, made into a singleton list, is returned in line 13, indicating that the rule

```
1   -- applyOr t = the list of tableau states derived from t by
2   -- a single application of the union rule, if it is possible to apply this rule.
3   applyOr :: TableauTransformation
4   applyOr t = transform toDo
5     where toDo = [(n,c) | n <- nodes t,
6                      c <- concepts n, orConcept c (concepts n)
7                   ]
8         -- Verify the firing conditions of the union rule.
9         orConcept (c1 `Or` c2) cs =
10            (c1 `notElem` cs) && (c2 `notElem` cs)
11        orConcept _ _ = False
12        -- Perform a single union rule, if applicable.
13        transform [] = [t]
14        transform ((n,c1 `Or` c2) : _) =
15          [t {nodes = n1 : nodes'}, t {nodes = n2 : nodes'}]
16            where n1 = n {concepts = c1 : cs}
17                  n2 = n {concepts = c2 : cs}
18                  cs = concepts n
19                  nodes' = removeNode (nodes t) (nid n)
```

Figure 6.6. Applying the union rule to a tableau.

---

[8] Note that, in line 19, the expression (ineqs t) is supplied as the list of edges of the graph to be coloured. This list contains all distinct node pairs, not just those occurring in the successor list rss. This is not a problem, as the function colourings is not sensitive to such superfluous edges.

did not fire. If the `toDo` list has at least one element, we perform the union transformation for the first node–concept pair in the list (node n and concept c1 `` `Or` `` c2 in line 14). As prescribed by the ⊔-rule, we return a list of two tableaux (line 15). These two tableaux differ only in the first node of their node list: in the first tableau this node is derived from n by adding the concept c1 to its label, while in the second the concept c2 is added (lines 16 and 17).

Recall that Haskell is a lazy language. This means that no elements of the `toDo` list are generated after the first has been obtained, as the remaining elements are discarded (see the use of the character _ in line 14).

Note that the function `applyOr` performs just one possible transformation out of the many that are possible. This is in contrast with most earlier transformation functions, which were asked to do as much work as possible. The reason for the change is to allow other rules to be executed before the next union rule is applied. For example, detecting a clash as early as possible can save a lot of unnecessary computation.

We have not used any heuristics or optimisation techniques in this implementation of the union rule. However, it must be noted that an efficient implementation of this rule is vital, because the size of the search space depends to a great extent on the number of choice points created by this rule.

To conclude this subsection we will show how simple it is to add the optimisation technique called *semantic branching* to the source code in Figure 6.6. This technique will be discussed in Subsection 7.9.5. In order to apply this optimisation, only a single line of the code has to be modified. In lines 16 and 17 we build the two nodes, n1 and n2, in which the two tableaux produced by the union rule differ:

```
16  n1 = n {concepts = c1 : cs}
17  n2 = n {concepts = c2 : cs}
```

To introduce semantic branching we add the negation of the first member of the union, c1, brought to negation normal form, to the label of the node n2:

```
16  n1 = n {concepts = c1 : cs}
17  n2 = n {concepts = nnf (Not c1) : c2 : cs}.
```

Exercise 6.21: Modify the program so that the function `applyOr` applies the ⊔-rule transformation on all nodes where this is possible, and compare its behaviour with the original version.

6.6.6. The existential restriction rule

The final two rules to be discussed are *expansion rules*, i.e. rules that add new nodes and edges to the tableau. To prepare for this, let us implement a function which extends a tableau with a new edge and returns the extended tableau (Figure 6.7).

```
1  -- newEdge t dnodes pid r c = the tableau derived from t by adding
2  -- a new r-successor to the node with the identifier pid, where
3  -- the label of the r-successor contains the concept c. Also,
4  -- the list of the inequalities of the tableau is extended so
5  -- that the new node is distinct from any of the nodes
6  -- whose identifiers are supplied in the list dnodes.
7  newEdge ::
8      Tableau -> [Id] -> Id -> RoleName -> Concept -> Tableau
9  newEdge t dnodes pid r c =
10     t {nodes = n : nodes t, edges = e : edges t,
11        nextId = newid + 1, ineqs = ineqs'
12       }
13     where n = Node newid [c,tboxConcept t]
14           e = Edge pid r newid
15           newid = nextId t
16           -- The list of inequalities of the tableau t is extended
17           -- with pairs (newid,id'), for each id' in dnodes.
18           ineqs' = addIneqs newid (ineqs t) dnodes
19
20  -- addIneqs id ieqs ids = inequalities ieqs extended with all
21  -- (id,id') pairs where id' is an arbitrary element of ids.
22  addIneqs :: Id -> [(Id,Id)] -> [Id] -> [(Id,Id)]
23  addIneqs id = foldl op
24      where op x id' = (id',id) : x
```

Figure 6.7. Adding a new edge to a tableau.

The function newEdge has the following arguments:

- t denotes the tableau which is to be extended with a new node;

- dnodes is a list containing the identifiers of the nodes that have to be made distinct from the new node;

- pid is the identifier of the parent of the new node;

- r is to be used as the role label of the edge running from the node pid to the new node;

- c is the concept which is to be placed in the label of the new node and which is assumed to be in negation normal form.

We build the new tableau in lines 10–12 of Figure 6.7. Here, the node list is extended with the new node n, the new edge e is added to the edge list, the nextId field is incremented by 1 and the inequalities field is set to ineqs'. The variables used here are defined in the **where** clause in lines 13–18.

To build the new node n in line 13, we use the constructor function **Node**, as supplied in the definition of the node datatype, followed by the expressions providing the values of the fields. Note that the second field, i.e. the list of concepts to appear in the label of the node, contains the concepts c and tboxConcept, where the latter is the internalised form of the TBox axioms. The new edge is built in line 14, using the constructor function **Edge**.

The new set of inequalities, `ineqs'`, is built in line 18 using the auxiliary function `addIneqs`, as defined in lines 23 and 24. It is interesting to note that the last two arguments are not named in the code of this function, since `addIneqs` is simply defined as the repeated application (by means of the function `foldl`) of the operation `op` specified in line 24. Also note that the inequality invariant is automatically ensured by our placing the new node identifier as the second member of the inequality pair. The reason is that the new node identifier is larger than any of the older ones, and thus the first member of the inequality pair is bound to be smaller than the second.

This concludes the discussion of the function `newEdge` which is to be used in both expansion rules. Let us now deal with the first of these, the ∃-rule.

For the ∃-rule to fire we need a node x whose label contains a concept of the form $∃R.C$ and which does not have an R-successor y such that $C \in \mathcal{L}(y)$. When the rule fires, a new R-successor is created for x, with a label containing the concept C (in addition to the internalisation concept, to be placed in each new node). The ∃-rule is implemented as the function `applyExists` in Figure 6.8.

```
1   -- applyExists t = a list containing a single tableau state
2   -- derived from t by applying the exists rule at all nodes
3   -- where the rule is applicable.
4   applyExists :: TableauTransformation
5   applyExists t = [foldl makeEdgeAndNode t toDo]
6     where ns = nodes t
7           es = edges t
8           -- toDo = a list of pairs (id,exc), where id is
9           -- the identifier of a node whose label contains
10          -- the existential concept exc, for which
11          -- the exists rule has to be applied.
12          toDo = [(nid n,c) | n <- ns, nonBlocked n ns es,
13                  c <- concepts n, match n c
14                  ]
15          -- match n c = true iff the exist rule fires for
16          -- the concept c appearing in the label of node n.
17          match :: Node -> Concept -> Bool
18          match n (Exists r c1) =
19              all (notElem c1)
20                  [(concepts node) |
21                   id' <- successors (nid n) r t,
22                   node <- findNode ns id'
23                  ]
24          match _ _ = False
25          -- makeEdgeAndNode t (id,exc) = the tableau derived
26          -- from t by the application of the exists rule for
27          -- the concept exc and the node with the identifier id.
28          makeEdgeAndNode t (id,Exists r c) =
29              newEdge t [] id r c
```

Figure 6.8. Applying the existential restriction rule to a tableau.

Just as for some of the previous transformations, the function `applyExists` first collects a `toDo` list: see lines 12–14. The elements of this list specify the changes to be made to the tableau. Changes are performed by the function (`foldl makeEdgeAndNode`) (line 5), where the function `makeEdgeAndNode` executes the ∃-rule for a single node and concept; see lines 28 and 29.

The built-in function `all`, used in line 19 within the function `match`, requires some explanation. It can be invoked in the form `all f lst`, where `f` is a function returning a **Bool** value and `lst` is a list whose elements have the same type as the argument of `f`. The expression `all f lst` is true if, and only if, for each element `x` of the list `lst` the expression `f x` evaluates to **True**.

Let us now discuss the function `match`, defined in lines 18–24. This function takes a node `n` and a concept `c` appearing in the label of `n`. The function decides whether the ∃-rule is applicable for the concept `c` at the node `n`. To accomplish this, it checks that `c` is of the form **Exists** `r c1` (line 18) and furthermore that `c1` does not appear in the label of any `r`-successor of `n` (lines 19–23). The latter condition is checked by the function `all`, whose second argument is the list comprehension in lines 20–23, which evaluates to the list of the labels of all `r`-successors of `n`.

Finally, we discuss how the `toDo` list is built in lines 12–14. First we simply enumerate all the nodes, selecting those that are not blocked (line 12). Next we enumerate all the concepts in the node label and check, by means of the function `match` (line 13), whether the ∃-rule is applicable. As regards blocking, we use the function `nonBlocked`, which is responsible for implementing subset blocking (as defined in Subsection 5.4.2). This function will be presented in Section 6.7. For the present, it is enough to know that the value of the expression `nonBlocked n ns es` is true if, and only if, the node with identifier `n` is not blocked in the tableau containing the nodes `ns` and the edges `es`.

Exercise 6.22: Modify the program so that the function `applyExists` applies the ∃-rule transformation on only a single node, and compare the behaviour of the modified version with the original version.

6.6.7. The at-least restriction rule

The firing condition of the ⩾-rule (see Figure 5.10) requires that there is a node x in the tableau such that: its label $\mathcal{L}(x)$ contains the concept $(\geqslant k R)$; x is not blocked; and x has fewer than k *distinct* (i.e. non-identifiable) R-successors. If this is the case then the ⩾-rule generates k R-successors of x such that the $\neq$ relation holds between any two of them, i.e. the newly generated nodes are pairwise distinct.

In the implementation we use a slightly different firing condition; the requirement

$$\text{"}x \text{ has fewer than } k \text{ } distinct \text{ } R\text{-successors"} \tag{6.3}$$

is replaced by the condition

$$\text{"}x \text{ has fewer than } k \text{ } R\text{-successors".} \tag{6.4}$$

If the new condition (6.4) holds then so does the original version, but this is not true the other way round. It is easy to see that this change does not break the tableau algorithm. Since the new version fires less often than the original version, it is obvious that the termination and completeness of the algorithm still hold. To ensure its soundness, one has to show that model construction still works when the new firing condition is used. This is left to the reader, via the following exercise.

Exercise 6.23: Reconsider Exercise 5.20. Solve task (d) of this exercise for the case when the firing condition (6.3) for the ⩾-rule is replaced by (6.4).

We now proceed to discuss the function `applyAtLeast` (see Figure 6.9), implementing the at-least rule. To understand how the function works, let us first examine the local definitions, starting at line 6. In lines 6 and 7 we extract the node and edge lists from the tableau `t` and store them in the variables `ns` and `es`.

The `toDo` list in line 10 holds triples of the form `(id,r,k)`, such that `id` is the identifier of a node containing a concept **AtLeast** `k r` to which the ⩾-rule should be applied. The list comprehension defining the value of the `toDo` variable works as follows. We consider an arbitrary node `n` of the tableau which is not blocked (line 11). Next, we check that the label of `n` contains a concept of the form **AtLeast** `k r` (line 12). Finally we check the remaining firing condition, namely that the node `n` has fewer than `k r`-successors (line 13) using the function `successor` defined in Subsection 6.6.4.

```
1   -- applyAtLeast t = a list containing a single tableau state
2   -- derived from t by applying the at-least restriction
3   -- rule everywhere possible
4   applyAtLeast :: TableauTransformation
5   applyAtLeast t = [foldl (addEdge []) t toDo]
6       where ns = nodes t
7             es = edges t
8             -- toDo = the list of the successor nodes to create,
9             -- each as a triple (identifier,edge label,count)
10            toDo = [(nid n,r,k) |
11                    n <- ns, nonBlocked n ns es,
12                    AtLeast k r <- concepts n,
13                    k > length (successors (nid n) r t)
14                   ]
15            -- addEdge dnodes t (pid,r,k) =
16            -- tableau t after adding k successor nodes that
17            -- are connected to the node with identifier pid by
18            -- edges with r in their label. The new nodes are
19            -- pairwise distinct and also distinct from all the
20            -- nodes in the list dnodes.
21            addEdge dnodes t (pid,r,k) =
22                if k < 1 then t
23                else addEdge (nextId t : dnodes) t' (pid,r,k - 1)
24                where t' = newEdge t dnodes pid r Top
```

Figure 6.9. Applying the at-least restriction rule to a tableau.

The toDo list is used in line 5. It is processed by the function foldl (addEdge []), i.e. by repeatedly applying the function that is the result of the invocation of addEdge on the empty list. The function addEdge is defined in lines 21–24. It takes three arguments:

- dnodes, the list of successors generated so far;

- t, the tableau to which the transformation is to be applied; and

- (pid,r,k), a triple specifying the edges to add to the tableau.

Since foldl in line 5 uses the partial application addEdge [], dnodes is initially empty; only the recursive invocations receive a non-empty list in the dnodes argument.

The function addEdge uses the function newEdge, see line 24, to add one new edge and then calls itself recursively (line 23) to add the remaining edges. Here, we make use of the fact that the new node added by newEdge t ... has the identifier nextId t. This expression is used in line 23 when extending dnodes, the list of successor nodes.

Exercise 6.24: Modify the program so that the function applyAtLeast applies the transformation on only one node, and compare the behaviour of the modified version with the original version.

6.7. Blocking

In this section we present the implementation of *subset blocking* used in the $\mathcal{ALCN}$ tableau algorithm. We showed in Subsection 5.4.2 that subset blocking ensures the termination of the $\mathcal{ALCN}$ tableau algorithm in the presence of a non-empty TBox.

Let us recall the definition of subset blocking. A node y is considered blocked if it has an ancestor x in the tableau such that the label $\mathcal{L}(y)$ is the subset of the label $\mathcal{L}(x)$. Transformation rules that add new nodes to the tableau are not applied to blocked nodes.

The notion of blocking involves solely the nodes and edges of the tableau state. Therefore, the two main functions defined in this section have arguments ns and es, denoting the nodes and edges of the tableau state in question. When referring to these two arguments we will often use the phrase "the tableau specified by ns and es".

In order to determine whether the blocking condition holds for a node, we need to generate the list of its ancestor nodes (as defined in Subsection 5.4.3). This is accomplished by the function ancestors shown in Figure 6.10.

The function ancestors relies on the local function ancestorIds, which collects the list of identifiers of the ancestor nodes. Given this, the list of ancestor nodes is computed in a straightforward way by the list comprehension in lines 4–6, which relies on the function findNode to convert a node identifier to the corresponding node.

The function ancestorIds is defined in lines 9–16. It receives a node identifier id and returns the list of identifiers of its ancestors. In line 15 we collect the list of the parents of id, which is bound to have at most one element (as the tableau graph is a tree). Line 9 states that if the node in question has no parents then it has no ancestors either. In line 10 we handle the case when the node id does have a parent: we build a list the head of which is the identifier of the parent while the tail is the list of ancestor identifiers of the parent, calculated by a recursive invocation of the function ancestorIds. When calculating the

```
1  -- ancestors n ns es = the list of ancestors of n
2  -- in the tableau specified by ns and es.
3  ancestors :: Node -> [Node] -> [Edge] -> [Node]
4  ancestors n ns es = [anc | ancid <- ancestorIds (nid n),
5                             anc <- findNode ns ancid
6                            ]
7    where -- ancestorIds id = the list of identifiers of the
8          -- ancestor nodes of the node with the identifier id.
9          ancestorIds id = if null pids then []
10                           else pid : ancestorIds pid
11             where -- pids = the singleton list containing the
12                   -- identifier of the parent of the node with
13                   -- the identifier id;
14                   -- or [], if no such parent exists.
15                   pids = [parentId e | e <- es, childId e == id]
16                   pid = head pids
```

Figure 6.10. Determining the ancestors of a tableau node.

parent identifier pid we rely on the laziness of Haskell: head pids in line 16 will not be called if null pids in line 9 evaluates to true, i.e. if pids is empty.

Given the function ancestors, checking whether subset blocking holds is quite easy. To this end we define the function nonBlocked, which takes three arguments, a node n, a node list ns and an edge list (es), and returns **True** if n is not blocked and **False** otherwise. This function is used in the implementation of the ∃- and ⩾- rules.

```
1  -- nonBlocked n ns es = node n is not blocked by
2  -- any of its ancestors in the tableau
3  -- specified by ns and es.
4  nonBlocked :: Node -> [Node] -> [Edge] -> Bool
5  nonBlocked n ns es =
6        not (any (blocks (concepts n)) (ancestors n ns es))
7    where -- blocks cs anc = True if, and only if, every
8          -- concept in the list cs is also found in
9          -- the label of the node anc.
10         blocks cs anc = all isIn cs
11            where isIn x = x `elem` (concepts anc)
```

The function nonBlocked is defined by a negated expression in line 6. This states that node n in question is not blocked if none of its ancestors blocks it. Thus we first obtain the list of ancestors (ancestors n ns es). Next, we invoke the function blocks with concepts n, i.e. the list of concepts in the label of the node n as its first argument and with each ancestor node as the second argument. If none of these calls returns **True** then nonBlocked itself returns **True**.

The local function blocks is defined in lines 10 and 11. It simply checks whether each concept in the list cs appears in the label of the ancestor node in question. If this is so then the label of the node n is a subset of the ancestor label, and so n is blocked.

6.8. Auxiliary functions

In this section we implement two auxiliary functions used by the reasoning algorithm. Since the task of these functions is not connected in any way with tableau reasoning, we have so far treated them as black boxes. We supplied the necessary specifications as regards their usage but did not deal with their implementation. In our view these implementation details would have distracted the reader's attention from understanding how the tableau algorithm works.

To make the description of the tableau reasoner complete, however, we now present the functions usort and colourings.

6.8.1. The function usort

Let us start with the implementation of the function usort, used in Subsections 6.6.2 and 6.6.4. This function sorts the elements of a list and removes identical elements. We will build on the function sort of the Haskell module **Data.List** in the implementation of usort. In order to use the function sort, we have to import it:

```
import Data.List (sort)
```

The type of the function sort is **Ord** a **=>** [a] **->** [a]. This is different from the function types encountered so far. It has a prefix **Ord** a **=>** which specifies that the *type variable* a has to implement the operations of the **Ord** class. Note that most main data types used in this chapter, such as **Node** and **Edge**, do indeed provide operations of the **Ord** class.

The part of the above type specification after the prefix is very much like other function types encountered earlier in this chapter but, instead of some concrete type, it uses the type variable a. Thus sort maps a list of arbitrary elements, whose type implements the operations of the **Ord** class, to a list of elements of the same type. Note that the type variable a can denote any type, but every occurrence of the variable then refers to the same type.

The function sort sorts the elements of the list passed to it, making use of operations of the **Ord** class.

In order to implement usort, let us first write a function, called unique, which removes all elements of a list that are equal to their right-hand neighbour in the list. If we apply the function unique to a sorted list, where duplicate elements stand after each other, all but the last occurrence of each element will be removed.

The function unique drops the head of the list if the first two elements are equal and keeps it otherwise. Next, it continues by recursively calling itself in order to filter the duplicates from the tail of the list.

```
-- unique lst = the list obtained from lst by replacing
-- any maximal sequence of equal elements by a single
-- member of the sequence.
unique :: Eq a => [a] -> [a]
unique (x : y : lst) = if x == y then unique (y : lst)
                       else x:unique (y : lst)
unique lst = lst
```

Here, the type of the function includes the **Eq** a **=>** prefix. This specifies that the types of the elements of the function argument are derived from the **Eq** class, because we have made use of the `==` operator in the function. Note that any type derived from the class **Ord** is automatically derived from the class **Eq** as well.

Finally, let us present the function `usort`:

```
1  -- usort lst = a sorted list containing the
2  -- distinct elements of lst.
3  usort :: Ord a => [a] -> [a]
4  usort = unique . sort
```

The "`.`" operator is the function composition operator. It is usually denoted by $\circ$ in mathematical formulae and is used to create composite functions: $(f \circ g)(x) = f(g(x))$. Similarly, given the list `lst`, we have

$$\text{usort lst} \rightarrow (\text{unique . sort}) \text{ lst} \rightarrow \text{unique (sort lst)}.$$

Thus the function `usort` is defined as the composite function `unique . sort`. This applies `sort` to its argument, passes the sorted list to `unique` and returns the value of the latter. This is exactly what we require from the function `usort`.

6.8.2. The function `colourings`

The function `colourings` computes all possible colourings, with *exactly* k colours, of a graph specified by a list of nodes `ns` and a list of edges `es`. It was used in Subsection 6.6.4 in the implementation of the at-most restriction. Its task is to colour a graph the nodes of which are tableau node identifiers. Since the type of the latter is a synonym of **Int**, we use the type **Int** for the nodes of the graph to be coloured.

Recall that an element of the list returned by the function `colourings`, i.e. a *colouring*, is a list of *colour partitions*. A colour partition is a list containing nodes that have the same colour.

Since nodes are represented by their integer identifiers, the types of colourings and partitions are specified by the following type synonyms:

```
1  type Partition = [Int]
2  type Colouring = [Partition]
```

We now present the function `colourings`:

```
1   -- colourings k ns es = the list of all colourings, using
2   -- exactly k colours, of the graph whose sets of
3   -- nodes and edges are ns and es, respectively.
4   colourings :: Int -> [Int] -> [(Int,Int)] -> [Colouring]
5   colourings k ns es = map first (pcolourings ns pcs0)
6      where pcs0 = [([],k,length ns)]
7            first (a,_,_) = a
8            pcolourings [] pcs = pcs
9            pcolourings (n : ns) pcs =
10                  pcolourings ns
11                      [pc' | pc <- pcs,
12                             pc' <- colourNode pc n es
13                      ]
```

The function `colourings` takes the nodes of the graph one by one and places them in *partial colourings*. A partial colouring is a data structure which contains:

- the partitions of nodes already coloured;
- the number of colours not yet used; and
- the number of nodes not yet coloured.

Note that the sum of the colours not yet used and the number of node partitions always equals `k`, since each partition corresponds to a colour.

A partial colouring is implemented as a triple (`cps,ac,an`), where `cps` holds the list of colour partitions, `ac` is the number of *available colours*, i.e. the colours not yet used, and `an` (*available nodes*) denotes the number of nodes yet to be coloured. The type of partial colourings can thus be described by the following type synonym:

```
type PartialColouring = ([Partition],Int,Int)
```

We construct the initial partial colouring, (`[],k,length ns`), in line 6 of the function `colourings`. This has no colour partitions, all the `k` colours are still available and all nodes are yet to be coloured. This initial partial colouring is made into a singleton list and named `pcs0`. The latter variable is then passed to the local function `pcolourings` in line 5.

The function `pcolourings` takes a list of nodes `ns` and a list of partial colourings `pcs`. Its task is to add each node in `ns` to each partial colouring in `pcs`, in all possible ways allowed by the graph to be coloured (i.e. the list of edges `es`). The value of the function `pcolourings` is a list of all such extended partial colourings, where all `k` colours are used. Notice that this list, produced by `pcolourings`, is actually the list of all possible (complete) colourings, just wrapped into triples. Thus, to obtain the value of the function `colourings`, all we have to do is to extract the first member of each triple in the list returned by `pcolourings`. This is performed by the function `map first` (line 5). The local function `first`, which extracts the first member of a partial colouring triple, is defined in line 7.

Let us now discuss the definition of the function `pcolourings`. If there are no nodes to be added (line 8), the function just returns the partial colourings obtained so far. Otherwise we take `n`, the first element of the list of nodes to be added, and build a new list of partial colourings in which each partial colouring in `pcs` is extended with the node `n` in all possible ways. This is accomplished by the list comprehension in lines 11–13. Here we use an auxiliary function `colourNode` that takes a partial colouring `pc`, a node `n` and the edge list `es` and then returns the list of all extensions of the partial colouring `pc` in which node `n` is coloured, observing the graph-colouring principles, as specified by the edge list `es`. The list comprehension, which collects all such extended partial colourings, is passed as the input argument to the recursive call of the function `pcolourings` (line 8), which then adds the remaining nodes to the list of partial colourings.

Note that we do not need to supply the list of edges to the function `pcolourings` as an argument, because the local definitions in the **where** part can refer to the variables defined anywhere in the function. Thus the argument `es` of the function `colourings` is visible in the body of the local function `pcolourings`.

Let us now turn our attention to the function `colourNode`. The value of the expression `colourNode pc n es` is a list of all possible partial colourings in which n is included in the partial colouring `pc`. Here n can be put into an existing partition in `pc` or used to start a new partition. If the colouring of n turns out to be impossible, i.e. the node cannot be put into any existing colour partition,[9] and no more colours are available then the function returns an empty list. There is another case for which the return value is an empty list: it occurs when the number of available nodes is less than the number of colours to be used. This makes it impossible to use up all colours, i.e. the graph can be coloured only with fewer than k colours, which is not allowed.

Before dealing with the function `colourNode`, let us first introduce two auxiliary functions.

The function `select` serves to select an arbitrary element of a list together with the list of the remaining elements. It takes an input `1st` and produces a list of pairs. The first member of each pair is an element e of `1st`, while the second member of the pair is the list containing all elements of `1st` except for the selected occurrence of e. The value of `select 1st` contains pairs of the above format for all elements of `1st`. For instance, we have

$$\text{select } [1,2,3] \;\rightarrow\; [(1,[2,3]),(2,[1,3]),(3,[1,2])].$$

The function is as follows:

```
 1  -- select 1st = the list of all pairs (e,1st') where e is
 2  -- an element of 1st and 1st' is obtained from 1st by removing e.
 3  select :: [a] -> [(a,[a])]
 4  select [] = []
 5  select (head : tail) = (head,tail) : map sel (select tail)
 6     where sel (elem,1st) = (elem,head : 1st)
```

We also need a function for deciding whether a node `id` can be added to a given colour partition containing nodes `ids`. This can be done if `id` has no neighbour amongst the nodes `ids`, i.e. no edge runs between `id` and any of the nodes `ids`. This condition is checked by the function `noEdge`:

```
 1  -- noEdge id ids es = True iff the node with identifier id
 2  -- does not share an edge with any of the nodes with identifiers in ids,
 3  -- given the list of edges es.
 4  noEdge :: Id -> [Id] -> [(Id,Id)] -> Bool
 5  noEdge id ids es = all noEdge' ids
 6     where noEdge' id' = (pair id id') `notElem` es
```

We now discuss the implementation of the function `colourNode` (Figure 6.11). We have included detailed comments in this piece of code, thereby making further explanations unnecessary. Here we just note that the somewhat cryptic variable name `newp` refers to a partial colouring in which the current node is used to start a **new p**artition, while `exps` names the list of those partial colourings in which the current node is added to an **ex**isting **p**artition.

---

[9] This is the case if, for each existing colour partition in pc, there is an edge in the graph to be coloured which links n with a node in the given partition.

```
1  -- colourNode pc0 n es = the list of all partial colourings that
2  -- can be derived from pc0 by colouring the node n, observing
3  -- the constraints given by graph edges es.
4  colourNode ::
5      PartialColouring -> Int -> [(Int,Int)] -> [PartialColouring]
6  colourNode pc0 n es =
7          -- We have fewer nodes than colours available,
8          -- thus the graph cannot be coloured:
9          if (an < ac) then []
10         -- Colours and nodes available are equal in number,
11         -- so we have to put n into a new partition:
12         else if (an == ac) then [newp]
13             -- We still have colours to use, so we can start a
14             -- new partition, or extend an existing one:
15             else if (ac > 0) then newp:exps
16                 -- There are no more colours to use,
17                 -- we have to extend an existing partition:
18                 else exps
19     where (cps,ac,an) = pc0
20         -- newp = pc0 extended with a new singleton
21         -- partition [n].
22         newp = ([n] : cps,ac - 1,an - 1)
23         -- exps = the list of all possible partial colourings
24         -- where n is put into an existing partition of pc0.
25         exps = foldl ins [] (select cps)
26         -- ins exps (cp,cps) = add the partial colouring
27         -- in which n is put into the partition cp to the list
28         -- exps, if this partial colouring is allowed.
29         -- Otherwise return exps unchanged.
30         ins exps0 (cp,cps) =
31             -- If n does not share any edge with any other node
32             -- in cp, given the edge list es,
33             if noEdge n cp es
34             -- then build a new partial colouring,
35             -- where n is put into the partition cp,
36             -- and prepend it to exps0;
37             then ((n : cp) : cps,ac,an - 1) : exps0
38             -- otherwise return exps0 itself.
39             else exps0
```

Figure 6.11. Colouring a node of a graph.

Exercise 6.25: Are the types of the functions colourings, colourNode, select, noEdge and pair as general as they possibly could be? If not, generalise them as much as possible.

6.9. Challenges

The program described in the preceding sections is far from efficient. Our goal was to present an implementation which is as simple as possible yet fast enough to solve interesting problems. In this section we offer some ideas for its improvement, in the form of exercises. Note that these exercises are substantially more complex (and less clearly specified) than those encountered so far in this chapter. Think of these exercises as small projects when considering how to solve them.

We will discuss two kinds of suggested improvement. First we try to make the present algorithm perform better, by using slightly different programming techniques and data structures. Next we suggest new approaches for solving some sub-tasks in the implementation of the reasoning engine.

6.9.1. Techniques and data structures

In Section 6.6 we put forward an alternative representation for the values returned by the functions performing tableau transformations.

Exercise 6.26: Modify the program to use the type defined in Exercise 6.13. Compare the performance of the new version with that of the original program.

The current implementation uses only very simple data structures, such as tuples and lists. It is very likely that the use of more complex data structures could improve the performance. For example, one could use search trees or hash tables for looking up edges belonging to nodes or for representing sets of concepts.

Exercise 6.27: Devise and use efficient data structures for representing the tableau graph.

(a) Collect the types of operations used on various parts of the tableau.

(b) Try to find those which are executed most often.

(c) Choose data structures which support the most frequent operations.

(d) Define these data structures and modify the program to use them. You might need to rewrite parts of the program first to make it easier to experiment with various data structures.

6.9.2. New approaches

When implementing the tableau algorithm, concepts may be represented in lexical normal form instead of negation normal form. The lexical normal form and its advantages are explained in Subsection 7.9.2.

Exercise 6.28: Change the program to use lexical normal form instead of negation normal form.

(a) Implement a function producing the lexical normal form of a concept expression.

(b) Change the program to use lexical normal form.

After you have read Section 7.9, consider the final exercise of this section.

Exercise 6.29: Implement as many optimisation techniques discussed in Section 7.9 as you can.

6.10. Summary

In this chapter we have presented an implementation of a description logic *inference program*. The knowledge-representation formalism used by this system is the $\mathcal{ALCN}$ language; the program can carry out reasoning tasks on $\mathcal{ALCN}$ concepts with respect to an $\mathcal{ALCN}$ TBox. The implementation is written in the *Haskell language*, which is a concise and easy-to-read functional programming language that has a notation very close to the usual mathematical formalism.

First, we demonstrated a few examples of how to run the reasoning engine. We then described the *data structures*, i.e. the representation of description logic *concept expressions* and *roles* and of the *tableau state*, which is the main data structure used in the course of reasoning. Then we wrote down our first Haskell function, which transformed an $\mathcal{ALCN}$ concept into the *negation normal form* required by the tableau algorithm.

Next, we presented the framework of the reasoning algorithm. We defined the possible *query types* that the reasoning algorithm has to be able to answer. We reduced all these inference tasks to the problem of *concept satisfiability*, which we could decide using the tableau algorithm. By repeatedly executing the transformation rules, the tableau algorithm keeps transforming the initial tableau state until a complete and clash-free tableau is created or until a contradiction is found in each branch reachable from the initial state.

We then dealt with the *transformation rules*, one by one, and presented a Haskell function for each. These functions generate a list of tableau states from an input tableau state. In the case of deterministic transformation rules, such as the ⊓-rule, the ∀-rule, the ∃-rule and the ⩽-rule, a list with at most one element is generated. In the case of non-deterministic rules, such as the ⊔-rule and the ⩾-rule, the list may have more than one element, each corresponding to a branch of a choice point. In our implementation, *clash* detection also takes the form of a transformation rule. If a clash has been detected in the input tableau state then the generated tableau state list is empty.

We completed the presentation of the reasoning system by describing the implementation of a *blocking condition*, which ensures the termination of the algorithm.

Two custom-made auxiliary functions, `usort` and `colourings`, were described in a separate section, because the implementation details of these functions are not necessary for understanding the behaviour of the reasoning engine.

Finally, we presented a few challenging problems for the reader to tackle.

Chapter 7

The $\mathcal{SHIQ}$ tableau algorithm

In this chapter we present a variant of the tableau algorithm that can accommodate the $\mathcal{SHIQ}$ language. We first summarise the elements of the tableau reasoning that have been introduced so far. Next, we discuss the techniques to support each new construct of the $\mathcal{SHIQ}$ language: transitivity, role hierarchy, inverse roles, functional restrictions and qualified number restrictions. Finally we describe the full $\mathcal{SHIQ}$ tableau algorithm, first only for TBox inference and then for reasoning over ABoxes and TBoxes together. The chapter is concluded with a discussion of optimisation techniques for the $\mathcal{SHIQ}$ tableau algorithm.

The discussion follows the papers [63, 60], although parts of the formalism have been simplified. Detailed proofs of the properties of the algorithm can also be found there.

7.1. An outline of the $\mathcal{SHIQ}$ tableau algorithm

First we reiterate the main characteristics of the $\mathcal{ALCN}$ tableau algorithm with respect to a possibly non-empty TBox (see Section 5.4). The purpose of this discussion is to highlight the most important features that will be reused in the $\mathcal{SHIQ}$ algorithm.

(1) The goal of the tableau algorithm is to decide whether a *root concept* C_0 is satisfiable w.r.t. a (possibly empty) TBox $\mathcal{T}$. To make the following discussion simpler, we will often omit the reference to the TBox.

(2) The algorithm works by repeatedly applying transformations to so-called tableau states, until a state is reached for which no transformation is applicable. Such a tableau state is called *complete*.

(3) A tableau state $\mathbf{T} = \langle V, E, \mathcal{L}, I \rangle$ consists of a finite, directed, labelled graph $\langle V, E, \mathcal{L} \rangle$ and a set of node inequalities I. This graph is a tree, except when used for ABox reasoning.

(4) Each tableau state $\mathbf{T}$ can be mapped to an ABox $\mathcal{A}_{\mathbf{T}}$ in a natural way: the nodes of the graph become individual names, the labels associated with the nodes give rise to concept assertions and the edges are mapped to role assertions, as described in (5.18)–(5.20).

(5) A tableau transformation rule can be applied at a tableau state **T** if its *firing conditions* hold. The transformation rule, when applied to **T**, returns a set of tableau states S_T. There are six transformation rules in the $\mathcal{ALCN}$ tableau algorithm; see Figures 5.4 and 5.10.

(6) The tableau algorithm, as shown in Figure 5.5, performs a non-deterministic search where the search tree contains tableau states. If a transformation rule returns a single new state, the execution continues deterministically from this new state. If multiple states are returned then a choice point is created and each new state is explored through backtracking until one such non-deterministic branch leads to a positive answer.

(7) Alternatively, the tableau algorithm can be viewed as a sequence of transformations on a set S of tableau states; see Figure 5.6. In this interpretation a rule can be applied to an arbitrary element of the set S, and the new set is formed by replacing the selected element with the output of the transformation rule. Thus the set S contains those tableau states of the search space to which no transformation rule has yet been applied.

(8) Each transformation rule preserves satisfiability: the input state **T** is satisfiable if, and only if, the output set of states, S_T, is satisfiable, (5.25). Here a tableau state **T** is said to be satisfiable if, and only if, the corresponding ABox $\mathcal{A}_T$ is satisfiable, and a set of tableau states is called satisfiable if, and only if, one of its elements is satisfiable.

(9) The initial tableau state contains a single node with the root concept C_0 in its label. Accordingly, the initial state is satisfiable if, and only if, the root concept C_0 is satisfiable.

(10) So-called clash conditions are defined for a tableau state. Should any of these conditions hold, the ABox associated with the tableau state is trivially unsatisfiable.

(11) Blocking conditions, which forbid the application of certain transformation rules, prevent the tableau algorithm from falling into an infinite loop.

(12) The tableau algorithm terminates with a positive answer (i.e. it reports that C_0 is satisfiable) if a complete and clash-free state is found.

(13) The tableau algorithm terminates with a negative answer (i.e. it reports that C_0 is not satisfiable) if a clash is found in every branch of the search tree.

(14) A negative answer is justified by the fact that the transformation rules preserve satisfiability, (8), and that a clash trivially means unsatisfiability, (10).

(15) To show that the positive answer is correct, so-called *model construction* is used. This procedure takes the ABox corresponding to a complete and clash-free tableau state and builds an interpretation which demonstrates that the concept C_0 is satisfiable. The model construction technique relies on transforming this ABox into a self-realising one, i.e. an ABox whose natural interpretation satisfies both the ABox and the TBox in question.

(16) To prove that the tableau algorithm terminates we show that the number of possible tableau states is finite, for any given input. Furthermore, every transformation rule is monotonic in the following sense: if $T' \in S_T$ then the ABox $\mathcal{A}_{T'}$ has $\mathcal{A}_T$ as its subset. Thus the algorithm cannot revert to an earlier state.

The tableau algorithm for the language $\mathcal{SHIQ}$ is also founded on the above principles. The global control flow of the algorithm does not change, i.e. Figures 5.4 and 5.10 remain effective. However, in order to support the new language elements the following changes have to be made:

- Certain transformation rules change and new rules have to be added.

- New clash conditions need to be taken into consideration.

- New, stronger, blocking conditions have to be introduced in order to be able to construct a model from the complete and clash-free tableau.

Recall that the $\mathcal{SHIQ}$ language family is based on the $\mathcal{ALC}$ language (see Section 4.5). We thus start our transition from the $\mathcal{ALCN}$ to the $\mathcal{SHIQ}$ tableau algorithm by removing those parts of the algorithm which deal with number restrictions (denoted by the letter $\mathcal{N}$). Number restrictions will be reintroduced in a more general form – as qualified number restrictions, denoted by $\mathcal{Q}$ – in the final language extension step.

Number restrictions are handled by the $\leqslant$- and $\geqslant$-rules. Note that the fourth component of the tableau state, the set of inequalities I, is made necessary only by these rules.

In Chapter 5 we discussed a tableau algorithm for empty TBoxes and later extended it to cater for non-empty TBoxes, where blocking was introduced. In the present chapter we assume a possibly non-empty TBox from the very start, as even $\mathcal{S}$, the simplest language discussed here, requires blocking to prevent infinite loops (see Section 7.2).

We thus start from an $\mathcal{ALC}$ tableau algorithm for non-empty TBoxes. This can be obtained from the algorithm discussed in Subsection 5.4.3 by restricting it to the $\sqcap$-, $\sqcup$- and $\forall$-rules (see Figure 5.4) and the $\exists$-rule (see Figure 5.10). This variant will be referred to as the *base algorithm*.

In the following sections we first discuss, one by one, the extensions to the tableau algorithm made necessary by the new language features denoted by $\mathcal{S}$, $\mathcal{H}$, $\mathcal{I}$, $\mathcal{F}$ and $\mathcal{Q}$. We then give a full description of the $\mathcal{SHIQ}$ tableau algorithm for TBoxes and for ABoxes.

When discussing the individual extensions, we will focus on the new elements of the $\mathcal{SHIQ}$ tableau algorithm and the corresponding techniques required for model construction (which forms the basis of a proof of the soundness of the algorithm). Proving other properties – such as termination, see list point (16), and the preservation of satisfiability, see list point (8) – requires arguments very similar to those given for the case of the $\mathcal{ALCN}$ tableau algorithm in Chapter 5. The discussion of these properties is postponed until Section 7.7, where the full $\mathcal{SHIQ}$ TBox tableau algorithm is covered.

7.2. Transitive roles; the language $\mathcal{S}$

The language $\mathcal{S} = \mathcal{ALC}_{\mathcal{R}^+}$ is the extension of $\mathcal{ALC}$ to include transitive roles. This means that we allow axioms of the form $\mathsf{Trans}(R)$, which express the fact that R is a transitive role. For example, the transitivity axiom $\mathsf{Trans}(\mathsf{hasDescendant})$ states that a descendant of a descendant of an individual is also a descendant of the said individual.

7.2.1. Supporting transitivity

If we wanted to capture the semantics of transitivity explicitly, the following transformation rule would have to be added to the tableau algorithm:

If R is a transitive role and there is a node x with an R-successor y, which itself has an R-successor z, then z has to be made an R-successor of x, i.e. an edge must be added from x to z with label R.

This rule has several disadvantages. First, it is more complex than the earlier rules because it involves three "levels" of the tableau tree. Second, it is obvious that the tableau graph will cease to be a tree after application of this rule. Third, if there is a chain of R-successors consisting of n individuals, the number of edges to be added by this rule is proportional to n^2.

Because of these drawbacks let us try to handle transitivity implicitly, i.e. without adding the edge $x \to z$ to the tableau for each pair of adjoining edges $x \to y$ and $y \to z$. Let us consider how the presence of the edge $x \to z$ (which we do not want to add) would influence the further operation of the algorithm. Notice that such implicit edges in practice affect $\forall$-rules only. If the label of x contains a concept of the form $\forall R.C$ where R is transitive then, because of the implicit edges, the concept C should be added to the label of all descendants of x which can be reached through a chain of adjoining edges labelled with the role R. This leads to the following generalisation of the $\forall$-rule (which still does not represent our final solution for handling the transitivity problem):

If R is a transitive role and a concept of the form $\forall R.C$ appears in the label of a node x then the concept C should be added to every node reachable from x by a chain of adjoining edges bearing the label R.

This rule is even more complex than the previous one, since chains of R-successors of *arbitrary* length have to be taken into consideration. Notice, however, that the desired effect can be achieved in a much simpler way. Rather than generalising the $\forall$-rule we introduce an additional rule, called the *transitivity rule* for value restrictions, or the $\forall_+$-rule for short:

If R is a transitive role and a concept of the form $\forall R.C$ appears in the label of a node x then the concept $\forall R.C$ should be added to every R-successor.

This new rule makes the concept $\forall R.C$ appear in the label of all nodes reachable from x through R-chains. Because of the "old" $\forall$-rule the concept C will also appear in the label of all such nodes, which is exactly what we would like to achieve.

The following exercise shows that the use of the $\forall_+$-rule is justified.

Exercise 7.1: Assume that R is a transitive role and that an individual x is an instance of the concept $\forall R.C$. Show that if y is an R-successor of x then y belongs to $\forall R.C$.

7.2.2. Blocking

Because of the new $\forall_+$-rule, the presence of a concept (of the form $\forall R.C$) in a node label may cause the same concept to appear in the label of its successor. Thus it is no longer true that the maximal role depth of the concepts in a label decreases when one is going downwards in the tableau tree. This means that blocking may be required in order to avoid an infinite loop, even in the absence of concept inclusion axioms. For example, let us check the satisfiability of the concept

$$\exists \mathsf{hasDescendant}.\top \sqcap \forall \mathsf{hasDescendant}.\exists \mathsf{hasDescendant}.\top, \qquad (7.1)$$

where hasDescendant is transitive. Having unfolded this expression using the ⊓-rule, the ∃-rule fires for the first concept in the intersection, creating a hasDescendant-successor. Next, the concept ∃hasDescendant.⊤ is added to the label of this successor, owing to the ∀-rule in the base algorithm. The new ∀$_+$-rule also fires, extending the label of this new successor with the concept

$$\forall \text{hasDescendant}.\exists \text{hasDescendant}.\top.$$

The last three rule applications thus produce a successor whose label is the same as that of the predecessor node. This obviously leads to an endless loop unless blocking is applied.

7.2.3. The tableau algorithm for the language $\mathcal{S}$

Summing up our observations, we now define the tableau algorithm for the language $\mathcal{S}$, for checking the satisfiability of a concept w.r.t. a TBox.[1]

The tableau algorithm for the language $\mathcal{S}$ is obtained by extending the base algorithm by the ∀$_+$-rule introduced above. The precise definition of the ∀$_+$-rule is shown in Figure 7.1.

Recall that the tableau is a data structure of the form $\mathbf{T} = \langle V, E, \mathcal{L}(,I) \rangle$,[2] and that the description of a transformation rule lists only the altered components of the tableau state. Thus the ∀$_+$-rule, as described in Figure 7.1, only changes the label of the node y in question.

Exercise 7.2: Use the $\mathcal{ALCN}$ tableau algorithm to decide the satisfiability of the following concept C w.r.t. an empty TBox:

$$C = (\exists \text{hasFriend}.\exists \text{hasFriend}.\neg \text{Optimist}) \sqcap (\forall \text{hasFriend}.\text{Optimist}).$$

Next, use the tableau algorithm for the language $\mathcal{S}$ to decide the satisfiability of the concept C w.r.t. the TBox $\{\text{Trans}(\text{hasFriend})\}$.

7.2.4. Model construction

Consider a complete and clash-free tableau state $\mathbf{T} = \langle V, E, \mathcal{L}(,I) \rangle$, derived by the tableau algorithm for the language $\mathcal{S}$. We can associate an ABox $\mathcal{A}_\mathbf{T}$ with $\mathbf{T}$ in the usual way:

$$\mathcal{A}_\mathbf{T} = \{C(x) \mid x \in V, C \in \mathcal{L}(x)\} \tag{7.2}$$
$$\cup \{R(x,y) \mid \langle x,y \rangle \in E, R = \mathcal{L}(\langle x,y \rangle)\}. \tag{7.3}$$

∀$_+$-**rule**	
Condition:	$(\forall R.C) \in \mathcal{L}(x)$, $\text{Trans}(R) \in \mathcal{T}$ and there is a $y \in V$ such that $\mathcal{L}(\langle x,y \rangle) = R$ and $(\forall R.C) \notin \mathcal{L}(y)$.
New state $\mathbf{T}'$:	$\mathcal{L}'(y) = \mathcal{L}(y) \cup \{\forall R.C\}$.

Figure 7.1. The ∀$_+$-rule of the tableau algorithm for the language $\mathcal{S}$.

---

[1] As blocking is needed anyway, the absence of concept inclusion axioms would not make the algorithm simpler. Therefore we do not deal separately with the case of a TBox containing transitivity axioms only.

[2] The state component I is put in parentheses because, in the absence of number restrictions, it will always be the empty set.

The above definition differs from the analogous formulae (5.18)–(5.20) for the language $\mathcal{ALCN}$ only in that here we are not concerned with the inequality system I.

We need to show that the ABox $\mathcal{A}_\mathbf{T}$ constructed from the complete and clash-free tableau $\mathbf{T}$ is satisfiable. If we confine ourselves to the $\mathcal{ALC}$ language, that is, we ignore transitive roles and blocking, then this ABox is *self-realising* (as defined in Subsection 5.3.4). However, this is not the case in the presence of the two new elements of the tableau algorithm: blocking and transitivity.

We have already dealt with blocking for an $\mathcal{ALCN}$ tableau with TBoxes (Subsection 5.4.3). We discussed there the problem of "missing edges", i.e. that a blocked node has no outgoing edges while some concepts in its label, such as $\exists$hasChild.$\top$, may require the existence of edges to make the ABox self-realising. In Subsection 5.4.3 we solved this problem by adding new edges to certain blocked nodes, which led to appropriate successors of the blocking nodes. Here we can use a simpler ABox transformation, thanks to the absence of number restrictions. We can simply identify each blocked node with the blocking node, i.e. omit the blocked node from the ABox and "redirect" the edge leading to it so that it points to the blocking node.[3] Informally, this redirection is justified because the label of the blocking node is a superset of the label of the blocked node (since subset blocking is used). Because of this, the blocking node belongs to all concepts of which the blocked node is expected to be an instance.

Let $\mathcal{A}$ be an ABox whose individual names are the nodes of the tableau $\mathbf{T}$ ($\mathcal{A}_\mathbf{T}$ is obviously such an ABox). We now formally define the ABox transformation $IdBlock_\mathbf{T}$, which identifies two nodes if one of them blocks the other in the tableau $\mathbf{T}$:

$$IdBlock_\mathbf{T}\ \mathcal{A} = \mathcal{A} \cup \left\{ a = b \ \middle|\ \begin{array}{l} a \text{ and } b \text{ occur in } \mathcal{A} \text{ and} \\ a \text{ blocks } b \text{ according to tableau } \mathbf{T} \end{array} \right\}. \tag{7.4}$$

Rather than adding equalities to the ABox, we can make this identification more explicit by defining an auxiliary function $mapB$:

$$mapB(b) = \begin{cases} b & \text{if } b \text{ occurs in } \mathcal{A} \text{ and } b \text{ is not blocked in the tableau } \mathbf{T}; \\ a & \text{if } a \text{ and } b \text{ occur in } \mathcal{A} \text{ and } b \text{ is blocked by } a \text{ in the tableau } \mathbf{T}. \end{cases}$$

The expression $mapB(x)$ thus denotes x itself if x is not blocked; otherwise it denotes the node which blocks x. Using this function, we can provide an alternative definition of the transformation $IdBlock_\mathbf{T}$:

$$IdBlock_\mathbf{T}\ \mathcal{A} = \{C(mapB(a)) \mid C(a) \in \mathcal{A}\}$$
$$\cup \{R(mapB(a), mapB(b)) \mid R(a,b) \in \mathcal{A}\}. \tag{7.5}$$

The two alternative definitions produce ABoxes which are obviously equivalent w.r.t. satisfiability.

Note that while speaking of an ABox transformation we referred to notions relating to the tableau such as edges, blocked nodes etc. We can do this since the elements of the tableau and those of the corresponding ABox are in one-to-one correspondence. We will use the

---

[3] Please note that the notion of identifying blocked nodes in model construction has nothing to with the identification of nodes in the $\leqslant$-rule of the tableau algorithm.

term *redirected tableau* for the tableau counterpart of the ABox $IdBlock_{\mathbf{T}} \; \mathcal{A}_{\mathbf{T}}$ (i.e. a tableau in which the edges going to a blocked node are redirected to the blocking node).

Exercise 7.3: Show that the ABox $IdBlock_{\mathbf{T}} \; \mathcal{A}_{\mathbf{T}}$ is self-realising, assuming that the tableau **T** is complete and clash-free and there are no transitive roles. Follow the argument outlined in Exercise 5.20.

Unfortunately, the statement in the above exercise is not true in the presence of transitivity axioms. We chose to make transitivity implicit in the tableau graph (see Subsection 7.2.1), i.e. tableau edges labelled with a transitive role do not necessarily form a transitive relation. Obviously, the same holds for the role assertions of the above ABox. However, this problem can be solved easily by replacing each role declared to be transitive by its transitive closure. This is implemented by the following ABox transformation:

$$ClosT_{\mathcal{T}} \; \mathcal{A} = \mathcal{A} \cup \left\{ R(a_1, a_n) \; \middle| \; \begin{array}{l} \mathsf{Trans}(R) \in \mathcal{T}, n > 2, \text{ and} \\ \{R(a_1, a_2), \ldots, R(a_{n-1}, a_n)\} \subseteq \mathcal{A} \end{array} \right\}. \qquad (7.6)$$

By applying the above two transformations we obtain a self-realising ABox. To sum up, a complete and clash-free tableau state **T** is satisfiable w.r.t. the TBox $\mathcal{T}$ because the interpretation

$$\mathcal{I}_{\mathbf{T}} = \mathcal{I}^{nat}(ClosT_{\mathcal{T}} \; IdBlock_{\mathbf{T}} \; \mathcal{A}_{\mathbf{T}}) \qquad (7.7)$$

is a model of the ABox $\mathcal{A}_{\mathbf{T}}$ w.r.t. the TBox $\mathcal{T}$.

Equation (7.7) is best read backwards: we first take the ABox $\mathcal{A}_{\mathbf{T}}$ and apply the transformation $IdBlock_{\mathbf{T}}$ to it. Next, we perform $ClosT_{\mathcal{T}}$ on the output of the previous transformation. Finally, the natural interpretation of the resulting ABox is constructed. To make the evaluation order more explicit one can use additional pairs of parentheses:

$$\mathcal{I}_{\mathbf{T}} = \mathcal{I}^{nat}(ClosT_{\mathcal{T}}(IdBlock_{\mathbf{T}}(\mathcal{A}_{\mathbf{T}}))).$$

Because we believe that the first formula, with fewer parentheses, is more readable, we will normally omit parentheses around the arguments of ABox transformations.

7.3. Role hierarchies – extension $\mathcal{H}$

This section deals with the language extension $\mathcal{H}$, introducing role inclusion axioms of the form $R \sqsubseteq S$.

Recall that the technique of internalisation, see Subsection 4.7.2, makes it possible to eliminate all concept axioms, assuming transitivity and role hierarchy axioms are allowed. Since from now on we discuss languages which allow these two constructs, we will only consider TBoxes with no concept axioms, i.e. those containing only role axioms.

7.3.1. An example inference involving role hierarchies

Let us first consider an example in which we examine the satisfiability of the concept $C = \exists \mathsf{hasChild}.\neg \mathsf{Blonde} \sqcap \forall \mathsf{hasRelative}.\mathsf{Blonde}$, w.r.t. the TBox

$$\mathcal{T}_0 = \{\mathsf{hasChild} \sqsubseteq \mathsf{hasRelative}\}. \qquad (7.8)$$

Clearly, C is not satisfiable: if an individual belonged to C then it would have to have a non-blonde child but at the same time all its relatives, including its children, would have to be blonde, which is an obvious contradiction.

When the tableau algorithm is applied to this satisfiability problem, a hasChild-successor c of the root node b is created, where c has the label $\{\neg\text{Blonde}\}$:

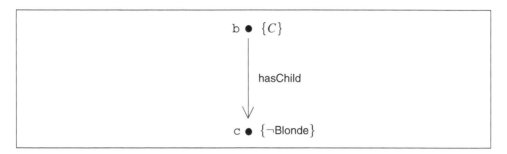

The $\forall$-rule, in its original form, cannot be applied to the above tableau graph because the role hasRelative in the concept expression $\forall$hasRelative.Blonde is not the same as the edge label hasChild. However, we must take into account the TBox $\mathcal{T}_0$, which states that any hasChild relationship is also a hasRelative relationship. Using this knowledge the algorithm should be able to view the pair $\langle\text{b},\text{c}\rangle$ as belonging to the hasRelative relation. From this, using the $\forall$-rule, the algorithm can infer that c is an instance of the concept Blonde, resulting in a clash as expected.

There are several ways to modify the tableau algorithm so that the role hierarchy is taken into account. For example, the $\exists$-rule could be extended so that each time it fires for a node x, creating an R-successor y, it adds multiple edges between x and y: for each role S such that $R \sqsubseteq S$ holds, y is made an S-successor of x.

This approach is not reasonable, as it significantly increases the size of the tableau graph. Instead, we will handle role inclusions implicitly, i.e. rather than modifying the $\exists$-rule, which *constructs* the tableau graph, we alter the $\forall$- and $\forall_+$-rules, which *use* it.

7.3.2. Closing the role hierarchy

Before examining how to modify these rules, let us have a look at the role inclusion axioms. In the previous example, (7.8), the TBox $\mathcal{T}_0$ contained a single axiom, hasChild $\sqsubseteq$ hasRelative. Let us extend this TBox with another statement: hasSon $\sqsubseteq$ hasChild. Consider an arbitrary model of the extended TBox. Here, it is clear that the axiom hasSon $\sqsubseteq$ hasRelative also holds, because role inclusion is transitive. Although the TBox does not contain this last statement, it should be taken into account as well as the two original statements.

Accordingly, we include a preprocessing stage in the $\mathcal{SH}$ tableau algorithm for checking the satisfiability of a concept C w.r.t. a TBox $\mathcal{T}$ (now consisting of role axioms only). The preprocessing stage creates a TBox $\mathcal{R}_{\mathcal{T}}$ which is an extension of $\mathcal{T}$ with new role inclusion axioms. For any role R occurring in either C or $\mathcal{T}$ we add the axiom $R \sqsubseteq R$ to $\mathcal{R}_{\mathcal{T}}$, because role inclusion is obviously reflexive. Furthermore, if we have a chain of role inclusion axioms in $\mathcal{T}$

$$\{R_1 \sqsubseteq R_2, \ldots, R_{n-1} \sqsubseteq R_n\} \subseteq \mathcal{T}, \qquad n > 2,$$

then, because of the transitivity of role inclusion, we add the axiom $R_1 \sqsubseteq R_n$ to $\mathcal{R}_{\mathcal{T}}$. Thus the extended TBox $\mathcal{R}_{\mathcal{T}}$ contains the transitivity axioms of $\mathcal{T}$ plus the reflexive–transitive closure of the $\sqsubseteq$ relation defined in $\mathcal{T}$.

For example, let us consider the task of checking the satisfiability of the concept $C_1 = \exists$hasFriend.$\forall$hasDescendant.Tall w.r.t. the TBox $\mathcal{T}_1$:

$$\mathcal{T}_1 = \{\text{hasSon} \sqsubseteq \text{hasChild}, \text{hasChild} \sqsubseteq \text{hasDescendant}, \text{Trans(hasDescendant)}\}.$$

Here, the extended TBox $\mathcal{R}_{\mathcal{T}_1}$ will contain the following statements:

hasSon $\sqsubseteq$ hasChild, hasChild $\sqsubseteq$ hasDescendant, hasSon $\sqsubseteq$ hasDescendant,

hasSon $\sqsubseteq$ hasSon, hasChild $\sqsubseteq$ hasChild,

hasDescendant $\sqsubseteq$ hasDescendant, hasFriend $\sqsubseteq$ hasFriend,

Trans(hasDescendant).

Notice that in the above example the role hasFriend occurs only in the concept C_1. Nevertheless, we include the reflexivity axiom hasFriend $\sqsubseteq$ hasFriend in the extended TBox $\mathcal{R}_{\mathcal{T}_1}$. This example highlights the fact that the notation $\mathcal{R}_{\mathcal{T}}$ is slightly imprecise since the extended TBox depends on the concept C in question. However, for the sake of simplicity this dependence is not shown.[4]

7.3.3. The $\mathcal{SH}$ tableau algorithm

Let us now discuss the modifications to the tableau algorithm needed to support role hierarchies. As we saw in the introductory example, the $\forall$-rule must fire if a node bearing the label $\forall R.C$ has an S-successor for which $S \sqsubseteq R \in \mathcal{R}_{\mathcal{T}}$. Rather than modifying the $\forall$-rule, we will change the definition of an R-successor, as follows.

A node y is said to be the R-successor of a node x w.r.t. a TBox $\mathcal{T}$ if there is an edge with the label S from x to y (that is, $\mathcal{L}(\langle x, y \rangle) = S$), where $S \sqsubseteq R \in \mathcal{R}_{\mathcal{T}}$.

We can now see why the reflexivity axioms $R \sqsubseteq R$ were included in $\mathcal{R}_{\mathcal{T}}$: because of this, the endpoint of an edge bearing the label R is still considered to be an R-successor. Also note that the modified definition is conservative in the following sense: if $\mathcal{T}$ contains no role inclusion axioms then the definition of *successor*, as modified for $\mathcal{SH}$, is the same as the original definition for the language $\mathcal{S}$. The reason is that in this special case the $\sqsubseteq$ relation becomes equality, so *only* the endpoints of edges with label R will be considered R-successors, even in $\mathcal{SH}$.

The modification to the $\forall_+$-rule is somewhat more complex, because two role inclusion axioms might be involved. Assume, for example, that the label of a node contains the concept $\forall$hasRelative.Blonde and that this node has a hasChild-successor where the role hierarchy is the following:

$$\text{hasChild} \sqsubseteq \text{hasDescendant}; \tag{7.9}$$

$$\text{hasDescendant} \sqsubseteq \text{hasRelative}. \tag{7.10}$$

---

[4] We might as well assume that every role occurring in the concept in question also appears in the TBox $\mathcal{T}$, for example, within a trivial axiom such as $R \sqsubseteq R$.

$\forall$-**rule**	
Condition:	$\forall R.C \in \mathcal{L}(x)$ and x has at least one R-successor y for which $C \notin \mathcal{L}(y)$.
New state **T$'$:**	$\mathcal{L}'(y) = \mathcal{L}(y) \cup \{C\}$.
$\forall_+$-**rule**	
Condition:	$(\forall R.C) \in \mathcal{L}(x)$, there is a role S such that $\mathsf{Trans}(S) \in \mathcal{R}_{\mathcal{T}}$ and $S \sqsubseteq R \in \mathcal{R}_{\mathcal{T}}$; furthermore, x has an S-successor y for which $(\forall S.C) \notin \mathcal{L}(y)$.
New state **T$'$:**	$\mathcal{L}'(y) = \mathcal{L}(y) \cup \{\forall S.C\}$.

Figure 7.2. The modified rules of the tableau algorithm $\mathcal{SH}$.

Assume, furthermore, that the hasDescendant relation is transitive but hasRelative is not. Because of the role inclusion (7.10), the node in question should be considered as belonging to the concept $\forall$hasDescendant.Blonde. This makes the $\forall_+$-rule applicable for the given node. However, the role inclusion (7.9) makes the $\forall_+$-rule applicable along the edge bearing the label hasChild.[5]

Figure 7.2 presents those rules of the $\mathcal{SH}$ tableau algorithm that have been modified w.r.t. the base algorithm. Note that the formulation of the $\forall$-rule is exactly the same as in the base algorithm: we have repeated it here only to draw attention to the fact that the meaning of the notion "R-successor" has changed.

Exercise 7.4: Let a TBox $\mathcal{T}$ contain the role inclusion axioms (7.9) and (7.10) together with the transitivity axiom Trans(hasDescendant), and let

$$C = (\exists \mathsf{hasChild}.\exists R.\neg \mathsf{Blonde}) \sqcap (\forall \mathsf{hasRelative}.\mathsf{Blonde}).$$

Execute the $\mathcal{SH}$ tableau algorithm to decide the satisfiability of the concept C w.r.t. Tbox $\mathcal{T}$ for each of the following substitutions for the role R:

(a) $R = $ hasChild;

(b) $R = $ hasDescendant;

(c) $R = $ hasRelative.

7.3.4. Model construction

Model construction for the language $\mathcal{SH}$ involves

- making the implicit transitivity explicit, as in the language $\mathcal{S}$, and
- making the implicit role hierarchy explicit as well.

We start again from the ABox $IdBlock_{\mathbf{T}}\,\mathcal{A}_{\mathbf{T}}$, as defined by (7.2)–(7.5). This ABox, in which every blocked node is identified with the node that blocks it, already contains the necessary concept assertions but it does not necessarily satisfy the role axioms. However, all we have to do is to devise a closure operation which, when applied to this ABox, will ensure that

---

[5] Because of (7.9), the given hasChild-successor is considered to be a hasDescendant-successor as well, according to the modified definition of the *successor* relationship.

all transitivity and role hierarchy axioms hold in the natural interpretation of the ABox thus modified. The transformation $ClosT$ which closes the ABox w.r.t. the transitivity axioms has already been introduced in the previous section; see (7.6). Below we introduce the operation $ClosH$, where the letter H refers to (role) hierarchies. This operation extends the ABox with the statements that follow from the role-hierarchy axioms in $\mathcal{T}$:

$$ClosH_{\mathcal{T}} \, \mathcal{A} = \mathcal{A} \cup \{R(a,b) \mid (S \sqsubseteq R) \in \mathcal{R}_{\mathcal{T}}, S(a,b) \in \mathcal{A}\}. \qquad (7.11)$$

The inclusion axioms are obviously true in the natural interpretation of the ABox $ClosH_{\mathcal{T}} \, \mathcal{A}$, and the transitivity statements are true in that of $ClosT_{\mathcal{T}} \, \mathcal{A}$. However, we need an ABox where both kinds of axiom are true. It is easy to verify that the following three-step transformation[6] is appropriate for this purpose:

$$ClosHT_{\mathcal{T}} \, \mathcal{A} = ClosH_{\mathcal{T}} \, ClosT_{\mathcal{T}} \, ClosH_{\mathcal{T}} \, \mathcal{A}. \qquad (7.12)$$

The $ClosH_{\mathcal{T}}$ transformation has to be applied a second time in order for those roles to be interpreted correctly that are not transitive themselves but that contain transitive roles.

Exercise 7.5: Show that, given an arbitrary ABox $\mathcal{A}$ and TBox $\mathcal{T}$ containing $\mathcal{SH}$ role axioms only, the natural interpretation of $ClosHT_{\mathcal{T}} \, \mathcal{A}$, as defined above, satisfies every axiom in $\mathcal{T}$.

Putting everything together one can see that the ABox $ClosHT_{\mathcal{T}} \, IdBlock_{\mathbf{T}} \, \mathcal{A}_{\mathbf{T}}$ is self-realising. Thus we can conclude that a complete and clash-free tableau state $\mathbf{T}$, obtained in the tableau algorithm for the language $\mathcal{SH}$, is satisfiable w.r.t. to a TBox $\mathcal{T}$ since the interpretation

$$\mathcal{I}_{\mathbf{T}} = \mathcal{I}^{nat}(ClosHT_{\mathcal{T}} \, IdBlock_{\mathbf{T}} \, \mathcal{A}_{\mathbf{T}})$$

is a model of the ABox $\mathcal{A}_{\mathbf{T}}$ w.r.t. the TBox $\mathcal{T}$.

7.4. Inverse roles – extension $\mathcal{I}$

In the language extension $\mathcal{I}$ we introduce inverse roles. For example, the axiom hasParent $\equiv$ hasChild$^-$ can be formulated and inverse role expressions (e.g. hasParent$^-$) can be used within concept expressions.

7.4.1. Supporting inverse roles

With the introduction of inverse roles, a new phenomenon appears in the tableau graph, namely that information can be propagated not only top down but also the other way round. To see how, let us examine the construction of a tableau for the intersection $C \sqcap \neg$Blonde, where $C = \exists$hasChild.$\forall$hasChild$^-$.Blonde. This formalises the question whether there can be someone who is not blonde and has a child all of whose parents are blonde.

In the tableau state below we have created a hasChild-successor c for the root node b. A value restriction for the inverse role hasChild$^-$ appears in the label of c. No edge bearing

---

[6] This operation is given a name here because it will be used several times later.

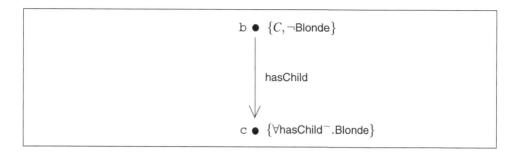

the label hasChild$^-$ departs from the node c (it has no outgoing edges at all), but there is an edge with the label hasChild that goes towards c. In the presence of inverse roles, the origin of this edge has to be considered a parent of c (i.e. b is hasChild$^-$-related to c). This should make the $\forall$-rule fire, causing a clash and thus showing that the concept $C \sqcap \neg$Blonde is not satisfiable, as expected.

Another new feature is that edges labelled with inverse roles can be created in the tableau graph. Consider, for example, the following concept: "a tall parent who has a child who in turn has a parent who is not tall". This is formalised as follows: $D =$ Tall $\sqcap$ $\exists$hasChild.$\exists$hasChild$^-$.$\neg$Tall. When this concept is tested for satisfiability, we obtain the following complete and clash-free tableau:

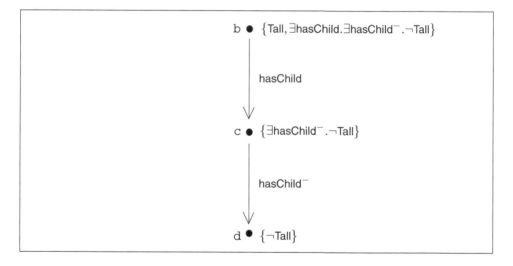

In the model corresponding to this tableau, c is the common child of b and d.

Let us now extend the root node of the tableau with the concept "people all of whose children have only blonde parents". This means that we are about to decide the satisfiability of the concept $D \sqcap \forall$hasChild.$\forall$hasChild$^-$.Blonde. Having obtained the above tableau we apply the $\forall$-rule at node b for this new concept and so the concept $\forall$hasChild$^-$.Blonde is added to the label of node c. When we apply the $\forall$-rule to the latter concept, it affects the tableau in two directions: the *target* of the outgoing edge with the label hasChild$^-$, i.e. node d, has to be extended with the concept Blonde and the same has to be done to the *origin* of the incoming edge bearing the label hasChild, i.e. to node b.

To keep the transformation rules simple, we will introduce a new notion: a node y is said to be an *R-neighbour* of a node x if either y is the R-successor of x or x is the $\text{Inv}(R)$-successor of y in the given tableau **T**. In the last example-tableau the nodes b and d have a common hasChild-neighbour, namely c, while c has two hasChild$^-$-neighbours: b and d.

It is important to note that whenever the tableau graph is extended (currently this can only happen through the application of the ∃-rule), a new edge is added from the already existing node x to the new node y. A new edge can never be added from a new node y to an old node x. In other words, the new node will always be the successor of the old node and not the other way round.

Apart from this case, the neighbour relation is used instead of the successor relation in every other situation, treating the "upper" and "lower" neighbours in the same way. This is relevant when the label of the *neighbour* nodes is extended by the ∀- and ∀$_+$- rules and also when we examine whether a given concept appears in any *neighbour* node as a precondition of the ∃-rule.

Before describing the precise transformation rules of the $\mathcal{SHI}$ tableau algorithm, we need to revise the notion of blocking.

7.4.2. Dynamic blocking and equality blocking

Subset blocking is not appropriate in the presence of inverse roles because in some cases no model can be built for a complete and clash-free tableau graph. For example, let us examine the satisfiability of the concept $(\forall\text{hasChild}^-.\neg\text{Tall}) \sqcap \text{Tall}$ w.r.t. the axiom $\top \sqsubseteq \exists\text{hasChild}.\text{Tall}$. We get the following tableau state after applying the $\sqcap$- and ∃- rules:

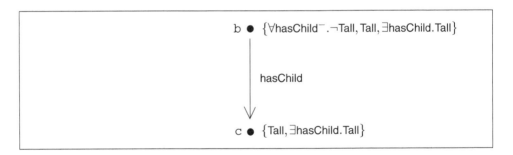

The label of node c is a subset of that of the node b. So we can apply subset blocking and the tableau becomes complete. However, the usual model construction does not work for this tableau because, when the edge pointing to c is redirected to the blocking node b, b "goes wrong" in the following sense: it is no longer an instance of the concept "all his parents are not tall" ($\forall\text{hasChild}^-.\neg\text{Tall}$)), because it becomes its own parent and is itself Tall.

The problem is that when the blocked node is identified with its blocker, the latter inherits the "upper" neighbours of the blocked node (this did not happen when there were no inverse roles, because then there were only lower neighbours, i.e. successors). These new, inherited, neighbours can cause the blocking node to cease to be an instance of a concept in its label.

However, if *equality blocking* is used, i.e. when we require the labels of the blocking and blocked nodes to be equal, the two nodes to be identified will belong to the same concepts and the identification cannot cause a clash.

In our example, this modification implies that another $\exists$-rule fires, creating a successor d for c with the same label, which – according to the rules of equality blocking – is blocked by node c. Therefore, the model $\mathcal{I}$ will contain two individuals, b and c: both are Tall and the hasChild relation holds between b and c and also between c and c itself.

The other important change concerning blocking is that the blocking condition is now *dynamic* owing to the possible presence of inverse roles (see Subsection 5.4.2), because concepts can now propagate upwards in the tableau graph and thus a blocked node can cease to be blocked (owing to the change in its label). It might also happen that a non-blocked node becomes blocked. In the case of static blocking, a blocked node was always a leaf of the tableau tree since no successor could be added to such a node. Now dynamic blocking can make a node become blocked even though it already has successors.

The tableau tree can be divided into three parts with respect to blocking. The upper part contains non-blocked nodes, that is, nodes for which no node above them has the same label. Going downwards, there can be nodes whose label is equal to that of one of their ancestors – the topmost of these is said to be *directly blocked*. Finally, there can be nodes under directly blocked nodes. These are called *indirectly blocked*, regardless of their label. Tableau transformations can be applied to the upper part of the tree (i.e. to the non-blocked nodes) with no restrictions. No transformation rules are allowed to fire for the nodes indirectly blocked, i.e. those in the bottom part of the tree. One could say that these nodes are useless in the current blocking setup. Nodes which are directly blocked form a frontier in the middle of the tableau graph. No expansion rules can be applied to these nodes to prevent the tree from growing indefinitely, but other rules are allowed.

The exact definitions of the different blocking states are given in Figure 7.3. Here we use the relation "ancestor-of", introduced in Subsection 5.4.3, the formalised version of the relationship "is above in the tree". Blocking affects the tableau algorithm in two ways: the expansion rules are applicable when the node in question is *not blocked* whereas other rules are applicable if the node is *not indirectly blocked*, that is, does not belong to the set of

---

The base condition of blocking (for *equality blocking*) The base condition of blocking is said to hold between a node y and one of its ancestors x if the labels of these two nodes are the same, i.e. $\mathcal{L}(y) = \mathcal{L}(x)$.

Directly blocked nodes A node y is *directly blocked* if it has an ancestor x such that the basic blocking condition holds for x and y but does not hold for any two ancestors of y. In this case y is said to be blocked by x.

Indirectly blocked nodes A node is *indirectly blocked* if it has an ancestor which is directly blocked.

Blocked nodes A node is *blocked* if it is directly or indirectly blocked.

Figure 7.3. Definitions regarding equality blocking.

indirectly blocked nodes. The latter condition is true if the node in question either is not blocked or is directly blocked.

7.4.3. The $\mathcal{SHI}$ tableau algorithm

To summarise the discussion so far, we now present the $\mathcal{SHI}$ tableau algorithm. The algorithm still assumes that the TBox $\mathcal{T}$ contains only role axioms (role inclusion and transitivity), but these axioms can now involve inverse roles too. Because of this, the construction of the TBox $\mathcal{R}_\mathcal{T}$ containing $\mathcal{T}$ and its consequences has to be modified. To build $\mathcal{R}_\mathcal{T}$, we first add to $\mathcal{T}$ statements of the form $\mathsf{Trans}(\mathsf{Inv}(R))$ for every axiom $\mathsf{Trans}(R)$ in $\mathcal{T}$. Next, $\mathsf{Inv}(R) \sqsubseteq \mathsf{Inv}(S)$ is included for each axiom $R \sqsubseteq S$. Finally, the reflexive–transitive closure of the resulting $\sqsubseteq$ relation is built, as discussed in Subsection 7.3.2.

Exercise 7.6: To justify the above construction of $\mathcal{R}_\mathcal{T}$, show that:

(a) $\mathsf{Trans}(R)$ implies $\mathsf{Trans}(\mathsf{Inv}(R))$.

(b) If $R \sqsubseteq S$ is known to be true then $\mathsf{Inv}(R) \sqsubseteq \mathsf{Inv}(S)$ also holds.

The rules of the $\mathcal{SHI}$ tableau algorithm are given in Figure 7.4. These rules have only changed to the extent that has already been discussed: the "neighbour" relationship is used instead of "successor" wherever necessary, and each rule is extended with an appropriate blocking condition (see Figure 7.3).

Exercise 7.7: Consider a TBox $\mathcal{T}$ containing the following two axioms:

$$\top \sqsubseteq \exists\mathsf{hasChild}.\mathsf{Tall},$$
$$\top \sqsubseteq \forall\mathsf{hasChild}^-.\mathsf{Blonde}.$$

Using the $\mathcal{SHI}$ tableau algorithm execute the following reasoning tasks:

(a) Is ¬Blonde satisfiable w.r.t. $\mathcal{T}$?

(b) Is Blonde satisfiable w.r.t. $\mathcal{T}$?

Try various rule orders, such as giving the ∀-rule a higher priority than the ∃-rule, or the other way round. Keep track of the blocking status of the nodes and pinpoint situations when a directly blocked node becomes unblocked.

7.4.4. Model construction

An important change now has to be made in the process of model construction. In the presence of dynamic blocking a tableau $\mathcal{T}$ can contain indirectly blocked nodes. The processing of such nodes stopped when one of their ancestors became directly blocked.

When the ABox $\mathcal{A}_\mathbf{T}$ is constructed from such a tableau $\mathcal{T}$, the assertions relating to indirectly blocked nodes may not be satisfiable. The reason is that such a node may have contradicting concepts in its label that did not actually cause a clash since the processing of the node was abandoned. Fortunately, indirectly blocked nodes are not needed in the model construction and so all assertions relating to such nodes can and must be removed from $\mathcal{A}_\mathbf{T}$.

⊓-**rule**	
Condition:	$(C_1 \sqcap C_2) \in \mathcal{L}(x)$, x is not indirectly blocked and $\{C_1, C_2\} \not\subseteq \mathcal{L}(x)$.
New state **T′**:	$\mathcal{L}'(x) = \mathcal{L}(x) \cup \{C_1, C_2\}$.
⊔-**rule**	
Condition:	$(C_1 \sqcup C_2) \in \mathcal{L}(x)$, x is not indirectly blocked and $\{C_1, C_2\} \cap \mathcal{L}(x) = \emptyset$.
New state **T$_1$**:	$\mathcal{L}'(x) = \mathcal{L}(x) \cup \{C_1\}$.
New state **T$_2$**:	$\mathcal{L}'(x) = \mathcal{L}(x) \cup \{C_2\}$.
∃-**rule**	
Condition:	$(\exists R.C) \in \mathcal{L}(x)$, x is not blocked and
	x has no R-neighbour y such that $C \in \mathcal{L}(y)$.
New state **T′**:	$V' = V \cup \{y\}$ ($y \notin V$ is a new node),
	$E' = E \cup \{\langle x, y \rangle\}$, $\mathcal{L}'(\langle x, y \rangle) = R$, $\mathcal{L}'(y) = \{C\}$.
∀-**rule**	
Condition:	$(\forall R.C) \in \mathcal{L}(x)$, x is not indirectly blocked and
	x has an R-neighbour y such that $C \notin \mathcal{L}(y)$.
New state **T′**:	$\mathcal{L}'(y) = \mathcal{L}(y) \cup \{C\}$.
∀$_+$-**rule**	
Condition:	$(\forall R.C) \in \mathcal{L}(x)$, x is not indirectly blocked and,
	for some S, $\mathsf{Trans}(S) \in \mathcal{R}_\mathcal{T}$ and $S \sqsubseteq R \in \mathcal{R}_\mathcal{T}$; furthermore,
	x has an S-neighbour y such that $(\forall S.C) \notin \mathcal{L}(y)$.
new state **T′**:	$\mathcal{L}'(y) = \mathcal{L}(y) \cup \{\forall S.C\}$.

Figure 7.4. Transformation rules of the tableau algorithm $\mathcal{SHI}$.

The following transformation *Base*$_\mathbf{T}$ is defined for this purpose:

$$Base_\mathbf{T}\; \mathcal{A} = \{R(a,b) \mid R(a,b) \in \mathcal{A}, a \text{ and } b \text{ are not indirectly blocked in } \mathbf{T}\}$$
$$\cup \; \{C(a) \mid C(a) \in \mathcal{A} \; a \text{ is not indirectly blocked in } \mathbf{T}\}. \qquad (7.13)$$

Here $\mathcal{A}$ is an arbitrary ABox whose individual names form a subset of the nodes of tableau **T**. The ABox $\mathcal{A}_\mathbf{T}$ is obviously of this form.

Given a complete clash-free tableau **T**, we first build the ABox $\mathcal{A}_\mathbf{T}$ as usual. Next, we apply the above transformation (7.13), producing the ABox *Base*$_\mathbf{T}$ $\mathcal{A}_\mathbf{T}$. Subsequently we identify each blocked node with the node which blocks it, using the transformation *IdBlock*$_\mathbf{T}$, (7.5). Then, to make the ABox self-realising w.r.t. inverse roles, we add $\mathsf{Inv}(R)(b,a)$ for each role assertion $R(a,b)$ in the ABox, as the former is a trivial consequence of the latter. The formal definition of this inverse closure transformation *ClosI* is the following:

$$ClosI\; \mathcal{A} = \mathcal{A} \cup \{\mathsf{Inv}(R)(b,a) \mid R(a,b) \in \mathcal{A}\}.$$

We thus obtain an extended ABox *ClosI IdBlock*$_\mathbf{T}$ *Base*$_\mathbf{T}$ $\mathcal{A}_\mathbf{T}$, which is closed with respect to role inversion. We now apply the transformation *ClosHT*, introduced in (7.12).

This ensures that the role hierarchy and transitivity axioms hold. The result remains closed with respect to role inversion, because the inverse consequences of role axioms were added to the extended TBox $\mathcal{R}_T$. Thus the ABox obtained here is self-realising. To sum up, the interpretation

$$\mathcal{I}_\mathbf{T} = \mathcal{I}^{nat}(ClosHT_T \; ClosI \; IdBlock_\mathbf{T} \; Base_\mathbf{T} \; \mathcal{A}_\mathbf{T}) \tag{7.14}$$

is a model of the ABox $Base_\mathbf{T} \; \mathcal{A}_\mathbf{T}$, i.e. this ABox is satisfiable.

Earlier, in Subsection 5.3.4, when discussing the soundness of the $\mathcal{ALCN}$ tableau algorithm we built the ABox $\mathcal{A}_\mathbf{T}$ and then mentioned two possibilities for proving the satisfiability of the concept C in question. First, we argued that the transformation rules preserve satisfiability and, since we had shown that $\mathcal{A}_\mathbf{T}$ is satisfiable, so then must be the concept C. Second, we showed that the natural interpretation of $\mathcal{A}_\mathbf{T}$ in itself demonstrates that C is satisfiable.

The first line of argument is no longer appropriate because now, owing to the possible presence of indirectly blocked nodes, we can only show that a *subset* of $\mathcal{A}_\mathbf{T}$, namely $Base_\mathbf{T} \; \mathcal{A}_\mathbf{T}$, is satisfiable. However, we can still use the second line of argument: the interpretation constructed in (7.14) clearly satisfies the concept C (because the root node of the tableau is an instance of this concept) and, at the same time, it is a model of the TBox $\mathcal{T}$ because of the closure transformation $ClosHT$.

Exercise 7.8: Consider a complete tableau **T** obtained as a solution to Exercise 7.7(b). Using the transformations described above, build progressively a model from this tableau, i.e. construct the series of ABoxes $\mathcal{A}_0 = \mathcal{A}_\mathbf{T}$, $\mathcal{A}_1 = Base_\mathbf{T} \; \mathcal{A}_0$, $\mathcal{A}_2 = IdBlock_\mathbf{T} \; \mathcal{A}_1$ and $\mathcal{A}_3 = ClosI \; \mathcal{A}_2$. Notice that there is no need to apply the transformation $ClosHT_T$, as there are no role hierarchy or transitivity axioms in the TBox of the given example.

7.5. Functional restrictions – extension $\mathcal{F}$

The language extension $\mathcal{F}$ introduces concept expressions of the forms $(\leqslant 1R)$ and $(\geqslant 2R)$. This kind of number restriction – which is even weaker than the construct denoted by $\mathcal{N}$ – is especially interesting, because it leads to a language which does not have the so-called *finite-model property*. A DL language does have this property if, whenever a concept C is satisfiable, i.e. there is a model in which C's meaning is a non-empty set, then there exists a *finite* model in which C has a non-empty meaning. In the language $\mathcal{SHIF}$ one can formulate a concept expression which is satisfiable but for which all models satisfying it are infinite; i.e. this language does not have the finite-model property.

7.5.1. Finite and infinite models

When we examine the satisfiability of an $\mathcal{ALCN}$-concept w.r.t. an empty TBox, we require only a finite number of conditions to be satisfied by the model being built. Recall that in this case the tableau tree itself can serve as a model. Therefore, this class of reasoning tasks has the *finite-tree model property*, i.e. the role relationships in the model form a finite tree.

If concept axioms are allowed then we can formulate a reasoning task (even using just $\mathcal{AL}$) which requires an infinite chain of role connections. For example, if we examine the satisfiability of the $\top$ concept w.r.t. the $\top \sqsubseteq \exists$hasChild.$\top$ axiom (everyone has a child), we are actually asking whether there can exist a chain of (not necessarily different) objects x_i, in which every adjacent pair is in a hasChild relation:

$$x_1 \text{ hasChild } x_2 \text{ hasChild } \cdots \text{ hasChild } x_n \text{ hasChild } x_{n+1} \text{ hasChild } \cdots \qquad (7.15)$$

Obviously, this infinite chain can be satisfied using an infinite model. However, we can also create a finite model, by forming a cycle, so that we identify x_i with an x_k (for some $k < i$), x_{i+1} with x_{k+1} etc. When a model is built from a tableau in which subset or equality blocking occurs then, in fact, a similar infinite chain is "cut short".

To enforce the existence of an infinite chain one can use transitivity instead of concept axioms. Recall one of our previous examples, (7.1). This was formulated in the language $\mathcal{AL}_{\mathcal{R}^+}$ and examines the satisfiability of the concept

$$\exists \text{hasDescendant}.\top \sqcap \forall \text{hasDescendant}.\exists \text{hasDescendant}.\top,$$

w.r.t. the Trans(hasDescendant) axiom. Thus the question is whether an infinite hasDescendant chain (similar to the previous hasChild chain) can exist. The answer, returned by the tableau algorithm, is again a finite model which contains a loop involving the hasDescendant relation.

By using the $\mathcal{SHI}$ model construction described in the previous section, we can build a *finite* model for every satisfiable concept. Thus, up to now, we have managed to "cut short" all infinite chains and so have proved that (any sublanguage of) $\mathcal{SHI}$ has the finite-model property.

However, with the introduction of functional restrictions we can form requirements that prevent us from identifying elements in infinite chains. Consider the following satisfiability problem, which uses the language $\mathcal{ALIF}$: examine the satisfiability of the concept $C_0 = \forall$hasChild$^-$.$\bot$ (has no parent) w.r.t. the TBox

$$\{\top \sqsubseteq \exists \text{hasChild}.\top \sqcap (\leqslant 1 \text{ hasChild}^-)\}. \qquad (7.16)$$

Informally, this TBox states that "everyone has a child and at most one parent".

Suppose that the above concept is satisfiable w.r.t. the given TBox using a finite model, which has, say, n elements. In this model at least n different hasChild relationships hold, because every object has a child. According to the TBox, however, it is also true that every individual has at most one parent. Furthermore, because the concept C_0 is satisfiable there has to be an individual that has no parent. This means that there can be at most $n - 1$ instances of the hasChild$^-$ relationship, which is clearly a contradiction. Thus we have shown that the concept C_0 cannot have a finite model w.r.t. the TBox (7.16).

However, an infinite model can be constructed in an obvious way. If we form an infinite chain of hasChild connections (just as in formula (7.15)), the first object will have no parent and the condition described by the TBox (7.16) is met. Thus, we have shown that in the $\mathcal{ALIF}$ language one can formulate a concept satisfiability problem which can be satisfied, although all its models are *infinite*.

These infinite models, however, are cyclic in the sense that they can be *described in a finite way*. For example, the chain (7.15) can be built by taking the x_1 hasChild x_2 edge, then copying this edge (viewed as a subgraph) to node x_2 (hence forming an x_2 hasChild x_3 edge), then copying the initial edge to node x_3 etc. This subgraph copying constitutes the basic idea of model construction for the $\mathcal{SHIF}$ and $\mathcal{SHIQ}$ tableaux.

Let us consider a slightly more complicated example, where we examine the satisfiability of a concept $C = \exists\mathsf{hasChild.Blonde} \sqcap \exists\mathsf{hasChild.Tall} \sqcap \exists\mathsf{hasChild.Thin} \sqcap (\leqslant 1\,\mathsf{hasChild}^-)$ w.r.t. the following TBox:

$$\mathsf{Tall} \sqsubseteq C. \tag{7.17}$$

If we examine the satisfiability of the concept C on its own, ignoring the axiom (7.17) for the moment, we obtain the complete tableau shown in Figure 7.5.[7]

Now consider the subsumption axiom (7.17), and create its internalised form: $\neg\mathsf{Tall} \sqcup C$. We need to add this concept to all the nodes of the tableau. The $\sqcup$-rule succeeds on its first branch by choosing $\neg\mathsf{Tall}$, unless the node label in question contains the concept Tall. This is the case for node d, where the first alternative of the union causes a clash and the tableau algorithm is forced to use the second alternative, extending the label of d with the concept C. Subsequently, this generates a subtree rooted at this node that is identical to the one in Figure 7.5. Figure 7.6 shows the tableau state obtained this way, in which node g is blocked by node d above it, as indicated by the broken arrow.

At this point the tableau algorithm terminates. Let us build a model from this tableau state. As node d blocks node g, the model-construction technique applied so far prescribes that these two nodes are to be identified. This would mean that the $\mathsf{hasChild}$ edge from d to g is "redirected" to d itself, i.e. it goes from d to d. However, this redirection would imply that d has two parents (two $\mathsf{hasChild}^-$ neighbours), thus violating the $(\leqslant 1\,\mathsf{hasChild}^-)$ condition present in the label of node d, as unfolded from the concept C.

As the redirection-based model construction technique therefore cannot be applied, we will use a so-called *copy-in* technique. This involves copying the complete subgraph under the blocking node (which, in our example, is identical to that in Figure 7.5) into the blocked

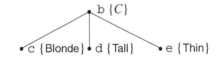

Figure 7.5. The tableau of concept C viewed on its own.

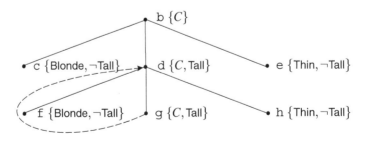

Figure 7.6. The complete tableau of the example.

[7] Note that in Figure 7.5 all edges are implicitly labelled with the role hasChild.

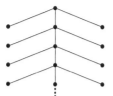 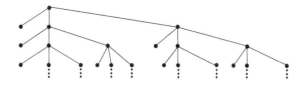

Figure 7.7. Infinite models: one-way and two-way repetition.

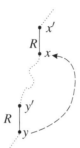

Figure 7.8. The pairwise blocking scheme.

node. Next, we repeat this procedure for the copy of the blocked node, and so on. The result will be an infinite tree, shown on the left-hand side of Figure 7.7. Naturally, if there are multiple blocked nodes then this infinite repetition has to be performed for them all.

For example, let us extend the TBox in question with the axiom Thin $\sqsubseteq$ C. In this case the concept C will also appear in the nodes on the right-hand side of the tableau; hence the branches on the right-hand side will also begin to "reproduce". In this case the complete tableau will be much larger, and a number of further blocking situations will appear, but sooner or later every branch will be blocked. If we apply the copy-in technique for the complete tableau, we obtain a model with infinite repetitions in two directions. The scheme of this model is shown on the right-hand side of Figure 7.7.

A formal description of the copy-in method will be discussed in Subsection 7.5.4, after our presentation of the $\mathcal{SHIF}$ tableau algorithm.

7.5.2. Pairwise blocking

In the preceding subsection we showed that the introduction of functional restrictions may require infinite models, which are built using the copy-in method. Up to now we have used equality blocking, which was originally introduced for the $\mathcal{SHI}$ language. However, the copy-in model construction method requires a stronger kind of blocking, so-called *pairwise blocking*.

In the case of pairwise blocking, equality of the labels of the blocked and blocking nodes is no longer enough. Figure 7.8 shows the scheme of pairwise blocking. The nodes shown in the figure are the following: y is the blocked node, y' being its predecessor, x is the blocking node and x' is its predecessor (here, y' and x are not necessarily different). The base condition of blocking, described in Figure 7.3, is now modified as follows.

The base condition for (pairwise) blocking We say that the base condition for blocking holds between a node y and its ancestor x if x has a predecessor x', y has a predecessor y' and the following statements hold for these nodes:

- $\mathcal{L}(y) = \mathcal{L}(x)$;
- $\mathcal{L}(y') = \mathcal{L}(x')$;
- $\mathcal{L}(\langle y', y \rangle) = \mathcal{L}(\langle x', x \rangle)$.

Thus, the base condition prescribes that the labels of the blocked and the blocking nodes are the same and that this also holds for their predecessors. Furthermore, the labels of the edges leading to the blocked and the blocking node are required to be the same.

Earlier, in Figure 7.3, we presented the definitions for direct and indirect blocking. These definitions remain unchanged; however, they now include the pairwise-blocking base condition presented above (as opposed to the equality-blocking condition used previously).

Despite the fact that the new base condition is much stronger than that of equality blocking, it still achieves its primary aim, namely preventing the tableau algorithm from looping. To understand why this is so, consider the following three parameters of an edge in a tableau graph: the labels of the two endpoints of the edge and the label of the edge itself. When we examining the satisfiability of a given concept w.r.t. a given TBox, find that only a finite number of such triples can be formed. The reason is that both the edge and node labels can only take values that are subsets of a fixed finite set (which, of course, depends on the reasoning task at hand). As only a finite number of such triples can exist, on any infinite branch of the tableau graph there must be a triple that occurs twice. This leads to pairwise blocking, which means that the branch cannot be continued forever.

Let us now examine what makes the introduction of the new blocking method necessary. We have already seen that the number restrictions introduced by the language extension $\mathcal{F}$ require the building of infinite models, for which the copy-in method is used. It is this technique that necessitates pairwise blocking.

To show that it is the copy-in technique which makes pairwise blocking necessary, we will consider the following satisfiability problem in the language $\mathcal{SHI}$. We will show that equality blocking is no longer sufficient when the copy-in method is used for building a model from a complete clash-free tableau.

Let us thus examine the satisfiability of the concept Tall w.r.t. a singleton TBox $\{\top \sqsubseteq C_0\}$, where $C_0 = \exists hC.\exists hC^-.\text{Tall}$. Here, the role name hC is shorthand for hasChild and so the TBox states that everyone has a child with a tall parent. The tableau algorithm first creates an hC-successor c for root node b, with the label $\exists hC^-.\text{Tall}$ as prescribed by C_0. It is important to note that the $\exists$-rule does not fire for this label, as c already has a hC^--neighbour with the Tall label, namely the node b above it. Because of the TBox, node c acquires the label C_0 as well, and this triggers the execution of the $\exists$-rule creating a node d, with a label identical to that of c. This tableau state is shown in Figure 7.9.

If we use equality blocking then node c blocks node d in this tableau state. When we use the redirection-based model construction method of the $\mathcal{SHI}$ tableau algorithm, in which the edge going from c to d is redirected to c itself, we obtain the following interpretation $\mathcal{I}: \Delta^\mathcal{I} = \{b, c\}$, $\text{Tall}^\mathcal{I} = \{b\}$, $hC^\mathcal{I} = \{\langle b, c \rangle, \langle c, c \rangle\}$. Obviously, $\mathcal{I}$ proves that the concept Tall is satisfiable w.r.t. the TBox $\{\top \sqsubseteq C_0\}$. However, when the copy-in method is used, we build a model by copying the edge c $\to$ d infinitely many times, one after the other. Hence,

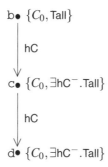

Figure 7.9. An example showing the necessity of using pairwise blocking.

we obtain a model, similar to the infinite interpretation shown in (7.15), in which only the starting node is Tall. Here, the axiom $\top \sqsubseteq C_0$ (everyone has a child with a tall parent) is clearly not met.

Let us now examine the difference between the two model-construction methods. In the redirection case, the blocked node d ceases to exist and the edge leading to it is redirected to node c instead. In contrast, when the copy-in method is used, d remains intact. For the model construction to be valid, the neighbourhood of d has to be the same as that of the blocking node c. The *downward* neighbours of d are identical to those of the blocking node c (as the former are copies of the latter). However, the labels of the upper neighbours of c and d may be different. In node c, it is the edge coming from above that ensures that c is an instance of the concept $\exists hC^-.\mathsf{Tall}$. As the hC^--neighbour of d is not Tall, this node will not have a tall parent in the copy-in model and as a result c will not belong to the concept C_0. In other words, the interpretation built by using the copy-in method will not be a model of the TBox $\{\top \sqsubseteq C_0\}$.

Let us consider again the tableau state in Figure 7.9 consisting of three nodes, and see what happens when pairwise blocking is used. Now d is not blocked by c, as the labels of their predecessors differ. Consequently, we must continue building the tableau graph: we have to add a Tall hC^--successor to d (call it e) and, because of C_0, we also have to add an hC-successor (call it f). The latter, labelled $\{C_0, \exists hC^-.\mathsf{Tall}\}$, will be blocked by d, according to the stronger, pairwise, blocking as the labels of the three hC-successor nodes c, d and f are the same. Similarly, node e will also acquire a successor but thereafter the conditions of pairwise blocking will be met on this branch as well. We leave it to the reader to fill in the precise details of this tableau construction, in the following exercise.

Exercise 7.9: Extend the tableau shown in Figure 7.9, using pairwise blocking, until it becomes complete.

The conditions of pairwise blocking extend those of equality blocking by the requirement that the "upper" neighbours of the blocking node x and the blocked node y are the same. Consequently, when the successors of node x (its "lower" neighbours) are copied under node y, the whole neighbourhood of y will be exactly the same as that of the blocking node x. This ensures that a model built from a complete tableau, using the copy-in method, is correct: every blocked node does indeed belong to each concept appearing in its label. In essence, this depends on the fact that the transformation rules examine and affect only the immediate neighbour nodes of the node in question.

Exercise 7.10: Assume that we are introducing an "optimised" version of the $\exists$-rule, which does not fire for a node labelled with $\exists R.\exists R.C$ provided that the node already has an R-neighbour having an R-neighbour labelled C. Using the tableau algorithm thus modified and the pairwise blocking condition, construct a complete tableau for which the copy-in method does not yield a proper model. What kind of blocking is needed to cater for the "optimised" $\exists$-rule?

The $\mathcal{SHI}$ example of Figure 7.9 can be easily extended to a $\mathcal{SHIF}$ reasoning task, which requires the use of the copy-in method; then pairwise blocking cannot be avoided. For this we only need a minor modification: consider checking the satisfiability of the concept Tall w.r.t. the TBox $\{\top \sqsubseteq C_1\}$, where $C_1 = C_0 \sqcap (\leqslant 1\,\text{hC}^-)$ (everyone has at most one parent). Here, the internalised concept to be added to each node contains the number restriction $(\leqslant 1\,\text{hC}^-)$. The only modification this causes in the tableau graph of Figure 7.9 is that the number restriction will appear in the labels of all three nodes. However, none of these changes will cause a rule to fire, as no node has two parents. Figure 7.9, thus modified, is still a complete tableau if equality blocking is employed. However, no model can be built from this tableau: the redirection method cannot be used, because of the number restriction, while the copy-in method, as in the case discussed previously, results in a model in which most nodes do not belong the concept C_1.

Again, the solution is to use pairwise blocking. Thus, the tableau state with three nodes is not considered complete and is further transformed, just as in the $\mathcal{SHI}$ example. Obviously, we have to take into account the new number restriction and so some nodes mentioned in the explanation of the $\mathcal{SHI}$ example, namely e and c – both an hC$^-$ neighbour of d – have to be identified. Working out the details of this tableau construction is again left to the reader; see Exercise 7.11 below.

7.5.3. The $\mathcal{SHIF}$ tableau algorithm

In Subsections 7.5.1 and 7.5.2 we discussed the two major problems raised by the language extension $\mathcal{F}$: the issues of infinite models and blocking. Before describing the $\mathcal{SHIF}$ tableau algorithm itself, we present an overview of further modifications which become necessary owing to the introduction of the new language elements mentioned at the start of the section.

Multiple edge labels. If a node has a label $(\leqslant 1\,R)$ and it has two R-neighbours then these – as for the $\mathcal{ALCN}$ tableau algorithm – have to be identified. However, the labels of the edges leading to these two R-neighbours might actually be different, owing to role hierarchy. For example, let us assume that a node x has a hasRelative-successor and a hasFriend-successor and that furthermore the concept $(\leqslant 1\,\text{knows})$ appears in the label of x, where hasFriend $\sqsubseteq$ knows and hasRelative $\sqsubseteq$ knows hold.[8] Owing to the number restriction the two successors

---

[8] Thus we are assuming that neither of the hasRelative and hasFriend roles subsumes the other, i.e. friends are not necessarily relatives and relatives are not necessarily friends.

have to be identified into a single node, which has to be both a hasRelative-successor and a hasFriend-successor of the node x.

Because of this, the data structure implementing the tableau graph has to be changed. Edges are no longer labelled with a single role but, instead, with a set of roles. The definitions of successor and neighbour are changed accordingly.

- A node y is an R-successor of a node x if there is an $S \in \mathcal{L}(\langle x, y \rangle)$ for which $S \sqsubseteq R \in \mathcal{R}_\mathcal{T}$ holds.

- A node y is an R-neighbour of x if y is an R-successor of x or x is an $\mathsf{Inv}(R)$-successor of y.[9]

Handling at-most restrictions. New rules have to be introduced to deal with the $\leqslant$ and $\geqslant$ concept constructors. The $\leqslant$-rule fires if the $(\leqslant 1 R)$ concept appears in the label of a node which has at least two R-neighbours. In this case, one R-neighbour inherits the concepts in the label of the other, and its edge label is extended with the roles in the label of the other edge. At the same time this other edge is erased, along with the whole subtree below it.

This approach differs from that used in the description of the $\mathcal{ALCN}$ tableau algorithm (Figure 5.4). There, the $\leqslant$-rule transferred the edges (and the subtrees rooted there) from the node being eliminated to the node that survives. In the $\mathcal{SHIF}$ tableau algorithm, presented now, we do not relocate subtrees; this keeps the rules as simple as possible and does not cause any problems, as the surviving node inherits the labels of the eliminated node and consequently will be able to regenerate the necessary subtrees. Naturally, one may use this subtree-relocation technique in an actual implementation, to improve the efficiency of the algorithm.

The elimination of a subtree of the tableau graph is actually carried out by setting the label of the uppermost edge of the subtree in question equal to the empty set $\emptyset$. All nodes below an edge labelled with $\emptyset$ are considered indirectly blocked and from now on will remain in this state. This means that the tableau algorithm will never again examine the eliminated part of the tableau graph.

Handling at-least restrictions. The task of the $\geqslant$-rule is to create two distinct (i.e. non-identifiable) R-successors for every node with a $(\geqslant 2 R)$ label. To ensure that the successors cannot be identified with each other, the transformation rule uses A_{spec} as the label of the first node and $\neg A_{spec}$ as that of the other. Here, A_{spec} is a fixed atomic concept that does not appear in the concept C being examined. Note that this form of the $\geqslant$-rule is inefficient, as the subtrees being built at the two nodes will be identical (except for the A_{spec} and $\neg A_{spec}$ concepts in the node labels).[10] The reason for choosing this form of the rule is that the properties of the tableau algorithm, such as the soundness of model construction, are then easier to prove.

---

[9] Note that the wording of this definition is the same as in Subsection 7.4.1, where the notion of *neighbour* was introduced. However, the meaning is different as the present definition uses the modified notion of an R-successor.

[10] The $\mathcal{SHIF}$ tableau algorithm can be made more efficient by creating only a single R-successor in the $\geqslant$-rule and at the same time introducing a new clash condition; the appearance of the concepts $(\geqslant 2 R)$ and $(\leqslant 1 R)$ together in the same label is now considered as a clash; see Subsection 7.9.1.

∃-rule

Condition:　　　$(\exists R.C) \in \mathcal{L}(x)$, x not blocked, and

　　　　　　　　x has no y R-neighbour for which $C \in \mathcal{L}(y)$.

New state **T′***:*　$V' = V \cup \{y\}$ ($y \notin V$ a new node),

　　　　　　　　$E' = E \cup \{\langle x,y \rangle\}$, $\mathcal{L}'(\langle x,y \rangle) = \underline{\{R\}}$, $\mathcal{L}'(y) = \{C\}$.

⩾-rule

Condition:　　　$(\geqslant 2\,R) \in \mathcal{L}(x)$, x not blocked, and

　　　　　　　　x has no y R-successor for which $A_{spec} \in \mathcal{L}(y)$.

New state **T′***:*　$V' = V \cup \{y,z\}$ ($y,z \notin V$ new nodes),

　　　　　　　　$E' = E \cup \{\langle x,y \rangle, \langle x,z \rangle\}$,

　　　　　　　　$\mathcal{L}'(\langle x,y \rangle) = \{R\}, \mathcal{L}'(\langle x,z \rangle) = \{R\}$,

　　　　　　　　$\mathcal{L}'(y) = \{A_{spec}\}, \mathcal{L}'(z) = \{\neg A_{spec}\}$.

⩽-rule

Condition:　　　$(\leqslant 1\,R) \in \mathcal{L}(x)$, x not directly blocked, and

　　　　　　　　x has two R-neighbours, y and z, where x is not a successor of y.

New state **T′***:*　$\mathcal{L}'(z) = \mathcal{L}(z) \cup \mathcal{L}(y)$.

　　　　　　　　$\mathcal{L}'(\langle x,y \rangle) = \emptyset$,

　　　　　　　　$\mathcal{L}'(\langle z,x \rangle) = \mathcal{L}(\langle z,x \rangle) \cup \mathsf{Inv}(\mathcal{L}(\langle x,y \rangle))$ if x is a successor of z,

　　　　　　　　$\mathcal{L}'(\langle x,z \rangle) = \mathcal{L}(\langle x,z \rangle) \cup \mathcal{L}(\langle x,y \rangle)$ if x is not a successor of z.

Figure 7.10.　The modified and new transformation rules of the $\mathcal{SHIF}$ tableau algorithm.

The tableau algorithm.　　Figure 7.10 presents the ∃-, ⩾- and ⩽- rules of the $\mathcal{SHIF}$ tableau algorithm. The other rules are the same as their $\mathcal{SHI}$ counterparts. The ∃-rule is only slightly modified, to reflect the change of edge labels: the label of the edge created is now a singleton set of roles rather than a single role (this change is indicated by underlining).

The ⩾-rule, which generates new nodes, like the ∃-rule, fires only if the node in question is not blocked. The phrase "has no y R-successor for which $A_{spec} \in \mathcal{L}(y)$", which appears in the condition part of the rule, ensures that the rule can be applied at most once to every node. Note that the "successor" relationship is used here, instead of "neighbour", as a node may have an upper neighbour with A_{spec} in its label even if the ⩾-rule has never been applied to it.

Since the ⩽-rule does not create new nodes, it can be applied to both non-blocked and directly blocked nodes. The last two lines of Figure 7.10 represent alternative branches, which correspond to two different topologies:

- the case of an upper and a lower neighbour;
- the case of two lower neighbours.[11]

In the condition part of the rule, the following text appears: "x has two R-neighbours, y and z, where x is not a successor of y." The final "where ..." phrase represents a naming convention

---

[11] The tableau graph is actually a tree, hence the root has zero upper neighbours, the other nodes having exactly one upper neighbour.

rather than a proper condition. It simply requires that if either y or z is an upper neighbour of x then this upper neighbour should thenceforth be denoted by z. The last two lines of the rule handle the merging of the edge labels: the first deals with the case when z is an upper, while the second when z is a lower neighbour, of x. Notice that in the last but one line the Inv operation is applied to a set of roles $\mathcal{S} = \mathcal{L}(\langle x,y \rangle)$ (as now the edges are labelled with sets). Here, $\mathsf{Inv}(\mathcal{S})$ denotes a set whose elements are obtained by applying the Inv syntactical transformation to the elements of $\mathcal{S}$, one by one.

Exercise 7.11: Using the $\mathcal{SHIF}$ tableau rules described above check the satisfiability of the concept Tall w.r.t. the TBox

$$\{\top \sqsubseteq \exists hC.\exists hC^-.\mathsf{Tall}\} \sqcap (\leqslant 1\, hC^-).$$

Note that this task was discussed briefly in Subsection 7.5.2.

7.5.4. Model construction

In this section we present the formal description of the copy-in model construction method. We start with the example tableau shown in Figure 7.6, which is complete and clash-free. The left-hand side of Figure 7.7 shows the infinite tree structure that we would like to obtain using the copy-in method. In order to formalise the process, let us try to systematically assign names to the nodes of the infinite tree structure, using the node names of the original tableau. Figure 7.11 shows two such naming schemes, both using the non-blocked nodes of the tableau for naming the nodes of the infinite tree.

On the left-hand side of Figure 7.11 the copies are distinguished using indices. In this simple, linear, example, it can be done easily. However, in a more complex case, with multiple occurrences of blocking, such a solution quickly becomes difficult to follow. On the right-hand side of Figure 7.11, the nodes are marked with letter sequences representing the path from the root to the given node. These paths can be derived from the redirected version of the original tableau as well (Figure 7.6). In the resulting graph, the finite paths starting at the root can be easily mapped to the nodes of the infinite tree on the right-hand side of Figure 7.11. For example, node f_2 can be obtained by following the path b–d–d–f (here, the second edge starts from d and then reaches the blocked node g, through which it goes to the

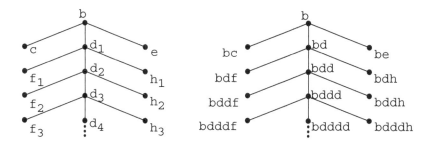

Figure 7.11. Naming schemes for infinite trees.

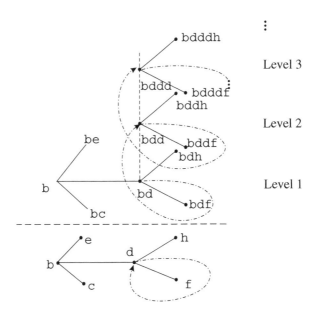

Figure 7.12. Infinite tree structure represented by a spiral.

blocking node, which is again d). Thus, the node f_2 on the left-hand side tree of Figure 7.11 is called bddf in the right-hand side tree.

The construction of an infinite tree can be visualised in three dimensions, as shown in Figure 7.12. Here the parts of the infinite tree that are the copies of the same subtree of the tableau are positioned one above the other. In the process of copying in, whenever we reach an edge going to a blocked node, instead of following that edge we go to a *copy* of the subtree rooted at the blocking node, placed one level higher. At the bottom of the figure, we see the projection of an infinite spiral. This is actually the redirected version of the tableau in question (it corresponds to the ABox $IdBlock_{\mathbf{T}}\ \mathcal{A}_{\mathbf{T}}$, where $\mathbf{T}$ is the tableau of Figure 7.6).

To proceed with the general case, let us consider a complete and clash-free $\mathcal{SHIF}$ tableau $\mathbf{T} = \langle V, E, \mathcal{L}(, I)\rangle$, built for checking the satisfiability of a concept C w.r.t. the extended TBox $\mathcal{R}_{\mathcal{T}}$. The nodes blocked indirectly are again removed using the $Base_{\mathbf{T}}$ transformation, as defined in (7.13). Our task is to show the satisfiability of the ABox $Base_{\mathbf{T}}\ \mathcal{A}_{\mathbf{T}}$ by building a model. Just as before, the model is created using further transformations. The instances of our initial ABox are named using *sequences* of names of the tableau nodes. To be more precise, we collect sequences representing a path originating from the root node within the redirection-based closure of the tableau.[12]

To define such paths, we introduce the following notation: a node $y \in V$ is an R-heir of a node $x \in V$ in a tableau $\mathbf{T}$ if neither x nor y is blocked in $\mathbf{T}$ and if

---

[12] This also means that we are now speaking about infinite ABoxes. At first glance, this might seem problematic, as so far we have considered the ABox as an input parameter of the reasoning task, which is obviously finite. However, in the definition of the ABox and the concepts related to it, we neither noted, nor used, its finiteness. In order to avoid the introduction of a new mathematical structure, we continue to prove the satisfiability of the model using transformations of (by now, infinite) ABoxes.

- either $R \in \mathcal{L}(\langle x, y \rangle)$, i.e. there is an edge from x to y, labelled R,

- or there is a node z such that y blocks z and $R \in \mathcal{L}(\langle x, z \rangle)$, i.e. there is an edge labelled R from x to a node z which is blocked by y.

Furthermore, we will say that a node $y \in V$ is an heir of a node $x \in V$ if there is an R for which y is an R-heir of node x. For example, in the tableau shown in Figure 7.6, node d is an hC-heir of b, because of the first alternative,[13] whilst d is also an hC-heir of itself according to the second bullet point in the above definition (as d has an hC-successor g that is blocked by d). The lower part of Figure 7.12 – which is the projection of the upper part – can be viewed as a graph representing the "heir" relationship: a solid edge corresponds to the first bullet point, while the broken and dotted edge corresponds to the second bullet point.

Exercise 7.12: Show that the statement "y is an R-heir of x" is true in a tableau $\mathbf{T}$ if, and only if, the ABox $IdBlock_{\mathbf{T}} Base_{\mathbf{T}} \mathcal{A}_{\mathbf{T}}$ contains the statement $R(x, y)$.

Building upon the "heir" relationship, we can now proceed to describe the formal definition of the infinite copy-in ABox corresponding to a $\mathcal{SHIF}$ tableau $\mathbf{T}$. This ABox is named $\mathcal{A}_{\mathbf{T}}^{cp}$, where the upper index cp indicates *copy*.

First, we define the set of instance names of the ABox as follows:

$$Dom_{\mathbf{T}}^{cp} = \{[x_0, \ldots, x_n] \mid \text{the root of } \mathbf{T} \text{ is } x_0, x_0 \text{ has an heir } x_1,$$
$$x_1 \text{ has an heir } x_2, \ldots, x_{n-1} \text{ has an heir } x_n\}. \tag{7.18}$$

Thus, the entities in the ABox are finite lists (of unbounded length), whose first element is the root of the tableau $\mathbf{T}$ and whose adjacent elements are in the "heir" relationship.

Let us denote by $last(X)$ the last element of a list $X = [x_0, \ldots, x_n]$, i.e. $last(X) = x_n$. Furthermore, let the expression $X \oplus Y$ denote the concatenation of two lists X and Y. To be more precise, $X \oplus Y = [x_0, \ldots, x_n, y_0, \ldots, y_k]$, assuming that X is as defined above and that $Y = [y_0, \ldots, y_k]$. Using this latter notation, $last(X)$ might also be defined in the following way: $last(X) = x$ if there is a list U for which $U \oplus [x] = X$.

Using the above notation, we define an infinite copy-in ABox as follows:

$$\mathcal{A}_{\mathbf{T}}^{cp} = \{C(X) \mid X \in Dom_{\mathbf{T}}^{cp}, last(X) = x \text{ and } C \in \mathcal{L}(x)\}$$
$$\cup \{R(X, Y) \mid X, Y \in Dom_{\mathbf{T}}^{cp}, X \oplus [y] = Y \text{ and } y \text{ is an } R\text{-heir of } last(X)\}.$$

In this ABox, the concept assertions depend only on the endpoint of the path. Notice that this means that the nodes above each other in Figure 7.12 always belong to the same concept.

Exercise 7.13: Build the ABox $\mathcal{A}_{\mathbf{T}}^{cp}$ for the example tableau $\mathbf{T}$ of Figure 7.6. Show that this ABox is *self-realising*, i.e. its natural interpretation is a model of the ABox.

Let us now finalise the construction of a model for the ABox $\mathcal{A}_{\mathbf{T}}^{cp}$ w.r.t. $\mathcal{T}$. The statement of the above exercise, i.e. that $\mathcal{A}_{\mathbf{T}}^{cp}$ is self-realising, is true in general, assuming that there are no transitive or inverse roles and that no role hierarchy is present in the reasoning task.

---

[13] Note that edge labels are not shown in Figure 7.6 for the sake of simplicity, as each is labelled with $\{hC\}$.

However, when an ABox uses such language elements, the appropriate closure operations, as introduced earlier, have to be applied to it. It can easily be demonstrated that the appropriate closure of the ABox is in fact self-realising; i.e. the interpretation

$$\mathcal{I}_{\mathbf{T}} = \mathcal{I}^{nat}(ClosHT_{\mathcal{T}}\ ClosI\ A_{\mathbf{T}}^{cp})$$

satisfies concept C w.r.t. the TBox $\mathcal{T}$.

7.6. Qualified number restrictions – extension $\mathcal{Q}$

The language extension $\mathcal{Q}$ introduces the $(\leqslant n R.C)$ and $(\geqslant n R.C)$ qualified number restrictions. In this section we give an informal overview of the modifications in the tableau algorithm which are required for this extension. The precise details of the $\mathcal{SHIQ}$ tableau algorithm will be presented in the next section.

In Section 5.3 we described the $\leqslant$- and $\geqslant$- rules in the context of the $\mathcal{ALCN}$ tableau algorithm. Recall that – in comparison with the *unqualified* number restrictions of $\mathcal{N}$ – extension $\mathcal{Q}$ makes it possible to place restrictions on the number of successors *belonging to a specific concept*. For example, with the qualified number restriction $(\geqslant 2\,\mathsf{hasChild.Tall})$ we can require the existence of two tall children, as opposed to the unqualified case, where we could request the existence only of two children of whatever kind.

Thus the $\leqslant$- and $\geqslant$- rules of the $\mathcal{SHIQ}$ tableau algorithm differ from their $\mathcal{ALCN}$ counterparts only in that they now speak about neighbours which are labelled with the concept specified in the qualified number restriction.

- The $\leqslant$-rule fires for a concept $(\leqslant n R.C)$ if it finds $n+1$ R-neighbours that all have the label C, and it performs an appropriate identification in this case.

- The $\geqslant$-rule fires for a concept $(\geqslant n R.C)$ if it does *not* find n R-neighbours that all have the C label, and in this case it creates n instances of non-identifiable R-successors labelled with the concept C.

The last component of the tableau quadruple – the inequality store I, containing node-pairs that cannot be identified – will be used again in the $\mathcal{SHIQ}$ tableau algorithm. This approach is more general and more efficient than that previously used in the $\mathcal{SHIF}$ algorithm, where a special A_{spec} concept was introduced to avoid identification of the two successors created by a $\geqslant$-rule.

Earlier, when the inequality store was introduced for $\mathcal{ALCN}$, we had to define a new clash condition. Now, a similar new condition has to be defined for $\mathcal{SHIQ}$: if a tableau node has a label $(\leqslant n R.C)$, and at the same time it has $n+1$ successors with the label C, no two of which can be identified with each other, then the tableau is said to contain a clash.

The set of rules introduced thus far is not sufficient. The reason is that one can define a concept which is obviously unsatisfiable, but for which no clash is produced by the tableau algorithm as described so far. For example, let us examine the satisfiability of the concept $(\geqslant 3\,\mathsf{hasChild.\top}) \sqcap (\leqslant 1\,\mathsf{hasChild.Blonde}) \sqcap (\leqslant 1\,\mathsf{hasChild.\neg Blonde})$. The first member of the intersection will create three hasChild-successors with empty labels. The $\leqslant$-rule only fires if it finds two nodes with either Blonde or $\neg$Blonde appearing in their labels – but these labels are now empty. In conclusion there is no rule to apply, and no clash is detected. At the same time, the concept is clearly unsatisfiable.

One might experiment with more complex clash conditions, designed to detect inconsistencies similar to the above. As a generalisation of the example, one could consider introducing a clash condition which states that the appearance of the concepts $(\geqslant kR)$, $(\leqslant nR.C)$, $(\leqslant mR.D)$ represents a clash, assuming that $C \sqcup D \equiv \top$ and $n + m < k$.[14] However, deciding whether $C \sqcup D \equiv \top$ holds represents a challenging reasoning task on its own.

Instead of introducing a new clash condition, a simpler solution will be adopted. A new transformation rule is introduced, the so-called *choice rule*. This rule fires if an arbitrary qualified number restriction $(\bowtie nR.C)$ appears in the label of a node, where $\bowtie$ denotes either the $\leqslant$ or the $\geqslant$ sign. In effect, for every R-successor of the node we create a choice point. On the first branch of the choice point we add the concept C to the label of the given R-successor and on the second branch, the negation of C. In our example this means that the choice rule will fire three times, once for each hasChild-successor. In each case it will extend the label of the given successor either with the concept Blonde or with the concept ¬Blonde. As soon as two successors receive the same label (which will happen on all branches, sooner or later), our newly introduced clash condition is met. Hence, after checking all possibilities the algorithm will return a "not satisfiable" answer, as expected.

Exercise 7.14: Draw a search tree of tableau states, similar to that shown in Figure 5.7, for the reasoning task discussed above, i.e. for checking whether the concept

$$(\geqslant 3 \, \mathsf{hasChild}. \top) \sqcap (\leqslant 1 \, \mathsf{hasChild}.\mathsf{Blonde}) \sqcap (\leqslant 1 \, \mathsf{hasChild}.\neg\mathsf{Blonde})$$

is satisfiable. After each firing of the $\bowtie$-rule, check whether the $\leqslant$-rule is applicable. How many choice points are there in this search tree?

Note that the choice rule requires that the *negation* of the concept C appearing in the number restriction is included in the label of some successors. Recall that the tableau algorithm relies on concepts being in negation normal form, so at this point $\neg C$ has to be transformed to this normal form.

Thus far, the labels of the tableau graph contained only the subconcepts of the concept in question. With the introduction of the choice rule, the node labels may include the negations of such subconcepts, transformed to negation normal form (and the subconcepts of these and their negations etc.). This larger set is still finite, however, so our earlier claim, that on each infinite branch of the tableau tree blocking will occur sooner or later, still holds.

We do not include here a formal description of the extensions of the tableau algorithm made necessary by number restrictions, as the whole $\mathcal{SHIQ}$ tableau algorithm is fully described in the next section.

7.7. The complete $\mathcal{SHIQ}$ tableau algorithm

This section gives a detailed definition of the tableau algorithm for the $\mathcal{SHIQ}$ language. To make the section self-contained, all elements of the algorithm and all related definitions are given.

---

[14] In fact, one should state a generalisation of this clash condition for an arbitrary number of concepts, the union of which is $\top$.

7.7.1. The task of the algorithm

The task of the algorithm is to determine whether an $\mathcal{SHIQ}$ concept expression C, formulated in negation normal form, can be satisfied w.r.t. a TBox $\mathcal{T}$ containing only role axioms.

In Subsection 4.7.2 we showed that, by internalisation, the satisfiability check of an $\mathcal{SHIQ}$ concept w.r.t. a TBox $\mathcal{T}$ can be reduced to a satisfiability check of another concept w.r.t. a TBox that only contains role axioms.

An expression is of negation normal form if the negation constructor $\neg$ only appears before atomic concepts within the expression. The equivalent negation normal form of any $\mathcal{SHIQ}$ concept can be formed easily by repeatedly applying the rules shown in Figure 7.13. (Similar rules for the $\mathcal{ALCN}$ language were shown in Figure 5.2.)

Exercise 7.15: Transform the following concepts to negation normal form:

(a) $C_1 = \neg\exists\mathsf{hasChild}.(\geqslant 2\,\mathsf{hasFriend}.(\mathsf{Blonde} \sqcap \neg\mathsf{Tall}))$;

(b) $C_2 = \forall\mathsf{hasChild}.(\leqslant 1\,\mathsf{hasFriend}.\neg(\mathsf{Blonde} \sqcap \neg\mathsf{Tall}))$;

(c) $C_3 = \neg\forall\mathsf{hasChild}.(\geqslant 1\,\mathsf{hasFriend}.\neg\mathsf{Optimist})$;

(d) $C_4 = \neg\forall\mathsf{hasChild}.(\neg\forall\mathsf{hasFriend}.\mathsf{Optimist})$.

Are any two of these concepts equivalent?

Given that internalisation reduces an arbitrary concept-satisfiability problem to another having role axioms only and that the arbitrary concepts can be brought to negation normal form, we conclude that the $\mathcal{SHIQ}$ tableau algorithm can be used to decide the satisfiability of an *arbitrary* concept w.r.t. an *arbitrary* TBox.

7.7.2. The tableau algorithm

Let C be a $\mathcal{SHIQ}$ concept expression in negation normal form and let $\mathcal{T}$ be a TBox containing only role axioms. The algorithm decides whether C is satisfiable w.r.t. $\mathcal{T}$.

The main data structure of the tableau algorithm is the *tableau state*. This consists of a labelled graph, called the tableau graph, and an inequality store. The nodes of the tableau

$$\neg\neg C \Rightarrow C,$$
$$\neg(C \sqcap D) \Rightarrow \neg C \sqcup \neg D,$$
$$\neg(C \sqcup D) \Rightarrow \neg C \sqcap \neg D,$$
$$\neg(\exists R.C) \Rightarrow \forall R.\neg C,$$
$$\neg(\forall R.C) \Rightarrow \exists R.\neg C,$$
$$\neg(\leqslant n R.C) \Rightarrow (\geqslant m R.C) \qquad \text{where } m = n+1,$$
$$\neg(\geqslant 1 R.C) \Rightarrow \forall R.\neg C$$
$$\neg(\geqslant n R.C) \Rightarrow (\leqslant m R.C) \qquad \text{where } m = n-1 \text{ and } n > 1.$$

Figure 7.13. Transforming $\mathcal{SHIQ}$ concepts to negation normal form.

graph are labelled with sets of concept expressions, while the edges are labelled with sets of role expressions. Tableau states are modified by the application of tableau transformation rules.

Preliminaries.   Let $\sim D$ stand for the negation normal form of the concept expression $\neg D$. Given an arbitrary concept expression D, we define the set $subneg(D)$ to be the smallest set containing D which is closed with respect to both the $\sim$ operation and the subconcept relation.[15] Furthermore let $roles(D)$ denote the set of roles appearing in D.

Exercise 7.16: Let a concept C be the negation normal form of $C_1 \sqcap C_3$, where the latter concepts are defined in Exercise 7.15(a), (c). Build the sets $subneg(C)$ and $roles(C)$.

The node labels in the tableau graph are subsets of $subneg(C)$, because the initial tableau graph contains the concept C only and the tableau transformation rules have the property formulated in the following exercise.

Exercise 7.17: Consider all tableau transformation rules defined so far. Verify that whenever a tableau transformation rule introduces a new concept, the latter is derived from a concept already present in the tableau graph by either selection of a subconcept or application of the $\sim$ operation.

The edge labels can contain only role expressions which appear in the concepts in the node labels, i.e. those appearing in $subneg(C)$.[16] Note that the set of roles appearing in $subneg(C)$ is the same as that appearing in C, as no new role expressions are introduced when $subneg(C)$ is formed from C. Thus the edge labels are subsets of $roles(C)$.

Extending the TBox.   In the course of the tableau algorithm, as well as the role axioms explicitly present in the TBox $\mathcal{T}$, we also need to take into account the axioms which can be inferred from these. This extended TBox is denoted by $\mathcal{R}_\mathcal{T}$ and is defined as the smallest set satisfying the following conditions.

    (a) If $\mathcal{T} \in \mathcal{T}$ then $\mathcal{T} \in \mathcal{R}_\mathcal{T}$.

    (b) If R is a role name appearing in $\mathcal{T}$ or $R \in roles(C)$ then $R \sqsubseteq R \in \mathcal{R}_\mathcal{T}$.

    (c) If $\text{Trans}(R) \in \mathcal{R}_\mathcal{T}$ then $\text{Trans}(\text{Inv}(R)) \in \mathcal{R}_\mathcal{T}$.   (7.19)

    (d) If $R \sqsubseteq S \in \mathcal{R}_\mathcal{T}$ then $\text{Inv}(R) \sqsubseteq \text{Inv}(S) \in \mathcal{R}_\mathcal{T}$.

    (e) If $R \sqsubseteq R' \in \mathcal{R}_\mathcal{T}$ and $R' \sqsubseteq R'' \in \mathcal{R}_\mathcal{T}$ then $R \sqsubseteq R'' \in \mathcal{R}_\mathcal{T}$.

Clearly, the set $\mathcal{R}_\mathcal{T}$ depends not only on $\mathcal{T}$ but also on the concept C at hand. For the sake of simplicity, this dependence is not reflected in the notation.

---

[15] In other words, $S = subneg(D)$ implies $D \in S$, and, if $D' \in S$, then both $\sim D' \in S$ and $sub(D') \subset S$ hold. Furthermore, S is the smallest set satisfying these conditions.

[16] The TBox $\mathcal{T}$ might contain roles other than those in $subneg(C)$, but these will not appear in the tableau data structure.

The tableau state.   Formally, the tableau graph is a triple $\langle V, E, \mathcal{L} \rangle$, where V is the set of nodes, $E \subseteq V \times V$ is the set of edges and $\mathcal{L}$ is a function that assigns *labels* to the nodes and edges. The labelling function $\mathcal{L}$ maps every node $x \in V$ to a set of concepts $\mathcal{L}(x) \subseteq subneg(C)$ and every edge $\langle x, y \rangle \in E$ to a set of roles $\mathcal{L}(\langle x, y \rangle) \subseteq roles(C)$. In addition to the graph, we also store a set I consisting of inequalities of the form $x \not\approx y$, where $x, y \in V$ are nodes of the graph. We say that nodes x and y are *identifiable* if $x \not\approx y \notin I$ and $y \not\approx x \notin I$.

Thus, a tableau state $\mathbf{T}$ can be described by a quadruple $\langle V, E, \mathcal{L}, I \rangle$.

The structure of the tableau graph.   The basic positional relationships between the nodes of a tableau graph are defined as follows.

- A node y is said to be an *R-successor* of a node x if there is a role expression $S \in \mathcal{L}(\langle x, y \rangle)$ for which $S \sqsubseteq R \in \mathcal{R}_{\mathcal{T}}$. In this case, we also say that y is a successor of x.

- A node y is an *R-neighbour* of a node x if it is an R-successor of x or if x is an $\mathsf{Inv}(R)$-successor of y.

- A node x is a *predecessor* of a node y if y is a successor of x.

- A node x is an *ancestor* of a node z if x is a predecessor of z or if x is a predecessor of a node y such that y is an ancestor of z.

- A node z is a *descendant* of a node x if x is an ancestor of z.

Following normal English usage, the statement "node x has a successor (neighbour, ...) y" is equivalent to the sentence "node y is a successor (neighbour, ...) of x".

Blocking.   We now define the base condition for pairwise blocking and three kinds of blocking condition for a tableau $\mathbf{T}$.

- We say that the base condition for (pairwise) blocking holds between a node y and its ancestor x if x has a predecessor x', y has a predecessor y' and the following statements hold for these nodes:
  - $\mathcal{L}(y) = \mathcal{L}(x)$;
  - $\mathcal{L}(y') = \mathcal{L}(x')$;
  - $\mathcal{L}(\langle y', y \rangle) = \mathcal{L}(\langle x', x \rangle)$.

- A node y is *directly blocked* if it has an ancestor x such that the base condition for blocking holds between y and x and, furthermore, y has no two ancestors for which the condition holds. In this case we also say that y is blocked by x (or that x blocks y).

- A node y is *indirectly blocked* if it has a predecessor x which is either directly blocked or for which the label of the edge from x to y is empty, i.e. $\mathcal{L}(\langle x, y \rangle) = \emptyset$ (the latter condition can hold only when node y has been identified with another node and hence is of no further interest to the algorithm). Furthermore, a node is indirectly blocked if it has an ancestor which is indirectly blocked.

- A node is *blocked* if it is directly or indirectly blocked.

Clashes.   We now describe the conditions under which a tableau state is considered to be inconsistent. A tableau state is said to contain a *clash* if the tableau graph contains a node x for which

- $\perp \in \mathcal{L}(x)$, or

- $\{C, \neg C\} \subseteq \mathcal{L}(x)$, or

- $(\leqslant nR.C) \in \mathcal{L}(x)$ and x has $n+1$ R-neighbours $y_0, \ldots, y_n$ such that $C \in \mathcal{L}(y_i), i = 0, \ldots n$, and no two of the nodes $y_0, \ldots, y_n$ are identifiable.

Initialisation.   The initial state of the tableau algorithm is $\mathbf{T}_0 = \langle \{x_0\}, \emptyset, \mathcal{L}_0, \emptyset \rangle$. Here, the set of inequalities is empty: the graph has no edges and only a single node x_0, which is called the *root node*. The label of the root node is $\{C\}$, i.e. $\mathcal{L}_0(x_0) = \{C\}$ where C is the root concept, i.e. the concept expression whose satisfiability is being investigated.

The tableau transformation rules.   Figures 7.14 and 7.15 show the transformation rules of the $\mathcal{SHIQ}$ tableau algorithm. A given rule can be applied in a tableau state $\mathbf{T} = \langle V, E, \mathcal{L}, I \rangle$ for an arbitrary node $x \in V$ if the firing condition stated in the rule is met. The application of a rule results in one or more new tableau states $\mathbf{T}' = \langle V', E', \mathcal{L}', I' \rangle$. These are preceded by the label "***New state:***" in the figure. The specification of a new state mentions only those components which are modified by the rule. Thus, if a rule does not provide the "new" value of V', E' or I' then $V' = V$, $E' = E$ and $I' = I$, respectively. Likewise, the labelling function changes only for the arguments explicitly mentioned in the rule. Thus $\mathcal{L}'(X) = \mathcal{L}(X)$ if the

⊓-**rule**	
Condition:	$(C_1 \sqcap C_2) \in \mathcal{L}(x)$, x is not indirectly blocked and $\{C_1, C_2\} \nsubseteq \mathcal{L}(x)$.
***New state* T′:**	$\mathcal{L}'(x) = \mathcal{L}(x) \cup \{C_1, C_2\}$.
⊔-**rule**	
Condition:	$(C_1 \sqcup C_2) \in \mathcal{L}(x)$, x is not indirectly blocked and $\{C_1, C_2\} \cap \mathcal{L}(x) = \emptyset$.
***New state* T₁:**	$\mathcal{L}'(x) = \mathcal{L}(x) \cup \{C_1\}$.
***New state* T₂:**	$\mathcal{L}'(x) = \mathcal{L}(x) \cup \{C_2\}$.
∃-**rule**	
Condition:	$(\exists R.C) \in \mathcal{L}(x)$, x is not blocked and x has no R-neighbour y for which $C \in \mathcal{L}(y)$.
***New state* T′:**	$V' = V \cup \{y\}$ ($y \notin V$ is a new node), $E' = E \cup \{\langle x, y \rangle\}$, $\mathcal{L}'(\langle x, y \rangle) = \{R\}$, $\mathcal{L}'(y) = \{C\}$.
∀-**rule**	
Condition:	$(\forall R.C) \in \mathcal{L}(x)$, x is not indirectly blocked and x has an R-neighbour y for which $C \notin \mathcal{L}(y)$.
***New state* T′:**	$\mathcal{L}'(y) = \mathcal{L}(y) \cup \{C\}$.
∀₊-**rule**	
Condition:	$(\forall R.C) \in \mathcal{L}(x)$, x is not indirectly blocked and there is an S for which $\mathsf{Trans}(S) \in \mathcal{R}_{\mathcal{T}}, S \sqsubseteq R \in \mathcal{R}_{\mathcal{T}}$; furthermore x has an S-neighbour y for which $(\forall S.C) \notin \mathcal{L}(y)$.
***New state* T′:**	$\mathcal{L}'(y) = \mathcal{L}(y) \cup \{\forall S.C\}$.

Figure 7.14.   The transformation rules of the $\mathcal{SHIQ}$ tableau algorithm, part 1.

$\bowtie$- **rule**	
Condition:	$(\bowtie nR.C) \in \mathcal{L}(x)$, where $\bowtie$ is one of the symbols $\geq$ or $\leq$, x is not indirectly blocked and x has an R-neighbour y for which $\{C, \sim C\} \cap \mathcal{L}(y) = \emptyset$.
New state $\mathbf{T}_1$:	$\mathcal{L}'(y) = \mathcal{L}(y) \cup \{C\}$.
New state $\mathbf{T}_2$:	$\mathcal{L}'(y) = \mathcal{L}(y) \cup \{\sim C\}$.
$\geq$-**rule**	
Condition:	$(\geq nR.C) \in \mathcal{L}(x)$, x is not blocked, it is not the case that there exist nodes $y_1, \ldots, y_n$ such that no two of them are identifiable and, for every i, y_i is an R-neighbour of x and $C \in \mathcal{L}(y_i)$ holds.
New state $\mathbf{T}'$:	$V' = V \cup \{y_1, \ldots, y_n\}$ ($y_i \notin V$ new nodes), $E' = E \cup \{\langle x, y_1 \rangle, \ldots, \langle x, y_n \rangle\}$, $\mathcal{L}'(\langle x, y_i \rangle) = \{R\}$, $\mathcal{L}'(y_i) = \{C\}$, for every $i = 1 \leq i \leq n$, $I' = I \cup \{y_i \neq y_j \mid 1 \leq i < j \leq n\}$.
$\leq$-**rule**	
Condition:	$(\leq nR.C) \in \mathcal{L}(x)$, x is not indirectly blocked, x has $n+1$ R-neighbours $y_0, \ldots, y_n$ such that $C \in \mathcal{L}(y_i)$ holds for every i and there exist y_i and y_j ($i \neq j$) that are identifiable.
	For every $(0 \leq i < j \leq n)$, where y_i and y_j are identifiable, let $\{y, z\} = \{y_i, y_j\}$ such that x is not a successor of y.
New state $\mathbf{T}_{ij}$:	$\mathcal{L}'(z) = \mathcal{L}(z) \cup \mathcal{L}(y)$, $\mathcal{L}'(\langle x, y \rangle) = \emptyset$, $\mathcal{L}'(\langle z, x \rangle) = \mathcal{L}(\langle z, x \rangle) \cup \mathsf{Inv}(\mathcal{L}(\langle x, y \rangle))$ if x is a successor of z, $\mathcal{L}'(\langle x, z \rangle) = \mathcal{L}(\langle x, z \rangle) \cup \mathcal{L}(\langle x, y \rangle)$ if x is not a successor of z, $I' = I[y \rightarrow z]$ (each occurrence of y is replaced by z).

Figure 7.15. The transformation rules of the $\mathcal{SHIQ}$ tableau algorithm, part 2.

value of $\mathcal{L}'(X)$ is not explicitly prescribed by the rule, where X stands for either a node u or for a pair of nodes $\langle u, v \rangle$.

Note that a rule can never be applied twice for a specific assignment of nodes and concepts appearing in the rule, because the condition of each rule is formulated in such a way that it ceases to hold for the given parameter assignment after the rule has been applied.

To sum up, the two figures describing the tableau transformation rules should be interpreted in the following way. We assume a given tableau state $\mathbf{T}$, a node x in $\mathbf{T}$ and a transformation rule whose firing conditions are met. Given these, the application of the transformation rule creates a *set* of new tableau states $S_{\mathbf{T}}$. In the case of the $\sqcup$- and $\bowtie$- rules, $S_{\mathbf{T}}$ will be the set $\{\mathbf{T}_1, \mathbf{T}_2\}$, where $\mathbf{T}_1$ and $\mathbf{T}_2$ are the two new states specified in the description of the rule. In the case of the $\leq$- rule, a new state is built for each pair of identifiable nodes selected from the node set $\{y_0, \ldots, y_n\}$ specified in the conditions of the rule. Thus

$$S_{\mathbf{T}} = \{\mathbf{T}_{ij} \mid 0 \leq i < j \leq n, \; y_i \text{ and } y_j \text{ are identifiable}\},$$

where $\mathbf{T}_{ij}$ is the state described in the description of the $\leq$-rule. Here, $S_{\mathbf{T}}$ is a finite nonempty set, as the conditions require the presence of at least one identifiable pair of nodes.

Finally, for the deterministic rules (i.e. for all rules other than $\sqcup$, $\bowtie$ and $\leqslant$), $S_{\mathbf{T}}$ is the single-ton set $\{\mathbf{T}'\}$, where $\mathbf{T}'$ is the new state specified in the appropriate section of Figures 7.14 and 7.15.

The execution of the tableau algorithm. A tableau state is called *complete* if no transfor-mation rule can fire in this state.

The execution of the $\mathcal{SHIQ}$ tableau algorithm follows the same scheme as the algorithm for the $\mathcal{ALCN}$ language. The two versions of the algorithm shown in Figures 5.5 and 5.6 are applicable here, provided that each reference to Figure 5.4 (which gives the $\mathcal{ALCN}$ rules) is replaced by a reference to Figures 7.14 and 7.15 (which give the $\mathcal{SHIQ}$ rules). The first, recursive, version presents the algorithm as an exploration of a search space in which the applications of non-deterministic rules represent the choice points and where each of the multiple states returned offers an alternative exploration path. The second, iterative, version relies on a variable S containing a set of tableau states to be explored. Let us now briefly revisit this second version.

At the start of the algorithm, the variable S is a singleton set containing the initial state $\mathbf{T}_0(C)$.

In each iteration, a state $\mathbf{T} \in S$ is selected, and a rule is chosen (together with its node and concept parameters) in such a way that the firing condition of the rule holds in the tableau state $\mathbf{T}$. Subsequently $\mathbf{T}$ is replaced by $S_{\mathbf{T}}$ in S, i.e. a new set $S \setminus \{\mathbf{T}\} \cup S_{\mathbf{T}}$ is formed where $S_{\mathbf{T}}$ is the set of transformed tableau states prescribed by Figures 7.14 and 7.15. The iteration continues with the variable S now containing this new set.

If a complete and clash-free tableau state appears as an element of S, the algorithm ter-minates and returns the answer that "C is satisfiable w.r.t. $\mathcal{T}$". The tableau algorithm also terminates if all tableau states in S contain a clash. In this case it returns the answer "C is not satisfiable w.r.t. $\mathcal{T}$".

7.7.3. Properties of the $\mathcal{SHIQ}$ tableau algorithm

We now discuss the three main properties of the tableau algorithm: termination, soundness and completeness.

The tableau algorithm terminates. This is a simple consequence of the fact that the tableau graph handled by the algorithm is actually a labelled tree, and an upper bound can easily be given for the tree depth, the tree branching factor and the number of possible labels in the tree. These upper bounds are functions of certain properties of the root concept, i.e. the concept C whose satisfiability is being investigated.

We use the same arguments as those given for the termination of the $\mathcal{ALCN}$ tableau algorithm in Subsection 5.3.4. In the $\mathcal{SHIQ}$ algorithm we have edges labelled with sets of roles (rather than with single roles) and a larger set of concepts possibly appearing in node labels (*subneg*(C) rather than *sub*(C)), but the size of these sets is still bounded.

If C is the root concept then the label of a node (resp. edge) is a finite subset of *subneg*(C) (resp. *roles*(C)). Thus $m = |subneg(C)|$ and $n = |roles(C)|$ are upper bounds on the number of concepts and roles that can appear in the labels of the tableau tree for the concept C. Let us assume that there exists a path of length $p = 2^{2m+n} + 2$ in the tableau tree. We claim that this path has to contain a pair of nodes for which the upper node directly blocks the lower.

For pairwise blocking we have to consider a node, its predecessor and the edge between these two nodes. The number of possible label combinations for such a triple is 2^{2m+n}, as the numbers of different node and edge labels are 2^m and 2^n, respectively. Our path of length p contains $2^{2m+n}+1$ triples and thus there have to be two occurrences of the same triple on the path, which means that the base condition for pairwise blocking is satisfied. Thus we have shown that the depth of the tableau tree is bounded.

A bound for the branching factor of the tableau tree can be calculated in exactly the same way as for the $\mathcal{ALCN}$ tableau algorithm: it is the sum of the numbers appearing in the $\geqslant$-expressions in C plus the number of existential restrictions in C.

Since the depth, the branching factor and the size of the labels is limited, so is the number of possible tableau trees for a given concept. Furthermore, as there is an upper bound on the number of tableau nodes, the set of possible inequalities (characterised by node pairs) is also limited. Consequently there exists an upper bound on the number of possible tableau states.

The remaining arguments, regarding the lengths of possible paths in the search tree and regarding the branching factor of the search tree, are exactly the same as for the case of the $\mathcal{ALCN}$ tableau (see Subsection 5.3.4). Since both these measures have an upper bound, the $\mathcal{SHIQ}$ tableau algorithm terminates.

The tableau algorithm is complete.   The fundamental idea behind the proof of completeness is again the same as that for the $\mathcal{ALCN}$ tableau algorithm: we associate ABoxes with tableaux. A $\mathcal{SHIQ}$ tableau state $\mathbf{T} = \langle V, E, \mathcal{L}, I \rangle$ is mapped to the following ABox $\mathcal{A}_{\mathbf{T}}$:

$$\begin{aligned}
\mathcal{A}_{\mathbf{T}} = {} & \{D(x) \mid x \in V, D \in \mathcal{L}(x)\} \\
& \cup \{R(x,y) \mid \langle x,y \rangle \in E, R \underline{\in} \mathcal{L}(\langle x,y \rangle)\} \\
& \cup \{x \neq y \mid x \neq y \in I\}.
\end{aligned} \tag{7.20}$$

There is only a small difference between the above formulae and their $\mathcal{ALCN}$ counterparts (5.18)–(5.20). In $\mathcal{SHIQ}$ an edge label is a set of roles and so it is mapped to multiple role assertions. Accordingly, in the above formula (7.20), an underlined $\in$ relation sign appears in place of the equality sign in the $\mathcal{ALCN}$ version.

We call a tableau state $\mathbf{T}$ satisfiable w.r.t. a TBox $\mathcal{T}$ if the corresponding ABox $\mathcal{A}_{\mathbf{T}}$ is satisfiable w.r.t. $\mathcal{T}$. We call a set of states S satisfiable if it has at least one element which is a satisfiable state.

The transformation rules of the $\mathcal{SHIQ}$ tableau algorithm define the possible transitions from a tableau state $\mathbf{T}$ to a set $S_{\mathbf{T}}$ of states. For each rule, it is easy to see that $\{\mathbf{T}\}$ is satisfiable w.r.t. $\mathcal{T}$ if, and only if, $S_{\mathbf{T}}$ is satisfiable. Because of this, it also holds that if a set of states S' can be reached from S through repeated application of transformation rules then S and S' are equivalent in terms of satisfiability.

By definition, the initial set of states of the tableau algorithm, $S_0 = \{\mathbf{T}_0\}$, is satisfiable w.r.t. $\mathcal{T}$ if, and only if, the ABox $\mathcal{A}_{\mathbf{T}_0}$ is satisfiable. The latter consists of a single concept assertion $C(a)$, whose satisfiability w.r.t. $\mathcal{T}$ is equivalent to the satisfiability of the concept C w.r.t. $\mathcal{T}$ (see the end of Subsection 4.8.2).

Hence, the concept C is satisfiable if, and only if, the initial state set S_0 is satisfiable, and this latter is satisfiable if, and only if, each set S' of states created during the tableau algorithm is satisfiable.

The tableau algorithm returns the answer "C is not satisfiable" if it reaches a state set S' in which every element contains a clash. If there is a clash within a tableau state then it cannot be satisfiable, as there is an obvious contradiction in the ABox to which it is mapped. Because every element of S' contains a clash, S' is not satisfiable; hence C is also unsatisfiable.

The tableau algorithm is sound – the model construction for $\mathcal{SHIQ}$.   The tableau algorithm returns the answer "C is satisfiable" if it reaches a set of states in which there is a complete and clash-free tableau $\mathbf{T}$.

Using this complete and clash-free tableau state $\mathbf{T} = \langle V, E, \mathcal{L}, I \rangle$ we now build an interpretation in which the meaning of the root concept C is non-empty and which is a model of the TBox $\mathcal{T}$. This gives a justification for the positive answer of the tableau algorithm, i.e. proves that the algorithm is sound.

The model construction for $\mathcal{SHIQ}$ is similar to that for $\mathcal{SHIF}$. Thus we first build an infinite interpretation $A_{\mathbf{T}}^{cpQ}$ which satisfies C.[17] Next we perform the transformations necessary to make this interpretation a model of the TBox $\mathcal{T}$ as well.

The domain of our initial interpretation – just as in the case of the $\mathcal{SHIF}$ tableau algorithm, discussed in Subsection 7.5.4 – contains finite paths beginning at the root of the tableau state $\mathbf{T}$. However, the construction has to be modified since a node now may have multiple successors with identical labels.

As an example, let us examine the satisfiability of the concept $\top$ w.r.t. the TBox $\mathcal{T}_0 = \{\top \sqsubseteq C_0\}$, where $C_0 = (\geqslant 2\,\mathsf{hC}) \sqcap (\leqslant 1\,\mathsf{hC}^-)$. The complete and clash-free tableau for this reasoning task can be seen in Figure 7.16. Each edge of the tree is labelled with the set $\{\mathsf{hC}\}$, while each node has the label $\{C_0, (\geqslant 2\,\mathsf{hC}), (\leqslant 1\,\mathsf{hC}^-)\}$. The (pairwise) blocking relationship is shown as a broken arrow which points to the blocking node. If we follow the model construction method used in the $\mathcal{SHIF}$ tableau algorithm (7.18), the domain of our interpretation will consist of lists:

$$\{[b], [b,c], [b,d], [b,c,c], [b,d,d], \ldots\}.$$

The statement $\top \sqsubseteq (\geqslant 2\,\mathsf{hC})$ is obviously false on this domain, as, apart from $[b]$, every domain element has a single hC-successor. To understand the issue, let us consider how the path $[b,c]$ is extended. This path can be continued in two different ways, through the node e or through the node f. However, in both cases we get back to the same blocking node, namely c, which means that in both cases we obtain $[b,c,c]$ as the extended path.

An obvious solution is to include the blocked node in the path, i.e. the two hC-successors of the instance $[b,c]$ are denoted by the lists $[b,c,e,c]$ and $[b,c,f,c]$. This construction solves our problem but has a minor technical flaw: the formation of successors is non-uniform. Namely, $[b]$ has a successor $[b,c]$, where the latter is formed by adding a single element c to the former, because c is not blocked. However, a successor of $[b,c]$ is represented by $[b,c,f,c]$, formed by adding two list elements, the blocked and the blocking node. To make the representation of the successor relationship uniform, the authors of [63] proposed to name the elements of the domain using lists of *pairs*. Whenever we go through a non-blocked node y, the list is extended with the pair $\langle y, y \rangle$. However, if we extend the path through a

---

[17] In the notation $A_{\mathbf{T}}^{cpQ}$ the first two letters of the upper index cpQ refer to the copy-in method and the letter Q indicates that this ABox construction supports the $\mathcal{SHIQ}$ language.

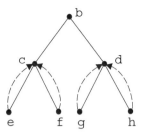

Figure 7.16. A simple example for $\mathcal{SHIQ}$ tableau.

blocked node z to a node y which directly blocks z then the list is extended with the pair $\langle y,z \rangle$. The following lists represent the paths of length 2 in the tableau of Figure 7.16:

$$[\langle b,b \rangle, \langle c,c \rangle, \langle c,e \rangle], [\langle b,b \rangle, \langle c,c \rangle, \langle c,f \rangle],$$
$$[\langle b,b \rangle, \langle d,d \rangle, \langle d,g \rangle], [\langle b,b \rangle, \langle d,d \rangle, \langle d,h \rangle].$$

In this tableau, lists of the form $[\ldots, \langle c, \ldots \rangle]$ can be extended with the pairs $\langle c,e \rangle$ and $\langle c,f \rangle$ while those of the form $[\ldots, \langle d, \ldots \rangle]$ can be extended with the pairs $\langle d,g \rangle$ and $\langle d,h \rangle$. Thus we obtain an infinite *binary* tree, where every node is an instance of the concept $(\geqslant 2\,\mathsf{h}\mathsf{C})$.

For a formal description of our method, the "heir" relationship, introduced in the discussion of the $\mathcal{SHIF}$ tableau algorithm, has to be slightly modified. Consider a tableau **T** and nodes $x,y,z \in V$. We now say that the pair $\langle y,z \rangle$ is an R-heir of the node x in the tableau **T** if neither x nor y is blocked and if

- either $R \in \mathcal{L}(\langle x,y \rangle)$, i.e. there is an edge with from x to y with R in its label, and $z = y$;

- or y blocks z and $R \in \mathcal{L}(\langle x,z \rangle)$, i.e. there is an edge from x to z, labelled R.

Furthermore, we say that $\langle y,z \rangle$ is an heir of a node x if there is an R such that that $\langle y,z \rangle$ is an R-heir of x. We denote this relationship by $x \mapsto \langle y,z \rangle$.

Let x_0 denote the root node of the tableau **T**. We now define the set of instance names of the ABox as follows:

$$Dom_{\mathbf{T}}^{cpQ} = \left\{ [\langle x_0,x_0 \rangle, \langle x_1,u_1 \rangle, \ldots, \langle x_n,u_n \rangle] \left| \begin{array}{l} x_0 \mapsto \langle x_1,u_1 \rangle, \\ x_1 \mapsto \langle x_2,u_2 \rangle, \ldots, \\ x_{n-1} \mapsto \langle x_n,u_n \rangle \end{array} \right. \right\}.$$

Given a list of pairs $X = [\langle x_0,u_0 \rangle, \ldots, \langle x_n,u_n \rangle]$, let us denote by $last_1(X) = x_n$ the first component of the last pair in the list. Using this notation, we define the $\mathcal{SHIQ}$ version of the infinite copy-in ABox in the following way:

$$\mathcal{A}_{\mathbf{T}}^{cpQ} = \{C(X) \mid X \in Dom_{\mathbf{T}}^{cpQ}, last_1(X) = x \text{ and } C \in \mathcal{L}(x)\} \cup$$
$$\{R(X,Y) \mid X,Y \in Dom_{\mathbf{T}}^{cpQ}, X \oplus [\langle y,u \rangle] = Y$$
$$\text{and the } R\text{-heir of } last_1(X) \text{ is } \langle y,u \rangle\}.$$

The ABox $\mathcal{A}_{\mathbf{T}}^{cpQ}$ satisfies the concept C, but the role axioms in $\mathcal{T}$ do not necessarily hold. To satisfy $\mathcal{T}$ we have to employ the closure operations introduced in the previous sections, as for the $\mathcal{SHIF}$ construction. It is easy to demonstrate that the ABox formed using these operations is self-realising: that is, the interpretation

$$\mathcal{I}_\mathbf{T} = \mathcal{I}^{nat}(ClosHT_\mathcal{T}\ ClosI\ A_\mathbf{T}^{cpQ})$$

satisfies the concept C w.r.t. the TBox $\mathcal{T}$. Consequently, if the algorithm returns the answer "C is satisfiable w.r.t. $\mathcal{T}$" then C is in fact satisfiable w.r.t. $\mathcal{T}$.

For the sake of completeness, we repeat the definitions of the transformations used in the construction of the above interpretation:

$$ClosI\ \mathcal{A} = \mathcal{A} \cup \{ \mathsf{Inv}(R)(b,a) \mid R(a,b) \in \mathcal{A} \},$$
$$ClosH_\mathcal{T}\ \mathcal{A} = \mathcal{A} \cup \{ R(a,b) \mid (S \sqsubseteq R) \in \mathcal{R}_\mathcal{T}, S(a,b) \in \mathcal{A} \},$$
$$ClosT_\mathcal{T}\ \mathcal{A} = \mathcal{A} \cup \left\{ R(a_1,a_n) \,\middle|\, \begin{array}{l} \mathsf{Trans}(R) \in \mathcal{T}, n > 2, \text{ and} \\ \{R(a_1,a_2),\dots,R(a_{n-1},a_n)\} \subseteq \mathcal{A} \end{array} \right\},$$
$$ClosHT_\mathcal{T}\ \mathcal{A} = ClosH_\mathcal{T}\ ClosT_\mathcal{T}\ ClosH_\mathcal{T}\ \mathcal{A}.$$

7.8. The $\mathcal{SHIQ}$ tableau algorithm for ABoxes

The tableau algorithm introduced in the previous section can be used to solve ABox reasoning tasks as well. As in the $\mathcal{ALCN}$ ABox tableau algorithm (Subsection 5.5.1), we use the ABox to construct the initial tableau state. This initial state may be an arbitrary graph, as opposed to the tree-shaped tableau states used in TBox reasoning. Next, we apply the $\mathcal{SHIQ}$ transformation rules shown in Figures 7.14 and 7.15 to this graph. The only exception is the $\leqslant$-rule, because special care is required when identifying the nodes corresponding to instances of the original ABox. The structure of the tableau state is also slightly modified, in that the component I stores not only inequalities ($x \neq y$) but equalities ($x \doteq y$) as well.

The task of the ABox tableau algorithm is to decide the consistency of an ABox $\mathcal{A}$ w.r.t. a TBox $\mathcal{T}$ containing role axioms only. This latter condition is not a proper restriction; we showed in Subsection 4.8.3 that all concept axioms can be eliminated from the TBox by the technique of internalisation. The algorithm relies on the reflexive–transitive closure $\mathcal{R}_\mathcal{T}$ of the TBox $\mathcal{T}$, just as does the tableau algorithm for checking concept satisfiability (Subsection 7.7.2). Reflexivity now means that the axiom $R \sqsubseteq R$ is added to $\mathcal{R}_\mathcal{T}$ for every role R appearing in $\mathcal{A}$ or $\mathcal{T}$.

Suppose that the assertions of the ABox $\mathcal{A}$ contain the instance names $a_1,\dots,a_n$. The initial tableau state $\mathbf{T}_0 = \langle V_0, E_0, \mathcal{L}_0, I_0 \rangle$ is built in the same way as in the $\mathcal{ALCN}$ tableau algorithm (Subsection 5.5.1):

$$V_0 = \{a_1,\dots,a_n\},$$
$$E_0 = \{\langle a,b \rangle \mid \text{ there is an } R \text{ such that } R(a,b) \in \mathcal{A}\},$$
$$\mathcal{L}_0(a) = \{C \mid C(a) \in \mathcal{A}\},$$
$$\mathcal{L}_0(\langle a,b \rangle) = \{R \mid R(a,b) \in \mathcal{A}\}.$$

The I_0 component contains inequalities of the form $a_i \neq a_j$ ($1 \le i < j \le n$), provided that the unique name assumption (UNA) applies; otherwise it may contain a subset of these

---

$\leqslant$-rule

Condition: $(\leqslant nR.C) \in \mathcal{L}(x)$, x is not indirectly blocked,

                      x has $n+1$ R-neighbours $y_0, \ldots, y_n$ such that $C \in \mathcal{L}(y_i)$ holds for every i

                      and there exist y_i and y_j ($i \neq j$) that are identifiable.

For every $(0 \leq i < j \leq n)$, where y_i and y_j are identifiable:

Branch A: At least one of y_i and y_j is not a root node.

Let $\{y,z\} = \{y_i, y_j\}$ such that x is not a successor of y and y is not a root node.

New state $\mathbf{T}_{ij}$: $\mathcal{L}'(z) = \mathcal{L}(z) \cup \mathcal{L}(y)$,

                      $\mathcal{L}'(\langle x,y \rangle) = \emptyset$,

                      $\mathcal{L}'(\langle z,x \rangle) = \mathcal{L}(\langle z,x \rangle) \cup \mathsf{Inv}(\mathcal{L}(\langle x,y \rangle))$ if x is a successor of z,

                      $\mathcal{L}'(\langle x,z \rangle) = \mathcal{L}(\langle x,z \rangle) \cup \mathcal{L}(\langle x,y \rangle)$ if x is not a successor of z,

                      $I' = I[y \to z]$ (every occurrence of y is replaced by z).

Branch B: Both y_i and y_j are root nodes.

Let $y = y_i, z = y_j$.

New state $\mathbf{T}_{ij}$: $\mathcal{L}'(z) = \mathcal{L}(z) \cup \mathcal{L}(y)$,   (1)

                      $\mathcal{L}'(\langle z,u \rangle) = \mathcal{L}^*(\langle z,u \rangle) \cup \mathcal{L}(\langle y,u \rangle)$ for each u s. t. $\langle y,u \rangle \in E$,   (2)

                      $\mathcal{L}'(\langle u,z \rangle) = \mathcal{L}^*(\langle u,z \rangle) \cup \mathcal{L}(\langle u,y \rangle)$ for each u s. t. $\langle u,y \rangle \in E$,   (3)

                      $V' = V \setminus \{y\}$,   (4)

                      $E' = E \setminus \{\langle u,v \rangle \mid \langle u,v \rangle \in E$, and either $u = y$ or $v = y\} \cup$

                              $\{\langle z,v \rangle \mid \langle y,v \rangle \in E\} \cup \{\langle u,z \rangle \mid \langle u,y \rangle \in E\}$,   (5)

                      $I' = \{y \doteq z\} \cup I[y \to z]$ (every occurrence of y is replaced by z).   (6)

Figure 7.17.   The modified rule of the $\mathcal{SHIQ}$ tableau algorithm supporting ABoxes.

inequalities, as prescribed by the ABox. The nodes of the initial tableau $\mathbf{T}_0$ are called root nodes.

Having constructed the initial tableau state, we repeatedly apply the $\mathcal{SHIQ}$ ABox tableau rules. These consist of the modified $\leqslant$-rule shown in Figure 7.17 and the remaining rules inherited from the TBox tableau algorithm, as presented in Figures 7.14 and 7.15. Note that the $\leqslant$-rule has two branches, depending on whether there is a non-root among the two nodes to be identified.

Branch A handles the situation when at least one of the nodes being identified is not a root node. In this case we proceed exactly in the same way as in the $\mathcal{SHIQ}$ tableau algorithm for TBoxes, i.e. this branch is identical to the $\leqslant$-rule shown in Figure 7.15. Branch B deals with the case when two root nodes have to be identified. The node to be eliminated is denoted by y while z is the node which remains in the tableau graph. Here we use some new notation: $\mathcal{L}^*(\langle u,v \rangle)$ denotes the label of the edge $\langle u,v \rangle$ if this edge occurs in the tableau graph, otherwise it denotes the empty set:

$$\mathcal{L}^*(\langle u,v \rangle) = \begin{cases} \mathcal{L}(\langle u,v \rangle) & \text{if } \langle u,v \rangle \in E; \\ \emptyset & \text{otherwise.} \end{cases}$$

Let us list the transformations to be performed on Branch B one by one.

(1) Node z inherits all concepts in the label of node y.
(2) Node z inherits all outgoing edges of y.
(3) Node z inherits all incoming edges of y.
(4) The node y is removed from the graph.
(5) The edges going to y are removed and replaced by edges that are directed to z instead.
(6) The equality $y \doteq z$ is added to the component I, and all other occurrences of y (in inequalities) are replaced by z.

The main difference between the two branches of the $\leqslant$-rule is that Branch A simply ignores the edges going to or coming from node y (i.e. the node being removed), while Branch B relocates these edges to node z. The simpler behaviour of Branch A is made possible by the fact that y is a non-root node and all concepts in its label are added to the label of the remaining node z. This means that the tableau algorithm is able to regenerate the edges removed. However, on Branch B, y is a root node and some of its edges may go to or come from other root nodes. Such edges were created from the initial ABox, and the tableau algorithm is not able to regenerate them; hence the need for relocation of the edges.

Note that equalities are added to the tableau component I in Figure 7.17. However, these equalities are never used in the algorithm. They can be considered as part of the output of the algorithm: the consistency of the ABox requires that the equalities collected by the algorithm hold for the individual names concerned.

The tableau algorithm supporting ABoxes can be shown to terminate and to be sound and complete. This can be proved using techniques similar to those used when we were discussing similar properties of the TBox tableau algorithm (Section 7.7).

7.9. Optimisation of the tableau algorithm

The tableau algorithm, as described in the preceding sections, was not geared towards efficiency. Our aim was to present an algorithm in a simple and easy to understand way and to ensure that the main properties of the algorithm could be proved fairly straightforwardly. To obtain acceptable performance a number of optimisation techniques (such as those described in [56, 54]) should be employed.

In this section we consider a variant of the tableau algorithm using depth-first search (see Figure 5.5) where the non-deterministic transformation rules give rise to *choice points*, explored using *backtracking*. We now present a variety of techniques, implementation tricks and considerations that improve the efficiency of the reasoning algorithm. We do not aim for completeness, nor for an in-depth analysis; we just sketch a few important and interesting ideas, following Horrocks [56].

An important issue is the need for a reduction in the number and branching factor of choice points, as the execution time of the tableau algorithm very much depends on these factors. This reduction, addressed by several optimisations, can be achieved e.g. by delaying the creation of specific choice points, by the early recognition of clashes, by the clever handling of union concepts, or any combination of the three.

In Subsection 7.9.1 we discuss optimisations which involve finding appropriate rule execution ordering. Next, in Subsection 7.9.2, we introduce the lexical normal form of concepts, which – while being somewhat more difficult to handle – has several advantages over the negation normal form used so far. Subsection 7.9.3 presents optimisations relying on prepro-cessing, i.e. the transforming of DL axioms to a form which can be handled more efficiently by the reasoning algorithm. Subsection 7.9.4 examines how to detect clashes as early as possible, while the next two subsections present optimisations for handling union concepts. Subsections 7.9.7 and 7.9.8 discuss optimisations regarding the exploration of the search tree, while Subsection 7.9.9 presents some ideas about caching the node labels of the tableau graph. In the final subsection we discuss optimisations specific to the task of the classification of TBox concepts.

7.9.1. Ordering rules

In this subsection we confine ourselves to description logic languages that do not contain inverse roles. To simplify the discussion we focus our attention on the $\mathcal{ALCN}$ language, although several optimisations can be extended to more complex languages.

The absence of inverses means that no rule of the tableau algorithm changes the label of an ancestor of the node to which the rule was applied. In other words, a transformation rule triggered by a concept appearing in the label of a node x affects only the subtree rooted at x. For this reason, it is practical to postpone the application of those transformation rules that create new successors or modify the labels of the successor nodes in the tableau. Thus all successors of a node can be generated at once, after all transformation rules that do not create new successor nodes have been applied.

An important optimisation can be applied to the $\geqslant$-rule. This rule can be modified so that a *single* R-successor is created by an $(\geqslant nR)$ concept and only if no R-successors are created by the $\exists$-rule for the given node; if the $\exists$-rule creates an R-successor for a node then there is no need to create another successor using the $\geqslant$-rule, because the label of the node created by the $\geqslant$-rule is a subset of the label of the node created by the $\exists$-rule. Hence, whenever a clash occurs while the subtree rooted at the former node is being explored, the same clash is bound to appear when the node created by the $\exists$-rule is being processed. If no R-successors are created for a node by the $\exists$-rule then it is still sufficient to create a single successor node by the $\geqslant$-rule. If n distinct successor nodes were created, their labels would be identi-cal: each would contain the TBox axioms and the concepts added by the application of the $\forall$-rule. The processing of these nodes would mean an unnecessary repetition of the same task n times.

However, the above simplifications make the clash condition involving $\leqslant$-concepts unus-able. This condition states that the presence of a $(\leqslant nR)$ concept in the label of a node x, together with the presence of $n+1$ pairwise-distinct R-successors, constitutes a clash. Notice that the only way for these pairwise-distinct successors to be created is through the applica-tion of a $\geqslant$-rule to node x, where the concept $(\geqslant mR)$ appears in the label of x and $m \geq n+1$. Hence the clash condition can be reformulated in the following way: a clash is detected if a node label contains the concept expressions $(\geqslant mR)$ and $(\leqslant nR)$, where $m > n$. Because of the above modifications the tableau-state data structure can also be simplified: there is no need to store the $\neq$ inequality relation between pairs of nodes.

These considerations lead to the following ordering of the rules. We examine the concepts in the label $\mathcal{L}(x)$ of a node x one by one and apply the $\sqcap$- and $\sqcup$ rules to these. As it is worth delaying the creation of choice points, the application of the $\sqcap$-rule should have a higher priority. During the transformation we examine the clash conditions in every step to detect possible contradictions as early as possible. When these two transformation rules cannot be applied further, the label of x is fixed, i.e. it cannot change. The reason is that all other rules create or modify successor nodes only. As the label of x is finalised, we can check whether the node x is blocked. If this is so then the examination of the subtree of the tableau rooted at x is complete; we can continue with the other branches of the tableau. If x is not blocked then we process every concept within $\mathcal{L}(x)$ which creates new nodes in the tableau or modifies the label of an existing successor node.

For the $\mathcal{ALCN}$ language, the rules can thus be ordered along the following lines.

- The highest priority should preferably be given to the $\sqcap$-rule as it is a deterministic transformation rule, modifying only the label in which the precondition of the rule is present.

- Afterwards the $\sqcup$-rule can fire, since this has no effect on the labels of successor nodes.

- By applying the $\exists$-rule we create appropriate successor nodes.

- With the $\leqslant$-rule, for each $(\leqslant nR)$ concept we check whether the given restriction is met regarding the successors just created. Should the $\exists$-rule create more R-successors than is allowed by the $\leqslant$-rule, some pairs of R-successors should be identified (non-deterministically, in all possible ways), so that only n different R-successors remain.

- The modified $\geqslant$-rule is applied, potentially creating a single new successor for the given node.

- By applying the $\forall$-rule the label of every R-successor is extended with appropriate concepts: if $\forall R.C \in \mathcal{L}(x)$ then the concept C is added to the label of every R-successor of x.

Recall that each tableau transformation rule contains a condition forbidding repeated application of the rule. If the above rule order is used, checking these conditions becomes unnecessary. For example, all applications of the $\exists$-rule at a node x can be done in a single action by scanning the concepts in the label of x and applying the transformation prescribed by the $\exists$-rule whenever an existential restriction is encountered.

Also notice that once the above actions have been carried out for a node x, no transformation rule will ever be applied to x. Thus the following issue arises: to save space, can we get rid of some concepts in a node label once we know that no transformation rule will fire for the given node? The answer, in general, is negative because we still need the node label for checking blocking conditions. However, this space-saving optimisation can be performed for the union and intersection concepts. Recall that the $\sqcap$-rule prescribes that the concept expressions C and D have to be added to the label of the given node, assuming that the label contains the concept $C \sqcap D$. If the $\sqcap$-rule is applied repeatedly while this is possible and then all the concepts of the form $C \sqcap D$ are removed, no information is lost since the smaller set of concepts is obviously equivalent to the larger set. One can argue in a similar way to show that $C \sqcup D$ can be removed from the node labels once the $\sqcup$-rule has been applied.

An alternative form of this optimisation would be to remove the concept expressions $C \sqcap D$ and $C \sqcup D$ immediately after applying the $\sqcap$- and $\sqcup$- rules, respectively. However, this simpler form has its drawbacks. For example, a node label may contain the two $\sqcap$-concepts C and $D \sqcap C$ (here C itself is of the form $\cdots \sqcap \cdots$). If we apply the simpler rule and remove C from the label immediately after it is processed then we will have to repeat the process when C is encountered for the second time, within the concept expression $D \sqcap C$. However, the original tableau algorithm will unfold $D \sqcap C$, adding D and C to the set of concepts in the node label, and will thus notice that there is no need to unfold C for the second time. Hence, it is beneficial to remove the $\sqcap$- or $\sqcup$- concepts from the node label only when the $\sqcap$-rule or the $\sqcup$-rule cannot be applied further to the node.

Exercise 7.18: Execute the tableau algorithm, using the optimisations and rule ordering discussed above, for the following reasoning tasks:

(a) the example discussed in Subsection 5.3.3;

(b) the problem presented in Exercise 5.17.

7.9.2. Lexical normal form

In the standard presentation of the tableau algorithm it is assumed that the concepts are in negation normal form. The major advantage of this approach lies in the simplicity of the algorithm. However, the $\bowtie$-rule of the $\mathcal{SHIQ}$ tableau algorithm requires the building of $\sim C$, which is the normal form of $\neg C$. When C is a large complex concept, building $\sim C$ is a time-consuming operation. Furthermore there are some optimisations which require the formation of concept negations. Therefore it may be worthwhile to introduce an alternative normalisation, the so-called *lexical normal form*, in which forming the negation of a concept is a quick, constant-time, operation.

The principal idea of the lexical normal form is the removal of redundant concept constructors. Each concept of the $\mathcal{SHIQ}$ language can be expressed using only the following four constructors: $\forall$, $\neg$, $\sqcap$ and $\geqslant$. When transforming a composite concept to lexical normal form, each concept operand is (recursively) transformed to lexical normal form, and then the following rules are used to eliminate the disallowed concept constructors:

■ $C \sqcup D \longrightarrow \neg(\neg C \sqcap \neg D)$;

■ $\exists R.C \longrightarrow \neg \forall R.\neg C$;

■ $(\leqslant nR.C) \longrightarrow \neg(\geqslant n+1 R.C)$.

In order to simplify further the representation of concepts, a common practice is to disallow some concept patterns, e.g. $C \sqcap C$ or $\neg\neg C$, which can obviously be replaced by simpler equivalents. A few such simplifications are listed below:

■ $\neg\neg C \longrightarrow C$;

■ $\top \sqcap C \longrightarrow C$;

■ $\bot \sqcap C \longrightarrow \bot$;

■ $C \sqcap C \longrightarrow C$;

■ $C \sqcap \neg C \longrightarrow \bot$;

■ $\forall R.\top \longrightarrow \top$;

■ $\forall R.C \sqcap \forall R.D \longrightarrow \forall R.(C \sqcap D)$;

■ $(\geqslant 0R.\top) \longrightarrow \top$;

- $(\geqslant m R.C) \sqcap (\leqslant n R.C) = \bot$, if $m > n$;

- $(\geqslant m R.C) \sqcap (\geqslant n R.C) = (\geqslant m R.C)$, if $m > n$.

In the lexical normal form, negation can appear in front of any concept. This is in contrast with the negation normal form, where only atomic negation is allowed. When lexical normal form is used, building the negation C_{neg} of a concept C is thus a constant-time operation:

$$C_{neg} = \begin{cases} C_0 & \text{if } C = \neg C_0; \\ \neg C & \text{otherwise.} \end{cases} \qquad (7.21)$$

Normalisation is important for making the transformation rules simpler. However, it also makes the algorithm more efficient by mapping equivalent concepts to the same form. This is useful e.g. when a concept is added to a node label which already contains the given concept, possibly in a different formulation. Like the negation normal form, the lexical normal form transforms several equivalent concept patterns to the same format. For example, it is easy to see that the concepts $\exists R.\neg(\geqslant 3 R.C)$ and $\neg\forall R.\neg(\leqslant 2 R.C)$ are equivalent, as both are mapped to $\neg\forall R.(\geqslant 3 R.C)$ when transformed to lexical normal form.

There is an additional form of ambiguity in concept representation owing to the commutativity and associativity of the $\sqcap$ and $\sqcup$ operations. For example, let C, D and E be arbitrary (possibly composite) concepts. The concept expression $(C \sqcap D) \sqcap (E \sqcap D)$ is obviously equivalent to $D \sqcap (E \sqcap C)$. Both concept expressions are in lexical normal form. To make concept representation unique in this respect, it is worth using unary $\sqcap$ and $\sqcup$ operations, whose single argument is a set of concepts. For example, the above two concepts are both mapped to $\sqcap\{C,D,E\}$.

A similar problem appears in the case of the equivalent concept expressions $\forall R.C \sqcap \forall R.D$ and $\forall R.(C \sqcap D)$. A possible solution has already been shown above: concepts of the form $\forall R.C \sqcap \forall R.D$ should be simplified to $\forall R.(C \sqcap D)$.

When switching from negation normal form to lexical normal form only slight modifications are needed in the formulation of the transformation rules, as concept expressions in lexical normal form can be handled similarly to those in negation normal form.

- No modification is needed for transformation rules which handle concept expressions of the form $\forall R.C$, $C \sqcap D$ and $(\geqslant n R.C)$.

- The concept expression $\neg(C \sqcap D)$ is equivalent to the concept expression $C_{neg} \sqcup D_{neg}$, hence the $\sqcup$-rule can be applied. Here C_{neg} and D_{neg} are the lexical normal forms of the concepts $\neg C$ and $\neg D$; these can be obtained using the simple procedure described in (7.21).

- The concept expression $\neg\forall R.C$ is equivalent to the concept expression $\exists R.C_{neg}$, hence the $\exists$-rule can be applied.

- The concept expression $\neg(\geqslant n R.C)$ is equivalent to the concept expression $(\leqslant n-1 R.C)$, hence it should be handled using the $\leqslant$-rule.

The use of the lexical normal form, on its own, does not significantly reduce the execution time of the tableau algorithm. The reason is that only the representation of the concepts is affected, which has a minimal impact on the runtime. The simplification rules listed above might accelerate the reasoning, as subconcepts become simpler, union concepts disappear etc. It may even happen that the process of normalisation results in a reduction of the concept at hand to $\bot$, which makes the execution of the tableau algorithm unnecessary. In general, however, the changes introduced here do not cause significant speed-ups. However, the use of lexical normal form is a prerequisite for several other optimisation techniques which can significantly improve the speed of the tableau algorithm.

Exercise 7.19: Reformulate the following tableau transformation rules in such a way that they use lexical normal form instead of negation normal form:

(a) the $\sqcup$-rule (Figure 7.14);

(b) the $\exists$-rule (Figure 7.14);

(c) the $\leqslant$-rule (Figure 7.15).

7.9.3. Transforming terminological axioms

As discussed in Subsection 4.7.2, the usual method of handling concept axioms of the TBox is by internalisation. Concept axioms can be assumed to be of the form $C \sqsubseteq D$. The internalisation of each such axiom is the union concept $\neg C \sqcup D$. The TBox is handled by adding its internalisation, i.e. the intersection of all the union concepts formed from the TBox axioms, to each node of the tableau graph. In practice there is no need to form the intersection concept, which is to be immediately unfolded anyway. Instead, the internalised form of all axioms is added to each node.

In the case of large TBoxes containing thousands of concept axioms, this results in unacceptably large execution times. Each such union concept has to be unfolded at every node, and at least one side of the union has to be added to the node label. All these union concepts have to be processed by the algorithm, in spite of the fact that most axioms might not be needed at a given node.

For example, let us investigate whether the subsumption Lion $\sqsubseteq$ Mammal $\sqcap$ Predator is met in a terminology which describes knowledge about the flora and fauna of the Earth. Our intuition says that the axiom defining the concept Cactus, as well as many other concepts unrelated to lions, will not be needed for answering this question. However, the internalisation of the TBox does indeed contain the union concepts corresponding to such axioms; each will produce a choice point and unfold at least one of the two sides of the union. The concepts obtained this way may also trigger the execution of further tableau transformation rules. This suggests that the efficiency of the tableau algorithm could be significantly improved by a method capable of intelligently selecting the axioms relevant for the given node rather than blindly adding every axiom to every node.

There is a special case of the general concept-inclusion axiom $C \sqsubseteq D$ in which the left-hand side C is a (possibly negated) atomic concept. Let us call such an axiom *primitive*. A primitive axiom needs to be taken into consideration only at nodes whose labels contain the left-hand side C (which can be either A or $\neg A$, where A denotes an atomic concept). The reason is that unfolding the internalised form of the above axiom, $\neg C \sqcup D$, to its first member cannot produce a clash in the absence of a C in the node label. This axiom can influence the tableau algorithm only when a C appears in the node label: a clash is produced when the left-hand side of the union concept is unfolded, and so the right-hand side of the union, D, is added to the node label.

Using this observation, let us divide the TBox into two disjoint parts. The subset $\mathcal{T}_p$ of a TBox $\mathcal{T}$ only contains primitive axioms while the rest of the axioms belong to $\mathcal{T}_g = \mathcal{T} \setminus \mathcal{T}_p$, which thus contains the non-primitive general concept inclusion (GCI) axioms. Furthermore, the following restrictions are imposed on $\mathcal{T}_p$:

- The left-hand side of the axioms in $\mathcal{T}_p$ is unique, i.e. no two axioms in $\mathcal{T}_p$ can have the same concept expressions on their left-hand side: $\{A \sqsubseteq C, A \sqsubseteq D\} \subset \mathcal{T}_p \Rightarrow C = D$.

- The TBox $\mathcal{T}_p$ is acyclic (as defined in Subsection 4.6.1).

The first restriction can easily be overcome by merging any two axioms of the form $C \sqsubseteq D_1$ and $C \sqsubseteq D_2$ into the axiom $C \sqsubseteq D_1 \sqcap D_2$; see Exercise 7.20(a) below. The reason for the second restriction is the danger of an endless loop: an axiom is added to a node label because of the presence of a (possibly negated) atomic concept and this may lead to the appearance of the same concept later, which forces a repeated addition of the same axiom etc. The requirement that $\mathcal{T}_p$ is acyclic can often be relaxed; for example, in the case of the cyclic concept A, defined by the axiom $A \equiv \exists R.A$, blocking prevents the formation of an infinite loop [56].

Exercise 7.20: Prove the following statements, where C, D and E are arbitrary concept expressions.

(a) The TBoxes $\{C \sqsubseteq D, C \sqsubseteq E\}$ and $\{C \sqsubseteq D \sqcap E\}$ are equivalent.

(b) The axioms $C \sqcap D \sqsubseteq E$ and $C \sqsubseteq \neg D \sqcup E$ are equivalent.

(c) The axioms $\neg C \sqsubseteq \neg D$ and $D \sqsubseteq C$ are equivalent.

When a TBox is divided into two parts according to the above principles, we continue to use internalisation for the axioms in $\mathcal{T}_g$. However, the axioms in $\mathcal{T}_p$, which are of the form $A \sqsubseteq C$ or $\neg A \sqsubseteq C$, where A is an atomic concept, can be handled much more efficiently. When the tableau algorithm processes node x the following steps are taken.

1. We first unfold all the union and intersection concepts in the label of node x.

2. If the label of x contains a possibly negated atomic concept, which appears on the left-hand side of an axiom in $\mathcal{T}_p$, then the right-hand side of this axiom is added to the label of node x. Otherwise no further axioms of $\mathcal{T}_p$ need to be taken into account at node x at the moment and we proceed with the normal tableau algorithm.

3. We return to point 1, so that before any processing of further axioms the freshly added concept is unfolded.

It is worthwhile to transform the axioms in the TBox so that as many axioms as possible can be placed in $\mathcal{T}_p$ as possible. For example, the axiom $A \sqcap C \sqsubseteq D$ is not primitive, but it can be reformulated to $A \sqsubseteq \neg C \sqcup D$ (see Exercise 7.20(b)), which is a primitive axiom provided that A is an atomic concept.

A generic TBox $\mathcal{T}$ contains concept inclusion and concept equivalence axioms. An equivalence axiom $(C \equiv D) \in \mathcal{T}$ is transformed to two subsumption axioms: $C \sqsubseteq D$ and $\neg C \sqsubseteq \neg D$. Earlier, instead of the second axiom we used $D \sqsubseteq C$.[18] However, the two forms are clearly

---

[18] See, for example, Subsection 4.3.1, where this transformation was first discussed.

equivalent, as stated in part (c) of Exercise 7.20. The format suggested has the advantage
that a definition of the form $A \equiv D$ (where A is an atomic concept) is transformed into two
primitive axioms.

A definitional TBox (i.e. a TBox consisting of a definitional axioms only, see Subsection 4.6.1) can thus be located fully within the $\mathcal{T}_p$ part, assuming that it is acyclic. If, however,
there are cycles in it then these can be broken by leaving out some axioms. The axioms that
are left out become part of $\mathcal{T}_g$; all the other primitive axioms go into $\mathcal{T}_p$.

Let us now consider an arbitrary TBox $\mathcal{T}$ of concept axioms in which the equivalence
axioms have been replaced by subsumptions as specified above. We now present an algorithm which transforms the TBox $\mathcal{T}$ into an equivalent set of axioms, partitioned into an
acyclic set of primitive axioms $\mathcal{T}_p$ and a set of general inclusion axioms $\mathcal{T}_g$.

Let $\mathcal{T}_p$ and $\mathcal{T}_g$ be empty at the beginning. For every subsumption axiom $C \sqsubseteq D \in \mathcal{T}$,
perform the following steps (the sign $\neg$ in parentheses denotes an optional negation).

(1) We proceed to the next step, unless $C = (\neg)A$ where A is an atomic concept. If there is
a cycle in the TBox $\mathcal{T}_p \cup \{C \sqsubseteq D\}$ then we also proceed to the next step. If there is an
axiom of the form $C \sqsubseteq E \in \mathcal{T}_p$ then this latter axiom is replaced by the merged axiom
$C \sqsubseteq D \sqcap E$ in $\mathcal{T}_p$; otherwise the original axiom $C \sqsubseteq D$ is added to $\mathcal{T}_p$. In both cases the
processing of the axiom is complete.

(2) If $D = (\neg)A$ where A is an atomic concept then the axiom $\neg D \sqsubseteq \neg C$ is added to $\mathcal{T}_p$,
according to step 1.

(3) If $C = C_1 \sqcup C_2 \sqcup \cdots \sqcup C_N$ then for each C_i, which is a possibly negated atomic concept, we
add the axiom $C_i \sqsubseteq D$ to $\mathcal{T}_p$, according to step 1. Let the set of unprocessed subconcepts
of C be $\{C_{j_1}, C_{j_2}, \ldots, C_{j_L}\}$. From these we build the axiom $C_{j_1} \sqcup C_{j_2} \sqcup \cdots \sqcup C_{j_L} \sqsubseteq D$ and
proceed to the next step.

(4) If $D = D_1 \sqcap D_2 \sqcup \cdots \sqcap D_N$ then we examine the axiom $\neg D \sqsubseteq \neg C$ instead of the axiom
$C \sqsubseteq D$ and proceed according to step 3.

(5) If $C = C_1 \sqcap C_2 \sqcap \cdots \sqcap C_N$, where $C_{i_1}, C_{i_2}, \ldots, C_{i_K}$ are all, possibly negated, atomic concepts and $K > 0$ then for every index $i \in \{i_1, \ldots i_K\}$ we build an axiom $C_i \sqsubseteq \neg C_1 \sqcup$
$\neg C_2 \sqcup \cdots \sqcup \neg C_{i-1} \sqcup \neg C_{i+1} \sqcup \cdots \sqcup \neg C_n \sqcup D$, which is equivalent to the original one. Any
of these axioms can be added to $\mathcal{T}_p$ according to step 1. However, the axiom selected for
addition to $\mathcal{T}_p$ should be such that $\mathcal{T}_p$ remains acyclic after this extension. Furthermore,
those axioms which can be merged with a primitive axiom in $\mathcal{T}_p$ should be preferred to
others, so that the number of axioms in $\mathcal{T}_p$ is kept as small as possible.

(6) If $D = D_1 \sqcup D_2 \sqcup \cdots \sqcup D_N$ then we replace $C \sqsubseteq D$ by $\neg D \sqsubseteq \neg C$ and perform step 5.

(7) If we reach this point, i.e. none of the preceding points were successful in converting
the axiom $C \sqsubseteq D$ to primitive axioms, then $C \sqsubseteq D$ is a GCI axiom and goes to $\mathcal{T}_g$.

Exercise 7.21: Consider the the TBox containing only the axiom $A \sqcap \forall R.\neg C \sqsubseteq B \sqcap \exists S.B$,
where A, B and C are distinct atomic concepts. Transform this TBox to the acyclic
set of primitive axioms $\mathcal{T}_p$ and a set of general inclusion axioms $\mathcal{T}_g$, using the above
algorithm.

The technique outlined above is one of the most powerful optimisations and reduces the number of choice points drastically. As in human thinking, it deterministically adds the right-hand side of appropriate axioms to the node label and thus avoids the need for the costly processing of union concepts.

7.9.4. Lazy unfolding of concepts

A tableau graph is obviously unsatisfiable when both C and $\neg C$ are present in a node label. However, such clashes are detected only if C is an atomic concept, and this is a major source of inefficiency in the tableau algorithm. No matter which normal form is used to represent the concepts, it is quite expensive to decide whether two composite concepts are negations of each other. First, one concept has to be negated and then the equality of the two concepts has to be checked. If lexical normal form is used, performing the negation is a constant-time operation. However, checking the equality of two composite concepts can take a time proportional to the size of the concepts.

A technique for addressing this problem is to replace composite concepts in the TBox by atomic concepts and to add new axioms to the TBox; using these new axioms, atomic concepts can be unfolded. For example, the concept $C \sqcap D$ can be substituted by a new atomic concept Aux_1 not appearing elsewhere in the TBox, provided that we extend the TBox with the axiom $Aux_1 \equiv C \sqcap D$. Naturally, care should be taken to hide Aux_i from the user; for example, such a concept should not appear in the concept hierarchy produced by the TBox classification algorithm.

As discussed in Subsection 4.6.1, definitorial TBoxes can be expanded by replacing all the name symbols with the right-hand sides of their definitions. However, the size of the expanded TBox might be exponential in comparison with that of the original; hence expansion is not an efficient technique. The lazy unfolding of concepts is a transformation in the opposite direction: it ensures that composite concepts which can take part in clashes are replaced by name symbols, at the cost of adding appropriate definitions.

The equality of two composite concepts can be decided efficiently using the above lazy unfolding transformation. However, the number of axioms in the TBox can significantly increase. Thus it is important to include only those composite concepts which can take part in clashes. Consequently a concept can be excluded from this transformation if it does not occur in the TBox both with and without a negation, unless it is present within a number restriction.[19] Thus, the number of added axioms is reduced, yet there is still no need to check the equality of composite concepts.

If the TBox axioms are handled by the technique of internalisation, the benefits of lazy unfolding are offset by the increase in execution time needed to handle the internalised axioms; however, lazy unfolding cooperates efficiently with the transformation of axioms described in the previous subsection, as the latter technique prevents the creation of unnecessary choice points. A further disadvantage of lazy unfolding is that a preprocessing step is needed to select the composite concepts for which a name should be introduced. This

---

[19] When executing the $\bowtie$-rule, the concept within the number restriction is added to node labels both with and without a negation.

involves the enumeration of all subconcepts that appear in the TBox axioms and comparing these with each other.

Exercise 7.22: Perform a lazy unfolding optimisation on the $\mathcal{ALCN}$ tableau reasoning example discussed in Subsection 5.3.3. Which subconcepts should be named? How does this affect the execution of the tableau algorithm?

7.9.5. Semantic branching

As we stated earlier, the most important issue in improving the efficiency of the tableau algorithm is the reduction of the number of choice points created. This is the aim of the optimisation, discussed in this subsection, called *semantic branching*.

Let us assume that the label $\mathcal{L}(x)$ of a node x contains the concept $C \sqcup D$, but neither C nor D appears in the label of x. Here the tableau algorithm creates a choice point and adds concept C to $\mathcal{L}(x)$, then continues the reasoning. Should the algorithm detect a contradiction in this branch, it backtracks to the choice point and tries the alternative branch by adding D to $\mathcal{L}(x)$. However, we lose some information here, namely that adding C to the label of the node leads to a clash. This knowledge can be expressed by adding $(\neg C)$ to $\mathcal{L}(x)$.

The idea outlined above can be generalised as follows: when an expression $C_1 \sqcup C_2 \sqcup \cdots \sqcup C_n$ is unfolded and the ith branch of the choice point is examined then, in addition to adding C_i, the concept expression $\neg C_{i-1}$ is added to the label of the node, in normalised form. This addition is justified by the fact that the concept C_{i-1} has already been examined by the algorithm and has been found to lead to a contradiction.[20] Note that this optimisation is costly if negation normal form is used (owing to the non-constant time cost of normalising the concept expression $\neg C_{i-1}$); therefore lexical normal form should be used.

The information that adding a certain concept to the label leads to a clash can be used in the early detection of certain contradictions appearing in subsequent branches of the choice point. Let us assume that semantic branching optimisation is applied in the processing of the concept expression $C \sqcup D$ and that of the unfolding of this union to C produces a clash. This means that the tableau algorithm continues to add both D and $\neg C$ to the node label. During the subsequent tableau transformations the concept C may be added to the label of the examined node by a transformation rule (for example, a TBox axiom $D \sqsubseteq C$). Thanks to the semantic branching optimisation the presence of $\neg C$ in the node label triggers a clash, which would have gone unnoticed if the optimisation had not been applied. Here, for the sake of simplicity we assume that C is an atomic concept; a contradiction can be discovered in case of composite concepts as well, but the application of further transformation rules might become necessary.

The drawback of semantic branching is that the negated concepts added to the node labels trigger the execution of further tableau transformation rules, possibly leading to the creation of new choice points or even new nodes.

---

[20] As opposed to C_i, $\neg C_{i-1}$ is placed in the node label in such a way that it remains there even after further backtracks to the given choice point. However, all $\neg C_{i-1}$ expressions, $i = 2, \ldots, n$, are removed when a clash occurs in the last branch of the given choice point and thus the choice point is discarded.

Exercise 7.23: Consider a tableau graph with a node x whose label contains the concept $C \sqcup (\exists R.\forall R^-(C \sqcap D))$. Assume that unfolding this union concept to C produces a clash. Show that this implies that unfolding the union concept to its right-hand side also produces a clash. Can semantic branching improve the performance of the tableau algorithm in this example?

7.9.6. Boolean constraint propagation

When handling disjunctions (i.e. union concepts), it is worth examining the label of the node at hand before creating a new choice point since the union might be deterministically expandable. For example, consider a disjunction $C_1 \sqcup C_2 \sqcup \cdots \sqcup C_n$ in a node label, where all but one of the concepts C_i are negations of concepts appearing in the same label. In this case, adding any of these concepts would result in a contradiction. The concept C_k whose negation does not appear in the label of the node can be added deterministically to the label without creating a choice point. If the negation of all concept expressions C_i is present in the node label, a clash should be signalled. The main advantage of Boolean constraint propagation is that it reduces the size of the search space, since fewer choice points are created. However, there is the overhead of checking whether Boolean constraint propagation is applicable. To reduce this overhead it is worth using appropriate complex data structures.

Boolean constraint propagation can be generalised and incorporated into the $\sqcup$-rule in the following way. The $\sqcup$-rule first inspects the union concept at hand and removes any disjuncts whose negation is present in the label of the given node. The reason for this is obvious: if the union concept were unfolded to such a disjunct, this would immediately produce a clash. Next, if no disjuncts remain in the union concept then a clash is signalled; if exactly one disjunct remains then it is unfolded deterministically; if there are multiple disjuncts then the original non-deterministic $\sqcup$-rule is applied to the remaining disjunction.

Note that Boolean constraint propagation requires a decision to be made about whether the negation of a (possibly composite) concept is present in a node label. In Subsection 7.9.4 we discussed lazy unfolding optimisation, which improves the efficiency of deciding the equality of two concepts. Hence it is advisable to use lazy unfolding optimisation together with the Boolean constraint propagation.

Exercise 7.24: Reconsider the tableau reasoning example of Subsection 5.3.3. Execute the tableau algorithm for this example using Boolean constraint propagation together with some optimisations discussed earlier:

- rule ordering and the simplification of the $\geqslant$-rule, as discussed in Subsection 7.9.1, see Exercise 7.18(a);
- lazy unfolding optimisation, see Subsection 7.9.4 and Exercise 7.22.

Show that the tableau algorithm can solve the given reasoning task without creating any choice points if all the above optimisations are applied together.

7.9.7. Dependence-directed backtracking

Let us consider a tableau graph with a node x whose label $\mathcal{L}(x)$ includes the concept expressions $C_1 \sqcup D_1, C_2 \sqcup D_2, \ldots, C_n \sqcup D_n$ and $\exists R.(C \sqcap D), \forall R.\neg C$. Before creating the R-successor of x, the union expressions are processed and thus n choice points are created. Next, the $\exists$-rule creates an R-successor node with the label $C \sqcap D$, the $\forall$-rule adds the concept $\neg C$ to the label of this successor and then the $\sqcap$-rule unfolds the first concept in the label of the successor. At this point a clash appears, as both C and $\neg C$ are present in the label of this R-successor. Hence we backtrack to the last choice point and add D_n to the label of x instead of C_n, creating an R-successor again etc. Since exactly the same concepts will appear in the label of the R-successor, we again reach a contradiction. As there are n binary choice points, the above process – the creation of an R-successor and the detection of a clash in its label – is unnecessarily repeated 2^n times.

The source of the problem is that the cause of the clash is independent of the choice points created by the union concepts. Backtracking to these choice points is bound to result in a contradiction again and again. Unnecessary computations arise because we do not backtrack far enough to remove the *source* of the contradiction.

A solution to this problem is to make the backtracking more intelligent, e.g. by storing, for every concept expression in every node, references to the choice points on which it *depends*. A concept expression C at node x depends on

- the choice point at node x if C was added to the label $\mathcal{L}(x)$ by the $\sqcup$-rule or the $\leqslant$-rule;

- the choice point at node z, if C was added to the label $\mathcal{L}(x)$ by the firing of a transformation rule for a concept D at node y and if the concept D at node y depends on the choice point at node z.

In other words, a concept added by the $\sqcup$-rule at a given node depends on the given choice point and, whenever a concept C is added to a node by the firing of a rule for a concept D, C inherits all dependences of D.

Exercise 7.25: Consider the tableau search tree shown in Figure 5.7. There are three choice points in this tree, namely, below the tableau states T_5, T_6 and T_7. For each concept occurrence in the nodes of tableau states T_6 to T_{13} determine on which choice point it depends.

Upon detecting a clash we can determine the most recent choice point to which backtracking is necessary by using the dependences of the concepts taking part in the clash. Having performed the backtracking, computation is continued on the next branch of that choice point. Using this technique we can avoid exploring the choice points irrelevant to the given clash, hence reducing the size of the search space. The only drawback of dependence-driven backtracking is that the dependences have to be calculated and stored for every concept expression, which increases the time and space requirements of the algorithm. However, in most cases the search space becomes much smaller and hence the total execution time is significantly reduced.

7.9.8. Heuristics-based disjunctive branching

A concept that is the union of n subconcepts gives rise, in general, to a choice point with n branches. By eliminating branches which necessarily contain a clash, Boolean constraint propagation reduces the branching factor of appropriate choice points. If one cannot pinpoint branches that are known to contain a contradiction, one can still apply some heuristics to reduce the number of branches produced by disjunctions.

We will first discuss the MOMS heuristic (the *maximal number of occurrences in disjunctions of minimal size*) known from propositional calculus [42]. As the name of this heuristic suggests, it selects the concept which occurs the maximal number of times in disjunctions having the smallest size. Let us assume, for example, that the minimal disjunctions in the tableau are those that contain just two disjuncts. Let C be one of the disjuncts whose number of occurrences within the binary disjunctions is maximal. If a binary disjunction containing C is unfolded to C, this "neutralises" all other disjunctions in the given node which contain C, in the following sense: the ⊔-rule will not fire for the these disjunctions owing to the presence of C. However, if this unfolding of C happens to produce a contradiction then – assuming semantic branching is used – the presence of $\neg C$ in the other branch will cause the other disjunctions containing C to unfold deterministically.

The MOMS heuristic works well when it is used with semantic branching and Boolean constraint propagation. When a concept appearing in many short disjunctions turns out to be unsatisfiable, semantic branching adds its negation to the node label examined. Subsequently, the Boolean constraint propagation deterministically unfolds those disjunctions in which there is only one term which does not lead to a clash. When the MOMS heuristic is used, exactly these concept expressions are selected first, as they appear in disjunctions containing only a few elements.

The MOMS heuristic would seem to be a promising optimisation technique. However, it does not always fulfil expectations, as it was geared to solve problems in propositional calculus. In propositional calculus it is much more common for variables to appear in many disjunctions than in the case of concepts in the disjunctive expressions in description logics. The reason is that a propositional problem normally contains a small number of variables and a comparatively large number of disjunctions. In a DL knowledge base, however, concepts (which are not necessarily atomic) are the counterparts of propositional variables and the number of concept expressions used is often much larger than the number of disjunctions.

Another disadvantage of the MOMS heuristic is that it sometimes interacts badly with dependence-directed backtracking. In experiments with the FACT system it was discovered that the reasoning engine performed much worse with the MOMS heuristic than without it [54], the reason being that the MOMS heuristic does not take into account dependences, and it tends to select disjunctions with relatively recent dependences, which results in a much larger search space being explored.

Instead of – or together with – MOMS, other heuristics can be employed to improve the interaction with dependence-directed backtracking. The *oldest-first* heuristic selects the disjunction which depends on the least recent choice point. Thanks to this, in the case of a clash the algorithm is likely to backtrack to an early choice point instead of unnecessarily expanding more recent choice points.

When introducing heuristics, there is an obvious overhead of evaluating the heuristic function. Furthermore, in some cases heuristics can lessen the effects of other optimisation techniques. For example, while the MOMS heuristic interacts well with Boolean constraint propagation, it interferes with dependence directed backtracking. However, when used together with other appropriately selected optimisations, in general heuristics improve the overall performance of tableau reasoners.

7.9.9. Caching

During reasoning, the tableau algorithm might create numerous descendant nodes. It can happen that there are nodes amongst these whose labels are identical. Consider the concept expression $\exists R.C \sqcap \exists S.C$ present in a node x. The $\exists$-rule creates two successors for x, say y and z, whose labels are identical (assuming that the $\forall$-rule applications, if any, extend the labels of y and z with the same concepts). Hence the concept C, which appears in the labels of both y and z, is unfolded twice and so are the axioms of the TBox. The same successor nodes are created for y and z, and this can give rise to further identical nodes etc. If no clash was found when transforming y and its successors, it seems reasonable not to repeat the same transformations for z and just to assume that expanding z does not lead to a clash. In general, one could set up a cache memory which stores node labels together with the result of their evaluation.

A node x is said to be *satisfiable* if, and only if, all its descendant nodes are satisfiable, no tableau transformation rule can be applied to x and the label of x does not contain a clash. The cache memory is then used to remember whether a node with a given label is satisfiable. If an identical node label is encountered later, we reuse the satisfiability result stored in the cache memory.

There are certain limitations to using the cache memory. As for cache memories in general, provisions should be made to handle the situation when a new entry has to be added to a cache which is full and so cannot accommodate this new entry. In such cases a suitable replacement policy has to be used to remove a certain older item, e.g. the item used least recently or the item used least frequently.

The presence of inverse roles also brings in some complications. Recall that the $\forall$-rule can affect not only the labels of successors but also the label of the predecessor node, if inverse roles are used. Thus tableau transformations can change the label of the predecessor of a node, possibly causing a clash. For example, let y be an R-successor of a node x and let $\neg C \in \mathcal{L}(x)$ and $\forall R^-.C \in \mathcal{L}(y)$. Furthermore, let us assume that the cache memory has an entry noting that a node with the label $\mathcal{L}(y)$ is satisfiable. Here, it would be improper to consider y satisfiable without further investigation, as in doing so the presence of a clash would remain unnoticed. When y is properly expanded, the concept C is added to the label of x because of the concept $\forall R^-.C$ in the label of y. This causes a clash, as both C and $\neg C$ are now present in $\mathcal{L}(x)$. A cache can still be used with description logic languages supporting inverse roles; however, the algorithm becomes more complicated and the time and space requirements also grow.

When the technique of caching is applied, attention should be paid to blocked nodes, because it might happen that a blocked node is qualified as satisfiable despite the fact that it would be unsatisfiable were another node not blocking it [83]. For example, assume that a node y is blocked by its ancestor x, as $\mathcal{L}(y) \subseteq \mathcal{L}(x)$ holds (subset blocking). In this case y

is declared to be satisfiable although it may happen that a contradiction is found in another descendant of x, which would make x unsatisfiable; thus y would be blocked by an unsatisfiable node, from which it does not follow that y is satisfiable. Hence, when recognising a blocking, the blocked node should not be written to the cache.

More generally, consider the following situation. Assume that we have just obtained a complete clash-free subtree rooted at a node x and that there is a node y in this subtree which is blocked by an ancestor of x. Obviously, the fact that the node x is satisfiable depends on the presence of an ancestor with the given label. This should be taken into account when caching this result.

If there are no inverse roles in the given description logic language, the size of the search space can be further reduced with a slight modification of the above technique. This essentially means that the node labels in the cache are examined using the subset relationship rather than equivalence. That is, a node x is considered satisfiable if a label $\mathcal{L}(y)$ can be found in the cache for which y is satisfiable and $\mathcal{L}(x) \subseteq \mathcal{L}(y)$. In other words, if there is no clash in a subtree rooted at y then there is no clash in the subtree rooted at x either. Similarly, if the above subsumption holds between the labels of the nodes x and y, and the subtree rooted at x contains a clash, then the subtree rooted at y is also unsatisfiable because the concepts which resulted in a clash in the subtree of x also appear in the label of y.

7.9.10. TBox Classification

The task of the TBox classification algorithm is to arrange the atomic concepts occurring in the TBox in a hierarchy according to the $\sqsubseteq$ relation. A trivial solution for this is to check, for every pair of concepts, whether one contains the other. If both concepts contain the other then the two concepts are equivalent. This algorithm requires the checking of $n(n-1)$ concept subsumptions, assuming that n atomic concepts are present in the TBox. Each concept subsumption can be decided by a separate invocation of the tableau algorithm. As the execution of the tableau algorithm is rather expensive, it is worthwhile reducing the number of invocations by using an optimised classification algorithm.

In building the concept hierarchy a *directed acyclic graph* is used whose nodes are labelled with sets of atomic concepts present in the TBox and whose edges are directed according to the $\sqsubseteq$ relation. Equivalent concepts are represented in the graph by a single node whose label contains all such equivalent concepts. The graph is acyclic, because the presence of a cycle would indicate that any two nodes in the cycle contain each other; hence they would be equivalent and thus the cycle would need to be merged into a single node. The graph also includes nodes labelled with the top $\top$ and bottom $\bot$ concepts. The concept $\top$ subsumes all atomic concepts, as $\top^{\mathcal{I}} = \Delta^{\mathcal{I}}$, and, for every concept C, $C^{\mathcal{I}} \subseteq \Delta^{\mathcal{I}}$. Thus $\top$ is the root of the directed acyclic graph representing the concept hierarchy. Similarly, the concept $\bot$ is subsumed by every concept C, as $\bot^{\mathcal{I}} = \emptyset$ and $\emptyset \subseteq C^{\mathcal{I}}$.

Initially, the graph contains the edges $(\{\top\}, \{C\})$ and $(\{C\}, \{\bot\})$ for every atomic concept C, as shown in Figure 7.18. Note that whenever the $\top$ and $\bot$ concepts have to be merged, this means that the TBox is inconsistent, i.e. it has no model.[21]

---

[21] By definition, the domain of an interpretation cannot be an empty set. As the equivalence of $\top$ and $\bot$ would imply that $\Delta^{\mathcal{I}} = \top^{\mathcal{I}} = \bot^{\mathcal{I}} = \emptyset$, this cannot hold for any interpretation $\mathcal{I}$.

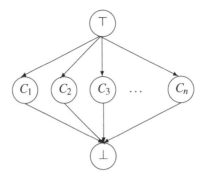

Figure 7.18. Building a concept hierarchy: the initial state.

In the process of TBox classification we frequently use the fact that the relation $\sqsubseteq$ is transitive. If there is a path between node x, labelled with concept A, and node y, labelled with concept B, then it is unnecessary to check the validity of the subsumption relation between these two concepts, as this relation follows from the transitivity of $\sqsubseteq$. One should strive to make as much use of this observation as possible by choosing a suitable order for checking the subsumption relations between atomic concepts.

Initially, atomic concepts are only connected with the concepts $\top$ and $\bot$. This initial graph is then refined by finding where the concepts are placed in the hierarchy, one by one. We thus select a concept and remove it from the graph. Next, we determine which concepts are subsumed by it and which concepts subsume it and then reinsert the concept into the graph: we add incoming edges from concepts subsuming the given concept and outgoing edges to concepts subsumed by it. We then repeat this procedure for all atomic concepts in the TBox.

To find the correct place for concept C in the hierarchy we have to collect those concepts that can be shown to subsume C as well as those which can be shown to be contained in C. In this process it is important to make use of the part of the concept hierarchy that is already known. Hence, instead of looking for all concepts which subsume C, we will focus our search on the least general ones amongst these, i.e. those furthest down from concept $\top$ along the known hierarchy of subsumptions. We thus systematically explore the hierarchy, starting from concept $\top$ and going downwards. When we reach the first concept, say D, which does not subsume C then we can stop, because all concepts below D in the hierarchy are contained in D and so these concepts cannot subsume C; see Exercise 7.26(a) below. We thus add the concept preceding D in our present exploration, which is the last concept to subsume C, to our result set and proceed with the traversal of the hierarchy until all such nodes, corresponding to the least general concepts subsuming C, are collected. The search outlined above is called the *top-down* phase, because we begin from the concept $\top$, i.e. the root of the concept hierarchy, and proceed downwards.

Next we perform the *bottom-up* phase: beginning from the concept $\bot$ we follow the edges upwards and examine which concepts are contained in the concept C. If the subsumption relation $D \sqsubseteq C$ does not hold for a concept D then it also does not hold for any ancestor of D, because the transitivity of the relation $\sqsubseteq$ would not be met otherwise; see Exercise 7.26(b). The concept immediately preceding such a D is a least specific concept contained in C, which is then added to the result set of the second phase, and the bottom-up traversal continues.

Let *TD* and *BU* denote the result sets obtained in the top-down and bottom-up phases, respectively. The two phases having been completed, the concept C is reinserted into the hierarchy by

- adding the subsumption $C \sqsubseteq D$ for each $D \in TD$; and
- adding the subsumption $D \sqsubseteq C$ for each $D \in BU$.

Exercise 7.26: Using the transitivity of the subsumption relation $\sqsubseteq$ show the following statements.

(a) If $C \not\sqsubseteq D$ and $E \sqsubseteq D$ then $C \not\sqsubseteq E$ also holds.

(b) If $D \not\sqsubseteq C$ and $D \sqsubseteq E$ then $E \not\sqsubseteq C$ also holds.

In addition to transitivity, the structure of the axioms in the TBox can also be used to draw useful conclusions allowing us to avoid some tableau algorithm calls. If the axiom $A_1 \sqsubseteq A_2$ holds between the atomic concepts A_1 and A_2 then it is unnecessary to call the tableau algorithm to examine whether the subsumption relation holds between them, since this subsumption is explicitly stated in the TBox. As a generalisation, if the TBox contains the axiom $A \sqsubseteq A_1 \sqcap A_2 \sqcap \cdots \sqcap A_n$, where A and A_i are atomic concepts, then, for every i, $A \sqsubseteq A_i$ holds. Similarly, the axiom $A_1 \sqcup A_2 \sqcup \cdots \sqcup A_n \sqsubseteq A$ entails that, for every i, the subsumption $A_i \sqsubseteq A$ is valid. These subsumptions should be transformed to edges to be added to the graph prior to starting the search for the exact location of the atomic concepts.

Exercise 7.27: Consider the following TBox, where A, B, C, D, E and F are atomic concepts:

$$B \sqcup C \sqsubseteq A;$$
$$\neg C \sqsubseteq \exists R. \neg A;$$
$$D \equiv B \sqcap C;$$
$$E \sqsubseteq \forall R.A;$$
$$D \sqsubseteq F;$$
$$F \sqsubseteq \exists R^-.E.$$

Build the initial concept hierarchy using the techniques outlined in the preceding paragraph. Next, find the exact location of all concepts by performing the top-down and bottom-up searches described above.

Once the concept hierarchy is obtained from the TBox classification algorithm it can also be used to answer the question whether the TBox is *coherent*. The concepts appearing in the same node as the concept $\perp$ are all equivalent to the concept $\perp$, and as such, are unsatisfiable. A TBox is coherent if, and only if, there is no unsatisfiable atomic concept in it. So, if the algorithm does not result in an atomic concept being made equivalent to the concept $\perp$ then the TBox is coherent.

The classification algorithm is often used to measure the performance of the tableau algorithm, because it requires a large number of tableau algorithm invocations: in general this number is proportional to the square of the number of atomic concepts.

7.10. Summary

In this chapter we have presented a tableau algorithm for the language $\mathcal{SHIQ}$. We took, one by one, the components of the language $\mathcal{SHIQ}$ and discussed the techniques needed for handling them. Having reiterated the principles of the $\mathcal{ALCN}$ tableau, we introduced the algorithm for the language $\mathcal{S}$. We then progressively extended this algorithm to support the languages $\mathcal{SH}$, $\mathcal{SHI}$, $\mathcal{SHIF}$ and $\mathcal{SHIQ}$. We also showed how to extend the $\mathcal{SHIQ}$ TBox tableau algorithm to support ABox reasoning tasks.

The basic ideas of these algorithms follow those of the $\mathcal{ALCN}$ tableau discussed in Chapter 5. We decide the satisfiability of a concept C with respect to a (possibly empty) TBox $\mathcal{T}$ by trying to build a model of the concept. Such an interpretation is constructed using a so-called *tableau graph*, the nodes of which, in the simplest cases, form the domain of the interpretation while the edges correspond to the role relations. The nodes are labelled with sets of concept expressions and the edges with role expressions or sets of these. When qualified number restrictions are introduced, a set of inequalities also needs to be maintained in addition to the tableau graph. Thus, in the general case, these two data structures together form the so-called *tableau state* handled by the algorithm.

For the more complex languages of the $\mathcal{SHIQ}$ family new types of blocking were considered. The weakest form, *subset blocking*, was used before inverse roles were introduced. From this point on we had to use a stronger variant, called *equality blocking*. Finally, because of functional restrictions, the most complicated type, *pairwise blocking*, had to be presented.

As the languages supported become more and more complex, the process of *model construction* has to be adjusted too. Initially, for simpler languages that do not allow functional restrictions, a model can be constructed using *redirection:* the blocked nodes are omitted from the interpretation and their incoming edges are redirected to the blocking node. With functional restrictions, there can be satisfiable concepts which have no finite model. For these cases the *copy-in* method is used: the whole graph under the blocking node has to be copied into the blocked node, then this has to be repeated for the newly created copy of the blocked node and so on.

In the last section of the chapter we dealt with the *optimisation* of the tableau algorithm. We showed how to reduce the size of tableau graphs and how to make the handling of terminological axioms efficient. We also demonstrated several methods to reduce the size of the non-deterministic search space and the number of backtracks. We discussed how using a cache memory can improve the reasoning performance, and, finally, showed the optimisations applicable in the task of building a concept hierarchy.

Part III

Ontologies and the Semantic Web

Chapter 8

The Web Ontology Language

In this chapter we focus on heavyweight ontologies and on the role they play in the Semantic Web. We introduce the Web Ontology Language OWL, which is based on Description Logic and which was created as an extension of the RDF schema language (discussed in Section 2.6).

In Section 8.1 we give an introductory overview of the OWL language. Next, in Section 8.2, we present the details of the first OWL standard. Finally, in Section 8.3, we discuss the recently released extension of OWL, the OWL 2 standard.

Unless stated otherwise, we will use the term "OWL" when discussing the features present in both the initial and the recent standards.[1] The terms "OWL 1" and "OWL 2" are used to refer to the first and the recent variant of the Web Ontology Language, respectively.

8.1. The language OWL – an introduction

The deficiencies of RDF schema and increasing demand led to the development of a large number of ontology languages. At the end of the last millennium, the two most significant languages were the *OIL* (Ontology Interface Layer) [37] and the *DAML-ONT* (DARPA Agent Markup Language) [52] languages. The former was developed by the University of Manchester, the latter by the United States Department of Defense (DoD). Both languages were designed with Description Logic in mind; OIL, in particular, is suited for the FaCT reasoner [55] and hence it realises the $\mathcal{SHIQ}$ language class. Because of their DL background, documents written in OIL and DAML can easily be translated into DL TBoxes and ABoxes. This makes reasoning on them very convenient and straightforward.

The DAML+OIL language [29] was born at the end of 2001. It unified the advantages of both DAML and OIL and was created by a joint European–American ad hoc team involving the main developers of the two languages. The DAML+OIL language was submitted to the W3C office for discussion. Later, it formed the basis of the W3C official ontology language,

---

[1] There was also an intermediate standard, OWL 1.1, which is not discussed here.

the so-called *Web Ontology Language* (OWL). The name OWL is not a typo; as is well known, owls are wise, so this seemed to be a fitting name for a knowledge representation language.

The OWL 1 language was released as a W3C recommendation on 10 February 2004 [7], while OWL 2 was announced on 27 October 2009 [86]. The RDF and RDF schema languages also became recommendations on the same day as OWL 1. That was not a coincidence, as these technologies are built upon each other: RDF is a generic framework for connecting meta-information to resources. The RDF schema is a collection of RDF resources to be used for describing lightweight ontologies. The OWL language continues this line as it can be considered an RDF-based ontology language suitable for writing heavyweight ontologies.

The W3C recommends OWL for those cases where the capabilities of the RDF schema are inadequate. OWL, similarly to RDF schema, can be regarded as a set of URIs. The URIs belonging to this set identify resources that help us to create terminological systems using normal RDF descriptions. The meaning of these resources is formalised and, most of all, standardised. We can use them to describe the equivalence or disjointness of classes, the transitivity or cardinality of properties etc.

In the following, however, we will regard OWL as an ontology language. This means that, for example, we can say that "the union of two classes can be given using the `owl:unionOf` property", without elaborating on the fact that the property is actually only a resource identified by a URI. From this point of view, OWL is a language with RDF syntax: OWL documents should be easily understandable with sufficient RDF knowledge.

8.1.1. An introductory example

The introductory example shown in Figure 8.1 defines three classes and one property. The class `FatherOfGirls` is similar to the concept introduced in Subsection 4.3.1, formula (4.1). However, to save some space, here we do not require that such a father has at least one child. Furthermore we explicitly define the class `Female` as a subclass of humans. So actually we are stating that an instance of `FatherOfGirls` is someone who is human and not female, *all* of whose children are female.

Our example is a standard RDF description: the OWL constructs are referred to using the special `owl` namespace. Note that it is not the name of the namespace that is important, but the corresponding URI (`http://www.w3.org/2002/07/owl#`). This URI is used by an OWL-compliant application to indicate that the namespace identifies the RDF schema describing OWL. As an example, the class called `Class` in the OWL namespace (used throughout Figure 8.1) is defined in the following way (we use XML entities for compactness):

```
<rdfs:Class rdf:ID="Class">
  <rdfs:label>Class</rdfs:label>
  <rdfs:subClassOf rdf:resource="&rdfs;Class"/>
</rdfs:Class>
```

We can see that the class `owl:Class` is actually a subclass of `rdfs:Class`. This means that RDF schema classes are not necessarily classes in the OWL sense.

```
<?xml version="1.0" encoding="ISO-8859-1"?>
<rdf:RDF
  xml:base  = "http://swexpld.org#"
  xmlns:rdf = "http://www.w3.org/1999/02/22-rdf-syntax-ns#"
  xmlns:rdfs= "http://www.w3.org/2000/01/rdf-schema#"
  xmlns:owl = "http://www.w3.org/2002/07/owl#">

  <owl:Class rdf:ID="Human" />

  <owl:Class rdf:ID="Female">
    <rdfs:subClassOf rdf:resource="#Human" />
  </owl:Class>

  <owl:ObjectProperty rdf:ID="hasChild">
    <rdfs:domain rdf:resource="#Human" />
    <rdfs:range rdf:resource="#Human" />
  </owl:ObjectProperty>

  <owl:Class rdf:ID="FatherOfGirls">
    <owl:intersectionOf rdf:parseType="Collection">
      <owl:Class rdf:about="#Human" />
      <owl:Class>
        <owl:complementOf rdf:resource="#Female" />
      </owl:Class>
      <owl:Restriction>
        <owl:onProperty rdf:resource="#hasChild" />
        <owl:allValuesFrom rdf:resource="#Female" />
      </owl:Restriction>
    </owl:intersectionOf>
  </owl:Class>
</rdf:RDF>
```

Figure 8.1. An introductory OWL example: the father of girls class.

As another example consider the property owl:complementOf, also used in Figure 8.1. This property is described in the RDF schema of OWL in the following way:

```
<rdf:Property rdf:ID="complementOf">
  <rdfs:label>complementOf</rdfs:label>
  <rdfs:domain rdf:resource="#Class"/>
  <rdfs:range rdf:resource="#Class"/>
</rdf:Property>
```

This specifies that the property owl:complementOf connects OWL classes with OWL classes. Note that although OWL has its own RDF schema, the limited expressivity of the RDF schema language does not allow one to properly capture the meaning of the different OWL constructs. For example, the above piece of RDF schema does not express the fact that `complementOf` describes the complement of a class. The W3C have provided several documents to describe fully the semantics of the OWL language [94].

The OWL language also allows us to talk about instances. Using our introductory example we may say that Bob is a human, Ryan is a father of girls and Annie is a child of Ryan:

```
<Human rdf:ID="Bob" />

<FatherOfGirls rdf:ID="Ryan">
  <hasChild rdf:resource="#Annie" />
</FatherOfGirls>
```

Finally, we should note that from the RDF point of view the class `owl:Class`, for example, is just like any other class that we have described in a domain-specific RDF schema: we did very similar things when we defined the classes for buildings and bungalows in Section 2.6. In this RDF sense, OWL can be considered simply as a specific RDF schema, which defines classes and properties that can be used in RDF descriptions by anyone.

Exercise 8.1: Use an OWL editor, such as Protégé [104], to visualise the example in Figure 8.1. Add some instances to the ontology, similar to `Bob` and `Ryan` above. Build the class hierarchy and list the individuals belonging to the class `FatherOfGirls`.

8.1.2. Important characteristics of OWL

All OWL documents are valid RDF descriptions: an RDF parser should be able to read them without any problem. As regards parsing, the only thing we have to note is that OWL descriptions often use the `rdf:parseType` attribute with the value `Collection`, which may not be supported by older RDF parsers. The `rdf:parseType` attribute, which was introduced in Subsection 2.4.3, is a general tool for changing the interpretation of the property element to which it belongs. If its value is `Collection`, the property element must be interpreted as an RDF collection. In Figure 8.1 we used this collection to enumerate the classes whose intersection defines the class `FatherOfGirls`.

Similarly to RDF schema, OWL also maintains the open world assumption (see Subsection 4.8.4). From the viewpoint of building OWL ontologies this means that anyone can make new statements concerning classes, properties and individuals described by us. For example, someone else may state new facts about Ryan, such as the titles he holds. Such extra information can complement our statements but it may also contradict them. For example, suppose that somebody states that Peter, who is a man, is also a child of Ryan. The semantics of the OWL language is normally based on a monotonic logic, which means that all conclusions that can be drawn at a certain point remain valid when new pieces of information are added to the knowledge base. Accordingly, OWL provides no means for "deleting" or "invalidating" OWL statements, even those that others have added without our consent to our knowledge base.

Like DL languages with concrete domains (see Subsection 4.10.1), OWL distinguishes between the $\Delta^{\mathcal{I}}$ and the Δ_D domains, that is, the sets containing *individuals* and *values*. These sets may sometimes overlap. In connection with these two sets, we can distinguish object properties and datatype properties. The former connect individuals with individuals, and thus correspond to (abstract) roles in Description Logic; the latter connect individuals with values, and so correspond to *concrete* roles. OWL properties will be discussed in Subsection 8.2.3.

Finally, it is important to note that OWL does not make the unique name assumption (see Section 4.8) since this would not be feasible in a web environment, where each resource may be referred to in many different ways; that is, different URIs may refer to the same instance. Note that several widely used DL reasoners actually do make the unique name assumption, which may cause problems when using them for OWL-based ontologies.

8.1.3. OWL 1 sublanguages

As regards expressivity, OWL 1 defines three sublanguages: OWL Full, OWL DL and OWL Lite. Whether a specific OWL description belongs to a certain sublanguage depends on *which* OWL constructs it uses, and *how*. Note that OWL 2 completely redefines the system of sublanguages (see Section 8.3 below). Therefore the present subsection applies to OWL 1 only.

OWL Full

The OWL Full sublanguage does not put any restriction on the use of OWL: any RDF construct may be used in any way that is allowed by RDF. For example, in OWL Full we may state that a certain class is an instance of another class. For this, we only need two appropriate RDF triples, such as the following:

```
[ex:Airbus_A380],[rdf:type],[owl:Class]
[ex:Airbus_A380],[rdf:type],[t:Aeroplane]
```

The first triple states that the resource identified by `ex:Airbus_A380` is an OWL class, and the second states that the same resource is an aeroplane. The idea here is that on one hand we would like to view the resource `Airbus_A380` as a set of aeroplanes. The instances of this class are the actual aeroplanes used by an airline. We can make statements about these, describing their state, the time of last maintenance etc. On the other hand, we would also like to view the resource `Airbus_A380` as an instance of a class describing the types of aeroplanes.

As a matter of fact, this modelling freedom of OWL Full is not that surprising, as we already have this without OWL, using simple RDF schema descriptions. In the more expressive OWL, however, this kind of usage raises serious issues from the point of reasoning, and it is just why other OWL sublanguages, such as OWL DL, do not allow such constructs.

OWL Full is not equivalent to any DL language. To do reasoning on OWL Full documents we need first-order reasoning capabilities and, even in this case, many "tricks" are needed to transform OWL Full documents to first-order logic statements [59].

Finally, OWL Full, in contrast with Description Logic, does not distinguish *clearly* between the domains $\Delta^{\mathcal{I}}$ and Δ_D, that is, the individuals and the values corresponding to data types. The fact that something may be an element of both these sets has serious consequences, as described in Horrocks and Patel-Schneider [59].

OWL DL

The OWL DL language is a sublanguage of OWL Full that directly corresponds to Description Logic. It supports all OWL constructs, but their use is somewhat limited. OWL DL requires the set of classes, the set of datatypes, the set of object properties, the set of datatype properties, the set of annotation properties, the set of ontology properties,[2] the set of instances, the set of values and the set of URIs identifying built-in classes and properties *to be pairwise disjoint.* Accordingly, in OWL DL a resource cannot be both an instance and a class: it is always clear whether a property connects instances with instances or instances with values etc. Other details and consequences will be discussed in the following sections, dealing with specific OWL constructs.

Documents in the OWL DL language can be transformed into the $\mathcal{SHOIN}(\mathbf{D})$ DL language [58]. In addition to the usual constructs of the $\mathcal{S}$ language, $\mathcal{SHOIN}(\mathbf{D})$ supports role hierarchies ($\mathcal{H}$), nominals ($\mathcal{O}$), the inverse construct ($\mathcal{I}$), (unqualified) number restrictions ($\mathcal{N}$) and datatypes ($\mathbf{D}$).

OWL Lite

While OWL DL supports (albeit in a limited way) all the OWL constructs that OWL Full supports, the OWL Lite sublanguage lacks some constructs completely. The basic idea behind OWL Lite was to develop an ontology language which is more expressive than RDF schema but which is only a small step towards the more expressive ontology languages. This may prove useful from the viewpoint of application builders. In the envisioned scenario, the existing applications that are already able to process RDF schemas will extend their abilities step by step: first, they will support OWL Lite; then, at some point later, they can move towards the more expressive OWL sublanguages.

The most narrow DL language able to capture the semantics of OWL Lite documents is $\mathcal{SHIF}(\mathbf{D})$ [58]. In comparison with OWL DL, the $\mathcal{SHIF}(\mathbf{D})$ language lacks the ability to describe nominals and supports only functional restrictions ($\mathcal{F}$) instead of proper cardinality restrictions.

Exercise 8.2: Determine to which OWL 1 sublanguage the example in Figure 8.1 belongs. You may use any available web-based OWL validator or the Protégé [104] editor itself (in the current version this functionality can be found in the Tools menu).

8.2. The ontology language OWL 1

In this section we discuss the OWL features allowed by the OWL 1 standard. We first introduce the different types of OWL *class descriptions*, then we discuss how to create so-called OWL *axioms* based on these descriptions.

When introducing the OWL constructs we also show how they are related to Description Logic. In this way those readers who have already read the corresponding chapters can easily

---

[2] The annotation and ontology properties are not covered in this book. They are discussed in more detail in the OWL specification [7].

couple the DL and OWL elements. However, the section should be understandable on its own, without any knowledge of Description Logic.

8.2.1. OWL class descriptions

The OWL 1 language distinguishes between six kinds of *class description*. Class descriptions denote sets of individuals and they actually correspond to concept expressions in DL languages. For the sake of simplicity, where it will not cause confusion, in the following we will refer to class descriptions simply as classes. Accordingly, OWL allows us to create the following kinds of class:

(1) a *named class*;

(2) an *enumeration class*;

(3) a class given with a *property restriction*;

(4) a class given as an *intersection* of classes;

(5) a class given as a *union* of classes;

(6) a class given as the *complement* of a class.

Named classes are the only classes having a URI. The others are unnamed classes and pose restrictions on which individuals can be their instances. An enumeration class, for example, explicitly states which individuals belong to it. A class that has a property restriction filters its instances on the basis of the value, existence or cardinality of certain properties. The last three kinds of class are created from existing classes by appropriate set operations. Using these we are able to create arbitrarily complex class descriptions.

Named classes are represented as instances of `owl:Class`, as shown below:

```
<owl:Class rdf:ID="Human"/>.
```

As a reminder, the above description corresponds to the RDF triple

```
{[#Human], [rdf:type], [owl:Class]}.
```

In the case of named classes, the class in question is represented by the subject node of the single available triple. A class of any other kind is represented by a set of RDF triples in which a blank node corresponds to the class being described.

OWL has two named classes built into it. The class `owl:Thing` is the top class: in OWL DL, all instances belong to this class and, because of this, `owl:Thing` is a superclass of all OWL DL classes. Thus, `owl:Thing` corresponds to the $\top$ (top) construct in description logics, the interpretation of which is the whole $\Delta^{\mathcal{I}}$ domain. In OWL Full, `owl:Thing` is the same as `rdfs:Resource`: all instances, values and other resources belong to the class `owl:Thing`.

The other built-in class is `owl:Nothing`. This class has no instances and, as such, is a subclass of all OWL classes. Thus, `owl:Nothing` corresponds to the $\bot$ (bottom) concept in Description Logic, whose interpretation is the empty set. For more about $\top$ and $\bot$ see Section 4.3.

All other class descriptions have the following structure, where "..." stands for the actual description of the given class:[3]

```
<owl:Class>
...
</owl:Class>
```

In the following we describe the different kinds of OWL classes in detail.

Enumeration

We can create a class by explicitly enumerating the instances it contains. For this purpose we can use the property `owl:oneOf` offered by OWL. The domain of this property is the class `owl:Class` and its range is an RDF collection of individuals. To represent such a list we use the `rdf:parseType` attribute, which makes the definition of RDF collections fairly easy. As introduced earlier, in Subsection 2.5.4, this is only syntactic sugar as collections are always built up from the `rdf:List`, `rdf:first` etc. elements.

Below we give an example of an enumeration class that contains the days of the week:

```
<owl:Class>
  <owl:oneOf rdf:parseType="Collection">
    <owl:Thing rdf:about="#sunday" />
    <owl:Thing rdf:about="#monday" />
    <owl:Thing rdf:about="#tuesday" />
    <owl:Thing rdf:about="#wednesday" />
    <owl:Thing rdf:about="#thursday" />
    <owl:Thing rdf:about="#friday" />
    <owl:Thing rdf:about="#saturday" />
  </owl:oneOf>
</owl:Class>
```

In graph form, our example contains a blank node from which two edges originate. One edge is labelled `rdf:type` and points to a node with the `owl:Class` URI as a label, i.e. this resource is the instance of the class `owl:Class`. The other edge is labelled `owl:oneOf`. This edge points to a node describing the given RDF collection, as described in Subsection 2.5.4.

The elements of our collection are instances. For now, we will say only that they are instances of the class `owl:Thing`. We cannot spoil anything by doing this, as all individuals are instances of `owl:Thing`.

In such a class description an entry for an individual can contain other information besides its name. We get a perfectly valid OWL description if we change the last entry in the example above to the following, more complex, description:

```
<owl:Thing rdf:about="#saturday">
  <rdfs:comment>The last day of the week</rdfs:comment>
</owl:Thing>
```

---

[3] For classes defined using property restrictions, instead of `owl:Class` we will use its subclass `owl:Restriction`.

The `owl:oneOf` construct cannot be used in OWL Lite at all. It may be used in OWL DL if all the elements of the given collection are from the $\Delta^{\mathcal{I}}$ domain (i.e. all elements are individuals) or if all these elements are from the Δ_D domain (i.e. all elements are values). In the latter case, the `owl:oneOf` property is connected to a node having `owl:DataRange` as its type. The `owl:DataRange` class is the subclass of `owl:Class` and is discussed in detail in Subsection 8.2.5. In the following, whenever we talk about a resource having the type `owl:DataRange` we are actually thinking of it as a set of values.

DL equivalent of the `owl:oneOf` construct uses nominals, as introduced in Subsection 4.10.2. Accordingly, the example above is equivalent to the following DL concept: {sunday, monday, tuesday, wednesday, thursday, friday, saturday}.

Exercise 8.3: Describe in OWL a class containing your family members and another containing your colleagues. Load the descriptions into your favourite ontology editor to verify your work.

Property restriction

Classes described by *property restrictions* are unnamed classes whose instances satisfy certain constraints with respect to a given RDF property: the constraints restrict the value or the cardinality of the property in question. These are called *value* and *cardinality constraints* respectively.

The general form of such classes is the following (P is the URI of the property to be used in the restriction, for example `#hasChild`):

```
<owl:Restriction>
  <owl:onProperty rdf:resource="P" />
  ... restriction on the value or cardinality of the property ...
</owl:Restriction>
```

The class `owl:Restriction` is a subclass of `owl:Class`. A class description such as that above corresponds to three triples, where the subject is shared: the blank node represents the class itself. The first triple states that the `rdf:type` of the blank node is `owl:Restriction`. The second has the predicate `owl:onProperty` with object P that can identify either an object property or a datatype property (for more on this, see Subsection 8.2.3 below). The last triple specifies the value or cardinality constraint itself.

Notice that when we define a class in this way, the domain or range of property P is not restricted at all (as it would be if we used `rdfs:domain` or `rdfs:range`). We are simply stating that the unnamed class in question contains those individuals that comply with the given condition. Nothing is stated about the applicability of property P in general.

Value constraints. Here we present the three types of value constraint that can be used when specifying `owl:Restriction` classes. They are `owl:allValuesFrom`, `owl:someValuesFrom` and `owl:hasValue`.[4]

---

[4] Note that the term *value constraints* is broader than the DL term *value restriction*, which corresponds to the `owl:allValuesFrom` construct only.

The universal restriction. The `owl:allValuesFrom` property can be used to spec-ify the first kind of value restriction. The right-hand side of this property is an OWL class description `C` or an `owl:DataRange`, i.e. a set of values. In the former case the value restriction means that all individuals belonging to the class `owl:Restriction` must be such that the right-hand sides of all the `P` properties connected to them belong to the given class `C` or, more precisely, to the set defined by this class. In other words, an individual `x` is an instance of the class defined by a universal restriction if it holds that whenever a pair `(x,y)` belongs to property `P` then `y` is an instance of the class description `C`.

If there is a set of values on the right-hand side of `owl:allValuesFrom`, the meaning can be obtained by an obvious reformulation of the definition above.

Let us now consider the following example:

```
<owl:Restriction>
  <owl:onProperty rdf:resource="#hasChild" />
  <owl:allValuesFrom rdf:resource="#Blonde" />
</owl:Restriction>
```

In this example we have defined a class whose instances are those individuals who have only blonde children (more precisely, all of whose children belong to the class `#Blonde`). It is important to note that individuals having no children at all also belong to this class, as we only require that *if* someone has a child then the child should be blonde.

The fact that there can be an arbitrary class description on the right-hand side of `owl:allValuesFrom` also means that we can use more complex class descriptions instead of named classes (such as `Blonde` in the example above). Below, we define the class of those individuals who like certain kinds of film. We assume that there exists a class `t:MovieType` that has instances such as `#comedy`, `#sci-fi`, `#horror`, `#drama` and so on:

```
<owl:Restriction>
  <owl:onProperty rdf:resource="#favourite_movie_type"/>
  <owl:allValuesFrom>
    <owl:Class>
      <owl:oneOf rdf:parseType="Collection">
        <t:MovieType rdf:about="#horror"/>
        <t:MovieType rdf:about="#sci-fi"/>
        <t:MovieType rdf:about="#action_movie"/>
      </owl:oneOf>
    </owl:Class>
  </owl:allValuesFrom>
</owl:Restriction>
```

The individual `#Jane`, for example, may belong to this class if she does not like movies at all or if she likes some, which cannot be different from those in the definition above. It is possible that she likes all three types, or any two or only one.

We note that we could have simply written `owl:Thing` instead of `t:MovieType` in the example above.

In OWL Lite, the `owl:allValuesFrom` construct can be used only in a restricted way: there can be only named classes or named datatypes on the right-hand side of owl:allValuesFrom. Owing to this, our example above does not belong to the OWL Lite sublanguage, this is reinforced by the fact that it uses the owl:oneOf construct.

The owl:allValuesFrom property restriction corresponds to the value restriction construct in Description Logic, i.e. to the $\forall R.C$ concept constructor (see Section 4.3). According to this, our first example is equivalent to the $\forall$hasChild.Blonde DL class expression.

Exercise 8.4: Describe in OWL the classes whose instances are respectively those individuals who:

(a) have only happy parents;

(b) have only daughters;

(c) are unmarried (hint: individuals whose spouses belong to owl:Nothing);

(d) have no children.

Existential restriction. The owl:someValuesFrom property is similar to the property owl:allValuesFrom; its right-hand side is an OWL class description C or an owl:DataRange. Here again we discuss only the meaning of the first case, as the second case can be treated analogously.

The meaning of the restriction is the following: exactly those individuals will belong to the owl:Restriction class which have at least one P property that has an individual belonging to the given class description C on its right-hand side. That is, all x individuals belong to the class for which there exists at least one y such that P contains the (x,y) pair and y is an instance of class C.

The example below describes the set of individuals that have at least one blonde child:

```
<owl:Restriction>
   <owl:onProperty rdf:resource="#hasChild" />
   <owl:someValuesFrom rdf:resource="#Blonde" />
</owl:Restriction>
```

It is possible that, although #Steve is an instance of this class, he has a child who is not an instance of the #Blonde class. This is not a problem as long as #Steve has at least one blonde child. It is important to note that individuals having no children will not be instances of the unnamed class described above (as opposed to the case of the owl:allValuesFrom property).

The owl:someValuesFrom property can also be used for creating more complex classes, as there may be an arbitrary class description on its right-hand side. In the following, we describe a class whose instances know at least one person who has only strong children.

```
<owl:Restriction>
   <owl:onProperty rdf:resource="#knows"/>
   <owl:someValuesFrom>
     <owl:Restriction>
       <owl:onProperty rdf:resource="#hasChild" />
       <owl:allValuesFrom rdf:resource="#Strong" />
```

```
      </owl:Restriction>
    </owl:someValuesFrom>
</owl:Restriction>
```

To understand the example, let us first notice that the "embedded" class represents those people who either have no children or, if they have, all of whose children are strong. Then we are interested in those individuals who know at least one instance of this class.

OWL Lite restricts the usage of `owl:someValuesFrom` in the same way as in the case of `owl:allValuesFrom`: there can be only named classes or datatypes on the right-hand side of `owl:someValuesFrom`. Accordingly, the above example can be described only in OWL DL and OWL Full.

The `owl:someValuesFrom` construct corresponds to the full existential restriction in Description Logic, i.e. to the $\exists R.C$ concept constructor (see Section 4.4). According to this, the DL equivalent of our first example is the expression $\exists$hasChild.Blonde, while the equivalent of the second is $\exists$knows.($\forall$hasChild.Strong).

Exercise 8.5: Describe in OWL the classes whose instances are respectively those individuals who:

(a) have a child;

(b) have a daughter;

(c) have a grandchild (use only the `hasChild` property);

(d) have a sibling having a child;

(e) have a sibling all of whose children are female.

Concrete restriction. The right-hand side of the `owl:hasValue` restriction is an individual or a value, i.e. an element of the $\Delta^{\mathcal{I}}$ or the Δ_D domain. The meaning of the restriction is that the instances of `owl:Restriction` are those individuals that have at least one P property having an individual or value on the right-hand side that is *semantically equivalent* to the given individual or value.

Two *individuals* are semantically equivalent if they are identified by the same URI or if their equivalence has been stated (see Subsection 8.2.4) or if their equivalence has been inferred. Two *values* are equivalent if they represent the same value regardless of their lexical form (e.g. the numbers 2.5 and 2.50 are semantically equivalent).

In our first example we describe the set of people having #Steve as their child, i.e. we determine the class of #Steve's parents:

```
<owl:Restriction>
    <owl:onProperty rdf:resource="#hasChild" />
    <owl:hasValue rdf:resource="#Steve" />
</owl:Restriction>
```

This class will most likely contain two individuals, but – depending on the interpretation of the #hasChild relation – we may get more than two parents (e.g. it is possible that the ontology also regards stepchildren as children).

The `owl:hasValue` construct can be replaced by the appropriate use of `owl:oneOf`. That is, if we define a class with a single instance, i.e. a nominal, then we can replace `owl:hasValue` with `owl:someValuesFrom`. Accordingly, our previous example can be written in the following way:

```
<owl:Restriction>
   <owl:onProperty rdf:resource="#hasChild" />
   <owl:someValuesFrom>
    <owl:Class>
      <owl:oneOf rdf:parseType="Collection">
        <owl:Thing rdf:about="#Steve"/>
      </owl:oneOf>
    </owl:Class>
   </owl:someValuesFrom>
</owl:Restriction>
```

In the example we describe a class having only `#Steve` as an instance, and then we select those individuals who have a child belonging to this class.

The `owl:hasValue` construct cannot be used in OWL Lite as in Description Logic it actually corresponds to the use of nominals in existential restrictions. Accordingly, the previous example can be written as ∃hasChild.{Steve}.

Exercise 8.6: Describe in OWL the classes whose instances are respectively those individuals who:

(a) know `Bob`;

(b) know somebody who knows `Bob`.

Cardinality constraints. By using cardinality constraints we can define classes with instances having a restricted number of individuals connected to them via a given property. In OWL we can use three kinds of cardinality constraint to create `owl:Restriction` classes: `owl:maxCardinality`, `owl:minCardinality` and `owl:cardinality`.

Before we go into details, we would like to remind the reader that RDF does not restrict the number of RDF statements in which a certain resource happens to be in a subject position. In other words, a resource can have an arbitrary number of properties attached to it. This is of course very advantageous, as it makes feasible a fundamental idea of the RDF framework, i.e. "anyone can say anything". The cardinality constraints of OWL pose no restrictions on such freedom of speech. These constraints only influence the classification of individuals: they do not limit in any way the number of edges that originate from a given resource.

We now proceed to describe the cardinality restrictions allowed by the OWL 1 language. These correspond to the unqualified number restrictions of Description Logic (Subsection 4.4.4). The OWL 2 language allows a wider variety of cardinality restrictions, namely those corresponding to qualified number restrictions; see Subsection 8.3.1.

Maximal cardinality. The right-hand side of `owl:maxCardinality` is a non-negative integer. This is syntactically represented in OWL as a typed literal (see Subsection 2.5.5) where the value of the `rdf:datatype` attribute is set to the URL of the XML schema datatype `nonNegativeInteger`. In the examples below we refer to the XML schema using the `xsd` XML entity.

The meaning of the `owl:maxCardinality` restriction is that instances of the `owl:Restriction` class can have *at most* a given number of P properties which have semantically different right-hand sides. For example, it can be used to describe the concept of a *very small company* (a company with at most three employees), as follows:

```
<owl:Restriction>
   <owl:onProperty rdf:resource="#hasEmployee" />
   <owl:maxCardinality rdf:datatype=
        "&xsd;nonNegativeInteger">3</owl:maxCardinality>
</owl:Restriction>
```

Let us now consider a resource with two #hasEmployee properties connected to it, with different URIs on their right-hand side. The question is whether an OWL reasoner should classify this resource as a small company. As OWL does not maintain the unique name assumption, these employees may turn out to be the same. We may say that this does not matter: either way, our company has fewer than three employees so it should be an instance of the class described above. We must not forget, however, that because of the open world assumption we cannot know for sure that our company does not have any more employees. Thus, an OWL reasoner actually should not classify the resource as a small company.

In OWL Lite, `owl:maxCardinality` can be used only with the values 0 or 1. In the first case we state that the instances of the class being described cannot have any P property attached to them; in the latter case, we allow at most one occurrence of P.

The example above corresponds to the $(\leqslant 3\,\mathsf{hasEmployee})$ DL concept expression.

Minimum cardinality. The right-hand side of `owl:minCardinality` is a non-negative integer. Like `owl:maxCardinality`, this is represented as a typed literal in the RDF/XML serialisation. The meaning of `owl:minCardinality` is that instances of the `owl:Restriction` class must have *at least* a given number of P properties with semantically different right-hand sides. For example, `owl:minCardinality` can be used to describe the class of large companies. We consider a company large if it has at least 50 employees, thus:

```
<owl:Restriction>
   <owl:onProperty rdf:resource="#hasEmployee" />
   <owl:minCardinality rdf:datatype=
        "&xsd;nonNegativeInteger">50</owl:minCardinality>
</owl:Restriction>
```

Let us consider the following individual, which physically has 51 #hasEmployee properties connected to it:

```
<owl:Thing rdf:ID="Future2100 Inc">
   <hasEmployee rdf:resource="#Bob"/>
   <hasEmployee rdf:resource="#Rudy"/>
   <hasEmployee rdf:resource="#Bob"/>
   ...
   <hasEmployee rdf:resource="#George"/>
```

```
<hasEmployee rdf:resource="#Rudolph"/>
</owl:Thing>
```

Should we consider #Future2100 as a large company? It seems that the open world assumption does not affect our answer here, since if we know for sure that a company has more than 50 employees then the exact number irrelevant. The question is, can we be sure that #Future2100 has at least 50 workers?

On the basis of the URIs it is apparent that two workers are the same. In real life this would certainly not be so explicit, but, for example, two different sources would state that #Bob is a worker of the company. Let us assume that the other URIs are pairwise different. Now we have a resource that has 50 employees with different URIs; can we classify it as a large company?

No, because the lack of a unique name assumption means that some employees may still turn out to be the same so we cannot be sure that #Future2100 has more than 50 employees. Note that such a behaviour cannot be expected from a DL reasoner using the UNA, because the UNA does not allow two individuals with different names to denote the same domain element.

The owl:minCardinality construct may be used in OWL Lite only with the values 0 or 1. In the first case practically nothing is stated; in the latter, we require that each instance of the class being described must have at least one other individual connected to it via the P property.

The example above may be written as $(\geqslant 50\,\mathsf{hasEmployee})$ in DL formalism.

Exact cardinality. Syntactically, owl:cardinality is very similar to the cardinality constraints introduced above. The meaning of it is that instances of the owl:Restriction class must have *exactly* a given number of P properties having semantically different right-hand sides. For example, we can define the class of individuals with two children in the following way:

```
<owl:Restriction>
    <owl:onProperty rdf:resource="#hasChild" />
    <owl:cardinality rdf:datatype=
        "&xsd;nonNegativeInteger">2</owl:cardinality>
</owl:Restriction>
```

The owl:cardinality construct is actually only syntactic sugar, as it can be replaced by the simultaneous use of owl:maxCardinality and owl:minCardinality. An example of this is shown later.

In OWL Lite, owl:cardinality may be used only with the restriction that we give it either the value 0 or the value 1. In the first case we require that instances of the class being described have no P property attached to them. In the second case we specify that exactly one occurrence of P is present. This latter construct can be used to describe attributes in the sense of the object-oriented approach, such as the *name* attribute of the *person* object. The constraint that a *person* object is required to have exactly one *name* attribute can be described using an owl:cardinality restriction with the value 1.

Our earlier OWL example, about individuals with exactly two children, corresponds to the DL concept $(\leqslant 2\,\mathsf{hasChild}) \sqcap (\geqslant 2\,\mathsf{hasChild})$.

Exercise 8.7: Using cardinality restrictions, describe in OWL the classes whose instances are respectively those individuals who:

(a) have more than two children;

(b) have at most three children;

(c) have no children at all (hint: individuals having at most zero children);

(d) have exactly two parents.

Intersection

The fourth kind of OWL class-building operator constructs a new class from the intersection of class descriptions. We can use the property `owl:intersectionOf` for this purpose; it connects an instance of `owl:Class` with a list of class descriptions. The class described this way contains the individuals that are instances of *all* the given class descriptions in the list.

In the simplest case, the list contains named classes. In the following example we describe the class of individuals who are both tall and blonde.

```
<owl:Class>
  <owl:intersectionOf rdf:parseType="Collection">
    <owl:Class rdf:about="#Tall"/>
    <owl:Class rdf:about="#Blonde"/>
  </owl:intersectionOf>
</owl:Class>
```

As the list may contain arbitrary class descriptions, we do not need to use named classes only. For example, the next example class contains the tall individuals from the set George, Bob and Caroline:

```
<owl:Class>
  <owl:intersectionOf rdf:parseType="Collection">
    <owl:Class rdf:about="#Tall"/>
    <owl:Class>
      <owl:oneOf rdf:parseType="Collection">
        <t:Human rdf:about="#George"/>
        <t:Human rdf:about="#Bob"/>
        <t:Human rdf:about="#Caroline"/>
      </owl:oneOf>
    </owl:Class>
  </owl:intersectionOf>
</owl:Class>
```

In the above example we create the intersection of two classes, one of which is a named class while the other is an enumeration class.

Using the intersection operator we can show that the `owl:cardinality` constraint is actually only syntactic sugar. For example, the class of individuals having exactly two children may also be specified without using `owl:cardinality`, as follows:

```
<owl:Class>
  <owl:intersectionOf rdf:parseType="Collection">
    <owl:Restriction>
      <owl:onProperty rdf:resource="#hasChild" />
      <owl:minCardinality rdf:datatype=
        "&xsd;nonNegativeInteger">2</owl:minCardinality>
    </owl:Restriction>
    <owl:Restriction>
      <owl:onProperty rdf:resource="#hasChild" />
      <owl:maxCardinality rdf:datatype=
        "&xsd;nonNegativeInteger">2</owl:maxCardinality>
    </owl:Restriction>
  </owl:intersectionOf>
</owl:Class>
```

Here we describe a class whose instances fulfil two criteria: on the one hand, each individual must have at least two distinct children, while on the other it must have no more than two distinct children. Consequently, an instance of this class must have exactly two distinct children.

Using intersection we can easily describe the class of blue-eyed people: humans intersected by those individuals having blue eyes. This can be seen below.

```
<owl:Class>
  <owl:intersectionOf rdf:parseType="Collection">
    <owl:Class rdf:about="#Human"/>
    <owl:Restriction>
      <owl:onProperty rdf:resource="#hasEyeColour" />
      <owl:hasValue>Blue</owl:hasValue>
    </owl:Restriction>
  </owl:intersectionOf>
</owl:Class>
```

In the example above, the colour blue is represented as a literal this is the result of a modelling decision. We could have also used an individual for this purpose: an instance of the class of colours, for example.

Our concluding example creates the intersection of two enumeration classes:

```
<owl:Class>
  <owl:intersectionOf rdf:parseType="Collection">
    <owl:Class>
      <owl:oneOf rdf:parseType="Collection">
        <owl:Thing rdf:about="#George" />
        <owl:Thing rdf:about="#Bob" />
        <owl:Thing rdf:about="#Alex" />
      </owl:oneOf>
```

```
    </owl:Class>
    <owl:Class>
      <owl:oneOf rdf:parseType="Collection">
        <owl:Thing rdf:about="#Thomas" />
        <owl:Thing rdf:about="#George" />
      </owl:oneOf>
    </owl:Class>
  </owl:intersectionOf>
</owl:Class>
```

This example is interesting because of the lack of a unique name assumption in OWL. At first sight one would expect that the resulting class consists of a single instance, as #George is the only individual present in both given classes. However, in OWL different URIs may identify the very same resource. Thus, it may turn out that #Bob and #Thomas identify the same person, and so this instance must also belong to the class above.

OWL Lite restricts the use of the intersection construct: the class descriptions in the list must be named classes or classes described using property restrictions.

The owl:intersectionOf resource corresponds to the intersection construct in Description Logic (see Section 4.3). Accordingly, our very first example above can be written as Tall ⊓ Blonde.

Exercise 8.8: Describe in OWL the following classes:

(a) people with only happy parents;

(b) fathers with more than three children;

(c) mothers having only daughters;

(d) lawyers who know Steve.

Union

Using the owl:unionOf property we can create a new class by specifying it to be the union of two or more other classes. Syntactically, owl:unionOf connects a class to a list of class descriptions. The meaning of this construct is the following: the class on the left-hand side contains exactly those individuals which are instances of *at least one* of the given class descriptions in the list on the right-hand side.

As an example, let us consider the class description below, which specifies a set containing individuals that are blonde or blue-eyed or female.

```
<owl:Class>
  <owl:unionOf rdf:parseType="Collection">
    <owl:Class rdf:about="#Female"/>
    <owl:Class rdf:about="#Blonde"/>
    <owl:Class rdf:about="#BlueEyed"/>
  </owl:unionOf>
</owl:Class>
```

The class above is created as the union of three other classes: the `#Female` class, containing women; the `#Blonde` class, containing individuals with blonde hair; and the `#BlueEyed` class, containing individuals with blue eyes. Naturally, a man also can have blonde hair, and somebody who has blue eyes can also have dark hair etc.

The same concept can be modelled differently by defining what is meant by blonde and blue-eyed individuals. For this we use composite class descriptions instead of simple named classes, as follows:

```
<owl:Class>
  <owl:unionOf rdf:parseType="Collection">
    <owl:Class rdf:about="#Female"/>
    <owl:Restriction>
      <owl:onProperty rdf:resource="#hasHairColour" />
      <owl:hasValue>Blonde</owl:hasValue>
    </owl:Restriction>
    <owl:Restriction>
      <owl:onProperty rdf:resource="#hasEyeColour" />
      <owl:hasValue>Blue</owl:hasValue>
    </owl:Restriction>
  </owl:unionOf>
</owl:Class>
```

OWL Lite does not allow the use of the union operator. The `owl:unionOf` property corresponds to the union constructor in description logic (see Section 4.4). Accordingly, our first example can be written as Female ⊔ Blonde ⊔ BlueEyed.

Exercise 8.9: Describe in OWL the following classes:

(a) a man or woman;

(b) a person who is blonde or has a blonde child;

(c) people who are rich or happy.

Complement

The last kind of OWL class description defines a new class as the complement of another. For this, OWL offers the `owl:complementOf` property, which connects a class with exactly one class description. The class described in this way contains individuals that are *not* instances of the class description on the right-hand side.

The example below describes the class of non-blonde people or, more precisely, the set of those instances that are not in the `#Blonde` class:

```
<owl:Class>
  <owl:complementOf>
    <owl:Class rdf:about="#Blonde"/>
  </owl:complementOf>
</owl:Class>
```

However, it is likely that we do not really want a sofa, for example, to be the instance of our class just because it is not in the #Blonde class. Therefore it seems to be more practical to use the following description:

```
<owl:Class>
  <owl:intersectionOf rdf:parseType="Collection">
    <owl:Class rdf:about="#Human"/>
    <owl:Class>
      <owl:complementOf>
        <owl:Class rdf:about="#Blonde"/>
      </owl:complementOf>
    </owl:Class>
  </owl:intersectionOf>
</owl:Class>
```

Thus the class above represents the set of non-blonde humans.

Generally, there can be arbitrary class descriptions on the right-hand side of owl: complementOf. Accordingly, the following piece of valid OWL code describes the class of people who do not have blue eyes:

```
<owl:Class>
  <owl:intersectionOf rdf:parseType="Collection">
    <owl:Class rdf:about="#Human"/>
    <owl:Class>
      <owl:complementOf>
        <owl:Restriction>
          <owl:onProperty rdf:resource="#hasEyeColour" />
          <owl:hasValue>Blue</owl:hasValue>
        </owl:Restriction>
      </owl:complementOf>
    </owl:Class>
  </owl:intersectionOf>
</owl:Class>
```

The complement operation cannot be used in OWL Lite. The owl:complementOf construct is equivalent to full – i.e. not necessarily atomic – negation in Description Logic (see Section 4.4). Accordingly, the class of non-blonde people can be written as Human ⊓ ¬Blonde.

Exercise 8.10: Describe in OWL the following classes:

(a) non-violent movies (hint: use the property contains);

(b) people having unhappy children;

(c) non-female people all of whose children are female;

(d) lawyers not knowing Steve.

8.2.2. OWL axioms

The class descriptions introduced above form a basis for the formulation of OWL *axioms*. Axioms can be created using three kinds of OWL property. The left- and right-hand sides of these properties are class descriptions (note that none of the properties introduced so far allows class descriptions on its left-hand side). The three properties are:

1. `rdfs:subClassOf`;
2. `owl:equivalentClass`;
3. `owl:disjointWith`.

Using `rdfs:subClassOf` we can describe subclass–superclass relationships. Formally, we can state that the interpretation of the class description given as the subject is a subset of the interpretation of the class description given as the object. Equivalence is allowed in this "subset" relation, i.e. non-proper subsets are also allowed. The reader should already be familiar with the `rdfs:subClassOf` construct, as it was discussed when we introduced RDF schemas (see Section 2.6). There we used it to describe the subsumption relation between two named classes. In OWL we have the option of using arbitrary class descriptions instead of simple named classes.

Using `owl:equivalentClass` we can state that the interpretation of the class description given as the subject is the same as the interpretation of the class description given as the object. Thus we can assert that the two class descriptions have equivalent sets of instances.

The last kind of OWL axiom, `owl:disjointWith`, can be used to state that the interpretation of the class description given as the subject and that of the class description given as the object have no common elements.

The above OWL axioms correspond to the concept axioms of Description Logic (see Section 4.2). Concept axioms form the basis of TBoxes, as they describe a fundamental subsumption relationship between two concept expressions. The `rdfs:subClassOf` construct captures exactly this relationship. The other two OWL axioms are actually only syntactic sugar: equivalence can be formulated as a two-way subsumption and disjointness can be transformed into a subsumption axiom where, on the left-hand side, we have the intersection of the two classes and on the right-hand side there is `owl:Nothing`.

However, it is very useful that both the equivalence and disjointness of classes can be specified explicitly. Within these axioms it is quite common to have complex unnamed class descriptions, which give rise to rather cumbersome OWL specifications when transformed to subsumptions. If we insist on using subclass relations to express equivalence then the best solution is to name certain intermediate classes, but this may reduce the readability and increase the size of our ontology.

OWL axioms are also important as they help establish connections between different ontologies. Namely, we can use the `owl:equivalentClass` to state the equivalence of a class in our ontology to some other class in an external ontology.

Subclasses

As discussed above, in OWL the subsumption relation can be given using the `rdfs:subClassOf` property. The meaning of `rdfs:subClassOf` is that the set of individuals that belong to the class description given as the subject is the subset of the set of individuals that belong to the class description given as the object. The `rdfs:subClassOf` property is transitive and reflexive. Its transitivity means that if A is a subclass of B, and B is a subclass of C, then it is certain that A is also a subclass of C. The fact that `rdfs:subClassOf` is reflexive means that every class is subsumed by itself: we consider a set as a subset of itself.

In the simplest case both the subject and the object are named classes. This is a subsumption that we could already express using pure RDF schema. As an example, let us consider the following axiom, where we state that houses are buildings:

```
<owl:Class rdf:ID="House">
  <rdfs:subClassOf rdf:resource="#Building">
</owl:Class>
```

A class can have an arbitrary number of `rdfs:subClassOf` properties (i.e. it can participate in multiple axioms), and the right-hand side of these can be any kind of class description. For example, someone may give the following additional description about the class #House above:

```
<owl:Class rdf:about="#House">
  <rdfs:subClassOf>
    <owl:Restriction>
      <owl:onProperty rdf:resource="#hasWindow" />
      <owl:minCardinality rdf:datatype=
      "&xsd;nonNegativeInteger">3</owl:minCardinality>
    </owl:Restriction>
  </rdfs:subClassOf>
</owl:Class>
```

Here we also specify that a house has at least three windows. This is achieved by stating that the class of houses is the subclass of an unnamed class containing individuals that have at least three windows. We do not claim that if something has at least three windows then it is a house: think about a ship, an aeroplane and so on. All we are saying is that whenever a resource is classified as house it should fulfil this criterion about the number of windows.

In the following example we state that, if the construction materials of a house are given, these can only be #brick, #clay or #wood (we could also restrict the number of materials that may be used in a house by setting an appropriate cardinality restriction):

```
<owl:Class rdf:about="#House">
  <rdfs:subClassOf>
    <owl:Restriction>
      <owl:onProperty rdf:resource="#hasMaterial" />
      <owl:allValuesFrom>
        <owl:Class>
          <owl:oneOf rdf:parseType="Collection">
            <t:Material rdf:about="#brick"/>
            <t:Material rdf:about="#clay"/>
            <t:Material rdf:about="#wood"/>
          </owl:oneOf>
        </owl:Class>
      </owl:allValuesFrom>
```

```
        </owl:Restriction>
    </rdfs:subClassOf>
</owl:Class>
```

What makes really interesting descriptions possible is that we are not confined to simple named classes on the left-hand side of `rdfs:subClassOf`. Let us consider the example in Figure 8.2. We state that an unnamed class, described by a property restriction, is the subclass of another class. More specifically, we state that everyone who has a rich child is happy. It is important to see that we have not created a new class with this statement; we have merely stated that, in our world, every individual that has a rich child is an instance of the class `#Happy` (see the general concept inclusion axioms in Subsection 4.6.1.)

In Figure 8.2 we also see that `#George` has a child, who is in fact rich. From these facts, an OWL reasoner can prove that `#George` is happy.

An example of such a reasoner is the RacerPro [47] system, which is one of the most up-to-date DL inference engines. RacerPro is capable of reading OWL descriptions, so we can use the example in Figure 8.2 directly. This is exactly what we do in the first line below. In the subsequent lines we ask Racer to enumerate all the individuals, then we ask for the happy individuals:

```
<?xml version="1.0"?>
<rdf:RDF
  xml:base = "http://swexpld.org#"
  xmlns = "http://swexpld.org#"
  xmlns:rdf = "http://www.w3.org/1999/02/22-rdf-syntax-ns#"
  xmlns:rdfs = "http://www.w3.org/2000/01/rdf-schema#"
  xmlns:owl = "http://www.w3.org/2002/07/owl#">

  <owl:Class rdf:ID="Rich" />
  <owl:Class rdf:ID="Happy" />
  <owl:ObjectProperty rdf:ID="hasChild" />

  <owl:Restriction>
    <owl:onProperty rdf:resource="#hasChild" />
    <owl:someValuesFrom rdf:resource="#Rich" />
    <rdfs:subClassOf rdf:resource="#Happy" />
  </owl:Restriction>

  <Rich rdf:ID="Katy" />

  <owl:Thing rdf:ID="George">
    <hasChild rdf:resource="#Katy"/>
  </owl:Thing>
</rdf:RDF>
```

Figure 8.2. Complex class description as a subject.

```
(owl-read-file "axioms.owl")
(all-individuals)
(concept-instances |http://swexpld.org#Happy|)
```

As an answer, we get that #George and #Katy are both individuals but only #George is happy.

```
(ALL-INDIVIDUALS) -->
  (|http://swexpld.org#George|
   |http://swexpld.org#Katy|)
(CONCEPT-INSTANCES http://swexpld.org#Happy) -->
  (|http://swexpld.org#George|)
```

OWL Lite restricts the use of rdfs:subClassOf in the following way: the subject can only be a named class and the object must be either a named class or a class given with property restriction.

As mentioned before, the DL equivalent of a rdfs:subClassOf axiom is a general concept inclusion axiom (cf. Subsection 4.6.1). The example in Figure 8.2 can be written in DL as ∃hasChild.Rich ⊑ Happy.

Exercise 8.11: Describe in OWL the following axioms.

(a) Tigers are mammals.

(b) A human having an alcoholic friend is non-alcoholic.

(c) Somebody is happy if they have a rich child all of whose children are happy.

(d) Those having at least three cars are rich.

(e) Every human has a name.

Equivalence

Using the owl:equivalentClass property we can state that the instances of two class descriptions are the same sets in any possible interpretations. A significant difference compared with rdfs:subClassOf is that owl:equivalentClass gives a *necessary and sufficient* condition for an individual to be in a given class. In the simplest case, we state the equivalence of two named classes:

```
<owl:Class rdf:about="http://swexpld.org#Woman">
  <owl:equivalentClass rdf:resource="#Beautiful"/>
</owl:Class>
```

Here, we have stated that all women are beautiful and everyone who is beautiful is also a woman. The literature usually emphasises that the equivalence of two classes does not mean that they have the same *intensional* meaning, i.e. denote the same abstract concept. Specifically, this means that the concepts #Woman and #Beautiful are not the same. We have merely stated that we are considering only those worlds where it is true that all individuals that belong to one class also belong to the other class: i.e. their *extensions* are the same.

Using owl:equivalentClass we can give names to unnamed classes, e.g. the class containing the days of the week may be described in the following way (see the enumerations in Subsection 8.2.1):

```
<owl:Class rdf:ID="DayOfTheWeek">
  <owl:equivalentClass>
    <owl:Class>
      <owl:oneOf rdf:parseType="Collection">
        <owl:Thing rdf:about="#monday" />
        <owl:Thing rdf:about="#tuesday" />
        <owl:Thing rdf:about="#wednesday" />
        <owl:Thing rdf:about="#thursday" />
        <owl:Thing rdf:about="#friday" />
        <owl:Thing rdf:about="#saturday" />
        <owl:Thing rdf:about="#sunday" />
      </owl:oneOf>
    </owl:Class>
  </owl:equivalentClass>
</owl:Class>
```

In this example we introduce a new class by enumerating its instances. Note that owl:equivalentClass actually connects two classes: one is the named class DayOfTheWeek and the other is a complex unnamed class description. This kind of usage of owl:equivalentClass corresponds to the definitional axioms in Description Logic (see Subsection 4.6.1).

With owl:equivalentClass we can restructure the example in Figure 8.2. Instead of starting an rdfs:subClassOf edge directly from an unnamed class, we can first name it and then apply the subclass relation to it. The OWL description below illustrates this:

```
<owl:Class rdf:ID="ExceptionalParent">
  <owl:equivalentClass>
    <owl:Restriction>
      <owl:onProperty rdf:resource="#hasChild" />
      <owl:someValuesFrom rdf:resource="#Rich" />
    </owl:Restriction>
  </owl:equivalentClass>
  <rdfs:subClassOf rdf:resource="#Happy" />
</owl:Class>
```

We know two facts about the class #ExceptionalParent: (1) the individuals who have a rich child are members of this class (and the other way round); (2) all members of this class are necessarily happy. Thus if we ask for happy persons, we will get George as an answer, as having a rich child makes him the instance of class #ExceptionalParent and, owing to this, he is also a member of the class #Happy.

We consider the above definition of #ExceptionalParent easier to understand, and better structured, than the semantically equivalent version in Figure 8.2. Therefore, as a general principle we recommend using named classes on the left-hand sides of OWL axioms, when building ontologies.

Although there can be more than one `owl:equivalentClass` property connected to a class description, we must be careful about this. For example, if we state that a given class is equivalent to both the class of women and the class of men, we may get undesirable global effects: this would actually mean that the classes of men and women are equivalent, which probably is a modelling error.

Here we mention a simplification offered by the OWL language. OWL allows us to name unnamed classes described by enumeration, intersection, union or negation (but not classes defined with property restrictions), without using `owl:equivalentClass`. To achieve this, it is enough to include the given class description as a child element of a named class. Semantically, this is the same as stating the equivalence of this named class and the given class description; something we have just discussed.

As a matter of fact, we have already used this option in our introductory example, shown in Figure 8.1. In the class describing fathers of girls we used the `owl:intersectionOf` property directly as the child element of this named class, instead of using the `owl:equivalentClass` OWL axiom to connect `FatherOfGirls` with the unnamed class given as the intersection of classes.

According to this, the spelled-out version of the class `FatherOfGirls` in our introductory example actually takes the following form:

```
<owl:Class rdf:ID="FatherOfGirls">
  <owl:equivalentClass>
    <owl:Class>
      <owl:intersectionOf rdf:parseType="Collection">
        <owl:Class rdf:about="#Human" />
        <owl:Class>
          <owl:complementOf rdf:resource="#Female" />
        </owl:Class>
        <owl:Restriction>
          <owl:onProperty rdf:resource="#hasChild" />
          <owl:allValuesFrom rdf:resource="#Female" />
        </owl:Restriction>
      </owl:intersectionOf>
    </owl:Class>
  </owl:equivalentClass>
</owl:Class>
```

Using this simplified form, the definition of the class `#DayOfTheWeek` can also be rewritten, in the following way:

```
<owl:Class rdf:ID="DayOfTheWeek">
  <owl:oneOf rdf:parseType="Collection">
    <owl:Thing rdf:about="#monday" />
    <owl:Thing rdf:about="#tuesday" />
    <owl:Thing rdf:about="#wednesday" />
    <owl:Thing rdf:about="#thursday" />
    <owl:Thing rdf:about="#friday" />
    <owl:Thing rdf:about="#saturday" />
    <owl:Thing rdf:about="#sunday" />
```

```
  </owl:oneOf>
</owl:Class>
```

Once again we must draw attention to the fact that this simplification cannot be used in the case of classes given with property restrictions. In such cases, `owl:equivalentClass` must still be used explicitly.

In OWL Lite, the left-hand side of `owl:equivalentClass` can only be a named class but the right-hand side can be either a named class or a class given with property restrictions.

The construct that corresponds to the `owl:equivalentClass` property in Description Logic is the concept equivalence axiom (see Section 4.2). Thus, for example, the OWL class `#ExceptionalParent` can be described by the two axioms ExceptionalParent $\sqsubseteq$ Happy and ExceptionalParent $\equiv \exists$hasChild.Rich.

Exercise 8.12: Transform to OWL the following statements.

(a) Humans are exactly those whose parents are also human.

(b) Lawyers are exactly those who work for a law company and have a degree in law.

(c) The books by Steve are exactly those books whose author is `Steve`.

Disjointness

The last kind of OWL axiom is `owl:disjointWith`. Using such an axiom we can state that the sets of instances of two class descriptions are disjoint, in all models. For example, we may state that women and men are disjoint, as shown below:

```
<owl:Class rdf:about="#Man">
  <owl:disjointWith rdf:resource="#Woman"/>
</owl:Class>
```

The axiom above does not give a necessary and sufficient condition for being a man or a woman, i.e. not being a woman does not imply being a man or the other way round. If we would like to achieve such a condition, we may introduce the concept *person*, as in the following:

```
<owl:Class rdf:about="#Person">
  <owl:unionOf rdf:parseType="Collection">
    <owl:Class rdf:about="#Woman"/>
    <owl:Class rdf:about="#Man"/>
  </owl:unionOf>
</owl:Class>

<owl:Class rdf:about="#Man">
  <owl:disjointWith rdf:resource="#Woman"/>
</owl:Class>
```

Here we state that a person can be either a woman or a man and that the latter two classes are disjoint. In this way we can give a sufficient criterion for belonging to these classes: if someone is known to be a person but not a woman, we can conclude that he is a man.

The `owl:disjointWith` property connects two arbitrary class descriptions. Thus we may state that one class is disjoint from another that contains individuals having dark hair (see the `owl:complementOf` property), as follows:

```
<owl:Class rdf:about="#Albino">
  <owl:disjointWith>
    <owl:Restriction>
      <owl:onProperty rdf:resource="#hasHairColour" />
      <owl:someValuesFrom rdf:resource="#DarkColour" />
    </owl:Restriction>
  </owl:disjointWith>
</owl:Class>
```

OWL Lite does not support the `owl:disjointWith` axiom. This OWL axiom actually corresponds to a special form of concept inclusion axiom in Description Logic (see Subsection 4.6.1). For example, knowledge about the class of albinos given by the OWL description above can be represented using the DL formalism in the following way: $\text{Albino} \sqcap (\exists \text{hasHairColour}.\text{DarkColour}) \sqsubseteq \bot$.

Exercise 8.13: Formalise the following statements in OWL.

(a) Somebody having no children cannot be a parent.

(b) Those having at least three cars cannot be poor.

8.2.3. OWL properties

In OWL we distinguish *object properties* from *datatype properties*. Object properties connect individuals with individuals, while datatype properties connect individuals with values. That is, object and datatype properties correspond to abstract and concrete roles, i.e. these are interpreted as subsets of $\Delta^{\mathcal{I}} \times \Delta^{\mathcal{I}}$ and of $\Delta^{\mathcal{I}} \times \Delta_D$, respectively.

Object properties are instances of the class `owl:ObjectProperty`; datatype properties are instances of `owl:DatatypeProperty`. In OWL DL, both these classes are subclasses of `rdf:Property` and are disjoint, e.g. an object property cannot be a datatype property at the same time. In OWL Full we do not have such a separation.

As we have already seen, the OWL language offers a wide variety of possibilities for creating class descriptions. This is not the case for properties, at least within OWL 1; we cannot define a property based on other properties. For example, OWL 1 does not make it possible to state that the property #hasAunt is a composition of the properties #hasParent and #hasSister.[5]

Basically, the only thing we can do is to state that a given property exists by instantiating it from the appropriate built-in OWL class. We will illustrate this for properties #hasChild and #hasSize:

```
<owl:ObjectProperty rdf:ID="hasChild"/>
<owl:DatatypeProperty rdf:ID="hasSize"/>
```

---

[5] This is made possible in OWL 2; see Section 8.3.

Later, we will use the property #hasChild to connect people with people and the property #hasSize to connect things with values. This is the reason why above we used the classes owl:ObjectProperty and owl:DatatypeProperty, respectively.

Although OWL does not offer property constructors, it provides several *property axioms*. Some of these axioms resemble class axioms, as they run between two properties; others simply define additional characteristics of the properties. The OWL specification classifies property axioms into four groups:

(1) RDF schema constructs;

(2) equivalence and inverse axioms;

(3) global cardinality constraints;

(4) property characteristics.

In the first group we have axioms describing the hierarchies of the properties and constructs that restrict the domain and range of a property. The axioms in the second group can be used to state the equivalence of two properties or to express the fact that one property is the inverse of another. The global cardinality restrictions describe whether a property represents a function or the inverse of a function. Finally, the property characteristics can be used to express the fact that a property is transitive or symmetric.

Notice that although the R^- inverse role constructor of Description Logic is not supported as such, we can state that one named property is the inverse of another. Thus if we want to use the inverse of a property, we have to name it.

As with RDF schema, the instances of a property are pairs. For example, if we take a specific interpretation, the #hasChild property may have the (#George,#Katy) instance.

In the following we describe each group of OWL property axioms in detail.

RDF schema constructs

Here we discuss the OWL-specific use of some resources already introduced in the context of RDF schemas.

Subproperties. The property–subproperty relationship can be described in OWL exactly as in RDF schema: the left- and right-hand sides of rdfs:subPropertyOf are both property descriptions. The meaning of rdfs:subPropertyOf is that the set denoted by the property given as the object contains the set denoted by the property given as the subject.

As an example, let us describe the fact that the property #hasFather is a subproperty of #hasParent. That is, in every case when we know that two resources are related to each other via the #hasFather property, we can be sure that the #hasParent relationship also holds between them:

```
<owl:ObjectProperty rdf:ID="hasFather">
  <rdfs:subPropertyOf rdf:resource="#hasParent" />
</owl:ObjectProperty>
```

In the case of OWL DL and OWL Lite there can only be properties of the same kind on the two sides of rdfs:subPropertyOf. Accordingly, we cannot state that an object property is the subproperty of a datatype property, or the other way around.

The `rdfs:subPropertyOf` corresponds to the role inclusion axiom in Description Logic (see Section 4.2). Thus the example above can be formulated as hasFather ⊑ hasParent.

Domain and range restrictions.   The `rdfs:domain` and `rdfs:range` restrictions connect a given property with certain OWL classes. Using such axioms we can express the constraint that the individuals on the left- or right-hand side of the property must belong to a given class. For example, in the case of the property `hasFavouriteDrink` we can state that it connects people with drinks. Thus:

```
<owl:ObjectProperty rdf:ID="hasFavouriteDrink">
  <rdfs:domain rdf:resource="#Person" />
  <rdfs:range rdf:resource="#Drink" />
</owl:ObjectProperty>
```

We can use a variety of class constructors in such restrictions. In the following example we restrict the range of the property `#hasBank` to a given enumeration class:

```
<owl:ObjectProperty rdf:ID="hasBank">
  <rdfs:range>
    <owl:Class>
      <owl:oneOf rdf:parseType="Collection">
        <s:Bank rdf:about="#OTP Bank"/>
        <s:Bank rdf:about="#Citi Bank"/>
        <s:Bank rdf:about="#Erste Bank"/>
        <s:Bank rdf:about="#CIB Bank"/>
      </owl:oneOf>
    </owl:Class>
  </rdfs:range>
</owl:ObjectProperty>
```

If the above axiom regarding the property `#hasBank` is included in an OWL ontology then this property may by applied to an arbitrary resource, but only the given individuals (`#OTP Bank`, and so on) are allowed on its right-hand side.

A property can have multiple `rdfs:domain` and `rdfs:range` restrictions. In such cases we must use the intersection of the class descriptions to determine the effective domain and range. In OWL we may also explicitly use the `owl:intersectionOf` constructor as an alternative to giving multiple `rdfs:domain` or `rdfs:range` restrictions. Below we give the explicit form of the `hasMaidenName` property introduced in Subsection 2.6.5:

```
<owl:ObjectProperty rdf:ID="hasMaidenName">
  <rdfs:domain>
    <owl:Class>
      <owl:intersectionOf rdf:parseType="Collection">
        <owl:Class rdf:about="#Person"/>
        <owl:Class rdf:about="#Female"/>
      </owl:intersectionOf>
    </owl:Class>
  </rdfs:domain>
</owl:ObjectProperty>
```

On the right-hand side of `rdfs:range` we may put the name of a datatype. Below, we state that the property #hasSize connects shoes with positive integers:

```
<owl:DatatypeProperty rdf:ID="hasSize">
  <rdfs:domain rdf:resource="#Shoe" />
  <rdfs:range  rdf:resource="&xsd;positiveInteger"/>
</owl:DatatypeProperty>
```

The constructs `rdfs:domain` and `rdfs:range` correspond to specific concept inclusion axioms in Description Logic (see Section 4.2). Accordingly, the previous example can be expressed using the following axioms: $\exists$hasFavouriteDrink.$\top \sqsubseteq$ Person (anyone who has a favourite drink is a person) and $\top \sqsubseteq \forall$hasFavouriteDrink.Drink (it is true, for all individuals x, that if x has a favourite drink it is an instance of the class Drink). Alternatively, we could have written our axioms as $\top \sqsubseteq \forall$hasFavouriteDrink$^-$.Person or $\exists$hasFavouriteDrink$^-$.$\top \sqsubseteq$ Drink.

Exercise 8.14: Transform the following DL axioms to OWL DL:

(a) $\top \sqsubseteq \forall$hasLocation$^-$.(Event $\sqcap$ Activity);

(b) $\top \sqsubseteq \forall$hasLocation.(Building $\sqcup$ Country).

Equivalence and inverse

We now discuss how to describe the equivalence of properties and how to express that one property is the inverse of another.

Equivalence.   As with classes, we can also state the equivalence of properties. The `owl:equivalentProperty` axioms can be used to express the fact that the meaning of two properties is the same set of pairs in all models. While an `rdfs:subPropertyOf` axiom gives only a sufficient condition for a pair of individuals to be an instance of a property, `owl:equivalentProperty` gives a *necessary and sufficient* condition for this.

In the example below we assume that the properties #hasChild and #hasKid are already defined, perhaps in different ontologies. The following construct states that these two properties denote the same set of pairs:

```
<owl:ObjectProperty rdf:about="#hasChild">
  <owl:equivalentProperty rdf:resource=
  "http://swexpld.org#hasKid"/>
</owl:ObjectProperty>
```

As in the case of the equivalence of classes, we must also emphasise that the equivalence of sets of instances does not mean that the relations denoted by the properties have the same intensional meaning.

In OWL Lite and OWL DL, only properties of the same type can be on the two sides of the `owl:equivalentProperty`; for example we cannot state that an object property is equivalent to a datatype property.

The DL equivalent of the `owl:equivalentProperty` construct is the role equivalence axiom (see Section 4.2). The example above can be written as hasChild ≡ hasKid.

Inverse. OWL gives us the option of stating that a property is the inverse of another property. The `owl:inverseOf` axiom can be used for this purpose. This axiom connects two properties, and the meaning of it is that if the pair `(a,b)` belongs to the property on the left-hand side then the pair `(b,a)` has to belong to the property on the right-hand side, and the other way round. Below we state that everyone is a parent of her own children:

```
<owl:ObjectProperty rdf:about="#hasChild">
  <owl:inverseOf rdf:resource="#hasParent"/>
</owl:ObjectProperty>
```

Because the inverse relation is symmetric, when we state that the inverse of `hasChild` is `hasParent` it follows that the inverse of `hasParent` is `hasChild`. Thus the example above also expresses the fact that everyone is a child of her own parents.

OWL Lite and OWL DL require that `owl:inverseOf` is used only for object properties. The reason for this is simply that in OWL Lite and DL a value cannot be the subject of a triple, which would happen if we defined an inverse of a datatype property.

The `owl:inverseOf` axiom can be mapped to Description Logic by using a role equivalence axiom involving the inverse role constructor (see Section 4.2). Accordingly, the example above can be written as hasChild⁻ ≡ hasParent or equivalently as hasChild ≡ hasParent⁻.

Exercise 8.15: Formalise the following statements in OWL.

(a) Those with no parents are orphans (use only `hasChild`).

(b) The relation `hasParent` is the inverse of the relation `hasChild`.

Global cardinality restrictions

Using global cardinality restrictions we can give some specific restrictions on the number of individuals on the left- or right-hand side of a certain property. Actually we have already introduced cardinality restrictions, for example `owl:cardinality` (see Subsection 8.2.1). These restrictions, however, are local in nature as they restrict a property only in the scope of a given class, not globally.

OWL has two types of global cardinality restriction: the functional and inverse functional properties. These are discussed now.

Functional properties connect only one object to any given subject. This means that if x and y are semantically different individuals then the functional property, viewed as a set of pairs, cannot contain the two pairs (a,x) and (a,y) for any instance a. In OWL, properties that are instances of the class `owl:FunctionalProperty` are called functional properties.

As a simple example of a functional property consider the relation #hasFather; it is fairly reasonable to assume that every individual has only one father. The following OWL construct describes this, together with the domain and range restrictions for this property:

```
<owl:ObjectProperty rdf:ID="hasFather">
  <rdf:type     rdf:resource="&owl;FunctionalProperty" />
  <rdfs:domain rdf:resource="#Person" />
  <rdfs:range   rdf:resource="#Person" />
</owl:ObjectProperty>
```

We have used the class `FunctionalProperty` to express the fact that the property `#hasFather` is functional. This class is actually a subclass of `rdf:Property`. This is the reason why we needed to state that `#hasFather` is both an object property and a functional property. Of course we could have changed the order of these instantiation statements, the important thing being that there must be two `rdf:type` edges connected to the resource representing a functional property.

Not only object, but also datatype, properties can be functional: we can express the fact that everybody can have only one birthday. This is shown below, where we use a syntactic variant different from the above for stating that a property is functional:

```
<owl:DatatypeProperty rdf:ID="hasBirthDay">
  <rdfs:domain rdf:resource="#Person" />
  <rdfs:range   rdf:resource="&xsd;nonNegativeInteger" />
</owl:DatatypeProperty>
```

```
<owl:FunctionalProperty rdf:about="#hasBirthDay" />
```

One may find many other examples of functional properties, such as the primary address of someone, eye colour etc. However, sometimes it is good to be cautious, as, for example, the property `#hasWife` is only functional in certain cultures. Of course this is not a problem, as it exactly shows one of the main points of any formal representation: we can unambiguously describe what we mean by certain concepts.

Naturally, not all properties are functional. Someone may have several favourite foods or films, someone else may have several houses, a firm normally has more than one employee etc. In some of these examples the opposite also holds: a food or a film may be the favourite of more than one person or someone may be employed by several companies simultaneously. However, in the case of houses and their owners, one can use a model in which a house must have at most one owner (the situation of multiple owners can be modelled by using a collection of owners in the place of a single owner). If such model is adopted then any single house can occur only once on the right-hand side of the `hasHouse` property,

Such properties are called *inverse functional properties*. An inverse functional property can connect only one subject with a given object. In other words, if q and w are semantically different individuals then the inverse functional property, viewed as a set of pairs, cannot contain the two pairs (q, b) and (w, b) for any instance b. Inverse functional properties are instances of the class `owl:InverseFunctionalProperty`.

For example, we can use the following piece of OWL code to state that the property `#hasHouse` is inverse functional; thus we state that no house can have multiple owners as follows:

```
<owl:InverseFunctionalProperty rdf:about="#hasHouse" />
```

The property `owl:InverseFunctionalProperty` is a subclass of the class of object properties. This has two consequences. First, it is not necessary to use two `rdf:type` edges when defining an inverse functional property (see the discussion of functional properties above). Second, in OWL Lite and OWL DL we cannot state that a datatype property is inverse functional.

A functional property in OWL corresponds to a functional role in Description Logic. Such a role can be described by terminological axioms using (unqualified) number restrictions (see Subsection 4.4.4). According to this, the fact that the property #hasFather is functional can be expressed in Description Logic as $\top \sqsubseteq (\leqslant 1\,\text{hasFather})$ ($\top$ is a subset of the set of individuals having at most one father).

The inverse functional property can also be expressed by an appropriate terminological axiom. For example, we can use the axiom $\top \sqsubseteq (\leqslant 1\,\text{hasHouse}^-)$ to state that the property #hasHouse is inverse functional (everything belongs to the set of individuals having at most one incoming #hasHouse edge).

Property characteristics

A relation may have several characteristics, among which OWL 1 supports the description of symmetry and transitivity.[6] We now discuss these two characteristics.

Symmetry. *Symmetrical* properties hold in both directions between two resources. In other words, if a pair (a,b) belongs to a symmetric property then the pair (b,a) also has to belong to this property. An example of a symmetric property is the property #hasSibling: if we know that George has a sibling, Sophie, we also know that Sophie has George as a sibling.

Syntactically, symmetric properties are represented in OWL as instances of the class owl:SymmetricProperty. This class is a subclass of owl:ObjectProperty, which means that in OWL Lite and OWL DL we may state the symmetry only of object properties (the reason is similar to why we cannot express the inverse of a datatype property: a value cannot be in subject position). Our example above can be represented in OWL as follows:

```
<owl:SymmetricProperty rdf:ID="hasSibling">
  <rdfs:domain rdf:resource="#Person"/>
  <rdfs:range  rdf:resource="#Person"/>
</owl:SymmetricProperty>
```

A symmetric property can actually be considered as a property that is equivalent to its own inverse. Accordingly, we can describe the above example in Description Logic as the role axiom $\text{hasSibling} \equiv \text{hasSibling}^-$, which states that hasSibling is a symmetric role.

Transitivity. A property is considered to be transitive if it is true that whenever both (a,b) and (b,c) belong to it then (a,c) belongs to it too. A good example of a transitive property is the #hasAncestor relation, as the ancestor of an ancestor is, in fact, an ancestor. Similar things can be said about properties describing partitive relationships. For example,

---

[6] There are other characteristics, such as reflexivity, that can be used to describe, for example, the statement that everyone loves himself or herself. See Section 8.3 for further characteristics supported by OWL 2.

if we know that a spoke is #partOf a wheel and a wheel is #partOf a bicycle, we may rightfully conclude that the spoke is #partOf the bicycle.

Transitive properties can be specified in OWL using owl:TransitiveProperty. This is a subclass of owl:ObjectProperty, just like the class used for specifying symmetric properties. Thus the transitivity of a datatype property can be expressed only in OWL Full.

Our example concerning the #partOf relation above can be described in OWL as follows:

```
<owl:TransitiveProperty rdf:ID="partOf" />
```

OWL Lite and OWL DL do not allow the modeller to pose any cardinality restrictions on transitive properties, on their superclasses or on their inverses. Thus, a transitive property in OWL DL cannot be, for example, functional. This limitation also appears in Description Logic, building on the notion of simple roles (see Subsection 4.5.4).

The idea of transitivity used in OWL corresponds to the transitivity axiom used in Description Logic (see Section 4.2).

8.2.4. Instances

Unlike RDF, OWL does not introduce any new notation for the description of instances. However, we have already mentioned that OWL does not maintain the unique name assumption, which effectively means that several URIs may identify the same resource. An OWL reasoner must take this possibility into account during execution.

For modelling reasons and also to guide the reasoning process, OWL provides facilities for stating that two URIs actually represent the same resource or that, on the contrary, they represent different resources. In the following we introduce the constructs that allow us to describe the equality or distinctness of instances.

The owl:sameAs property can be used to state that two instances identified by different URIs are actually the same, i.e. two URIs refer to the same individual. In the following example we state that #Rudy and #Rudolph are the same person:

```
<rdf:Description rdf:about="#Rudy">
  <owl:sameAs rdf:resource="#Rudolph"/>
</rdf:Description>
```

Regarding instances, we note that in OWL Full all resources are also instances, i.e. owl:Thing is equivalent to rdfs:Resource. As a consequence, owl:sameAs can be used to state the identity of two classes, for example. This is quite different from expressing the equivalence of classes (see Subsection 8.2.2), since with owl:sameAs we indicate that two classes have the same *intensional* meaning.

The fact that some individuals are different (i.e. the corresponding URIs refer to different domain elements) can be expressed with two OWL constructs. One can use the property owl:differentFrom to state that two individuals are different, while the resource owl:AllDifferent serves for stating that the members of a collection are pairwise different.

Below we state that the movies identified by the URIs #Fifth_Element and #Pulp_Fiction are different:

```
<t:Movie rdf:ID="Fifth_Element"/>

<t:Movie rdf:ID="Pulp_Fiction">
  <owl:differentFrom rdf:resource="#Fifth_Element"/>
</t:Movie>
```

Naturally, in the case of OWL Full we may state about any two resources that they are different. For example, we state below that the classes of men and women are different:

```
<owl:Class rdf:about="#Man">
  <owl:differentFrom rdf:resource="#Woman"/>
</owl:Class>
```

Note that this is quite different from stating that these two classes are disjoint (see Subsection 8.2.2). Indeed, this example states nothing more than the fact that the above two URIs are not the same resource. As far as the statement in the example goes, the extensions of these two classes could be the same.

An individual can have several owl:differentFrom properties connected to it. Thus, for example, we can express that the Quentin Tarantino movie *Kill Bill* is different from the previous two movies shown above:

```
<t:Movie rdf:ID="Kill_Bill">
  <owl:differentFrom rdf:resource="#Fifth_Element"/>
  <owl:differentFrom rdf:resource="#Pulp_Fiction"/>
</t:Movie>
```

If we have a large set of instances then using the above notation for stating their pairwise distinctness is very cumbersome and error-prone. Thus OWL provides the construct owl:AllDifferent for stating that a collection of individuals is pairwise distinct. This construct is also useful in cases when the unique name assumption should be enforced for a given OWL ontology: all we have to do is to build a collection of all instances and state that these are pairwise distinct. This is supported by state-of-the-art ontology editors, for example Protégé [104].

Using owl:AllDifferent might seem to be a bit tricky at first. Here we express the fact that the three movies introduced above are pairwise different:

```
<owl:AllDifferent>
  <owl:distinctMembers rdf:parseType="Collection">
    <t:Movie rdf:about="#Fifth_Element">
    <t:Movie rdf:about="#Pulp_Fiction">
    <t:Movie rdf:about="#Kill_Bill">
  </owl:distinctMembers>
</owl:AllDifferent>
```

The owl:AllDifferent resource is actually a class. In the example we create an unnamed instance (a blank resource) of this class and build an outgoing link using the property owl:distinctMembers. The right-hand side of this property is the collection whose elements are stated to be pairwise different.

Exercise 8.16: Describe in OWL the following statements.

(a) The parents of `Steve` are `Kate` and `Bill`.

(b) `Kate` is not the same person as `Bill`.

(c) The soccer players `Giggs`, `Rooney`, `Ronaldo`, ... (pick your favourites) are pairwise different.

8.2.5. OWL datatypes

Datatypes can be used in OWL in the same way as in RDF (see Subsection 2.5.5). That is, the type of the object of an RDF statement can be specified using the `rdf:datatype` attribute. The value of this attribute is the URI identifying the datatype.

We now state that the size of the individual `#myShoe` (which is an instance of the class `#Shoe`) is an integer with the value 42:

```
<Shoe rdf:ID="myShoe">
  <hasSize rdf:datatype="&xsd;int">42</hasSize>
</Shoe>
```

What is new here is that in OWL we are able to define enumeration classes that have (typed or untyped) literals as elements. In other words, we may name a subset of Δ_D (see Subsection 8.1.2). These special kinds of enumeration classes, called *enumeration datatypes*, are the instances of `owl:DataRange` having the `owl:oneOf` property connecting to them. One thing worth noting is that to describe the collection on the right-hand side of `owl:oneOf` we must use the `rdf:List` construct explicitly, since `rdf:parseType` can only be used to simplify the description of collections containing individuals.

In Figure 8.3 we describe a datatype property called `#hasTshirtSize` with an enumeration datatype as its range. We actually state that only the literals `S`, `M`, `L` and `XL` are allowed on the right-hand size of `#hasTshirtSize`.

Exercise 8.17: Formalise in OWL the following statements by using enumeration datatypes.

(a) Laptops may have screens of size 10, 13, 15 or 17 inches.

(b) Restrict the domain of the property `hasTennisScore` to `TennisGame` and its range to the the list of integer values {0, 15, 30, 40}.

8.2.6. Local property restrictions in OWL

RDF schema allows us to create *global property restrictions*. In other words, we can restrict the domain and range of a given property, i.e. we can specify the classes whose instances are allowed to be on the left- and right-hand sides of the property. To describe these restrictions we use the `rdfs:domain` and `rdfs:range` axioms. As we saw before, OWL also uses these RDF schema constructs, with the extension that their values can be arbitrary class descriptions and not just named classes (see Subsection 8.2.3). We call these restrictions global because we restrict the domain independently of the range, and the other way around.

```
<owl:DatatypeProperty rdf:ID="hasTshirtSize">
  <rdfs:domain rdf:resource="#T-shirt"/>
  <rdfs:range>
    <owl:DataRange>
      <owl:oneOf>
        <rdf:List>
            <rdf:first>S</rdf:first>
            <rdf:rest>
              <rdf:List>
                <rdf:first>M</rdf:first>
                <rdf:rest>
                  <rdf:List>
                    <rdf:first>L</rdf:first>
                    <rdf:rest>
                      <rdf:List>
                        <rdf:first>XL</rdf:first>
                        <rdf:rest rdf:resource="&rdf;nil" />
                      </rdf:List>
                    </rdf:rest>
                  </rdf:List>
                </rdf:rest>
              </rdf:List>
            </rdf:rest>
        </rdf:List>
      </owl:oneOf>
    </owl:DataRange>
  </rdfs:range>
</owl:DatatypeProperty>
```

Figure 8.3.   The property hasTshirtSize connects T-shirts with their sizes.

Let us reconsider the property #hasSize, introduced in Subsection 8.2.3:

```
<owl:DatatypeProperty rdf:ID="hasSize">
  <rdfs:domain rdf:resource="#Shoe" />
  <rdfs:range   rdf:resource="&xsd;positiveInteger"/>
</owl:DatatypeProperty>
```

This property connects shoes with positive integers regardless of the context. For example, if we define an OWL class containing T-shirts whose sizes (i.e. the right-hand sides of the hasSize properties attached to them) are string literals, we should suspect that something has gone wrong: either this class has no instances or the instances will most likely violate the rdfs:domain restriction that belongs to the property.

The biggest problem with global restrictions is that using them we cannot effectively model certain situations. We cannot formalise the knowledge, for example, that the value of the property #hasSize must be an integer when it is applied to shoes *but a literal* when it is used for T-shirts. Our only option is to declare a new property (with a different name), similar to that shown in Figure 8.3.

In OWL we are able to formulate so-called *local property restrictions*. In the example below we state that every instance of the class Shoe has positive integers on the right-hand sides of the outgoing #hasSize edges. Here we use a one-way implication; we do not claim that if the size of something is a positive integer then it is necessarily a shoe, i.e. we do not give a sufficient condition for being an instance of the class #Shoe.

```
<owl:Class rdf:ID="Shoe">
 <rdfs:subClassOf>
  <owl:Restriction>
    <owl:onProperty     rdf:resource="#hasSize"/>
    <owl:allValuesFrom rdf:resource="&xsd;positiveInteger"/>
  </owl:Restriction>
 </rdfs:subClassOf>
</owl:Class>
```

The term "local property restriction" refers to the fact that we restrict the use of hasSize *locally*, namely in the context of the class Shoe. One may find this term actually somewhat misleading, as we are doing nothing new here: we are simply using a universal restriction introduced in Subsection 8.2.1 to describe an unnamed class and then using this class in an rdfs:subClassOf axiom. This is better illustrated by the DL equivalent of the example:

$$\text{Shoe} \sqsubseteq \forall \text{hasSize.positiveInteger}.$$

A good practice to follow when building OWL ontologies is to apply global restrictions on the domain or range of a property very sparingly and use local property restrictions for expressing the stronger constraints. Apart from the modelling advantages we obtain in this way, we are also it easier for others to use our properties.

We conclude the section with an example where we define the classes Shoe and T-shirt and the property hasSize, as shown in Figure 8.4. This example demonstrates the advantages of using local property restrictions since, for example, we can use the *same* property to specify the sizes of a T-shirt and of a shoe.

Exercise 8.18: Formalise in OWL the following statement: if the subject of the property hasScore belongs to the class TennisGame then the object must belong to the set of integer values {0, 15, 30, 40}.

8.3. Revision of the OWL language: OWL 2

The widespread use of the OWL language revealed some of its weaknesses. In 2005 the design of OWL 1.1 started, and this resulted in a W3C member submission. It was used as a starting point for a new W3C Working Group officially formed in 2007. As the new proposal contained important extensions and re-engineering, the Working Group decided to call it OWL 2. This language became an official W3C recommendation on 27 October 2009.

A primary concern about OWL was the lack of expressiveness of the language. Although OWL Full allows a lot of modelling freedom it lacks several constructs that are necessary

```
...
<owl:Class rdf:ID="Thing" />

<owl:Class rdf:ID="Shoe">
  <owl:disjointWith rdf:resource="#T-shirt" />
  <rdfs:subClassOf rdf:resource="#Thing" />
  <rdfs:subClassOf>
    <owl:Restriction>
      <owl:onProperty rdf:resource="#hasSize"/>
      <owl:allValuesFrom rdf:resource=
        "&xsd;positiveInteger"/>
    </owl:Restriction>
  </rdfs:subClassOf>
</owl:Class>

<owl:Class rdf:ID="T-shirt">
  <rdfs:subClassOf rdf:resource="#Thing"/>
  <rdfs:subClassOf>
    <owl:Restriction>
      <owl:onProperty rdf:resource="#hasSize"/>
      <owl:allValuesFrom rdf:resource="&xsd;string"/>
    </owl:Restriction>
  </rdfs:subClassOf>
</owl:Class>

<owl:DatatypeProperty rdf:ID="hasSize">
  <rdfs:domain rdf:resource="#Thing"/>
</owl:DatatypeProperty>

<T-shirt rdf:ID="myRunningShirt">
  <hasSize rdf:datatype="&xsd;string">L</hasSize>
</T-shirt>

<Shoe rdf:ID="myShoe">
  <hasSize rdf:datatype="&xsd;positiveInteger">42</hasSize>
</Shoe> ...
```

Figure 8.4. An example of local property restrictions.

for modelling complex domains. Moreover: (1) no reasoner has so far been implemented for OWL Full; (2) formalising knowledge in OWL Full leads to undecidability [85]. These issues made OWL Full an unviable option in many scenarios. As a response, attention turned towards extending the most expressive, but still decidable, language of the OWL framework, OWL DL.

As mentioned in Section 8.1, OWL 1 DL documents can be transformed into axioms of the $\mathcal{SHOIN}(\mathbf{D})$ DL language. Since the initial design of the OWL DL language the DL research community has managed to increase the number of concept and role constructors that can be added to a DL language without seriously affecting its core computation properties. The idea is that those constructors that are practically useful as well as feasible from the implementation point of view should definitely be part of the OWL language.

OWL 2 supports a language whose expressivity is equivalent to the $\mathcal{SROIQ}(\mathbf{D})$ DL language [57]; see Subsection 4.10.4.

We now discuss the new features of OWL 2 in turn.

8.3.1. New class constructs in OWL 2

Recall that the cardinality restriction of OWL 1 corresponds to the unqualified number restriction of Description Logic. In contrast with this, OWL 2 provides support for qualified cardinality constraints. These allow us to describe a class with instances having a restricted number of individuals connected to them, which, in turn, all belong to a certain class. In this way we can describe a company employing at least three Engineers, as shown below.

```
<owl:Restriction>
   <owl:minQualifiedCardinality
        rdf:datatype="&xsd;nonNegativeInteger">3
   </owl:minQualifiedCardinality>
   <owl:onProperty rdf:resource="#hasEmployee" />
   <owl:onClass rdf:resource="#Engineer" />
</owl:Restriction>
```

Similarly, constraints involving owl:maxQualifiedCardinality (owl:qualifiedCardinality can be used to describe the class containing those individuals that have at most (exactly) a given number of outgoing edges leading to instances of a given class. Qualified cardinality constraints correspond to the qualified number restriction constructs of Description Logic (see Subsection 4.5.4).

OWL 2 also introduces a new construct corresponding to $\exists R.\mathsf{Self}$, which can be used to express local reflexivity, e.g. to express that somebody likes herself: $\exists\mathsf{likes.Self}$. This is demonstrated below in RDF syntax:

```
<owl:Restriction>
   <owl:onProperty rdf:resource="#likes" />
   <owl:hasSelf rdf:datatype="&xsd;boolean">
        true
   </owl:hasSelf>
</owl:Restriction>
```

Exercise 8.19: Describe in OWL the following statements.

(a) Those having at least three expensive cars are rich.

(b) Every person has exactly one human mother.

(c) Cars with at most two faulty components are acceptable.

(d) A reliable system is not faulty if it has at most one faulty component.

8.3.2. New property constructs in OWL 2

OWL 2 supports the use of complex role inclusion axioms of the form $S \circ R \sqsubseteq S$ or $R \circ S \sqsubseteq S$ (see Subsection 4.10.3). Such role axioms are widely used in medical ontologies. Moreover, OWL 2 DL also allows a generalisation of such role inclusions which makes it possible to describe that the brother of somebody's parent is an uncle, i.e. hasParent $\circ$ hasBrother $\sqsubseteq$ hasUncle. This is shown in the following snippet, where we use the owl:propertyChainAxiom construct to define the hasUncle property:

```
<rdf:Description rdf:about="#hasUncle">
  <owl:propertyChainAxiom rdf:parseType="Collection">
    <owl:ObjectProperty rdf:about="#hasParent"/>
    <owl:ObjectProperty rdf:about="#hasBrother"/>
  </owl:propertyChainAxiom>
</rdf:Description>
```

This example states that given two individuals i and j where (1) j is the parent of i and (2) j has a brother k we can conclude that (3) k is the uncle of i, i.e. the hasUncle(i, k) relation holds.

The chain can contain an arbitrary number of properties, which allows us to describe relations such as hasGreatGrandfather:

```
<rdf:Description rdf:about="#hasGreatGrandfather">
  <owl:propertyChainAxiom rdf:parseType="Collection">
    <owl:ObjectProperty rdf:about="#hasParent"/>
    <owl:ObjectProperty rdf:about="#hasParent"/>
    <owl:ObjectProperty rdf:about="#hasFather"/>
  </owl:propertyChainAxiom>
</rdf:Description>
```

Beside property chains, OWL 2 DL supports the universal property and negative property assertions and it also allows us to state that properties are pairwise disjoint. For example, below we state that Will is definitely not working for Future2100 – which is an example of a negative assertion:

```
<owl:NegativePropertyAssertion>
  <owl:sourceIndividual rdf:resource="Future2100 Inc"/>
  <owl:assertionProperty rdf:resource="hasEmployee"/>
  <owl:targetIndividual rdf:resource="Will"/>
 </owl:NegativePropertyAssertion>
```

The built-in owl:topObjectProperty connects all possible pairs of individuals (cf. the universal role), while owl:propertyDisjointWith can be used to describe property disjointness, e.g. to say that parents and spouses are different:

```
<rdf:Description rdf:about="hasParent">
  <owl:propertyDisjointWith rdf:resource="hasSpouse"/>
 </rdf:Description>
```

Exercise 8.20: Describe in OWL the following statements.

(a) The enemy of an enemy is a friend.

(b) Suzie does not like Will.

8.3.3. OWL 2 sublanguages

Beside expressivity concerns, the OWL 1 framework suffers from some other weaknesses. One such weakness is that the OWL Lite sublanguage has still very high computational complexity despite the severe restrictions posed by the OWL specification. The problem is that most disallowed constructs can be described by other means. For example, `owl:disjointWith` is not supported in OWL Lite, but the fact that the classes Man and Woman are disjoint can still be described by OWL Lite axioms:

```
<owl:Class rdf:about="#Man">
  <rdfs:subClassOf>
    <owl:Restriction>
      <owl:onProperty rdf:resource="#hasSomething" />
      <owl:allValuesFrom rdf:resource="owl:Nothing" />
    </owl:Restriction>
  </rdfs:subClassOf>
</owl:Class>

<owl:Class rdf:about="#Woman">
  <rdfs:subClassOf>
    <owl:Restriction>
      <owl:onProperty rdf:resource="#hasSomething" />
      <owl:someValuesFrom rdf:resource="owl:Thing" />
    </owl:Restriction>
  </rdfs:subClassOf>
</owl:Class>
```

Here hasSomething is a newly introduced property that does not appear anywhere else in our ontology. We are basically saying that no man should have any hasSomething attached to him, while every women has at least one such property. This makes these two classes disjoint. Note that the above OWL description corresponds to the DL axioms Man $\sqsubseteq$ $\forall$hasSomething.$\perp$ and Woman $\sqsubseteq$ $\exists$hasSomething.$\top$.

OWL 2 solves this problem by completely redefining the structure of OWL sublanguages. Beside the complete OWL 2 DL, OWL 2 provides three sublanguages for different application scenarios or *profiles*. One profile is aimed at describing large terminologies where classification of the ontology concepts is the main focus. Another profile is suitable for ontologies having relatively simple terminology but large amounts of instances. Finally, a third profile is designed to eliminate the need for reasoning with anonymous individuals. Such anonymous individuals may come to exist when, for example, an `owl:someValuesFrom` restriction appears on the right-hand side of an `rdfs:subClassOf` axiom.

8.4. Summary

In this chapter we introduced the OWL approach, which extends RDF schema towards heavyweight ontology management.

Shortcomings of RDF schema have led to the development of more complex ontology languages. One of these is the OWL language, which, like RDF schema, is a set of resources. Accordingly, OWL documents are ordinary RDF descriptions, with the difference that certain identifiers have fixed meanings. The OWL 1 standard defines three sublanguages, which differ in expressive power. To which sublanguage an OWL description belongs depends on which OWL constructions it uses and how it does this. The strongest OWL sublanguage does not place any restriction on the use of OWL resources. The other OWL sublanguages contain restrictions but, in turn, ensure higher efficiency in reasoning.

Unlike RDF schema, OWL lets us specify *class descriptions*. In this way one can create enumeration classes, classes with property restrictions or classes defined as intersections, unions or complements of other classes. We have described the RDF/XML form of each of the above constructions, as well as their DL equivalent.

Using class descriptions, *axioms* can be formulated. For example, we can state that a class is a subset of another class. This essentially corresponds to a DL *general concept inclusion* axiom.

In OWL, *object properties* and *data type properties* can be distinguished. The former properties associate individuals with individuals, while the latter associate individuals with values. OWL supports several axiom schemes for expressing our knowledge about properties. Besides constructions already used in RDF schema, OWL lets us state that properties are equivalent or that one property is the inverse of another. Additionally to these, global number restrictions can be specified and property features such as transitivity and symmetry can be declared.

An important feature of OWL is that it allows us to specify not only global property restrictions, which are already present in RDF schema, but also their *local* variants.

In 2009 the Web Ontology Language was revised. The new language, called OWL 2, introduces several new features in addition to the constructors and axioms summarised above. Most importantly, OWL 2 supports complex role inclusion axioms, crucial for medical and engineering ontologies.

References

[1] Aduna BV. Sesame. Accessed 30 March 2013. URL: http://www.openrdf.org.

[2] Apache Software Foundation. Formatting object processor. Accessed 30 March 2013. URL: http://xml.apache.org/fop.

[3] Apache Software Foundation. Jena toolkit. Accessed 30 March 2013. URL: http://jena.apache.org.

[4] Franz Baader, Diego Calvanese, Deborah L. McGuinness, Daniele Nardi and Peter F. Patel-Schneider, editors. *The Description Logic Handbook: Theory, Implementation, and Applications, Second Edition.* Cambridge University Press, 2007.

[5] Franz Baader and Ulrike Sattler. Expressive number restrictions in Description Logics. *Journal of Logic and Computation,* **9**(3):319–350, 1999.

[6] Sean Bechhofer, Ian Horrocks, Carole Goble and Robert Stevens. OilEd: a Reason-able ontology editor for the Semantic Web. In *Proceedings of KI2001, Joint German/Austrian Conference on Artificial Intelligence,* volume 2174 of Lecture Notes in Computer Science, pp. 396–408. Springer-Verlag, September 2001.

[7] Sean Bechhofer, Frank van Harmelen, Jim Hendler *et al.* OWL Web Ontology Language reference. Accessed 30 March 2013. URL: http://www.w3.org/TR/owl-ref, February 2004. W3C recommendation.

[8] Dave Beckett. Turtle – terse RDF triple language. Accessed 30 March 2013. URL: http://www.w3.org/TeamSubmission/turtle, December 2006.

[9] Dave Beckett and Art Barstow, editors. N-triples. Accessed 30 March 2013. URL: http://www.w3.org/2001/sw/RDFCore/ntriples, 2001. W3C RDF core WG internal working draft.

[10] David Beckett. The design and implementation of the Redland RDF application framework. In *Proceedings of WWW '01, the 10th International Conference on*

World Wide Web, pp. 449–456. ACM Press, 2001. Accessed 30 March 2013. URL: `http://citeseer.ist.psu.edu/viewdoc/summary?doi=10.1.1.21.312`.

[11] Dave Beckett, editor. RDF/XML syntax specification (revised). Accessed 30 March 2013. URL: `http://www.w3.org/TR/rdf-syntax-grammar`, February 2004. W3C recommendation.

[12] Tamás Benkő, Gergely Lukácsy, Attila Fokt, Péter Szeredi, Imre Kilián and Péter Krauth. Information integration through reasoning on meta-data. In *Proceedings of IJCAI'03 Workshop "AI Moves to IA, Workshop on Artificial Intelligence, Information Access and Mobile Computing", Acapulco, Mexico*, pp. 65–77, August 2003.

[13] Anders Berglund, editor. Extensive Stylesheet Language (XSL) Version 1.1. Accessed 30 March 2013. URL: `http://www.w3.org/TR/xsl`, December 2006. W3C recommendation.

[14] Robin Berjon, Travis Leithead, Erika Doyle Navara, Edward O'Connor and Silvia Pfeiffer, editors. HTML 5: a vocabulary and associated APIs for HTML and XHTML. Accessed 30 March 2013. URL: `http://www.w3.org/TR/html5`, December 2012. W3C candidate recommendation.

[15] Tim Berners-Lee. Ideas about Web architecture – yet another notation, Notation 3. Accessed 30 March 2013. URL: `http://www.w3.org/DesignIssues/Notation3.html`, August 2005.

[16] Tim Berners-Lee, Roy T. Fielding and Henrik Frystyk. RFC1945 – Hypertext Transfer Protocol 1.0. Accessed 30 March 2013. URL: `http://www.w3.org/Protocols/rfc1945/rfc1945`, May 1996.

[17] Tim Berners-Lee, Roy T. Fielding and Larry Masinter. RFC3986 – uniform resource identifiers (URI): generic syntax. Accessed 30 March 2013. URL: `http://www.ietf.org/rfc/rfc3986.txt`, January 2005.

[18] George S. Boolos, John P. Burgess and Richard C. Jeffrey. *Computability and Logic, Fifth Edition*. Cambridge University Press, 2007.

[19] Alexander Borgida and Peter F. Patel-Schneider. A semantics and complete algorithm for subsumption in the CLASSIC Description Logic. *Journal of Artificial Intelligence Research*, **1**:277–308, 1994.

[20] Per Bothner. Compiling XQuery to Java bytecodes. In *Proceedings of the 1st International Workshop on XQuery Implementation, Experience and Perspectives*, pp. 31–36, June 2004. Accessed 30 March 2013. URL: `http://per.bothner.com/papers/Qexo04/index.html`.

[21] Tim Bray, Jean Paoli, C. M. Sperberg-McQueen, Eve Maler and François Yergeau, editors. Extensible markup language (XML) 1.0, Fifth Edition. Accessed 30 March 2013. URL: `http://www.w3.org/TR/xml`, November 2008. W3C recommendation.

[22] Dan Brickley and R.V. Guha, editors. RDF Vocabulary Description Language 1.0: RDF Schema. Accessed 30 March 2013. URL: `http://www.w3.org/TR/rdf-schema`, February 2004. W3C recommendation.

[23] Sergey Brin and Lawrence Page. The anatomy of a large-scale hypertextual Web search engine. *Computer Networks and ISDN Systems*, **30**(1–7):107–117, 1998. Accessed 30 March 2013. URL: `http://citeseer.ist.psu.edu/viewdoc/summary?doi=10.1.1.109.4049`.

[24] Diego Calvanese, Maurizio Lenzerini and Daniele Nardi. Description Logics for conceptual data modeling. In Jan Chomicki and Günter Saake, editors, *Logics for Databases and Information Systems*, pp. 229–264. Kluwer Academic Publishers, 1998. Accessed 30 March 2013. URL: `http://citeseerx.ist.psu.edu/viewdoc/summary?doi=10.1.1.5.2743`.

[25] Peter Pin-Shan Chen. The entity-relationship model – toward a unified view of data. *ACM Transactions on Database Systems*, **1**(1):9–36, 1976.

[26] James Clark and Steve DeRose, editors. XML Path Language (XPath). Accessed 30 March 2013. URL: `http://www.w3.org/TR/xpath`, November 1999. W3C recommendation.

[27] Kendall Grant Clark, Lee Feigenbaum and Elias Torres, editors. SPARQL protocol for RDF. Accessed 30 March 2013. URL: `http://www.w3.org/TR/rdf-sparql-protocol`, January 2008. W3C recommendation.

[28] James Clark, editor. XML transformations (XSLT). Accessed 30 March 2013. URL: `http://www.w3.org/TR/xslt`, November 1999. W3C recommendation.

[29] Dan Connolly, Frank van Harmelen, Ian Horrocks, Deborah L. McGuinness, Peter F. Patel-Schneider and Lynn Andrea Stein. DAML+OIL reference description. Accessed 30 March 2013. URL: `http://www.w3.org/TR/daml+oil-reference`, March 2001. *W3C Note*.

[30] Willem Conradie. The Beth property for the modal logic of graded modalities, with an application to the Description Logic $\mathcal{ALCQ}$. In *Proceedings of the 8th ESSLLI Student Session*, pp. 59–68, 2003. Accessed 30 March 2013. URL: `https://sites.google.com/site/willemconradie/files/Conradie1.pdf`.

[31] CoreFiling Ltd. XML schema validator. Accessed 30 March 2013. URL: `http://www.corefiling.com/opensource/schemaValidate.html`.

[32] Dublin Core Metadata Initiative. Dublin Core. Accessed 30 March 2013. URL: `http://dublincore.org`.

[33] Michael Eisfeld. Model construction for configuration design. In *Proceedings of the Workshop on Applications of Description Logics*. Technical University of Dresden, Germany, 2002. Accessed 30 March 2013. URL: `http://citeseerx.ist.psu.edu/viewdoc/summary?doi=10.1.1.5.649`.

[34] English Words of Hungarian Origin. Accessed 30 March 2013. URL: `http://en.wikipedia.org/wiki/List_of_English_words_of_Hungarian_origin`.

[35] Christiane Fellbaum, editor. *WordNet: An Electronic Lexical Database*. The MIT Press, 1998. Book review: Accessed 30 March 2013. URL: `http://citeseer.ist.psu.edu/viewdoc/summary?doi=10.1.1.14.2583`.

[36] Dieter Fensel, Katia Sycara and John Mylopoulos, editors. *The Semantic Web – ISWC 2003, Proceedings of the 2nd International Conference*, volume 2870 of *Lecture Notes in Computer Science*. Springer-Verlag, October 2003.

[37] Dieter Fensel, Frank van Harmelen, Ian Horrocks, Deborah L. McGuinness and Peter F. Patel-Schneider. OIL: an ontology infrastructure for the Semantic Web. *IEEE Intelligent Systems*, **16**(2):38–45, 2001.

[38] Mary Fernández, Ashok Malhotra, Jonathan Marsh, Marton Nagy and Norman Walsh, editors. XML Query (XQuery). Accessed 30 March 2013. URL: http://www.w3. org/TR/xpath-datamodel, December 2004. W3C recommendation.

[39] JSON RDF Task Force. JSON+RDF. Accessed 30 March 2013. URL: http:// www.w3.org/2011/rdf-wg/wiki/TF-JSON, September 2011.

[40] Fourthought, Inc. 4suite: an open-source platform for XML and RDF processing. Accessed 30 March 2013. URL: http://foursuite.sourceforge. net.

[41] Ned Freed and Nathaniel S. Borenstein. RFC2045 – multipurpose internet mail extensions (MIME). Accessed 30 March 2013. URL: http://www.ietf.org/rfc/ rfc2045.txt, November 1996.

[42] Jon William Freeman. Improvements to propositional satisfiability search algorithms. Ph.D. thesis, University of Pennsylvania, 1995. Accessed 30 March 2013. URL: http://citeseerx.ist.psu.edu/viewdoc/summary?doi=10. 1.1.43.255.

[43] Glasgow Haskell compiler. Accessed 30 March 2013. URL: http://www. haskell.org/ghc.

[44] Google. Google Scholar. Accessed 30 March 2013. URL: http://scholar. google.com.

[45] R.V. Guha. rdfDB: an RDF database. Accessed 30 March 2013. URL: http:// guha.com/rdfdb.

[46] R.V. Guha, Ora Lassila, Eric Miller and Dan Brickley. Enabling inferencing. In Marchiori [77]. Accessed 30 March 2013. URL: http://www.w3.org/TandS/QL/ QL98/pp/enabling.html.

[47] Volker Haarslev and Ralf Möller. *RACER User's Guide and Reference Manual Version 1.7.19*. Montreal, Canada, 2003. Accessed 30 March 2013. URL: http://www.sts.tu-harburg.de/ r.f.moeller/racer/racer- manual-1-7-19.pdf.

[48] Peter Haase, Jeen Broekstra, Andreas Eberhart and Raphael Volz. A comparison of RDF query languages. In *Proceedings of ISWC 2004, the 3rd International Conference on The Semantic Web*, volume 3298 of Lecture Notes in Computer Science, pp. 502–517, November 2004. Accessed 30 March 2013. URL: http:// citeseer.ist.psu.edu/viewdoc/summary?doi=10.1.1.105.8731.

[49] Steve Harris and Andy Seaborne, editors. SPARQL 1.1 query language. Accessed 30 March 2013. URL: http://www.w3.org/TR/sparql11-query, November 2012. W3C proposed recommendation.

[50] David Hawking and Nick Craswell. Very large scale retrieval and web search. In Ellen Voorhees and Donna Harman, editors, *TREC: Experiment and Evaluation in Information Retrieval*, pp. 199–231. MIT Press, 2005. Accessed 30 March 2013. URL: `http://es.csiro.au/pubs/trecbook_for_website.pdf`.

[51] Kevin Hemenway. Amphetadesk – syndicated news aggregator. Accessed 30 March 2013. URL: `http://www.disobey.com/amphetadesk`.

[52] James Hendler and Deborah L. McGuinness. The DARPA agent markup language. *IEEE Intelligent Systems*, **15**(6):67–73, 2000.

[53] Bernhard Hollunder. Consistency checking reduced to satisfiability of concepts in terminological systems. *Annals of Mathematics and Artificial Intelligence*, **18**:95–131, 1996.

[54] Ian Horrocks. Optimising tableaux decision procedures for Description Logics. Ph.D. thesis, University of Manchester, 1997. Accessed 30 March 2013. URL: `http://www.cs.ox.ac.uk/ian.horrocks/Publications/download/1997/phd.pdf`.

[55] Ian Horrocks. The FaCT system. In Harrie de Swart, editor, *Automated Reasoning with Analytic Tableaux and Related Methods: International Conference on Tableaux'98*, volume 1397 of Lecture Notes in Artificial Intelligence, pp. 307–312. Springer-Verlag, 1998. Accessed 30 March 2013. URL: `http://www.cs.ox.ac.uk/ian.horrocks/Publications/download/1998/Horr98b.pdf`.

[56] Ian Horrocks. Implementation and optimization techniques. In Baader *et al.* [4], pp. 306–346.

[57] Ian Horrocks, Oliver Kutz and Ulrike Sattler. The even more irresistible $\mathcal{SROIQ}$. In *Proceedings of KR 2006, the 10th International Conference on the Principles of Knowledge Representation and Reasoning*, pp. 57–67. AAAI Press, 2006. Accessed 30 March 2013. URL: `http://www.cs.ox.ac.uk/ian.horrocks/Publications/download/2006/HoKS06a.pdf`.

[58] Ian Horrocks and Peter F. Patel-Schneider. Reducing OWL entailment to Description Logic satisfiability. In Fensel *et al.* [36], pp. 17–29.

[59] Ian Horrocks and Peter F. Patel-Schneider. Three theses of representation in the Semantic Web. In *Proceedings of WWW2003, the 12th International World Wide Web Conference*, pp. 39–47. ACM Press, May 2003. Accessed 30 March 2013. URL: `http://www.cs.ox.ac.uk/ian.horrocks/Publications/download/2003/p50-horrocks.pdf`.

[60] Ian Horrocks and Ulrike Sattler. A Description Logic with transitive and inverse roles and role hierarchies. *Journal of Logic and Computation*, **9**(3):385–410, 1999. Accessed 30 March 2013. URL: `http://www.cs.ox.ac.uk/ian.horrocks/Publications/download/1999/090385.pdf`.

[61] Ian Horrocks and Ulrike Sattler. Ontology reasoning in the $\mathcal{SHOQ(D)}$ Description Logic. In *IJCAI'01: Proceedings of the 17th International Joint Conference on Artificial Intelligence*, volume 1, pp. 199–204. Morgan Kaufmann Publishers,

2001. Accessed 30 March 2013. URL: `http://www.cs.ox.ac.uk/ian.`
`horrocks/Publications/download/2001/ijcai01.pdf`.

[62] Ian Horrocks and Ulrike Sattler. Decidability of $\mathcal{SHIQ}$ with complex role inclusion
axioms. LTCS Report LTCS-02-06, Dresden University of Technology, Germany,
2002. Accessed 30 March 2013. URL: `http://www.cs.ox.ac.uk/ian.`
`horrocks/Publications/download/2002/HoSa02b.pdf`.

[63] Ian Horrocks, Ulrike Sattler and Stephan Tobies. A Description Logic with transitive
and converse roles, role hierarchies and qualifying number restrictions. LTCS Report
LTCS-99-08, LuFG Theoretical Computer Science, RWTH Aachen, 1999. Accessed
30 March 2013. URL: `http://www.cs.ox.ac.uk/ian.horrocks/`
`Publications/download/1999/HoST99b.pdf` (revised version).

[64] Ian Horrocks, Ulrike Sattler and Stephan Tobies. Practical reasoning for expressive
Description Logics. In *Proceedings of LPAR'99, the 6th International Conference on
Logic for Programming and Automated Reasoning*, volume 1705 in Lecture Notes in
Artificial Intelligence, pp. 161–180. Springer-Verlag, 1999. Accessed 30 March 2013.
URL: `http://citeseerx.ist.psu.edu/viewdoc/summary?doi=10.`
`1.1.36.5145`.

[65] Paul Hudak, John Peterson and Joseph H. Fasel. A gentle introduction to Haskell
98, 1999. Accessed 30 March 2013. URL: `http://www.haskell.org/`
`tutorial`.

[66] David Huynh, Stefano Mazzocchi and David Karger. Piggy bank: experience the
Semantic Web inside your web browser. In *Proceedings of ISWC 2005, the 4th
International Conference on the Semantic Web*, volume 3729 of Lecture Notes in
Computer Science, pp. 413–430. Springer-Verlag, 2005.

[67] Internet Archive. Accessed 30 March 2013. URL: `http://www.archive.org`.

[68] ISO Prolog standard ISO/IEC 13211-1. Accessed 30 March 2013. URL: `http://`
`webstore.ansi.org/RecordDetail.aspx?sku=INCITS%2fISO`
`%2fIEC+13211-1-1995+(R2007)`, 1995.

[69] Graham Klyne and Jeremy J. Carroll, editors. Resource Description Framework
(RDF) concepts and abstract syntax. Accessed 30 March 2013. URL: `http://`
`www.w3.org/TR/rdf-concepts`, February 2004. W3C recommendation.

[70] Martijn Koster. A method for web robots control. Accessed 30 March 2013. URL:
`http://www.robotstxt.org/robotstxt.html`, 1996. Technical report,
Internet Engineering Task Force (IETF).

[71] Daniel Krech. RDFLib Python library. Accessed 30 March 2013. URL: `https://`
`github.com/RDFLib`.

[72] Ora Lassila. Enabling Semantic Web programming by integrating RDF and
Common LISP. In *Proceedings of SWWS'01, 1st Semantic Web Working
Symposium*, pp. 403–410, July 2001. Accessed 30 March 2013. URL: `http://`
`citeseer.\penalty\z@ist.\penalty\z@psu.\penalty\z@edu/`
`\penalty\z@viewdoc/\penalty\z@summary?\penalty\z@doi=10.`
`1.1.21.\penalty\z@3921`.

[73] Dik L. Lee, Huei Chuang and Kent Seamons. Document ranking and the vector-space model. *IEEE Software*, **14**(2):67–75, 1997.

[74] Gergely Lukácsy. Intelligent handling of RDF sources (in Hungarian). M.Sc. thesis, Budapest University of Technology and Economics, 2003.

[75] Ashok Malhotra and Neel Sundaresan. RDF query specification. In Marchiori [77]. Accessed 30 March 2013. URL: http://www.w3.org/TandS/QL/QL98/pp/rdfquery.html.

[76] Massimo Marchiori. Metalog. Accessed 30 March 2013. URL: http://www.w3.org/RDF/Metalog. W3C research paper.

[77] Massimo Marchiori, editor. *Proceedings of QL'98, the Query Languages 1998 Conference*. World Wide Web Consortium, December 1998. Accessed 30 March 2013. URL: http://www.w3.org/TandS/QL/QL98.

[78] Oliver A. McBryan. GENVL and WWWW: tools for taming the web. In *Proceedings of the 1st World Wide Web Conference (WWW-1)*, pp. 79–90. Elsevier Science Publishers, 1994.

[79] Jim Melton and Subramanian Muralidhar, editors. XML syntax for XQuery 1.0 (XQueryX), Second Edition. Accessed 30 March 2013. URL: http://www.w3.org/TR/xqueryx, December 2010. W3C recommendation.

[80] Libby Miller. Inkling: RDF query using SquishQL. Accessed 30 March 2013. URL: http://swordfish.rdfweb.org/rdfquery, February 2005.

[81] Libby Miller, Andy Seaborne and Alberto Reggiori. Three implementations of SquishQL, a simple RDF query language. In *Proceedings of ISWC 2002, the First International Conference on the Semantic Web*, volume 2342 of Lecture Notes in Computer Science, pp. 423–435. Springer-Verlag, 2002.

[82] Ryan Moats. RFC2141 – URN syntax. Accessed 30 March 2013. URL: http://www.ietf.org/rfc/rfc2141, May 1997.

[83] Ralf Möller. Expressive Description Logics: foundations for practical applications, 2001. Habilitation thesis, University of Hamburg. Accessed 30 March 2013. URL: http://citeseerx.ist.psu.edu/viewdoc/summary?doi=10.1.1.94.4283.

[84] Graham Moore and Andy Seaborne. RDF net API. Accessed 30 March 2013. URL: http://www.w3.org/Submission/2003/SUBM-rdf-netapi-20031002.

[85] Boris Motik. Reasoning in Description Logics using resolution and deductive databases. Ph.D. thesis, Universität Karlsruhe (TH), Karlsruhe, Germany, January 2006. Accessed 30 March 2013. URL: http://www.cs.ox.ac.uk/boris.motik/pubs/motik06PhD.pdf.

[86] Boris Motik, Peter F. Patel-Schneider and Bijan Parsia, editors. OWL 2 Web Ontology Language, structural specification and functional-style syntax, Second Edition. Accessed 30 March 2013. URL: http://www.w3.org/TR/owl2-syntax, December 2012. W3C recommendation.

[87] National Institute of Standards and Technology. Text Retrieval Conference Series. Accessed 30 March 2013. URL: `http://trec.nist.gov`.

[88] Bernhard Nebel. Terminological cycles: semantics and computational properties. In John F. Sowa, editor, *Principles of Semantic Networks*, pp. 331–362. Morgan Kaufmann Publishers, 1991. Accessed 30 March 2013. URL: `http://citeseerx.ist.psu.edu/viewdoc/summary?doi=10.1.1.49.6816`.

[89] Netscape. Open directory project. Accessed 30 March 2013. URL: `http://www.dmoz.org`.

[90] Natalya Fridman Noy, Ray W. Fergerson and Mark A. Musen. The knowledge model of Protégé-2000: combining interoperability and flexibility. In *Proceedings of EKAW2000, the 12th International Conference on Knowledge Engineering and Knowledge Management. Methods, Models, and Tools*, volume 1937 of Lecture Notes in Computer Science, pp. 17–32. Springer-Verlag, October 2000.

[91] OpenGALEN Foundation. GALEN (generalised architecture for languages, encyclopaedias and nomenclatures in medicine). Accessed 30 March 2013. URL: `http://www.opengalen.org`.

[92] Lawrence Page, Sergey Brin, Rajeev Motwani and Terry Winograd. The PageRank citation ranking: bringing order to the web. Technical report, Stanford Digital Library Technologies Project, 1998. Accessed 30 March 2013. URL: `http://citeseer.ist.psu.edu/viewdoc/summary?doi=10.1.1.31.1768`.

[93] Shankar Pal, Istvan Cseri, Oliver Seeliger *et al.* XQuery implementation in a relational database system. In *Proceedings of VLDB'05, the 31st International Conference on Very Large Data Bases*, pp. 1175–1186. ACM Press, 2005.

[94] Peter F. Patel-Schneider, Patrick Hayes and Ian Horrocks, editors. OWL Web Ontology Language semantics and abstract syntax. Accessed 30 March 2013. URL: `http://www.w3.org/TR/owl-semantics`, February 2004. W3C recommendation.

[95] Polymeta – a meta search engine using query expansion. Accessed 30 March 2013. URL: `http://www.polymeta.com`.

[96] Eric Prud'hommeaux and Andy Seaborne, editors. SPARQL query language for RDF. Accessed 30 March 2013. URL: `http://www.w3.org/TR/rdf-sparql-query`, January 2008. W3C recommendation.

[97] Yves Raimond and Mark B. Sandler. Evaluation of the music ontology framework. In *Proceedings of ESWC2012, the 9th Extended Semantic Web Conference*, May 27–31, 2012, volume 7295 of Lecture Notes in Computer Science. Springer, 2012.

[98] RDFizers. Accessed 30 March 2013. URL: `http://simile.mit.edu/wiki/RDFizers`.

[99] Alberto Reggiori. RDFStore – Perl/C RDF storage and API. Version 0.51. Accessed 30 March 2013. URL: `http://rdfstore.sourceforge.net`, 2006.

[100] RSSOwl – a newsreader for everyone. Accessed 30 March 2013. URL: `http://www.rssowl.org/overview`.

[101] Manfred Schmidt-Schaubss. Subsumption in KL-ONE is undecidable. In *Proceedings of the First International Conference on Principles of Knowledge Representation and Reasoning*, pp. 421–431. Morgan Kaufmann Publishers, 1989.

[102] Manfred Schmidt-Schauss and Gert Smolka. Attributive concept descriptions with complements. *Artificial Intelligence*, **48**(1):1–26, February 1991.

[103] Additional materials for this book, *The Semantic Web Explained*. Accessed 30 March 2013. URL: `http://www.swexpld.org`.

[104] Stanford Medical Informatics. Protégé. Accessed 30 March 2013. URL: `http://protege.stanford.edu`.

[105] Danny Sullivan. Checking your listing in search engines. In *Search Engine Watch*. Accessed 30 March 2013. URL: `http://searchenginewatch.com/webmasters/article.php/2167861`, October 2001.

[106] Alfred Tarski. The semantic conception of truth and the foundations of semantics. *Philosophy and Phenomenological Research*, **4**(3):341–376, 1944. Accessed 30 March 2013. URL: `http://www.jstor.org/stable/2102968`.

[107] Henry S. Thompson, David Beech, Murray Maloney and Noah Mendelsohn, editors. XML Schema Part 1: Structures, Second Edition. Accessed 30 March 2013. URL: `http://www.w3.org/TR/xmlschema-1`, October 2004. W3C recommendation.

[108] Unified Modeling Language. Accessed 30 March 2013. URL: `http://www.uml.org`.

[109] Stuart Weibel, Jean Godby, Eric Miller and Ron Daniel. OCLC/NCSA Metadata Workshop report, Dublin, Ohio, USA. Accessed 30 March 2013. URL: `http://dublincore.org/workshops/dc1/report.shtml`, March 1995.

[110] Jan Wielemaker, Guus Schreiber and Bob Wielinga. Prolog-based infrastructure for RDF: performance and scalability. In Fensel *et al.* [36], pp. 644–658.

[111] World Wide Web Consortium. RDF validator. Accessed 30 March 2013. URL: `http://www.w3.org/RDF/Validator`.

[112] World Wide Web Consortium. Semantic Web activity. Accessed 30 March 2013. URL: `http://www.w3.org/2001/sw`.

[113] Yahoo! Inc. Yahoo! Accessed 30 March 2013. URL: `http://www.yahoo.com`.

[114] Jeonghee Yi, Neel Sundaresan and Anita Huang. Using metadata to enhance web information gathering. In *Proceedings of WebDB2000, the 3rd international Workshop on the World Wide Web and Databases*, volume 1997 of Lecture Notes in Computer Science, pp. 38–57. Springer-Verlag, May 2001.

Index